THE GAY REVOLUTION

THE STORY OF THE STRUGGLE

LILLIAN FADERMAN

SIMON & SCHUSTER

New York   London   Toronto   Sydney   New Delhi

Simon & Schuster
1230 Avenue of the Americas
New York, NY 10020

First Simon & Schuster hardcover edition September 2015

SIMON & SCHUSTER and colophon are
registered trademarks of Simon & Schuster, Inc.

For information about special discounts for bulk purchases,
please contact Simon & Schuster Special Sales at
1-866-506-1949 or business@simonandschuster.com.

The Simon & Schuster Speakers Bureau can bring authors to your live event.
For more information or to book an event, contact the
Simon & Schuster Speakers Bureau at 1-866-248-3049
or visit our website at www.simonspeakers.com.

Interior design by Ruth Lee-Mui

Manufactured in the United States of America

3   5   7   9   10   8   6   4   2

Library of Congress Cataloging-in-Publication Data
Faderman, Lillian.
The gay revolution : the story of the struggle / Lillian Faderman.
      pages   cm
Includes bibliographical references and index.
1. Gay rights—United States—History.   2. Gay liberation movement—United States—
History.   3. Gays—United States—History.   I. Title.
HQ76.8.U5F33   2015
306.76'60973—dc23   2015007285

ISBN 978-1-4516-9411-6
ISBN 978-1-4516-9413-0 (ebook)

For Phyllis, who is—and always has been—necessary to it all

CONTENTS

PART 9: LGBT AMERICAN CITIZENS

PART 10: "WHAT JUSTIFICATION COULD THERE POSSIBLY BE FOR DENYING HOMOSEXUALS THE BENEFITS OF MARRIAGE?"

PROLOGUE

On the morning of May 26, 1948, Professor E. K. Johnston was standing at the rostrum in a University of Missouri auditorium. The annual awards ceremony for the School of Journalism was in full swing. Best columnist, best sports writer, best feature writer—each award winner was called up to the stage, where Professor Johnston shook his hand and said kind and appropriate words as he bestowed a trophy of recognition. The professor had been on the University of Missouri faculty since 1924 and was now fifty years old, a man distinguished and comfortable in middle age, dressed formally in a light summer suit, spectacles balanced low on the bridge of his nose.

Professor Johnston had taken a place of honor on that stage because that academic year he'd served as acting dean of the School of Journalism. The elderly permanent dean, Frank Mott, had been on leave, and Professor Johnston was an apt choice as his temporary replacement: E. K. Johnston was a full professor, he was much loved and respected by students and colleagues alike,[1] and he had a national reputation as a multiterm president of a professional fraternity for those working in the relatively new discipline of the science of newspaper advertising.[2] Indeed, it was assumed by many at the University of Missouri that when the present dean retired, Professor Johnston would be named his permanent successor.

But as Professor Johnston was fulfilling his academic duties by shaking hands and wishing the aspiring young journalists continued success, he knew there was a warrant out for his arrest, issued by the county prosecutor.[3] He suspected too that the charge against him was commission of sodomy. But for the moment, he wanted only to get through the awards ceremony—to fulfill his last duty of the academic year to the students in his charge—and he did.

When the ceremony was over, Professor Johnston drove himself downtown, walked into the county prosecutor's office, and gave himself up. At his arraignment, he pleaded innocent. Thrown into the Boone County jail until he could raise bail, he spent two days behind bars.[4]

The county prosecutor, Howard Lang, had started the investigation six months earlier. There'd been a robbery, and a man was apprehended and brought in for questioning. It was he, Prosecutor Lang told the newspapers, who talked about a "homosexual ring" there in Columbia, Missouri, that carried on sex orgies. As happened often during police interrogations of homosexuals in the mid-twentieth century, police detectives grilled the robber until he named names. One of the names was Willie Coots, a thirty-nine-year-old gift shop employee. Coots was then brought in and was made to name more names. Each man that Willie Coots named was dragged in for questioning and grilled. A police department secretary took down in shorthand what each arrestee said, and she compiled a list of thirty names.[5]

Of all the men Coots named, the most interesting to the Columbia police, because of his prominence, was Professor E. K. Johnston. Coots confessed that he and the professor had lived together for ten years as lovers and for the last six years as friends. The police wanted more facts. Had he and Johnston held homosexual parties in their shared apartment? Yes, they had. More names; other homosexuals who'd had illegal congress with Johnston. Yes, he did remember some: just a few days earlier, there was a man named Warren Heathman. Heathman was a thirty-five-year-old World War II veteran who had fought overseas; he'd earned a master's degree in agriculture from the University of Missouri and was now an instructor for the Veterans Administration's farm training program.

Heathman could not be found at his home address, so the Columbia police sent out an all-points bulletin for his arrest. He was picked up by state highway patrolmen in Rolla, Missouri, about two hours away, and locked up overnight in Jefferson City's Cole County Jail. In the morning, patrolmen shackled him and drove him to the jail in Columbia, and he too was grilled. This was serious business, they told him. Perjury is a felony for which he could be incarcerated for five years. Willie Coots had mentioned a big fish: a professor at the university. Did Heathman know E. K. Johnston? When had he last seen him? Where?

Heathman, disoriented and scared, did not take long to answer every question they threw at him. Yes, he and Johnston engaged in homosexual activities. Yes, on an average of every other week. Yes, usually in Johnston's apartment. Yes, he'd been to homosexual parties not only in that same apartment but also at a cabin near Salem, Missouri. ("Mad parties of a homosexual cabal," the newspapers would report.[6]) Just as Willie Coots had done, Heathman signed a statement implicating Johnston as the leader of the "homosexual ring."

Heathman and Coots both waived their preliminary hearings; they did not want to drag out their ordeal. Because neither one was the supposed kingpin of the "homosexual ring," their bail was set at $2,500 apiece, $1,000 lower than Johnston's.[7] The professor, however, was not as easily intimidated. He had gone himself to the police station and demanded to know why there was a warrant out for his arrest. When police detectives took him into a room to interrogate him, he knew his rights. He would say nothing to his inquisitors except "I want to talk to my lawyer." He was permitted to call his attorney, Edwin Orr, who advised him not to sign any statement and not to waive his preliminary hearing.

From the Boone County Jail, he contacted his half brother in Kansas City, and a friend in Sedalia, Missouri, and borrowed money for the $3,500 bond.[8] In their coverage of the story, local newspapers were sure to name both Howard Johnston, the brother, and Fred Hildebrandt, the friend, shaming them for having aided and abetted a homosexual.

Family newspapers within a thousand-mile radius of Columbia all seemed to pick up the story, which was covered by the wire services of the Associated Press as well as the United Press International. The local papers embellished their articles with sensational headlines. "Missouri Professor Held for Sodomy: Termed Principal in Homosexual Ring" was the *Pottstown (PA) Mercury* headline.[9] The headline in Arkansas's *Hope Star* was simply "Homosexual," which was shocking enough all by itself in 1948.[10]

It was not until his temporary release from jail that Johnston learned that he'd been found guilty even before he was tried. "In view of the nature and gravity of the charges that have been made against Professor E. K. Johnston," the president of the university, Frederick Middlebush, told reporters, "he has been relieved of his duties as a member of the university."[11] Hysteria spread. The superintendent of the State Highway Patrol, Colonel Hugh Waggoner, announced not only to the university's board of curators but also to the media that Johnston was only the tip of the iceberg.[12]

The board of curators panicked. Allen McReynolds, its president, immediately called a press conference to promise the public, "The board will take such action as it deems necessary to protect the interests of the university." McReynolds added defensively that homosexuals were "a public problem, and one that ought to be solved."[13] Missouri's governor, Phil Donnelly, weighed in, assuring Missourians that he had ordered the president of the board of curators to confer with State Highway Patrol officials about the homosexuals they'd discovered and to make sure such people had no place on the university's faculty or among the student body.[14]

On November 17 Johnston stood before Judge W. M. Dinwiddie of the Boone County Circuit Court. Johnston's lawyer, Edwin Orr, had advised him that the prosecutor held in his hands multiple signed statements. He must throw himself at the mercy of the court. Johnston must have struggled to resign himself to this: How could he relinquish into perpetuity the image of the man he once was? How could he claim as his the character of a criminal? Orr promised that he would call witnesses who would talk about Johnston's good character and plead for clemency. The witnesses would tell the judge there was no point in sending a man like Johnston to jail. The ex-professor was by now emotionally and physically exhausted. He'd lost his job, his good name, his beloved students, his entire career— even his pension. He was fifty years old. What would he live on for the rest of his life? He had no more fight left in him. And if he did not confess to the world of being guilty of sodomy and then throw himself at Judge Dinwiddie's mercy, he would be locked in jail for who knew how many years to come.

Johnston pleaded guilty and did not open his mouth again for the rest of the trial. The principal witness for the defense was Dr. Edward Gildea, head of the Department of Psychiatry at Washington University in Saint Louis. Asked whether E. K. Johnston would be a menace to society if he were placed on probation, the psychiatrist said no, "though in my judgment he *is* a homosexual." He was followed by a long line of character witnesses. Each confirmed that Johnston had been widely respected and liked; that a penitentiary sentence would not help him nor serve society; that he could be turned free without detriment to society.[15]

The pleas for clemency were not without effect. Judge Dinwiddie wouldn't send the defendant to jail, he announced. He'd put him on probation for four years. Johnston must have felt a surge of relief, even joy. But the judge was not through. Johnston was required to post a $2,000 bond. It was his obligation to pay all court costs. Judge Dinwiddie ordered him to report regularly to Wayne Ballard, the state probation officer. Finally, Judge Dinwiddie concluded, "Your order of probation includes your cessation of all homosexual practices."[16]

There's a Women's Memorial at Arlington National Cemetery. It was erected in 1997 to honor the two million women who have served in the American military, past and present. It sits on the grand four-acre ceremonial entrance; and its elegant structure, with its lofty classical design and its arced ceiling made of glass tablets, is worthy of the solemn site. There's also an auditorium at the Women's Memorial, where ceremonies are held to recognize the outstanding achievements of female military personnel. In that auditorium, army colonel Tammy Smith was pinned with two stars: one on each epaulet, making official her promotion to brigadier general. A ceremony that celebrates a woman's rise to the rank of general is certainly rare, though not unheard of: there'd already been about fifty women generals or admirals serving in the US military. But the auditorium of the Women's Memorial had never yet seen quite such a ceremony as the one that took place on August 10, 2012.[17]

At four o'clock, as a soloist sang "The Star Spangled Banner," Smith, a short, slight, bespectacled woman who'd once been a senior parachutist and an airplane jump master, marched onto the stage together with her commanding officer, Major General Jack Stultz. Media cameras rolled and clicked. In General Stultz's ceremonial remarks he talked about why Smith had been promoted to her elevated position: she'd racked up a fruit salad of medals in her distinguished twenty-six years of service in the army, which included a stint in Afghanistan as chief of army reserve affairs. General Stultz praised "the values she epitomized" and her ability as a leader. She is, he said, "a quiet professional who just knows how to come in and take over."

Then the general introduced the guests of honor: first Smith's elderly father and then her spouse and her in-laws. Traditionally, the stars on a new general's epaulets are pinned by the two individuals most meaningful to that person. Smith stood at attention while her father pinned on one side and her spouse pinned on the other. Her in-laws too had an official role in the ceremony: they were chosen to remove the colonel's shoulder boards from Smith's uniform and replace them with a general's shoulder boards. Next, father and spouse unfurled a flag—red with a white star—which is to be flown wherever Smith will be stationed to announce that a general is present.

There was little about this traditional ceremony that was unique— except that the spouse, Tracey Hepner, was a woman. It was a brave act, not because Smith might be in danger of discharge or losing her new rank, but because never before in the entire history of the US military had it been done.

Smith had told General Stultz well in advance that she wanted her wife to be part of the pinning ceremony. "He didn't blink an eye," she recalled; nor did the Department of Defense. "This is your story. It's a good story. Don't be afraid to tell it," DOD officials said in encouraging her to respond to media requests for interviews about the inclusion of her wife in her promotion ceremony. "Tell them why it's important to have Tracey pin your star. Tell them what it means to you."[18]

What it meant, General Smith told the media, was that finally, with the repeal of "Don't Ask, Don't Tell," she was able to feel "full, authentic, and complete" by no longer having to keep secret who she was. She had no desire to grandstand—to make political "coming-out" declarations. Her wife's prominent role in the ceremony was Smith's clear and simple statement that "this is my *family*." Since Don't Ask, Don't Tell has been overturned, sexual orientation is considered a private matter by the Department of Defense. It's a private matter for General Smith as well—but, she said, participating with family in traditional ceremonies, such as the pinning ceremony, is both common and expected of a leader. By including her wife, she was doing no more and no less than what military leaders have always done at such ceremonies.

What long-fought battles, tragic losses, and hard-won triumphs have brought us as a country from the days when a much-loved and gifted professor could be disgraced, thrown in jail, and hounded out of his profession as soon as his private life was revealed, to the days when a military officer could marry the woman she loves in broad daylight and be promoted, in a very public ceremony, to the rank of general with her wife by her side? How does the amazing evolution in image and status of gays and lesbians, as well as bisexual and transgender people, affect all Americans? And what remains to be done before they will truly be first-class American citizens? These are the stories *The Gay Revolution* will tell.

A BRIEF HISTORY OF
CHANGING TERMINOLOGY

To nineteenth-century sexologists such as Richard von Krafft-Ebing and Havelock Ellis, men and women who were attracted sexually to the same sex, and those whose gender identity didn't match their anatomical sex, were all "sexual inverts." In the twentieth century, the sexologists' conflation of sexual orientation and gender identity was reflected in popular culture. For instance, the protagonist of Radclyffe Hall's 1928 novel, *The Well of Loneliness*, Stephen Gordon, who'd be considered "transgender" in our day, became the most famous fictional "lesbian" of the era.

Homosexual, another umbrella term coined by the sexologists in the nineteenth century, came into popular use in the twentieth century; it too made no distinctions, though in argot, all "effeminate male homosexuals" were called "queens"; "masculine female homosexuals" were called "butches," regardless of the *degree* of their male gender identity. Midcentury civil rights organizations, wanting to take the emphasis off the "sexual" of homo*sexual*, coined the term *homophile*.

Gay became an underground synonym for "homosexual" in the early twentieth century, encompassing men who were attracted to men, lesbians, people who'd later be called transgender, and bisexuals when they were acting homosexually. The first literary use of *gay* appeared in Gertrude

Stein's short story "Miss Furr and Miss Skeene," written in 1908, about the tumultuous lesbian relationship between two of her acquaintances, Ethel Mars and Maud Hunt Squire. When Stein published the story in *Vanity Fair* in 1922, few readers would have known the underground meaning of gay, though homosexuals active in the burgeoning subculture would have recognized that Stein's story, which plays with the word *gay* throughout, was an in-joke. The Stonewall generation, which preferred to describe itself as "gay," brought the term from the underground into popular consciousness in the 1970s.

About the same time, feminism prompted women who were sexually attracted to other women to distinguish themselves from male counterparts by bringing into popular use the term *lesbian* (from Lesbos, birthplace of Sappho). As the movement for civil rights grew in the 1980s, "gay and lesbian" became practically one word, which was also intended to imply transgender people.

The term *transgender* had been in occasional use since the 1970s; in the 1990s, *queer* was becoming the term of choice for many young people. In the late 1990s, the acronym *LGBT* (lesbian, gay, bisexual, transgender) came into use, as did LGBTQ, though "gay-and-lesbian" remained the most frequent descriptor, and was meant to be inclusive into the twenty-first century.

With the growing visibility of transgender people and the increasing willingness of bisexuals to identify themselves, LGBT became a popular term by the second decade of the twenty-first century. Other groups, in demanding recognition, have stretched the acronym as far as LGBTQQ-IAAP (which also includes Questioning, Intersex, Asexual, Allies, and Pansexual).

I've chosen to call this book *The Gay Revolution* because *gay* is still most widely understood as an umbrella term for a diverse community. However, in aiming for historical precision, I've tried to use the terms that were most current in each era I depict: whether *homosexual, homophile, gay, lesbian, lesbian feminist, gay-and-lesbian, LGBT,* and so on.

PART 1

SCAPEGOATS

Chapter 1

LAWBREAKERS AND LOONIES

"HOMOSEXUALIST PSYCHOPATHIC INDIVIDUALS"

Dr. Carleton Simon was an enlightened man. Though special deputy police commissioner for New York State since 1920, he opposed the death penalty, and he advocated the rehabilitation of criminals. He opened a psychiatric clinic to serve the mentally disturbed down-and-out of the Bowery; and he disputed the use of the "water cure," a torture technique devised by the US Army to interrogate prisoners during the occupation of the Philippines in World War II. He was a star among law enforcement officials and the medical establishment, and among society's upper crust, too.[1]

But Dr. Simon had his idiosyncrasies and prejudices. The bald, hulking doctor dabbled in phrenology. He assured his formidable audiences, including the New York Academy of Medicine and the New York State Association of Chiefs of Police, that a criminal could be identified even before he committed a crime by a drooping eyelid or a hanging corner of the mouth.[2] Simon was also an expert on race. "Negro criminals," he opined, were "dishonest, shiftless, and unreliable."[3] His 1947 lecture to the International Association of Chiefs of Police on "Homosexuals and Sex Crimes," a model of bigotry and flawed logic, passed for science that lay people accepted uncritically. The "born-male homosexualists," he asserted, are easy to spot by their female characteristics: their walk, body contour, voice, mannerisms, texture of skin, and also their interest in housekeeping and theatrical productions. The "women homosexualists" are fickle, always eager to add to their list of conquests, and are extremely jealous of the object of their lusts.

Though Simon granted that some homosexualists live as "decent members of society," many, he insisted, have psychopathic personalities, are indifferent to public opinion, and become "predatory prostitutes." He extolled the state of Illinois's treatment of "homosexualist psychopathic individuals" and recommended it be adopted everywhere. In Illinois, convicted "homosexualists" could be held as psychiatric prisoners until they "recovered." If they "recovered," they were then tried for having committed sodomy, which was punishable in that state by up to ten years in prison.[4]

Dr. Simon had influential counterparts all over the country, such as Dr. Arthur Lewis Miller, a Nebraska physician who was state health director. From that position of authority, Dr. Miller disseminated his theory about the homosexual's cycles of uncontrolled desire, which were as regular as women's menstrual cycles. "Three or four days in each month, the homosexual's instinct [for moral decency] breaks down, and he is driven into abnormal fields of sexual practice." Because the homosexual can't control himself, the doctor told the Nebraska State Medical Association, science must step in. "Large doses of sedatives or other treatment" were what Dr. Miller recommended to help the homosexual "escape from performing acts of homosexuality."[5]

When Dr. Miller was elected to the US Congress, he brought his ideas with him to Washington. As Congressman Miller, he authored a Sexual Psychopath Law for the District of Columbia.[6] The Miller Act, as it was called, passed both the House and the Senate without difficulty. It made sodomy punishable by up to twenty years in prison. It also mandated that anyone accused of sodomy (defined as either anal *or* oral sex) had to be examined by a psychiatric team. The psychiatrists would determine whether the accused was a "sexual psychopath"—one who through "repeated misconduct in sexual matters" had shown himself to be unable to control his sexual impulses. If a man were picked up several times by the DC police for cruising in Lafayette Park, for instance, the psychiatric team could diagnose him to be a "sexual psychopath," and he could be committed to the criminal ward of the District of Columbia's St. Elizabeth's psychiatric hospital, even before being allowed his day in court. Under section 207 of the bill, he would remain there until the superintendent of St. Elizabeth's "finds that he has sufficiently recovered." The Senate Committee on the District of Columbia called the Miller Act a "humane and practical approach to the problem of persons unable to control their sexual emotions."[7]

President Harry Truman signed Dr. Miller's bill into law in June 1948. Five months earlier, Alfred Kinsey's *Sexual Behavior in the Human Male* had been published. No one who was reasonably informed could have escaped knowing about Kinsey's book because it was reviewed in every major newspaper and magazine in the country. Kinsey's name became a household word. He and his team had interviewed 5,300 men, asking each of them over three hundred questions: the Kinsey Study found that 46 percent of American males admitted that as adults they'd "reacted" sexually to both males and females; 37 percent admitted to having had *at least* one homosexual "experience" as an adult; 10 percent said that as adults they'd been "more or less exclusively homosexual" for at least three years.[8]

Even those who chose to believe that Kinsey's numbers were inflated had to admit the likelihood that vast numbers of the male population were having sex with other men. But, in a stunning disconnect, lawmakers and the medical doctors who influenced them preferred to insist that people who engaged in such acts comprised a tiny distinct group, different from the rest of humanity. These "homosexuals" were lawbreakers and loonies, and they must be controlled.[9]

CONTROLLING THE LAWBREAKERS

About ten o'clock on the evening of September 4, 1959, Thomas Ferry, a strikingly well-built young man in tight jeans and a form-fitting T-shirt, walked into Tiger's, a beer-and-wine bar on Los Angeles's Sunset Strip. The routine wasn't new to him; he'd been in Tiger's five times in the last weeks. He sat down at the end of the long bar so that he could see the action, and he ordered a beer. Ten o'clock was early for a Friday night, and the crowd was thin. As Ferry sipped from his glass, he idly watched a shirtless man in his twenties, eyebrows penciled and eyes mascaraed, stand at the jukebox and feed it dimes, and then walk back to his seat with an exaggerated swishing of his hips. Ferry hadn't taken more than a few sips of his beer before the bartender placed in front of him another full glass. The bartender nodded in the direction of a man sitting a few stools away. The man, in his thirties perhaps, was smiling at Ferry. Ferry had been in Tiger's no more than ten minutes, but he knew he'd already caught his fish.

Ferry got up and walked over to where the man was sitting. "Thanks for the beer," he said. "Do I know you?" "No, but I'd like to know you," the man said. He introduced himself as Jim Cannon and offered his hand. Ferry shook hands warmly, and then pulled a business card from a back pocket and gave it to Cannon. The card said that the affable young man was Tom Ferry, a salesman. "Well, pleased to meet you, Tom," Cannon said, putting the card in his wallet.

"Let me buy *you* a drink now," Ferry said, standing close to Jim Cannon's bar stool.[10]

Two of Jim Cannon's friends who'd just come back from San Francisco walked into Tiger's and, spotting Cannon, came over to chat about their gay adventures up north. Ferry stood there patiently, listening. "Why don't you sit down," Cannon suggested, and Ferry took the stool next to him. In the dark of the bar, Cannon, still talking with his friends, put a hand on Ferry's knee. Ferry sat there. Cannon squeezed his thigh, stroked his pubic area, and Ferry still didn't move away.

After Cannon's friends went off to find a table, Ferry said casually, "Well, it's too dead in here for me. I think I'll leave. Do you want to go? My car's across the street."

"Yeah, swell!" Cannon said, flattered by the buff younger man's willingness. They left and crossed the street together. Officer Martin Yturralde, who was waiting in the unmarked car, got out to witness Thomas Ferry flash his officer's badge at James Cannon, pull out his handcuffs, and make the arrest. Officers Ferry and Yturralde deposited the stunned Cannon into the back of the car and drove him to the Hollywood police station, where he was asked to take out his wallet and show his identification. Officer Ferry plucked his "salesman" card from Cannon's wallet because he knew he'd be using it again.[11] James Cannon was charged under Penal Code 647.5: Vaglewd, which covered vagrancy as well as lewd and lascivious conduct.

Ferry's report was added to the record the Department of Alcoholic

Beverage Control had been building for months—reports of dozens of visits to Tiger's by undercover agents and officers. After the deputy attorney general of California examined their testimonies, he affirmed the ABC's recommendation. The bar's license was revoked.[12]

The California Department of Alcoholic Beverage Control had actually been created because of homosexuals. Before 1955, there was only an Alcoholic Beverage Commission, under the Board of Equalization. In 1951 the California Legislature authorized and pledged to finance a four-year study on "Sexual Psychopath Legislation" in twenty-three states and the District of Columbia.[13] Four years later, horrified (as they'd expected to be) by what the study told about homosexuals and their "victims," the legislators passed a constitutional amendment that created a Department of Alcoholic Beverage Control and added a section to the Business and Professions Code that said that a liquor license could be revoked if a place was a "resort" where "sexual perverts" congregated.[14]

The newly created ABC was charged with maintaining public safety in establishments that served alcohol—and homosexuality, the legislature and most of America agreed, was intensely injurious to the public. Undercover agents and vice squad police were sent out on fishing expeditions, to find any evidence that the ABC could use to close the doors of homosexual bars. In San Francisco, by the late 1950s, there were so many undercover officers and agents that some nights they made up 25 percent of the people in the bar. For several months in 1959, for instance, agents were sent to a small, sedate bar on Geary Street, the Criterion Lounge. According to the hearing transcript of the agents' testimony, one evening there were sixteen patrons and four undercover officers in the bar—each officer waiting for a patron to do something lewd to him.[15]

Lesbians were less likely than homosexual men to make a sexual move on a stranger after a brief conversation, but women agents and undercover officers were sent into lesbian bars as spies.[16] Almost as soon as the Alcoholic Beverage Control was established in 1955, vice squad officer Marge Gwinn was sent with another undercover policewoman, Helen Davis, to do surveillance on Pearl's, a lesbian bar that catered mostly to Latinas, for whom the place was like a social club. Gwinn passing for butch in boy's pants and short pomaded hair, and Davis passing for her femme, hit pay dirt after only a few nights. Lorinda Pereira, a young woman in a dress and high heels, plopped herself down on the lap of short-haired Dorothy Gardner, who was decked out in a man's shirt and fly-front trousers. Gardner petted Pereira's leg and then rested her hand somewhere near Pereira's pubic area—and Officers Gwinn and Davis quietly summoned their Oakland Police Department colleagues for a 1:30 a.m. raid. With a nod to the raiding police, the two officers identified the two women whose behavior was "injurious to public welfare and morals." Pereira and Gardner were the first to be taken out to the paddy wagon. At the station, they were charged under Penal Code 647.5, "vag-lewds," and were given suspended sentences of thirty days. Their "misconduct" was the heart of the ABC case to revoke Pearl Kershaw's liquor license and shut the bar down.[17]

At a time when bars were the only public place where homosexuals could congregate, the loss of any gay bar was no small thing. Yet there was almost no public protest among gay bar-goers when Pearl's was lost; nor when the North Coastal Area administrator of the ABC, Sidney Feinberg, declared a "vigorous" campaign to revoke the licenses of *all* gay establishments in the region. Feinberg, an imposing figure with a booming voice,[18] announced publicly that he'd put a dozen undercover agents to work, "gathering evidence."[19] But to protest, homosexuals would have had to admit they were part of a group called "perverts" and "psychopaths." Everywhere, homosexual anger was tamped down by shame and fear.[20]

If you let your homosexuality show, the streets were even more unsafe than the bars. George Barrett was a police officer with New York's Sixteenth Precinct. "Germs," "degenerates," and "perverts" he called the homosexuals and "other lawbreakers" he ran into on his beat around Times Square, an area he dubbed "the sewer." Barrett admitted to being "obsessed" with cleaning up the sewer and getting rid of the "germs." His language, and his looks too, were a caricature of the hard-boiled film noir cop: "If I can't get the best of a guy with punches, I'll kick him, and if he's a better kicker than I am, I'll go with the stick or the jack, and if I have to, I'll use my gun," he told James Mills, a reporter for *Life* magazine in 1965. Mills described him in a long, illustrated feature article as having eyes as cold as gun metal and a jaw as hard and square as a brick. Barrett liked the description. "My wife says I got a mean look too," he boasted. Most nights, Barrett roamed the area between Forty-Third and Forty-Fifth Streets, looking to bust homosexual prostitutes and their clients. He relished his work so much that he invited Mills to come along and watch the perverts with him.

"These animals, I'll eat them up!" he told the reporter, who shadowed him up and down the streets. Barrett pointed out a group of five women standing together in a doorway: prostitutes and heroin addicts, all of them lesbians, he snarled. On a side street off Broadway, Barrett stopped when he saw a knot of six young men, two of them in a heated altercation. "Are you males?" he growled, though he knew they were. "Yes," they said, startled by the sudden appearance of a cop. "Are you homosexual?" "Yes," they admitted. "Well, you germs walk up this street to Broadway and get lost. Don't come back." To the one who was the most aggressive, a black man, Barrett said, "I'm going to walk you around the corner to the subway, and you're going to run down that hole and get out of here, and if you ever come back, I'm going to drill you right between the eyes, you understand that?"

Even reporter James Mills was taken aback at Officer Barrett's violent threat to the young man. "Yeah, I was rough on him," Barrett agreed. "But I won't be hearing from his lawyers because the guy is an admitted homosexual."[21] Not one of *Life*'s millions of readers wrote to express their disapproval.[22]

CONTROLLING THE LOONIES

Poor or well-off; black, brown, or white; male or female—homosexuals were criminals or crazies or both. Vice squad officers Grimm and Beaudry spent the summer of 1962 cruising around the streets of downtown San Diego, protecting young sailors stationed at the naval base from the pitfalls of vice during their R & R. On the afternoon of July 1, they'd gotten a complaint, they said later, that "two Negro males" were extorting money from sailors by promising to hook them up with a female prostitute. At six o'clock the officers spotted a black man, Eldridge Rhodes, who fit the description of one of the supposed pimps. He was walking on Fifth and Market Streets in the company of Thomas Earl, a young white man who, though dressed in civvies, might be a sailor. Grimm and Beaudry parked their police car and tailed the two on foot for a block and a half, to one of the shabby downtown hotels. The plainclothes officers lingered in the doorway and saw the two men take the stairs up to a room on the second floor. The officers flashed their badges to the unnerved desk clerk and got the men's room number.

The door to room 214 was closed, but through an open transom Officers Grimm and Beaudry heard a bed squeaking and "kissing-type" noises. Grimm discovered that the door didn't fit tightly against the door frame, and there was a gap in the molding. Peering in, he could see the two men sitting on a bed, naked, embracing and kissing. When the men moved out of Grimm's sight line, Beaudry gave him a boost so he could peer through the transom for a better view. Oral copulation.

Beaudry, too heavy for a boost, rushed back downstairs to the desk clerk and demanded a stool; he needed to confirm what Grimm had seen.[23]

Thomas Earl and Eldridge Rhodes were tried in 1963, a decade and a half since Drs. Simon and Miller had called for the psychiatric institutionalization of those found guilty of homosexual crimes. By now in many states, facilities had been built and mechanisms put in place. In California, there was Atascadero State Hospital, constructed in 1954 at the cost to taxpayers of over $10 million (almost $100 million in today's money). Atascadero was a maximum-security psychiatric prison on the central coast where mentally disordered male lawbreakers from all over California were incarcerated. Inmates were treated at Atascadero by a variety of methods, including electroconvulsive therapy, lobotomy, sterilization, and hormone injections. Anectine was used often for "behavior modification." It was a muscle relaxant, which gave the person to whom it was administered the sensation of choking or drowning, while he received the message from the doctor that if he didn't change his behavior he would die.[24]

Earl and Rhodes were found guilty of violating Penal Code section 288a, which made oral copulation a crime in California that was punishable by up to fifteen years in prison.[25] A district court sent them to Atascadero for an indeterminate period. Thomas Earl fought to get a retrial on the grounds that Officers Grimm and Beaudry did not have a warrant when they spied on him and Rhodes and broke into their hotel room. An appeals court ruled that looking through a gap in a door and listening to noises that came through a transom did not violate legal procedures, and once the officers saw what they saw, they were right to break into the room.[26]

• • •

Sally Taft Duplaix[27] was a sophomore in 1956 at Smith, the rich-girl's college. Classy all-American girl looks, stylish, and smart too, Sally had even
been valedictorian at her posh high school. She seemed to fit perfectly into
the Smith environment, until another student reported to the dean that
she'd caught Sally and her roommate *in flagrante delicto*. Though wealthy
whites, especially females, didn't generally get arrested and committed to
state hospitals for being homosexual, as did people like Thomas Earl and
Eldridge Rhodes, they weren't unscathed by the widespread assumption
that homosexuality was a sickness and needed curing. A few years earlier, in
1952, that assumption had been made official in the American Psychiatric
Association's first *Diagnostic and Statistical Manual of Mental Disorders*, the
psychiatrist's bible. Homosexuality was "pathological behavior," the *DSM*
stated. Sally Duplaix was sent to the Smith College doctor, who informed
her parents that they must put their daughter under a psychiatrist's care.[28]

Duplaix's parents weren't uneducated, but they knew no more about
homosexuality than did most other straight people at midcentury. Their
knowledge on the subject came mostly from popular media—magazines
such as the widely read *Collier's*, which called homosexuality "the biggest
taboo," and associated it with "sexual maladjustment and sex crimes that
twist the lives of tens of thousands of people into patterns that are as pitiful
as they are ugly."[29] A flood of books and popular articles by psychoanalysts
such as Irving Bieber, Charles Socarides, and Edmund Bergler promised
that rescue was possible. With enough psychoanalysis (and the money to
pay for it) homosexuals could be transformed into heterosexuals. Duplaix's
parents found a psychoanalyst for her in Manhattan, and five days a week
she was to take the train in from the suburbs in order to be cured.[30]

Duplaix showed up dutifully, but she was uninterested and uncoopera-
tive, the doctor said. He told her parents she'd do better in a residential facility. He recommended Silver Hill Hospital in New Canaan, Connecticut,
a place that looked like a five-star hotel on a country estate. As well off as
Duplaix's parents were, they had to take out a second mortgage on their
home to afford the treatment. The facility specialized in super-rich alcoholics who came to dry out, but the doctor thought Duplaix would benefit from the multihour seven-day-a-week regimen of private and group
therapy. She didn't. She refused to stop saying that she was a homosexual

and was not ashamed. The Silver Hill staff recommended that she be sent to a private mental hospital, the Elmcrest Psychiatric Institute in Portland, Connecticut.

There Duplaix was heavily medicated. She received both insulin-shock and electroshock treatments. She was told that if she didn't behave, she'd be transferred to Littleton, the state asylum in the next town, which was far worse. She'd heard that lobotomies were sometimes performed to cure people of homosexuality, and she feared she'd be lobotomized.[31] "Little Miss Spoiled in the Snake Pit," she later said of her helplessness and dread at Elmcrest.

One evening Duplaix managed to escape, running through the autumn fields in search of a pay phone. She found one in a café not far from the hospital. She wanted to call her parents and beg them to get her out of Elmcrest. But the café was the first place the Elmcrest attendants looked for her. Before she could tell the telephone operator she wished to make a collect call, the attendants had bundled her into the hospital van and brought her back. From that point on, she was allowed to dress only in nightgown, bathrobe, and slippers, to assure she wouldn't attempt another escape.

In December 1956, after five months of shock treatments and heavy medication, Duplaix was released to her parents, who again put her in psychoanalysis. She died in July 2012, at the age of seventy-six, still a lesbian.

The "malevolent monsters of the 'mental health' establishment," she'd called the psychiatrists who treated her. But she'd overcome her anger toward her parents for throwing her to the monsters by telling herself that was what loving parents with some money and some sophistication did in the 1950s. It was no better and no worse, she theorized, than what poor or unenlightened parents did: they threw their homosexual children out into the streets.[32]

Chapter 2

AMERICA HUNTS FOR WITCHES

SCANDAL ON A TRAIN

On September 15, 1940, William Bankhead died. He was Speaker of the US House of Representatives and father of movie star Tallulah. After a memorial service in Washington, Bankhead's body was shipped to Jasper, Alabama, to be buried in his family's plot. President Franklin Delano Roosevelt ordered his entire cabinet to come with him to the burial. By thus honoring a southern politician Roosevelt was hoping to make a peace offering to the conservative Southern Democrats who were furious because he'd recently chosen as his running mate in the upcoming election the Left-leaning Henry Wallace. But on the presidential train returning to the capital, an incident occurred that would be distressing in the extreme to FDR.

The president's security men learned of it shortly after it happened, but they kept it secret from him. He heard about it anyway, directly from the Federal Bureau of Investigation head J. Edgar Hoover, and he worried. If the public learned of the incident, his chances of being reelected could be seriously damaged. No word of it leaked before the election seven weeks later, and FDR won an unprecedented third term. But the incident on the train triggered huge repercussions for decades after.

Secretary of State Cordell Hull had been unable to attend Bankhead's burial because he was ill, but the undersecretary had been sent in his stead. Sumner Welles was Harvard-educated and the scion of an aristocratic family that included a senator, two governors, a fabulously wealthy Astor, and even a Roosevelt. He was a tall, slender, patrician-looking man who sported Bond St. suits, silver-headed walking sticks, and a neatly trimmed moustache. He'd married appropriately (three times) and had two sons. He'd entered the US Foreign Service on the advice of FDR, at whose 1905 wedding Welles, then a twelve-year-old in short pants, had been a page. Early in his career, he negotiated protections for American investors in the Dominican Republic and he made peace among warring factions in Honduras. So it was not surprising that when Roosevelt became president, he named his old friend and distant relative to be ambassador to Cuba. When a feared socialist revolution was averted because the dictatorial Cuban president, Gerardo Machado, was persuaded to step down, Welles got the credit.[1]

That same year, 1933, Roosevelt nominated Welles to be undersecretary of state, and he easily won congressional approval. A short while later, he acted as the architect of the US–Latin American Good Neighbor Policy, which pledged that the United States would cease intervening in Latin American affairs but also strengthened lucrative trade agreements between the continents. By now it was widely agreed that Sumner Welles had a golden diplomatic touch, and it was assumed that when the perennially ailing secretary of state, Cordell Hull, retired, Welles would succeed him.[2]

On the night of September 17, 1940, on the presidential train back to Washington after Bankhead's interment, Sumner Welles had joined Henry Wallace and several other top Roosevelt men for dinner in the dining car. Drinking whiskey after whiskey to unwind from the long, hot day, Welles was more than a little tipsy when he staggered back to his sleeping compartment. He did not sleep. About four o'clock he rang for a porter. John Stone, a black man who was the senior Pullman porter on the train, answered the ring. Welles offered him money for sex. Stone politely turned him down and retreated. But the very drunk Welles would not stop ringing the buzzer that led from his room to the porters' quarters. Another porter finally came, and Welles made a move on him too and was refused. Again Welles rang the buzzer, and the fiasco was repeated with a third porter. In the porters' quarters, the men shared their stories, and then the three went together to report the incidents to the conductor, who informed the Secret Service men on board.[3]

The following spring, William Bullitt, a presidential advisor to FDR, showed up at the Oval Office brandishing a sheaf of documents. They were about the Pullman porter affair. He wanted the president to read them. Bullitt had found out about the scandal because one of the porters had filed a complaint with the Southern Railway Company that was headquartered in Bullitt's hometown of Philadelphia. The judge who received the documents supposedly implored Bullitt on his deathbed to make the story public.[4]

William Bullitt, a contentious and darkly brooding man, had several reasons for animosity to Undersecretary Welles. As a diplomat, Bullitt had negotiated relations between the United States and the Bolshevik regime, he'd been the first US ambassador to the Soviet Union and the ambassador to France, and he'd been Cordell Hull's special assistant—all of which had given him high hopes that he might someday be the one to succeed Hull as secretary of state. And then Sumner Welles became the man of the hour and dashed his dreams. But Bullitt had even more personal reasons to be resentful of Welles. Homosexuals had ruined his life. Ten years earlier, he'd learned that his wife, Louise Bryant, was having a lesbian affair with the English sculptor Gwen Le Gallienne. Bullitt and Bryant had a bitter divorce. He'd had to sue for custody of their daughter so the girl wouldn't be contaminated by "bad and dangerous company."[5] And now the State Department, in which he'd had a long proprietary interest, was in very "bad and dangerous company."

Roosevelt read the first page of what Bullitt handed him, said, "I know about this already," and handed back the documents.

Bullitt, puzzled that FDR wasn't more upset, blurted, "But Welles's actions open the way to criminal charges . . . This could menace the presidency by provoking a public scandal. He will be your Achilles heel."

Roosevelt answered that he was confident that no newspaper would publish anything about the affair,[6] and he'd make sure there'd be no criminal charges. At J. Edgar Hoover's suggestion, he'd already assigned a "bodyguard" to go around with Welles and prevent him from propositioning any more men.[7]

"Mr. President, you're thinking of asking Americans to die in a crusade for all that's decent in human life," Bullitt kept on. "You can't have among the leaders of that crusade a criminal like Welles." Bullitt's list of reasons why the president must get rid of Sumner Welles went on and on. FDR, appalled and sickened, would hear no more. He ended the meeting. He canceled the rest of his appointments for that day and went back to the presidential bedroom to lie down.[8]

Bullitt found a more open ear in the secretary of state. Cordell Hull was resentful of Sumner Welles, who shared blue bloodlines and a deep friendship with the president and seemed always to be favored by him. Since FDR would not act himself to put Welles down, Hull ordered the very-willing Bullitt to pass the Pullman porter documents on to Republican senator Owen Brewster of Maine. Brewster, an adversary of FDR's, did what Hull and Bullitt had hoped he would: he threatened the president with a senatorial inquiry unless Welles was fired.[9] The president, contemplating a run for a fourth term, knew his enemies would revel in the enormous scandal.

As soon as Sumner Welles, ever a faithful friend to the president, understood what was at stake, he didn't have to be asked to turn in his resignation.[10]

But FDR had a chance to vent his rage on William Bullitt. Sometime later, when the former ambassador to France was hoping to make a run for the job of mayor of Philadelphia, he asked for the president's endorsement. FDR famously responded to the outrageously tone-deaf request, "If I were the angel Gabriel, and you and Sumner Welles should come before me seeking admission into the Gates of Heaven, do you know what I'd say? I would say, 'Bill Bullitt, you have defamed the name of a man who toiled for his fellow man, and you can go to hell.' And that's what I tell you to do now!"[11] To the Democratic leaders in Philadelphia, Roosevelt said, "Cut his throat!"[12] Bullitt lost the mayoral race by a wide margin.

But satisfying as FDR's rage-fest must have felt to him, the Sumner Welles incident with the Pullman porters became the ripple that began the tidal wave of Washington's homosexual witch hunts.

KEEPING OUR NATION SAFE

Vice President Harry Truman assumed the presidency after FDR's death in April 1945. He inherited the virulent animosity of the Right and their smear campaigns about "creeping socialism" from which Roosevelt had suffered. Truman realized that if he hoped to be elected in 1948, he would have to show himself to be as good a Cold War Warrior as any conservative Republican or Southern Democrat. To that end, on March 21, 1947, he signed Executive Order 9835, the Federal Employee Loyalty Program, which established review boards to work within all government agencies in order to fire any employee or not hire any job applicant suspected of being in any way "disloyal" to the United States.

John Peurifoy had been named assistant to the undersecretary of state the year before Truman signed Executive Order 9835. Unlike many State Department officials whose youths had been spent at Groton and Harvard (such as the effete Sumner Welles), Peurifoy had been a South Carolina farm boy. He prided himself on being a self-made man. Peurifoy had had to work as a night cashier in a restaurant to support himself when he was young, but his dreams were always grandiose. He would someday be the president of the United States, he'd announced in his high school yearbook.[13] When Peurifoy first came to Washington, he'd spent his days toiling as an elevator operator in the US Senate Building and his evenings sitting in college classes. In 1938, at the age of thirty-one, he landed a job at the State Department as a $2,000-a-year clerk, but a few years later he'd quadrupled his salary and was raring for further advancement.

The wildly ambitious Peurifoy, given to wearing flamboyant neckties that a *Saturday Evening Post* reporter described as capable of "blinding a prairie dog at fifty paces,"[14] ostensibly saw his main chance in the galloping postwar paranoia about threats to American safety, security, and normalcy. A clerk during the Sumner Welles debacle, he remembered the panic at State that homosexuals could be blackmailed by foreign powers to give up state secrets—and how FDR had virtually tied Cordell Hull's hands. Now Peurifoy blasted the State Department's Division of Security and Investigations for still being dangerously lax. He asked for and got permission from Secretary George Marshall to do what should have been done years ago: deal "in a direct and forthright manner" with the problem of homosexuality among State Department employees.[15] Truman's 1947 executive order gave Peurifoy the firepower he needed.

Peurifoy started an investigation of an unmarried, dandified State Department employee who, scuttlebutt said, had proclivities like those of Sumner Welles. Like the interrogation of Willie Coots in Columbia, Missouri, that led to the downfall of Professor E. K. Johnston and many more Columbia homosexuals, the first homosexual grilled was forced to cough up the names of all the homosexual employees he knew, and those were forced to cough up the names of all whom they knew.[16] Peurifoy ordered that two investigators on the staff of the Security Division be assigned full-time to do nothing but detect homosexual employees and make "thorough and comprehensive inquiry" into their lives.

A couple of years later, Secretary of State George Marshall elevated John Peurifoy to the position of undersecretary of state for administration, the third-ranking position in the entire department. He was given complete jurisdiction over hirings, firings, and the "elimination of Communists and other dubious characters" from State.[17] He excelled in his duties, especially with regard to "dubious characters." If a male applicant was unmarried or in the least effeminate, Peurifoy ordered that his history be scrutinized—friends, coworkers, employers, all would get visits from State Department investigators trained in finding out whether the applicant was a pervert. Ninety-one employees were soon fired. "The Man Who Runs the State Department," the *Saturday Evening Post* called Peurifoy in 1949, and observed that he was "looked upon with favor, even affection, by both Republicans and Democrats."[18]

February 1950: Dean Acheson, who had succeeded George Marshall as secretary of state, was asked to appear before the Senate Appropriations Subcommittee. He was accompanied by John Peurifoy as his hiring-and-firing man. Acheson thought he'd been invited to speak in support of his department's request for appropriations. But instead, he was ambushed. For two hours, Republican senators William Knowland, Styles Bridges, and Homer Ferguson—sworn foes of President Truman and Truman's appointees—rancorously accused Acheson of tolerating disloyalty because he wasn't quick enough to condemn his friend Alger Hiss as a Communist spy.[19]

"Would a friend of a person who is a member of a Communist front be a security risk?" Bridges asked, impugning Acheson's loyalty. "Would a person known to associate with members of a Communist front be a security risk?" Bridges kept on, intending to humiliate the now seething Acheson. The senators demanded Acheson turn over the State Department's "loyalty files" to their crony Senator Joseph McCarthy, who'd grabbed headlines a few weeks earlier when, speaking to the Republican Women's Club in Wheeling, West Virginia, he waved a piece of paper in the air and shouted, "I have here in my hand a list of two hundred five Communists who are still working for the State Department!"[20]

John Peurifoy, hoping to give his besieged boss a respite, asked to speak and offered a distracting token. The State Department had, in fact, already gotten rid of 203 people who seemed to be security risks, he told the senators. Ninety-one of them were in the "shady category, mostly homosexuals."[21]

It created a conflagration. Ninety-one homosexuals in the State Department. Who had hired them, and how many more were there? And where else in government were they? Two Senate Appropriations Subcommittee members immediately volunteered to do a preliminary study: Republican Kenneth Wherry and Southern Democrat Lister Hill. They would hold closed hearings on the extent of the problem of homosexuals on US government payrolls. "We have a chance for an educational job about sexual deviations comparable to what the Surgeon General's Office has done on venereal disease," Hill told the press. Homosexuality needed eradicating no less than syphilis.[22]

Wherry and Hill interviewed more than a score of government officials about homosexuals, or "moral weaklings" as they were alternately dubbed in Wherry's report to the Appropriations Subcommittee.[23] The star of their interviews was "tough, old Lt. Roy E. Blick," as *Newsweek* called him[24]—an eighteen-year veteran of the DC police department, a true believer in the evils of perversion, whose "Pervert Elimination Squad" employed four men to do nothing but detect and arrest homosexuals.

"Out of your eighteen years' experience, how many homosexuals do you think there are in the District of Columbia?" Wherry asked the lieutenant.

"There are 3,750 perverts employed by government agencies,"

Lieutenant Blick declared confidently—though he later admitted that his precise figure was really "a quick guess,"[25] based on his "own judgment" that there were about 5,000 homosexuals in DC and about 75 percent of them worked for the government.[26] In the hysterical popular press, Blick's figure grew exponentially: "There are at least 6,000 homosexuals on the government payroll," the book *Washington Confidential* announced, "and these comprise only a fraction of the total of their kind in the city."[27] The *New York Post* didn't settle for guesstimates: the Office of Naval Intelligence had the exact number, the *Post* announced: 7,859.[28]

"Is a homosexual, because he is a moral pervert, one that is an easy prey for blackmail?" Senator Wherry prodded Lieutenant Blick to expound on the dangers homosexuals posed to national security.

The lieutenant cooperated. "I would say that anything I want from an individual who is a pervert, I could get," he answered. "I could get it quicker by the approach of exposing him than I could by offering him money."

With such evidence in hand, Senator Wherry declared breathlessly to the Appropriations Subcommittee that "the guarding of government secrets upon which the life of our Republic may depend is lax. This sordid situation will shock the American people when they are given these facts!"[29]

Members of the subcommittee read Wherry's report and concurred. They wasted no time in making a unanimous recommendation to the Senate. The entire executive branch of government must be thoroughly investigated for homosexuals—and a system must be put in place so that if an employee is fired from his job because he is homosexual, he won't be able to turn around and find work in another government agency; he will be forever debarred from all federal jobs.[30]

The Senate agreed with Appropriations. A new Senate subcommittee was formed, with Clyde Hoey of North Carolina as its head. Republican senator Margaret Chase Smith, the only woman in the Senate, would serve as well. "Pervert Inquiry Ordered," the *New York Times* announced to the public.[31]

Members of the House of Representatives weighed in too. Dr. Arthur L. Miller—the physician-congressman from Nebraska whose Miller Act threw convicted DC homosexuals into St. Elizabeth's for indeterminate periods—ignited his fellow lawmakers by emoting on the House floor about what he'd been told by "a gentleman from the CIA": "Mr. Göring of Germany had a complete list of all the homosexuals in the State Department, Department of Commerce, and Department of Defense. They knew who to contact when they came over here on espionage missions," Miller asserted. "The danger of spies, the danger of blackmail, the fear of blackmail, has caused these people to sabotage our government!" No one among his listeners interrupted to ask for evidence: "And the Russians have the same list of homosexuals! They know who to contact when they come over here too!" he declaimed.[32]

The general public, fed on news of the ninety-one firings and hints of even more pervasive perversion at State, weighed in daily. A *Washington Post* reporter doing an inquiry of people standing in line for concert tickets asked one man where he worked. "The State Department," the man answered sheepishly. Everyone in earshot burst into sniggering laughter. Another reporter got into a taxi and said, "Take me to the State Department, please." The driver turned around in his seat to caution his passenger, "Fruits, the whole place is full of fruits."[33]

The State Department stepped up its homosexual hunts; the Civil Service Commission pitched in. Together they scrutinized the files of the FBI, the vice squad, and the DC Park Police, and they created a master list of homosexuals to be purged. "Panic on the Potomac," *New York Post* writer Max Lerner called it in a multipart series in July 1950.

By November 1950, five hundred more federal employees, not just in DC but in offices all over America, had been fired or forced to resign.[34] That was only the beginning. In December Senator Hoey and his subcommittee issued their report: a spectacular conglomeration of pseudoscience, circular reasoning, moralism, prejudice, and scapegoating. The committee had consulted "eminent" psychiatrists and physicians, the report said, and they agreed that the indulgence in sexually perverted practices is a sign of a personality which has failed to reach sexual maturity. The subcommittee also took testimony from representatives of the FBI, CIA, and the intelligence services of the army, navy, and air force. All concurred that homosexuals constituted a security risk since homosexual acts are criminalized under federal, state, and municipal statutes; persons who commit such acts are violators and outcasts; and because acts of sexual perversion weaken the moral fiber, homosexuals will give in to blandishments by foreign espionage agents and to blackmail. On top of all that, homosexuals have a "corrosive effect" on other government workers because "these perverts will frequently attempt to entice normal individuals to engage in perverted practices."[35]

To his fellow senators Hoey granted that when hunting for homosexuals, errors might be made, some employees might be falsely accused and fired; nevertheless, he said, for the sake of the nation's security, "the American people are entitled to have errors of judgment on the part of their officials resolved on the side of caution"—that is, better to get rid of whatever number of "innocents" than to allow real homosexuals to slip through the cracks.[36]

President Truman was largely silent on the issue. Even if he thought that Washington was running amuck in mass hysteria, there was little he could say. It was as deadly to be soft on homosexuals as it was to be soft on Communists.[37]

HOUSECLEANING

Truman's successor was not silent. "Let's Clean House with Ike and Dick" was a major campaign slogan of Republican presidential candidate Dwight D. Eisenhower (nicknamed Ike) and his running mate, Richard Nixon. One of Eisenhower's first presidential acts, in April 1953—he'd been in office barely three months—was to sign into law Executive Order 10450. The order specifically named as "security risks" not only Communists and subversives but those who behaved badly—the dishonest, the immoral, drunks and drug users, and sexual perverts.

Liberal Republican senator Clifford Case from New Jersey—a strong supporter of civil rights for Negroes and a passionate critic of Senator McCarthy's Communist witch hunts—complained on CBS's *Face the Nation* that the executive order did not go far enough. Homosexuals, because they were immoral and illegal, should be removed not just from sensitive positions where there was concern about blackmail, Senator Case said, but from *all* government positions.[38]

•   •   •

In the first half of the twentieth century, middle-class lesbians, who rarely went to gay bars or walked the streets in male garb, were seldom hassled by police or anyone else. If you didn't hang out in dangerous places or look like a butch stereotype, a little discretion was all that was needed to stay safe. Until the lavender witch hunts, when middle-class lesbians who were employed in the few professional jobs open to women—teacher, social worker, nurse, government worker—became victims, too.

When Betty Deran was twenty years old, she signed up for the Women's Army Corps (WAC). It was 1951. There was a war going on in Korea, she was very patriotic, she wanted to see the world—and she'd just sat through an alarming closed-door meeting with the dean of women at Northwestern University, where she was a student. A jealous roommate had told the housemother in their dorm that Deran was having a lesbian affair with another student. It was true. The housemother spoke to the dean, who summoned Deran and her lover to come to her office posthaste. The dean leveled charges, and the two young women denied them. Nothing was provable, so they were warned but not expelled. But Deran was so shaken that she left Northwestern for the WAC.[39]

In the military, she was an aide to a WAC major who, Deran sensed, was "a little bit too fond of me." But the major was ordered by the general to whom she reported to break up a "nest of lesbians" in her company, and she did. Deran thought that those who were caught "were just damn stupid to be so blatant and open." She left the military with an honorable discharge and went back to school on the GI Bill of Rights. In 1961 she got a PhD in Economics from the University of Michigan.

It was a time when there were few women PhDs and almost none in so male-dominated a field. But with her superlative credentials, Deran was hired by the Treasury Department as a tax economist. It was a plum job, reserved for PhDs from the most elite universities—virtually unheard of for a female in that era. With the woman who'd become her lover, Alma Routsong (who would later write the lesbian classic *Patience and Sarah* under the nom de plume Isabel Miller[40]), Deran moved to Washington, DC. Effervescent and outgoing, deservedly sure of herself and her talents, Deran kept her lover a secret and fit in well at Treasury, despite being the only woman in her department and a head shorter than any of her colleagues.

She'd been at the Treasury Department several months, and things were going swimmingly. She was working with eminent economists, people who'd come to Treasury from professorships at Yale and Harvard, such as Stanley Surrey, who was considered the greatest tax scholar of his generation. John F. Kennedy was president, and once in a while Deran's boss, Harvey Kooten, dropped by her office with an exhilarating tidbit such as, "Well, I was talking to JFK. He liked your memo." Deran's only worry—a niggling bit of anxiety—was when she realized she still hadn't been notified that her security clearance had been okayed.

When she'd come to DC for an interview, she was told that everyone employed at Treasury must get clearance—it was merely routine, they'd said. But month after month went by, ten months, and Deran still had no word about having been cleared. "Do you realize I haven't gotten my clearance yet?" she finally told Harvey Kooten over coffee. She'd known before she took the job that being homosexual could be a problem if one worked in a "sensitive" government position. But it never occurred to her that working for the Treasury Department, making decisions about mineral taxation, "would be a job considered vital to the security of the United States."[41]

"Well, the holdup on your clearance must just be some bureaucratic tangle," Kooten told her. But a few days later, he came into her office and closed the door behind him. He was visibly upset. "I just discovered that your clearance papers have been sitting in the code box." That meant she was being investigated. "For homosexuality," he was told. He had no idea what triggered the investigation. Nor did she. Had a Civil Service Commission check turned up the Dean of Women—that unsettling meeting at Northwestern when Deran was twenty years old? Since the early 1950s, when John Peurifoy started the policy at State, if anything about a federal employee in a professional position aroused suspicion—male effeminacy, short hair on a woman, no spouse—investigators questioned landlords, past bosses, acquaintances, people from the employee's childhood even. They even placed employees under surveillance to determine whether they frequented "homosexual places" or associated with "known homosexuals."[42]

"Betty, please be careful," Kooten said. He was clearly on her side. But she *had* been careful. She wasn't "blatant and open," like the WACs in her unit who'd been caught. She didn't go to bars or hang out with obvious types or even talk about being gay to anyone she didn't know well.

"Couldn't we just send Dr. Deran to a psychiatrist or something to keep her?" Stanley Surrey (who'd become assistant secretary of the Treasury that year) suggested when he learned of the problem.

She ended up leaving the Treasury Department and going to New York to take a job for which a bachelor's degree was enough qualification—and where everyone knew "the only reason they could hire me was because I was gay and couldn't get a clearance, and I didn't have much choice."[43]

Witch-hunt fever didn't infect every politician in Washington, but those who tried to fight it were sorely defeated—even seasoned men like Senator Millard Tydings of Maryland. Tydings was first elected to the legislature in 1922, when he was thirty-two years old. In July 1950, when he'd been there almost thirty years, he headed a Senate subcommittee to examine McCarthy's allegations of the infestation of subversives at the State Department. In a thunderously angry two-and-a-half-hour speech, which the *Washington Post* described as "one of the bitterest and most bare-fisted personal denunciations ever delivered on the Senate floor," Tydings warned his colleagues that they'd been "hoaxed" by McCarthy's "false and vile charges." He implored them to take "remedial action." He called McCarthy's henchmen, such as Wherry and Hoey, "men of little character who would prefer to serve their own ends rather than their country." When his speech was over and the senators got up to leave, the incensed Kenneth Wherry, bumping into a member of Tydings's subcommittee at the door, hurled an "unprintable epithet" at him, as the *Washington Post* reported; and when the Democratic senator from Texas, John Connally, admonished Wherry "not to do such things on the Senate floor," Wherry slugged him.[44]

But that was nothing compared to what the McCarthy faction cooked up over the next few months, when Tydings was running for reelection: it distributed all over Maryland a doctored photograph that spliced together two separate pictures: one of Tydings taken in 1938, and one of Earl Browder, a former leader of the Communist Party USA, taken in 1940. The picture they manufactured appeared to be one of Tydings cozying up to Browder, whom he'd never met personally. In the paranoid climate of post–World War II America, the phony photo did the trick. After three decades in the legislature, Tydings was defeated in that November's election.[45]

McCarthy tactics were disturbing even to some conservative

Republican politicians such as Harry Cain, senator from Washington State, who'd been a friend and early supporter of Joseph McCarthy and had even served on the Subversive Activities Control Board. By the mid-1950s, Cain was disgusted. McCarthy's skill in "whipping his audience into a frenzy" reminded Cain of another orator he'd seen in 1935 in Germany, Adolf Hitler. Investigations of government employees who were "messenger boys, grain inspectors, librarians, and cancer specialists" were "sheer foolishness," Cain warned. In an article in the mass-circulation magazine *Coronet*, he objected that "any suspicion of sex deviation" was bringing on a corps of security investigators and even a full-scale FBI check. He told of two young women whose jobs had nothing to do with protecting the nation's security, but they were anyway being "hideously tortured" by a security officer who asked them "the most intimate and revolting questions and bullied them mercilessly." It was "gestapo tactics," or like a "lynching bee," Cain protested. And he pleaded that the government come to its senses and stop hounding people who were not even employed in sensitive positions.[46] Cain's protests in a national magazine had no effect whatsoever. Investigations for homosexuality spread far outside the Beltway.

Tens of thousands of people lost their jobs.[47] The firing of homosexual workers from nongovernmental positions was so ubiquitous, and their chances of being hired after losing a job so slim, that by 1956 the incipient homophile press was lamenting the "tragic plight" of many of its readers. They'd come to the end of their unemployment benefits, their savings had run out, and no matter their talents or training or work experiences, they couldn't get a job because "their character investigation didn't stand up."[48]

Investigation fever seized even small businesses that had not the slightest connection to the government. National companies sprang up whose sole function was to serve employers by snooping into the background of employees or would-be employees and reporting anything that hinted at homosexuality or other undesirable traits such as drunkenness and dope addiction. One such company, Fidelifacts, made up of former FBI agents, sold their skills with a panic-inducing brochure that demanded "Do You Know Who You Are Hiring?" America had succumbed to "morality" hysteria.

Chapter 3

NO ARMY OF LOVERS: TOWARD
A HOMOSEXUAL-FREE MILITARY

A RETIRED REAR ADMIRAL MAKES HISTORY

For weeks during the winter of 1957, four agents from the Office of Naval Intelligence commandeered a house on Coronado, a little island off San Diego. They were engaged in a security mission, they told the owners. Through holes in a fence, the intelligence officers peeked beyond the bird-of-paradise plants and bougainvillea bushes in the neighboring garden and spied into the suspect's living room. To see what was happening in an apartment above the garage, they went up to the second floor of the home they'd taken over and used binoculars and periscopes to peer through windows.[1]

What they saw the first night was a fine foretaste of what they'd hoped to see: not a rogue sailor selling state secrets to the Russians, but a retired rear admiral, Selden Hooper, dancing with Roscoe Braddock, a twenty-two-year-old seaman who lived with Hooper when Braddock wasn't at sea. The two men kissed. Then Hooper turned out the lights.

The intelligence agents agreed it was worth coming back a second night. They were disappointed that nothing of interest happened that night, or the following one; but their job entailed infinite patience. On the fourth night, they were rewarded. The slim and still-dashing six-foot-tall Hooper was having dinner with two young men: Braddock and enlisted sailor John Schmidt.

Roscoe Braddock left after dinner, and the sailor and Hooper went out to walk Hooper's dog. The four intelligence officers waited patiently. Then the sailor and Hooper came back and had a few drinks. Then they watched television. The four intelligence officers waited some more. Finally, Hooper and Schmidt kissed, and undressed, and turned off the lights. That was quite a bit already, but the intelligence officers wanted even more. They returned night after night, peering through cracks and binoculars and periscopes, and taking notes and pictures.

In April retired rear admiral Selden Hooper was officially notified by navy counsel that the commandant of the Eleventh Naval District, Rear Admiral Charles Hartman, was filing charges against him for having violated the Uniform Code of Military Justice. He was being charged under Article 125 (sodomy), Article 134 ("conduct of a nature to bring discredit on the armed forces"), and Article 135 ("conduct unbecoming to an officer and a gentleman").

Three weeks later, Hooper was called to the US Naval Station on the mainland, where he had to sit in the courtroom and listen as one witness after another testified in front of a court-martial board. Hooper was making history. Retired admirals had never before been brought up in front of a court-martial board and prosecuted under the Uniform Code of Military Justice.

The military had been Hooper's life since 1921, when at the age of seventeen he left his San Francisco high-society mother and stepfather to enlist in the National Guard. Two years later, the handsome and gentlemanly Hooper entered the US Naval Academy in Annapolis. Upon graduating, he joined the US Navy as an ensign; he made lieutenant in good time. Then in 1937, at thirty-three, still a bachelor when most American men were married by twenty-five, he took a wife, the daughter of a wealthy paper manufacturer in the east. Their marriage, a high-profile society wedding,[2] ended four years later when America entered into the war. He was made commander of the newly built naval destroyer *Uhlmann*, and he saw action in Okinawa, Formosa, and the Philippines.

On August 12, 1944, on a moonless, overcast night, Japanese bombers and torpedo planes attacked Hooper's task group in the waters around the Philippines. He ordered his ship's antiaircraft guns to open fire on enemy planes. Under his command, seven Japanese aircraft were downed during that one night. Captain Hooper was credited with having averted a crippling attack on a crucial fleet of American amphibian ships that were supporting allied positions.[3] Secretary of the Navy James Forrestal pinned the Silver Star on Hooper's chest, which took its place among two bronze stars, an American Defense medal, a Philippine Liberation medal, and a rainbow of commendation ribbons and valor ribbons. After the war, he became head of the Naval Reserve's Eleventh Naval District, which included Arizona, New Mexico, Nevada, and Southern California. At his retirement in 1948, at the age of forty-four, Selden Hooper was bumped up to the rank of rear admiral, a "tombstone" recognition, as the military called it, of his exceptional performance in active combat and his twenty-five years of distinguished service.

But a few years later, a young sailor, caught by the law in one of the usual ways—entrapped in a bar or on a street or spied on in a men's room—was grilled by the authorities and made to name names. In a familiar scenario, one of the names he named was a man of some prominence. The young sailor's inquisitors were thrilled. A big fish would be caught— a rear admiral who threw parties in his home for "persons known to be sexual deviates."

Hooper was no longer on active duty. His lawyers demanded to know what jurisdiction the military could possibly have over what he did in the privacy of his own home. The navy's lawyers responded that even though Hooper had retired, he'd been entitled to wear the uniform and draw the pay of a naval officer. And retired officers are part of the nation's national defense effort; therefore they're subject to court-martial the same as active-duty officers.[4] To assure there was no way Hooper could wriggle loose, Rear Admiral Hartman, the commandant who'd initiated the court-martial proceedings, ordered that Hooper be nominally reinstated to active-duty status.

Witnesses were called to testify against Hooper at a court-martial panel. Roscoe Braddock was forced to admit under oath that he and Hooper had shared a bed. (Intelligence agents had already supplied that information to the panel.) But they'd never engaged in sodomy, Braddock insisted. Then he chose to take any punishment the court would mete out to him rather than say more.[5] Others, young men who'd been scared into baring all they knew, testified they'd seen Hooper embracing men, or they'd seen two men kissing in Hooper's home. Some gave graphic details about their own acts of sodomy with Hooper.[6]

Hooper's lawyer called scores of character witnesses to counter those damning testimonies: Hooper had a sterling record in the military. He was an upstanding citizen. They called members of the Kiwanis Club, the Lions Club, the American Red Cross, the chamber of commerce, all organizations to which Hooper belonged, and the witnesses testified that he'd worked unstintingly to help rehabilitate juvenile delinquents and serve the community. The lawyers called Hooper's elderly mother, Rose Hooper, at that time a well-known painter of society women's portraits. She lived in an apartment in her son's home, she told the panel, and she was certain he was not a homosexual. They called a psychiatrist from San Diego County Hospital who also testified that Hooper was not a homosexual.

Rear Admiral Hartman sat in the courtroom through all of it, unsmiling but confident. A couple of years earlier, he'd stripped the rank and benefits of an honorably discharged naval lieutenant who'd been accused of joining leftist organizations after he left the service. An appeals court upheld Hartman. "Whatever may be the guarantees of civilian life," the court declared, "the armed forces are not required to tolerate the typical tergiversations of the alleged subversive,"[7] and if he was drawing a military pension, he had to abide by military rules, no matter that he was no longer on active duty. Rear Admiral Hartman could be sure of the strength of his case against Selden Hooper now because homosexuals were even lower than subversives in the court's regard.

An officer of flag rank, as Hooper was, cannot be court-martialed without the agreement of a Military Board of Review and the Court of Military Appeals. Both bodies affirmed the decision of the court-martial panel. Even retired officers form a vital segment of our national defense, the chief appeals judge agreed in explaining his court's 3-to-0 decision. "The salaries they receive are not solely recompense for past services but a means devised by Congress to assure their availability and preparedness in future contingencies."[8] That meant that Hooper could be stripped of his pension and all other veterans' benefits, too.[9]

The final decision rested with the commander in chief of the armed forces, president and former general Dwight Eisenhower. But he'd declared "sexual perverts" enemies of the nation's security within his first months in office; his opinion was predictable. Selden Hooper became the only admiral of the US Navy to be convicted by court-martial.

SERIOUS AND NOT-SO-SERIOUS HOMOSEXUAL-HUNTING IN THE ARMED FORCES

The American military had been homosexual hunting since 1919, when the assistant secretary of the navy, thirty-seven-year-old Franklin Delano Roosevelt, assigned special investigators to the Intelligence Office at the Naval Training Station in Newport, Rhode Island. Roosevelt had gotten complaints that sailors were engaging in "scandalous conduct" with male civilians at the Newport Art Club and the YMCA, and he ordered the investigators to ferret out homosexual behavior by conducting "a most searching and rigid investigation," in which the very zealous investigators didn't scruple to entrap the homosexuals by indulging in sex acts with them, to the point of ejaculation.[10] This was the first massive "sexual pervert" witch hunt in America.

The following year, 1920, the military code of conduct, Articles of War, officially criminalized the commission of any homosexual act by a service member;[11] but few people were charged. In the army, for instance, only about seventy-five soldiers were court-martialed for sodomy each year.[12] It was only with the start of World War II that the US Selective Service tried to get serious about eliminating all men with "homosexual proclivities." At induction centers, recruits were asked whether they were homosexual, made to bend over and spread their cheeks, and observed for feminine mannerisms. Five thousand were weeded out.[13] But as the war progressed and manpower was desperately needed, scrutiny became halfhearted. Most men with "homosexual proclivities" slipped through. So did most lesbians who wanted to enlist.[14]

In the middle of the war, War Department Circular 3 made the military's ambivalent policy toward homosexuals clear. Those homosexuals who were "reclaimable" were to be hospitalized and treated; if the treatment was successful, they were to be restored to duty. The Circular emphasized that "the mere confession by an individual to a psychiatrist that he possesses homosexual tendencies will not in itself constitute sufficient cause for discharge."[15] At a time when bodies were sorely needed for the war effort, the military would not easily let go of anyone. The next year, 1944, a new regulation, 615-360, section 8, mandated that homosexuals, whether self-identified or identified by others, must be examined by psychiatrists. But the psychiatric examination was to reveal the malingerer—the man "simu-lating homosexuality in order to receive a discharge"—at least as much as it was to reveal the "genuine chronic homosexual."[16]

After World War II, there was a sea change in military policy. From 1947 to 1950, the number of military personnel shrank by almost 90 percent of what it had been at the height of the war, but the number of homosexuals who were discharged tripled. Serious screening began soon after the war. In directives of staggering ignorance, officers and military doctors were encouraged to spot the homosexuals by telltale signs of inappropriate gen-der behavior or appearance, and by inquiring into personal histories. Male homosexuals, for instance, would have a history of "shunning girls after puberty" and "abnormal attachment to mother."[17]

In October 1949 the newly established Department of Defense issued a memorandum that left no doubt about how rigid the policy regarding ho-mosexual men and women would be: "Homosexual personnel, irrespective of sex, should not be permitted to serve in any branch of the Armed Forces in any capacity, and prompt separation of known homosexuals from the Armed Forces is mandatory."[18] The various branches of the military got to work on implementation. In 1950, Army Regulation 600–443 delineated three kinds of homosexuals—all of them to be gotten rid of: aggressive homosexuals (those who forced attention on others) must be immediately court-martialed; nonaggressive homosexuals could avoid court-martial by resigning or accepting a dishonorable discharge; those with "homosexual tendencies," against whom there was no hard evidence, must be removed from the military but could receive a general or honorable discharge.[19]

But in June of that year, America entered the Korean War, and bodies were again needed. The number of discharges shrank and remained low until the armistice was signed in 1953. Then it soared.[20] The years that fol-lowed saw the most brutal homosexual-hunts in US military history.

CLEARING OUT THE LESBIANS

Women made up only 2 percent of the postwar military. But the percent-
age of lesbians among the women who did serve was huge. For obvious
reasons: the social climate of the 1950s indoctrinated females to strive for
3.4 children and a house with a white picket fence. Few straight women
were willing to serve their country instead. And women who were already
married or had children under the age of eighteen weren't allowed to
enlist. Most lesbians had none of those disqualifications. Also, they knew
they'd never have a man to support them. The military offered training
that could be used to make a living in civilian life; it offered the GI Bill for
advanced education, too. Common sense suggests that the WAC, WAVES
(Women Accepted for Volunteer Emergency Service), WAF (Women in
the Air Force), and Marine Corps Women's Reserve were full of lesbians—
despite the resolute decree of the Department of Defense that "Homosexual personnel, irrespective of sex, should not be permitted to serve in
any branch of the Armed Forces."

From the very beginning, Carlita Durand liked everything about the WAF:
learning to carry out orders (no questions asked); the disciplined neatness
(skirts and blouses starched so well that they stood up by themselves, nylons
perfectly rolled, bras folded and put in the drawer in a specified way); the
high moral standards (you weren't even supposed to go to a bar in uniform). She liked especially being a team member. It was the best possible
training anyone could have, she thought, and was honored to be part of it
all. She was made a squad leader and was allowed to carry the flag. She was
twenty years old, and her ambitions soared. "There's something in me that
would make a good officer," she thought.[21]

Shortly before she'd joined the WAF, Durand had a brief relationship
with another girl, Winn. It was right after her father died. One night she
and Winn and a few friends had gotten a little high on Budweiser, and they
sentimentally snipped locks of one another's hair for mementoes. Durand
kept Winn's. She put it in the glove compartment of her car, together with
a smiling picture of her.

But Durand wasn't sure she was a lesbian. She thought she might be
straight. She didn't know what she was. Wiry and athletic, she sometimes

liked to wear jeans and a boy's shirt, and sometimes a dress and high heels. At her enlistment physical, the doctor asked her point-blank, "Do you like women?" "No," she said. "Do you date?" "Yes," she said. When a young man in the Medical Corps showed interest in her, Durand started going out with him. When a bunch of other WAFs invited her to go to Corpus Christi, Texas, to loaf on the beach and swim in the bay, she did that, too.

She finished her six-month medical training: setting IVs, drawing blood, cleaning tracheostomy tubes, lugging medical equipment while crawling under barbed-wire fences. Then she was assigned to work in the squadron orderly room until an appropriate spot opened for her elsewhere. "Airman Durand has been an outstanding airman in all respects and can be relied upon to do all tasks assigned to her promptly and efficiently, to the best of her ability. Her appearance and barracks area are always commendable," her commander, Captain Barbara Pratt, wrote in an evaluation.[22]

One day, at work in the orderly room, Durand was summoned to report to the reception area of the barracks. Two men dressed in plain clothes were waiting for her. The badges they flashed said they were agents from the Air Force Office of Special Investigations. "We're here to investigate you," one told her without preliminaries.

"What for?" she asked.

"Homosexuality," the other said. "Let's go up to your room."

They were emotionless, tall. Giants, in Durand's head. She thought they'd come to put her in jail or court-martial her. "This is what it means to be scared out of your mind," she thought. People were walking by. She was humiliated.

In her room, they went through everything as she stood there. They turned all the pockets of her skirts and pants and jackets inside out. They opened her locker and all her drawers. Everything she'd neatly rolled according to regulations they unrolled, even her nylons and bras. They found her address book. They looked through every page, demanded she tell them about her relationship with every female listed. Then they confiscated it. "Take us to your car," they told her. They left her clothes and everything else strewn about the bed and floor.

They looked under the seats of the car; they took off the inside door panels. She had to stand there while they did it. People walking by turned their heads to watch. They took every piece of paper out of her glove compartment and examined it minutely. Then they found the lock of hair and Winn's picture. "Here's your girlfriend," they said. "We need to contact this person."

"No, we're just friends!" Durand protested. They told her they knew she'd gone to a lesbian party in Corpus Christi. "Nobody told me it was a lesbian party," she said. "Nothing went on there!"

She racked her brain to think of why this was happening. She remembered that one of the women with whom she'd gone to Corpus Christi was later investigated on charges of homosexuality and was kicked out of the air force. She must have named Durand when they made her name names.

They came back every few days to ask the same questions again and again. How many lesbian relationships? What did she do in them? Who were the other lesbians on base? Who were the lesbians she'd known before she enlisted? They ordered that she be sent for a psychiatric examination. The chief of the Lackland Air Force Base Medical Center Psychiatry Service reported that "at this time she was found to be free of mental defect, disease, or derangement and is not suffering from any condition which would warrant separation from the Air Force."[23] But she was not allowed to go to her duty post. She was confined to the barracks and assigned to a cleaning detail, scrubbing floors, picking up garbage outside the buildings. She was kept on base while the OSI men finished building their case against her.

She knew she'd be discharged. Captain Pratt, who was not unsympathetic, had told her, "Lee, this is not going to go away." But the captain promised she'd recommend an honorable discharge. Durand feared that if she fought, they'd try to dredge up real "evidence." She could be court-martialed. She was stunned and frightened and after three weeks of harassing investigations didn't feel strong enough to fight.

Finally, the staff sergeant (whom Durand knew to be "one of the girls," but who never got investigated) came to her to say, "Put all the air force property in your duffel bag. We have to go check them off." Again she was led across the base. Again humiliated. She was being discharged under the DOD directive that said "known homosexual individuals are military liabilities and security risks who must be eliminated."[24]

The honorable discharge Captain Pratt had promised was denied. She was given a general discharge, which meant that the world would know she'd been booted out of the military as unsuitable.[25]

Officers weren't as easily expendable. But if they were homosexual, they not only had to stay in the closet, they also had to be complicit in the military's harassment of other homosexuals. In 1953, at the end of the Korean War, Sue Young applied for a commission in the navy and was sent to the Women Officers Indoctrination School at the Naval Training Station in Newport. She'd grown up during World War II, her two older brothers had been soldiers, and she'd learned patriotism at the dinner table every night. Before entering the navy, she'd had four years of college at the University of Arkansas, but she hadn't lost her Ozark Hills twang. Blond, five foot eight, and 120 pounds, she looked like a Coca-Cola poster of a 1950s college coed.[26]

She'd had crushes on girls since she was five years old but had never had a lover. Her company officer, Barb, a bright young woman only five or six years older than Young, had breezy, all-American girl looks and overwhelming charm. Young was quickly smitten. It was a wonder to Sue Young that when she was invited to a cocktail party on board a visiting ship, Barb was there too. And sat next to her. When she was invited with three classmates for a week's vacation in Boston, Barb offered to take them, saying she had to get her new car serviced there. When Young was invited for Thanksgiving in New York, Barb said she was going in that direction and could drive her. That Thanksgiving weekend, they became lovers.

On the drive back that Sunday night, Barb stopped the car on a dark street, a few blocks away from the naval station. "I have to tell you something," she said. "I'm giving a lecture tomorrow in your personnel administration class. It's about how officers need to handle things if someone is reported to them for being a lesbian."

Young listened in stunned silence as Barb went into detail about the instructions she would have to deliver the next day about what officers were obliged to do with lesbian personnel and the discharge procedures. "But don't worry," Barb said. Official policy was one thing, and personal life was something else.

Months later, Young finished Women Officers Indoctrination School and waited with the rest of her class for assignments to be doled out.

Barb, good friends with the assignment officer (who was also a lesbian), asked the officer to assign Young to a nearby post. The arrangement lasted for years, during which Barb taught Young strict rules about how to survive as a lesbian officer in the navy: Don't trust anybody unless you have absolute knowledge of him or her. Never let anyone see you upset when homosexuals are getting harassed or being discharged. Be ladylike, wear makeup; if you can stand it, date men for cover. Be "neat and discreet"—that one a private talisman, to be chanted daily by lesbian officers everywhere.

A LEFT-HANDED VICTORY

Fannie Mae Clackum was a Georgia girl—pretty and feminine, friends said of her. Soon after she graduated from Marietta High School in 1948, she entered the air force as a reservist and was sent to Barksdale Air Force Base in Louisiana. There she met Grace Garner, and they became inseparable. They were promoted together from privates to corporals, and by 1950, they were seen so often together around the base that they aroused suspicion. The Korean War had started, and witch hunts of homosexuals had slowed, but they hadn't stopped entirely. When an obvious "pair" such as Clackum and Garner came to the attention of the Office of Special Investigations, the Office pursued with fervor.

In this case, OSI staged a sting operation using a decoy, another air force woman who befriended Clackum. The decoy and her "partner," one of the other reservists, were going to visit an aunt in Dallas for the Easter holiday. She invited Clackum and Garner to come along, stay at the aunt's spacious house, and go sightseeing in Dallas. When the "aunt" was nowhere to be found, the decoy told Clackum and Garner that she'd foot the bill for two motel rooms. They accepted, and the two "couples" checked into a Dallas motel.[27]

Soon after the Dallas trip, the decoy supplied the OSI with testimony that Clackum and Garner were a pair. They were called before their commanding officer and an OSI investigator and accused of violating the military's prohibition against homosexuality. Clackum and Garner denied they were a couple and denied they were homosexual. Denial didn't help. The OSI began its obsessive investigation of them, tearing apart their rooms looking for incriminating evidence, summoning them for repeated long and brutal interrogations.[28]

In October, their commanding officer told Clackum and Garner they must resign. They refused. They stuck to their story. They were friends and not homosexual lovers. They demanded to see documented evidence against them. When it wasn't forthcoming, Clackum, the feistier of the two women, called the OSI's bluff. She demanded a court-martial. That would force the military to produce whatever evidence it thought it had. It was a breathtakingly bold move: she'd grabbed the upper hand by challenging the OSI. No one had dared to do it before.

In November the commanding officer demanded that Clackum be examined by a psychiatrist. After twenty or thirty minutes, the psychiatrist concluded that Clackum was "a sexual deviate manifested by homosexuality latent."[29] She and Garner were both demoted back to private; and on the same day, January 22, 1952, they were given dishonorable discharges. Clackum demanded a hearing before the Air Force Discharge Review Board.

At the hearing, she brought in witnesses—acquaintances, clergymen, past employers. They testified to her "ladylike manner" and claimed it was "impossible to believe that she is a homosexual." The OSI countered that it had solid evidence of her homosexuality. But except for the psychiatric report, it presented nothing. "What evidence?" Clackum's lawyer demanded. He scoffed at the "absurdity" of the "oracular" psychiatric pronouncement that Clackum was a homosexual on the basis of a twenty- to thirty-minute exam. But the Air Force Discharge Review Board confirmed that both women were to be given dishonorable discharges.

The two women left Barksdale Air Force Base and went to live in Clackum's hometown of Marietta. As though they had nothing to hide, or as though they were thumbing their noses at the OSI, or as though they really were lovers, the two got an apartment together and then waged war on the air force.

Eight years later, still living together, their case finally went to the United States Court of Federal Claims. Judge J. Warren Madden tore into the discharge board. Due process had been violated, he rebuked them. "The evidence upon which the case was decided was not present at the hearing, unless the undisclosed dossier which contained it was in the drawer of the table at which the board sat," Judge Madden declared sarcastically in his written opinion.[30] The women won their suit. They were granted back pay and all veterans' benefits.

But homosexual witch hunts continued. The Clackum case was no victory for the right of lesbians and gay men to serve in the military. The judge's major complaint had been that Clackum was, *without evidence*, "officially branded as an indecent woman."[31] If the OSI had presented credible proof that she and Garner were lovers, the Court of Federal Claims's judge would have upheld the discharge board's decisions.

The outcome of *Fannie Mae Clackum v. United States* does prove, however, that the witch hunters didn't always have proof that could stand up under scrutiny. Those who were discharged were almost never caught *in flagrante delicto*: someone had been frightened into naming names, or they hung out with suspicious company, or they wore their hair the wrong length. But to challenge the Office of Special Investigations took more confidence than most young lesbians or gays had at a time when the government, the law, the church, the psychiatric profession, all colluded to tell homosexuals they were guilty just by being who they were. There was no one to encourage them to believe that they were innocent because homosexuality in and of itself is innocent.

Chapter 4

AMERICA PROTECTS
ITS YOUNGSTERS

"NEW MORAL MENACE TO OUR YOUTH"

A mass hysteria hit Boise, Idaho, in fall 1955: almost 10 percent of the male population—bank vice presidents, high school teachers, shoe repairmen—were accused of having seduced young boys.[1] It was symptomatic of bogeyman fears all over America. An article in the popular *Coronet* magazine titled "New Moral Menace to Our Youth" warned, "No degenerate can indulge in his unnatural practices alone. Each year thousands of youngsters of high school and college age are introduced to these unnatural practices by inveterate seducers."[2] Professors and teachers whose jobs threw them into regular contact with "youngsters" were suddenly being scrutinized for degeneracy. After E. K. Johnston's arrest, the witch hunts at the University of Missouri expanded even to students—dozens were kicked out to prevent "contagion."[3] Witch hunts spread to colleges and universities across America: UCLA,[4] the University of Michigan,[5] the University of Wisconsin,[6] Smith College,[7] the University of Massachusetts,[8] the University of Texas.[9] The über–witch hunt, which targeted Florida educators and students, was carried out from 1958 to 1965 at the cost of millions of dollars to state taxpayers.[10]

Florida state senator Charley Johns billed himself as a populist, a supporter of the much put-upon "little man." Johns's father was a sheriff who'd been killed in the line of duty,[11] and one of Johns's first proposals as a new senator in 1947 was that the state should purchase a portable electric chair that could be transported by truck, along with an electric generator. The chair could be set up in front of any jailhouse, and when a capital offender's time had come, anyone who wished could witness his execution, just like in the days of public hangings.[12] His proposal failed, but the former railroad conductor and insurance agent from the rural town of Starke (population four thousand) was not daunted. Eventually he became leader of the "Pork Chop Gang," a group of twenty segregationist Democratic senators from north Florida. The Pork Chop Gang managed to get Johns elected president of the Senate in April 1953. Florida didn't have a lieutenant governor; so when Governor Dan McCarty died in office five months later, Charley Johns became acting governor.

Johns ran for governor on his own the following year and lost to the less flamboyant Senator LeRoy Collins, but his rural constituency reelected him to the Senate in 1955. "Communist people are behind a lot of this Negro agitation. We're going to stop it, and let the chips fall where they may," the fire-eating Johns proclaimed to the voters of his district.[13] The Supreme Court ruling in *Brown v. the Board of Education* the year before be damned, Johns pledged; he'd fight to keep Florida schools—and all of Florida—segregated.

In 1956, in the midst of the Negro bus boycott in Tallahassee, Senator Johns announced that there were subversive organizations that were violating the laws of the state by carrying on Communist-influenced activities. He proposed that a Florida Legislative Investigation Committee be formed to investigate those organizations. His fellow politicians voted to appropriate money for salaries, per diems, office supplies, long-distance telephone charges, travel,[14] even honoraria for spies. FLIC (or the Johns Committee, or "Florida's Little McCarthy Committee," as it came to be called by those who finally fought it[15]) began by investigating the National Association for the Advancement of Colored People (NAACP) for its subversive support of the bus boycott. The committee also investigated troublemaking individuals such as a black woman in Senator Johns's hometown who'd been going out with a white man[16] and a University of Florida botany professor who gave "integrated parties" in his home.[17]

But the Johns Committee hit a snag with the NAACP when it demanded that the head of the Miami chapter, black Episcopalian minister Theodore Gibson, and the white vice president, librarian Ruth Perry, hand over membership lists. They refused. Perry informed Senator Johns, "This committee's demand constitutes an invasion of the rights of free speech and association of the NAACP, its members, and myself—all of which I claim and assert."[18] Johns's committee then subpoenaed three more NAACP officials, all of them black, and accused them of having ties to the Florida Communist Party. They wouldn't answer any of the committee's questions either.[19]

"If blacks refuse to testify, they should be forced to. And if they still refuse, we should put them in jail!" Johns proclaimed.[20]

The NAACP fought Johns all the way to the US Supreme Court, and it won. "The NAACP could file anything, and that court would grant it!" the fuming Senator Johns told the *Miami News.*[21] He was sitting on a pile of money earmarked for investigations, and as long as the Supreme Court was telling civil rights groups they didn't have to answer his questions, he had nothing to investigate.[22]

But when a rabidly anticommunist professor at the University of South Florida alerted Johns that "known Communists" were being invited to speak on campus,[23] the senator found a new focus for his committee. He and his team traveled up and down Florida interviewing students to find out if their professors had "Communist ideas." They scrutinized reading lists and discovered that the young were being taught subversive and obscene material, such as *The Grapes of Wrath, Brave New World*, and Beat poetry. But faculty committees and the American Association of University Professors obstinately upheld the tenets of academic freedom and fought Johns's attempts to censor what they taught.[24] Again the senator had to look elsewhere to spend the bulk of his committee's investigative money.

In the fall of 1958, the senator's son, Jerome, who'd been a student at the University of Florida, told his father that he'd observed quite a few homosexual professors on campus. Coincidentally, when Johns's chief investigator, R. J. Strickland, a former head of the Tallahassee vice squad, went to the University of Florida the following week to investigate Communist professors, he was told by his informants that there weren't many of those, but the place was packed with homosexual professors. Strickland called Johns to relay what he'd learned.

"Well, get back there and take care of the problem!" the excited Johns ordered.[25] Here was a fine use for the money the legislature had given the Johns Committee. Florida had a "crimes against nature" law, which made all homosexuals criminals. No court or professors' union would dare tell Johns that homosexuals didn't need investigating.[26] Hundreds of homosexual professors, university students, and public school teachers were summoned by the Johns Committee to be interrogated; no one came to their defense—not even homosexuals themselves.[27] They couldn't say, as NAACP vice president Ruth Perry did, "This committee's demand constitutes an invasion of my rights, which I claim and assert." They knew that under Florida law, there was no "right" to be homosexual.

Remus James Strickland—R. J., or "Sergeant," as Charley Johns called him[28]—had been the head of the Tallahassee vice squad and had a lot of experience in getting at the truth when a homosexual arrestee was intractable. He applied the techniques he'd perfected to the grilling of Florida educators and students at the University of Florida; the University of South Florida; Florida State University; the state's Negro college, Florida Agricultural and Mechanical University; and at junior colleges and elementary and secondary schools all over Florida. University presidents and school principals cooperated. Senator Johns, they knew, could influence state funding.[29]

"Have you had homosexual relationships with anybody since you've been on the faculty over there?" Strickland questioned a man who taught English at the University of Florida.[30]

"No sir, no sir!" answered the rattled professor. He was married and the father of three children, ages five, twelve, and seventeen.[31] He'd been plucked out of class in the middle of teaching freshmen students how to structure a paragraph; and now he found himself sitting in a room at the Manor Motel, a modest little inn not far from the university. The room, which had been rented by the Johns Committee, was where suspected homosexual professors and students were brought to be interrogated. Before the quizzing, Johns Committee counsel Mark Hawes, a pudgy, stern-looking lawyer from Saint Petersburg, "duly cautioned" suspects about the law against perjury, and then he swore them in.[32] A stenographer sat in a corner of the room. A uniformed officer, John Tileston of the University of

Florida Police Department, stood at the door.[33] It was Tileston who'd accompanied the English professor from his classroom.

"You have not had homosexual relations?" Strickland continued.

"No, sir. I've been . . . I've had affectionate relationships with some of my students," the professor answered, clearly grasping to figure out why he'd been brought to this motel room.

"What do you mean by 'affectionate'?"

"Well, I've given them a hug, something like that, but I don't think that . . . there's anything wrong with that."

Strickland, well practiced in the language that flustered, quickly came in for the kill: "Have you ever taken another man's penis in your mouth and given him what is commonly referred to as a blow job?"

"No, sir!"

"Did you meet a man in the urinal in the restroom on the second floor of the library, standing at the urinal, you standing there, and he standing there"—Strickland gestured proximity—"with both of you having an erection, and did you ask him if he wanted to go to your office, and did you take him to your office?" Strickland was reading now from notes the stenographer had made earlier. "And did you lock the outer door and take him into the little room in your office and lock both doors to that, and there perform a homosexual act on him?"

"No! No, sir!" The professor was vehement.

"Bring him in," Strickland told Officer Tileston.

The man Tileston led into the room a moment later repeated the details of the on-campus encounter, and Strickland reiterated to the professor that perjury and homosexual acts were both serious crimes, offenses punishable by five to twenty years in Raiford State Prison. But he would not prosecute someone who told the truth, Strickland assured the professor: "This is not a criminal investigation, this is a civil inquiry. The legislature just wants to find out the extent of this problem out here as it affects this university."[34] However, if the subject would not cooperate, Strickland warned, he would personally make sure that he was charged with sodomy under Florida law.

It was a Hobson's choice: go to state prison for sodomy compounded by perjury, or admit guilt (and name others) and slink away from the university. He gave them one other choice, too—equally diabolical: "If you don't want to talk to me here in private, you don't have to. It's your right to demand a public trial," he told them. Of course, if they did demand a trial, the whole world would know they'd been accused of committing shameful homosexual acts. Most of the accused chose to slink away.

There were few women on university faculties in the late 1950s and early 1960s. Those who were lesbians pretended that partners were friends and male friends were fiancés, and they glued their feet to the closet floor. Most escaped detection. Of the fourteen faculty members terminated for homosexuality at the University of Florida, for instance, only one, a library science instructor,[35] was female.[36] Determined to nail lesbians too, Strickland turned his attention to elementary and high school teachers. In October 1959 he wrote the Johns Committee claiming that "admitted homosexuals" had informed him that fully 30 percent of the school teachers in the Tampa, Pinellas, and Sarasota areas were homosexual.[37] He got permission to expand his witch hunts to the Florida public schools.

It wasn't easy to catch lesbian teachers.[38] They hardly ever engaged in sex in public places, so Strickland's vice squad savvy didn't help him much. Intent on finding them but having no idea how to go about it, he quizzed lesbians who'd gotten in trouble with the law, hoping they'd drop some teachers' names. He even went to Florida's Lowell State Prison for Women to ask inmates if they'd known any lesbian teachers. "I want you to be truthful with me, so we might help some small child," he told them.[39] Saint Petersburg Police Department sergeant David Hooper brought him an unemployed twenty-year-old female he'd arrested, who was a habitué of gay girls' bars. "Have you had any occasion where teachers' names have been mentioned to you as far as homosexuality is concerned, that you remember?" Strickland asked hopefully during his interrogation of her.

"No, this is something I never heard anything of," the puzzled young woman told him.

Strickland didn't give up: "Would you be willing to make an effort to see what you could find out?"

What could the young woman say? In trouble already, hoping her punishment might be mitigated, she promised, "Yes. If I thought it could be of some help, I would. I don't know how I'd go about it, but I guess I could figure out some way."[40]

•　　•　　•

TRAP LAYING

With the blessings of Senator Johns's committee, Strickland paid people to be informants, such as a nineteen-year-old Tampa hustler, Dwight Evans,[41] who often plied his trade at the Greyhound bus terminal. The investigators set up shop in Tampa, in a room at the Hawaiian Village, a cheap motel landscaped with tikis and bits of synthetic thatch. There they queried Evans, asking for detailed descriptions of the University of South Florida students and faculty he picked up at the terminal. They wanted specifics about the acts Evans committed with those men; and, if they took him to their homes, their addresses and the make, model, and color of their cars.

"Well, there isn't anything I can think of now," Evans declared after a long debriefing in which he named multiple names. "Probably later there will be, because, as I said, I do know quite a few people you'd be interested in here in Tampa. But I have talked quite a bit here, and I'm gonna have to think a little bit. I know some more." Young Evans was a man who knew well how to tantalize his paying customers and make them come back for repeats.[42]

Strickland also paid female informers to help entrap lesbians. At Florida State University, an eighteen-year-old woman student, May,[43] had read in the newspapers about R. J. Strickland's homosexual hunts, and in September 1959, she phoned him. She offered her services, explaining that her close friend Cathy had become involved with lesbians and had been wooed away to West Virginia by them. Through Cathy's suffering, May had seen up close, she claimed, "how destructive it was." For that reason, she was "making an effort to do something about it."[44]

May was full of ideas about how to help the Johns Committee investigators find lesbians on her campus: for instance, a girl she knew, Carol Lee Palmer, had been kicked out of FSU by the dean of women, Katherine Warren, for being a lesbian. Palmer was now living in West Virginia, but May could encourage her to come visit and bring her present girlfriend, and the investigators could arrest them and get Palmer to name all the lesbians at FSU.

Strickland didn't seem to care that the eighteen-year-old's story hinted at the vengeance of a spurned lover. He and State's Attorney Mark Hawes cooperated completely with her on her bizarre scheme (financed, of course, by the taxpayers of Florida). She would write Carol Lee Palmer in West Virginia and say that she was herself interested in "becoming converted" to homosexuality, and that she was involved with a girl, but they were still "sitting on the fence." Could Palmer come back to Tallahassee for a weekend with her present partner, Ruby Kelly, and "show us your side of the fence?" May and her "girlfriend" (also on the Johns Committee payroll) and Carol and Ruby could all stay for free at the Sunset Motel, May wrote Carol Lee Palmer. Her girlfriend's mother had rented two rooms for out-of-town relatives who'd had to cancel their visit, she explained.[45]

That Saturday night of the visit, Attorney Hawes and Leon County sheriff William Joyce were listening at Carol and Ruby's motel room window; when they "figured that the time was ripe, they broke through the door." It was a bit precipitous: the two lesbians were only kissing. But that was enough. They were arrested for "crimes against nature" and taken to Leon County Jail.[46]

When Carol Lee Palmer was interrogated in jail, she couldn't think of many names of lesbians to give Strickland, but she did say she'd heard a rumor that Katherine Warren, the dean of women at FSU—who'd been responsible for having her expelled—"was around some woman all the time and was living with some woman."[47]

The proficiency of informants at snagging homosexuals helped to justify R. J. Strickland's reimbursement requests for spy expenses. For example: "Enclosed you will find a voucher for informants' fees in amount of $223.13, which includes $5.30 for confidential telephone calls for the month of July and $12.90 for the month of August," he wrote to the chairman of the Johns Committee. He was anxious to protect his spies, and he imposed cagey secrecy on the committee: "It would be detrimental for those telephone toll tickets to become part of the public records in the Comptroller's Office," he warned the committee chairman in his request that the reimbursements be paid under the table.[48]

SWAN SONG

As much as Charley Johns and R. J. Strickland strived for secrecy and kept the public ignorant about their use of spies, word did eventually get out about the excesses of their tactics, and in 1963, moderate legislators tried to put an end to the funding for the Johns Committee. Charley Johns announced that if they had a gripe with him, he would gladly step down— but the work of the committee must not be stopped. He harangued his colleagues about the committee's accomplishments: "Scores of homosexual school teachers and university people have already been flushed out," he declared, and if the committee would be allowed to continue, "scores more would soon be gotten rid of." And on top of that good work, the committee had "uncovered a ploy among homosexuals," Johns announced. Homosexuals had planned to kidnap the eleven-year-old son of Municipal Judge John Rudd to get back at him because he'd been tough in sentencing them for their immoral acts, but their plan was nipped in the bud thanks to the committee's chief investigator. "If R. J. Strickland never does another thing, that earned him every dime the committee has paid him," Johns proclaimed dramatically.[49]

The majority of the legislature agreed. The committee was granted another $155,000 for the next two years and given an extended mandate: to ferret out homosexuals from *all* state-funded agencies. Charley Johns, R. J. Strickland, and Mark Hawes receded into the background, but nothing changed significantly.[50]

The committee, called more often by its formal name, the Florida Legislative Investigation Committee, after Johns's departure, got its coup de grace the following year when an outlandish misstep revealed just how wacky its tactics were. In January 1964 the committee spent $720 to print a few thousand copies of a booklet titled *Homosexuality and Citizenship in Florida*. It came to be called "the Purple Pamphlet" because of its contents as well as the color of its paper cover. "Although this report has been prepared . . . primarily for the benefits of state administrators and personnel officers, it can be of value to all citizens," the Purple Pamphlet declared. "[E]very parent and every individual concerned with the moral climate of the state should be aware of the rise in homosexual activity noted here, and be possessed of the basic knowledge set forth."[51] The pamphlet's price as stated on the front cover was 25 cents; but bulk discounts were available for orders of one hundred copies or more.

The fetching picture on the cover of the booklet was of two buff young men in a lip-lock, both naked to the pubes. Inside was a picture of a handsome blond boy, sporting nothing but a piece of black silk over his genitals, arms akimbo, and muscled chest bound loosely with a rope. There were pinup pictures of pretty young boys glancing seductively at the camera. And there were sexually graphic tales about homosexual misdoings, and a glossary of gay argot, with terms such as "69 queen" and "browning queen." FLIC hoped to demonstrate that Florida needed to pass a Homosexual Practices Control Act because homosexuals engaged in disgusting practices, like looking at pictures such as those reproduced in the booklet.

The Dade County state attorney, Richard Gerstein, threatened to sue for obscenity if the booklet was distributed anywhere in his area.[52] "State-sponsored pornography," the media called the Purple Pamphlet. It was reprinted by a homosexual book club in Washington, DC, and became a bestseller on the homosexual streets of New York.[53]

In 1965, after nine years of hunting for witches (seven of those years focused especially on homosexuals), the committee disbanded because the legislature cut off its funding. But the demise of Charley Johns's committee was not the end of the persecution of Florida homosexuals. Richard Gerstein, the state's attorney who in June 1964 had banned the Purple Pamphlet in his county, worried that the public might think he was soft on deviates. In July 1964 he announced a drive to rid Miami of homosexuals, claiming it was because *Life* magazine—in an alarming article that asked, "Do the Homosexuals, Like the Communists, Intend to Bury Us?"[54]—had identified the city as one of six in the United States that had "established homosexual societies."[55] "Homosexuals recruit youth," Gerstein proclaimed, echoing Charley Johns. "It's a growing problem, and anyone who says it isn't is ignoring the obvious."[56]

Gerstein's drive to rid Miami of homosexuals succeeded no more than did FLIC's drive to rid education of homosexuals. Despite Gerstein, despite the Johns Committee, despite Thomas Bailey—the state superintendent for public instruction, who continued to purge homosexual teachers even after the death of FLIC—homosexuals kept flourishing in Florida. But those Floridians who wanted to get rid of them wouldn't give up. In the next decade, they spearheaded a hysterical campaign, dubbed with the heart-tugging moniker "Save Our Children," which spread throughout America. Its message was culled from Charley Johns's rhetoric: the lifeblood of homosexuals depended on their seduction of innocent youngsters.

PART 2

THE HOMOPHILES

Chapter 5

MATTACHINE

"WE ARE AN OPPRESSED CULTURAL MINORITY"

Harry Hay had a love/hate relationship with his wealthy, despotic father and with most authority. Hay spent a couple of years at Stanford University in the 1930s. Then he quit and rebelled against his conservative Republican parent in every way he could think of. He tried to organize migrant farm workers and longshoremen into unions. In 1934 he participated in the San Francisco General Strike to protest the capitalists' treatment of labor. He joined the NAACP. He registered Mexican Americans to vote in the barrios of East Los Angeles. He joined the Communist Party.

Yet as a devout member of the party, Hay bowed to its dictates. Six feet three inches tall, with an elfish face that seemed to belie his height, Hay had known he was homosexual since adolescence. Party dogma said that homosexuality was a decadent by-product of capitalism and would die out with the demise of that loathed system. Hay, an original thinker, well read, with an encyclopedic mind, nevertheless took to heart the comrades' knee-jerk distaste for homosexuals because party members expressed it as rational fear. Homosexuality was illegal all over America, they pointed out. It would attract closer government scrutiny of the CP and would jeopardize them all. So in 1938 Harry Hay looked around for a wife.

Anita Platky, with whom he'd participated in party political protests, caught his eye. She seemed a plausible choice to Hay. They both had strong social consciences. They shared artistic interests. She was tall, strong jawed, with a Prince Valiant haircut and a boyish air. She'd even once played an Amazon onstage. They adopted two daughters. The twenty-six-year-old Hay became a family man, though he couldn't stop being homosexual in heart and secret deed.[1]

Ten years later, still married, two things happened to cause Hay to question both the life he'd made for himself and the party's view of homosexuals as a dangerous handful of degenerates who must be expelled and ostracized. He'd been one of sexologist Alfred Kinsey's 5,300 interviewees, and when *Sexual Behavior in the Human Male* came out in January 1948, he purchased a copy immediately. He was elated to realize that based on Kinsey's statistics, there must be many millions of homosexuals in America. He carried the Kinsey Report with him everywhere, like a religious zealot carrying around a Bible.[2] Then, a few months later, in the summer of 1948, he heard that a purge had begun of homosexuals who worked in the State Department. "These are the next scapegoats, to replace Negroes and Jews," he thought. Negroes were being integrated into the armed forces and labor organizations. Truman and the United Nations had recognized the new Jewish state of Israel, and news of the horrors perpetrated by Hitler had put an end to anti-Semitism for the time being. Both Negroes and Jews had defenders.[3] But no one would stand up for homosexuals, and they couldn't stand up for themselves because they lived isolated lives. They were the one group of disenfranchised people who didn't even know they were a group.

Hay had spent years agitating for minorities and underdogs. Now he realized that despite his dutiful attempts to blend into society, he too belonged to a minority; and its members were underdogs, just as surely as were racial and ethnic minorities. He would make the multitudes of homosexuals like him understand who they were: a minority that must band together and struggle against the outrageous persecution of their tribe.

Hay wasn't the first to think of organizing homosexuals to fight for their rights. But he didn't know at the time about the Scientific-Humanitarian Committee that Magnus Hirschfeld had started in Germany in 1897 with the hope of changing the laws that criminalized male homosexuality.[4] He'd heard a little about the Society for Human Rights, which was started in Chicago in 1924 by Henry Gerber—someone had told him that the group had been dangerous, was shut down by police only weeks into its existence, and "brought everyone to bad ends."[5] He'd never heard that its express purpose was to protect homosexuals from those who would deprive them of "their legal pursuit of happiness which is guaranteed them by the Declaration of Independence."[6] There was a New York group, too, the Veterans Benevolent Association, which had been started in 1945 to fight the mistreatment of homosexual veterans who'd received less-than-honorable discharges and thus were denied the GI Bill.[7] The Veterans Benevolent Association was still going in 1948, though its numbers were small, and, being frustrated in its battle for rights, it morphed into a social organization. Hay had heard nothing of it either.[8]

He described his own conviction that homosexuals must organize as an epiphany that came to him one hot night in July 1948. He'd been invited to a beer bust near the University of Southern California by a homosexual student he'd cruised. Henry Wallace, who'd been vice president during FDR's third term, was running for president as a Progressive Party candidate. As Hay and everyone else at the beer bust cooled off by guzzling quantities of Schlitz, it hit him suddenly that the time was propitious: "We've got to start a group," he told the knot of homosexual young men who'd gathered round him. Hay had always been a charismatic speaker, and now his ideas flowed as freely as the beer. They could fight to make the Progressive Party include in its platform a plank for "a modernization of sexual legislation." They'd need to be a little careful, of course. They could call themselves American Bachelors for Wallace—that would give them the cover that was crucial. Hay's fellow beer drinkers slapped his back. "Brilliant plan!" they hollered, and they spun the idea even further. When Wallace got elected, their new group could agitate for a constitutional amendment against discrimination.

Hay went home in a delirium of excitement and stayed up past dawn, writing a ten-page treatise on Bachelors for Wallace. It was a call to action. The organization would champion the long-suffering homosexual minority. It would offer support socially, culturally, and politically. He thought big. It would have educational programs, counseling services, an organized campaign of legislative reform. The plan was exhilarating.[9]

At a decent hour of the morning, he called his student friend to get the telephone numbers of those who'd cheered his idea at the beer bust; then he called each of them. But sober, the homosexual progressives considered the dangers. Hay couldn't get a single one of them interested. "A bubble of yeasty fantasy had soared," he wrote later, "only to burst promptly in dawn's early light."[10]

Hay continued to be a husband and father and secret homosexual, but the epiphany he'd had that hot July night didn't leave him. Then two years later, in July 1950, at his daughter's dancing school, he met Rudi Gernreich, an Austrian Jew who, with his mother, had escaped Hitler's annexation of Austria in 1938, when Gernreich was a teenager. Gernreich had had ambitions as both a dancer and a fashion designer, though he hadn't yet designed the thong or the single-piece topless monokini that would catapult him to fame in the 1960s. The two men happened to be sitting together while Hay waited for his daughter to finish rehearsing for a recital. They found themselves agreeing about the foolishness of the recently started Korean War. They shared stories of their life on the Left. "Beautiful creature," Hay was thinking all the while about the lithe, dark-eyed younger man.[11] They made a date for dinner the next week, and they soon became lovers.

Hay's hope to start an organization for homosexuals made perfect sense to Gernreich. He'd heard about Magnus Hirschfeld's work in Europe on behalf of homosexual rights: the Scientific Humanitarian Committee and then the Institute for Sexual Research, which had been destroyed by the Nazis when they came to power. But why shouldn't there be a group like that in America? His enthusiasm buoyed Hay, and together they hatched plans to proselytize others.

Armed with Communist Party–sponsored petitions demanding that US troops be recalled from Korea, they descended on Malibu Beach and the beach below the Pacific Palisades. Throngs of homosexuals gathered in those places on sunny weekends. The petitions would give Hay and Gernreich an excuse to approach the sunbathers, and as they were signing, Hay or Gernreich would say something like, "Would you also be interested in joining a group to talk about Kinsey's findings on sexual deviancy?" They plied their wares every weekend for two months. Five hundred homosexuals agreed to sign the Communist Party–sponsored petition; but not one of them agreed to join a group to talk about sexual deviancy. Clearly they understood what was the more dangerous in 1950.

Hay and Gernreich were vexed but not vanquished. The multitalented Hay had taught a course, "Music, the Barometer of Class Struggle," at the People's Education Center, a Los Angeles night school for union members.[12] He told Gernreich about an interesting young man: a pianist who gave up his music career to make a living as a chemist. He'd enrolled repeatedly in Hay's class. Hay was certain that the very blond and youthful-looking Bob Hull was a homosexual. Why not give this Bob Hull a copy of the treatise Hay had written two years earlier? Gernreich suggested.

Hull, long enamored of his teacher's brilliance, was swept away by the treatise. The beginning had come. He shared the treatise with his former lover and now roommate Chuck Rowland. He shared it also with a some-time lover, Dale Jennings, a writer who was working in his family's business while he tried to sell his screenplays. Hull and Rowland had been active in Communist organizations; Jennings was a libertarian, but a sometime fellow traveler.[13] All had spent years fighting for the underdog and against injustice. Hay's call for the oppressed homosexuals to organize, they now agreed ecstatically, resonated with their sentiments exactly.

One afternoon when Hay's wife and daughters were out, the five men met to discuss their next steps in Hay's handsome old house overlooking the sparkling Silver Lake. But first, as Dale Jennings recalled, fearing spying eyes, they pulled down the shades. Then they locked the door. They spoke in modulated tones, too.[14] "What is our theory?" Chuck Rowland wanted to know. As a Communist, he believed, he said, that "you've got to work with a theory." The Coke-bottle glasses he always wore gave him an intellectual air. "What is our basic principle that we're building on?" he demanded of the group.

Hay had long possessed the answer and had been waiting for two years to share it: "We are an oppressed cultural minority," he said simply.

"That's exactly it!" the others—even Dale Jennings, who was by nature a contrarian[15]—agreed. No one before Harry Hay had articulated those words—that homosexuals were "an oppressed cultural minority."[16]

They would meet regularly in discussion groups and invite others to join them. But what would they discuss? Since they were all well versed in Marxist theory, they agreed that before they could talk about how to ameliorate homosexual suffering, they had to come to some theoretical understandings. Why did homosexuals have an inferior status in the world? Why could they be made scapegoats so easily? Injustice and oppression don't come simply from prejudice and misinformation, they said. They're embedded in the structure of society. They would figure out how that worked.[17]

It was their unanimous hope to attract to their discussions both men and women, black and white. They plunged into the venture. In December 1950 they asked various homosexual acquaintances to come to a meeting. Eighteen people showed up: sixteen white men, one black man, and one woman—a blond fashion model friend of Rudi Gernreich's, a lesbian by the name of Flo. Pessimistic about the possibility of homosexuals doing much of anything as a group, she never returned. Gernreich invited another lesbian model to later meetings—Katherine Cassidy—but she didn't last long either. It was hard for women to see how the group's discussions, which centered on male homosexuality, could fix whatever oppressions lesbians faced.[18] But not many men came back either. The talk was far too cerebral for most people. What good would such talk do in helping them cope with the very real problems of being homosexual in an unfriendly, punitive world?

In April 1951 two motorcyclists showed up at a discussion group: Jim Gruber,[19] a twenty-four-year-old ex-marine who was studying for his teaching credential at Occidental College, and his lover Konrad "Steve" Stevens, a twenty-six-year-old photographer. They alone of the new people came back for several meetings in a row. Brunette Steve Stevens and blond Jim Gruber were so much of one mind that the group christened them "Stim." The two brought with them a youthful vigor that energized the five regulars. They also brought with them a bisexual woman friend, German-born Ruth Bernhard[20] (who would later become one of the most famous photographers of the female nude). At forty-six, with prematurely silver hair, Bernhard was much older than most of the early members. She was one of the few women who didn't mind that the group's discussions seemed to take for granted that male and female homosexuals shared all the same problems. She too returned for meeting after meeting, and, along with Gruber and Stevens, she became part of the inner circle for a short while.[21] Stim and Bernhard, untutored in Marxist theory, forced the discussions to be less abstract and speculative. They brought with them several new people, who also came back.

The group had been calling itself by the easily misunderstood name Society of Fools. No one really liked it. Harry Hay had thought at different times of names such as International Bachelors Fraternal Order for Peace and Social Dignity, Social Minorities United for Civil Security, Bachelors Anonymous, Androgynes Anonymous (which he compared with Alcoholics Anonymous).[22] But those names were dreary, or they didn't say what he and the other members hoped the organization would be. One evening Hay pulled from his vast and random store of knowledge the history of the *Société Mattachine*, a secret fraternity of the medieval and early Renaissance eras in France. Young bachelors—the *Société Mattachine*'s members—used to join together in clandestine dances and rituals during the vernal equinox, Hay told the discussion group. They would also appear in public dressed in motley and masks, and, using satire as their weapon, they would speak truth to power and challenge the oppressive church and state.[23]

Most of Hay's listeners were enchanted with the story. Gruber and Stevens called out, "That's gotta be our name! Mattachine!" Dale Jennings (who played contrarian to many of Hay's ideas after his initial fascination wore off) claimed later that it was Hay alone who wanted to name the group "after a passel of medieval clowns."[24] But the name did suggest appealing parallels. Twentieth-century homosexuals also were a secret fraternity. They also lived in disguise and met clandestinely. They also had to find ways to challenge tyrannical oppression. The Mattachine Society, the group would call itself.

Harry Hay's wife divorced him. She'd accepted from the start that he was a homosexual; but Mattachine was beyond acceptance. "It's inimical as far the children are concerned," she told him.[25] As long as he'd kept his homosexuality a secret, the children couldn't be harmed. But everyone would know about it now because he'd started an organization for homosexuals. News of such a bizarre group would surely make the papers; the girls would be ostracized. Hay didn't contest the divorce, nor did he protest when the court awarded sole custody of their daughters to Anita Platky. He agreed to alimony and child support. He divorced himself from the Communist Party too. He would not endanger the party by his homosexual activities, nor would he be hindered by the party's hostility to homosexuality. He was also free now to lead the personal life he'd always known was most natural to him, and to lead the organization he'd birthed.

In July 1950—when Mattachine was still only a glint in Hay's eye—he concocted a complex plan. The group would be a secret society, a cross between the Masons and the Communist Party cell structure of the 1930s. There'd be five degrees, Hay decreed, each having its own insignia, from the first, Order of Fools, to the highest, Order of Pharaoh (later named the Order of Parsifal). He described that Fifth Order as "the historic personification of the Androgynous Ideal." The cell structure would not only optimize secrecy but also define the working groups. There would be study groups, welfare groups, even first-aid squads (sort of hotlines—"to provide therapy, guidance, or counsel on a 24-hour basis to members in emotional or psychological distress").[26] People would use made-up names, too. That way, everyone would be kept safe. When Mattachine was born the next year, it adopted a lot of its parent's guidelines.

To throw hostile forces off the track even further, when members of the Mattachine Society's Fifth Order decided to register the organization with the state of California as a nonprofit corporation, they changed its name to Mattachine Foundation Inc. and listed as its board of directors three heterosexual women. The president of the board was Mrs. Henry Hay, the name of Harry Hay's widowed mother, Margaret—who loved her son unconditionally and never gave a thought to the sexuality of "homophiles."[27] Mrs. D. T. Campbell and Romayne Cox, Konrad Stevens's supportive mother and sister, were the other "board members." The three women had no role at all in the group other than to help mask its membership and purpose. Mattachine Foundation Inc.'s official address was for several months Margaret Hay's home address.

Secrecy and convolution had a purpose. They helped insure Mattachine's safety at a time when mighty enemies—from the Federal Bureau of Investigation[28] down to the local vice squad—made it dangerous to be a homosexual. But secrecy and convolution added drama and intrigue, also. No one even got as far as attending a cell meeting unless he or she was invited by Fifth Order members. The process of invitation too was complicated. Mattachine held semipublic formal discussion groups in the homes of people whom the Fifth Order knew well and knew could be trusted.

The Fifth Order was always there, acting as surreptitious scouts, identifying likely members by the aptness of what they said and how well they said it. The scouted never knew the scouts were Pharaohs or Parsifals.

But the discussions at these semipublic affairs were often stiff and oddly judgmental—such as one on "Sense of Value" ("The homosexual has a false sense of value, especially concerning money. The heterosexual is concerned with what money can do to enhance his life; the homosexual tends to make a fetish of money," the discussion note taker wrote down dutifully),[29] and another on "Social Directions of the Homosexual" ("Homosexuals need to be concerned about developing ethical standards to curb licentious conversations").[30] Such moralizing wasn't likely to draw eager throngs. So though the Fifth Order was out scouting, membership that first year remained sparse. What happened in the spring of the second year changed everything.

"*NOW* IS THE TIME TO FIGHT!"

Mattachine's Fifth Order member Dale Jennings was a slight, studious-looking man. The wire-rimmed glasses he wore occasionally gave him a monkish appearance. He'd been married briefly to women—three times—but by his midthirties, his romances were all with men. In February 1952, he'd broken up with his lover and fellow Fifth Order member Bob Hull. He'd been living alone for a while, but now he was lonely. One evening he left his Echo Park apartment and went on foot in search of a good movie to fill a few empty hours. There were several theaters a couple of miles away, bordering Westlake Park. Jennings had studied cinema for two years at the University of Southern California and was trying to write screenplays. He'd become something of a film aficionado, even a bit of a snob, and the first two theaters he passed were showing movies that didn't interest him. He cut across Westlake Park and headed to a theater on the other side. But Jennings had been walking for a while, and nature called. He stopped off at one of the park's public toilets—to do nothing, he claimed subsequently, other than what "the city architect had in mind when he designed the place."[31]

Jennings's version of the story, which he told in court, was that when he left the toilet, he was followed by a big, rough-looking man who caught up with him and wanted to know if he had a light, and wasn't it a nice night, and where was he heading. Jennings answered, "No," "Yes," and "To the movie theater right over there." But the movie that was posted on the marquee was one that Jennings had already seen, and it wasn't worth a second viewing. Instead of buying a ticket, he turned around and headed home. He felt panic, he told the jury, when he saw that the same thuggish-looking man who'd tailed him out of the restroom was still right behind him. Jennings was sure he'd be robbed. He walked fast, he took detours, but he couldn't lose the fellow. Finally home, Jennings fumbled to unlock his apartment door. The man ran up and pushed his way in.

The scene that followed was surreal, as Jennings described it. The man sprawled on Jennings's divan, touched his own private parts, and made lewd proposals. (Jennings "flitted wildly" all the while, the prosecutor told the jury; Jennings said he "flitted" because he was so unnerved that he couldn't think how to get rid of the guy.) When the man finally strolled to the back bedroom, Jennings thought, "Now I can telephone the police," but the man commanded him loudly, "Get in here!" and Jennings obeyed. The man was sprawled on the bed, his jacket off, his shirt unbuttoned. "So what kind of work do you do?" he asked Jennings incongruously. "How much do you make? What's the rent here?" He slapped the bed, ordering Jennings to sit down.

"You have the wrong guy," Jennings claimed he said.

"Hey, I know you're a homosexual. Let down your hair," the man told him. "I was in the navy. All us guys played around."

"You have the wrong guy," Jennings repeated. That was when the man grabbed Jennings's hand and tried to force it down the front of his trousers. Jennings struggled to pull away, he recalled for the jury. And that was when a badge loomed in his face, and then the undercover officer pulled out his handcuffs and locked Jennings's wrists together. "Maybe you'll talk better to my partner outside," the officer said.[32]

The partner wasn't outside. The officer led the handcuffed Jennings through the streets for eight or ten blocks.[33] People turned their heads to see what a perp looked like. The partner was found on a dark side street near the park, sitting with another policeman in an unmarked car. Jennings was forced into the backseat; the man who'd tried to entice him to sex climbed in with him. The three policemen carried on shop talk and laughed a lot while they sat in the parked car with their handcuffed prisoner. They ignored Jennings for minutes at a time, and then suddenly a voice would boom at him in the dark: "How long you been this way?" "Where do you work?" "What do you get paid?"

Finally, the driver started the car. It crept along the streets at ten miles per hour, toward the nearby Lincoln Heights Jail, and then past it; then the driver doubled back, and then passed the jail again. Jennings was sure he'd be taken out to a deserted country road and be shaken down or beaten up. But again the driver doubled back toward the jail. "Plead guilty, and you'll be all right," all three officers advised him as they led him in to be booked. The ordeal in the car had taken almost ninety minutes.[34]

Jennings refused to sign anything. He demanded to know the specific charges against him. He said he would make no statement without a lawyer.[35] By now it was eleven thirty. He asked to be allowed to make a telephone call. At two in the morning, he was finally permitted to use the phone.

It was Harry Hay whom Jennings called, though for the last year, they'd often been snarly with each other. ("He's got all the humor of Moses striding down the mountain with that dratted Decalogue," Jennings once said of Hay.[36]) But Harry Hay was the only person Jennings knew to have a checkbook.[37] "They're asking me fifty dollars for bail," Jennings told him.

Hay showed up with the money at six thirty that morning. "Let me take you to breakfast at the Brown Derby over on Wilshire Boulevard," he told Jennings—because he'd recognized already that this incident could be the start of something momentous for Mattachine. They sat in a small booth at the café that was shaped like a man's derby hat. Hay put heavy hands on Jennings's shoulders and spoke in hushed, solemn tones, "You'd have nothing to lose, Dale. You're working in your family's business. They won't fire you."[38] The courts had already decided that wiretapping and speed entrapment violated a citizen's Fifth Amendment rights. Jennings could argue that sexual entrapment violates those same rights. Mattachine would be standing behind him every minute.[39]

Jennings wasn't sure he wanted to be made a cause célèbre. And he resented Hay staring down at him "in his best Screen Actors Guild style."[40]

But Hay went on. They'd demand a jury trial. Jennings would admit he was a homosexual. But he would contest the charge that he'd made advances to the undercover officer. He would argue that the officer tried to entrap him. Hay had every step figured out. They'd try to get the American Civil Liberties Union to take the case.[41] But if the ACLU wouldn't, Mattachine would do something that had never been done before: ask other homosexuals for money to support a homosexual cause. Mattachine would point out that in the past it had been impossible to find a homosexual with courage and conviction who would stand and fight. But such an opportunity was now being offered: Jennings was ready to fight for the sake of them all.[42]

Jennings, suspicious as always of Hay, nevertheless said yes.

"Okay!" Hay jumped to his feet. "I'm going home and calling an emergency Fifth Order meeting, eight o'clock, your apartment," he told Jennings.

Not a man of them missed the meeting. Jennings would be a test case, they agreed. They would form a Citizens Committee to Outlaw Entrapment. They would print leaflets and distribute them in homosexual bars and anywhere else homosexuals went. They would send them to homosexuals they knew all over the country. They'd raise the necessary legal fees, and, even more important, they'd get the word out that Mattachine was fighting to make clear to the world that homosexuals were not ipso facto lewd and dissolute.

"NOW Is The Time To Fight," the leaflets proclaimed. "The issue is CIVIL RIGHTS," they declared. Almost nobody ever before had dared to suggest that homosexuality might have anything to do with "civil rights." The leaflets emphasized that what had happened to Jennings could happen to anyone. "How will *YOU* prove your innocence when a friendly stranger strikes up a conversation with you and turns out to be a member of the vice squad arresting you for lewd and indecent conduct?" the leaflets inquired provocatively before making the "ask": "funds are urgently needed at once to conduct the trial in the local courts and eventually, if need be, in the higher courts."[43] When had homosexuals ever read such fighting words? Pledges of funds poured in. Mattachine hired George Shibley, a liberal lawyer from nearby Long Beach, who'd defended labor unionists and a dozen young Mexican Americans in the famous Zoot Suit murder case in the 1940s.

• • •

It had been universally true: when a man was arrested under "vag-lewd," he would plead guilty or nolo contendere. Then he'd pay his fine and walk out of the police station with the fervent hope that he'd put the awful incident behind him. But not this time. "Yes, my client is a homosexual," attorney Shibley said in his opening statement to the jury on June 23, 1952. "But homosexuality and lasciviousness are not the same thing." He declared that his client was innocent of lasciviousness. "The only true pervert in this courtroom is the arresting officer," Shibley proclaimed, and he described Jennings's version of the man's bizarre attempts to get Jennings to have sex with him. The trial went on for three days. Shibley called one witness after another to tell the jury at length what it was like to be a homosexual in the sociopolitical climate of 1952.[44]

The jury deliberated for thirty-six hours and ended in deadlock. Eleven jurors found Jennings innocent. The chairman of the jury ("The bastard of the ballad," Hay called him[45]) dissented. Jennings was without a doubt guilty, the chairman insisted, and vowed that he'd "hold out till hell freezes over." The city attorney—frustrated by the hung jury and reluctant to put the city through the expense of another trial—declared he would not continue prosecuting so trivial a case, and he moved for dismissal, which the judge granted.

But the case was not trivial: Jennings had actually admitted to a court to being a homosexual—and still he went free.[46] It was the first time in California history that an admitted homosexual was exonerated after being charged as "vag-lewd." Mattachine knew it must use that fact to make political hay immediately, and it worked. Hundreds of people began attending Mattachine discussion groups. Many were selected to be Mattachine members. Groups sprang up all over Southern California, and then Northern California, and then Central California. Homosexuals in Saint Louis, Chicago, and New York wrote to Hay to say they were interested in establishing Mattachine discussion groups there, too.[47] They wrote to ask for help with their own entrapment cases. In early 1953, when Bayard Rustin (who would become Martin Luther King's chief strategist a couple of years later) was arrested by the Pasadena police and charged with having sex with two men in a parked car, his defenders immediately turned to Mattachine: Might it have been entrapment? they wanted to know, and "Is there any way he can be saved?"[48]

•   •   •

Dale Jennings had been given unprecedented support by the homosexual community. But he wasn't "abjectly grateful," he announced. By joining his fight, homosexuals had served themselves as much as they'd served him: "A bond of brotherhood is not mere blind generosity. It is unification for self-protection. Were all homosexuals and bisexuals to unite militantly, unjust laws would crumble in short order."[49] That was precisely the point Mattachine needed to drive home, the Fifth Order realized: unjust laws would crumble if homosexuals united. That was the tack to make Mattachine grow. "This small victory alone will not suffice," Mattachine's leaflets proclaimed after Jennings won his case. "We must have more victories and in the highest courts."[50]

"HATH NOT A HOMOSEXUAL EYES?"

The success of Harry Hay's group led directly to its failure. Mattachine had been cast into prominence at the height of the government's hunt for subversives. When no one was paying attention, it didn't much matter that its founding members were politically as well as sexually subversive. But now, as a result of their victory, a spotlight was beating down on them. Suddenly there were twenty-seven active Mattachine discussion groups nationally and letters of inquiry from European cities, too. A movement of consequence was at stake.

So when an article appeared in a Los Angeles newspaper naming Harry Hay as a Marxist,[51] the others in the Fifth Order called a meeting. To Hay's dismay, they asked him to stop representing the Mattachine Foundation in public. They had to disavow one "subversion" in order to take heat off the other. Hay could continue to write on behalf of Mattachine, but only under a pseudonym he'd used in the past, Eann MacDonald. He felt whipped.[52] But he agreed that "Harry Hay" would disappear entirely from Mattachine Foundation Inc. In February 1953 the Fifth Order published an official policy statement: "The sole concern of the Mattachine Foundation is with the problems of sexual deviation. The Foundation has never been, is not now, and must never be identified with any 'ism,' political, religious or otherwise."[53]

The Jennings's win and Mattachine's mushrooming fame had whetted the Fifth Order's appetite. They decided to take another unprecedented step. They'd remind politicians that homosexuals were legion, and that they were voters, and that they wanted their rights as citizens. During campaign season for the 1953 Los Angeles city elections, Mattachine Foundation sent letters to city council candidates to introduce the organization and ask them about their views on civil rights for homophiles. They sent letters to school board candidates, too, to tell them that "the sexual hygiene programs in City Schools must be modernized to meet the needs of potential sexual deviates."[54] Those plucky (and touchingly foolhardy) moves were the beginning of the end.

One of the letters fell into the hands of Paul Coates, a columnist for the Los Angeles tabloid the *Daily Mirror*. Coates specialized in lurid topics, from B-girls to religious quacks. "The already harassed and weary candidates for office were whacked with a broadside from a strange new pressure group," Coates wrote now with sensationalistic flair. Though ignorant of the Communist histories of the founders, he'd learned that Fred Snider, the attorney who'd drawn up the articles of incorporation for Mattachine Foundation Inc., had been called before the House Un-American Activities Committee when it met in Los Angeles in October 1952. Snider had taken the Fifth, a sure sign he was hiding Communistic activities, Coates implied. It didn't matter to Coates that just a month earlier the Mattachine had disavowed all "isms." What mattered was that the organization claimed there were as many as two hundred thousand homosexuals in the Los Angeles area—and they were in bed with a Red. "Eventually homosexuals might swing tremendous political power," Coates proclaimed. "A well-trained subversive could move in and forge that power into a dangerous political weapon."[55]

Marilyn Rieger, nicknamed Boopsie, was a large, energetic businesswoman, a recent recruit to Mattachine, who'd brought a number of lesbians with her. She was developing philosophical ideas about the homosexual's place in the world, and, as an ardent joiner, she was pleased to find a group on whom she might try them out. A couple of weeks before the Coates editorial appeared, she'd led a discussion group in the affluent Beverly Glen section of Los Angeles on "Why Homosexual Marriages Fail," and, as was customary, she'd forwarded the notes of what had been said to the Mattachine Foundation. Harry Hay, more secretive than ever about the identity of the leadership but keen to encourage the new members, wrote back under the guise of "Mrs. Henry Hay," telling Rieger that her detailed notes were "about the finest we have ever received." Rieger, flattered, replied, "I hope I will be called upon again to perform any service I can for the Foundation."[56]

So when Marilyn Rieger read Paul Coates's statement about a "well-trained subversive" moving in and controlling Mattachine, she—a successful entrepreneur who had no quarrel with capitalism—was personally offended. She'd attended about twenty-five Mattachine discussion group meetings, she informed Coates in an outraged letter the day after his piece appeared, and she could vouch that "there is no political aim of the Mattachine Foundation Inc. other than to fight for the right of man. *It is definitely and absolutely non-partisan.*"[57] She received no reply.

But Coates's allegations troubled her. They made her begin to think that perhaps she'd jumped into the organization without sufficient circumspection. Why, for instance, was there such an emphasis on secrecy? Eight days after the Coates editorial appeared, her Beverly Glen discussion group met again. With Rieger's urging, the eighteen men and ten women voted to set aside the scheduled topic and talk about the editorial instead. She found that others in the group were likewise troubled. They authorized her to write to the Mattachine Foundation on their behalf and demand some answers. "Who are the people who make policy for the Mattachine Foundation Inc.?" she asked in a March 23 letter. "Who is the Board of Directors? Who are Mrs. Henry Hay, Mrs. D. T. Campbell, and Romayne Cox? . . . What are the political affiliations of the Board of Directors?" Most of all, Rieger wanted to know whether she and the other Beverly Glen discussion group members were being made dupes.[58]

Three weeks later, Rieger got a reply from "Mrs. Henry Hay." Writing again in his mother's name, Harry Hay assured Rieger that the true purpose of Mattachine was just as its literature stated, and that the board was in no way subversive—and then "she" added, "Personally, I have been a Republican for over fifty years. Incidentally, my husband was once a partner of Herbert Hoover, and we often visited the Hoovers in New York."[59] An idiot might have been taken in by this comically bogus letter; but Rieger was no idiot, and she now set out in earnest to rip the mask from the Wizard of Oz.

She was joined by a slew of other Mattachine members, such as Ken Burns, a well-spoken, formal young man who favored Brooks Brothers suits and worked as a safety engineer for the Carnation Company.[60] Burns and the Mattachine group he presided over were bothered from the beginning by the secrecy of the organization's leaders and the rumors that they were subversives. Burns's group also questioned, as Rieger did, Mattachine's most basic precept: that homosexuals were a "cultural minority." They scoffed at the simpleminded notion that there was a "culture" all homosexuals shared. And homosexuals were in no sense a "minority," they argued. The only difference between homosexuals and heterosexuals was that homosexuals chose romantic and sexual partners of the same sex.

The old order was standing in the way of the organization's growth in power and influence, too, it seemed. Dr. Richard Gwartney, a psychologist who worked at Norwalk State Hospital and one of the few professional people in Mattachine, held out tantalizing promises. Acquaintances of his, other homosexual professional men, would start chapters in Chicago and Saint Louis and would help Mattachine become a strong and politically influential organization—but only if Mattachine could guarantee "that there be no red influence at all and that steps be taken to prevent infiltration." The well-connected doctor declared that Mattachine must be an open organization, "like one of the large church groups."[61]

In the San Francisco Mattachine, too, there were pockets of rebellion. Hal Call, a businessman, had come to San Francisco only the year before. He'd been a student at the University of Missouri School of Journalism when Professor E. K. Johnston was put through his ordeal. After graduation, he'd worked out of the *Kansas City Star*'s Chicago office, but he lost his job when he was arrested on a vag-lewd charge. He'd been made to pay $800 ($400 to an attorney, $200 to the judge, and $200 to the arresting officer) to "fix" his case.[62] Call joined the Mattachine in San Francisco because Dale Jennings's victory had cheered him. But he'd always distrusted the mystery of the Mattachine hierarchy. The new rumors about Communists in the leadership, who could endanger the very existence of the organization, riled him. He, Marilyn Rieger, and Ken Burns soon formed a troika of the discontented, and they led a mutiny.

•   •   •

The organization that Harry Hay and the others of the Fifth Order had started was morphing beyond recognition. Hay, still reeling from his comrades' silencing of him, wasn't up to bloody battles with other homophiles; and neither was the rest of the Fifth Order. Evolution wasn't unhealthy, they agreed. They'd bend a bit to the pressures. They'd end secrecy and identify themselves to the entire membership. "We believe that the time is right for a democratic organization of all individuals interested in the problems of sexual equality," they'd announce. Using their real names, they'd call a "Constitutional Convention" where the members could ratify a democratic constitution for Mattachine.[63]

The progressive ministers of LA's First Unitarian Church had always welcomed people that the rest of the world judged outré, so it wasn't astonishing when Reverend Steve Fritchman opened the church's grand Renaissance-revival-style building to Mattachine's constitutional convention. April 11–12, 1953, was the first time in America that a hall full of homosexuals came together for political purposes. Harry Hay was at first tickled by the numbers of homophiles who showed up: five hundred, he estimated. (Jim Kepner, a new member, who'd saved the vote tallies, said there were actually fewer than 150.[64]) But the fate of the old order was soon sealed. Ken Burns was elected chair of the constitutional convention by acclamation; Marilyn Rieger was eventually elected secretary.

Chuck Rowland was the convention's first speaker. Tattooed and wearing a crew cut, he stuck out among the many male delegates who were dressed in business garb and sported man-in-the-gray-flannel-suit-type haircuts. Rowland adhered still to the theory that had gotten everything started in Harry Hay's Silver Lake home in 1950. He compared homosexuals to Negroes, Jews, Mexican Americans, Japanese Americans: "Whether we like it or not, we are a minority!" he proclaimed with a tremor in his voice, because he knew that new members had no interest in being part of a "minority culture"; they wanted only that homosexuals be allowed to integrate with the straight world. His passionate oratory prefigured gay militant rhetoric by fifteen years: "I say with pride, 'I am a homosexual!'" Rowland shouted. He was eerily prophetic, too: "The time will come," he declared, "when we will march down Hollywood Boulevard arm in arm, proclaiming our pride in our homosexuality!"[65]

But the majority of the middle-class convention delegates were not roused.

In 1953 they, like most homosexuals, couldn't imagine ever marching to proclaim homosexual pride. Their homosexuality was no more something to have pride in than it was something to be ashamed about. They just wanted to get on with their lives without having to worry about being entrapped by a vice squad cop, fired from their job, thrown out of their apartment. They wanted to be allowed to live just like any other citizen, and not to be told they were different from their fellow Americans. They'd joined Mattachine because the organization had made the Jennings victory possible, and they wanted more such victories.

They weren't assured by Harry Hay's speech, either. Had he declared his patriotism and disavowed the alarming possibilities that the *Daily Mirror* editorial had raised, he might have allayed the suspicions of the new members. But Hay was incapable of such straightforwardness. "Are You Now or Have You Ever Been a Homosexual?," he titled his speech, parodying the McCarthy witch hunts of Reds. "To be one hundred percent pro-American," Hay declared, "one is required to be not only one hundred percent anti–New Deal but also one hundred percent antihomosexual."[66] Instead of dispelling qualms, his speech raised more doubts among those who abhorred radicalism.

Leery of the politics of the old order, suspicious of its past secrecy, disliking its doctrine that homosexuals are different from the rest of humanity, the delegates debated on and on, and no constitution was approved before the weekend came to an end. The only consensus the delegates arrived at was that they'd meet again within six weeks.

May 23–24, 1953: The Burns-Rieger-Call camp came to the next convention meeting armed with an alternate constitution that cut the *Foundation* out of Mattachine altogether. Hal Call, angry and persuasive, spoke about "a free society," which was necessary for homosexual "integration." Where are the laws against homosexuals "the most brutal and restrictive"? he asked rhetorically. In Russia, under Communism! he answered, and he proposed a resolution that Mattachine would not be infiltrated by "the extreme left."[67] It passed.

Marilyn Rieger's contribution that day was to circulate a statement she'd penned that attacked everything the old order had stood for. It captured the sentiments of the majority of the delegates. Borrowing Shylock's lines from William Shakespeare's *The Merchant of Venice*—"Hath not a Jew eyes? . . . fed with the same food, hurt with the same weapons?"—Rieger demanded, "Hath not a homosexual eyes?" And, she proclaimed, "We know we are the same, no different from anyone else. Our only difference is an unimportant one to heterosexual society, unless we make it important!"

Outraged still by the old order's secrecy—and its silly mendacities—Rieger also proposed that homosexuals must "come out into the open." The purpose of "coming out," she said, was not to flaunt the homosexual's difference before the world but rather to upend misconceptions by showing homosexuals to be simply "men and women whose homosexuality is irrelevant to our ideals, our principles, our hopes and aspirations."[68] Like Rowland's call to feel "pride," Rieger's call to "come out" was revolutionary—though who could do it in 1953, when homosexuals were persecuted as "moral perverts" and "sexual psychopaths"? But realistic or not, Rieger moved the delegates as Rowland and Hay had failed to.

The Fifth Order understood by that evening that Mattachine was no longer theirs. They met the next morning to discuss their course. On Sunday afternoon, when the delegates reassembled, the seven men marched up on the stage, identified themselves as the once-clandestine Fifth Order, and announced their resignations.

Ken Burns became the president of Mattachine, and when Hal Call succeeded him in 1956, he moved Mattachine headquarters to San Francisco. Marilyn Rieger, who'd urged Mattachine to focus on the high-minded advancement of homosexuals, was disgusted when she learned that Mattachine men were throwing parties that devolved into sexual affairs. Before the year was over, she left the homophile movement to become active in Paramahansa Yogananda's worldwide Self-Realization Fellowship. Mattachine continued to have chapters in a half dozen or so cities, but it never grew larger than a few hundred members nationally at any given time. In 1961 Hal Call declared that Mattachine would cease to be centralized. A few independent groups around the country continued to use the name Mattachine and hung on into the early 1970s.

Harry Hay went through a period of deep depression. He withdrew from those with whom he'd "been through hell and paradise," as Chuck

Rowland described their three-year journey.[69] In 1970, in the wake of a radical gay revolution, Hay founded the Radical Faeries, which, to this day, embraces "faerie culture" and resists the notion that homosexuals are "no different from anyone else." But he never got over the hurt of having been cast out by the organization he'd fathered with such love; he almost gloated that Mattachine had not amounted to much after the old order left. Those who remained, he said, "were interested in being middle class. They were all going to rush up to Sacramento and pound on the doors and tell the legislators to change the law—but otherwise be respectable. So the moment they became as good as the middle class, the dream was gone, and the movement died. And nothing was reborn until the late sixties."[70]

The riots at the Stonewall Inn, the birth of the radical Gay Liberation Front, Hay's Radical Faeries—those were to him beloved heirs to what he'd started. He disdained, to his death in 2002, the "assimilationist" goals of the successors to Mattachine. That bitter clash in 1953—radicals who'd regarded homosexuals as a different species from heterosexuals, versus assimilationists who'd insisted homosexuals and heterosexuals were almost exactly the same—augured the big internal clashes that would divide lesbian and gay communities even into the twenty-first century.

Chapter 6

THE DAUGHTERS

SORORITY

In 1950 Del Martin had just been hired as an editor for a Seattle trade journal, *Daily Construction Report*, and she moved up to Washington from San Francisco. She was a stocky woman with thick black hair, who wore gabardine suits and open-toed high-heel shoes and carried a briefcase to work. She was twenty-nine years old and not at all unhappy to leave the city where she'd been born. She'd recently given up custody of her eight-year-old daughter to her ex-husband and his new wife because they'd convinced her that a child needed a normal home and the presence of both a mother and father.[1] Martin would eventually become a fierce advocate for the rights of lesbian mothers[2]—but now she was still reeling from her painful decision. It was good to get away.

Phyllis Lyon, another displaced San Franciscan, was an associate editor at a sister trade journal, *Pacific Builder and Engineer*, which shared a suite of offices with *Daily Construction Report*. She'd never before seen a woman carrying a briefcase. It grabbed her attention right away. But she regarded herself as a straight lady—long haired and lipsticked—and was dating men (though she was already twenty-six years old and had never been married). Lyon lived close to the office of the two journals and offered to throw a little welcome-to-the-company party for her interesting new colleague. When Del Martin spent most of the evening in the kitchen talking to the guys and smoking cigars with them—they also tried to teach her how to tie a Windsor knot in a necktie—Lyon thought it a little curious.

But the two women became friends. They liked to go to the Seattle Press Club after work and sip martinis together. One evening over martinis the subject of homosexuality came up, and Martin expatiated like an expert. "How do you know so much about it?" a third woman in their party wanted to know. "Because I am one," Martin told them. That truly grabbed Lyon's attention. But nothing more came of it until 1952, when she invited Martin to her apartment for dinner and announced that she was leaving Seattle to go with her sister on an extensive road trip around America. Sitting together on the divan, they recalled later, Martin "made a half-pass"; Lyon "completed the other half." That evening, they became lovers.[3]

They moved back to San Francisco the next year. In a city crammed with aspiring writers, it was virtually impossible in the fifties for women to get jobs in any kind of journalism. Martin took work as a bookkeeper for Mayflower Moving and Storage, and Lyon was hired as an office worker in an import-export company. In 1955 they bought a home in a neighborhood adjoining the Castro district, which was not yet the gay mecca it would become in the next decade. The modest little house was perched on a hill in the Noe Valley area. Out the living-room window was a sweeping, romantic view of downtown, Twin Peaks, and Telegraph Hill.

But their lives were lonely. They felt isolated.[4] They couldn't tell their parents about the bliss of their coupledom. Their parents were as ignorant and hostile toward homosexuals as was the rest of America. ("If a child is a homosexual, the parents are to blame," Martin's mother had opined already. "She looks like a queer," Lyon's father had already told his wife about his daughter's housemate.[5]) Hoping to make friends, the two women started going to bohemian North Beach's lesbian bars, "gay girls' hangouts," as such places were called:[6] Mona's, the Paper Doll, Miss Smith's Tea Room (which never served tea). But they were ignored by the other gay girls, who all seemed to be in airtight cliques. And anyway, those girls were rougher and scruffier than the sorts of people Martin and Lyon wanted for friends. Even worse, Martin and Lyon had heard that homosexual bars could be raided. It wasn't easy to relax if you thought a paddy wagon might pull up in front of the place any minute. Nor was it easy to relax when straight tourists invaded the bars to ogle the queers, as often happened.

But having no place but the bars to be at least in the proximity of other lesbians, that summer they ventured into still another "gay girls' hangout": Tommy's on Broadway. They went with fear and trembling because an earlier iteration of Tommy's, located a few blocks down, had been the site of a huge raid the year before. Yet the place was nicer than most: tables for two scattered around the perimeter; droll posters and photographs decorating the walls.[7] The chatty gay male bartender made friendly conversation and introduced them to his partner, a female impersonator. Through them Martin and Lyon finally met another lesbian, Rose Bamberger, a short, brown-skinned woman who came from the Philippines and wanted to be known in those dangerous times as "Marie."[8] At the end of the summer, she telephoned Lyon and Martin to say that she and five other lesbians were tired of being gawked at by straights and worrying that they might be swept up in a bar raid. They were putting together a group, a secret lesbian society. Would Lyon and Martin like to be part of it? Of course they would. It was what they'd been looking for since they settled together in San Francisco.

Four lesbian couples showed up at the home of Rose and her partner, Rosemary Sliepen, for that first meeting. What they wanted, they all agreed, was a safe space to meet and dance and share a drink, and maybe occasionally go bowling or horseback riding. They could get together weekly in each other's homes. The group could be like a secret sorority, with colors (sapphire blue and gold), insignia (a triangle), motto ("*Qui Vive*"—Be Vigilant), a mission statement—articles of incorporation, even. Most of the women at the meeting were in their twenties; Lyon and Martin, both in their thirties, had *gravitas*. Martin was elected president. Lyon was elected secretary. The group should spend a few weeks drawing up a constitution and bylaws, Martin and Lyon suggested. They needed a name, too, of course—something that wouldn't reveal too much about who they were. They rejected Amazons, Musketeers, Two.

The fourth meeting, a month later, was in the small Fillmore Street apartment of a couple who wanted to be called "Nancy" and "Priscilla." (Nancy's real name was Noni Frey. Her partner, "Priscilla," was Mary, the lone Mexican American in the group.) "Nancy," the biggest reader among them, though she worked in a factory, whipped out a book. It was a translation of collected works by the French author Pierre Louÿs, and it included a cycle of 143 poems called "Songs of Bilitis." In 1894, when Louÿs first issued those poems, he'd claimed they'd been found by an archeologist on the walls of a tomb in Cyprus, and that he, Louÿs, was merely their translator. They were written, he said, by a Greek courtesan, a contemporary of Sappho who, like the poet of Lesbos, had had romantic and sexual relations with both men and women. Louÿs's forgery was revealed almost immediately, but the titillating poems had anyway been popular in his day, and from time to time, they were brought back into print.

Nancy was reading a 1951 edition. "Why don't we call ourselves Daughters of Bilitis?" she suggested. None of the other seven women at the meeting had read the poems, but they liked the name. It sounded like a straight women's organization—like the ultraconservative Daughters of the American Revolution or like the female auxiliary to the Shriners, called the Daughters of the Nile. And if some smart aleck recognized "Bilitis" from Pierre Louÿs's poems, the women could always say they were a poetry club.[9]

The name Daughters of Bilitis was one of the very few things on which the eight founders agreed. When Martin and Lyon thought about it later, they decided the conflicts had been along class lines: The women who were blue-collar workers wanted a secret social club, like a sorority, with rites and rituals, open only to lesbians,[10] but they definitely didn't want dress regulations. To one early meeting, Nancy had invited four "very masculine-appearing types" whom she knew from the factory and from bars. The white-collar workers, particularly Martin and Lyon, were uncomfortable with that. They wanted an official dress code that declared, "If slacks are worn to a meeting, they must be women's slacks." They were soon thinking, too, that maybe the club's purposes shouldn't be limited to holding dances and chili feeds and going horseback riding. They'd found out about Mattachine a few months after Daughters of Bilitis started. The headquarters was right there in San Francisco. Maybe they could have public forums together with Mattachine. Maybe Daughters of Bilitis could publish a newsletter, too.

Those plans scared the others who'd signed on for a secret social club. Rose Bamberger and her partner pulled out first. Then Nancy and her partner pulled out, and Nancy started a club mostly for working-class lesbian mothers and their partners. (The literary Nancy called her new club Quatrefoil, inspired by James Barr's 1950 novel about homosexual men.) A few more members joined DOB, which grew to twelve; and then shrank back to six. By the end of the first year, there were fifteen members, but of the original eight, only three remained.[11]

By then, they'd formulated their purpose: first of all, they would educate "the variant," their euphemism for "lesbian," "to enable her to understand herself and make her adjustment to society." They'd advocate to her "a mode of behavior and dress acceptable to society." To educate her, they'd maintain a library; and they'd have public discussions in which "leading members of the legal, psychiatric, religious, and other professions" would address her (and would also lend seriousness and respectability to Daughters of Bilitis). It was a goal similar to that of post–Harry Hay Mattachine. DOB would also supply research subjects ("female variants") to "duly authorized and responsible" psychologists, sociologists, and the like, so those "experts" could study them, as psychologist Evelyn Hooker had studied the men of Mattachine.[12]

Like Mattachine, too, Daughters of Bilitis pledged it would work to support changes in the penal code "as it pertains to the homosexual."[13] But that sort of battle wasn't what Daughters of Bilitis did best. Del Martin and Phyllis Lyon took personally another DOB aim, "to help the individual lesbian overcome isolation and fear."[14] Young lesbians in San Francisco usually lived in apartments. They had reason to fear not only that bars might be raided but also that neighbors might call the police if they saw bunches of short-haired women coming to visit. Before there was such a thing as LGBT community centers, the Lyon and Martin house high on a hill in Noe Valley became a sort of lesbian center.[15]

In 1956, to reach lesbians outside of San Francisco, the Daughters began publishing a magazine. They chose the name *The Ladder* to suggest the magazine's purpose—to encourage the lesbian to strive to pull herself up the ladder of social tolerance; the magazine would show her how, too. But Martin and Lyon were very aware that putting out a lesbian magazine at a time when homosexuals were being witch hunted was a scary proposition. Simply receiving a copy of *The Ladder* could trigger panic. A Tacoma,

Washington, woman had carelessly put her friend, a WAC, on the mailing list—and then had to write a hasty, pleading letter to Del Martin: "Please do all you can to keep the next issue from being sent to Marion Bales. There is a big investigation going on at Fort Lewis, and she is quite involved. It is very serious as every possible suspect may be ousted from the army . . . It would be very incriminating to have the magazine in her possession."[16]

In that atmosphere of justified worry, Lyon decided that as editor she'd use the name "Ann Ferguson." Her anonymity lasted for three issues. In the fourth *Ladder* she announced, "*Ann Ferguson is dead!*" and told readers her real name. She accused her "other self" of not having "practiced what I preached"[17]—but she knew she didn't dare ask other lesbians to use their real names. Even with the protection of an alias most were nervous. Lesbians who feared they had too much to lose, such as those with professional jobs, seldom subscribed to *The Ladder* or joined DOB, even under a false name.[18]

"WE ARE NOT A POLITICAL ORGANIZATION"

Phyllis Lyon, desperate to bring readers to the magazine, promised that the mailing list would never "fall into the wrong hands." "Your name is safe!" she wrote repeatedly in editorials.[19] But that promise proved false. The FBI was contacted about Daughters of Bilitis by "a confidential source who has furnished reliable information in the past." Whoever the woman was,[20] she kept Bureau agents regularly apprised of all the organization's doings. She also forwarded to the FBI copies of *The Ladder*. FBI agents read them cover to cover. "This is a group that is active in educating the public to accept the homosexual into society," they reported in their memos.[21] They also declared, with not an iota of evidence, that Daughters of Bilitis "appears to have been infiltrated by certain Communists."[22]

The Bureau went into high gear in 1964, when, informed by "a member of the Cleveland chapter of Citizens for Decent Literature" that Daughters of Bilitis, which by now had a few small chapters on the East Coast and in Chicago, was planning a national convention in New York. Memos, classified "Secret" by the Federal Bureau of Investigation, flew back and forth from the Cleveland office to the DC office to the New

York office to the San Francisco office, as agents tracked convention plans. But intelligence faltered: FBI agents in New York reported that the Hotel New Yorker had refused to host the "Daughters of Beletis [*sic*] convention."[23] Where were the lesbians planning to go? Agents checked with the New York Convention Bureau, which reported "no knowledge as to where the Daughters of Belitus [*sic*] were to hold their convention."[24] All signs of the lesbian convention had vanished. Apparently neither FBI agents nor their informants read the *New York Times*, which covered in some detail the June 21–22 conference of "Homosexual Women" (as attendees were called in the *Times* headline). One hundred of them, the newspaper announced to anyone who had the twenty-five cents to buy it, were at a two-day meeting in New York's Barbizon-Plaza Hotel.[25] The FBI, oblivious to its agents' fumbles, continued to keep track of DOB, as best it could, into the 1970s.

Despite its fixation, the Bureau really didn't have much to worry about in Daughters of Bilitis. The founders had never had a romance with the Left. "We are not a political organization," Phyllis Lyon assured DOB members and *Ladder* readers.[26] There were never battles over "isms," as there'd been among Mattachine members. Yet if Daughters avoided politics altogether, the group would be no more weighty than the dancing-dining-horsey sorority that Rose Bamberger and Nancy had wanted it to be. Martin and Lyon had envisioned a serious lesbian organization. But in those early years, they were ambivalent about politics.

In 1960 Del Martin read an article in the *New York Post*: "Elections and the Homosexual," by Murray Kempton, future Pulitzer Prize winner and Left-leaning gadfly who'd modelled his journalistic style after H. L. Mencken. Kempton had proclaimed, not quite accurately, that right-wing politicians had stopped persecuting homosexuals because "some bright young man in Republican headquarters had dipped into the best-selling Kinsey Report," and he'd put the word out that "there must be several million homosexuals of voting age." That meant, Kempton said, it was almost as dangerous for the Republican Party to be considered the antihomosexual party as to be considered the anti-Negro or anti-Polish or anti-Jewish party.

Del Martin quoted Kempton's article at length in *The Ladder*. People were finally noticing that a homosexual vote could influence elections, she exulted. "Let us do our utmost to make this a powerful factor," she declared passionately. "We do have a voice in the affairs of the community and the nation. Let us make it a strong voice."[27]

In the early years, she tried to rev up *Ladder* readers and DOB members. In her editorials, she protested raids on gay bars, urged revision of the vag-lewd and sodomy laws, and declared that homosexuals "are citizens of the United States, and as such are entitled to those civil rights set forth in the Constitution."[28] But the women who joined DOB wanted to stay out of the bars; and the vag-lewd laws and sodomy laws, it seemed to them, affected gay men, not lesbians. Martin backed off of militancy when it became apparent that most members were less interested in fighting for civil rights than in the Gab 'n' Java meetings: "rap sessions" that she and Lyon hosted in their living room.

On the rare occasions that a Gab 'n' Java session did turn to politics, it was only to disavow homosexual political action. Two years after Del Martin had beseeched homosexuals to "do our utmost" to make the homosexual vote powerful, she reported in *The Ladder* that it was agreed at a recent Gab 'n' Java that lesbians should not vote for a candidate "simply because he was homosexual, or was sympathetic toward the problem." Anyway, Gab 'n' Java–goers opined, a homosexual voting bloc was "nonexistent." And campaigns to try to create such a bloc, they said, would be "harmful."[29]

Political action even more militant than suffrage was out of the question for DOB. In 1961 Dorr Legg proposed that a ONE Midwinter Institute,[30] which brought together representatives of the homophile groups, be devoted to drawing up a "Homosexual Bill of Rights." Legg, lanky and bland looking, was the business manager of *ONE*, a homophile magazine that grew out of LA Mattachine. He liked to call himself "one of the few radical Republicans in existence,"[31] and would later be a founding member of the Log Cabin Republicans. Legg was also perhaps the most urbane and intellectual of the homophiles, and he was a far-sighted strategist too.[32] A Homosexual Bill of Rights, Legg declared, would remind the American government that homosexuals were citizens too, and it would make demands: the right to full first-class citizenship, the right to be free from discriminatory statutes, the right to be free from police surveillance, the destruction of all government records on any citizen's homosexual behavior, the right to equal treatment before the law, the right to custody of one's own children, the right to adopt.[33] It was the first time that homophiles had dared spell out in detail what civil rights for homosexuals might be. It was a daring and revolutionary proposal.

Daughters of Bilitis abhorred it. Even before the institute meeting, Del Martin mocked the notion of a Homosexual Bill of Rights in an all-caps editorial: "We Can Only Ask—How Far Out Does The Homosexual Want To Go? How Ludicrous Can We Get? Such A 'Bill Of Rights' Is Unnecessary, Irrelevant, And Likely To Set The Homophile Movement Back Into Oblivion."[34]

Jaye Bell, the national president of DOB, agreed. Bell (nicknamed Shorty because she was close to six feet tall), had plenty of reason to be angry about her second-class citizenship. She'd been dishonorably discharged from the military as a lesbian—before she even knew she *was* a lesbian.[35] But militancy troubled Bell. She waited for the institute's evening banquet before seizing the microphone. Her organization would "officially dissociate" itself from any Homosexual Bill of Rights, she announced, because the bill "*demanded* that people have the attitudes we prescribe for them." DOB's approach was to *educate* people to have the right attitudes; to help psychologists and other experts undertake scientific studies of homosexuals that would tell the straight world that homosexuals weren't monsters. That was the only way to change the position of the homosexuals. "One cannot demand or legislate attitudes," she lectured Legg and his supporters.[36]

"Homosexual Bill of Rights Sizzles and Fizzles," a *Ladder* headline gloated.[37]

May 1960, the first Daughters of Bilitis National Conference: The organizers were exhilarated to see over one hundred lesbians gathered in the Vista Room of San Francisco's genteel Hotel Whitcomb, waiting to be addressed by a psychiatric authority, a minister, a legal expert, and a high representative of the law. On the morning panel called "Why the Lesbian?" the psychiatric authority, Dr. Norman Reider, told his listeners that the answer lay in "psycho-pathology and developmental psychology." The luncheon speaker, Reverend Fordyce Eastburn, Episcopal chaplain at St. Luke's Hospital, addressed the question "Can the Practicing Homosexual Be Accepted

by the Church?" by admitting that during his twenty-six years in the ministry, he'd met only one homosexual. But his paucity of real knowledge
didn't stop him from spouting his views: homosexuals were afflicted with
a disorder of nature. They must stay away from their sources of temptation,
and they should take therapy and attempt to make a heterosexual adjustment to life. "The minister served up our damnation with our dessert," one
DOB member lamented.[38] Yet there were no shouts of "Bigot!" and no
overturning of lunch tables.

In the early afternoon, the eager DOB conventioneers were told by the
staff council of the ACLU that his progressive organization "found nothing unconstitutional in the federal government's security risk program,"
which persecuted homosexual employees.[39] The late-afternoon speaker
was Sidney Feinberg, the bombastic and bullying head of the North Coast
Area office of the Alcoholic Beverage Control—the same Sidney Feinberg
who'd announced the year before that he'd "put a dozen undercover agents
to work to root out homosexual bars."[40] If the DOB organizers had fan-
tasized that he'd magically transformed in the last year, they were roundly
disappointed. Feinberg proclaimed that homosexual bars were under surveillance because law enforcement authorities had a responsibility "to keep
their eyes on the criminal elements in society."[41]

One hundred–plus lesbians sat listening to the string of insults, but consistent with DOB's policy of decorum, "The audience rumbled but had the
good sense not to erupt."[42]

Despite insults from the experts, DOB continued on its course. Del
Martin insisted in 1962 that DOB was not formed as "a crusade" to change
laws. What DOB was about was helping the lesbian "make her adjustments
to self and society." It was about giving the lesbian "knowledge of herself"
by encouraging researchers to study her, so she could "move into the world
at large as a more secure, self-assured, and productive citizen." It was about
helping her climb a ladder. It was not about antagonizing the public with
"the beating of the drums—and gums."[43]

But the following year, 1963, *The Ladder* got a new editor. To Martin's
and Lyon's discomfort and even fury, she scorned DOB's notions about
climbing ladders, using lesbians as research guinea pigs, and stifling beating
drums and gums. She helped shift the homophile movement in a whole
new direction.

ADULTS ONLY

Barbara Gittings was a bright young woman with a mellifluous voice and beautiful diction. She was born in Vienna, Austria, in 1932, the daughter of a US diplomat of *Social Register* forebearers, who brought his family back to the United States at the dawn of World War II. Big-boned, pale, serious, and serious looking, Barbara Gittings had been troubled before she entered Northwestern University as a freshman in 1949: she suspected she was homosexual and knew only that that was something one was not supposed to be. She spent her freshman year looking in the card catalog under "abnormal" and "perversion" and then haunting the library stacks, determined to find out what the taboo was all about. She was so busy searching for answers, she forgot to go to her classes and flunked out at the end of the year.

Gittings returned home to Delaware, but she couldn't bring herself to tell her family what had happened. When her father caught her reading *The Well of Loneliness*, he wrote her (though they were living in the same house) an unpleasant letter demanding that she <u>burn</u> the book. <u>Burn</u> was underlined because, he wrote, any other way of getting rid of the book might mean that someone else could find it and be infected. She hid the book; and she saved the money she earned in a clerical job so that she'd be able to leave home.

Gittings escaped to Philadelphia. There she found work as a music store clerk, lived in a rooming house, and subsisted on boiled eggs and plain cooked vegetables, which she fixed on a hot plate. Disguised as a boy, she hitchhiked every weekend to Greenwich Village, where she'd discovered the "gay girls" bar scene. Gittings didn't drink, so she'd sip ice water all evening, pretending it was gin on the rocks. She became "Sonny" because the habitués were calling themselves either butch or femme, and she felt silly in long hair and makeup; but she felt almost as silly being "Sonny." And worse, she could find no one in the bars who shared her interest in social issues or literature or medieval, Renaissance, and baroque music. About this time, she discovered Donald Webster Cory's 1951 book, *The Homosexual in America*. It was Cory's book that made her think that homosexuals ought to be defining themselves as a legitimate minority; they ought to start demanding rights, just as other minorities were doing.[44]

Her conception of how that might be done was vague, but her

determination was robust. Soon after reading *The Homosexual in America*, she wrote to Donald Cory,[45] asking where the organized homosexuals were. He referred her to *ONE* magazine in Los Angeles, and on her vacation from the music store in the summer of 1956, she hurried west. Through *ONE*, she found her way to Phyllis Lyon and Del Martin in San Francisco, and they invited her to a Daughters of Bilitis meeting the same day she arrived, rucksack still on her back.[46]

Gittings walked into the comfortable San Francisco home where the meeting was being held and saw a dozen to fifteen women sitting together in the living room of a nice house rather than in a Mafia-owned, liquor-permeated bar. She heard them planning the first issue of a lesbian magazine that would be called *The Ladder* and would come out that fall. She thought, for a while anyway, that she'd come home, even though she was critical of their abstruse and unpronounceable name, Daughters of Bilitis. The bespectacled twenty-six-year-old in her travel-stained sleeveless dress[47] told the members that their name hid the organization's identity behind a reference to a not-very-good book about an ancient fictional character who was not even lesbian but bisexual.[48]

Del Martin and Phyllis Lyon were quick to see that the outspoken newbie wasn't a typical recruit. Here was an unusually well-read, energetic young person who was looking for a way to combine her intense personal interest in the "homosexual condition" with a cause that would allow her to focus her considerable energies. They saw that she was someone "who was willing to take the bit and run a little."[49] They suggested she start a Daughters of Bilitis group in New York. Gittings was living in Philadelphia, but New York sounded like the sensible choice to her, too.

She found that New York already had a Mattachine Society, started in 1955 by two men: Cuban-born chemist Tony Segura, who'd also been fired up by Cory's book,[50] and psychologist Sam Morford, who'd learned of California's Mattachine through fellow psychologist Evelyn Hooker. In a small loft building on Sixth Avenue, in one of their postage-stamp-sized offices, Mattachine Society New York made space for the little group that Gittings pulled together.[51] Starting in 1958, she was taking the bus twice a month from Philadelphia to New York—she'd stopped hitchhiking by now—to run the first East Coast chapter of Daughters of Bilitis.

From the beginning, Gittings was bothered by DOB's stated goal to "educate" the lesbian to "adjust" to society, as though the lesbian were an unruly child that needed correction—"a scolding-teacher approach," she thought.[52] She hated *The Ladder*'s use of the term "sexual variant," as though *lesbian* needed a euphemism. She was against providing the "experts" with lesbian guinea pigs. And she became dismayed that "experts," usually straight people, were being invited to speak at DOB meetings about the "problems" of homosexuality. None of what DOB was doing had much to do with Donald Webster Cory's electrifying exhortation that homosexuals must demand their civil rights. But she hadn't any idea how to lead Daughters of Bilitis in a more meaningful direction, yet.

Del Martin had been editing *The Ladder* since Jaye Bell replaced her as DOB president in July 1960. After two and a half years, Martin thought it time to hand over her mantle. Barbara Gittings was the most literary person Martin knew, but Gittings was busy. At a picnic she organized in Rhode Island to try to get a DOB chapter started in the "Hope" state, she'd met Kay Tobin,[53] a petite redhead with whom she could share her passion for books, music, and homophile politics. Their promising relationship was less than two years old, and they were learning to live together. Also, Gittings was working full-time in a Philadelphia architectural firm, running its mailroom and mimeograph machine to make a living. She'd guessed that if you wanted to edit a magazine well, the editing would have to be your full-time job. "Okay," she finally told Martin, "I'll do it for a few months, until you find someone who can take it over permanently."

But a few months into her editorship, she attended a conference of the new East Coast Homophile Organizations (ECHO). Its founder, and main speaker at the conference, was Frank Kameny, the head of Washington, DC's Mattachine. Gittings thought him the most brilliant theoretician of homosexual rights she'd ever heard or met or read. Finally, she had a blueprint for how to begin doing what she'd dreamed of doing since she'd read *The Homosexual in America*.[54] Now that she had something to say, she would stay on as editor of *The Ladder*, Gittings decided. She quit her paying job and lived on a small trust fund: she'd been right that the unpaid editorship was a full-time position.

Under Gittings's editorship, *The Ladder* was transformed inside and out. In place of the insipid art that usually graced the cover, Gittings had her

partner, Tobin, who was an amateur photographer, persuade real live lesbians to be cover girls. Not only would it be a publishing breakthrough, but
also readers would be inspired to see actual healthy, happy-looking homosexual women.[55] She and Tobin wanted to portray the diversity of lesbians,
too—though there were practically no images of racial diversity even in
straight magazines in the early sixties. The November 1964 cover was of a
pretty Indonesian woman, Ger van Braam, who'd been writing stories for
The Ladder. The June 1966 cover was a headshot of the affable-looking vice
president of the New York chapter of DOB, Ernestine Eckstein, a black
woman; and the article that opened that issue was an eight-page interview
with Eckstein. It was the first time an out lesbian of color was featured in
any magazine.[56]

Gittings and Tobin also agreed it would be good to get rid of the title
The Ladder. They hopefully proposed more weighty names: Dialogue, Cata-
lyst, Vanguard, Counterpoint.[57] But the DOB powers made clear their attachment to the old title. Gittings bypassed them by adding to the cover a bold
subtitle, A Lesbian Review, hoping it would offset what she considered the
patronizing, mealymouthed name they'd stuck her with. A Lesbian Review,
she thought, was a proud proclamation of what the magazine was really
about, and it was an announcement to the world that lesbian was not unspeakable. With each issue, the words A Lesbian Review got larger while the
words The Ladder got smaller.

She ran into trouble pretty quickly. Martin and Lyon insisted that if
the word Lesbian was going to be on the cover, "For Sale to Adults Only"
needed to be there too. "That's offensive! It implies lesbian is salacious,"
Gittings protested. She called Kenneth Zwerin, DOB's pro bono lawyer
and an ex-president of San Francisco Mattachine, to ask whether an adults-
only warning was necessary. "If the contents are obscene, putting 'For Sale
to Adults Only' won't save you from being prosecuted," Zwerin told her.
"And if they're not obscene, you don't need the warning."[58] His professional opinion did not allay the DOB leadership's nervousness. "For Sale to
Adults Only" remained.

Even more important than the changes Gittings made to The Ladder's
covers were the changes she made to the content. She continued to run
lesbian book reviews as well as poetry and fiction; but the political shrewdness of articles soared. Her opinion pieces hit hard at the experts that the

Daughters had so revered. For example, she declared of a New York Academy of Medicine report characterizing homosexuality as a preventable and treatable illness: "It's a reminder of the sly, desperate trend to enforce conformity by a 'sick' label for anything deviant."[59] In the name of DOB, she sent the Academy of Medicine a letter, reprinted in the same issue of *The Ladder*, calling the authorities to task for their failure to substantiate their claims that homosexuality is an illness, and bringing to their attention the fact that there were other "experts," such as psychologist Dr. Evelyn Hooker, who disagreed with their careless assertion that homosexuals were sick.[60]

Gittings also opened a forum in *The Ladder* for her militant mentor, Frank Kameny. "Cringing meekness has taken its toll among homosexuals," he admonished the readers, who'd never before encountered the likes of his boldness. It is time for homosexuals to stop being "gentlemanly and lady-like," he rebuked them. They must move from "endless talk to firm, vigorous action."[61] Gittings gave room in the magazine, too, to a lengthy leaflet, written by Kameny, who was organizing homosexuals to picket the White House, the Civil Service Commission, the Department of Defense, the United Nations, and Independence Hall: "Homosexual American citizens have appealed repeatedly to their federal government for redress for their grievances," the leaflet announced. To Gab 'n' Java's annoyance, Kameny and his group *demanded* redress. "The Homosexual American citizen asks from his government what the founding fathers asked from the British government of their day: reasonable, constructive, meaningful action, taken in good faith."[62]

To prod her readers along, Gittings also ran a Cross-Currents column, in which she reported on homosexuals who were principals in court cases that the homophiles had thought could never be fought—such as Bruce Scott, a homosexual man who'd been denied employment by the Civil Service Commission and had filed suit in the US District Court.[63] Gittings reveled in such legal confrontations, in making political demands, in action. Almost as a direct rebuke to the Gab 'n' Java–goers who'd claimed that a homosexual voting bloc was "nonexistent" and that to try to create one would be "harmful," a headline by her partner Kay Tobin declared in a 1965 *Ladder*, "Homosexual Voting Bloc Puts Pizzazz in Politics."[64]

The coup de grace to the relationship between Gittings and the DOB founders came over issues of picketing. Gittings and Tobin worked at Kameny's side in organizing the pickets, and the three of them hoped to increase the numbers of protestors through ECHO, the coalition of organizations Kameny had started in order to bring homophile groups together for joint action. Del Martin and Phyllis Lyon, who kept seats on DOB's governing board, soon informed Gittings that Daughters of Bilitis was withdrawing from ECHO: "The bone of contention is over picketing programs," they wrote Gittings with indignation. DOB would never engage in direct action, they said, unless "there were support and involvement from the larger community [that is, from heterosexuals]."[65] Kameny jumped into the fray with rhetoric that, as usual, pulled no punches: "This is arrant nonsense. When one has reached the stage where picketing is backed by the larger community, such picketing is no longer necessary," he wrote Martin and Lyon and their governing board. "The entire force and thrust of picketing is as a protest on issues not yet supported or backed by the larger community."[66]

The relationship between Gittings and the DOB leadership had become irreparable. Despite the growth in circulation and distribution of the magazine under Gittings,[67] Martin and Lyon were waiting for an excuse to axe her. They got it in the months before the 1966 national DOB convention—she was missing deadlines,[68] she wasn't providing enough lead time for publicizing the convention.[69] Martin and Lyon's governing board fired Gittings just after the August 1966 issue went to press.

THE DAUGHTERS' RIPPLE EFFECT

At the height of McCarthy-era persecution, the founders of Daughters of Bilitis couldn't dream there'd be a time when lesbians would demand serious civil rights. Daughters of Bilitis existed mostly "to help the individual lesbian overcome the isolation and fear that are her worst enemy."[70] That goal wasn't hugely different from what Rose Bamberger had envisioned in 1955, when she called Lyon and Martin to ask if they'd like to join six other women to start a lesbian social group. Nor did Daughters of Bilitis ever have more than a few hundred members, including those in the small chapters of New York, Boston, Philadelphia, Los Angeles, Chicago, and Fanwood, New Jersey.[71] Its value, however, ought not be underestimated.

Through its magazine, *The Ladder*, it reached lesbians in the most unlikely places. It gave them comfort at a time when no one else would. Its existence had a ripple effect that kept going long after the organization died.

Lesbian activist Robin Tyler tells the story of herself when she was seventeen-year-old Arlene Chernick, born in Winnipeg, Canada, whose large Mennonite population set the tone of the city. She'd had crushes on girls for as long as she could remember, but without a name to put to her feelings she worried that she was a singular species. Then in 1959 Arlene happened into a small secondhand bookstore and there, inexplicably—in the social wilds of Canada—was a copy of *The Ladder*. The magazine told her that there was a name for her feelings, and that it didn't matter if people said those feelings were wrong, as long as they were right for her. That message was exactly what she needed, at a time when she really needed it. It beckoned her to the big cities of the United States, where she could live as a lesbian more easily. When she finally got to San Francisco, Del Martin and Phyllis Lyon were there at the airport to greet her. They welcomed and cossetted her, just as they had the many other lesbians whose lives had been changed by their organization and magazine.[72]

In 1979, twenty years after she'd discovered *The Ladder*, Robin Tyler, a well-known lesbian activist by then, called for the first March on Washington for Lesbian and Gay Rights.[73] It drew a hundred thousand people. In 1987 she was the rally producer of the second March on Washington for Lesbian and Gay Rights, which drew over six hundred thousand people. She was also a producer of the rally of the third march in 1993. That one drew almost a million.

Chapter 7

JOUSTS WITH THE
FOUR HORSEMEN

THE FIRST HORSEMAN: DORR LEGG
AND *ONE* TILT AT THE SOCIAL

October 1952: Dorr Legg was hosting a Mattachine Discussion Group in his living room. A former vice squad officer who'd quit the LAPD in disgust had been invited to give a talk. His subject was the dirty tactics that the police were using to entrap homosexuals. "Plainclothes officers even strap walkie-talkies under their jackets," he said. "That way, the cops waiting to make the bust can hear the homosexual agreeing to the undercover officer's proposition." It caused a huge stir among the twenty men who were there.[1]

"People don't know these things. We need to spread the word! We need a magazine!" one man stood up to say when the talk was over. A quarter of the audience was so swept away by the superb suggestion that they wanted to discuss it immediately. They'd start the first homophile magazine![2] While the rest of the audience agonized over how to outsmart dirty police tactics, they adjourned to Dorr Legg's kitchen.

Dale Jennings, the reluctant hero of the entrapment case that gave Mattachine its big boost, was one of the men who gathered around Legg's kitchen table. There was also Don Slater, an impish five-foot-six-inch-tall fellow with a gravelly voice and a bent for mocking humor. (He called Mattachine the Stitch and Bitch Club and refused to join, saying, "If any of these people had sex lives, they wouldn't sit around talking the subject to death."[3]) There was Martin Block, a plump, quick-witted New Yorker who'd been with Mattachine since the beginning but was a vociferous critic of "each and every one of their Communist enthusiasms."[4] Johnny Button, who'd said "We need a magazine!" was there, too. ("Little Pipsqueak" was Dorr Legg's inelegant moniker for him.) Button soon dropped out and left the magazine to the rest of the cantankerous crew.[5]

They decided that Martin Block, who owned a bookshop and was considered to be "a veritable encyclopedia of literary information," would be the first editor.[6] The magazine's title, *ONE*, was suggested at a later meeting by an elementary school teacher, Bailey Whitaker (aka Guy Rousseau), a young black man who became *ONE*'s official proofreader. Whitaker had been reading Thomas Carlyle's *Essays* and was moved by the sentence, "A mystic bond of brotherhood makes all men one." To raise money for the magazine Legg convinced a wealthy acquaintance with a huge Renaissance-style mansion—vaulted ceilings, eight-feet-high candelabras, rare tapestries covering the walls—to hold a benefit. The clean-up expenses were so high after two hundred people drank and cavorted that the still-unborn magazine netted just thirty-five dollars. They dinged friends for donations. *ONE*'s first issue finally came out in January 1953.[7]

Jim Kepner came on board soon after. He'd been a reporter for the *Daily Worker* and a Communist Party member until he was kicked out when he admitted he was a homosexual.[8] (Kepner avoided the subject of Communism when Block was around.) Now he supported himself by driving a cab and working in a milk-carton factory because such jobs didn't require the intellectual energy he wanted to save for his homophile work. As a writer for *ONE*, Kepner was "Lyn Pederson" "Dal McIntyre," "Frank Golowitz," and sometimes "Jim Kepner." He used pseudonyms to make readers think there were a lot more people writing for the magazine than there actually were.

Dorr Legg used pseudonyms, too, such as "Wendy Lane," because not many lesbians sent *ONE* their writing.[9] But in the spring of 1953, a lesbian couple—Irma Wolf (aka Ann Carll Reid) and Joan Corbin (aka Eve Elloree)—joined the staff after they heard Legg talk to a Mattachine group about the magazine.[10] Reid eventually became *ONE*'s editor, and Elloree, an artist, became the magazine's art director. They brought in a twenty-eight-year-old civil service employee, Stella Rush (aka Sten Russell).[11] But the magazine's readers continued to be mostly men, and most articles were aimed at them.

Dorr Legg had once remarked that homosexuals had four deadly enemies. The Four Horsemen of the Apocalypse, he called them: the Social, the Scientific, the Religious, and the Legal.[12] *ONE* would joust valiantly with the first and win some surprising victories.

ONE was headquartered on seedy South Hill Street, in a smoke-filled two-room office that was cluttered with orange-crate bookshelves and desks and chairs from the Goodwill store that was downstairs. One late July afternoon, soon after Sten Russell came to work in the magazine's office, the downstairs doorbell rang. She went out into the hall and watched two men in dark suits climb the creaky stairs. They showed her their IDs. They said they'd been sent by the Los Angeles postmaster, Otto K. Olesen, whose order of confiscation came from federal post office authorities. The cover of the August 1953 issue of the magazine had asked outrageously, "Homosexual Marriage?" It could not be mailed, the men said.[13]

If the post office refused to mail the magazine, *ONE* would be put out of business. Its staff needed a lawyer. Dale Jennings had recently been at a cocktail party in Malibu, where he was introduced to an interesting young attorney who was barely out of law school but had already been mentioned in a *Los Angeles Daily News* article about civil liberties.[14] He'd gotten a black man acquitted of drug possession and LAPD officers dressed down for police brutality.[15] Jennings, with Legg, Slater, and Kepner in tow, went to see the straight, very young-looking twenty-nine-year-old in his Beverly Hills office. "We're difficult, and we have no money," Dorr Legg admitted after telling Eric Julber about the confiscation. "I'm interested," Julber said.[16]

The post office actually had slim basis for a gripe against *ONE*. The "homosexual marriage" article, which asked "Marriage License or Just License?" presented no threat to society. Homosexuals had no interest in getting married, the writer declared—they despised monogamy, considered it "stuffy and hidebound." His conclusion was that "Rebels such as we demand freedom" and didn't care a whit for the privilege reserved for a man and woman.[17] The solicitor general to whom the ONE case was referred conceded that there was nothing "obscene" in the piece. Postmaster Olesen had to release the magazine for mailing.

The case hadn't been dramatic enough to assure Julber's big reputation as a civil liberties defender, but to the editors of ONE it was a solid tilt in the fight for homosexual rights. They hoped to use it to rally the troops. The post office decision was "historic," Dale Jennings declared. Never before had a big governmental agency had to admit that homosexuals might have legal rights. But there were still thousands of homosexuals being unjustly arrested, jailed, beaten, ruined—and now it was time to fight. "Want to help?" Jennings challenged ONE's readers.

Defiant as Jennings's editorial was, the board knew they'd be bullied again if they weren't vigilant. Eric Julber agreed to read every issue of the magazine carefully before it was sent off to the typesetter. "Depicting sex acts may be standard practice in heterosexual magazines and literature, but you can't do it in a homosexual magazine," Julber warned.[18] "No rubbing knees, feeling thighs, holding hands, soaping backs, or getting undressed. No 'That night, we made love.'"[19] For the October 1954 issue, he wrote a cover article, "'You Can't Print It!' by ONE's Legal Counsel," to explain why the stories in the magazine couldn't be hotter.

That same issue contained an innocuous ad for a Swiss homophile magazine, Der Kreis, which sometimes gave information about how to obtain pictures of naked men. There was also a campy, mock eighteenth-century poem about British homosexuals, "Lord Samuel and Lord Montagu," by "Brother Grundy," a philosophy professor at a Canadian university. (The poem had lines such as "His ins and outs with various scouts / Had caused a mild sensation.") And there was "Sappho Remembered" by "Jane Dahr" (pseudonym for James Barr, the homosexual author of Quatrefoil), a lesbian story about a twenty-year-old woman who spurns her loving fiancé and goes off with Pavia, her exotic thirty-year-old lesbian employer. The hottest line in "Sappho Remembered" was "Pavia touched the delicate pulse beat beneath the light golden hair on the child-like temple."

In late September 1954, the ONE staff lugged several hundred copies of the October issue to the post office. The next day, they were notified by Otto Olesen's office that the magazine contained material that was "obscene, lewd, lascivious, and filthy." It was not mailable under California and federal codes.[20]

Dorr Legg called Eric Julber. The magazine still couldn't afford to pay him, Legg explained. Accounts receivable that month totaled $1,428.89; accounts payable totaled $1,433.70.[21] No matter, Julber said. He'd help *ONE* sue the post office. They'd argue that the postmaster's refusal to mail the magazine was arbitrary, capricious, and an abuse of his discretionary powers. They'd argue that his action was unsupported by evidence, that it deprived *ONE* of equal protection of the laws, that it was a violation of *ONE*'s property and liberty without due process.

Julber, still fresh faced and young at the game, decided he'd try to get some heavyweight backup from the ACLU. This was, after all, a First Amendment issue. But the ACLU wasn't in the business of protecting homosexuals in 1954. "I don't think we'd be interested in a case like that," the director of the Southern California branch bluntly told Julber. He was on his own.[22]

By the time the Post Office had confiscated *ONE* for a second time, FBI agents were following the magazine avidly. The November 1955 issue featured an article by the old Mattachine's fiery Chuck Rowland, writing under the name David L. Freeman, titled "How Much Do We Know about the Homosexual Male?"[23] Rowland divided homosexual men into three groups. The "Tories" were the "elegant" ones. They wrote for magazines such as *Time* and *Newsweek*; they were in the Diplomatic Service; and "they occupy key positions with the FBI (It's true!)," Rowland claimed with a mischievous verbal wink. On January 26, 1956, FBI agent M. A. Jones forwarded the article to Associate Director Clyde Tolson. Tolson scribbled on the memo in dark, angry handwriting, "I think we should take this crowd on and make them put up or shut up," and he forwarded it to J. Edgar Hoover. Hoover wrote in his own furious hand, "I concur."[24] (If there's truth to the rumor that had been circulating since the 1940s—that Hoover and Tolson were lovers—that might have fueled their fury.)[25]

The next day, Hoover sent a memo to the director of the FBI's Los Angeles office: "You are instructed to have two mature and experienced agents contact David Freeman and William Lambert [Dorr Legg], chairman of the ONE board of directors, in the immediate future." The agents were to tell Lambert that "the Bureau will not countenance such baseless charges appearing in this magazine." They were to say he'd better "'put up or shut up!'" Hoover wrote, adopting his alleged lover's phrase.[26]

The Los Angeles office of the FBI did what it was ordered to do. Two agents descended on *ONE*'s shabby South Hill Street digs. David L. Freeman was nowhere to be seen, but Dorr Legg was sitting there, almost as though they'd had a date. He was ready for them. *ONE* and the homophile movement had been Legg's life. He'd been a professor of landscape architecture and an urban planner, but he'd sacrificed his career to the homophile cause. He was now working full-time on *ONE*. His Japanese American partner, John Nojima, paid their rent and bought their food. Legg wasn't about to be intimidated by two FBI hacks.

"He was sarcastic, refused to furnish any information regarding David Freeman, and he advised agents that *ONE*'s attorney, Eric Julber of Beverly Hills, approved everything that went into the magazine," the FBI men reported. This William Lambert, aka Dorr Legg—who obviously knew his rights—was as cool a customer as these "mature and experienced" FBI men had ever seen. "Do you have any objections to this interview being taped?" Dorr Legg had calmly asked the two. In their subsequent memo to their superior, the FBI men hastened to assure him that they'd been "extremely circumspect." (What went on in interviews where they hadn't been so "circumspect" can only be imagined.) The superior didn't have to worry, the agents kept on. They didn't believe the meeting was actually being recorded.[27] It's obvious who had the upper hand in this interview in *ONE*'s tiny office, and how astonishing that was to the two agents. "The interview shows that Lambert is strictly no good," one of the agents emoted in another memo about the encounter.[28]

A few weeks later, the US District Court judge Thurmond Clarke—a beefy former football player for USC—ruled that *ONE* was not mailable because "its filthy and obscene material was obviously calculated to stimulate the lust of the homosexual reader." Moreover, the judge declared, "The suggestion advanced that homosexuals should be recognized as a segment of our people and be accorded special privileges as a class is rejected."[29]

Julber told Dorr Legg that *ONE* must appeal. He promised to see the fight through though still there was no money to pay him. The appeal verdict was issued on March 1, 1957, by the Ninth Federal District Court of Appeals judges: "At the outset, it is well to dispel any thought that this court is its brother's keeper as to the type of reading to be indulged in," the judges said. They upheld "freedom of expression and the place of a free press in the world." They even waxed poetic: "Morals are not static like the everlasting hills, but are like the vagrant breezes to which the mariner must ever trim his sails."[30] So far, so good.

But the next line was a "nevertheless": "Sappho Remembered," they said, "is nothing more than cheap pornography calculated to promote lesbianism." As for "Lord Samuel and Lord Montagu," it "pertains to sexual matters of such vulgar and indecent nature that it tends to arouse a feeling of disgust and revulsion." Homosexuals aren't disgusted and revolted, the judges said, because the homosexual's "social and moral standards are far below those of the general community." But society doesn't have to put up with it: "Social standards are fixed by and for the great majority, and not by or for a hardened or weakened minority. Obscenity is not defined to fit the concept of morality of society's dregs." (So much for "vagrant breezes.") The appeals court upheld Judge Thurmond Clarke's decision.[31]

For four years, Eric Julber had taken nothing but an occasional small retainer fee from *ONE*. But, as he told Legg, he sincerely believed in *ONE's* right to publish and the homosexual's right to read. He also felt that if he could make something of this case his reputation as a civil rights lawyer would be made. With his own money, he bought a plane ticket to Washington, DC, and he filed a brief on behalf of *ONE* in the Supreme Court.

The Supreme Court had never in its history considered a case that dealt with homosexuality. It accepted Eric Julber's petition. The justices read his brief and declared they needed no further arguments. On January 13, 1958, five justices, led by Felix Frankfurter, voted to reverse the lower courts' decisions. *ONE's* major topic was homosexuality, but that didn't mean the publication was obscene or indecent, they concluded; and the Post Office had no right to confiscate the magazine. Though Julber didn't get to plead, the Supreme Court's reversal was a huge victory for him, and for Dorr Legg and all the *ONE* staff. Even more important, it made a remarkable social statement, tacit as it was. Homosexuality was not unspeakable.

THE SECOND HORSEMAN: EVELYN
HOOKER TILTS AT THE SCIENTIFIC

Evelyn Gentry Caldwell Hooker was almost six feet tall, a strong-looking woman with a chiselled face. She had a deep voice and a hearty laugh and liked to wear tailored suits. All that plus her professional interest in homosexuals made some in the community think she was a sister. She was careful to make it clear she was "hopelessly heterosexual."[32] She married twice.

In 1932 she received a PhD in Experimental Psychology from Johns Hopkins with a specialty in animal behavior—"rat psychology," she called it.[33] The UCLA Psychology Department, where she'd hoped to teach after receiving her doctorate, wouldn't hire her because they already had three women professors, and most of the men in the department thought that quite enough. It took years before she even got a job teaching classes at UCLA Extension. During the war, her brightest and most personable night-class student was Sammy From, who worked by day writing contracts between the air force and the Los Angeles–based aircraft industry. One evening, when her then husband, freelance writer Donn Caldwell, was unable to fetch her after class, Sammy From offered her a lift home, and they became friends. He eventually told her, "You have a moral responsibility to study my condition." "What's your condition?" she asked. "Homosexuality," he said. She told him she was "morally neutral" on the subject, but she didn't know anything about homosexuality. "In which case, you'll have to learn," he said.[34]

Sammy From introduced her to George, his partner of ten years, and to his friends, including two lesbians who threw gay parties in a big ramshackle house in the bohemian Silver Lake district of Los Angeles, not far from where Harry Hay would hold the first meeting of the group that became Mattachine. She thought these homosexuals were an impressive bunch. She was all the more intrigued by Sammy From's exhortation to study the homosexual "condition," because they seemed to have no "condition" at all in the usual sense of the term.

When she mentioned to a psychologist friend—Bruno Klopfer, a preeminent Rorschach expert—what Sammy From had suggested, he said, "You must do it! We don't know anything. What we know about are the sick ones."[35] She began her study by administering Rorschach tests to all the male homosexuals with whom Sammy From and his circle of friends could hook her up. But her project wasn't well conceived. She hadn't even thought about a control group. She was off to a false start—and she stopped. She also divorced Donn Caldwell and left Los Angeles to take a job at Bryn Mawr College. But she was restless and unsettled. She was "haunted," too, by her unfinished project. She returned to Los Angeles in 1951, remarried, and with the encouragement of her new husband, Edward Hooker, she started again.

In 1953 she applied to the National Institute of Mental Health for a grant to study homosexuals. The head of the grants division, John Eberhart, flew to Los Angeles from Washington, DC, to eyeball Hooker. NIMH had been established four years earlier, and Eberhart wanted to make no mistakes about who got funding. She introduced him to her husband. Her putative heterosexuality helped her "pass the test," as she acknowledged. Eberhart approved her grant; but even at the National Institute of Mental Health, homosexuality was so derided that Hooker's proposal was dubbed the "Fairy Project." Hooker never studied lesbians, she later admitted, because "a woman researcher—even a married one—could be undermined by critics who might question her sexuality."[36]

Hooker's project involved thirty homosexual men who were a 5 or 6 on the Kinsey scale—exclusively or predominantly homosexual; and thirty heterosexual men who were a 0 or 1. None of them was ever to have been in psychotherapy. She would give each subject an IQ test and then the three standard psychological projective tests: the Rorschach inkblot test; the Thematic Apperception Test (the subjects had to make up stories about human images); and the Make-a-Picture-Story Test (the subjects had to place cut-out figures in various settings and tell a story about them). Next, she would match homosexual with heterosexual for education and IQ. Then she would assign each subject a number and remove from his test all identifying information. Finally, she would get psychologists who were experts in each of the tests to try to distinguish between the matched pairs of homosexuals and heterosexuals. If the experts were able to discern from the tests who the homosexuals were, then homosexuality was legitimately a "diagnostic category." But if they couldn't discern—it wasn't.

Sammy From again helped Hooker get homosexual subjects from among his friends. He also introduced her to the reconstructed Los Angeles

Mattachine Society, headed by Ken Burns. Mattachine was now offering itself up to qualified researchers who wanted to study the homosexual. On June 24, 1953, Hooker made her pitch to Mattachine's Research Committee: she told them that no one had ever before done a systematic study of homosexuals who weren't in armed forces disciplinary barracks or institutionalized in prisons or insane asylums. She wanted to study the average homosexual. Mattachine agreed to supply all the men she needed. ONE would also cooperate, Dorr Legg said, and he offered himself.

It was harder to get the heterosexuals. She went to the personnel directors of labor unions. They wanted nothing to do with homosexuals, they told her. Her straight friend Herb Selwyn, a liberal lawyer who'd lectured to Mattachine on Homosexuals and the Law, offered himself.[37] But she still had twenty-nine heterosexuals to find. She asked maintenance men and a fireman who came to her home. ("No man who walks through these doors is safe," her husband teased.) She asked the policeman on the corner. She was studying the ways the average man functions, she told them as vaguely as she could. With great difficulty, she found her thirty heterosexuals.

Hooker lived in Brentwood, on a one-acre estate with a garden bungalow that was separate from the house. She did the testing there because once a man opened the garden gate, he was invisible to the neighbors. That guarantee of secrecy was important for the homosexuals who worried that people would know they were participating in a homosexual study.[38]

Hooker brought the finished tests to the three experts. Her friend Dr. Bruno Klopfer, professor of clinical psychology at UCLA, knew as much as Hermann Rorschach himself about the interpretation and scoring of the inkblot test. Another professor of clinical psychology, Dr. Edwin S. Schneidman, was the inventor of the Make-a-Picture-Story Test, which was widely used by clinicians everywhere. Dr. Mortimer Meyer was the chief psychologist at the Veterans Administration Mental Hygiene Clinic and an expert analyst of all "projective techniques," including the Rorschach and the Thematic Apperception Test. If anyone in the world could tell what's what from projective psychological tests, it was surely these three men.

But the judges' accuracy in discerning who was the homosexual and who was the heterosexual was no better than it would have been had they flipped a coin. The average psychological adjustment scores they gave to the homosexual and heterosexual samples were about the same. Dr. Klopfer and Dr. Meyer both looked at the sixty Rorschachs, but they agreed only sixteen times about who the homosexuals were—and most of the time, they were wrong. "There are no clues," they would say with the paired tests in front of them. "I just have to guess." "These are so similar."[39] Dorr Legg, they said, was definitely a heterosexual. Hooker called him that evening to tell him the interesting news.[40]

"Are you out to skin us alive?" Dr. Klopfer asked. (He was only half-joking.) He demanded to look at the Rorschachs again—but he was no more successful in identifying the homosexuals the second time. He had to admit that what he saw in these tests was nothing like what he saw in tests of homosexual *patients*. Dr. Meyer couldn't find the homosexuals through their Thematic Apperception Tests either. Dr. Schneidman scrutinized the Make-a-Picture-Story Tests and told Hooker, "If you showed me the protocol for thirty schizophrenics, I'd be surprised if I didn't get twenty-eight. But to identify the homosexuals . . ." He was convinced: "Homosexuality is not a diagnostic category."[41]

In 1956 Hooker presented the results of her research at the annual meeting of the American Psychological Association in Chicago. Homosexuality as a "clinical entity" simply does not exist, she told her fellow psychologists, because the homosexual population is as varied as the heterosexual population. A particular form of sexual desire and expression has little effect on personality and emotional development.[42] "We knew it all the time, but we needed empirical proof," a few psychologists in her audience said. "It absolutely can't be true. You must have had to search and search and search to find those guys," most of them told her.[43]

To the midcentury mental health professionals whose livelihoods depended on the notion that homosexuals were sick, Hooker's research made not one whit of difference. They continued with their prejudices intact, as did vice squads and McCarthyites—to whom all homosexuals were monsters and moral weaklings. But to those homosexuals who were beginning to challenge the prejudices, Hooker's findings were potent ammunition. Her work demonstrated clearly that none of the standard tests that showed who's mentally sick and who's mentally healthy could show who's homosexual and who's heterosexual. Here was concrete evidence that the mental health professions were wrong about homosexuality as an illness. It would be another two decades before the American Psychiatric Association would finally remove "homosexuality" from the *Diagnostic and Statistical Manual of Mental Disorders*—but Dr. Judd Marmor, an American Psychiatric Association president who participated in the APA discussions, recalled that Hooker's research was "the reference point to which we had to keep coming back."[44]

THE THIRD HORSEMAN: THE COUNCIL ON RELIGION AND THE HOMOSEXUAL TILTS AT RELIGIOUS BIGOTRY

In 1963 the board of the once-conservative Glide Memorial Methodist Church in San Francisco established the Glide Urban Center and hired a black head pastor, Cecil Williams, to minister to the disenfranchised, the poor, people of all races, and the countercultural of every stripe. They also hired a slightly offbeat thirty-one-year-old minister, Ted McIlvenna, whose job it would be to go into the high-crime area of the Tenderloin and reach out to young social castoffs.[45] McIlvenna had known the disenfranchised since childhood when he and his father, an itinerate minister, lived on American Indian reservations in the Pacific Northwest. As a young adult, McIlvenna took some time away from organized religion, thinking he might become an actor or a singer, or perhaps an art historian with a specialty in erotic art (because, he believed, sexuality was of the divine); but finally he got a degree in theology. He wasn't shocked to find that a lot of the Tenderloin castoffs were homosexual transvestites and hookers.

But he was profoundly disturbed by how abused they were by the police on the one hand and roughs on the other, and how alienated they were from organized religion. He needed to figure out how to approach them.

He'd heard of Mattachine, Daughters of Bilitis, and also two new groups in San Francisco that had started a year or so earlier. One of them, the League for Civil Education, was organized by Guy Strait, a fortysomething-year-old gay libertarian who was trying to get gay bar-goers excited about becoming a homosexual voting bloc.[46] The other, the Tavern Guild, was an association of gay-bar and gay-restaurant owners who'd agreed to "self-police" to get the Alcoholic Beverage Control Board off their collective backs, and also to donate to homophile concerns to show they weren't interested only in making money off of homosexuals.[47]

McIlvenna had heard of a few local celebrities, too. Drag entertainer Jose Sarria, known as the "Nightingale of Montgomery Street," had two claims to fame: his uproariously clever parodies of operas such as *Carmen*, which packed rooms at the Black Cat; and his 1961 bid for a seat on the San Francisco Board of Supervisors, when he ran as the first out homosexual political candidate in the country. (He didn't win but got 5,400 votes.) McIlvenna had heard also of Louise Lawrence, an early male-to-female transsexual patient of the pioneering endocrinologist, Dr. Harry Benjamin. Reverend McIlvenna invited Sarria, Lawrence, and leaders of the four homophile groups to a January 1964 dinner meeting.[48]

He wanted to organize a round-table discussion between them and religious leaders, he said, "an off the cuff exploration of homosexuality and the homosexual's response to the church." They could have a three-day retreat at a place owned by the United Church of Christ—White Memorial Retreat Center in Mill Valley. They could do it in the spring. "I could pull together the clergymen, and you could pull together the homosexuals . . . Glide has found sponsors to pick up the tab," he added.[49]

It was a breathtaking proposal. Totally unprecedented: churchmen sitting down with avowed homosexuals and listening to them. In the days when Del Martin and Phyllis Lyon were still steering Daughters of Bilitis to fight against the California sodomy law, they'd approached the two most likely assemblymen, Phillip Burton—who was so progressive he accumulated a six-hundred-page FBI file; and John O'Connell—loved by the Left as the assembly's most outspoken defender of the rights of the downtrodden. Martin and Lyon had asked them to introduce legislation in the assembly for repeal of the California sodomy law. "We'd be booted out of office if we did that," the assemblymen told them flatly. "The voters would say we were in favor of sin. Homosexuals need to work on the church first."[50] That "the church" would let itself be "worked on" had seemed farfetched to Martin and Lyon. But now, incredibly, it was happening.

McIlvenna had also sent feelers out to liberal clergymen who'd been active in civil rights. He told them about awful incidents he'd witnessed in his work. He'd been called to help two homosexual men whose genitals had been kicked in. They were writhing in pain. He telephoned the

Presbyterian Hospital for an ambulance, but the dispatcher refused to send one after McIlvenna mentioned the men were homosexuals. McIlvenna wanted to call the police, but the injured men stopped him. "It was the police who did the kicking," they said.[51] Homosexuals were being denied human dignity and civil rights just like black people were, McIlvenna told the clergymen. He convinced them—Methodist, Episcopal, Presbyterian, Lutheran, and Church of Christ ministers—to come to a three-day meeting and listen to what homosexuals had to say about their needs.

May 31–June 2, 1964: "Forget who you represent," McIlvenna told the men and women, who were all dressed, by his request, in lounging-about clothes. "We represent the human race. Let's start there."[52] They shared three days of wrenching talk—about how the Bible's condemnation of homosexuality encouraged hatred and injustice, how homosexuals had no reason to trust the church, how churchly people's attitude toward homosexuals was the real evil.[53]

Out of the retreat came the decision to start an organization. They would call it the Council on Religion and the Homosexual. No euphemisms. It would be the first organization to use the word *homosexual* in its title. Its stated purpose would be "to promote a continuing dialogue between the church and the homosexual."[54] Just as liberal ministers had been standing at the side of black people in their struggles for civil rights, they'd stand at the side of homosexuals; they'd actively welcome homosexuals into their churches. They'd spread the word to their fellow churchmen. They'd tell the hostile world of the homosexuals' humanity and demand justice for them.

The clergy of the CRH declared their intentions first to the leading magazine of mainline Protestantism, the *Christian Century*: they were "shattering a taboo," they proclaimed.[55] Eventually they even informed the magazine started by Evangelist Billy Graham—*Christianity Today*—about their "new theology," as the magazine called it: "Love is the ultimate and only norm of conduct," they told *Christianity Today*'s evangelical readers, and announced to them that they were "opening a channel from the churches to homosexuals."[56] They got Episcopal bishop James Pike to appoint a church committee on homosexuality that would support the repeal of sodomy laws and an end to the harassment of homosexuals by the police and other official authorities. They sent speakers to seminaries to spread their "new theology" to future ministers. They even opened discussions between priests and lay leaders in the Roman Catholic Church.[57]

It was what Del Martin and Phyllis Lyon had dreamed of: that such moral authorities, churchmen, respected and weighty pillars of society, would stick up for homosexuals. Completely won over by the Council on Religion and the Homosexual after an August meeting, Martin wrote to the Daughters of Bilitis Governing Board, "The Reverend Canon 'Bob' Cromey, assistant to Bishop James A. Pike of the Episcopal Diocese here, asked if the homophile organizations had any trouble with police pressure, and reminded us that if there were any trouble the clergy would go to the powers that be and speak up for us."[58] She'd been the one to argue passionately against DOB involving itself with other organizations. But this was different. "The Council has done more for DOB and the homophile movement in general, public relations-wise, in a few months than we have accomplished ourselves in ten years"; and if Daughters of Bilitis was uncomfortable with her involvement in another organization—well, "You may cancel my DOB membership."[59]

To raise money for all that the Council on Religion and the Homosexual hoped to do, the clergymen and the homosexuals agreed they'd hold a Mardi Gras ball on the first evening of 1965. The ministers were taking no chances: Ted McIlvenna and Cecil Williams requested a meeting with the chief of police, Thomas Cahill.

Despite their clerical collars, after they announced they were hoping to discuss a New Year's dance that would be sponsored by the Council on Religion and the Homosexual they didn't get to see Chief Cahill. They were told they could meet instead with the SFPD's Sex Crimes Detail.

On December 28, a roomful of vice squad officers listened with growing incredulity as Williams and McIlvenna announced their business: they were talking about a costume ball for *homosexuals*? Sponsored by *churches*? "What are the homosexuals going to do at the ball?" a detective wanted to know.

"We're going to have a party," Reverend McIlvenna answered.[60]

One detective, observing that both ministers wore wedding rings, said, "I see you're married. How do your wives accept this?"[61] Another said, "I don't understand why you ministers are interested in sex."

"We're interested because we want our brothers and sisters to fully participate in their rights as citizens," Reverend Williams answered patiently. The officers looked stony faced, disgusted, flabbergasted.

Finally, though, the Sex Crimes Detail could come up with no legal grounds on which to prohibit a ball, but the ministers were told that the Council on Religion and the Homosexual must do its own policing—make sure no hanky-panky went on. As Williams and McIlvenna were walking out the door, one of the detectives couldn't restrain himself. He called out to their backs, "There's going to be trouble. If you don't uphold God's will, we will!"[62]

The ministers took his threat as a heads-up. The council had three pro bono lawyers advising the group: Evander Smith and Herbert Donaldson, both homosexual; and Elliot Leighton, a straight man. McIlvenna and Williams called the lawyers as soon as they got back to the Glide office. Smith and Donaldson promised they'd be at the ball through the whole evening. They'd stand at the entryway and be witnesses should the police cause trouble. The reverends called the other ministers, too. "Bring your wife," they told each one, so the wives also could be witnesses if necessary.

The ball was to be held in California Hall, a once-elegant but by the 1960s dilapidated Bavarian-style building on Polk Street. On December 29 California Hall's manager (pushed by Sex Crimes officers[63]) informed Reverend McIlvenna that the rental agreement was canceled. The council's lawyers informed the manager that 1,500 tickets had already been sold, and that the Council on Religion and the Homosexual was ready to sue should he renege. He agreed to honor the contract.[64]

January 1, 1965: The scene was surreal. Fifty uniformed policemen set up cameras and klieg lights in front of California Hall. Helmeted riot police, batons in hand, stood on either side of the entrance. Newspaper reporters and their photographers stood directly opposite the entrance, ready to click away. Police photographers were there, too. Vans marked with TV-station logos had parked across the street long before California Hall's doors opened. Their mounted cameras were set to capture footage of the homosexual revelers as they arrived. By nine o'clock, squad cars were parked at the intersections of both ends of the street, their red and blue lights flashing.[65] "They couldn't be any better prepared if they were there to face gangsters with machine guns," attorney Evander Smith thought as he came down the street, ready to take his place at California Hall's entrance.[66]

When the 1,500 people who'd bought tickets to the ball approached 625 Polk Street decked out in Mardi Gras finery, nine hundred of them—seeing that even the church hadn't been able to guarantee their security—beat a path in the opposite direction. Only six hundred braved the gauntlet.

Three plainclothes vice squad officers came into California Hall at nine o'clock and stood against a wall near the door, glaring at the ticket taker and attorneys Smith and Donaldson and anyone who entered. "Do you have a search warrant?" Smith asked. "Do you have any reason to believe a felony is being committed on these premises?" Donaldson asked. The officers wouldn't answer.

About ten o'clock, eight more plainclothes officers barged in and stood with the other three in the ten-foot-wide hallway.[67] "You need to identify yourselves or get out," Smith and Donaldson told them. The officers said nothing. Smith told the Lutheran minister, who was standing by, to please call the chief of police. "Tell him that a bunch of hoodlums without the power of speech have invaded a private party, and we're requesting assistance from the police," Smith said.

Minutes later, the doors were flung open and six uniformed policemen stormed in—but not in answer to Reverend Colwell's phone call to Chief Cahill. They strong-armed the two lawyers out the door. "Are we under arrest?" Evander Smith asked.

"What does it look like?" a policeman said.[68]

Reverend Williams's wife, Evelyn Williams, who was standing by to witness, cried in outrage, "This is just like the South for black people!"[69]

"What are the charges?" both lawyers demanded of the policemen who were rushing them to the waiting paddy wagon.

"You're under arrest for obstructing our inspection of these premises for fire regulation violations," Chief Inspector Rudy Nieto answered. Cameras flashed as the lawyers were pushed into the wagon and onto the rusty steel benches.[70]

Nancy May, a straight woman married to a bisexual man, with whom she'd been one of the founders of a new homophile organization, Society for Individual Rights (SIR), had been at the door taking tickets. After the two lawyers were arrested, she called Elliot Leighton, the council's third lawyer, and told him he must come immediately. The officers returned. "You can't come in without a warrant," Nancy May said. "We're here to inspect," they said. "Well, you can't come in," May repeated. Attorney Leighton arrived in time to see the petite woman being rushed out the door by a burly policeman, and Reverend Cecil Williams pleading with him to stop. When Leighton protested to the policeman, he was dragged into the paddy wagon along with Nancy May.

It was the type of police conduct that homosexuals knew well; but before this night the police had never played their hand in front of average citizens. When the police had pronounced someone lewd and lascivious, a sanctimonious public had never questioned it. But now the clergy, who'd seen what went on, told the newspapers and TV reporters and even delivered sermons about it. They told the whole city that the SFPD had squandered a wad of public money in a major "criminal" operation which involved no criminals.[71]

Mayor John Shelley received more mail the week following the ball—almost all of it protesting police bullying and insane misuse of resources—than he'd gotten cumulatively in the several months prior.[72] As a result of all the bad publicity, Chief Thomas Cahill felt obliged to form a community relations board, to demonstrate that the police were willing to listen to the clergy, and to the homosexuals who were under church protection.

The Council on Religion and the Homosexual didn't stop there. With sights set on national media they issued "A Brief of Injustices." It went beyond what the clergy had witnessed to discuss the panoply of social injustices that homosexuals endured: police harassment, prosecution under inequitable laws, entrapment, discrimination in employment.[73] No group of men wearing the collar—no moral authority of any kind—had ever before pleaded the homosexual's case so well to the general public.

THE FOURTH HORSEMAN: THE COMMITTEE TO FIGHT EXCLUSION OF HOMOSEXUALS FROM THE ARMED FORCES TILTS AT THE LAW

By 1966 there were small homophile groups on both coasts and in a few Midwestern cities. Frank Kameny had started East Coast Homophile Organizations in 1963, to bring together groups from New York, Philadelphia, and Washington, DC. Now he and other ECHO members, dreaming big, called a national conference. They decided that to be more attractive to Midwest groups—and to avoid being accused of East Coast chauvinism by California groups—the National Planning Conference of Homophile Organizations would be held in Kansas City, Missouri, on the weekend of February 19, 1966.[74] Forty people came—representatives from fourteen organizations. All agreed that if they wanted a big national homophile presence, they needed something with the power to pull a lot more people into the movement. They needed a dramatic cause.

Phyllis Lyon and Del Martin had one to propose. They'd been reluctant to engage in direct action before,[75] but Martin was now on the board of trustees for the Council on Religion and the Homosexual. With the confidence that they had scores of clergymen behind them, they felt freer to be politically out front. The media was full of stories about the war escalation. There'd already been fierce battles between the United States and the North Vietnamese Army. The Vietcong had shown they were determined. More and more Americans would be needed to fight in Southeast Asia, and many of those drafted would be homosexual. On May 21, the next Armed Forces Day, all the homophile organizations should hold meetings "to consider the problem the homosexual encounters in connection with the military draft," Phyllis Lyon moved. There could be speakers who were vets, clergymen, lawyers—all condemning the military's policies on homosexuals.[76]

Don Slater was at the convention, representing his new magazine, *Tangents*. (He'd quit *ONE* the year before because of bitter battles with Dorr Legg, whom he accused of trying to control everything and everyone.) As soon as discussion on Lyon's proposal opened, the gruff and passionate Slater took to the floor. What this National Planning Conference needed to organize was more than a few polite town hall meetings. Homosexuals everywhere had to protest the injustice that the military always inflicted on homosexual men. They're drafted, they have to go serve, and then they get less-than-honorable discharges if their homosexuality is discovered.[77] The *hypocrisy* issue is what homophile groups had to deal with, Slater shouted into the microphone. It was like in World War II, when Slater himself had been drafted: the Selective Service turned a blind eye unless a man appeared for his physical in a tutu; but if a homosexual was caught while in

the military, he could be court-martialed. The military paid lip service to
the prejudice that homosexuals were unfit, but they sent homosexuals off
to fight and die anyway. Homophiles need to tell America that if homosexuals are to risk their lives for their country, the hypocritical laws and
regulations have got to be changed.[78]

There was consensus: on Armed Forces Day, there'd be simultaneous
dramatic protests in all the major cities the members represented.[79] Don
Slater, who became spokesman for the event, told the *New York Times*
News Service in April that the protests on May 21 would represent "the
first manifestation of a new militancy in the homosexual movement." He
promised "parades and demonstrations" everywhere.[80]

The "dramatic protests" were far tamer than Slater had hoped they'd be. In
San Francisco, there'd been talk about a parade complete with floats, but in
actuality about forty-five people from the various homophile groups[81] and
the Council on Religion and the Homosexual gathered at Federal Building Plaza and walked around with protest signs. Since it was a Saturday and
the Federal Building was closed, there were few spectators. In Philadelphia,
members of the Janus Society went to the Naval Yard to distribute leaflets
about the military's injustice to homosexuals. A measure of their success is
caught in a letter president Clark Polak wrote Slater: "At least nobody got
beat up."[82] In Kansas City, the Phoenix Society, which had been formed
months before, met to "discuss the issue." In DC, Frank Kameny led about
twenty people on a four-mile march from the White House to the Pentagon and then hopped on a plane to New York to speak at a small gathering
organized by Daughters of Bilitis.

In Los Angeles, Slater invited Harry Hay to be titular chair of the Los
Angeles Committee to Fight Exclusion of Homosexuals from the Armed
Forces. Hay actually loathed the military—in the seventies he would counsel men on how to get out of it—but he agreed to head the committee
because, he quipped, "You can't say 'Shaft the Draft' if you're excluded."[83]
Slater and the small group that worked with him would have liked to stage
dramatic demonstrations, but LA was so spread out. There was no central
area that gay people inhabited and no easy way to get the word out to
them. They decided on a quintessentially LA solution—a motorcade.

Every night for weeks, Slater and his team worked the dark streets near the gay bars, from Topanga Canyon in the north to Long Beach in the south. Under windshield wipers of all the parked cars, they stuck flyers. The Committee to Fight Exclusion of Homosexuals from the Armed Forces needed money and needed manpower, the flyers pled. Dancing-drinking-gay-bar-goers came back to their cars, pulled the sheet of paper off their windshield, maybe read it—then crumpled it and threw it away. To most homosexuals in 1966, a homosexual motorcade was unthinkable.

Slater was perplexed. Two years earlier, in 1964—the first time a big national magazine had done a major article on homosexuals, a twelve-page spread—the feisty Slater hadn't hesitated for a moment. He'd allowed himself, as the editor of *ONE*, to be photographed for *Life*'s eight and a half million readers. He'd made sure to look businesslike and "normal," in a crisp white shirt and dark tie; and his very respectable photo had given the lie to *Life* magazine's tired old proclamations about "the sad and sordid world" of gay people.[84] Why were most other homosexuals so afraid still to show themselves in daylight?

Dauntless[85] and optimistic, Slater and his volunteers constructed boxlike four-feet-tall signs. Those would be put on the roofs of the motorcade cars. They painted dozens of other signs for car trunks, hoods, and doors. "10% of All G.I.s Are Homosexual!" the signs read, or "Homosexuals Are the Most Moral People in the Service—They *Have* to Be!" or "Sex Belongs to Private Conscience!"

There were only thirteen vehicles in the motorcade. That afternoon, it was drizzling as the protestors took the scheduled twenty-mile route through Los Angeles, starting in Echo Park, near Slater's home. They covered huge areas of the city—down Cahuenga Boulevard, up Hollywood Boulevard, past the Hollywood Bowl, east on Sunset toward downtown, west through the Wilshire District. To be safe, Slater had notified Eric Julber, Herb Selwyn, and all the other lawyers he knew, asking them to stand by in case there was trouble. There was none.

Slater and Harry Hay were interviewed by several of the LA media. Columnist Paul Coates, now writing for the *Los Angeles Times*, used the interview as the basis of a mocking editorial in which he called the notion of homosexuals in the military "material for a burlesque skit." He also quoted the considered opinion of Colonel M. P. DiFusco, the assistant director of personnel management in the Office of the Assistant Secretary of Defense:

"We're responsible for a lot of kids. If we throw them in with homosexuals, we wouldn't have an army. We'd have chaos."[86]

After the motorcade, Slater approached the *Los Angeles Times* again, trying to get the city editor to do a story: this was, after all, the first gay motorcade in history. The editor informed Slater that he would consider the event newsworthy "only if someone was hurt."[87] Not even Don Slater could believe that the Committee to Fight Exclusion of Homosexuals from the Armed Forces had effected great changes.

Yet CBS News did a two-minute interview with Slater and other committee members that aired nationally at six and eleven. *Time* magazine sent a photographer. Thousands of Angelenos saw the committee's hand-lettered signs, and hundreds of thousands all over the country saw the *New York Times* News Service article in which Slater declared that hypocritical laws and regulations must be changed. "Millions of homosexuals have served honorably in the armed forces through all our wars," he said, and "all we are asking is that a man's sex life should be his own business."[88] Most people had never heard or read such things before.

PART 3

REVOLTS BEFORE THE REVOLUTION

Chapter 8

SLIVERS OF SPACE AND JUSTICE

A SLIVER OF SPACE

Los Angeles, May 1959: Almost ten years before the riots at the Stonewall Inn in New York, John Rechy, a muscular hustler who hung out between tricks at Cooper's Donuts, an all-night coffee shop in shabby downtown Los Angeles, sparked a gay rights brush fire. Cooper's was a home away from home to transients like Rechy, who earned their living on the streets, and to "queens":[1] mostly black and Latino, dressed in semidrag, their faces made up with lipstick and eye shadow. Cooper's patrons were regularly harassed by policemen who would walk through the coffee shop, stop in front of a random customer, and demand to see identification for no reason except for how the person looked. Every once in a while, the police would haul a few customers out of the restaurant and drive them down to the Sixth Street police station.

That May night, three men, including Rechy (who would immortalize his drag-queen and street-hustler friends four years later in his autobiographical *City of Night*), were ordered into the squad car. Perhaps it had happened one time too many, or perhaps it was because the good-looking, affable Rechy was so admired among Cooper's patrons—whatever the reasons, they staged a mini-riot, with drag queens and hustlers assaulting the police, turning donuts into flying missiles, flinging cups, sugar cubes, anything hurl-able, lobbing them at the heads of the offending officers. That had never happened before. The police ran to their cars to summon help. More squad cars, sirens blaring, hurried to the scene. In the confusion, Rechy managed to escape. The street was cordoned off for the rest of the night; several rioters were arrested.[2]

In the following year, 1960, television's nightly news brought into America's living rooms multiple stories of the Woolworth's sit-ins by "Negroes": black people protesting segregation by taking seats at all-white lunch counters in Greensboro, North Carolina; Atlanta, Georgia; Nashville, Tennessee; and a half dozen other southern cities. The black sit-ins resonated with some homosexuals because, like blacks, they too had to struggle for turf. Martin Luther King's March on Washington for Jobs and Freedom in August 1963, and the voting rights march from Selma to Montgomery, Alabama, in March 1965, were further dramatic reminders of what needed to be done in a serious fight for civil rights. But homosexuals, who had no Martin Luther King to bring huge numbers of them together, started small.

Downtown Philadelphia, around Rittenhouse Square, April 1965: Dewey's coffee shop was a favorite hangout for gay teens who were too young to get into the bars. But when the manager decided that the campy boys and butchy girls were driving away straight business, he ordered the staff not to serve them. That wasn't the first time gays were eighty-sixed from a favorite hangout, but the Woolworth's protests and Martin Luther King's Selma march were inspiration for two boys and a girl. When they were refused service, they sat; they wouldn't leave the coffee shop. The manager called the police, who dragged the three teens out. They were arrested and charged with disorderly conduct. The Janus Society, Philadelphia's homophile organization, sprang to life as it never had before.[3] Members mimeographed 1,500 leaflets about the discrimination at Dewey's and the arrest of the teens. Parading up and down in front of the coffee shop for the next five days, they handed out the leaflets to anyone about to go through Dewey's doors.

Dewey's manager, seeing how gay ire could really mess up business, reversed his policy. *Drum*, Janus's monthly magazine, called the gay teens' protest "the first sit-in of its kind in the history of the United States."[4]

But, unlike the black sit-ins and other black protests, the Cooper's revolt went unrecorded, and the Philadelphia story was noticed only by a couple of low-circulation gay magazines. The media blackout about gay protests permitted straight people to continue in their head-in-the-sand ignorance of gay grievances, Clark Polak, the frustrated chair of the Janus Society, complained. "We must make our protests unavoidable as news," Polak, himself a journalist, told a conference of homophiles in 1966. "How?" he asked. He answered his own question: "By civil disobedience and encouraging not so civil protests!" Gays needed to riot, to tear things up a bit, like black people were doing. Then the media would have to take notice. "In newspaper terms, no news is bad news; good news is no news; and bad news is good news. How about the movement becoming bad news?" Polak suggested.[5]

New York City, 1966: Dick Leitsch was a thirty-one-year-old Kentuckian, scion of tobacco planters. He was also the very serious-minded president of Mattachine Society New York. If potential members asked why his organization didn't have social events, he answered somberly that there were enough homosexual social clubs already; Mattachine's purpose was not entertainment but reform. Leitsch was so sincere about his reform work that he organized a "sip-in" through which he hoped to force the New York State Liquor Authority to stop harassing establishments that served homosexuals. He notified all the major New York City newspapers. "Send a reporter," he told city editors. "This will be an event of historic importance." The homosexual twist to the black sit-ins was novel enough so that several editors did send reporters. The *Times*, surprisingly, assigned one who seemed a promising choice: Thomas A. Johnson, the first black journalist in what had then been the *New York Times*'s hundred-year history.

Leitsch and two other Mattachine officers, John Timmons and Craig Rodwell,[6] planned their noontime sip-in at the Ukrainian American Village Restaurant in the East Village. They chose the place because of the sign displayed in the window: "If You're Gay, Please Go Away."[7] The three men showed up at the restaurant respectably dressed, just as the black Woolworth's protestors always were: conservative somber suits, starched shirts, tasteful ties. Leitsch even carried a black attaché case—"the picture of a

Madison Avenue executive," as the *Village Voice* reporter described him.[8] They were ready to ask for service and be refused. But one of the newspaper reporters arrived at the restaurant before the three men and announced he was there to cover a homosexual demonstration. The restaurant's manager cleared everyone out and closed down the place for the day.

Leitsch moved on to plan B. At a second bar, Howard Johnson's, he and his posse sat down, ordered, and then informed the bartender they were homosexuals. "I don't see you doing nothing homosexual," the bartender said and placed three bourbon-and-sodas down in front of them.[9]

Success finally came at Julius', which had been raided a week earlier after a minister was accused of soliciting sex there from an undercover officer.[10] Dick Leitsch and his friends knew they'd come to the right place when they saw that Julius' window even displayed the requisite shaming sign that warned the public that there'd recently been a raid of the premises. The young Mattachine members sat down at the bar and ordered. The bartender had already placed two of their drinks in front of them when Leitsch handed him a note on Mattachine stationery. It said, "We are homosexuals. We are orderly. We intend to remain orderly, and we are asking for service." Just as Leitsch had hoped, the bartender told the men that the State Liquor Authority forbade him from serving homosexuals, and he covered their glasses with his hand to prevent them from taking a drink. A *Village Voice* photographer obligingly captured the moment in a picture that Mattachine used in court.[11]

Thomas Johnson, writing the story for the *New York Times*, was just as snide about the homosexuals' efforts as white *Times* reporters had always been when writing about homosexuals. Johnson had made his name reporting on black civil rights protests. He abhorred the insinuation that a homosexual sip-in was as serious as a black sit-in. The headline of Johnson's back-page story announced his contempt: "3 Deviates Invite Exclusion by Bars." His article mocked the gay men for having to visit several bars before they succeeded in being turned down for service.[12]

But to Dick Leitsch, the sip-ins were no different from the black lunch-counter sit-ins. Both were about a First Amendment right, freedom of assembly. The right was supposed to be granted to all American citizens. He brought his complaint against the State Liquor Authority to both the New York Commission on Human Rights and the New York State Appellate

Court. And to everyone's astonishment, he won. The commission declared that city ordinances against sex discrimination meant that homosexuals had a right to be served in any licensed bar in the city. The judge of the New York State Appellate Court said that the Constitution supported even the homosexual's right to peaceful assembly, and the State Liquor Authority can't prohibit homosexuals from congregating in bars.[13] Leitsch's sit-in-inspired sip-in thus cleared the way for openly gay bars in New York to obtain state liquor licenses—though police harassment and gay bar raids didn't stop.[14]

San Francisco, summer 1966: Gene Compton's Cafeteria in the Tenderloin district was, like Cooper's Donuts in LA, beloved turf to black and Latino "queens" who considered the place, in the words of one of them, "fabulous—like the Wizard of Oz." With coffee at five cents a cup and a big bowl of oatmeal at twenty-five cents, Compton's was also a practical place for those who were down on their luck. Compton's management had been ignoring earlier police orders to shut down by midnight in order to discourage homosexuals and other "seedy types" from gathering after the bars closed at two in the morning.

Many of the Tenderloin queens who frequented Compton's had been at one time or another busted for violating the "masquerading" law, though not many of them tried to pass. They wore men's garb mostly, except perhaps for shirts that buttoned like blouses and lipstick and eye shadow. They'd long accepted harassment as the price of being who they were; but the night SFPD officers burst in and tried to evacuate them from Compton's, something changed. As a policeman approached a queen to demand identification, she threw hot coffee in his face. It sparked California's second homosexual brush fire—fifty young homosexuals hurling dishes, breaking windows, vandalizing a police car parked outside the cafeteria, setting a nearby newsstand on fire.

The next day, gay street teens staged a picket in front of Compton's to tell the police that harassment must stop. Most of the picketers had learned the idea of civil rights in a gay youth group called Vanguard, which had been meeting since 1965 at the ultraprogressive Glide Memorial Methodist Church.[15] Like the later rioters at the Stonewall Inn, the teens were demanding their sliver of space to be together for camaraderie, amusement, or sexual connection. Whether or not they articulated it, their protest against police harassment at Compton's was an important step toward a larger struggle for civil rights. If people can't congregate in public, they can't organize into a public movement.

Los Angeles again, New Year's Day, 1967: In 1966, landscape gardener and early leather man, twenty-seven-year-old Steve Ginsberg, had started a gay group called PRIDE (Personal Rights in Defense and Education). After a dozen policemen burst into the Black Cat, a Silver Lake district gay bar, swinging billy clubs and brandishing guns at the stroke of midnight on January 1, 1967, PRIDE organized a protest. Hundreds of PRIDE supporters overflowed the street on which the Black Cat was located. They marched and carried signs that said "Abolish Arbitrary Arrests" and "No More Abuse of Our Rights and Dignity." Ginsberg had mimeographed three thousand leaflets detailing police brutality, and the demonstrators handed them out to pedestrians and passing drivers. "The time has come when the love that dared not speak its name will never again be silenced," Jim Kepner of ONE announced hopefully.[16]

Policemen stationed themselves across the street from the Black Cat and quietly watched. They didn't dare interfere because Steve Ginsberg had invited lawyers and clergymen not only to address the demonstrators but also to bear witness to police brutality. The lawyers encouraged some of the gays who'd been arrested in the Black Cat raid to sue, and they even presented briefs to the US Supreme Court that asserted the rights of homosexuals to equal protection under the law.[17] SCOTUS was far from ready to consider such rights in 1967.

Los Angeles yet again, August 1968: Wilmington police raided the Patch, a gay bar in an LA suburb. Patrons who weren't arrested staged a gutsy flower-power demonstration, marching on the Harbor Division police station to bail the men out, carrying in their arms enormous bouquets of gladioli, mums, carnations, roses, daisies (but pointedly no pansies), and scattering flowers on the station floor.[18] The pioneering gay paper, *The Los Angeles Advocate*, speculated about the significance of the Patch demonstration, "If the reaction of the customers there that night is any indication, a new era of determined resistance may be dawning."[19]

•   •   •

A SLIVER OF JUSTICE

Threats to gay people's sliver of space sometimes did set in motion larger claims. Philadelphia, 1968: Rusty's was the favorite hangout of bar-going lesbians, but you wouldn't know it was there unless you knew it was there. Even the sign that identified the place didn't: it said "Barone's Variety Room." You got to Rusty's by going down Quince, an alley-like street, to a back door of a two-story building, then up a flight of wooden stairs and down a long hallway. At the door you paid $2 for a strip of drink tickets, and you could dance all evening or just sit with your lover or friends at one of the little tables that surrounded the floor.[20] You had to time your entrances and exits: Rusty's was right next to the rear door of the Forrest Theater, and you'd better be careful not to show yourself when a performance was letting out, or you might run into a straight theatergoing acquaintance. Rusty Parisi—eponymous to those in the know—was the bar's manager, a tough, handsome Italian butch with cropped bleach blond hair, who often showed up for work dressed in a button-down man's shirt and a dark man's suit. The femmes were thrilled by her panache and the butches strove to emulate it.[21]

Though Rusty's was not easy to find, one Friday night in March 1968 the police found it. Six or seven plainclothesmen burst into the dimly lit bar and ordered Rusty to turn on the lights. They unplugged the jukebox and fanned out around the room, checking IDs, accusing several women of being drunk and disorderly. Byrna Aronson, a twenty-two-year-old woman with cropped hair and keys on a chain hanging visibly at her side,[22] had leaned over to kiss her girlfriend on the cheek just as the police arrived. A man came over to Aronson and tapped her on the shoulder. Because he was wearing a suit and a porkpie hat, she didn't realize he was a policeman—and, anyway, all the Rusty's habitués were sure there'd never be a raid because the Mob that owned the place paid off the police.[23] "You're under arrest," the man said. "What for?" she asked. "Sodomy," he told her. She laughed until she saw he was serious.[24] Aronson, ten other lesbians, and Billy Schaefer, Rusty's gay male bartender, were rushed down the stairs and into a waiting paddy wagon.

Almost always it had been men's bars that the notoriously antihomosexual police commissioner, Frank Rizzo, had ordered raided; but Rusty's was the target on this night because Rizzo had supposedly gotten word that the bar was serving minors. None of the arrested women were minors—they weren't even asked to show their IDs to prove their age[25]—but they were taken to the police station anyway and locked up overnight. In the morning they appeared before a judge who dismissed the charges against them, as was usual in such arrests whose true purpose was to discourage homosexual establishments by hassling the patrons. The women were free to go; but no one apologized to them for the fear and humiliation they'd suffered because they'd been at a bar where lesbians congregated.

A Philadelphia branch of Daughters of Bilitis had begun meeting just the year before the raid at Rusty's. It was mostly a social group, though it made occasional small efforts to be political, such as writing letters of protest to the newspapers whenever articles characterized homosexuals as deviates and lowlifes.[26] Founding DOB member Ada Bello had left Havana in 1958 after President Fulgencio Batista's police quelled student unrest by killing the leaders at her university and shutting the university down. She'd wanted to make DOB more militant from the start. Her lover, Carole Friedman, who'd participated in black civil rights demonstrations, shared her ambitions; but they'd floundered around looking for a compelling cause.[27]

Byrna Aronson had coincidentally visited the DOB office for the first time on the day of the raid at Rusty's. When she and the other Rusty's lesbians were let out of jail, she brought them back with her. They told angry stories of being bullied and humiliated at the police station. "Are you gonna help us fight?" Aronson asked. "Yes!" Ada Bello said. She thought the Philadelphia police had just handed DOB a red-ribboned gift. Now the group had its compelling cause.

Carole Friedman, a recent Oberlin College graduate who'd done social work in a North Philadelphia slum-area settlement house, was chosen to compose an irate letter to the Philadelphia police inspector, demanding that he meet immediately with DOB. Once the letter was in the mailbox, DOB members felt a bit wacky: lesbians requesting to meet with the Philadelphia police, who had a long record of antihomosexual brutality? They calmed one another by saying their letter would probably get no answer anyway.[28] But it did: from the officer in charge of public relations for the Philadelphia Police Department. He would meet with two or three representatives of Daughters of Bilitis.

Carole Friedman went, and DOB president Edna Winans went, despite her terror that she might lose her job at IBM if the police informed her supervisor she was a lesbian. Ada Bello was afraid to go because she had not yet received her naturalization papers, and immigrants who were known to be homosexual were routinely denied citizenship; but she drove the others to the meeting. Friedman and Winans brought a representative from the ACLU with them—just in case there was trouble.

The officer in charge of public relations jotted notes on what the women said but offered no apology for the raid at Rusty's, nor for the arrest of a dozen patrons. Yet he took seriously their threat that they would make a public protest about police harassment of lesbians. On behalf of the Philadelphia police he went on the defensive, telling the *Philadelphia Inquirer* that "Homosexuals have been, are now, and will be treated equally with heterosexuals." It was a sign that the police department understood it was under scrutiny and that there were homosexuals willing to fight its abuse openly. Daughters of Bilitis had achieved a unique victory.

But the women couldn't continue to fight under the rubric of Daughters of Bilitis. Local chapters had to clear any intended action with national DOB president, Shirley Willer, and she was "a little nervous" that the Philadelphia group wasn't following protocol.[29] She was hard to get hold of, too. Plus, Bello and Friedman pointed out to other Philadelphia DOB members, if they wanted to fight for homosexual civil rights, why shouldn't they swell their numbers by working with gay men? That August, Philadelphia Daughters of Bilitis morphed into an independent, cogender organization, Homophile Action League. It was a name that satisfied everyone: "Action," its "middle name," was its reason for being; "Homophile," its first name, signaled there wouldn't be a complete rupture with past decorum.

The statement of purpose Friedman and Bello wrote for the Homophile Action League was ambitious and feisty. They made it clear that HAL had no interest in Daughters of Bilitis's goal to "uplift" the homosexual community: "It is our firm conviction that it is the heterosexual community which is sadly in need of uplifting," Bello and Friedman jibed. The league would "change society's legal, social, and scientific attitudes toward the homosexual in order to achieve justified recognition of the homosexual as a first-class citizen and a first-class human being." The league would assist homosexuals "in their battle to secure their constitutional rights and to deal effectively with all manner of publicly sanctioned discrimination against them." The league would use an arsenal of tools such as had never been used before in the fight for homosexual rights, like boycotts of businesses that discriminated against homosexuals.[30]

The Homophile Action League was one of the few homosexual action organizations founded by lesbians that succeeded in attracting gay men, though their numbers were never large.[31] The League's presidents were always lesbians, and—unusual for the times—two of the presidents, Ada Bello and Lourdes Alvarez, were Latinas. They helped tackle politicians such as gubernatorial candidate Milton Shapp and make them pay attention. Though Shapp had initially refused to speak at their community forum,[32] HAL's persistence got to him. As governor, he made Pennsylvania the first state to establish a Governor's Commission on Sexual Minorities, to recommend ways to end antigay discrimination. Shapp couldn't get his legislature to vote in favor of gay rights laws that he supported, but Pennsylvania became the first state to have any sort of pro-gay decree when he issued an executive order that ended discrimination against gays and lesbians in state employment. He was also the first governor to proclaim a Gay Pride Week, in 1976, though he had to battle the Pennsylvania Legislature again in order to do it.[33]

The Homophile Action League's other forays into fighting for lesbian and gay civil rights weren't as fruitful as their appeal to Shapp had been. The group had no real political expertise, no budget, no one who could devote themselves full-time to the battle. They tried to get Pennsylvania to repeal its sodomy law and Philadelphia to pass a gay rights ordinance. But by the time the city finally did pass an ordinance, in the 1980s, the organization was defunct.

In 1957 Randy Wicker, blue eyed and boyish looking, had a lover who was kicked out of the University of Texas for being homosexual. Wicker struggled with guilt because he was too scared to say anything that would get him kicked out, too. But he went to New York the next summer and looked for ways to be political. He saw through the example of the black civil rights movement that times were changing. Homosexuals, too, could be bolder and braver. To join Mattachine—which was the only game in town—Wicker had to lie about his age because he was a year short of the requisite twenty-one.[34]

Though he was the youngest member of Mattachine, he wouldn't keep his convictions to himself; and he didn't hesitate to lecture the older members, telling them that Mattachine needed to become aggressive. The more staid members were happy to see him go back to Texas when that summer was over. It had been prudence and hiding that let them survive in an era of witch hunts and entrapments. They had no doubt that their underground organization needed to stay underground.

But Wicker graduated from the University of Texas and returned to New York where he kept trying to light fires under Mattachine. Pre-Wicker, whenever Mattachine had guest speakers, the handful of members called a few friends and together they made up an audience of about twenty. But when a lawyer, Irwin Strauss, agreed to talk to the group about homosexuals and the law, Wicker couldn't bear to let a lecture on such a critical subject be wasted on an audience of twenty. He paid to have three hundred bright yellow signs printed at ten cents apiece announcing "Citizens: A Lawyer Discusses Homosexuality And The Law! Free Admission! Everyone Welcome!," and he went around Greenwich Village convincing people to hang the signs in their windows. An elderly lady who agreed to hang a sign told him, "It's about time those boys stood up for themselves." But the signs were as ambiguous as a Rorschach. A retired vice squad officer who agreed to hang a sign told him, "It's about time we really cracked down on those perverts."[35]

The lecture had to be moved from the tiny Mattachine headquarters on Forty-Eighth Street and Sixth Avenue to an auditorium at Freedom House, the majestic old Willkie Memorial Building on Fortieth Street, because more than three hundred people showed up. Most of Mattachine, and the closeted speaker, too, weren't charmed. Wicker had dragged the secret organization into the spotlight. When Mattachine was evicted from its offices shortly after the event, the members blamed him.

He finally gave up on pushing Mattachine to be bolder and in 1962 formed a side group, the Homosexual League of New York. Under its name, he could carry out more daring activities, like arranging for eight homosexuals to appear on a New York radio station to talk about homosexuality from their own perspective. That had never happened before. A *New York Times* headline announced with consternation, "Homosexuals Air Their Views Here: Radio Station Lets 8 Appear in Panel Discussion."[36] Jack

O'Brian of the *New York Journal-American* declared, "We've heard of silly situations in broadcasting but FM station WBAI wins our top prize for scraping the sickly barrel-bottom." O'Brian was certain his readers would share his disgust that the station had caved in to Wicker, whom he described as an "arrogant card-carrying swish" who'd convinced a program producer that homosexuals "have a right to be heard."[37]

Wicker wasn't intimidated. There'd be no progress until the subject of homosexuality was brought out from the closet. In 1963 he called for the first homosexual picket in America: a picket of the White House.[38] He could see no reason for homophile organizations if not to agitate for gay rights. But he couldn't get anyone to join him. In 1964 he again called for a picket: against the army's policy of informing employers and prospective employers when a homosexual was booted out of the military or rejected as 4-F. This time he was determined to see the protest through. But his Homosexual League never had more than a half dozen members, and he wanted a decent showing. He approached Mattachine, but the members would have nothing to do with a picket.

In 1964 there weren't many places to go in order to find people who would participate in a picket supporting homosexuals. Wicker asked the founder of the recently established Sexual Freedom League (who went by the name of Jefferson Fuck Poland) if his group would send bodies. The Sexual Freedom League was mostly heterosexual and fought for causes such as the legalization of prostitution and conjugal visits for prisoners. No ostensibly straight group had ever before supported homosexual rights, but Mr. Fuck Poland, who clearly enjoyed turning heads, promised to encourage members of the Sexual Freedom League to swell the picket line.

During a drizzly afternoon in September, a motley crew congregated in front of the Whitehall Induction Center near the East River and then marched up and down the street. The irrepressible Randy Wicker led; followed by twenty-four-year-old Craig Rodwell, who was elated that finally a group of homosexuals was making a serious public statement. Fuck Poland and his girlfriend and her baby, which she pushed along in its stroller, were there, too, as was one of Mattachine's few women members, Renée Cafiero, a newly minted twenty-year-old lesbian who brought along her lover, Nancy Garden. Both were modestly dressed in skirts.[39] Garden would go on to write the first young adult lesbian novel, the classic *Annie on my Mind* (1982), whose eponymous character bore some similarities to Cafiero; but now she and the other picketers were carrying picket signs: "Keep Draft Records Confidential!" "Homosexuals Died for the U.S. Too." "Love and Let Love." Two or three other gay protestors stood at the curb clutching flyers they hoped to distribute. The flyers were titled "The Army Invades Sexual Privacy" and explained that the army's policy made the men and women on whom they tattled permanently unemployable.

Wicker and the others wouldn't have been surprised if passersby shouted, "Commie freaks!" at them, or if toughs offered to beat them up. But no one did. Of course, it was a Saturday (the picketers chose the weekend because most of them worked during the week), and they were on a street where there was little foot traffic when offices were closed, and the weather was forbidding—so almost no one saw them. ("Too bad hardly anybody saw us," Cafiero thought—alternately with "Whew, I'm glad hardly anybody saw us."[40]) The media didn't deign to come see them, either, though Wicker alerted newspapers and TV. Nor did the Whitehall Induction Center change its policy of ruining homosexual lives.[41] Nevertheless, this was the first time that picketing was used as a tactic to demand a sliver of justice from the government on behalf of homosexuals.

These early battles for slivers of rights were limited by the political innocence and impotence of the participants. They didn't have a lot of time and resources; paid gay lobbyists or multimillion-dollar gay rights organizations were the stuff of fantasy. What an inchoate gay and lesbian civil rights movement sorely needed in order to wage war against the forces that defined them as criminals, crazies, sinners, and subversives was someone to dream big and to make others share the dream: if not a Martin Luther King at least a Bayard Rustin, King's chief strategist. The movement needed someone to persist single-mindedly and obsessively, until the enemy admitted, "<u>You</u> are right and we were wrong."[42]

Chapter 9

THROWING DOWN
THE GAUNTLET

A FALL FROM THE STARS

For two hours during a muggy afternoon on August 28, 1965, Paul Clark, a security officer at the US State Department, hid himself behind a pillar at Foggy Bottom, as State Department headquarters was metonymically called, and snapped photos. His subjects were a small group of conservatively dressed men and a few women, members of the Mattachine Society of Washington, DC, who were promenading in an elongated oval, silently picketing on the sidewalk in front of the imposing State building. Paul Clark sent the photos he took to an agent at the Federal Bureau of Investigation, and they became FBI records, showing the demonstrators carrying signs with confrontational messages such as "15 Million American Homosexuals Protest Treatment by State Department," "State Department Refuses Replies to Our Letters—Afraid of Us?," "Discrimination Against Homosexuals Is as Immoral as Discrimination Against Negroes and Jews," and "The State Department—the Last Bastion of McCarthyism!" The sign carried by the leader of the group, Frank Kameny, declared peremptorily, "Equal Opportunity for ALL—ALL Means ALL!"[1]

Kameny was a slight man with a voice nasal and booming. He had a rapid-fire speaking style and an accent that immediately marked him as a

New Yorker. He was not gifted with obvious charisma. But his vision and his words were brilliant, and they took the gay and lesbian rights movement further than any of the early homophiles could have even imagined it might go. Kameny had been a child prodigy and dreamed of becoming an astronomer from the time he was six years old. He entered Queens College in 1940 at the age of fifteen. His education was interrupted by World War II when he was drafted and sent to Germany as an army mortar crewman, but after the war he went through Harvard on scholarships and fellowships and in 1956 got a PhD in Astronomy. When Kameny was hired the following year for a civilian job with the Army Map Service, an agency of the Department of Defense, he kept secret a disturbing incident that he'd hoped he'd put behind him. Soon after receiving his PhD, he'd gone to San Francisco to deliver a paper at a meeting of the American Astronomical Society. On August 29, 1956, he found himself in the men's room of the San Francisco bus terminal, where, he later claimed, without invitation or solicitation on his part and without sexual response, a man touched his penis. Though Kameny was "immediately repelled and terminated the contact," he testified, two plainclothes policemen, in a sting that was common in the era, were watching through a ventilation grillwork, and he was arrested.[2]

At the police station, Kameny was advised by an officer that if he pled guilty, the matter would be quickly dismissed; but if he pled not guilty, he would have to go through a complicated rigmarole that would delay his return home. At the arraignment the next morning, he took the officer's advice. He was fined $50 and given six months' probation. And he was led to believe that at the end of his probation, the episode would be expunged from his record.[3] But in Washington, DC, only a few months after taking the job with the Army Map Service, he had a second problem. He was stopped by policemen as he walked late at night in Lafayette Park, a notorious homosexual cruising area, and he was taken by them to the police station.[4] To his relief, he was not charged and was released that same night. But his relief did not last long.

A short time after the incident, Kameny was sent on assignment to Hawaii. Almost as soon as he arrived, he received a call from his superior ordering him to fly back to Washington. Kameny must have known then that he was in trouble, but he put on an air of brashness that would become characteristic of him. At Army Map Service headquarters he was ushered into a small room where two Civil Service Commission investigators were waiting for him. "Information has come to the attention of the US Civil Service Commission that you are a homosexual," one of them told him without preliminaries and asked if it were true.[5] "That's none of your business," Kameny replied despite his alarm. He admitted to nothing and reiterated over and over, "That question is irrelevant to my job performance." A month later he received a letter from his superior informing him that he was fired on the grounds of homosexuality.

He was thirty-two years old, he'd spent his whole life training for a career in science, and now he was unemployed. Dismissed from a job at which he hadn't worked long enough to accumulate a nest egg, he was reduced to living on frankfurters and mashed potatoes. He moved to a cramped, dingy apartment with a bathtub in the center of the room, only a few feet away from his bed,[6] and he had to stave off his landlord's efforts to evict him for nonpayment of rent.[7] Kameny let himself wallow in shock only briefly. He got a $600 loan using his car as collateral, which allowed him to pay off his debts as he made appeals all over Washington—to the Department of Defense, the White House, Congress—complaining about his firing and asking to be reinstated. Washington, DC, homosexuals who'd been fired during the McCarthy era and its aftermath usually sneaked off into the night or committed suicide rather than call attention to their "disgrace." Kameny would not go quietly. To him, the real disgrace was the injustice perpetrated by the Army Map Service and the Civil Service Commission. But not only were his appeals ignored; he was also informed that his security clearance was revoked.

When President Eisenhower had announced that America was starting an aeronautics and space program to compete with Russia's Sputnik success, Frank Kameny had been sure that he would be chosen to be one of the country's first astronauts. And now the US government was stripping him of all his fine convictions about who Frank Kameny was and was destined to become. Since childhood, he'd been used to being the smartest person in the room, and his keen intelligence was matched by indomitable will. He was not a man to accept so huge an impediment to the future he'd envisioned for himself. "If society and I differ on something," he would later say, "I'm willing to give the matter a second look. If we still differ, then I am right and society is wrong, and society can go its way as long as it doesn't get in my way. But if it does, there's going to be a fight, and I'm not going to be the one who backs down."[8]

Kameny went to see Byron Scott, a former US congressman from California with a reputation as a liberal. Scott had become a lawyer after losing his reelection bid ten years earlier. Though Kameny had no money, Scott agreed to represent him. But when they lost in both a federal district court and an appeals court, Scott informed him that the case was hopeless.

The injustice Kameny had suffered at the hands of his government galled him. He couldn't let it go unchallenged. If Byron Scott wouldn't continue to fight for him, he'd have to figure out how to fight for himself. He asked Scott to tell him, at least, how to file a Supreme Court suit on his own. Kameny reasoned that if he could write a PhD dissertation in Astronomy at Harvard he could certainly write a petition to the Supreme Court. Scott gave him a booklet that outlined the procedure to be followed in order to request a Supreme Court hearing.

Homosexuals are a legitimate minority group, Kameny argued in his *Writ of Certiorari*. The government's discrimination against them "was no less illegal and no less odious than discrimination upon religious or racial grounds." The average homosexual is as well adjusted in personality as the average heterosexual, he declared; and even if the government regards homosexuality as "immoral conduct," a government employee has a right to practice it without fear, as long as it doesn't interfere with his ability to do his job. Kameny also told the justices that during World War II he didn't hesitate to shoot at the Germans, and he did it to help preserve for himself and others "rights and freedoms and liberties."[9] For sixty pages, he argued eloquently not only that he should be reinstated at the Army Map Service but also that prejudice against homosexuals had no rational basis.

The response he received was signed by Earl Warren, a great champion of equal rights for racial minorities and one of the most liberal chief justices in Supreme Court history. It was a curt form letter that said only that SCOTUS declined to hear Kameny's case. That was the beginning of Frank Kameny's life as a militant activist for gay and lesbian civil rights.

INVITATIONS TO A DUEL

Gays and lesbians in America have always been as varied in class, ethnicity, tastes, and political sentiments as America is in general. They are a group by virtue of their same-sex sexual preference and their common enemies. Period. Their diversity guaranteed that internecine quarrels and civil wars would start as soon as they began to organize and would continue to this day. Would-be leaders quickly find that leading them as a group is as difficult as the proverbial herding of cats. Divisive and contentious as they've been, they've never come to wide consensus about who to deem their most important historical leader; and no one gay leader of the past has been widely chronicled as having had the most foresight, the most spirited plans, and the most critical triumphs, without which contemporary LGBT people couldn't have won their own decisive civil rights victories. But if any one person deserves such credit, it is Frank Kameny.

Kameny didn't seem much like a militant with his conservative suits and ties, his precise speech, his penchant to intellectual elitism. But in his demand that the root causes of gay problems be attacked and that sweeping change be made, he was utterly radical. In these days of universal Levi's it's easy to mistake the costume of Kameny's era for a conservatism of thought and action and to overlook his pioneering militancy. But his legacy speaks for itself.

There was no homophile organization in Washington, DC, in 1961, but Kameny discovered that in New York there was a Mattachine group. He contacted its leaders to ask if they could help him start a homophile organization in his area, and he received from Mattachine Society New York a list of potential members living in DC. As was common in 1961, almost all the names on the list were aliases—including that of the police sergeant who was head of the Perversion section of the DC Police Department's Morals Division. The man showed up, undercover, at the Hay Adams Hotel on Lafayette Square, where Kameny had called an organizing meeting for his proposed group.

There in the small conference room, Ron Balin, one of the attendees who worked on Capitol Hill, whispered nervously in Kameny's ear, "That guy over there is a vice cop." He was nodding in the direction of Louis Fouchette. The police sergeant was known by sight to many gay men

because he'd shaken his penis at them in public restrooms all over downtown DC; and if they responded, they found themselves in handcuffs and
under arrest. Kameny kept an eye on Fouchette and spotted a gun and
holster under his suit jacket. Not in the mood to be intimidated, Kameny
strode over to Fouchette and told him, "I know who you are." The police
sergeant got up and walked quickly out the door. He hadn't stayed at the
meeting long enough to hear much discussion about the new group, but
he filed a report anyway, warning the Morals Division of the police department that homosexuals in DC were organizing.[10]

Frank Kameny didn't go to movies, he almost never drank, he had no
knowledge of spectator sports, he was uninterested in gossip or the love
lives of those around him (he had no ostensible love life himself), he knew
nothing of popular music; the one indulgence he allowed himself was classical music that he listened to while driving his car.[11] Jack Nichols, who
called himself "the second charter member of Mattachine,"[12] compared
Kameny to a self-propelled locomotive on a strict track, no amusing by-
ways.[13] After being fired from the Army Map Service, he never again held a
secure paying position. A couple of times in the years that followed he was
hired for jobs in which he could use his training as an astronomer, but as
soon as a security clearance check was run on him, his arrest record came
up and he was fired. He depended mostly on his mother, sister, and friends
for support.[14] The struggle for equality became his occupation and his life.

It didn't take him long to conclude that neither Mattachine Society
New York nor any of the other homophile organizations that were around
in 1961 were models for waging the collective battle he had in mind. He
had to invent a new model. His horrific experiences with the federal government had radicalized him.[15] What the homophile movement lacked and
must develop, Kameny declared every chance he got in the early days, was
"strong and definite positions, unequivocally held."[16] His organization's
statement of purpose promised to challenge every federal law that kept
homosexuals from full equality. Mattachine Society Washington would "act
by any lawful means to secure for homosexuals the right to life, liberty, and
the pursuit of happiness," its constitution announced. Kameny sent copies of the document not only to all the DC papers, but also to President
John Kennedy, Vice President Lyndon Johnson, the entire cabinet, all the

Supreme Court justices, and every member of the US Congress. Most of the recipients didn't deign to acknowledge receipt. A few did. The congressman from Missouri, Paul C. Jones, sent the document back with a handwritten note, angrily scrawled: "I am unalterably opposed to your proposal and cannot see how any person in his right mind can condone the practices which you would justify. Please do not contaminate my mail with such filthy trash."[17] The congressman from Michigan, Charles Chamberlain, was livid. "In all my six years of service in the United States Congress," he wrote Kameny, "I have not received such a revolting communication."[18]

But no one in Washington would escape Mattachine's "communications." Mattachine Society Washington published a newsletter, *Gazette*, which was distributed not only to Mattachine members and the executive and legislative branches of government, but also to the justices of the Supreme Court and Attorney General Robert Kennedy—who did not answer but sent the newsletter to the Federal Bureau of Investigation to be slipped into its "Mattachine Society Washington" file. Attorney General Kennedy need not have bothered because the FBI was already on Kameny's mailing list. Every month, J. Edgar Hoover received a copy of the *Gazette*, which Kameny himself ran off, working far into the night, on a mimeograph machine in the basement where he lived. Hoover sicced one of his agents on him. The FBI agent told Kameny that his boss "took a grave view" of being bombarded with the objectionable newsletter and demanded that he stop sending it immediately. Kameny informed the agent that the First Amendment protected his right to send public officials anything he pleased, as long as it was not threatening; and unless Hoover agreed to stop keeping an FBI file on Mattachine Society Washington, he would continue to be a recipient.[19] Hoover received copies of the Mattachine newsletter until his death in 1972.

Kameny became adept at tweaking the noses of the authorities to get them to duel. In July 1962, he decided that Mattachine Society Washington would apply to the District of Columbia Superintendent of Licenses and Permits for a "charity" license to enable the group to raise money. His application was explicit: Mattachine Society Washington intended to solicit funds to be spent on helping to procure for the homosexual equal status with his fellow man.[20]

The moment Superintendent C. T. Nottingham read it, he knew he was in a tough spot. The District of Columbia was under the direct jurisdiction of the US Congress, and there would be hell to pay if he granted the license, since Congress wholeheartedly sanctioned keeping homosexuals in pariah status. But the superintendent of licenses and permits had no legal grounds on which to refuse a license to Mattachine. As long as the organization avowed it would not engage in illegal activity—and raising money for the purpose of seeking civil liberties was not illegal—Nottingham had to grant the license. He did. "Group Aiding Deviates Issued Charity License," the *Washington Star* announced.[21] Kameny welcomed the stir. It gave him a platform to put civil liberties laws to the test.

Superintendent Nottingham tried to do damage control. He couldn't deny the license, but he talked tough, hoping to placate the public and especially the legislature. He was keeping an eye on those "deviates," he told the media. "If the group solicits as much as one dollar," he said, "I will order them to open their books and records for examination." And if such an order wasn't complied with, he promised, he would immediately revoke Mattachine's permit.[22]

But Nottingham's tough talk wasn't enough to placate Congress. East Texas Democrat John Dowdy, the ranking member of the House committee that oversaw the District of Columbia, already knew of Mattachine through Frank Kameny's mass mailings to all the congressmen. Dowdy was fuming. He complained on the House floor that licensing Mattachine was like licensing prostitutes. "The acts of these people are banned under the laws of God, the laws of nature, and are in violation of the laws of man!" he declared to his fellow congressmen, and he presented bill HR 5990 to revoke Mattachine's charity license.[23]

A few years later, Dowdy would be indicted for accepting a $25,000 bribe in return for sidetracking a Justice Department investigation, and he would do prison time for perjury.[24] But in the 1960 election, he'd hyped himself as "a responsible Christian gentleman,"[25] and he was out to prove his responsible Christianity by forcing Nottingham to revoke Mattachine's charity license. To his constituency back in Alto, Texas, he explained in his down-home manner about the "cancerous evil" of an organization like Mattachine that makes a mockery of the old virtues of "honesty, purity, duty, and honor." It was like "when a man starts by telling you there is no such thing as black or white in determining right from wrong, but only gray. When he gets you to believing that, the next stage is to tell you that black is right and white is wrong."[26]

Kameny was invited to appear before the House Subcommittee on the District of Columbia to tell why his organization's charity license should not be revoked. Nothing short of death could have kept him away. Dressed as usual in a dark suit and well-starched white shirt, oblivious to the brutal August humidity, he coolly reiterated to the congressmen what they would already have known if they'd read the statement of purpose he'd sent each one at Mattachine's founding: that Mattachine is strictly a civil liberties organization; homosexuals are a minority group, no different, as such, from other minority groups in America; and Mattachine Society Washington is working to achieve for the homosexual minority full equality with their fellow citizens.[27] John Dowdy sat glaring at Kameny. When Kameny misspoke, using the phrase "consensual behavior *among* adults," Dowdy pounced at the opportunity to tar homosexuals with promiscuity: "How many adults? Five? Fifteen? Fifty? Five hundred?"[28] But Kameny was not shakable. "We are NOT a social organization," he emphasized vehemently, and told his audience that even the group's constitution made that clear. "It is not a purpose of this organization to act as a social group or as an agency for personal introductions. We abide strictly by this prohibition."[29]

Despite Kameny's impassioned arguments, the House sided with Dowdy, and Mattachine's "charity license" was revoked. But Mattachine had gained more than it lost. Not all DC newspapers were swayed by the congressman's fulminations. A surprising editorial in the *Washington Post* titled "Piety by Fiat" mocked "the oddly inept little bill by that Master of Morality, Rep. Dowdy."[30] Mattachine members were elated. The *Washington Post* had just helped spread the word about the homophile cause more widely than they could possibly have done. Mattachine established an award for the public official who'd "done the most to advance the cause of homophile organizations." Congressman Dowdy won hands down.[31]

Nor was Mattachine Society Washington thwarted in its fund-raising by the Dowdy incident. Kameny discovered that a charity license was unnecessary for organizations that raised no more than $1,500 a year, which was far more than Mattachine had been raising. He claimed the last word by writing to the *Washington Post* to announce, "We will actively continue to solicit funds."[32]

•   •   •

April 28, 1963: Kameny and five other white men stood among 250,000 other people, mostly black, at Martin Luther King's March on Washington and held up signs that identified them as members of the Mattachine Society—an act less brave than it might seem since few would have known what "Mattachine" was.[33] (The men didn't realize, of course, that the march had been organized by Bayard Rustin, King's chief strategist, who was, like them, a homosexual and who, like Frank Kameny, had been arrested in California in the fifties on a homosexual morals charge.[34]) Mattachine member Jack Nichols, the twenty-five-year-old bohemian son of an FBI agent who'd threatened Nichols's life for putting his job in jeopardy, looked around at the crowd that stretched as far as he could see and wondered aloud, "Why aren't we gays having civil rights marches, too?"[35]

When an article appeared in the *New York Times* about Cuba's establishment of labor camps for homosexuals, Jack Nichols modified his idea: Mattachine could have a picket. In front of the White House. Protesting both Cuba's misdeeds toward homosexuals and America's, too. It took only awhile for Kameny to jump on the idea. Mattachine would organize homosexuals to play "Tweaking the Lion's Tail, or Constructive Fun and Games with Your Government," as he characterized it in the title of one of his talks. "And if nobody listens," he told Mattachine members, "we haven't lost anything. If somebody listens, we've gained."[36] During the next four years, Mattachine picketed the White House, the State Department, the Civil Service Commission, the Pentagon, and Independence Hall in Philadelphia, demanding that the US government acknowledge that homosexuals, as American citizens, deserved the same civil rights that all American citizens are guaranteed. Small though the number of picketers were, Don Slater, still writing for *ONE* magazine on the other side of the continent, very optimistically hailed the DC pickets as revolutionary, the end of "homosexual timidity and passivity, which have gained homosexuals almost nothing."[37]

Frank Kameny's single-minded focus came with downsides. He was prickly and snappish, and he did not suffer fools gladly. He was authoritarian, too. The president of Mattachine Society New York, Dick Leitsch, referred to him as a "führer."[38] Others complained that he "barked orders,"[39] and that he "had to control every bit of minutiae in the world."[40] He even kept tight control on his picketers' grooming. Men had to wear suits and ties and well-polished dress shoes, and their hair had to be cut short; women's hair must not be cut too short, and they had to wear skirts and stylish ladies' shoes, preferably with high heels—no matter that butch garb may have been their sartorial preference, or that they would have to march for two hours carrying picket signs. "If you're asking for equal employment rights, look employable," Kameny insisted.

But his conventional dress belied his unconventional rhetoric. On July 22, 1964, he was invited to speak at a public meeting in New York City. Coincidentally, it was the most violent night of a Harlem riot that had been going on since July 16, after an off-duty white police lieutenant shot and killed a black fifteen-year-old who'd lunged at him with a knife. While six hundred Harlem stores were being looted and a thousand rioters battled riot police in full gear, Frank Kameny, dressed in a business suit, was addressing an audience of homosexuals at Freedom House. His subject was "Civil Liberties: A Progress Report."

His authoritative podium style was more emotional than usual, perhaps because another kind of civil liberties drama was going on eighty-five blocks away. He told his audience that he scorned the homophile's useless attempts to "educate" the public about homosexuality. "Negroes tried for ninety years to achieve their purposes by 'educating' the public out of its prejudices," he declared. Their achievements during all that time "were nothing compared to those of the past ten years," when they became "vigorous" in their "social actions."[41] He also scorned, he said, the "social service" function of homophile organizations. "We can refer homosexuals to lawyers, we can find jobs for those who have lost jobs or have been denied them because of homosexuality, and we can assist them in other ways"—but such services "accomplished nothing of lasting value," and the homophiles' struggles would go on literally without end unless they adopted a more militantly activist strategy.[42] Kameny was exhorting his listeners to learn from the black example. Homosexuals needed to stop pushing the Sisyphean rock up the hill, and start throwing rocks, metaphorically at least.

"EVERY MOTHER'S DREAM
DAUGHTER": MATTACHINE SOCIETY
WASHINGTON'S FIRST LESBIAN

Lesbians who joined a homophile organization in the 1960s were most likely to choose Daughters of Bilitis because other homophile groups seemed focused on men's problems such as ending police entrapment in restrooms. As Eva Freund, who did join Mattachine Society Washington, complained even of that group, "We lesbians couldn't understand why the guys were in bathrooms having sex in the first place."[43] Lesbian presence in the other Mattachines—New York, Los Angeles, San Francisco, Denver, Detroit, Boston, Chicago—was negligible,[44] as it was in homophile groups such as the Society for Individual Rights in San Francisco and the tiny Athenaeum in Miami. But Frank Kameny was anxious to recruit lesbians for Mattachine. He understood long before "gay and lesbian" became a common phrase why it was good for the movement to bill itself as cogender: In a practical sense, it helped defuse the enemy's obsession with homosexual male promiscuity. In a principled sense, since Mattachine Society Washington's only raison d'etre under Kameny's design was to fight for first-class citizenship for all homosexuals, why would lesbians not be welcome?[45] There were ten marchers in the first Mattachine picket in front of the White House,[46] seven men and three women. Because Mattachine had so few women members, and Kameny believed female visibility was important for the cause, he encouraged a heterosexual and a bisexual woman to march along with Lilli Vincenz, the lone lesbian.[47]

Kameny planned the picket to coincide not only with the height of the tourist season, but also with a major anti–Vietnam War demonstration to protest the bombing in Southeast Asia—which, as he guessed, would attract an additional fifteen thousand to twenty-five thousand people to DC. On April 17, 1965, the day before Easter Sunday, tourists who came to gaze at the White House stared in astonishment at the unaccustomed sight of homosexuals carrying signs: "Cuba's Government Persecutes Homosexuals: U.S. Government Beat Them To It," "U.S., Cuba, Russia: United to Persecute Homosexuals"; "U.S. Claims No Second Class Citizens: What About Homosexuals?"

Incredulous tourists snapped pictures. Paul Kuntzler, one of the picketers, was especially worried about the press photographers. Thirty of them, having finished with the antiwar protest across from Lafayette Park, passed near the Mattachine demonstrators at the White House. He would lose his job if his picture appeared in the newspapers as a homosexual. As he walked the picket oval, Kuntzler hid behind his poster and Lilli Vincenz, whom cameras caught marching in front of him, her head held high.[48]

Lilli Vincenz was a wholesome-looking young woman with a radiant smile. The editor of *The Ladder*, Barbara Gittings, said she looked like "every mother's dream daughter" and was thrilled to put her on the cover of the January 1966 issue.[49] Vincenz grew up in Nazi Germany and was brought to America in 1949, when she was twelve years old. Gifted in languages, she received a master's degree in English from Columbia University in 1960 and then entered a PhD program supported by a fellowship. But by then, she was too anxious about who she was to focus on studying. It wasn't easy in those days for a middle-class young woman to explore her sexuality. At Columbia University's counseling center she'd been given the recently published *Voyage from Lesbos: The Psychoanalysis of a Female Homosexual*, by Dr. Richard Robertiello, a book about his success in "curing" a woman of her lesbianism. Vincenz was not sure what she wanted to do with her life, but she knew she had no interest in being "cured." She quit graduate school and joined the Women's Army Corps when some lesbians she encountered told her that the army was a "hotbed of gay people."

Her stint was brief. After she admitted to a heterosexual roommate that she was a lesbian, the roommate snitched. The next day, at work at Walter Reed Army Hospital in DC, where she was training as a neuropsychiatric technician, she was called off the ward. "We have information that you have engaged in homosexual behavior," her commanding officer told her. She'd been a star pupil in the neuropsychiatric training program, but she was given an administrative discharge anyway.[50]

Vincenz joined Mattachine a year after it was founded. Mattachine bylaws demanded that members assume a pseudonym, for their own protection, and she became Lilli Hansen.[51] Kameny, who'd been seeking lesbian members, was delighted with this bright, well-educated, personable young woman. He took her under his wing and made sure she was put on Mattachine's executive board. The admiration was mutual. Vincenz was awed by Kameny's clear-sightedness and the "bullet-proof arguments" he made for their cause.[52] But Kameny expected the same tethered-to-earth rationality and dedication from his disciples. When Jack Nichols took a leave from Mattachine to pursue a romance, Kameny was furious and complained that he "left the helm to go on a postadolescent spree."[53] Vincenz did not disappoint in that way. She took inconsequential jobs—a typist for a printing company, an editorial secretary for a trade association—in order to pay the rent and buy food, but her real work was Mattachine. It was impossible for her to refuse when Kameny asked her to become the editor of a new monthly magazine, the *Homosexual Citizen*.

It was impossible, too, for her to express any editorial philosophy but his. Every cover of the *Homosexual Citizen* announced the magazine's serious focus on "News of Civil Liberties and Social Rights." The articles were about battles with psychoanalysts who wanted to cure homosexuality, police who harassed homosexuals under the sodomy laws, ministers who preached "antihomosexualism," the government that denied homosexuals security clearances, the military that witch hunted and punished homosexuals. Kameny liked to boast that the *Homosexual Citizen* was activist, militant, and radical.[54]

But it lasted only seventeen months. Vincenz had made the acquaintance of a lesbian astrologer, and, thinking to offer the *Homosexual Citizen*'s readers a little relief from the usual sober fare, she solicited from the woman an article titled, "Astrology and the Homosexual." Kameny was not amused. He'd been furious when Dick Leitsch—whether out of mischief or a slip of the tongue—once introduced him to an audience as "a Harvard PhD in Astrology." Kameny wouldn't permit the piece to run, and Vincenz stepped down as editor.[55]

But Vincenz's work with and for Kameny didn't cease. Despite his pique over the astrology affair, he realized that Mattachine needed lesbian representation, and Vincenz, with her fresh-faced looks and poise, was a great asset. Though she was unhappy that Kameny couldn't loosen up, she never stopped being awed by his brilliance. She continued to devote herself to the movement as Kameny ran it, and he continued to utilize her for the movement's sake. In February 1967 he and Jack Nichols appeared on a call-in television program, *Controversy*, hosted by a local personality, Dennis Richards. The deceptively mild-looking Richards verbally assaulted the two men, screaming that all homosexuals are sick, child molesters, effeminate, sex obsessed. Kameny calmly corrected him. Nichols took the high ground, quoting Thomas Jefferson about "fighting tyranny over the mind of man." But Richards went ballistic. He pounded his on-set desk, yelling, "Get off my stage! Out of my studio, you vicious, perverted, lecherous people! You make me want to vomit!" His hysteria was disturbing even to the viewers. One called in to ask if he was overreacting because he was himself homosexual. Richards looked apoplectic. "No! I'm not! They are!" he shouted, jabbing his finger in the direction of Kameny and Nichols.[56]

Maybe the frenzied performance was good for ratings? Three weeks later, the producer phoned Kameny: Would he and Nichols appear again? By then, Kameny was appearing on TV more than he was watching it,[57] but he wouldn't give up a single opportunity to present his case for civil rights to a television audience, even if he had to go through a madman to do it. He agreed to another appearance; but this time he and Nichols brought along with them Lilli Vincenz—ladylike and neatly coifed, wearing a nice dress and high heels. She sat between Kameny and Nichols, which cleverly defused the incendiary image of a gay male couple and the sexual things they did. Maybe Richards's producer had admonished him to behave better this time, but he knew, too, that he couldn't credibly characterize Vincenz as a "vicious pervert." He gave the three Mattachine members space to make the arguments he'd earlier squelched.[58]

"THE MOTHER OF THE GAY CIVIL RIGHTS MOVEMENT": BARBARA GITTINGS

Barbara Gittings was another crucial find for Kameny. She met him at a conference of the recently founded East Coast Homophile Organizations (ECHO) soon after she became editor of the Daughters of Bilitis's monthly magazine, *The Ladder*.[59] ECHO, born in the winter of 1962–63, was the brainchild of Frank Kameny and Mattachine Society Washington. After Hal Call killed off Mattachine's national structure in 1961, the various groups around the country became independent entities; but Kameny believed the revolution might come quicker if they coordinated their battles against their common enemies. To start, in December 1962 he brought together in his living room representatives from New York and Washington Mattachines and announced that Donald Webster Cory, author of the much-revered *The Homosexual in America*, was coming to Philadelphia to give a lecture in January.[60] People from all the East Coast homophile groups, Kameny guessed, would be there. He proposed organizing them into a coalition: East Coast Homophile Organizations, they'd call it.[61]

ECHO held its first conference August 31–September 1, 1963, at the Drake Hotel in Philadelphia. (Public venues were so unused to hosting meetings of "homophiles" that they were unfamiliar even with the term. The sign in the lobby of the Drake Hotel announced a meeting of the "East Coast Hemophilia Organizations."[62]) The conference theme was "Homosexuality: Time for Reappraisal." Things did not go well. One of Kameny's main refrains from the beginning had been that homophiles were addicted to listening to "experts" and "authorities" about their mental health and moral acceptability. They needed to stop. "*We*, homosexuals, are the experts on ourselves," he reiterated, "and we need to be telling the experts that they have nothing whatsoever to tell homosexuals. We should be the ones telling *them*!" But the program planners of the first ECHO conference seem not to have heard Kameny's message.[63]

Fifty-year-old Dr. Albert Ellis arrived at the conference sporting on his arm a woman half his age[64]—intending perhaps to model normal behavior for his audience. The ECHO audience surely knew what to expect from Dr. Ellis because he'd spoken often at Mattachine and Daughters of Bilitis conventions in the past, and the homophile magazines looked to him as their premier expert. The cover of the April 1955 issue of *ONE*, for instance, announced as its main feature his article "Are Homosexuals Neurotic?" (The answer was a predictable "Yes.") Ellis's banquet speech contained no surprises. He was writing a new book, tellingly titled, *Homosexuality: Its Causes and Cures*, and his banquet speech was a foretaste. The gist of his message, which he repeated often to the packed room of homosexuals, was that the exclusive homosexual is a psychopath. Everyone in the banquet hall politely sat there, listening for an entire hour as the doctor rebuked them for their sexuality.[65]

Barbara Gittings sat in silence, too, remembering that was the way it always had been at the homophile conferences she'd attended: People from the law, the ministry, and the mental health professions were always invited to those conferences, and they accepted and almost always said nasty things. Yet the homophile leadership kept bringing them back because, as Barbara

Gittings understood it, "It was necessary to have people of respectability who were willing to come and address our meetings instead of ignoring us. It made us feel like that gave us some respectability too. And so we'd sit there not saying anything, and we'd applaud when they finished, and we'd go off to the social hour."[66]

But something was beginning to change. At the end of Ellis's banquet talk, a lesbian rose to her feet and called out, "Any homosexual who would come to you for treatment, Dr. Ellis, would *have* to be a psychopath."[67] Others in the audience dared think that too, though not many yet dared say it.

The next day, Gittings's partner, Kay Tobin, happened to be in the Drake's lobby where she saw a small knot of conference attendees listening to a man holding forth informally. She joined the group. It was Frank Kameny. Tobin had never heard someone speak so eloquently about what gay people needed to be doing to get their rights; she ran to find Gittings. "You've got to hear this guy," she told her, grabbing her arm, leading her to the lobby where he was still speaking to attentive listeners.[68] He was the next presenter on the conference program, too. The title of his talk was "The Homosexual and the U.S. Government," but he commented first, referring back to Ellis's banquet speech, that it was ludicrous to worry about what caused homosexuality. "I don't hear the NAACP worrying about which chromosome and gene produced a black skin," Kameny said as his audience tittered with relief and applauded loudly.

For Gittings, having been again subjected at the banquet to the old insults, Frank Kameny's talk was transporting. As he spoke she realized she'd never before heard a coherent philosophy of what a homosexual movement should be. She'd never before heard anyone so firm and uncompromising in defense of the homosexual, so insistent that homosexuality was as good as heterosexuality, and that the homosexual deserved all the rights granted to the heterosexual. His speech pulled her from the funk she'd been in since listening to Albert Ellis and, she believed, transformed her instantly into a militant ready to fight for homosexual civil rights. Gittings had been made editor of *The Ladder* just a few months before the 1963 ECHO conference, and Kameny became one of the few men who were not professional "experts" whose writing appeared in the pages of that lesbian magazine.

Gittings's admiration for Kameny was returned. They shared a single-mindedness and dedication to their cause; they shared the conviction that they were right and the world must be made to see it; they even shared personal tastes such as love of classical music. Gittings became an indispensable partner of Kameny's victories. Never given to modesty, Kameny liked to think of himself as the Father of the gay civil rights movement; eventually he would call Barbara Gittings its Mother.

Chapter 10

THE HOMOSEXUAL AMERICAN CITIZEN TAKES THE GOVERNMENT TO COURT

"I DO NOT BELIEVE THE QUESTION IS PERTINENT TO MY JOB PERFORMANCE"

The main purpose of Mattachine Society Washington, as far as Frank Kameny was concerned, was to fight for the rights of the "homosexual American citizen," a phrase he used often. He sought out victims on behalf of whom he and Mattachine might fight. He began with Bruce Scott, a Midwesterner with the face of a British aristocrat. Scott had had an un-blemished seventeen-year record as a Labor Department employee, inter-rupted only by World War II, when he'd served honorably in the military. In 1956, at the height of the McCarthy-era witch hunts, he was called into the office of his supervisor. The file that sat on the supervisor's desk was from the District of Columbia police, and it had been sent to the supervi-sor under the 1950s policy that mandated the ferreting out of homosexuals in the government employ.

The file showed that nine years earlier, in 1947, Scott had been arrested in the Lafayette Square men's room for "loitering"—the Morals Squad code word for hanging out somewhere in the hope of making a homo-sexual pickup. Denial was pointless. "Yes," he admitted, "I'm a homosexual. I've been one for as long as I can remember. I'm living with a man who is my lover."[1] Under Civil Service Commission policy, the supervisor had no alternative. If Scott didn't resign, he must fire him.

Five years after Bruce Scott was tossed out of the Labor Department, he read a brief article in the *Washington Star*. Another man, Frank Kameny, had also been thrown out of government service on the grounds of homosexual behavior, and he'd tried and failed to get his case heard by the Supreme Court. Scott, by then almost fifty years old, had not been able to find a decent job since he lost his Labor Department position. He contacted Kameny to commiserate.

Kameny had already been thinking by then that he would start an organization to fight for the civil rights of homosexuals. Bruce Scott became a founding member. His case would become Mattachine's first serious battle. "You apply again for a Labor Department job," Kameny plotted with Scott. "They'll turn you down on the grounds of your homosexual record, of course. And then we'll fight them."

On October 3, 1961, Scott applied for the position of management analyst. He had to take a qualifying exam, which he passed easily. But when an envelope arrived from the Civil Service he already knew there'd be no job offer inside. The letter invited him to a "voluntary interview" for the purposes of establishing his "qualifications and suitability for appointment."[2]

With few preliminaries, in a scene very much like the one Kameny had been through, the Civil Service Commission interrogator told Scott, "We have information indicating that you are a homosexual. Do you wish to comment on this matter?" Scott, having been coached by Kameny, responded: "I do not believe the question is pertinent insofar as my job performance is concerned."

That was the end of the interview. The following May, Bruce Scott was informed by letter that he was "ineligible for federal employment on the grounds of immoral conduct."[3] Now he and Kameny had grounds on which to make a test case.

"Let's assume, for the sake of argument, that I am a homosexual," Scott's appeal to the Civil Service Commission said. "But that is not evidence that I conduct myself immorally." Homosexuality and immoral conduct are not synonymous, he insisted, and he reiterated all of

Kameny's major themes: the sexual nature of an applicant has no relation to his fitness for the position; the Civil Service Commission has no right to ask whether an applicant is heterosexual, bisexual, or homosexual; the policy of the Civil Service Commission against homosexuals is discriminatory; the government has no business making itself an arbiter of morality and immorality.

The Civil Service Commission's Bureau of Personnel Investigations and the board of appeals turned a deaf ear to all of it. "There is convincing evidence that Mr. Scott engaged in homosexual conduct, which is considered contrary to generally recognized and accepted standards of morality," the board of appeals declared, and upheld the Civil Service Commission's refusal to consider him for employment.[4]

Kameny and Scott then went to the new DC chapter of the ACLU and asked for support. The ACLU hadn't been homosexual-friendly in the past,[5] but Kameny and Scott had reason to think that the DC president, attorney David Carliner, might be different. They were right. Carliner had been battling forces of injustice since 1934, when he was fifteen years old and picketed the German Embassy in protest over Hitler's policies. As a lawyer, he made a career in tackling cases that were unpopular or foolhardy, such as those involving miscegenation laws in the South. Bruce Scott's case was tailor-made for him. He got to work immediately.

Kameny made sure that the press was informed that homosexuals were fighting back and a suit against the Civil Service Commission was under way. He believed that any publicity was useful, even if reporters weren't fair. After all, Bruce Scott had found him by reading in the newspaper about his failed Supreme Court appeal. Kameny was particularly anxious that DC's major paper, the *Washington Post*, know of Scott's case. In the 1950s, the *Washington Post* regularly ran front-page articles with headlines such as "Names of 200 Perverts Listed for Firing by U.S. Agencies," which reported without agonizing that the "perverts" were being sacked as "unsuited for government work."[6] But something was clearly changing at the *Washington Post*, too. An editorial that appeared in the *Post* in April 1963, three months before *Scott v. Macy* went to court, was headlined "Misplaced Morality." The *Post* writer declared that homosexuals can and do lead "useful, successful, and apparently normal lives," and "to deny them all chance to work for their government is wholly arbitrary and unjust."[7] It was the most unequivocal statement a mainstream Washington paper had yet made supporting the rights of homosexual citizens.

Judge George L. Hart, who heard Scott's case in the district court, was not as sympathetic. He agreed with the Civil Service Commission attorneys' arguments that Scott had no legal *right* to employment, and that the commission officers did have a right to exercise their "discretion and judgment" to disqualify him. Bruce Scott had no case, Judge Hart decreed.[8]

Bruce Scott was discouraged. He'd been unemployed or underemployed for eight years, and it appeared he would never be able to make a living in Washington. He wanted to go back to Chicago, where he'd been raised. Illinois had gotten rid of its sodomy law in 1961, and he had reason to hope that there he could find a suitable job; but Kameny urged him to stay in DC and continue to fight.

Kameny's single-mindedness, which drove him to expend most of Mattachine's resources on battling the government, was not sitting well with members of his organization. He'd been founder and president since 1961, but a revolt was brewing. At the next election, several members ran against him—including, ironically, Bruce Scott, who'd served as both secretary and vice president. Kameny lost, though not to Scott. People had been unhappy about Kameny's insistence that Mattachine must not water down its focus on civil rights by being a "service" organization. Another charter member, Bob King,[9] had had thousands of leaflets printed on venereal disease prevention, and he organized Mattachine members to distribute them in bars, restrooms, theaters, anywhere gay men cruised. Such an action was far more useful than tilting at government windmills, many of Mattachine's members thought.[10] In 1965, Frank Kameny was out, and Bob King was in as president of Mattachine Society Washington.

Kameny was too focused on his fight for civil rights to bear a long grudge against either Bruce Scott or Mattachine. He pushed Scott to take his case to a US Court of Appeals.

George Hart, the district court judge who'd ruled that Scott had no case, was known in Washington as "an outspoken conservative with impeccable Republican credentials."[11] Kameny and Scott couldn't have been surprised that he would not rule against a government agency in favor of a homosexual. But they were surely surprised at their great good luck in finding themselves in the appeals court of Chief Judge David Bazelon, who was George Hart's polar opposite. Bazelon was well known for his decisions that championed the poor, the mentally ill, the underdog of various stripes, and for his view that it was a judge's duty to speak out on social issues. Now, opining about *Scott v. Macy*, he peered down from the bench over his half-glasses and declared to the federal attorneys for the Civil Service Commission that their charges against Bruce Scott were vague. Moreover, the government had to justify imposing disqualification for "immoral conduct." If there was no *nexus* between private conduct and job performance, conduct was irrelevant[12]—precisely what Kameny had been arguing since he himself was fired from the Army Map Service in 1957. The appeals court found in favor of Bruce Scott by a 2-to-1 decision (Warren Burger, who would become Chief Justice of the Supreme Court in 1969, was the dissenting vote), and declared that he must be considered eligible for federal employment. The *Washington Post*, now firmly in the corner of the homosexual, applauded the decision.[13]

When, two years later, the recalcitrant Civil Service Commission still had not declared him eligible for government employment, Scott filed a second appeal. The CSC would not give in. Bazelon's court had criticized the commission for its "vague charges"; so now it produced several specific charges against Scott. He did not meet the suitability and fitness standards for federal employment because he'd been arrested in 1947, and again in 1951, for "loitering"; and on top of that, he had "stood mute when a neighbor characterized him as a homosexual"; and when he'd been interrogated by the Civil Service Commission about whether he was a homosexual, instead of answering the question directly, he only said that his sexuality was not pertinent to his job performance.[14]

Scott's second appeal was heard in October 1967. Eleven months later, the court issued its verdict, which was an affirmation of the 1965 decision, with an additional opinion that US citizens had a right to privacy and did not have to answer questions about their sexuality. The Civil Service Commission had no grounds to refuse to consider Scott as an eligible applicant for employment. By that time, though, Scott, thoroughly discouraged by the pokey turning of the wheels of justice, had given up on trying to make a living in DC and returned to Chicago, where he immediately got a job with the State of Illinois.

"THE FEDERAL EQUIVALENT OF
GOVERNOR WALLACE"

The "Macy" of *Scott v. Macy* was John W. Macy Jr., who'd been the head of the Commission on Equal Opportunity in Hiring until President Kennedy promoted him in 1961 to chairman of the United States Civil Service Commission. Macy had a long and honored career as a devoted public servant, from the 1950s, when he worked in the Eisenhower administration, to his retirement in 1981 as the head of FEMA under President Carter. As the chairman of the Civil Service Commission, Macy was hugely influential. He kept a file of twenty thousand highly qualified Americans, and he had the ear of the White House when he made recommendations for presidential appointments and top civil service jobs. Lyndon Johnson called him "my talent scout" and "the best there is."

Macy, an avid liberal, was wholehearted in his support of the goals of LBJ's Great Society, particularly the goal of eliminating from American society the terrible demons of racial inequality and social injustice. He decreed that "affirmative attention" be given to attracting "Negroes and Spanish Americans and Puerto Ricans and Orientals and other minority group members to join us in the work of government,"[15] and he fought discrimination in federal hiring against women and the disabled, too. "The yeast in the dough of civil rights dissent and protest is the individual's desire to count for something, to explore his full potential as a human being. The stirrings are being felt in large groupings of minorities. Our society needs new patterns of participation, to make possible the constructive use of their abilities and personal attributes," Macy proclaimed.[16] Frank Kameny could not have said it better himself.

But when Macy spoke of the government making constructive use of those who had been stifled in the past, he most certainly did not mean homosexuals. Kameny had been trying to meet with him since August 1962, precisely to tell him that homosexuals, who were one of the "large groupings of minorities," also desired to count for something, to explore their full potential as human beings, to contribute their abilities and personal attributes to government service. Macy's first response to Kameny's request for a meeting was a curt letter saying that to meet with Kameny "would serve no useful purpose" because homosexuals were not suitable employees for federal civil service.

Through Mattachine, Kameny renewed his requests for a meeting in 1963 and again in 1964.[17] The answer he got, on US Civil Service Commission stationery, was *no*. Kameny dubbed John Macy "the federal equivalent of Governors [George] Wallace, [Ross] Barnett, and [Orval] Faubus," the obstructionists of Alabama, Mississippi, and Arkansas, respectively, who fought fiercely against racial integration. Like them, Macy was refusing to meet with "Homosexual American citizens" (a descriptor Kameny kept repeating like a mantra) to hear their legitimate grievances.[18]

Kameny again wrote John Macy after Mattachine members picketed the White House in April 1965, and asked that Macy change the commission's policy on homosexuals. In May Macy responded that the Civil Service Commission had, in fact, recently reconsidered the policy—and decided "to retain it unaltered."[19]

Kameny wrote back: "No homosexual citizens as such participated in the deliberations, as citizens in this country have a right to expect in matters affecting them!" No answer. He wrote Macy again to say that Mattachine Society Washington would be picketing in front of Macy's bailiwick on June 26, 1965; but, he said, it was not too late to call off the picket. All Macy had to do was agree to a meeting. Finally, Mattachine did receive an answer: "A meeting would serve no useful purpose," Macy reiterated his refrain on June 23.[20]

Though Kameny was no longer president of Mattachine, he was able to get twenty-five members to join the picket—a respectable number, two and a half times as many as those present at the first White House picket. For two hours on the afternoon of Saturday, June 26, 1965, seventeen men and eight women, dressed for balmy early-summer weather—the men in light suits, the women in sleeveless blouses and cotton skirts—marched in an oval in front of Civil Service Commission headquarters proclaiming "'Fair Employment' Applies to Homosexuals Too," "Government Should Combat Prejudice—Not Submit to It," and "Sexual Preference Is Irrelevant to Federal Employment." They were led by Lilli Vincenz and her bold, black-lettered picket sign, designed to tweak Chairman Macy's nose with the reminder that the civil service was already infiltrated by homosexuals, and not even his pusillanimous policies could keep them out: "A Quarter

Million Homosexual Federal Employees Protest Civil Service Commission Policy," her sign said.[21] To every passerby who would take it, the picketers distributed a three-page leaflet, "Why Homosexuals Are Picketing the United States Civil Service Commission," which complained of the commission's "un-American refusal" to meet with them.

Then Kameny went home and wrote a follow-up letter, again requesting a meeting with John Macy. Nothing. He sent another letter on August 15. This time he received a response from Macy saying that the Civil Service Commission's general counsel, Lawrence Meloy, and the director of the Civil Service Commission's Bureau of Personnel Investigations, Kimbell Johnson, would meet with a few Mattachine representatives. (Perhaps they'd hoped to pry out some of the names of the quarter million homosexual federal employees?) On August 28, Kameny, Jack Nichols, Lilli Vincenz, and Barbara Gittings stepped foot, as known homosexuals, into the halls of commission headquarters. They brought a married straight woman with them, too, the same one who was in the first Mattachine White House picket—to corroborate that not all heterosexuals felt contempt for homosexuals or would be uncomfortable working with them.[22] Johnson and Meloy listened for an hour and a half as the small contingent, Kameny leading the way, made their argument:[23] federal employment should be based on relevant background, training, on-the-job conduct, and nothing else—certainly not on off-the-job private sexual acts. "Morality and immorality are not the concern of the government and are not relevant to employment!" Kameny reiterated passionately.

"All the homosexuals I've come in contact with have been arrested for soliciting or they've been child molesters. What I can't stand is those people who take a youngster home, get him drunk, and seduce him," Meloy said flatly.[24]

"We don't condone things like that. We're not trying to make that legal. That has nothing to do with what we're talking about!" Kameny told him. It wasn't easy for Kameny to be patient with such ignorance.

When Meloy instructed the group to submit a formal written statement of their position—which they'd already presented verbally at great length—it felt like a stalling tactic.

But they'd leave nothing undone. In December Mattachine submitted a seventeen-page statement titled "Federal Employment of Homosexual

American Citizens," along with documents supporting Mattachine's position from the ACLU and the San Francisco Council on Religion and the Homosexual. For good measure, they stuck into the envelope the Mattachine leaflet, "Why Homosexuals Are Picketing the United States Civil Service Commission."

Two months later, Mattachine received a response—"a masterful stroke of illogic," Kameny called John Macy's long letter.[25] Macy rejected, first of all, Mattachine's most salient argument that homosexuals were a minority group comparable to racial or religious minorities. "Homosexual" isn't even a noun, Macy said, so the word can't refer to a person. It's an adjective and refers simply to deviate sexual behavior: and those who engage in such behavior are not suitable for civil service employment. Macy then listed the reasons why the government would not hire such people:

- the revulsion of other employees by homosexual conduct and the consequent disruption of service efficiency
- the apprehension caused other employees of homosexual advances, solicitations, or assaults
- the unavoidable subjection of the sexual deviate to erotic stimulation through on-the-job use of common toilets, showers, and living facilities
- the offense to members of the public who are required to deal with a known or admitted sexual deviate to transact Government business
- the hazard that the prestige and authority of a Government position will be used to foster homosexual activity, particularly among the youth
- the use of Government funds and authority in furtherance of conduct offensive both to the mores and the laws of our society[26]

Kameny declared himself doubly disgusted by the letter because John Macy had fervently vowed that as the head of the Civil Service Commission he would wage a "renewed attack upon prejudice itself, with the goal of eradicating every vestige of it from the federal service." That goal, Macy had pronounced in no uncertain terms, meant nothing less than "full acceptance of minority associates."[27] The duplicity of Macy's pronouncement renewed Kameny's outraged resolve to fight until the Civil Service Commission and all the other federal entities—the Justice Department, the Pentagon, the White House, the Supreme Court—admitted that homosexuals were indeed among those "minority associates."

"WHO IS THE CIVIL SERVICE COMMISSION TO MAKE OLYMPIAN PRONOUNCEMENTS ABOUT MORALITY AND IMMORALITY?"

Clifford Norton, for fifteen years a budget analyst for the National Aeronautics and Space Administration, had spent the evening of October 22, 1963, in a DC gay bar. He left about midnight and drove to Lafayette Square, where he pulled up to the curb and made eye contact with a young man by the name of Madison Monroe Procter. Procter ambled over to Norton's car, and Norton invited him in. They drove once around the square.

"Do you want to come to my apartment?" Norton asked.

"Drive me to my car, where you picked me up, and then I'll follow you," Procter said.

They were unaware that two Morals Squad officers had observed them, and now they, too, were following Norton's car to his home in southwest Washington.

Procter and Norton had gotten out of their cars and were walking together toward Norton's apartment house when the policemen pulled up in their unmarked car, jumped out, and told the two men they were under arrest. They were taken down to the police station, and each was led by an officer into a little room where he was interrogated for two hours about his sex history. Procter said under grilling that Norton had put his hand on Procter's leg as they drove around Lafayette Square.

Under grilling, Norton admitted that he worked for NASA. The interrogating policemen reported the information they'd extracted to the head of the Morals Squad, Lieutenant Roy Blick, who'd been a main force in witch hunting DC homosexuals since 1950. Blick released Madison Monroe Procter but telephoned NASA security chief Bart Fugler to say that Clifford Norton, a NASA employee, had been arrested for homosexual conduct.

Fugler arrived at the station at three o'clock in the morning. Blick showed him Norton's arrest record, and then let him listen incognito while Norton was interrogated for another twenty minutes. Norton continued to deny he'd made homosexual advances to Procter; and finally, he was told he would be released without being charged, though he was given a traffic ticket because he'd been driving forty-five miles per hour in a thirty-five-mile zone when the Morals Squad officers followed him.

But the ticket was the least of Norton's troubles. As he was about to leave the station, Fugler identified himself as the NASA Security Chief and ordered Norton to come with him. He was taken to a second-floor office of a deserted NASA building, where another NASA officer was already waiting for them. They questioned Norton until six in the morning. Exhausted by then (but not enough to spill all his beans), he admitted that he'd engaged in mutual masturbation with other males in high school and college, that he sometimes had homosexual desires when he drank, that a couple of times he blacked out after drinking and "suspected [he] might have engaged in some sort of homosexual activity," that he'd experienced a blackout when he met Procter and he remembered only that he'd invited him up for a drink. His interrogators produced a written statement that Procter had given the Morals Squad officer: "It would take an idiot not to be able to figure out that he wanted to have a sex act on me," Procter had said under questioning.

"Procter is a liar. I never made indecent advances on him," Norton insisted. "I never knowingly engaged in any homosexual activity during my entire adult life!" His denials did him no good. Fugler and the other NASA officer concluded that Norton did make advances to Procter, which amounted to "immoral, indecent, and disgraceful conduct," and that, based on his earlier admissions to them, they were convinced that Norton possessed "traits and character which render him unsuitable for further government employment."[28] He was fired from NASA, and both a civil service appeals examiner and the board of appeals and review upheld the firing.

Still reeling from shock, Norton remembered that the year before, he'd read in the *Washington Star* that Frank Kameny, president of Mattachine, had challenged Congressman Dowdy's attempt to revoke the homophile organization's license to raise money in order to fight for homosexual rights. Norton found Kameny's telephone number in the DC phone book, and he called.

Clifford Norton, who'd been fired from a job, was in a different situation from Bruce Scott, who was a job applicant; Norton's would be another important test case. Kameny worked with ACLU lawyers Glenn Graves and John Karr to build the case. Like *Scott v. Macy*, it ended up in the US Court of Appeals; and luck and coincidence were once more on the homophiles' side. The chief judge appointed to hear *Norton v. Macy* was again David Bazelon. "There is sufficient evidence that Norton made homosexual advances to Procter," Bazelon wrote in the majority opinion on *Norton v. Macy*. But, he wanted to know, how did that have any bearing on his performance as a budget analyst? "Who is the Civil Service Commission to make Olympian pronouncements about morality and immorality?" he scolded Macy and his subordinates. "Immorality covers a multitude of sins," he went on, expressing outrage at government hypocrisy. "Indeed, it may be doubted whether there are in the entire Civil Service many persons so saintly as never to have done any act which is disapproved by the 'prevailing mores of our society,'" he told the Civil Service Commission.[29]

Immediately after Judge Bazelon's court found in favor of Norton, the Civil Service Commission petitioned for rehearing. It was by now 1969. Clifford Norton had been fighting his case for six years. He could not get a job in Washington. While he awaited resolution of his case, he went to the other end of the continent and worked in Los Angeles until he was let go when the firm had to make cuts for economic reasons. He took a bus back across the country, stopping off in various places like Cincinnati to look for work. He found none. "I'm down to my last $4," he wrote Frank Kameny in July, while he was still waiting to hear whether the Civil Service Commission would be granted a rehearing.[30]

Coincidentally, the day after Kameny received Norton's letter he received another from a former coworker of Norton's at NASA saying that everyone in their office had been disturbed by his firing, and they all agreed that Norton had been a "well-liked and efficient worker."[31] Let the Civil Service Commission appeal their loss all the way to the Supreme Court, Kameny wrote Norton to cheer him—he and Norton could now provide concrete evidence about how well Norton fit in at NASA.[32]

But not many had Kameny's stomach for unlimited battle. Norton was tired of the fight. He wrote Kameny to say he was worried that the

Washington newspapers would use his name in reporting his victory over the Civil Service Commission. His brother, who worked in DC, might see the newspapers and tell his family that he was a homosexual.[33]

Kameny was furious. The year before, in 1968, he'd coined the slogan "Gay Is Good," which he would come to think of as his biggest contribution to the gay movement—even bigger than his victories over the federal government—because it had the power to make gays and lesbians strong. Norton's win over the Civil Service Commission had already made him a poster boy for the gay rights struggle. Kameny couldn't let him indulge in sniveling timidity. "You have fought the very government of the United States and won," he lectured Norton in a letter, fairly banging out his annoyance on the typewriter keys. "You have bearded the lion in his den. And you're still running from your family???!!! [sic] God knows, man—you stood up to the world and said, 'I am right and you are wrong'; and the world has said back to you (after a fight): 'Yes, you are right and we were wrong.' And you're still running from your family???!!! [sic] If I were you just now, impoverished and all, I'd be holding my head up in pride and looking anyone [sic] straight in the eye and saying, 'I'm a Homosexual and so what! Accept me on MY [sic] terms or you don't get me, and you'll lose more than I will.' And that includes your family. The closet is getting very stuffy. Come out. The fresh air and the sunshine are invigorating."[34]

Norton wrote thanking him for his advice, though his letter suggests he felt sorry for himself still. No word yet on whether the Civil Service Commission would be granted a rehearing. He'd settled for the time being in Boston and was eking out a little living, doing part-time work as a telephone solicitor.[35] The agony of his wait was alleviated somewhat by friends; he was staying with one of them in a fourteen-room restored town house in the gentrified South End.

But in a few months, Norton would be able to buy such a place for himself if he wished. The Civil Service Commission did petition for a rehearing; it was denied on October 20, 1969;[36] finally, the commission agreed to pay Norton $100,000 for wrongful termination and to provide him with a lifetime pension.[37]

And that was not the greatest victory of *Norton v. Macy*. As a direct result of losing this case in 1969 and the *Scott v. Macy* case the year before, the Civil Service Commission came to understand that it needed to give up on refusing to hire homosexual applicants and witch hunting homosexual employees. On December 21, 1973, the commission issued a bulletin to provide a guideline to all the agencies over which it had jurisdiction: "You may not find a person unsuitable for federal employment merely because that person is a homosexual or has engaged in homosexual acts; nor may such exclusion be based on a conclusion that a homosexual person might bring the public service into public contempt." The statement was a direct refutation of Chairman Macy's 1966 declarations that "homosexual" is not a noun, and that homosexuals should be barred from federal employment because their presence would offend the public.

In 1975 the guideline was formally codified in the Civil Service Commission's Regulations Relating to Suitability Disqualification.[38] A quarter-century-old policy of federal persecution of gay people who worked for, or hoped to work for, the US government, had come to an end. Frank Kameny, grandiose and bellicose, declared in inimitable Kameny style, "The US government surrendered to me on July 3, 1975."

FOG AND LIGHT: FOGGY BOTTOM, JUSTICE, AND DEFENSE

On August 27, 1965, President Lyndon Johnson's secretary of state, Dean Rusk, was holding a televised press conference. He was surrounded by reporters—a couple dozen men in suits and ties seated at desks with microphones, who raised their hands respectfully to be called on by the secretary: "Under what conditions would the US stop bombing North Vietnam?" they asked him, and "What hopes do you hold for French president Charles de Gaulle's attempts to settle the Vietnam conflict?" "Mr. Secretary, I understand that tomorrow a self-described 'minority group' will be picketing State Department headquarters. Would you care to comment on the personnel policies at issue?" one reporter called out from the back of the room.

Rusk smirked. "Well, you've been very gentle," he said, meaning that the reporter had not used the damning word for which he himself refused to substitute a less-offensive synonym: "Yes, I understand that we are being picketed by a group of *homosexuals*." Chuckles and guffaws. Rusk had been apprised of the picket a few days earlier, when Kameny informed the State

Department that Mattachine Society Washington would be willing to cancel plans to protest if the secretary of state would meet with members of the group to discuss routine firing of State Department employees who were found to be homosexual. Rusk did not dignify the request with an answer. "The policy of the department is that we do not employ homosexuals," he reiterated for members of the press. "If we discover homosexuals in our department, we discharge them. This has to do with problems of blackmail and problems of personal instability and all sorts of things. So I don't think we can give any comfort to those who might be tempted to picket us tomorrow," Rusk concluded[39] before he turned to a question from the front of the room: "Is it true that Hanoi has rebuffed a US peace proposal?"

Saturday, August 28, two o'clock in the afternoon: Mattachine pickets were there, just as promised. So were the AP and UPI wire services, which Frank Kameny had alerted, as well as reporters from CBS-TV, the *Kansas City Star*, the French News Agency, and a host of other media representatives[40] who learned of the picket from Rusk's comments in response to the reporter's question at the news conference. (It would not have been unlike Frank Kameny to have planted the reporter in the back of the room precisely for the purpose of getting the word out about the planned picket to a broader swath of print and television journalists.) As homosexuals picketed Foggy Bottom, television cameras caught them holding up neatly printed, bold-lettered signs—the perfect medium to get a message across, succinctly and instantaneously, to television viewers. The sign on which the cameras focused longest said:

WE WANT

STATE DEPARTMENT EMPLOYMENT OF HOMOSEXUALS

& CONFERENCES WITH STATE DEPARTMENT OFFICIALS

Kameny, sounding intelligent and looking very presentable, was also captured by CBS-TV's cameras. "Every American citizen has a right to be considered by his government on the basis of his own personal merits as an individual," he declared. Secretary Rusk had opened up for Kameny access to publicity venues that were priceless. Large numbers of people, straight and gay, in Nebraska and Alabama and Texas, who may not have known before that American homosexuals were making a demand to be treated like full-fledged American citizens, learned about it sitting in their living rooms and watching the nightly news.

But despite the nationwide coverage of the picketers' grievances, the secretary of state still did not deign to communicate with them. Mattachine's answer was to thumb its collective nose at Secretary Rusk. Kameny and a couple of other members of the group penned two circulars titled "How to Handle a Federal Interrogation" and "What to Do If You Are Arrested." They intended it for distribution everywhere that homosexuals congregated in DC, but first they invaded Foggy Bottom, walking up and down the halls to plaster the circulars all over State Department bulletin boards. They stuffed copies in holders, too, on which they wrote in red letters, "Take One!"[41]

Frank Kameny had been voted out as president of Mattachine; and almost to a person, members of the organization that he'd founded thought him arrogant and exhausting; but no one could deny that he was a dynamic, bold, and brainy tactician. As Eva Freund, one of Mattachine's few lesbians, observed, "Kameny was the only person I ever encountered who had an overarching perspective, who saw how all the pieces fit together, who knew the things you had to do to make social change happen."[42] Without an official title, he continued to be the group's chief strategist; and members continued to follow him into his various remarkable exploits.

He next waged a war of bombardment on the Justice Department's attorney general, Nicholas Katzenbach, and Assistant Attorney General Walter Yeagley, barraging them with Mattachine literature, notifying them whenever Mattachine planned to picket. He could have saved his envelopes and stamps. The Justice Department was keeping a file of the collected letters of Franklin Kameny—copies of all the correspondence he'd sent to US government officials.

But finally, astoundingly, it was the Justice Department that sent a letter to Kameny, informing him that he and Mattachine were being given a ninety-minute appointment. On January 25, 1966, they were to meet with Assistant Attorney General Yeagley in the Division of Internal Security. Yeagley's primary duties since the McCarthy years had been to flush out Communists and subversives. With common sense and chutzpah, Kameny took the offensive at the meeting. "The notion of homosexuals as a secu-rity risk is nothing but the creation of armchair theoreticians operating in ivory towers," he lectured Yeagley. "It's the government policies that are creating the real problems. The so-called 'problem' of homosexuals as a se-curity risk is nonexistent! There are no instances whatsoever of homosexu-als having been blackmailed to turn over American state secrets."[43]

The assistant attorney general let Kameny talk for most of the ninety minutes, but it's unclear why. In fact, it's unclear why Yeagley even agreed to a meeting—unless it was to see up close these people who were clut-tering up official mailboxes and creating a nuisance in front of public buildings. Kameny and the other Mattachine representatives learned from Yeagley only that the security clearance program was decentralized—and the Department of Justice had no direct responsibility for it. The Civil Service Commission was in charge of clearances for federal employees, based (as Mattachine already knew) on "suitability" standards; and the De-partment of Defense "set the tone" for clearances for employees in private industry that contracted with federal agencies.

The Department of Defense became the next target on Kameny's list. In May 1967 thirty-one-year-old Benning Wentworth, namesake and de-scendent of the first royal governor of New Hampshire,[44] received an of-ficial notification titled "Statement of reasons by the Defense Department for proposed revocation of security clearance." For seven years, Wentworth, an air force veteran and electronics technician, had had a clearance that permitted him to work with "secret" materials at Bell Laboratories in Murray Hill, New Jersey, a company which contracted with the federal government. Now the Defense Department was proposing the clearance be taken from him because "1. He has committed certain specified acts of sexual perversion over a specified period of time with a John Jerry Gaffney; and 2. Because of these acts, he is subject to blackmail."[45]

Gaffney, an eighteen-year-old high school senior when he met Went-worth in 1964, later enlisted in the air force, and in a crisis of panic admit-ted to both an air force chaplain and a psychiatrist that he had had sexual relations with men. Both his confessors informed the Air Force Office of Special Investigations, as they were required to do; and that triggered an interrogation of Gaffney. Investigators seized several of his "suspicious" belongings, including an address book in which they found Wentworth's telephone number and a jotting about their encounter. Thus began Wentworth's troubles, including long hours of questioning by security officers of the Department of Defense about the most intimate details of his sex life.[46]

By now frequent newspaper articles about Frank Kameny and his appearances on television had made his name familiar to anyone who was paying attention. Wentworth found him easily in the DC phone book, where Kameny let himself be listed for just this purpose. Yes, certainly, he would act as personal counsel to Wentworth.

"Look, I barely knew this kid Gaffney," Wentworth told Kameny quickly. "We had a brief half-hour encounter involving no sexual activity."[47]

"Okay," Kameny said, "but this is what our tactic has to be: First of all, it's strategically advisable to allow into the record that you're a homosexual and that you've never denied it. The admission will make it clear that you're in no way subject to blackmail. Secondly, instead of keeping the accusation against you secret, we're going to tell the whole world."

Barbara Gittings had by now lost her position as editor of *The Ladder* and had more time to assist in Mattachine Society Washington's civil liberties battles. Frank Kameny was thrilled. With her calm and cool speech and proper demeanor, she helped defuse the fevered associations between homosexuality and wildly illicit sex that lodged in the minds of those who upheld Defense Department policy. Kameny asked her to act as cocounsel for Benning Wentworth. He and Gittings wrote to the Security Clearance Review Office of the Defense Department, requesting that Wentworth be given a hearing. It was scheduled for November 24, 1967. At that hearing, Gittings and Kameny agreed, they'd admonish the Defense Department lawyers, "We do not come here as amateur lawyers, trying to act as professionals. We come as professional human beings, trying to teach our Defense Department to be the same."[48]

"We simply invited all the press services, all the major newspaper columnists and national magazines of importance, and the radio and TV networks, too, to attend the hearing and to report and broadcast freely," Kameny gleefully reported to Don Slater, who was then publishing the homophile magazine *Tangents* in Los Angeles. The press conference Kameny and Gittings arranged was held one hour before the hearing, immediately outside the hearing room doors. The purpose of the gathering was for Wentworth to announce to the press that he was indeed an active homosexual; and because his homosexuality was no secret, he could never be blackmailed for it. Barbara Gittings, wearing a big "Equality for Homosexuals" button on the collar of her neat dress, told the reporters—appropriating the rhetoric that was used against homosexuals and applying it to Wentworth's accusers: "We consider the very existence of this case to be part of the government's *improper, unethical,* and *immoral* effort to enter into the field of private morality."[49]

The media came out in full force because Wentworth's declaration and his public challenge to the Department of Defense were certainly news: never before had homosexuals whose security clearances were being revoked desired to spread the word about their trouble. Though some editors attached hostile headlines to the resultant articles, such as "Deviate, 31, Confesses in Bid to Retain Job,"[50] the public was also informed of Kameny's most crucial point of defense: Wentworth's willing admission to homosexuality made him immune to blackmail threats. Associated Press reporters stayed through every minute of the seven-and-a-half hours of the hearing. "They took many pictures," Kameny wrote Don Slater with satisfaction.[51]

As personal counsel, Kameny had the opportunity to feed leading questions to the slight and usually shy, but now defiant, Wentworth, who'd been coached well by Kameny and Gittings. "Do you know that under the law you are subject to criminal prosecution for having allegedly committed a homosexual act?" Kameny asked Wentworth who, though he was sitting on the witness stand with all eyes upon him, managed to control his nervousness enough to look composed. Wentworth was normally soft-spoken, but as instructed by his counsel, he answered loudly, "I would welcome a criminal prosecution because it would provide me with an opportunity, working with the ACLU and the Mattachine Society, to bring a Supreme Court test case and have the sodomy law struck down once and for all."

"Do you keep your homosexuality a secret? Do your fellow workers and supervisors know?" Kameny asked. "Everyone I work with knows," Wentworth answered. "When my security clearance was revoked, there was an article about it in the *New York Times*. A lot of my coworkers told me they saw it, and those who didn't see it heard about it. If anything, they seem to be going out of their way to be nice to me. It's a big company and I've had no adverse response whatsoever. Not even from my supervisors.

And now the whole world will know because I've just had a news conference announcing even on radio and television that I'm a homosexual."

"What about your family?" Kameny asked, again a question on which he and Gittings had coached Wentworth, who answered unflappably, "They're fine with it. Right after the *New York Times* article came out, I received two unsolicited letters, one from my mother and one from an aunt. They both said they were proud of me to be fighting for my rights. My mother said she was expecting me for Christmas dinner."

"So there's no fear whatsoever of adverse familial consequences," Kameny emphasized, reiterating for the fifth or sixth time that if everyone already knows that Wentworth is a homosexual, no one could blackmail him to turn over state secrets.[52]

Another major argument that the Defense Department used to bar homosexuals from security clearance was that they were emotionally unstable individuals whose sexuality was a manifestation of their severe neurosis. Defense Department attorneys called as an expert witness Dr. Charles Socarides, a Freudian psychoanalyst who had made a considerable reputation by curing, as he claimed, over seventy-five homosexuals. The attorneys' questions under direct examination allowed Socarides to coolly confirm that homosexuality was a sick adaptation to an unfortunate family constellation, that homosexuals were mentally unsound and unpredictable, that he'd never encountered a healthy homosexual, and that by their very nature, homosexuals were poor security risks.

Kameny and Gittings had their turn with Dr. Socarides in cross-examination. During the three hours of their questioning, Socarides's composure morphed to irritation and then agitation as it became clear that first Kameny and then Gittings were leading him into traps and knocking down his claims. They made his theories look so much like quackery that some weeks later Kameny was formally notified by the Defense Department that Dr. Socarides's name had been taken off the department's list of expert witnesses. But despite the logic of Kameny's and Gittings's arguments about an out homosexual being blackmail-proof, despite the bumbling ineptitude of the expert witness, the Security Clearance Review Office elected not to reinstate Benning Wentworth's clearance.

Wentworth appealed, and Kameny and Gittings again acted as cocounsel. The three showed up at the preliminary to the appeal hearing wearing

"Gay Is Good" buttons and ready to rumble. "We don't come into this case
as repentant and rehabilitated. We come wearing our slogans and holding
our heads high, and refusing to tolerate any transgression of our rights and
privileges," Kameny declared. At the actual hearing a week later, he argued
that standards of "morality" were evolving. He granted, "for the sake of argument," that some people still consider homosexuality to be immoral. But
so what? "A man has a right in this country to be unpopular; he has a right
to be unrespectable, disreputable, disgraceful, infamous, notorious, if he so
wishes, without adverse consequences of any kind from his government." It
was the government that was the monster and needed to be reformed, he
insisted. He was surely remembering his own sad history when he spoke
vehemently of the horrible injustices perpetrated on a man like Benning
Wentworth, "who has lived for years an honorable, honest, productive, useful life, respected—and properly so—by those around him, relied upon,
given responsibilities and trusts, which he has consistently shouldered and
met," only to find himself called "irresponsible, untrustworthy, unstable,
reckless, having poor judgment and integrity—all because in his personal,
private life he is unconventional."

Kameny concluded with a Shylock speech that aimed to convey the
humanity of the homosexual and the terrible inhumanity of the government's persecution of him. "We have our own sensitivities; we have our
feelings; we are human beings. You walk roughshod over those feelings
and sensitivities, with hobnailed boots, as if we were somehow less than
human—which is, of course, precisely the way all too many of you think
of us . . . You callously destroy people, needlessly, and then forget about
them."[53] But still the Department of Defense would not budge.

Kameny had by now conceived a clever tactic: "There are more of us than
there are [government] lawyers to cope with our cases, and we'll swamp
them and the courts with a tide of litigation," he declared.[54] He encouraged not only Benning Wentworth, but also Otto Ulrich and Richard
Gayer, two other homosexuals whose security clearances had been revoked,
to appeal to the district court. The trio was lucky enough to get as their
judge a man who was, like Judge David Bazelon, a staunch supporter of
civil rights. In 1972 Judge John H. Pratt—having just ruled that the Department of Health, Education, and Welfare must withhold federal funds

from 213 school districts that had failed to desegregate—now turned his attention to *Benning Wentworth v. Melvin Laird, Secretary of Defense*; and he ordered that Wentworth's security clearance be restored.[55]

Still, Defense Department lawyers would not concede wrong. Their next gambit was to appeal to the federal court. Wentworth's case was reviewed on that level in 1973. Senior Circuit judge Charles Fahy gave the majority opinion. He censured the Defense Department for the "shocking array of questions" that Wentworth had to endure when he was grilled by security officers six years earlier. He characterized their interrogation as "a wide-ranging fishing expedition, concerning the most intimate details of Mr. Wentworth's sex life." The entire administrative proceedings were tainted, the judge said, because Wentworth's questioners had flagrantly violated his First Amendment right to privacy. "Such unreasonable encroachments are indicative of the Defense Department's ill-defined approach to the problem," he scolded them. Moreover—Judge Fahy told Defense Department lawyers, reiterating co-counsels Kameny and Gittings's reproaches—they'd failed to establish a *nexus* between Mr. Wentworth's homosexuality and his ability to safeguard the nation's secrets. Therefore, the judge concluded, Benning Wentworth's security clearance had been erroneously revoked. And the Defense Department must rectify the error.[56]

Frank Kameny never, to the end of his life, stopped being indignant about what had been done to him as a young PhD working for the Army Map Service and dreaming he might become an astronaut. But his various victories over the federal government had done much to modify its cavalier and cruel treatment of gays and lesbians. Those victories must have given him great political satisfaction as well as considerable personal satisfaction. His personal satisfaction was surely made even sweeter in 2009, two years before his death, when he received an official letter from John Berry, director of the US Office of Personnel Management, the governmental organization that had morphed out of the Civil Service Commission in 1978. Berry apologized to Kameny for the Civil Service Commission's "shameful action" fifty-two years earlier when it fired Kameny. "With the fervent passion of a true patriot, you did not resign yourself to your fate or quietly endure this wrong," Berry wrote. The US government's eventual repudiation of its discriminatory policies was "due in large part to your determination and hard work," he added. He concluded by asking Frank Kameny to "please accept the gratitude and appreciation of the U.S. Office of Personnel Management for the work you have done to fight discrimination and protect the merit-based civil service system."[57]

Kameny, sometimes a man of surprisingly few words, wrote back: "Apology accepted."

PART 4

EARTHQUAKE: THE STONEWALL YEARS

Chapter 11

THE RIOTS

NIGHT OF A FULL MOON

The blacked-out windows and heavy door of the Stonewall Inn at 53 Christopher Street in Greenwich Village recalled a speakeasy—even to the peephole covered with a slide bar and a bouncer's eye that suddenly appeared to check whether a knock on the door was hooligans or the fuzz come to raid the place. The door opened easily for homosexuals with the three dollars to pay for tickets that could be exchanged for a couple of watered-down drinks. The cover charge was not trivial for the gay youngsters who were among the Stonewall Inn's main habitués; but they found a way to pay it because no gay bar in the Village had such a good dance floor, or such a varied and lively clientele. There were blacks, whites, Puerto Ricans, a few Asians, leather-clad hustlers, queens with made-up faces and fluffed-out hair or sometimes in full drag; there were chicken hawks who came to pick up street kids[1] and occasional "bougie" gays, as the kids called the Wall Street types in three-piece suits.[2] There were occasional fag hags, too, and butch dykes with or without femmes. Except for the chicken hawks, practically everyone there was in their teens or twenties and having an uninhibited ball in a place they could almost think of as home, if they forgot that the Genovese family held the deed and made the house rules—and couldn't keep the Stonewall safe.

About one in the morning on June 28, 1969, the bouncer was summoned to the peephole. He looked out and saw "Lily Law, Betty Badge,
and Peggy Pig," as policemen were called by campy Village queens, and
when police shouted, "Police! Open up!" a bouncer had to open up.[3] Six
officers of Manhattan's First Division Public Morals Squad invaded the
place. Two undercover policewomen were already inside. For more than an
hour they'd been sitting at the bar, pretending they were lesbians, and keeping their eyes open in the hopes of spotting homosexuals who were selling
or using drugs.

The Stonewall's dimly lit rooms, jammed with two hundred revelers,
were suddenly flooded with harsh light. The jukebox whirred to mute.
The patrons knew what that meant, and they froze. "Line up. Get your IDs
out and in hand," one of Deputy Inspector Seymour Pine's men ordered.
Those whose IDs showed they weren't minors or "masquerading" as the
other sex were shooed out the door. Several "drag queens"[4] said they were
"ladies" and were taken by the two policewomen to the toilet, where it was
determined they'd violated New York Penal Code 240.35 section 4, against
"unnatural attire or facial alteration." "You're under arrest," they were told.
A small knot of lesbian patrons were also singled out for special attention
when a couple of them got feisty, back-talking to the officers, yelling, "We
have a right to be here!"[5]

Police actions like this one were not uncommon in the gay bars of
Greenwich Village. The New York Court of Appeals had ruled after Dick
Leitsch's sip-in three years earlier that even homosexuals must be served in
drinking establishments, but in the two weeks before the Stonewall raid the
Public Morals Squad had found reasons to raid the Snake Pit,[6] the Tele-Star,
the Checkerboard, and the Sewer.[7] The excuse for the June 28 raid was that
though the Stonewall claimed to be a private club requiring membership
(people signed the "member book" with names such as Elizabeth Taylor,
Judy Garland, and Daffy Duck), liquor was being sold there and the bar did
not have a liquor license.[8] Regardless of the reasons for a raid, the history
of police harassment of gay bars was old enough so that gay people knew
what to do. If they were so lucky as to be shooed outside instead of carted
off to the police station and booked, they quickly skedaddled.

But on this night, they didn't. As patrons were released by the police,
they stood on the sidewalk in front of the bar waiting to see if friends still

inside would be set free; and as each new person came through Stonewall's door, those who waited applauded and cheered. The unexpected limelight proved irresistible to many of the liberated who made devil-may-care assertions of dignity by prancing out diva-style, striking a pose, curtsying and bowing, blowing kisses to the throng. "The whole proceedings took on the aura of a homosexual Academy Awards Night," an unfriendly and thoroughly baffled eyewitness reporter for the New York *Daily News* observed.[9] The festive crowd was soon swelled by Greenwich Village weekend tourists who came to see what the excitement was about.

A few doors down from the Stonewall, *Village Voice* reporter Howard Smith, who specialized in writing about sex, drugs, and rock and roll in the Greenwich Village counterculture, was working late in his office because he had a deadline to meet. Smith saw the commotion from his window and wondered whether there was some sort of story to be had. He wandered over to the scene. A rookie *Village Voice* reporter, Lucian Truscott, was already there. Truscott, a recent West Point graduate, son of a long line of military officers, had taken a summer job writing for the *Voice* that was to last until he had to report for duty at Fort Benning, Georgia, at the end of July. He'd had a late dinner in Chinatown and had gone for a nightcap to the Lion's Head, a writers' hangout two doors down from the Stonewall.[10] Seeing the commotion in front of the bar, Truscott changed his plans. Borrowing a pencil and pad of paper from someone in the Lion's Head, he hurried to the scene, where he hopped atop a lidded trash can from which he could get a good view of what was happening. He and Howard Smith would be the Richard Harding Davis and Ernie Pyle of the Stonewall riots.[11]

Howard Smith observed that when he first arrived the mood of the crowd had been a sort of "skittish hilarity." Then several violators of the masquerading law, as well as the Stonewall's bartender, the hatcheck girl, the doorman, and the men's room attendant, who was an elderly straight black man, were led outside in handcuffs and herded into a waiting paddy wagon. A few onlookers booed the policemen. But the real turning point, Smith and Truscott agreed, came after several policemen dragged a butch lesbian out of the bar.[12] They'd handcuffed her because she'd struggled with them. The paddy wagon was full, so the officers pushed the hefty, dark-haired woman who was wearing a man's dress suit[13] into one of the squad cars that were lined up on the street. But she wouldn't stay put. Three times she slid out the driver's-side back door and tried to run back into the Stonewall, perhaps to a lover still being questioned. The last time, as a beefy policeman wrestled her back toward the squad car, she yelled to the crowd, "Why don't you guys do something?"[14]

It was as though her question broke the spell that had, for generations, held gays and lesbians in thrall. "The crowd became explosive," Truscott jotted in his notepad.[15] "Police brutality!" "Pigs!" they shrieked.[16] They pelted the police with a rain of pennies (dirty coppers). Someone threw a loosened cobblestone. Beer cans and glass bottles followed. Bricks from a nearby construction site were hurled at the squad cars with baseball-player skill. A black drag queen, Marsha P. (for "Pay It No Mind") Johnson stuffed a bag with the bricks, then shinnied up a lamppost despite her high heels and tight dress. Taking aim at the windshield of a squad car parked below, she let fly and heard the satisfying shatter of glass.[17] Gays surrounded the paddy wagon and shook it as though they would rescue the prisoners trapped inside by pulling it apart. If some among the crowd suggested it was time to cut out, others answered—as purportedly did drag queen Sylvia Rivera—"Are you nuts? I'm not missing a minute of this. It's the revolution!"[18]

A white policeman grabbed a Puerto Rican man who was striking campy poses; the man struggled and the policeman raised his billy club to subdue him. "How'd you like a big Spanish dick up your little Irish ass?" the man screamed, and the policeman hesitated just long enough for his prisoner to slip away in the mass of rioters.[19] Two officers handcuffed twenty-eight-year-old Raymond Castro and pushed him into the paddy wagon. Hyped by the crowd's shouting, "Let him go! Let him go!" Castro sprang back and knocked both policemen down, superhero style.[20] A butch fellow set a fire in a nearby trash can, and when it blazed red and gold, he threw it through one of the Stonewall's plate-glass-and-plywood-backed windows. People rushed to phone booths to call other gays to join the fight; or they ran through the streets like Paul Revere, drawing gays and straights alike—and especially the Village radicals who had long been hoping and waiting for this night.

John O'Brien—a muscular twenty-year-old with an open Irish face, son of an immigrant woman who worked as a maid and a man who was a union janitor—had been a social activist since 1962. He'd been thirteen years old at that time and had seen a flyer put out by college students about helping black people fight for their rights. The students were going to march in Greene County, Alabama, and O'Brien ran off to join them. That was the start of his long career. He dropped out of high school as soon as he could and became a full-time radical in the civil rights movement, then in the antiwar movement, then in the abortion rights movement. He joined the Young Socialist Alliance, too, though he was kicked out of it in January 1969, when he refused to deny rumors that he was gay. Two or three months later, O'Brien began meeting with other radical young gays at Alternate U, on the second floor of a rundown old building that had once been a sweatshop, on Fourteenth Street and Sixth Avenue. Though the plaster was falling off the walls and the furniture was nothing but beat-up old couches, Alternate U was a favorite spot for counterculture types because it offered space and free classes to people interested in leftist politics, community organizing, or avant-garde art.

O'Brien's group—a half dozen gay kids in jeans and T-shirts, all in their early twenties—were repelled by New York Mattachine, "where everyone wore a suit and tie and you paid your dues and a couple of people politely represented you to the politicians." They were also furious about recent bar raids in the Village, about harassment by unfriendly business owners, and especially about a rumored police shooting of two gay kids near the docks where unguarded trucks that were used to haul meat during the day were taken over at night for a gay trysting area. In response to these recent incidents, O'Brien's little group of militants had written up circulars, gotten the War Resisters League to print them gratis, and posted them in cruising areas: "Gays Must Resist!" "It's Our Streets!" "Gays Must Fight Back Against The NYPD!"[21] That was earlier in June.

And now it was happening. That night, O'Brien had been talking radical politics at his usual hangout, on Eighth Street and Sixth Avenue, a block or so from the Stonewall. When he got the word that the revolution had started he came running, picking up bricks where he could and hurling them at police vehicles. (The second night of the riots, O'Brien led the charge, hurling bricks at the windows of nearby banks that had "shown their hatred of us," and especially at McDougall's, a record shop next to a Latino gay bar on Eighth Street. The owner liked to chase homosexuals with a baseball bat when they passed his shop.)[22]

Twenty-six-year-old Martha Shelley was in the Village that night, too. She was entertaining two Boston lesbians who'd come to New York to find out more about Daughters of Bilitis because they'd hoped to start a lesbian group in their city. Daughters of Bilitis was annoyingly conservative for Martha Shelley (who'd had to change her name from Martha Altman when DOB insisted that using a pseudonym helped keep members safe). But she'd belonged to the organization for two years and had even served briefly as its president. In Shelley's spare time, when she wasn't working as a secretary at Barnard, she was participating with the Columbia Student Homophile League in militant antiwar demonstrations; she was also representing the Daughters on panels and in classrooms, where her restrained and unspectacular message was "Homosexuals are not sick. Homosexuals just need equal rights." In the early hours of June 28, Shelley and the two Boston women left Gianni's, a lesbian bar a few blocks from the Stonewall. They first heard and then saw a brick-and-bottle-throwing crowd. "What's going on?" one of the Boston women asked Shelley. "Oh, it's probably an antiwar riot. We have them in the Village all the time," she answered, and they walked on. Because the *fact* was inconceivable, even to a committed activist: *this* time it was gay people who were rioting—not for other causes but for their own.[23]

Dick Leitsch, now executive director of New York Mattachine, was home doing some last-minute packing when the riot began. His partner was taking him on his first European vacation and they were to leave in a few hours. Leitsch had barely been listening to the all-news station WNEW that was playing in the background, but when he heard the newscaster announce a disturbance at the Stonewall Inn, he stopped packing and hurried out to find a cab.[24] By the time he got to the Village, the streets were so jammed with rioters that he jumped out on Fourteenth Street, more than a half dozen blocks away from the Stonewall. As he ran toward the bar, he thought, "This is what Lenin must have felt like at the revolution. It's the best thing that could happen for gays"—though the riot was soon to be the death knell for mannerly homophile groups such as his.

When the excitement was finally over for the night, Dick Leitsch went home, canceled his plane tickets, and began writing an article for the *New York Mattachine Newsletter*:[25] "The Hairpin Drop Heard Round the World."[26]

A LONG TIME COMING

Inspector Pine wanted to collar the perps and haul them off—but the paddy wagon and squad cars were already filled to capacity. He was astounded. He'd never seen a horde of fighting homosexuals. The officers of the Public Morals Division had always said that homosexuals were "easy arrests. They never gave you any trouble. Everybody behaved."[27] How had things changed so dramatically?

Howard Smith attributed the gay violence in the early hours of June 28 to the full white moon that illumed the night sky.[28] The summer heat might have had something to do with it, too: the black riots in New York and Philadelphia in 1964, in Watts in 1965, the 1966 riots in Cleveland and Omaha, the 1967 riots in Detroit and Newark—all of them took place in summer heat. Or perhaps gay people rioted at the Stonewall that June night because throughout the decade violent clashes with the police had been dramatizing the frustrations felt by the powerless of various stripes, including protesters against the Vietnam War and even students on college campuses. Riots brought media attention to the gripes of the disenfranchised as nothing else could. Emotions might have been stoked, too, by the multiple raids of Greenwich Village gay bars in the previous weeks, and by the circulars that John O'Brien's group had plastered all over Greenwich Village.

Nor were the actions of John O'Brien's jeans-wearing, radical-rhetoric-slinging group unique in the lead up to Stonewall. At the beginning of April, two months before the incipient gay militants of the Village began posting "Gays Must Resist!" circulars, Craig Schoonmaker had gotten officials at City College of the City University of New York to give approval to his student organization, *Homosexuals Intransigent!*, a name that was to appear always italicized and with an exclamation point, young Schoonmaker insisted. He scoffed at the "stupid, cowardly euphemism 'homophile'" that older organizations hid behind.[29] He scoffed, too, at the closet, and declared that anyone who wanted to join his group must be openly homosexual. Using City College student body funds, he mimeographed defiant flyers and posted them all over the campus. "Gay is a groove [as in "groovy"]," they announced, "not a rut or ditch!"[30]

Schoonmaker considered himself a "homosexual separatist" (cf. Black separatist), and to nongays, even bisexuals and sympathetic straights, he declared, speaking for *Homosexuals Intransigent!*: "Fuck off! Stay out of my life! . . . I view you with disgust." Nor did he spare lesbians: "I want to live my life among men and manly things! You don't belong!"[31] He hoped to convince masculine gay men to band together in all ways, but especially politically, to take over Manhattan's Nineteenth and Twentieth Districts, to vote "our own people in." "Blacks did it," he exhorted. "Puerto Ricans, Italians, Irish, others too. It works!"[32]

On the other coast, gay rhetoric was also heating up to boiling in the months before Stonewall. Gale Whittington, a baby-faced, blond, twenty-year-old accounting clerk, had been summarily fired from his job at the States Steamship Company in San Francisco because of a photo and story that appeared in the March 28, 1969, *Berkeley Barb*: Whittington, bare chested, being embraced by a thirty-six-year-old man, and above them the headline "Homo Revolt: Don't Hide It."[33] Before Whittington had agreed to pose and let an article be written that identified him as homosexual, he'd thought long and hard, and he concluded, "It was time for homosexuals to declare themselves."[34]

The older man in the photo, Leo E. Laurence, had been a writer for the underground New Left newspaper the *Berkeley Barb*. He'd also been on the board of directors of San Francisco's largest homophile group, the Society for Individual Rights, and was the editor of *Vector*, SIR's magazine, until he was booted out of his editorship because the photo in the *Berkeley Barb* had made SIR members uncomfortable.

But Laurence was more worried about Whittington than about losing his own job.[35] He'd gotten the news of the young man's firing late at night, and he couldn't sleep. He went down to an all-night coffee shop and there, on a paper napkin, sketched out plans for a new organization that would fight against injustices such as the firing of Gale Whittington for what he chose to do in his free time.

Laurence guessed that the Society for Individual Rights, despite its name, would not be likely to help. Never one to mince words, Laurence dubbed SIR members a bunch of "middle-class, uptight, bitchy old queens," whose main policy was "NOT to get involved in anything controversial."[36] Ironically, SIR had been started in 1964 because some San Francisco homosexuals thought the older homophile groups timid. SIR organized one of the first gay community centers in the country. They were able to get candidates for citywide political office to come speak to them. But as Laurence had predicted, when he and Gale Whittington approached SIR leaders to request help in picketing the States Steamship Company, they answered, "We're too busy getting things done to stop and make signs to carry."[37] That clinched Laurence's conviction that SIR was to homosexuals what the NAACP was to black militants. SIR was completely incapable of seeing that times were changing.[38] He decided to name his organization the Committee for Homosexual Freedom, and he worked with Gale Whittington to refine the plans he'd first designed on the coffee-shop napkin.

Laurence, who saw himself as a radical of the New Left, believed that the Committee for Homosexual Freedom needed to be like militant black groups. "The black man found self-respect and dignity when he said, 'Black is beautiful, and I am proud.' Now homosexuals are starting to say, 'Gay is good, and I too am proud,'" Laurence declared on behalf of the committee.[39] Through one of his associates on the *Barb*, Laurence got himself invited to Black Panther headquarters in the Fillmore, a black district of San Francisco; there, in a Victorian house lined on the inside with steel, he met Panthers leader Huey Newton, who encouraged him to fight fiercely for gays.[40] Laurence and Whittington wasted no time in organizing picketers who would help them send their militant message, and with more than a passing nod to the Black Panthers, they dubbed their picketers the "Pink Panthers."[41]

But though Laurence succeeded in getting a gay activist, Reverend Troy Perry—joined by a handful of other gays and several students from the Claremont College of Theology—to stage simultaneous pickets in front of the States Lines office in downtown Los Angeles,[42] there were no swells of public opinion nor masses of out homosexuals to boycott the company; and States Lines never bent. Despite that frustration, Laurence and his group carried on, holding demonstrations at Tower Records when it seemed that a homosexual employee was being discriminated against, at the San Francisco Examiner Building when a reporter wrote a disrespectful article about homosexuals, at Macy's when the store was complicit with the San Francisco police in entrapping gay men in its restrooms.[43] The organization also inspired a document that came to be considered "the bible of gay liberation." Carl Wittman, a member of Students for a Democratic

Society (SDS), and a war resister, was a participant in the pickets when he wrote "Refugees from Amerika: A Gay Manifesto." "Come out everywhere," Wittman exhorted gay people. "Initiate self-defense and political activity."[44]

The full moon, the heat, the police pulling the plug on the jukebox—all came together to create a perfect storm that brought on the riot at the Stonewall. But surely gay people would not have rioted that night if they hadn't watched for almost the entire decade as oppressed minorities angrily demanded to be treated like human beings and American citizens. Righteous ire stoked, irate gay rhetoric formulated, they understood the time had come for them to make demands just as other minorities had, and in the same way.

TRAPPED IN A GAY BAR

Inspector Pine had been in the Battle of the Bulge in World War II; he'd written a well-respected training manual on the subject of hand-to-hand combat. "But there was never any time that I felt more scared than I had that night," he later admitted.[45] There were only five other policemen and two policewomen with him at the Stonewall, and the mob had somehow grown to maybe a thousand.[46] More bad actors needed to be arrested as soon as possible, Pine thought, or the police would not regain control. He needed backup. He used his police radio to call Sixth Precinct headquarters, only a few blocks away—but inexplicably his calls would not go through.[47] It seemed he had no choice about what to do next. He dispatched the three squad cars and the paddy wagon packed with prisoners. "Hurry back!" he ordered the drivers. "Just drop them off at the Sixth Precinct and hurry back!"[48] The officers turned the squad car sirens on to shriek. Rioters pounded on the cars' hoods and screeched "Pigs!" as the police vehicles drove off.

The eight officers were left alone on the street with a mob that kept growing. "Let's get them!" somebody screamed.

"Back inside! We'll lock ourselves inside!"[49] Pine ordered his officers, and they beat a hasty retreat into the gay bar. Now they could hear the crowd screaming, "Kill the cops!" "Police brutality!" "We're not going to take this anymore!" "Let's get 'em!"[50]

A nearby parking meter had been loosened from the concrete some-time earlier by a bad driver. John O'Brien, together with a shirtless, buff man with curly brown hair, and a couple of other gays, rocked it till they pried it up. Then they ran with the phallic battering ram toward the Stonewall and crashed open its door.[51] Hurled beer cans and garbage followed. Blood spurted from under Patrolman Gil Weisman's eye when he was hit by a flung coin. The other officers grabbed their guns from their holsters. "We'll shoot the first motherfucker that comes through the door!" Inspector Pine yelled.[52] No one entered, and he pulled the broken door closed. A couple of the policemen went from room to room looking for a safe exit. They found a vent that opened out to the rear of the building. Only the more petite of the two women officers could slip out. She ran to a nearby firehouse, where she could call the Sixth Precinct for backup.[53]

But before backup arrived Pine and his crew may as well have been in a war zone. A hand reached in through the Stonewall's broken window, squirted lighter fluid that had been liberated from the United Cigar Store on Seventh Avenue, and dropped a match. Flames whooshed. A trash can, stuffed full with burning paper, landed inside with a thud. "Cook the pigs!" someone yelled.[54] The policemen grabbed the emergency hose from the back wall of the bar and put out the fires. Then three officers wedged the hose through a crack in the door and turned it on full force, hoping to douse the crowd and disperse them. A cold spray shocked the front-row rioters, but it didn't last long.[55] The hose was old and frayed, and when it split the water turned the Stonewall Inn into a small river, and police officers found themselves slipping and sliding on the concrete floor. Miserable and desperate, a couple of policemen again drew guns. Inspector Pine saw disaster looming. He walked up to each one of his officers, looked him in the eye, called him by name, and said, "If you fire that gun without me saying your name and the word 'fire,' you'll be walking a beat on Staten Island all alone for the rest of your career. Do you understand me?"[56]

Finally, at 2:55 a.m. police buses arrived carrying the Tactical Patrol Force, whose major job had been to quell New York City's race riots and out-of-control antiwar protests. Wearing riot helmets with long visors and carrying shields, they formed a phalanx like a Roman army. They were met by a Rockettes-style chorus line of queens who linked arms, kicked high, and to the tune of "Ta-ra-ra Boom-de-ay" bellowed sassily, "We are the Stonewall girls / We wear our hair in curls / We don't wear underwear / We show our pubic hair / We pick up lots of tricks / That's how we get our kicks / We wear our dungarees / Above our nelly knees." Officer Andrew Scheu of the Tactical Police Force tried to arrest one man, Wolfgang Podolski, who struck him in the left eye with a rolled-up newspaper. In the scuffle, Scheu fell down and broke his wrist—which, ironically, went limp.[57] Another officer, Charles Holmes, was bitten on the wrist when he tried to make an arrest, and he had to be taken to St. Vincent's Hospital for a tetanus shot.[58] But the rest of the Tactical Police Force cracked heads up and down Christopher Street until the rioters were finally dispersed at about four in the morning.[59]

The next day, the *New York Times*—not as astute as Sylvia Rivera claimed to be about the meaning of the night's events ("It's the revolution!")—reported the unprecedented melee on page 33 in a short article that bore the headline, "Four Policemen Hurt in 'Village' Raid."[60]

GAY POWER!

During the day on Saturday, exhausted rioters slept. But many gays who had not been there heard of the riot that morning on the "alternative" radio station, WBAI, which had been sympathetic to gays since the early 1960s. It was through WBAI that Frank Galassi, a closeted young college professor, learned there'd been a riot in his favorite gay bar. Galassi had been fired from St. John's College a couple of years earlier because it was suspected he was gay, and since then he'd tried to be very careful out in the world. But on nights when his partner, a male nurse, had to work, Galassi donned jeans and went to the Stonewall to dance. He loved the electric energy there, and the mix of ethnicities, and the exuberantly uninhibited dance moves he could learn nowhere else. Now, at about eleven o'clock on Saturday morning, Galassi hurried across town to the Stonewall. The WBAI commentator said the riots had been quelled, but Galassi was drawn to the site—just to see what was happening now, just to be there.[61]

There were traces of the riot—the shattered window, the broken door, the rubble on the street, the gray wooden sawhorses that announced "Police line. Do not cross." But there were no rioters, only a bunch of gays, ignoring the sawhorses' warning, walking in front of the Stonewall with signs that demanded "Equality for Homosexuals." Across the street at Sheridan Park, gay people were holding hands and kissing in broad daylight. Policemen were standing, hands on hips or arms crossed, watching it all. A couple of days earlier, the gaze of the police would have worried Frank Galassi. He'd never even have dared participate in one of Frank Kameny's pickets. Now he took up a sign and marched.[62]

Though the riot had been led by young street people, Galassi wasn't the only middle-class or professional gay person soon to feel liberated by it. Dr. Howard Brown lived in Greenwich Village, not far from the Stonewall. He'd served under Mayor Lindsay as the New York City health commissioner but resigned in 1967, when he heard that columnist Drew Pearson intended to out him in the pages of the *New York Times*.[63] Two years later, in the heat of the June night, Brown had heard through his open windows the rioters' roar. He went out to discover what the hubbub was about. The homosexuals he saw in front of the Stonewall were nothing like him. In fact, he thought, they were more like prisoners he'd seen on his official rounds of the Tombs, the municipal jail in Lower Manhattan—"obviously poor, most of them sort of limp wristed, shabby, or gaudy gays that send a shiver of dread down the spines of homosexuals who hope to pass as straight."

But, he had to admit, the scene brought to mind every civil rights struggle he'd ever witnessed. It was the riot that eventually "broke the spell" of his fears, Brown realized.[64] It enabled him sometime later, at a conference of six hundred medical people—a crowd of alerted reporters poised to jot down his words—to take the microphone and say, "I am publicly announcing my homosexuality in the hope that it will help to end discrimination against homosexuals." And to end silly stereotyping, too: "I have met more homosexual politicians than homosexual hairdressers," he informed his audience, challenging their willful ignorance about homosexuals in even the most "respected" walks of life, "more homosexual lawyers than homosexual interior decorators."[65]

Not all middle-class gays, of course, understood right away that the rioting of street-people types would be a good thing for them, too. An unidentified representative of Mattachine Society New York was quick to chalk a message on Stonewall's boarded-up window that betrayed the immediate response of many "respectable" gays: "We Homosexuals Plead

With Our People To Help Maintain Peaceful And Quiet Conduct On The Streets Of The Village."[66] But a new generation had just ushered in a new gay era, and the Mattachine plea for "peaceful and quiet conduct" seemed to them nothing short of laughable. For Village gays, the riot had been the equivalent of Rosa Parks taking a forbidden seat in the bus in Montgomery, Alabama. The rest of the world might not know it yet, but they knew that there was no going back to the way things had been.

Craig Rodwell, who'd opened the Oscar Wilde Memorial Bookshop a year after his 1966 Mattachine sip-in with Dick Leitsch, had pasted a "Gay Is Good" sticker in his store's window as soon as Frank Kameny coined the phrase in 1968; a few months later, Rodwell had coined a more militant-sounding slogan, "gay power." It was inspired by "black power," just as "Gay Is Good" had been inspired by "Black Is Beautiful."[67] Rodwell had been waiting for years for the spark that would ignite the fire. As a seventeen-year-old living in Chicago in 1958, he'd made a hundred flyers proclaiming "Homosexuals Unite! Tear Off Your Masks!" and had stuffed them into neighborhood mailboxes—nothing much happened except that two hairdressers were suspected of the deed and evicted from their apartment.[68] But when the riot started, Rodwell "recognized instantly that this was it!"[69] He ran through the streets screaming, "Gay power! Gay power!"[70] His cry was taken up by others among the rioters as they, too, ran around Greenwich Village.[71] (Lucian Truscott even headlined his *Village Voice* account of the riot, "Gay Power Comes to Sheridan Square.") "Support Gay Power!" someone chalked on the Stonewall window the next day. It captured the exhilarating anger that the rioters didn't forget even after they got some sleep.

That evening, they gathered again at the Stonewall. "Fat Tony" Lauria, the Stonewall's Mafia owner, had had a clean-up crew working all day, repairing whatever damage they could, though the main room was still charred and blasted and the only lights were dim, naked bulbs.[72] The jukebox had been destroyed, so a sound system was brought in and speakers placed around the room. To entice customers back, the management announced there would be no cover charge that night—and though liquor could not be sold until they straightened out the misunderstanding about a license, sodas would be free. The Stonewall was soon jammed, as was the street in front of it—not only with gays but also with the curious that had come to see the riot site.

What developed spontaneously was at first nothing more than a block party, with queens camping and posing for pictures and some gays shouting, "Gay power!" "We want freedom now!" "Equality for homosexuals!" But as the crowd grew, it spilled over from the sidewalk into the street and overflowed to Sheridan Square Park, and soon the streets were mobbed over a five-block area.[73] A bus driver, bringing his empty vehicle back to the car barn for the night, loudly honked his horn. Someone tore off a big cardboard advertisement from the bus's side and blocked the windshield with it. It was like a signal. The crowd beat on the bus thunderously and yelled, "Christopher Street belongs to the queens!" "Liberate the streets!" The bus was finally allowed to pass, but other vehicles were stopped and mounted by gays who danced on their roofs and hoods. When police cars arrived, rioters pelted them with garbage and a concrete block, pounded them with fists and feet, and knocked the flashing red light off one of the cars.[74] Four precincts were summoned for backup. By then, the crowd was about two thousand strong.

By the time the busloads of Tactical Police Force showed up, the second full-scale gay riot of the weekend was under way. TPF officers, riot visors already covering their faces, jumped from the buses, linked arms, and formed a flying wedge. They pushed the crowds before them until they got the rioters onto Tenth Street and Sixth Avenue. But some rioters circled back—and they showed up *behind* "Alice Blue Gown," as the queens jeeringly called their adversaries, taunting them with the Rockettes dance they'd perfected the night before. The Tactical Police Force pushed the crowds forward again, and again a troop of queens circled round the block, showed up behind the TPF, and kicked high in time to "We are the Stonewall girls / We wear our hair in curls . . ."

Some officers broke off from the wedge and, brandishing billy clubs, pursued rioters down side streets. At one point, two policemen chased a huge crowd of gays down Waverly Place—until someone shouted, "Hey, there are only two cops! Let's catch them and rip off their clothes and screw them!" The officers turned on their heels and ran back to their squad.[75] Lesbians who were in the lesbian bar Gianni's came out and joined the fray.[76] Jean Devente had been walking around the Village with Jimmy the Dyke, and when they saw the police knocking heads, they threw themselves into combat. Devente was felled by a policeman and kicked in the face. Marsha P. Johnson, back from the night before, took off her blouse and stanched the blood. "Get up, girl," the drag queen ordered the lesbian. "We got a fight on our hands."[77] It lasted until five thirty in the morning, when finally the TPF captain deemed the area "secured," and the officers could pile back into their buses and go home.

WILL THE SPARK DIE?

Sunday night: the Stonewall management again advertised a "free store." Hundreds of gays went inside the bar or milled around outside. Police were under orders to head off trouble and avoid a third night of riots that had already cost the city big bucks. With considerably more tact than they'd practiced in the preceding days, they tried to get people off the street. "It's okay, go on in," they urged those who stood outside the Stonewall. As Dick Leitsch observed with bitter amusement, "The citizenry was treated to the sight of the cops begging homosexuals to go inside the bar that they had chased everyone out of a few nights before."[78]

There were many more toughs in the Sunday night crowd, including a large "leather" contingent. A bunch of people tried to overturn a police car, and several were arrested.[79] But the energy to riot was not what it had been the previous two nights. Gays seemed to know they'd already won and now it was time to enjoy the fruits of winning. Many did go inside the Stonewall and reveled in a victory dance. Poet Allen Ginsberg and his friend Taylor Mead, the Andy Warhol star, dropped in at the Stonewall about one in the morning, after hearing tales about the two previous nights' riots. *Village Voice* reporter Lucian Truscott, still on his beat and recognizing the famous poet, followed them for the sake of the story. Ginsberg greeted Tactical Police Force members by flashing a two-fingered "V," the peace sign—or was it a victory sign? He danced with euphoric young gays, veterans of the riot, and he picked up the rapture of their mood.

"You know, the guys there were so beautiful. They've lost that wounded look that fags all had ten years ago," Ginsberg said to Truscott as they walked out together. "Defend the fairies!" he bid the reporter before they parted at Cooper Square.[80]

On Monday and Tuesday the streets of Greenwich Village were quiet. But the mood changed on Wednesday. The Village was overrun by Yippies and

Up Against the Wall/Motherfuckers[81] and Crazies (two New York–based anarchist groups), Black Panthers, and young toughs from street gangs all over New York and New Jersey—all ready to rumble: though it wasn't clear if they were there to fight the police or play "the old game of beating up queers";[82] and businesses that most Village gays would have protected were looted, such as a toy shop, the Gingerbread House, run by an elderly woman who was beloved on Christopher Street. Beer cans and bottles were again thrown at the police. Fires were set in trash cans. Again, the Sixth Precinct and the Tactical Police Force were called out to control the streets.[83] The conciliatory mood of Sunday night was gone. People were beaten so badly that Dick Leitsch, writing for the *New York Mattachine Newsletter*, observed that Seventh Avenue from Christopher to West Tenth Street "looked like a battlefield in Vietnam."[84]

But Leitsch wasn't alone in concluding that, despite cracked heads and broken limbs, victory belonged to the gays. Craig Rodwell and his lover, Fred Sargeant, printed up five thousand leaflets that they distributed everywhere gay people congregated in New York, proclaiming that the riots would "go down in history [as] the first time that thousands of Homosexual men and women went out into the streets to protest."[85] The government and police had been "put on notice that homosexuals won't stand being kicked around."[86]

However, the heady significance of the riots was clear mainly to those who'd been on the spot, rioting, and to a few gay newspapers. Outside New York, the Stonewall riots had been largely ignored—and even in New York, when the riot stories weren't relegated to the back page in mainstream newspapers, they were mocked with headlines such as "Homo Nest Raided, Queen Bees Are Stinging Mad."[87] It would be a huge challenge to figure out how to spread the word about what gay people had done in a little corner of New York at the start of the summer of 1969. Before that summer was over, Jack Nichols and his lover and coauthor, Lige Clarke, were nervously asking readers of a gay newspaper, "Will the spark die?"[88]

Chapter 12

SAY IT PROUD—AND LOUD: NEW GAY POLITICS

DEATH TO THE DODDERING OLDSTERS

July 4, 1969, one week after the start of the Stonewall riots: In Philadelphia, in front of Independence Hall, about forty lesbians and gay men marched in an oblong single file, just as they had every Fourth of July since 1965. It was the Annual Reminder Day Demonstration, sponsored by the Eastern Regional Conference of Homophile Organizations (ERCHO), which included the Janus Society and the Homophile Action League of Phila-delphia, the Mattachine Society New York and New York Daughters of Bilitis, and Frank Kameny's Mattachine Society Washington. The name of the event itself, "Annual Reminder Day," hinted at the infinite patience of these homophile groups. Yet again, they were reminding the country that things were still not right for some of its people.

As usual, the picketers handed out leaflets that decorously stated that July 4 was "a day for serious, solemn, and probing thought . . . a day to properly ask if we are guaranteeing to all our citizens [the promises inherent] in the Declaration of Independence, the Constitution, and the Bill of Rights."[1] As usual, too, they were dressed, as Len Lear, a reporter for the *Philadelphia Tribune* described them, to "look like they were going to church."[2] And they marched in silence, as usual. Except that something had changed.

The forty homophiles were joined by about thirty-five young demonstrators from New York. No one had told the young people that there was
a dress protocol at the Annual Reminders—and they probably wouldn't
have given up their jeans and T-shirts anyway. They'd come to Philadelphia
because they'd seen circulars posted on the streets of Greenwich Village or
an ad in the July 3 *Village Voice*. The announcements had been paid for by
Craig Rodwell in the name of his Homophile Youth Movement in Neighborhoods (HYMN), a small group he hadn't before been able to get off
the ground: "Gay Is Good," the announcements began and promised that
HYMN would be chartering buses to Philadelphia so that New York gays
and lesbians could support the Fifth Annual Reminder Day Demonstration. Round trip $5; for students only $4.[3] The young people who showed
up in Philadelphia with Rodwell were a different breed from the homophile picketers.

When Frank Kameny saw sandaled, bearded, and Zapata-mustachioed
homosexuals jump down from the buses and run to join the picket line, he
restrained himself from commenting other than to shout at them that the
rules were "No talking or chanting!" and "Walk in single file!" They obedi-
ently got in line with the homophiles, a rag-tag band trailing the mirror
image of Middle America.

The older homophiles didn't know it yet, but the parameters of *daring*
had been expanded exponentially by the events of June 28 to July 2. After
thirty minutes or so, two T-shirt-clad lesbians broke out of single file. Not
only did they walk side by side—they held hands. Kameny could no longer hold his tongue. Screaming, "You can't do that! You can't do that!" he
rushed over to them and slapped their hands apart. That gesture triggered
an uproar. Nineteen-year-old Bill Weaver found a black marker, crossed out
the meek "Equality for Homosexuals" message on the sign he was carrying
and wrote in its place "Smash Sexual Fascism!" Craig Rodwell, who'd been
walking just behind the two women, was so furious with Kameny that he
pulled his group into a caucus and got twenty of the young people he'd
brought with him from New York to break ranks and march in couples,
holding hands.[4] Frank Kameny may have fathered "Gay Is Good." He may
have fought Uncle Sam and squeezed crucial concessions from the US
Civil Service Commission. But he was a product of the repressive midcentury, and he was stodgy in his dress and manner. He hadn't experienced the

joyful intoxication of the Stonewall riots. He didn't understand that what happened there had already changed the world—or at least the world of urban gays. As far as Rodwell and the young people were concerned, the ways of the father were dead.[5]

Most of New York Mattachine Society was as bemused as Frank Kameny about what had suddenly made homophiles irrelevant. "What did the young ones mean by 'gay power' and 'gay liberation'?" "Price Dickenson," the pseudonymous editor of the *New York Mattachine Newsletter*, demanded to know. He concluded that what young gays were asking for was nothing more than what "us doddering oldsters who had been working quietly and steadily in the homophile movement for lo these many years had been striving for": Full equality for homosexuals. Repeal of sodomy laws. Municipal, state, and federal laws to prohibit discrimination. Laws that prohibit discrimination in private employment. Investigation of the police and other government officials for harassment. Prohibition of such harassment.[6] But in style and substance, "gay power" seemed to be beyond the understanding of Mattachine's newsletter editor with his heavy-handed "doddering oldsters" quip and his naivete in imagining that what these militant young people wanted could be reduced to a simplistic list of civil rights demands.

Yet Dick Leitsch, the executive director of Mattachine (who sometimes wrote under the name "Price Dickenson"), seemed to understand how Stonewall had changed the meaning of gay. He'd said as much the day after the first riot, when he coined the campy moniker "the hairpin drop heard round the world." Leitsch had on occasion seen himself as much more radical than his fellow homophiles. He'd been critical from the start about the style of Frank Kameny's orderly tactics. They won't get the attention of newspaper reporters and television cameras, Leitsch had warned Kameny in July 1965. "We need something to catch the public's imagination . . . The Negroes have King to talk, and that haunting 'We Shall Overcome.' . . . The suffragists dramatically chained themselves to lampposts . . . We've got to find something," Leitsch concluded—astutely presaging Stonewall by four years.[7]

He also told Frank Kameny to stop pretending all gays wanted to meet the criteria of middle-class respectability and their only problem was that the federal government wouldn't give them security clearances. At a San Francisco meeting of homophile leaders in September 1965,

Kameny had lectured about the importance of "packaging a good image" of the homosexual. Leitsch didn't like that either. "What is a good image? Young, attractive, well-dressed people who are almost no different than anyone else?" Leitsch lectured the older man. "The homosexual's concerns are wider. What about 'cruising,' 'drag,' and other issues which do not fit? [What about] sodomy charges in men's rooms and other 'distasteful' matters? "THEY ARE OUR PROBLEMS [*sic*]," he wrote, sounding very much like post-Stonewall gays in his disdain for anything that smacked of the conventional or careful.[8] "The homosexual freedom movement," he insisted (coining a phrase that augured "the gay liberation movement"), "is an attack on conformity."[9]

But by 1969, Dick Leitsch was in his midthirties, and he wore suits and ties, as all middle-class men of his generation did. A contemporary described him as looking like a "dependable Cartier salesclerk."[10] To young gays, he was indeed one of the "doddering oldsters." Craig Rodwell, who'd sat at Leitsch's side during the 1966 sip-in at Julius', now even accused him of being less interested in supporting militant tactics to empower gay people than in becoming "a mere politician"[11] toadying up to Mayor Lindsay—whose signed picture, which showed him to be as handsome as John Kennedy, Leitsch kept on his office wall.

Yet one young gay radical briefly saw Dick Leitsch differently. Michael Brown had been part of John O'Brien's group who'd met at Alternate U and had tried to get some radical gay action going in the weeks just before the explosion at the Stonewall. Now Brown read "The Hairpin Drop Heard Round the World" and came to Leitsch's Mattachine office with praise—and an idea. "Mattachine needs to build on the energy of the Stonewall riots," he told Leitsch, and offered to distribute copies of "The Hairpin Drop" all over the Village. The twenty-eight-year-old Brown, an activist with proud left-wing credentials, had spent years in the black civil rights movement and the antiwar movement. He told Leitsch he would help bring into Mattachine young gays and lesbians who'd honed their skills, as he had, by working for left-wing causes and who would apply what they'd learned to the homosexual movement.

His radical spiel about how gays needed to aid in a complete overhaul of society made Leitsch uncomfortable. Despite Leitsch's own dabbling on the Left,[12] for him Mattachine had only one purpose: to procure the rights of homosexuals. Nevertheless, Brown's idea of bringing energetic new blood into Mattachine had obvious appeal. For years Leitsch had thought that the movement needed to find dramatic ways to make homosexual demands known.[13] For that reason, he agreed: Michael Brown would bring together young activists like himself and start a group called the Mattachine Action Committee, which would meet at Freedom House, where all Mattachine meetings were now held.

Brown invited his friends, people in his own image. One of them was Martha Shelley—a self-described "red-diaper baby," given to wearing owl-eye eyeglasses and looking not at all like the "blue-eyed, blond stewardess" she thought you had to be to find a girlfriend in the bars. Shelley had joined Daughters of Bilitis to meet other lesbians, but the group was never a good fit for her. She was much more comfortable with her fellow workers in the antiwar movement and the feminist movement. Shelley loathed Dick Leitsch after she overheard him referring to the women in his presence with a silly remark that passed for wit among some homosexual men at the time: "Who opened the tuna fish can?"[14]

Lois Hart, another of Brown's invitees to the Mattachine Action Committee, was a former nun and then a follower of Timothy Leary and the Indian mystic Meher Baba. Pixie-ish in appearance, with light, bright eyes (but so tough that the drag queens of Greenwich Village called her "Louie Hard"),[15] Hart was an articulate, staunch feminist. She shared Shelley's intense dislike of Dick Leitsch, bitterly accusing him of male chauvinist piggery. Another friend whom Michael Brown invited to join the Mattachine Action Committee was Robert Martin, a bisexual who took the pseudonym Stephen Donaldson because his disapproving father, a naval officer, was also called Robert Martin. Donaldson had briefly been Martha Shelley's lover[16] and was now her political ally, even calling the cerebral Shelley his "political mentor." In 1967 he'd had an angry exchange with Leitsch over whether Donaldson had the right to use the Mattachine name for a homophile student group—the first of its kind—that Donaldson was starting at Columbia University. Because Mattachine's bylaws prohibited members under twenty-one, Leitsch vehemently opposed the Columbia group appropriating his organization's name.[17] Forced to name his own group the Student Homophile League, Donaldson never forgave Leitsch.

So, distrust and dislike of Mattachine's executive director was built into the Mattachine Action Committee; and other young radicals absorbed those opinions. The young people agreed that the committee should use Mattachine's paper and mimeograph machine, but they should have nothing else to do with the decrepit organization.[18]

If Leitsch suspected that Brown's group was brewing something inimical to Mattachine,[19] he tried to ignore it. He had visions of expanding Mattachine through a great influx of the gay youth who'd been excited by the riots, and he planned to use the next Mattachine "Town Meeting" to reel them into his organization. Flyers were distributed all over the village announcing a "Homosexual Liberation Meeting" on July 9 and touting the "new spirit" that had been born out of Stonewall. The flyers invited all the "homosexual community" to "come to this meeting and express yourselves about what we can do to secure our rights."

The meeting room in Freedom House was packed with 125 young people (and two police informers).[20] As Mattachine's executive director, Dick Leitsch ran the meeting. Things went south quickly when Michael Brown announced that gay people needed to show up in "power-to-the-people solidarity" at a forthcoming Black Panther demonstration. Leitsch blanched. Mattachine was formed to fight for the rights of the homosexual—period; and whether or not Leitsch was sympathetic personally to the struggles of other minorities, they were absolutely not the concern of Mattachine Society New York. When Martha Shelley raised her hand, Leitsch knew he had reason to worry again. She'd glowered at his attempts at humor in the past, and she was clearly of Brown's political bent.

Shelley waved her hand in the air until Dick Leitsch finally called on her. She was thinking as she waited for him to recognize her, "What kind of danger am I getting myself into? What if the kooks out there shoot at us?" But she was remembering too the courage of Martin Luther King, whose framed picture hung on her wall, and she forced herself to proceed.[21] She stood up and proposed a "Gay Power" rally in Washington Square Park to protest police treatment of homosexuals. It would be followed by a march to Sheridan Square Park, across from the Stonewall.

Leitsch had himself called for "dramatic action" on behalf of the movement a few years before—but was a march and rally the right sort of action now? Hadn't he been making fine headway in the last years by cultivating liberal alliances in the "Establishment" who gave him an "in" at city hall?

Under his leadership, Mattachine had gotten the police commissioner Howard Leary to order his officers to cease entrapping homosexuals.[22] He'd gotten the State Liquor Authority to reverse its policy of prohibiting licensed bars from serving homosexuals. With the help of the New York Civil Liberties Union, he and Mattachine had forced the Department of Social Services to reverse its decision against hiring two homosexual men as welfare case workers; and because of Mattachine's hard work, just two months earlier, in May, the New York Civil Service Commission had agreed that homosexuality "was no longer a barrier for all jobs under its jurisdiction."[23] Leitsch's methods had been undeniably effective for the last three years.

He had great misgivings about Shelley's proposal—yet he had no choice. "How many are in favor of a march and rally?" Dick Leitsch asked the crowded room.

Martha Shelley looked around and saw that every single person there was holding a hand up in the air.[24]

THE GAY LIBERATION FRONT

Dick Leitsch suggested that those interested in organizing a march and rally go off into a back room of Freedom House and come up with a plan. Perhaps Leitsch had hoped thereby to get a disruptive element out of the meeting. But it was the beginning of the end for homophile organizations.

The people who congregated in the back room—all in their twenties and all radicals—were of one mind. Just as Leo Laurence had concluded months before in San Francisco, they thought the homophiles were like the NAACP, and as gay radicals, they preferred to emulate the Black Panthers. To begin, they wanted to give themselves a title that would truly characterize them: something bold—something as politically confrontational as the "National Liberation Front," a name that had been used by revolutionary socialist and Communist movements all over the world since World War II.

Someone blurted out, "Gay Liberation Front!" Martha Shelley, perched on a table because there weren't enough chairs in the small room, cried, "That's it! That's it! That's it! We're the Gay Liberation Front!"[25] her palm banging the table on which she sat. It was a hot summer afternoon, and several people had brought their soda or beer bottles into the room with them. A bottle cap was lying on the table that Shelley pounded over and over as she shouted, "That's it!" She was so excited about the new name she didn't even feel it when the cap cut her hand. She bled profusely.[26]

Dick Leitsch put as good a face on things as possible. Mattachine, together with Daughters of Bilitis, placed an ad in the *Village Voice* announcing (in language not at all characteristic of either organization) that they were sponsoring a "Gay Power" march and rally in July to commemorate the one-month anniversary of the Stonewall raid.[27] Of course, neither organization had control over the tenor of the event. A crowd of about two thousand showed up that day in Washington Square Park. It was the largest planned congregation of gays and lesbians to that date.[28] Gay Liberation Front members ran around distributing lavender ribbons and arm bands. They'd brought no sound system because that would have required a permit from the NYPD, and all agreed that the less they had to deal with the police the better.

In tune with the burgeoning women's liberation movement, the Gay Liberation Front practiced gender parity. Martha Shelley was the woman chosen by the GLF to speak. Just five foot four, Shelley stood on a fountain rim to be seen better, and she spoke loud. "We're tired of being harassed and persecuted. If a straight couple can hold hands in Washington Square Park, why can't we? . . . Socrates was a homosexual! Michelangelo was a homosexual! Walt Whitman and Richard the Lion-Hearted were homosexuals!" Shelley shouted and was answered by energetic applause and whistles and cheers.[29]

Marty Robinson, the male rally speaker, proudly called himself "a hard hat":[30] a journeyman carpenter, though in hippie garb. The son of a doctor, Robinson had dropped out of Brooklyn College because, he said, he "couldn't find in books what he wanted to learn."[31] But he theorized and orated better than anyone among the Gay Liberation Front crowd. Robinson had been present at the Stonewall riots, and for him, this rally and march was step two—the necessary next move. "Gay power is here! Gay power is not a laugh!" he shouted to his Washington Square Park audience. "There are one million homosexuals in New York City, and we will not permit another reign of terror. Let me tell you, homosexuals: We've got to get organized. We've got to stand up. This is our chance!"[32]

The fired-up crowd marched toward Sheridan Square behind a big lavender banner decorated with both double male sex signs and double female sex signs. A young gay led a cheer for gay power: "Give me a G! Give me an A! Give me a Y! Give me a P! . . ." Traffic ground to a halt on Sixth Avenue as the marchers passed. Facing the Stonewall Inn, they bellowed out the words to "We Shall Overcome." New York had never yet seen anything like this.[33]

"Do You Think Homosexuals Are Revolting? You Bet Your Sweet Ass We Are!" was the headline of a flyer calling gay people to a meeting at Alternate U. Dick Leitsch had not yet fully understood that this new group (that promised in the same flyer, "We're going to make a place for ourselves in the revolutionary movement") had severed itself totally from Mattachine, and that in good Freudian fashion, the homophiles—fathers and mothers of gay libbers—had to be killed off.

The next month, August, the Gay Liberation Front showed up in Kansas City at the annual meeting of the North American Conference of Homophile Organizations. The homophiles had no notion that Stonewall had been the gays' storming of the Bastille and their Boston Tea Party all wrapped into one. The GLF-ers were there to let them know it. In 1968, the NACHO conference made a gesture toward militancy when it adopted the slogan coined by Kameny, "Gay Is Good." But that baby step of defiance was nothing to what Gay Liberation Front members were demanding.

GLF's Stephen Donaldson[34] presented to the forty other NACHO delegates at the Kansas City meeting a scathing criticism in the form of a manifesto that let the doddering oldsters know just how antediluvian they were. "The Homophile Movement Must Be Radicalized!" the manifesto was titled. The homophiles' long and dogged fight for homosexual rights was ineffectual and naïve. "Our enemies"—organized religion, business, and medicine were specifically named—"will not be moved by appeasement or appeals to reason and justice, but only by power and force," the manifesto lectured the homophiles. "If the detention camps are filled tomorrow with blacks, hippies, and other radicals, [homosexuals] will not escape that fate," no matter how hard the homophile organizations try to

"dissociate" themselves from "other victims of oppression and prejudice."
"A common struggle, however, will bring common triumph," the manifesto promised. Furthermore, it informed NACHO, the homophile movement had the responsibility to "totally reject the insane war in Vietnam and
refuse to encourage complicity in the war and support of the war machine,
which may well be turned against us."[35] Every part of "The Homophile
Movement Must Be Radicalized!"—even the language in which it was
couched—was over the top and insulting to NACHO. Members refused to
adopt the radicals' position.

But by the following year, there were radical gay groups, inspired by
Stonewall and the Gay Liberation Front, all across the country. At the 1970
NACHO convention in San Francisco, the "radical caucus" decided that
the time had come simply to declare that *it* was NACHO—and to take
over the organization. A rumor circulated among the homophile delegates
that one of the radicals had a gun and swore to use it if the radicals' resolutions were not adopted. On the third day of the convention, the radicals
marched into the plenary session waving banners with gay-power-to-gay-
people messages. Most of the homophile delegates walked or ran to the
nearest exit, and NACHO's chairman, Bill Wynne, adjourned the conference. The radical caucus took over the gavel and continued anyway.[36] The
first motion from the floor was that NACHO officially declare its support
for the Black Panther Party.

The motion passed. But that 1970 meeting was NACHO's last one. The
1971 convention was canceled, and in 1972 NACHO disbanded.

Radical gays also descended on the Eastern Regional Conference of
Homophile Organizations. Jim Fouratt, a colorful twenty-four-year-old
GLF-er with a leonine mane of blond hair, was their most hostile spokesman. He was disgusted with the fogeys. (The feeling was mutual.) Fouratt,
who was given to wearing leather pants, snakeskin boots, and a cowboy
hat, was described by an *Esquire* writer as looking like Billy the Kid.[37] He'd
been a rioter at Stonewall. He'd also been arrested in a 1965 Times Square
antiwar protest. He'd dreamed up a 1967 antiwar agitprop action on Wall
Street: Yippies, which he'd helped found, threw dollar bills from the balcony down onto the floor of the New York Stock Exchange to show their
disdain for the capitalist-financed war machine.[38] To Fouratt, there was
not much difference between Wall Street types and the ERCHO bunch.

"Lackeys of the Establishment!" and "Dinosaurs!" he bombastically dubbed ERCHO's chief leaders Frank Kameny and Barbara Gittings.[39] (Kay Tobin, Gittings's partner, had small stuffed dinosaurs made up as soon as possible, which the trio displayed with glee.)[40]

A scathing battle ensued when the radicals tried to get ERCHO to go on record as urging all homosexuals to participate in the antiwar Moratorium March on Washington. Homophiles popped up to the microphone to shout, "We can't do that! No group can dare speak for all homosexuals!" "ERCHO deals with the problems of homosexuals, not the problems of the world!" "Homosexuals are just like other people! We range from the most conservative to the most radical, and that's our right!" ERCHO would not take a stand on the Moratorium.

But one radical resolution did get passed at the ERCHO convention. It was drafted at a little dinner party in the Greenwich Village apartment that Craig Rodwell shared with his lover Fred Sargeant. A young lesbian couple, Linda Rhodes and Ellen Broidy, who'd made Rodwell's Oscar Wilde Memorial Bookshop a regular hangout in between classes at New York University, had been the dinner guests; and over dessert and coffee, the four wrote a resolution to be presented at ERCHO.

Rodwell had spearheaded the writing of the resolution, but he knew that by now he'd made himself so controversial among the homophiles that if he were the one to bring the resolution to the floor they'd see only the messenger and be deaf to the message. So he asked Broidy, an attractive, dark-haired twenty-three-year-old, to stand up and present the resolution as her own.[41] There on the floor of the convention of the eastern region homophiles, Broidy called for an official end to the Fourth of July Annual Reminder Day demonstration in Philadelphia. "Reminder Day has lost its effectiveness," she proclaimed, "because it's become just one of many demonstrations held at Independence Hall on that day." In its place, every year on the last Saturday of June there should be "Christopher Street Liberation Day" demonstrations nationwide to commemorate the 1969 Stonewall riots. And—very important to the four radicals who wrote the resolution—"no dress or age regulations shall be made for this demonstration."[42]

Not even those four could have predicted their resolution's enduring power, which would still be working decades later to mobilize hundreds of thousands of lesbians and gays in Pride Parades across the country every year, and to pull them out of the closet.

ERCHO, however, soon disbanded.

By the end of July 1969, Gay Liberation Front members formulated a statement of purpose whose tone mirrored the uncompromising militancy of groups such as the Black Panthers, with whom many of the GLF-ers, especially the men, had a spiritual romance.[43] GLF defined itself as a "revolutionary group of men and women" that had formed with the realization that "sexual liberation for all people cannot come about unless existing social institutions are abolished." GLF would do that, the statement of purpose declared, by creating new social forms based on "brotherhood, cooperation, human love, and uninhibited sexuality." But those peaceable forms couldn't be realized yet because "Babylon" (that is, "Amerika") was corrupt. So for the time being, GLF would be "forced to commit ourselves to one thing: revolution!"[44]

Every week, GLF-ers sat in a circle—GLF lesbians who admired the circle tradition among Native American cultures demanded that formation[45]—and they raised one another's consciousness about other groups who suffered oppression at the hands of Amerika, and about their own oppression as gays. Nikos Diaman had just been passing through New York, a San Franciscan on his way to Paris, where he'd planned to live for a year. The gay life he'd known before was in bars and bedrooms, and as a Catholic, he'd felt he was being eaten up by guilt. But after a New York friend took him to GLF, Diaman canceled his Paris plans. For the first time in his life, he found himself sitting with a group of gay people who were talking not about their cowering fear of police busts but about fighting police and being out and proud and guilt free. The personal part of consciousness raising was ecstatically empowering for Diaman and for many GLF-ers like him.[46]

But GLF had a stern sense of who belonged and who did not. One evening, a strange-looking couple showed up at a GLF meeting: a man and a woman who were older than the mostly twentysomethings. The couple stuck out, too, because they weren't dressed in unisex jeans, the uniform of GLF, but instead they wore bougie male and female clothes. The couple was Frank Kameny and Barbara Gittings, who'd come to New York to check out this new group that had taken over the homophile organizations, which Kameny and Gittings had so lovingly birthed and nurtured. "Who are you?" a GLF-er asked them. Kameny was taken aback that political gays didn't recognize him. "What are you doing here?" another GLF-er asked after he and Gittings gave their names. "I'm here because I'm a homosexual," Gittings said,[47] as though the mere fact of sexual identity should make her and Kameny welcome in GLF. It didn't.

To avoid hierarchy and hegemony, which GLF-ers despised, there were no official leaders of the Gay Liberation Front. The group grew quickly, but there were no membership rolls. Anyone who showed up (and wasn't dressed bougie) was a member in good standing and had a voice in making decisions. The plethora of voices at general meetings—the passionate pontificating, endless theorizing, disputatious debating—produced chaos.[48] Lois Hart, the Meher Baba devotee, argued that the group's "many mentalities, disparities, and persuasions" needed to be accommodated. That could be done, she suggested, by creating "cells," a structure based on the Communist model of carrying out tasks in small working groups. The cells would tap the best of its members' energies and talents by being attentive to their "needs, goals, and philosophies," and thus promote harmony. Everyone agreed.[49]

But then the cells fought one another ferociously. Lois Hart suggested that GLF try Communist-style "self-criticism" to hold in check the criticism that was directed at others. Everyone would sit in a circle and analyze aloud what he or she had done wrong.[50] But the hostility and paranoia didn't stop. Members of the Third World Revolutionary Cell told members of the 28th of June Cell, which produced the GLF magazine *Come Out!*, "You're running a white racist paper," and they issued a "nonnegotiable demand" that sections of the paper be devoted to them. Perry Brass, a usually mild-mannered poet who'd taken on the job of editor, agreed. But he asked that the Third World Revolutionaries help to sell *Come Out!* in the streets, since there were few stores that would distribute it. The Third World Revolutionaries thought that sales should not have to be their job—that's what the *Come Out!* cell was for. "That's insane!" Brass said. "You're a racist!" the TWR said.[51]

There was contention between affiliated GLF groups, too. The Street Transvestite Action Revolutionaries (STAR), which was formed by Marsha P. Johnson and Sylvia Rivera, couldn't be in the same room with the Radicalesbians. STAR stood up for the rights of effeminate street kids to be as girlie as they pleased, but Radicalesbians complained that their girlie-ness mocked women because they flaunted the worst stereotypes of femininity—and that violated GLF's supposed principles to fight against sexist oppression.

Harmony reigned, however, at GLF dances—at least for some. Perry Brass first heard about the Gay Liberation Front through an ad that advertised a "Gay Community Dance." He'd never before seen the word *gay* coupled with *community*—and that there should be a dance for the gay community was beyond his happiest dreams.[52] A grungy Mafia bar was no longer the only game in town because now every Saturday evening you could go up to the third floor of Alternate U. There you paid your mere buck fifty and walked into a paradise of wall-to-wall writhing muscled bodies, hundreds of them, shirtless and sexy and free, dancing to acid rock played on a tape deck in a huge room lit by swirling psychedelic light-show slides. And when you were thirsty, a beer was twenty-five cents, not the gauging prices of the bars. And your coat was checked for free. And when you were standing alone and lonely, a GLF "host" came around and encouraged you to grab a partner and dance.[53] What better way to build community and spread the word about the Gay Liberation Front and even raise a bit of money for the movement?

Except that lesbians felt excluded. About 15 percent of the attendees at the Alternate U Saturday nights were female, and, they objected, the Gay Community Dances did not make them feel they were part of the "Gay Community." Ellen Shumsky had thought she was a good fit with the Gay Liberation Front. She'd been to Cuba as a volunteer to work on a coffee plantation in 1968, a year before the Vinceremos Brigade brought other young leftist Americans to Cuba to help pick the harvests. Then she'd gone to Paris to study photography, and she'd interrupted her studies when she heard about Stonewall: Shumsky returned to New York to be the photographer of the gay revolution. But she resented that the dances "were conducted with a male sensibility." There was no place women could dance in groups, no place to talk. "Just bodies packed in and a lot of skin and a lot of contact." Most of the other lesbians of GLF agreed. They fought with the men until they finally managed to get money from GLF coffers to hold their own dance.[54]

• • •

Despite such dissensions, the idealistic image of revolutionaries banding together caught the imagination of young gays and lesbians who were brought up on the nightly news of civil rights and antiwar struggles. Gay Liberation Fronts sprang up not only in the coastal areas of the east and west but also in places such as Iowa City, Louisville, Atlanta, and Tallahassee (and in England, Germany, Denmark, and New Zealand, too). Some of the groups, less theoretical and philosophical than the parent GLF, were more focused as they went about the job of creating a more just world. The Los Angeles Gay Liberation Front, enraged by both the Vietnam War and the armed forces' mistreatment of gays in the military, encouraged all gay service members to get out as quickly as possible. "You Are Not Wanted in the Military," a GLF pamphlet announced, prodding gays to righteous anger because they "constitute the *only* minority against which the government and the military practice open and flagrant discrimination." Tragedy lurks if gays remain in the military, the pamphlet warned: "You are vulnerable to prosecution for being your loving self. You have only one alternative, and that is to see your local Gay Liberation Front."[55]

Gay Liberation Front groups around the country fought serious battles, but not always in serious style. John Singer had been a member of *Homosexuals Intransigent!* when he was a student at City College in New York; in 1970, after he moved to California, he joined San Francisco GLF. He changed his name to Faygele (the Yiddish word for "little bird" but also slang for *faggot*) ben Miriam (son of Miriam). Faygele ben Miriam did agitprop scenes on behalf of GLF, like the one at Macy's department store in San Francisco, where the SFPD had been entrapping gay men in the restrooms. Faygele and another GLF-er, wearing elaborate women's hats with huge feathers, started at the top floor of Macy's. They walked up to employees and offered to sell them a newspaper—*Gay Sunshine*—and when they got kicked off that floor, they peddled *Gay Sunshine* one floor down until they were asked to leave. And then they worked the next floor and the next, until employees on every floor of Macy's understood that the San Francisco Gay Liberation Front was incensed that Macy's management had let the police come into the store to arrest gay men.[56]

The next year, Faygele moved to Seattle and joined a Gay Liberation Front there. He was especially riled at Seattle police chief George Tielsch's practice of sending "pretty, young cops" to the parks for the old sting. If gays hit on them, they'd be arrested for propositioning a police officer. Faygele and Paul Barwick, another GLF member, organized a weekly agit-prop protest that would turn out a crowd of participants who came at least partly "because it was fun." Through a friend who worked at the telephone company, Faygele and Barwick found Chief Tielsch's address. Through another friend who had a livery service, they procured an old stretch limousine, which they loaded up with GLF activists, many in "scag drag" (dresses and beards). And they went in style to have a party—every week-end for two months—in front of Chief Tielsch's house, until they won a sweet victory: Tielsch admitted to the newspapers that he was taking a job in Garden Grove, California, "because of the situation that's arisen with the gay community."[57]

HOW TO GET THE WORD TO KINGSPORT, TENNESSEE

The mother of all GLF agitprops, the Alpine County prank that came out of the Los Angeles Gay Liberation Front, sent a message much more global than the usual protests against police harassment. The prank shined a giant spotlight on the silliness of antihomosexual hysteria. It was played out with the same mix of gleeful mischief and wrath as the Stonewall queens' game of outrunning their NYPD pursuers only to show up at their backs and torment them with a can-can dance. But the Alpine County agitprop got more immediate media attention than did the Stonewall riots. In 1970 and 1971, it brought word of the Gay Liberation Front into newspapers all over America and abroad, too. It apprised homosexuals everywhere that myriad gays and lesbians had come out and were fighting the good fight, and those still in the closet ought to join them. And that was the primary goal of the prank's organizers.

LA's Gay Liberation Front had begun three months after the New York group. Morris Kight, the man who was a midwife to its birth, was fifty, older by decades than the New York founders. But Kight had cut his activist teeth in 1967 by forming the Dow Action Committee against the chemical company that made the napalm and Agent Orange used in Viet-nam, and he resonated with New York GLF's radical position that the gay revolution had to be tied to a revolution of all the oppressed.[58]

Harry Hay—the man who'd been the founder of Mattachine, the group that pioneered the idea in 1950 that homosexuals were a legitimate minority and needed to organize—was the nominal first leader of the leaderless LA Gay Liberation Front. But less than a year after the Los Angeles GLF started, Hay and his lover, John Burnside, moved to San Juan Pueblo, New Mexico, where they eventually formed Radical Faeries, a queer spirituality group. Morris Kight donned Hay's elder statesman mantle and never took it off.

Kight's dazzling white hair and aristocratic nose; his erudite, polysyllabic, and excessively formal language (thieves were "brigands," men were "sir," women were "dear lady")—all made him seem an unlikely leader of a radical group. His critics thought him not only pompous but also egomaniacal for his trick of jabbing an elbow into other activists to grab the spotlight for himself at least as much as for the movement.[59] But he was almost always the guy with the most interesting ideas, and his followers followed.

Kight's Alpine County prank began as a serious plan after a Bay Area gay, Don Jackson, read Carl Wittman's "Refugees from Amerika: A Gay Manifesto," which was published in the *San Francisco Free Press* in December 1969. Jackson was inspired to imagine a "Stonewall Nation," run by gays and for gays. By the time he presented a proposal to a Gay Liberation Conference at Berkeley, Jackson had his plan down to specifics. He'd been thrilled to discover that Alpine County, a wonderland of pine forests and crystalline lakes nestled in the Sierra Nevada Mountains, had only 384 registered voters; and a new California law mandated that residency requirements for voters be reduced from one year to ninety days. If a mere four hundred gay people took up residency in Alpine County, within ninety days they could outvote the mountaineers, woodsmen, and fisherman who were its present residents. The entire local government could be recalled, and in its place, gays could put in a gay sheriff, a gay judge, gay council members—even a gay postmaster. Alpine would become "a national refuge for persecuted homosexuals." They'd live in utopian separatism. They'd create "a world center for the gay counter-culture and a shining symbol of hope to all gay people in the world," Jackson declared very solemnly in his Berkeley presentation.[60]

He teamed up with the head of the Psychedelic Venus Church, Jefferson Fuck Poland (the same Fuck Poland who'd helped swell the ranks

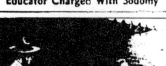

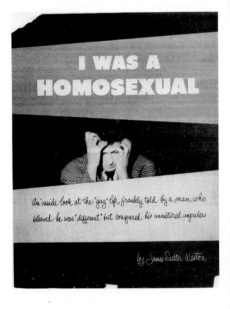

JAILED PROFESSOR RELEASED ON BOND

Educator Charged With Sodomy

E. K. Johnston, Charged With Sodomy, Relieved of Teaching Duties at Missouri U.

Columbia, Mo., May 28.—(AP)—A veteran University of Missouri journalism professor, charged with sodomy, posted $2,500 bond and was released from the Boone county jail late today.

The professor, E. K. Johnston, will have a preliminary hearing before Magistrate Temple Morgett here June 11. The hearing, originally set for June 3, was set back to give Johnston's attorney, Edwin C. Orr, time to study the case.

The bond was signed by Johnston's half-brother, Howard Johnston, of North Kansas City, and Fred Hildebrandt of Sedalia, Mo. Orr said Johnston will remain at his apartment here tonight and will go to North Kansas City tomorrow for a visit.

Earlier today the professor was relieved of his teaching duties.

Middlebush's Statement

Dr. Frederick Middlebush, president of the university, issued this statement:

"In view of the nature and gravity of the charges that have been made against Professor E. K. Johnston, he has been relieved of his duties as a member of the university faculty pending further determ...

[caption under photo] E. K. Johnston (right), 56-year-old University of Missouri journalism professor, leaves the Columbia, Mo., police station in custody of Trooper Lloyd Evans of the Missouri State Highway Patrol. Johnston, 56 years a member of the university faculty, is one of three men charged with sodomy in connection with what County Prosecutor Howard B. Lang Jr., termed a "homosexual ring." Johnston furnished $2,500 bail after reading in...

1. The arrest of Professor E. K. Johnston in 1948 triggered a witch hunt of homosexual faculty and students at the University of Missouri.

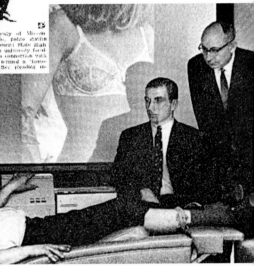

RIGHT: 2. Behavioral therapist Dr. Joseph Wolpe (right) and his assistant "converting" a homosexual to heterosexuality by "systematic desensitization."

I WAS A HOMOSEXUAL

An inside look at the 'gay' life, frankly told by a man who believed he was 'different' but conquered his unnatural impulses

by James Sutter Weston

LEFT: 3. Popular magazine articles in the 1950s presented homosexuals as sick, tormented, and eager to change.

RIGHT: 4. The 2011 military wedding of Major Tammy Smith and Tracey Hepner. Smith was promoted to brigadier general in 2012.

5. Del Martin (right) and Phyllis Lyon in 1954. In 1955 they cofounded Daughters of Bilitis, which was devoted to helping the lesbian "understand herself and make her adjustment to society."

6. The first homosexual picket, in 1964 at the Whitehall Induction Center in New York.

7. Harry Hay, pictured here ca. 1996, founded the Mattachine Society in 1950, for "an oppressed cultural minority."

8. A 1966 "sip-in" in Greenwich Village, inspired by black lunch-counter sit-ins. The State Liquor Authority forbade bartenders from serving homosexuals.

10. Homophiles picketing the White House in 1965. "If you're asking for equal-employment rights, look employable," organizer Frank Kameny told the picketers.

9. *The Ladder* boldly began featuring photos of lesbians on its covers, such as this one of Lilli Vincenz, "every mother's dream daughter."

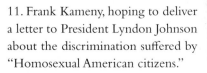

11. Frank Kameny, hoping to deliver a letter to President Lyndon Johnson about the discrimination suffered by "Homosexual American citizens."

12. Stonewall Inn habitués, camping it up before the second night of the June 1969 riots.

13. A New York Gay Activists Alliance Dance at the Firehouse in 1971: a grungy Mafia bar was no longer the only game in town.

LEFT: 14. Morty Manford in a paddy wagon, signaling other Gay Activists Alliance members to keep fighting, ca. 1971.

BELOW: 15. New York Gay Activists Alliance members picket the Board of Education.

BELOW: 16. GAA member Marty Robinson in a zap of Fidelifacts, a company that helped employers weed out homosexual applicants. Fidelifacts's owner had declared he could recognize homosexuals because "if one looks like a duck, walks like a duck, associates only with ducks, and quacks like a duck, then he is probably a duck."

ABOVE: 17. GAA member Arthur Evans zaps a New York Board of Examiners official.

18. Sylvia Rivera, co-founder in 1970 of the Street Transvestite Action Revolutionaries (STAR).

19. Jose Sarria (front and center), "drag performer" and the founder and Empress of the Imperial Court. Sarria became the first "gay" political candidate, running for the San Francisco Board of Supervisors in 1961.

20. Morris Kight (left), mastermind of the Alpine hoax, helped found one of the first gay community centers, in Los Angeles in 1971.

21. Jeanne Manford, marching beside her son Morty, in the 1972 Christopher Street Liberation Day March. After young gays and lesbians implored her to talk to their parents, she started the organization that became Parents and Friends of Lesbians and Gays (PFLAG).

22. Political buttons of the movement from the 1960s to the 1980s.

23. Radicalesbians zap a National Organization for Women conference in May 1970, after NOW's founder Betty Friedan called lesbians the "Lavender Menace" in the women's movement.

24. Jeanne Córdova (right), grassroots activist and editor of the *Lesbian Tide*, planning the first-ever national lesbian conference in 1972.

25. Two thousand lesbians gathered at UCLA in 1973 for the national lesbian conference.

of Randy Wicker's 1964 picket at New York's Whitehall Induction Center), and together they started the Alpine Liberation Front in Berkeley. The Front's primary purpose was to find a way to make the dream of the great gay migration to Alpine a reality. Jackson permitted an underground newspaper, the *Los Angeles Free Press*, to reprint his proposal in the hope it would attract future gay Alpiners. "Brother Don Has a Dream," the essay was called.[61]

That was when Morris Kight first heard of the Alpine plan. Kight had been exceedingly frustrated because for months the Los Angeles Gay Liberation Front had been conducting an agitprop a day to call attention to mistreatment of gays and lesbians in Los Angeles—but with the exception of underground papers, there'd been no media coverage. "You have to hit them over the head with a two-by-four before they'll pay any attention to our issues," Kight always complained.[62] A gay and lesbian takeover of a whole county: now, *that* would certainly be a two-by-four! "Alpine is freezing. It's no place where anyone gay would want to live," he told three of his most trusted henchmen with whom he shared a house. "But we'll *pretend* to be serious." Then he got on the phone to call the members of the press and inform them about what the Gay Liberation Front was "planning."

The media showed up as they never had before. "The Gay Liberation Front met and voted unanimously to take over Alpine—farms, ranches, crafts shops," Kight announced to reporters and rolling cameras. "And there'll be a university where gay and lesbian studies will be taught, too!" Yes, Alpine County would soon become a gay and lesbian "citadel of intellectual and activist activity," Kight promised.[63] He showed them a flyer GLF had printed up: "Come to Alpine County! The New Gay Mecca!"—and buttons in the spirit of the forty-niners, to be distributed to gay pioneers everywhere: "Alpine County or Bust!"

Gay became a household word as it never had been before: NBC Television News sent a crew out to Alpine. A star reporter, bundled to the nose but still shivering in the snow, announced, "We're standing on the land bought by the Gay Liberation Front [untrue, of course], and here they're going to build their homes." *Time* magazine sent a crew to interview Los Angeles GLF leaders. "We're doing what Governor Reagan and Richard Nixon and Spiro Agnew told us to do"—Kight had to swallow a chortle to say it—"If you're unhappy with the system, use your vote. It's the American way."[64] When Kight told newsmen that about a dozen Gay Liberation Front members would be on the steps of the Alpine County courthouse in Merkleeville to meet the sheriff, the chairman of the board of supervisors, and the postmistress, the Associated Press reported the story faithfully. "We already have applications from over a thousand homosexuals," Kight added with a poker face. "Our goal is to have six hundred located in the county by June 28, 1971!"[65]

The downside of the prank was that some gay people took the Alpine plan very seriously. Craig Schoonmaker, founder of *Homosexuals Intransigent!*, who'd called for homosexual separatism as a necessity in a homophobic world, thought that the takeover of a large piece of land like Alpine was exactly what was needed. It would be a homosexual homeland where gay men (lesbians would be excluded) could be "open and honest and take pride in themselves."[66] Don Jackson, the Alpine plan's first proponent, devoted himself night and day to the dream—which grew larger and larger to match Kight's reports of the multiplying numbers of (fictional) would-be pioneers.

Of course, Kight couldn't tell many people that as far as he was concerned, the Alpine takeover was a giant hoax. Someone might leak the truth to the press, and that would be the end of all the delirious attention that a gay issue was finally getting. So a split developed even in the Los Angeles Gay Liberation Front. Some wore their "Alpine or Bust" buttons as a huge joke. One elderly gay man came to every meeting with knitting needles and yarn, urging others to join him in knitting: "It's going to be cold in Alpine County," he said. "We'll need blankets to keep our brothers and sisters warm."[67]

Los Angeles GLF-ers who were in on the hoax were relishing the stick-it-to-'em pleasure. GLF member Don Kilhefner told the media, "Eventually Alpine County will become a mecca for homosexuals from all nations."[68] An Associated Press article reported that Herbert Bruns, an Alpine farmer and chairman of the board of supervisors, was beside himself with worry. "We have a real nice county here," Bruns lamented. "We don't know what we're going to do if they succeed. We'll try anything."[69] But the days of gays tolerating insults and intimidation were gone. Gay spokesman Lee Heflin apprised reporters firmly, "We plan to do this as peaceably as possible. But if there is vigilante action, we will defend ourselves in any way necessary."[70] A United Press International reporter, almost as jittery as Supervisor Bruns, reminded readers that "a district attorney, sheriff, and judge elected by a gay majority could determine which laws would be enforced."[71]

The prank was too delicious to be terminated. At Thanksgiving, three GLF members decided to picnic up at Alpine, and Kight was sure to inform the press that the three were a "scouting party," getting things ready for the gay invasion. UPI sent a photographer. He took pictures of Steve Beckwith, a Los Angeles accountant and spokesman for the "scouts," standing at the county courthouse door with Rod Gibson and June Herrle, the two bearded men flanking the petite lesbian, all three decked out in heavy winter jackets and smiling broadly.[72] "Thousands of gays have rallied to our cause [the number got bigger with every press coverage], and now we have international support," Beckwith proclaimed.[73]

Never before had the word *homosexual* or *gay* gotten so much media attention; never before had gays and lesbians in little towns all over America—Carroll, Iowa; Big Spring, Texas; Kingsport, Tennessee; Anderson, Indiana—been able to pick up their local papers and read that gay people were answering years of mistreatment with gay power. And when Kight thought the Alpine prank had gotten all the press coverage it was going to get, he moved on, announcing to the media the following year that though the gays and lesbians he represented were still considering a takeover of Alpine, they were now also planning to buy an entire Southern California town and seven Sacramento River villages. In fact, he said, homosexuals are already there: "They have quietly moved into those villages in considerable number and are gradually colonizing them."[74]

OUT OF THE CLOSETS AND INTO THE STREETS!

The resolution presented by Ellen Broidy at the final meeting of the Eastern Regional Conference of Homophile Organizations in 1969 had killed the Annual Reminder Day pickets in Philadelphia and replaced them with a march in New York to commemorate the Stonewall riots. June 28, 1970, was the first march. It was to start at Christopher Street and end up at Sheep Meadow in Central Park. The organizing committee had no idea what to expect. Would anyone show up? Would the marchers be beaten or spat at? Craig Rodwell's partner, Fred Sargeant, was at the front of the march, and as the parade began to move up Sixth Avenue, he looked back. As far as he could see, solid throngs of marching gays and lesbians. So many that no one would dare beat them or spit at them. To get a better perspective, Sargeant shinnied up a light pole. Stretched out to infinity, it seemed, were marchers, thousands and thousands, like a powerful army. Never in history had so many gay and lesbian people come together in one place and for a common endeavor. The Tactical Police Force that menaced gays on the night of the Stonewall riots were there too—at the tail end of the parade, three busloads of them, assigned to protect the marchers.

For the fifty-one blocks of the route, the marchers screamed the same chant over and over: "Say it clear! Say it loud! Gay is good! Gay is proud!"[75] It was a talisman to drive away the years of hateful propaganda, when the church, the cops, the priests, the government all colluded to tell homosexuals they were pariahs. It was a message to the straight world that gay people weren't buying that disinformation anymore. It was nose thumbing at the dozen Bible-thumpers who gathered on the route with signs that shouted "Sodom And Gomorrah" or proclaimed that homosexuals were going to hell.[76] It was a call to other homosexuals to come out of the closet and help fight the lies.

Craig Rodwell—who'd been waiting for years for the spark that would light the fire and who recognized immediately that the riot at Stonewall was what he'd been waiting for—had hoped there'd be sister parades all over America. Rodwell called gay leaders in big cities everywhere imploring them to commemorate Stonewall. But only media-savvy Morris Kight jumped on the idea. "Christopher Street West," the parade in Los Angeles would be called. At the same time as New York gays and lesbians marched down Sixth Avenue, Los Angeles gays and lesbians would be marching down Hollywood Boulevard, sending the same message to the straight world and making the same call to other homosexuals to come out.

But the Los Angeles parade almost didn't take place. The parade committee was obliged to obtain a permit from the Los Angeles police commissioner. They sent Reverend Troy Perry—who'd recently founded the gay Metropolitan Community Church—downtown to request it. Decked out in his clerical garb, Perry hoped for respect for the collar at least.

He didn't get it. Chief of Police Ed Davis—"Crazy Ed," he was called by homosexuals for his rabid use of the LA Vice Squad in bar raids and entrapment—snarled at Reverend Perry: "Do you know that homosexuality is illegal in the state of California?"

It wasn't—only certain sexual acts were illegal, and the reverend told the police chief so. They argued the point, until Davis, fed up with the facts, looked for an insult. "Well, I'd sooner give a parade permit to a bunch of robbers and thieves than to a bunch of homosexuals," he grumped.[77]

The police commissioners were just as hostile. "There'll be violence if homosexuals parade," one of them said. The others agreed and decreed that Christopher Street West would have to put up a $1 million bond to cover the "personal damages" that would result from the riots, and a $500,000 bond to cover property damages. Plus, before a parade permit would be given, they'd have to put up the money it would cost to hire extra policemen to protect the homosexuals from the anticipated outrage of the citizens.

Perry immediately got in his car and drove to the office of ACLU attorney Herb Selwyn, a heterosexual who'd been helping gay men fight unfair arrests since the early 1950s. Selwyn knew that after the Watts riots in Los Angeles, black nationalists had gotten city permission to hold a black parade and festival every summer, and they weren't assessed $1 million bonds and fees for extra policemen. It was good precedent. With only a few days left before the parade was scheduled to happen, Selwyn took Christopher Street West's case before Superior Court judge Richard Schauer.

At noon on Friday, two days before the parade, the judge lit into the police commissioners for their glaringly discriminatory double standards. No, Christopher Street West would not be obliged to post any bond nor pay any monies that were not required of other groups, Judge Schauer decreed. And yes, the police must protect the marchers. Because homosexuals are citizens of the state of California, and all citizens are entitled to equal protection under its laws.[78]

Chapter 13

LESS TALK AND MORE ACTION:
THE GAY ACTIVISTS ALLIANCE

IF I AM NOT FOR MYSELF . . .

John O'Brien recalls the New York Gay Liberation Front discussion: Shall we take the $500 we earned from our Alternate U dances and give it to the Committee to Defend the Black Panthers? "We wouldn't even be here if it weren't for the black civil rights movement. We owe it to them!" O'Brien rose to say.[1]

Of course, the $500 should be given to the Panthers defense fund, Bob Kohler agreed passionately. Kohler had come to the gay movement after being a Freedom Rider with the Congress for Racial Equality. He often told with relish about the time he, a young black woman, and a young black man jumped into an all-white public swimming pool in the South. The fifty whites who'd been enjoying a swim emptied out as though alligators had just dived in—and then the lifeguards rushed to drain the pool while the trio stood there, bathing suits dripping, arms clasped, singing emphatically "We Shall Overcome." Kohler had left CORE when it became clear that it was time for black people to handle the race battle by themselves, but he brought his intense convictions about political struggles with him into GLF. The Gay Liberation Front was not intended to be only about gay people, he preached to the converted. "Our fight is a people's movement, a class struggle with the rights of every oppressed person linked to one another."[2]

There was overwhelming consensus: the dance money would be given to the Black Panthers. When members of the Young Lords, a Puerto Rican nationalist group in Spanish Harlem, were jailed for actions such as piling up garbage and setting it ablaze in busy intersections to protest the scantiness of East Harlem social services, Gay Liberation Front members met, and again there was consensus: of course the group must dip into the kitty and this time bail the Young Lords out of jail.[3]

But a few New York GLF-ers, such as the group's treasurer, twenty-two-year-old Jim Owles, thought it was a crazy decision. The money needed to be going toward things like opening a gay community center, for instance—and not toward supporting organizations that were "viciously antihomosexual," he objected loudly.[4] Owles considered himself a "Eugene McCarthy liberal,"[5] not a radical leftist—though he'd had good credentials in thumbing his nose at the powers that be. He'd joined the air force in 1966 to avoid the draft and was assigned to Air Intelligence; but he was soon handing out antiwar leaflets to his fellow airmen, which got him a summary court-martial, a downgrade, and a transfer to a base in remote eastern Montana, a sort of "little Siberia," he called it. There he was assigned to the typing pool, though he could only type with two fingers. When he put those two fingers to use by typing letters to newspapers protesting the Vietnam War, his military career came to an abrupt end with a less-than-honorable discharge.[6] Most of Owles's fellow GLF-ers had liked that story very much, and they'd trusted him with the group's meager funds.

But Owles, unlike O'Brien and Kohler, hadn't been a founding member of GLF. He joined after its guiding principles were already established—and obviously he needed to be educated. Another one of the founders, Lois Hart, the former nun and Timothy Leary follower, waxed poetic about GLF's responsibilities to all suffering minorities: "Oppression is like a large tree with many branches, each branch being part of the whole," she pointed out. "They cannot be separated; they draw from each other."[7]

The faith that O'Brien, Kohler, and Hart had in making common cause with all the oppressed was richly rewarded by a "Letter from Huey [Newton] to the Revolutionary Brothers and Sisters on the Women's

Liberation and Gay Liberation Movements," in which the Black Panther leader admonished fellow Panthers: "Homosexuals might be the most oppressed people in the society. Whatever your personal opinions and your insecurities about homosexuality, we should try to unite with them in a revolutionary fashion."[8] But Newton's letter—and his caveats about "personal opinions"—were hardly sufficient to placate Owles and a few other GLF dissenters who were disgusted that the group was putting gay pennies and power into nongay organizations that were at best lukewarm about gay people.

Arthur Evans had been a radical activist since he was a teenager marching for black civil rights in York, Pennsylvania. At Brown University he made national news by leading a protest over compulsory chapel attendance; and when the devout Christian owner of a Pennsylvania paper company who'd funded Evans's four-year scholarship tried to withdraw it, twenty-one-year-old Evans got the Freethinkers Society of America to threaten legal action on his behalf.[9] The scholarship donor backed down, but Evans left Brown on his own. He'd been politically rambunctious but sexually timid and closeted, and he felt isolated in Providence, Rhode Island. When he read an article in a national magazine that said many homosexuals lived in Greenwich Village, it didn't take him long to pack his bags. In New York, Evans grew a beard and mustache, found a lover, finished his undergraduate work in political science at CCNY, started wearing the wire-rimmed glasses that stamped him as an intellectual, and in 1967 entered a PhD program in philosophy at Columbia University. But he dropped out before completing his degree: he'd realized he was far more excited by the 1968 student riots on campus than by his studies.[10]

In October 1969, four months after the Stonewall events (to which he'd paid no attention), Evans had been walking in Greenwich Village with his lover, Arthur Bell, when the two were handed a leaflet by a Little Orphan Annie–haired kid on Christopher Street.[11] It announced a meeting of a group they'd never heard of—the Gay Liberation Front. He and Bell casually thought they'd go see who would turn up in a group with such a name. Bell, a publicity director for Random House and later an out *Village Voice* columnist, was awed by the number of "hunky, chunky, big-basketed beauties dressed in radical motley" who squeezed into the upstairs meeting room at Alternate U.[12] Evans didn't mind the sight of the "beauties" either, but he also felt that he'd come home politically. Here was a roomful of homosexuals as passionate about radical politics as he, using familiar words such as *oppression, consciousness raising, liberation, pigs.* He hadn't known before that such homosexual beings existed, and he was soon swept up in the heady excitement of organizing a GLF Radical Study Group to examine the historical roots of homophobia and sexism. But his awe didn't last long. GLF members were "hysterical,"[13] he concluded; they were totally incapable of putting their passion to use. He was tired of listening to endless wishful thinking and jaw clapping about radical change, when what was needed was street activism, and the focus and discipline to make street activism effective.

Marty Robinson, who'd been GLF's chosen speaker at the Washington Square rally a month after the Stonewall riots, was also unhappy with the way things were going with the group he'd helped found. Robinson had been willing to give up a lot for the gay movement. The son of a successful medical doctor, who'd once wanted to be a doctor himself, he lived in a tub-in-the-kitchen apartment so he could work less at his job as a carpenter and spend more time on gay causes. "We've got to get organized. We've got to stand up. This is our chance!" he'd cried at the rally. But now he quit the Gay Liberation Front because he concluded that GLF-ers hadn't a clue about how to get organized or stand up for gays. He agreed with Owles that most of them were willing to make gay people cannon fodder for the revolution, and gay causes be damned.[14]

They weren't the only ones who were disillusioned. Kay Tobin was turned off when people in the Gay Liberation Front called her a fascist for wearing a John Lindsay button, and she loathed their sympathies with "every far-out radical cause that came along."[15] Others were turned off by the weekly character assassinations and the leaderless bedlam of the meetings where everyone could speak his or her mind at great length, no matter how confused or disputatious or inconsequential, and finally nothing was decided and nothing would get done.[16]

THE GAY ACTIVISTS ALLIANCE

On a rainy Sunday afternoon in early November 1969, Jim Owles, dressed in a Prussian army jacket as though ready for battle, showed up at Arthur Evans's apartment. He was furious about the latest GLF debacle. The Sunday before, a general GLF meeting was broken up when "some crazy" announced that the Electric Circus was discriminating against women, and half the people rushed out of the meeting to demonstrate against the Greenwich Village discotheque and show their outrage. Owles wanted to start a gay organization that would be an alternative to GLF—one that would focus just on gay and lesbian problems. One that would have some order and sanity. He'd already talked to Marty Robinson about it, and Marty had agreed. Evans and Arthur Bell wanted to be counted in.[17]

Just before Thanksgiving 1969, a dozen of the disillusioned New York GLF-ers met secretly in Jim Owles's apartment. Their new group's aim would be less about promoting gay "liberation" than about promoting gay rights. What to call it? "A name that really sings and says something," somebody suggested. They rejected "Homosexual Activist Movement," "Sexual Freedom Front," "Gay Scouts of America." They settled for "Gay Activists Alliance." It didn't sing, but at least its initials, GAA, said "Gay."[18] When Bob Kohler got wind of the new organization, he tarred it with the greatest insult he could think of: "It's a branch of the John Birch Society."[19]

But, in fact, all the founding Gay Activists Alliance members had been liberal to radical.[20] Several had participated in civil rights actions on behalf of blacks. All had been against the war, some even refusing to pay income tax to protest. Some had demonstrated at the 1968 Democratic National Convention in Chicago and taken knocks on the head from the Illinois National Guard. Now, though, most agreed that fighting for gay and lesbian rights didn't require tearing down the American system. They wanted only to open it up to gay people. They would fight for decriminalization by getting the state to repeal sodomy laws and getting the police to acknowledge that gays had the same rights to the pursuit of happiness as did other American citizens. They would fight for fair employment. They would fight for fair housing legislation.

To avoid the endless free-for-alls that GLF meetings always were, GAA meetings would be conducted by *Robert's Rules of Order*. But order would not mean timidity. They would work to become a powerful political bloc. They would be no less militant than the Gay Liberation Front, but the radical demands they would make would be for first-class American citizenship.[21]

"Assimilationists!" GLF-ers called them.

Arthur Evans never stopped believing that gays would need to join with other "oppressed people" to overturn what he called an "oppressive system," and his platform when he ran for GAA president was the promise to ignite in homosexuals everywhere the buried sense of anger at oppression. First they would be made political; and then they could be made into revolutionaries.[22] For most Gay Activists Alliance members, it sounded too much like Gay Liberation Front rhetoric, and Evans lost the presidency to Jim Owles.

It was Evans, though, who penned the preamble to GAA's constitution and brought into it what he called the "rhetoric of anger." Homosexuals have "the right to make love with anyone, anyway, anytime, provided only that such action be freely chosen by the individuals concerned." Homosexuals have "the right to treat and express our bodies as we will [and] to display and embellish them solely in the manner we ourselves determine, independent of any external control whatsoever."[23] Such declarations sounded very different from the Frank Kameny–Barbara Gittings[24] camp. And in style, GAA was very different. Unlike the super-serious Kameny and Gittings, the Gay Activists Alliance would make their demands with theatricality and a wicked sense of humor. But the primary goal of the Gay Activists Alliance was exactly what Kameny and Gittings had fought for: to claim a place at the American table as a bona fide family member, whether the rest of the family liked it or not.[25]

The founding members chose as the Gay Activists Alliance symbol the Greek letter *lambda*. "The Lacedaemonians, or Spartans, bore it on their shields, a people's will aimed at common oppressors," they explained bellicosely in a GAA leaflet.[26] Enemies of gays and lesbians, like Sparta's enemies, would cease to sleep peacefully in their beds at night. Homophobes in power would learn that they'd met their match. The Gay Activists Alliance would use "confrontation politics" to win civil rights: sit-ins, demonstrations, street theater, and especially meaningful monkey shines.[27]

ZAPPING

The Church of the Holy Apostles on Ninth Avenue was a progressive Episcopal parish that had started in the 1840s as an outreach to immigrants who worked on the Hudson River waterfront. During the Civil War it had been a stop on the Underground Railroad. In January 1970 it opened its doors as a meeting place for the Gay Activists Alliance. At the first meeting, Marty Robinson, wearing a new dark blue T-shirt with a big, bright yellow lambda insignia emblazed on the front like a Lacedaemonian shield, proposed what was to become the first step toward a place at the table. The Gay Activists Alliance would present a petition signed by thousands of people to Carol Greitzer, the New York councilwoman whose district included Greenwich Village. The petition would ask her to sponsor a bill that would add the words "sexual orientation" to a city ordinance that already prohibited discrimination in employment, housing, and public accommodations on the basis of race, religion, and gender.

For the next three winter months, Gay Activists Alliance members stood on street corners all over the city, collecting signatures from straights as well as gays. The collateral benefits of Robinson's petition drive, he'd explained, was that gay people would show themselves to all New Yorkers as out and proud and willing to stand up for their rights; and straight people would see that not all gays fit the homosexual stereotype. In early April Jim Owles gathered up the stacks of petitions that had been turned into GAA headquarters, and in the capacity of the organization's president he took them to city hall.[28]

"Councilwoman Greitzer, I have here between six and seven thousand signatures of New Yorkers who are asking you to sponsor a gay rights bill," Owles formally told the freshman councilwoman in her office, proffering the huge stack. Carol Greitzer had recently been elected chair of the newly established National Abortion Rights Action League. She'd just drafted a bill to outlaw discrimination against unescorted women in New York restaurants. Owles had good reason to believe that the liberal councilwoman would take the petitions and thank him.

"I have too much to do and too much to carry, and I can't lug those things home," she said instead and refused to accept them. Owles offered to help her carry the petitions, but she refused that too and told him that she would not sponsor a gay rights bill.[29] "Homosexuality is not my problem, so I don't quite understand it," she said.[30]

A few days later, three dozen gays and lesbians marched into a meeting of the Village Independent Democratic Club, whose members were Greitzer's base. "Carol Greitzer is antigay!" they screamed in unison. "If you're not," Arthur Evans yelled at her, "make a statement supporting the gay cause. And if you don't, we're staging a sit-in."

Greitzer was seated next to the Village Independent Democratic Club's platform chair Robert Egan. She turned to him and whispered, "I don't want to make a statement. Tell them I have a cold."

"You're guilty of the crime of silence!" Jim Owles shouted, and the three dozen chanted, "Guilty of the crime of silence! Guilty of the crime of silence!"[31]

Greitzer finally took the microphone to say, "Listen, the attorney general is the one who's done the most this past year with civil rights legislation. I can't get it done. There's no way of getting this through—not even with bombs."[32]

"Guilty of the crime of silence! Guilty of the crime of silence!" the three dozen kept chanting. Sylvia Rivera, the Latina drag queen, waved a menacing fist at the councilwoman.[33]

Greitzer surely feared that some members of the very progressive Village Independent Democratic Club would have sympathy with the homosexuals and she was being made to look bad. Not knowing what else to do, she said okay, she would accept the petitions. And, she added not too graciously, she would sponsor the bill, too.[34]

While Gay Activists Alliance members had been collecting signatures for the petition, GAA officers had been making numerous phone calls and sending countless letters and telegrams to New York's most influential political figure, Mayor John Lindsay. Lindsay was a very liberal Republican who, as New York congressman to the US House of Representatives, led a group of fellow Republicans to support the 1964 Civil Rights Act. As mayor of New York, he was so well liked and trusted by the black community that his appearance in Harlem after the assassination of Martin Luther King in 1968 averted race riots such as had erupted in big cities across the country. But when the Gay Activists Alliance asked Lindsay to make a public statement saying that he supported a gay rights law, he refused to dignify their request with a response.

Mattachine president Dick Leitsch continued to defend Lindsay. It was Lindsay who'd made the city "livable" for gay people by ending police entrapment, he said.[35] But the Gay Activists Alliance was asking much more of the mayor than what they said was a behind-closed-doors order to plainclothes cops to stop coming on to homosexuals and arresting them if they responded.[36] GAA wanted Lindsay to make clear to all of New York that he opposed discrimination against gays and lesbians in employment, housing, and public accommodations.

When the mayor was not forthcoming, he became GAA's chief target. Leitsch and Mattachine were outraged that with all the real enemies of gays and lesbians in New York, the Gay Activists Alliance chose to pick on a liberal mayor. But the reasoning of GAA's leaders was that conservative politicians were a lost cause—no use trying to pressure them. Liberal politicians (like Greitzer and Lindsay), who prided themselves on supporting the rights of minorities, could be made to understand that gay people were also a legitimate minority, whose rights they must champion no less than they championed the rights of black people.

Marty Robinson came up with another key idea: GAA would do agitprop, like the radical feminists did in the 1960s, when they invaded the Miss America Pageant in Atlantic City and brought with them "Freedom Trash Cans" into which they tossed bras, high heels, *Playboy* magazines, and cooking utensils. They held an "ogle-in" on Wall Street, dozens of women scrutinizing male butts, whistling, and catcalling. They released cages of mice at a bridal fair in Madison Square Garden. They "occupied" tables in restaurants that wouldn't seat unaccompanied women. "Zaps," Marty Robinson would call similarly impudent, high-spirited actions in which "the good guys publicly embarrass the bad guys."[37] They'd be mock warnings to the "bad guys," as in "Zap! You're dead!"

Zaps were soon GAA's trademark form of protest[38]—playful, mischievous, and dead serious, all at once. Mayor Lindsay became very familiar with the zap. In one of the first ones, a half dozen Gay Activists Alliance members posed as journalism students being taken on a civics junket by their professor (played by Ron Gold, a forty-one-year-old reporter for *Variety* who'd quit his day job and lived on an inheritance so he could be media director of GAA).[39] They went up to city hall's second-floor, where the mayor's office was located. Then they each whipped out a pair of handcuffs that were borrowed from GAA members who were into S&M, and they fastened themselves to the gate that blocked his office from public access. Their chants of derision and complaints against the mayor echoed in the marble halls and were heard by all the tourists and crowds of visiting school kids, until the police finally were able to sever the handcuffs from the gate and rush the zappers to the police station.[40] Lindsay didn't come out of his office to see the zap, though he undoubtedly heard it.

The next one, at the Metropolitan Museum of Art, forced a confrontation. On April 13, 1970, the museum held its one-hundredth birthday party, featuring the mayor. As Lindsay stood at a podium before a couple of hundred guests, extolling the contributions of the Metropolitan Museum to the cultural life of New York, Marty Robinson, intensity writ large on his earnest, handsome face,[41] ran up to Lindsay shouting, "I'm a member of the Gay Activists Alliance, Mr. Mayor. When are you going to speak out on homosexual rights?" Robinson was ungently hauled away by the mayor's bodyguards and kicked out.

But that wasn't the end of the zap. Gay Activists Alliance members had infiltrated the crowd, and wherever Lindsay went in the museum, they tailed him and tried to hand him a flyer that asked him to speak out about civil rights for gays and lesbians. That didn't end the zap either. It had been announced earlier that before Lindsay left the museum he would shake the hands of the first hundred people in a receiving line. GAA members rushed to take places throughout the line. "Mr. Lindsay, you have our flyer," each would say when the mayor got to him or her in the line and extended his hand. "Now when are you going to speak out on gay rights?" Lindsay would move his lips a bit to simulate a polite mumble; the GAA member would repeat, "When are you going to speak out on gay rights?" and wouldn't let go of the mayoral hand. Once the mayor's bodyguards saw what was up, they shadowed the mayor closely so they could bum-rush each activist out. It took three bodyguards to extricate Lindsay's hand from the grip of one of the activists. The tony museum supporters were thus put on notice that gays and lesbians had become tenacious in demanding their rights.[42]

GAA relentlessly zapped Lindsay all through the spring and summer. In the fall, the mayor and his dignified, blue-blood wife Mary, whom he called his most trusted advisor, were to be guests of honor for the opening night of a Broadway play, *Two by Two*. About twenty-five GAA members were already scattered among the high-society crowd when the couple arrived at the Imperial Theater. The gays waylaid the Lindsays in the lobby, shouting, "Mr. Mayor, when are you going to speak out on gay rights?" "Lindsay must speak out!" "Gay power!" "End police harassment!" John Lindsay responded just as he had throughout the spring and summer: he fixed his gaze on the distance and smiled a plastic smile. But Mary Lindsay, after hearing zap stories for six months, lost it. She kicked one zapper in the shins, punched another in the chest, and screamed like a fishwife, "Damn you! Get the hell out of here!" as the mortified mayor struggled to restrain her.[43]

In 1971 Mayor Lindsay declared himself a candidate for the US presidency. Because he suspected he was too socially liberal for Republican tastes, he and his wife both changed their party affiliations to Democrat. Lindsay had still not expressed support for gay civil rights, but the Gay Activists Alliance, after realizing that Carol Greitzer had no intention of keeping her extorted, halfhearted promise to sponsor a gay civil rights bill, was able to convince four other council members to be cosponsors. The city council was set to vote on the bill in January 1972. Both the policemen's union and the firemen's union campaigned hard against it, and it failed.

Rich Wandel, a former Catholic novitiate who'd jumped over the wall and come out shortly after the Stonewall riots,[44] had recently succeeded Jim Owles as president of the GAA. Wandel laid the blame for the bill's failure squarely at the mayor's feet, and he scoffed that Lindsay was campaigning for the Democratic nomination on the basis of his strong civil rights record. "He's touring the nation championing the rights of blacks, women, and Chicanos, which we applaud, but not one word about this country's twenty million homosexuals. Not one word about the oppression of eight hundred thousand gay New Yorkers," Wandel complained.[45]

He penned a flyer declaring that his organization was waging "Total War on John V. Lindsay." There were now activist gay groups in cities all over America, Wandel wrote, and the New York Gay Activists Alliance would inform every one of them that Lindsay was a civil rights phony. The war on Lindsay's presidential hopes would begin in New York's Radio City Music Hall, at a party to raise funds for his campaign—"6,000 people at $100 apiece."[46]

Allen Roskoff, chair of GAA's Municipal Government Committee, was a main organizer of the Radio City zap. Roskoff, hair down to his shoulder blades, had been a very out antiwar activist, but as a homosexual who was set to become a teacher he'd been totally closeted—until 1971, when he read a notice in the *Village Voice* about a Gay Activists Alliance meeting. For what seemed like hours, Roskoff had circled the blocks around Wooster Street. (After GAA members had appeared on *The David Susskind Show*, attendance at general meetings grew to over three hundred, too large for Holy Apostles's 1,800-square-foot meeting hall,[47] so GAA had recently moved to SoHo, into a 10,000-square-foot abandoned nineteenth-century firehouse with a spiral staircase and art nouveau decorations.) Roskoff was working up the courage to go into the Firehouse, as it was now called, though he couldn't stop worrying that he'd be harassed by men in high heels. When he finally entered the GAA meeting space, and saw the members and heard what they said and the smarts with which they said it, he knew that he'd found his people—and that the gay rights movement would be his life, even if it meant giving up his teaching career. The zaps he planned were labors of love.[48]

The afternoon before the fund-raiser, Roskoff, together with several other GAA members, bought tickets to the movie that was being shown at Radio City Music Hall that day, *The Hot Rock*, starring Robert Redford—coincidentally a film about an elaborate plan by good-guy outlaws who fight bad-guy policemen and break the law for a good cause. But relevant as the movie may have been, Roskoff and the others were too busy doing their job to see much of it. They were scoping out Radio City Music Hall, deciding who would sit in the balcony, who would sit in the orchestra, what the order of disruptions would be, where on the seats they might fasten their handcuffs . . . They would leave nothing to chance. Of course, they couldn't come up with hundreds of dollars to buy tickets for Lindsay's fund-raiser (nor would they have spent their money that way even if they'd had it). But Ron Gold had a connection: the head of the projectionist union (who never knew what Gold was up to) gave the former *Variety* reporter a small stack of complementary tickets to the evening's event.[49]

Now, how to present themselves at such a gala? Rich Wandel had been in the news too recently as president of GAA; he'd have to be disguised. "Okay, a dark suit and an Abraham Lincoln beard," Wandel promised. And the others would have to spiff up enough for this formal affair so they wouldn't call attention to themselves too soon. No lambda T-shirts here.[50]

The event that evening began with cigar-smoking comedian Alan King, who told New Yorker jokes for ten minutes, then introduced Lindsay's campaign manager, Richard Aurelio, with the prophetic quip, "That's like being the navigator on the *Titanic*."[51] Then King grandly introduced "the next president of the United States, John Lindsay!" Thunderous applause as the tuxedoed mayor walked onstage.

He'd barely opened his mouth before Morty Manford, stationed in the balcony where he'd affixed a sturdy rope, swung on it, Errol Flynn style, down to the orchestra, screaming, "Justice for homosexuals!"[52] Cora Perotta, a petite, vivacious Puerto Rican lesbian, veteran of many GAA zaps, and used to being arrested for them,[53] stood up from her seat in the orchestra and shouted, "Why are you contributing to homosexual oppression, Mr. Mayor?" She held up a siren that would sound an ear-splitting screech when the pin was pulled—and she pulled the pin. Then she threw pin and screech machine over the heads of the audience, as far as she could, and in opposite directions. She sat down again—and handcuffed herself to her chair, so that when the police arrived, there'd be an extra stir because they'd have to cut the handcuffs.

Then Roskoff stood up from his seat in the balcony, shouting, "There are twenty million gays in this country. Lindsay cannot run for president!" and he, too, held up a siren, pulled the pin, and threw siren and pin in opposite directions. He also flung hundreds of Gay Activists Alliance flyers down on the audience seated in the orchestra. "There are twenty million gays in this country. Lindsay cannot run for president!" the flyers proclaimed. Just as Perrotta had done, Roskoff quickly handcuffed himself to his chair. Then Wayne Sunday, another veteran zapper, and then Rich Wandel—one after another, they popped up from their seats in the orchestra or balcony, shouted their slogans, pulled the pins of their sirens, and chained themselves to their chairs. The noise of sirens and homosexuals barking and bellowing slogans ended Lindsay's speech. The candidate retreated from the stage. As the bemused audience filed out, the zappers kept yelling, "There are twenty million gays in this country. Lindsay cannot run for president!" and "Justice for homosexuals!" When the police finally arrived, they cut the zappers loose from their handcuffs, ushered them into a paddy wagon, and took them to the Midtown North Precinct Station for booking.

The next day, Mayor Lindsay, understanding that Wandel and GAA really would give no quarter in the war they'd declared on him, capitulated. He signed an executive order that said that the sexual orientation of city employees and job applicants for city jobs must be considered irrelevant. The executive order was not as good as a comprehensive gay rights bill that would give gays and lesbians fair treatment in employment, housing, and public accommodations, but it was a step in the right direction.

In fall 1972, Geoffrey Swearingen, a twenty-one-year-old college student, applied for a driver's job with the Dover Cab Company. All cab companies in New York were obliged to send their applicants to the Metropolitan Taxi Bureau to be tested for their suitability before they could be hired. Swearingen admitted under questioning that his draft classification was IV-F because the military examiners found he had "homosexual tendencies." His examiners at the Metropolitan Taxi Bureau were almost as leery of homosexuals as the military had been. They informed Swearingen that they could not approve him for work unless he got a letter from a psychiatrist stating that his sexual orientation would not interfere with his job performance.[54] Of course, Mayor Lindsay had issued an executive order six months earlier demanding that city agencies stop discriminating against homosexuals—and the bureau's insistence that Swearingen get cleared by a psychiatrist was certainly discrimination. But clearly not all agencies were taking Lindsay's executive order seriously.

The head of the Taxi and Limousine Commission was Michael Lazar (known as the "Taxi Czar"). He'd been in the audience at Radio City Music Hall when the Gay Activists Alliance zapped Mayor Lindsay off the stage,[55] so he'd already had a demonstration of the group's no-holds-barred tenacity. Now nine GAA members descended on his Wall Street headquarters, seven of them trailing Allen Roskoff and Arthur Bell, who carried a couch onto the freight elevator and got out on Czar Lazar's floor.

"We didn't order a couch!" Commissioner Lazar's startled secretary shrieked. "Who are you?" Allen Roskoff was decked out in a doctor's white smock, a stethoscope slung around his neck. "We are here to psychoanalyze Mr. Lazar. We must see if he is sane enough to be the taxi commissioner," a poker-faced Roskoff told her.[56]

Three days later, Lazar announced that the Taxi and Limousine Commission's policies had been reversed. Homosexual applicants would no longer be required to submit psychiatric certification, and homosexuals who had been given licenses would no longer be required to undergo semiannual psychiatric evaluations in order to keep them.[57] With no further ado, Geoffrey Swearingen received an unconditional license to drive a cab.

MAKING 'EM PAY ATTENTION

Gay Activists Alliance zaps didn't often yield such immediate payoffs, but GAA continued zapping. It was the organization's preferred tactic. It bullied the bullies—gave them a taste of their own medicine and made them understand that the days of impunity for oppressing homosexuals were gone. Even more important, zapping got the word *gay* into the media better than any previous technique had. *Life* magazine's December 31, 1971, issue, for example, announced to eight and a half million readers that homosexuals, a "hitherto silent majority," were "America's newest militants," and demonstrated the point by featuring photos of the GAA invasion of the New York City Clerk's office. He'd refused to issue wedding licenses to homosexuals. The zappers brought with them a big pot of coffee and a giant wedding cake that was decorated on top with two grooms and two brides in loving same-sex couples. On the side of the cake was the message "Gay Power to Gay Love," and over that was GAA's trademark lambda symbol. The *Life* article dubbed New York's Gay Activists Alliance "homosexual liberation's most effective organization."[58]

The zaps were most often about showing why a nondiscrimination ordinance was needed or putting pressure on public figures who were opposed to the ordinance. Marty Robinson and Jim Owles realized that tedious as the ordinance battles could be, they wouldn't be news for long unless GAA could promise the media a bit of entertainment or drama. And that it did. With as much humor as wrath, it took on Fidelifacts, for instance, a company whose obnoxious advertising come-on to corporations was, "Do you know who you are hiring?" Fidelifacts used former Secret Servicemen, IRS workers, and military intelligence officers to conduct background checks on job applicants. They examined criminal records, employment history, and military records, and then reported their findings to their client companies. They also reported whether they'd found a job applicant to be homosexual.

The Gay Activists Alliance got wind of Fidelifacts's services when its founder, Vincent Gillen, a former FBI agent, was invited to be luncheon speaker at the Association of Stock Exchange Brokers. As the Wall Street men digested their chicken a la king, the voluble Gillen merrily admitted about his company's tattling: "Establishing that someone is a homosexual is often difficult, but I like to go on the rule of thumb that if one looks like a duck, walks like a duck, associates only with ducks, and quacks like a duck, then he is probably a duck."[59]

GAA members worked with New York Daughters of Bilitis on the Fidelifacts zap. They tied up the company's phone lines all the next day, repeating the message, "Stop your offensive services now!" A delegation of fifteen GAA and DOB leaders also marched into Fidelifacts's sixth-floor office on Forty-Second Street—having first invited the press and WOR-TV to come along and watch gays and lesbians stage a sit-in.

"You're trespassing," two Fidelifacts employees told Jim Owles when he demanded to see Vincent Gillen.

"Fidelifacts is trespassing on the human rights of homosexuals and on the privacy of all Americans," Jim Owles solemnly lectured the employees—who shoved him hard against a wall. WOR-TV cameras caught the Fidelifacts men assaulting GAA's president and showed it on television that night, along with news of the homosexual sit-in. But that wasn't all the gays and lesbians provided for the media to see. As their delegation argued with Fidelifacts people upstairs, eighty more gays and lesbians picketed in the street below. Marty Robinson, dressed up in a bright yellow duck suit, led the picketers.[60]

The image of Marty Robinson, looking, walking, and quacking like a duck as he handed out leaflets telling why the protestors were there, was also captured in newspapers and by TV cameras, though reporters didn't fully appreciate what was happening. They presented the incident mostly as "another one of those funny gay demonstrations that we seem to be seeing more and more of"[61]—but the message that "more and more" gays and lesbians were demonstrating for rights and respect was just what GAA hoped to communicate to all the gays and lesbians who hadn't yet joined them, and to the straight world, too.

Chapter 14

A PARALLEL REVOLUTION:
LESBIAN FEMINISTS

"LESBIANS ARE *WOMEN*"

Hal Call, Mattachine Society's national president, learned how hostile lesbians were to his "boys' club" in 1959. That was the year he invited Del Martin and Phyllis Lyon, the most prominent female homophiles in the country, to Mattachine's Sixth Annual Convention in Denver. Perhaps he was still hoping that DOB would merge with his organization. At the evening banquet, he summoned Martin and Lyon up to the podium to present them with honorary Mattachine memberships.

Del Martin looked out over a sea of dark suits and ties—and instead of thanking the men of Mattachine for their gracious recognition, as they surely expected she would, she sternly rebuked them. "What do you men know about lesbians? You speak of the male homosexual and follow it with—'and incidentally, there are some female homosexuals, too, and because they are homosexual, all this should apply to them as well.'" Her taken-aback listeners sat quietly as she went on with her angry "lesson," as she called it. "Lesbians are *women*, and this twentieth century is the era of emancipation of women," she scolded. "Lesbians are not satisfied to be auxiliary members or second-class homosexuals."[1] The second wave of feminism wouldn't happen until the next decade, but this was militant feminist talk, spurred by homophile men's careless assumptions that their hopes and dreams were one and the same with lesbians' hopes and dreams.

Years later, irate lesbian feminists would make identical complaints about radical gay men. "Good-bye to all that,"[2] they told the men with whom they'd begun their work for the revolution. And for the next ten years or more, they went their separate way.

The lesbians in the Gay Liberation Front in 1969 were just as leftist, militant, and committed as the gay men. But they were a small minority of the group, 10 percent to 15 percent. From that, major gripes arose. At the GLF dances, lesbians were "like an afterthought in a roomful of men," GLF-er Arlene Kisner complained. She'd been in the radical feminist Redstockings when a long-haired hippie gay friend brought her to her first GLF meeting, soon after the group got started. She kept coming back because it seemed, at first anyway, like she was being drawn into an irresistible communal consciousness. She was awed by the collective energy. But at GLF dances she felt squeezed out by disturbingly rampant male sexuality.[3] Kisner wasn't alone among GLF women who resented that for the men at the dances "human contact was limited to groping and dryfucking."[4] The guys sucked up all the air in the room, the women felt. They couldn't breathe.[5]

The dance problem was barely the tip of the gripes. Ellen Shumsky, who'd gone to Cuba to help with harvests a whole year before the Students for a Democratic Society thought of forming the Venceremos Brigade, believed she knew as much as—more than—the GLF men; she couldn't bear their political diatribes, which were delivered as though only they had a pipeline to the truths of anarchism, Trotskyism, Leninism, Marxism, and everything else. And when women such as Martha Shelley or Lois Hart matched them in pontifications, the men resented it.[6]

It was the dawn of the radical feminist movement, and the radical feminist anger of GLF lesbians was growing apace. Lesbians were tired of fighting "for everyone else's cause while ignoring our own," Martha Shelley wrote in an essay she called "Stepin Fetchit Woman," which appeared in the first issue of the GLF magazine, *Come Out!* The feminism of lesbians is built into their being, she said. "I have met many feminists who were not lesbian, but I have never met a lesbian who was not a feminist."[7] She'd been a founder of GLF, but she concluded that the behavior of GLF men was intolerable to lesbians' feminist sensibilities.[8]

GLF lesbians were especially peeved when the group donated $500 to the Black Panthers.[9] "I don't remember agreeing to give the money to the Black Panthers," Flavia Rando complained at the next GLF meeting. She'd been brought into GLF by Martha Shelley. ("Want to come?" Shelley had asked. "Are you kidding? I've been waiting for this all my life!" Rando had answered.) Now she wanted to know why GLF wasn't donating money to abortion rights; and she wanted to know why the lesbians had to support the Panthers if the Panthers weren't supporting the lesbians.[10]

By the time GLF was six months old, they concluded that they'd all been radicals long before they hooked up with radical gay men; and they needed to put their radicalism into lesbian issues, women's issues. They'd meet on their own, without the men.[11]

That's what lesbians in the Gay Activists Alliance thought they needed to do, too. They were prodded to that conclusion by a young woman who a couple of years earlier had been a novitiate at the Sisters of the Holy Humility of Mary in Youngstown, Ohio. Jean O'Leary had jumped over the convent wall when she concluded—after she'd seduced a half dozen Sisters (wittingly and unwittingly)—that she was in the wrong place.[12] She got her father to drive her to New York, where she'd been accepted in the Organizational Development doctoral program at Yeshiva University. O'Leary finished the course work but never wrote her dissertation. She'd read an anonymous article in *Cosmopolitan* magazine (by its closeted entertainment editor Liz Smith, O'Leary later discovered), which said that Greenwich Village was where all the lesbians gathered. O'Leary found a gay man with whom to share a Village apartment. It was he who took her to a meeting of the Gay Activists Alliance. She was disappointed that less than 10 percent of those present were female, but she became a member anyway.[13]

Twenty-three-year-old O'Leary was attractive and articulate, and when she spoke people almost always listened. She had reason to be confident that she was a budding star; so she didn't take lightly the unaccustomed experience of being drowned out by the men in GAA. She was especially unhappy that whenever GAA held a press conference, the microphones would always go to the men. She was convinced by the feminist polemics she was reading that women didn't stand a chance of being heard in gatherings so dominated by testosterone. She flirted briefly with lesbian separatism.[14] Yet the Gay Activists Alliance seemed to be doing more to fight for rights than any lesbian group she knew—and political battles interested her far more than building a "women's culture," which is where lesbian separatists were investing their energy. She'd find a compromise, she decided. She announced at a GAA meeting that she wanted to start a new "committee." She wanted to call it the Lesbian Liberation Committee.

Even the name "Lesbian Liberation Committee" made GAA men nervous. They were suspicious of O'Leary's motives, despite the fact that every Tuesday in the preceding months, O'Leary, driving her little green Volkswagen with its missing headlight, had been leading a caravan up to the state capital of Albany to lobby hostile congressmen for a gay rights bill.[15] But how was "Lesbian Liberation" relevant to the purpose of the Gay Activists Alliance? "Lesbian Liberation" sounded as though the group would be about women's issues, not gay rights. Not even all the lesbians in GAA supported the idea. Kay Tobin, who, with her partner Barbara Gittings, had picketed the White House and Independence Hall with Frank Kameny and Mattachine Society Washington, thought that female homosexuals should be fighting first and foremost for homosexual rights. Nathalie Rockhill, head of GAA's Community Relations Committee, had no problem with the men in the Gay Activists Alliance. She'd never been in a gay group before she came to her first GAA meeting, and she'd been awed at the level of intelligent and orderly debate. "It was like being in Athens, like hearing Plato," she and her partner agreed. They'd been touched too that Jim Owles and Marty Robinson had rushed up to them afterward. "What did you think of the meeting?" they asked because they were so anxious to bring women into the organization. GAA had become Rockhill's emotional home. "I can be discriminated against for being a woman, but I can get beat up or worse for being gay," Nathalie Rockhill told Jean O'Leary.[16]

Finally, though, O'Leary's request to start a lesbian group in GAA was given a reluctant nod: she could hold her meetings and women-only dances and film nights at the GAA firehouse headquarters. But it didn't work. GAA men kept subverting the new "committee." Some of them showed up at the lesbian meetings and conspicuously sat. The women demanded they leave. Entertainment committee members were supposed to clean the kitchen or set up the movie projector. For lesbian events, they didn't.

Members of the Lesbian Liberation Committee were also unhappy that GAA allowed transvestites such as Sylvia Rivera and Marsha P. Johnson into the organization. Arthur Bell, a journalist and founder of GAA, wrote articles in the *Village Voice* that depicted them as heroes and took seriously the organization they started, Street Transvestite Action Revolutionaries.[17] Lesbian Liberation Committee members, like most feminists of the seventies, loathed that women were imprisoned in fashions such as high heels and short skirts that made them vulnerable; or tight dresses that revealed sex characteristics; or lipstick and eye shadow that encouraged frivolity. As lesbian feminists saw it, transvestites were mocking women by mimicking what demeaned them.

The 1973 New York Gay Pride rally in Washington Square: Sylvia Rivera, in a skin-tight woman's pantsuit and a comically tousled woman's wig, took over the stage and delivered a wild harangue about the gay community's neglect of gays in prison.[18] She was followed by entertainers Billie and Tiffany, two plump drag queens wearing big bonnets, inch-long eyelashes, and dowdy floral dresses, who did a singing sisters act. Jean O'Leary went up onstage and grabbed the microphone. She was there, she said, to deliver a message from the women of Lesbian Feminist Liberation—the old Lesbian Liberation Committee, which had by now completely severed itself from GAA. Lesbian Feminist Liberation had gotten wind the day before of the scheduled drag performance. Members had spent much of the night in O'Leary's living room, composing a furious protest. O'Leary shouted out the written statement, ignoring hisses and boos from the throngs of men who'd been happy to be entertained by Billie and Tiffany: "This is the exploitation of women by men! This is men trying to tell us who and what we are. This is men laughing with each other, telling us who *they* think *we* are."

RADICALESBIANS

In January 1970 Rita Mae Brown showed up at a Gay Liberation Front meeting. She had the seductive, dark good looks of a beautiful Italian boy, and she came to tell the GLF lesbians they belonged somewhere else.

Brown had been part of the Student Homophile League at Columbia University in 1967, but she dropped out because she'd discovered that gay men are just like straight men and "don't give a damn about the needs of women."[19] Though the 1969 rebellion at the Stonewall Inn was becoming iconic, Brown, already a feminist, proclaimed it a gay *men's* revolution. "For the great bulk of the lesbian community, it's just not all that significant," she insisted.[20]

As soon as she'd heard of the National Organization for Women (NOW), she found out where the New York group was meeting, and she joined. Her smarts and good looks led to hints by the leadership that she could have a place among them if she played her cards right.[21] But she quit NOW, too, because it was full of what she called "golden girls": stockbrokers, lawyers, art directors, and such. They did give a damn about women's needs, but mostly with regard to job discrimination and the pill. They also gave a damn about what the "white rich male heterosexual media found acceptable," which meant they sweated to keep NOW's image lesbian free.

Next, Brown found a radical socialist women's group, Redstockings. But what they gave a damn about were prostitutes and child care for single working mothers. Lesbians were off their radar. She didn't last long in Redstockings, either. By now, she decided, she was too tired and too wise to invest more energy on the "straight ladies."[22]

That's what brought her to a Gay Liberation Front meeting that night. With her bold rhetorical skills (of which she had no doubt) and her considerable lesbian sex appeal (of which she was even surer), she'd play the Pied Piper. ("There was energy around her that crackled and sparkled," the lesbians thought.)[23] She'd drag the GLF lesbians into an all-lesbian group that was feminist. It would heal the sense of alienation she suffered with male homophiles and heterosexual feminists of both the right and left wings; and it would be good for the lesbians, too.[24]

Rita Mae Brown's alluring performance at the first GLF meeting of the New Year became GLF lesbians' call to action. The most useful tool to promote radical awareness and constructive anger, Brown had learned in Redstockings, was consciousness raising;[25] and now, she announced to GLF, she'd be starting all-lesbian consciousness-raising groups. "Lesbian oppression and homosexual male oppression have less in common than you think," she goaded the women. In consciousness-raising groups, they'd learn why.[26]

• • •

By 1970, Betty Friedan, founder of the National Organization for Women, was getting very nervous about lesbians in the women's movement. Her worry had been set off by Ivy Bottini, a matronly suburban wife and mother of four who'd started the first chapter of NOW and was serving as its president. Friedan had been delighted with Bottini's average-American-housewife appearance and her wife-and-mother status. Ivy Bottini was just the sort of woman Friedan wanted to draw into NOW in great numbers, and she happily used Bottini as a speaker at NOW rallies—to show the media that NOW members were part of ordinary Middle America. But suddenly Bottini turned radical on her, leading her chapter members in a zap to drape the Statue of Liberty with a sign that proclaimed, "Women of the World, Unite!" Even worse, Bottini wanted to raise lesbian issues in NOW. Worst of all, she came out herself as a lesbian. Friedan arranged that her onetime poster mama be drummed out of the presidency. When it became clear that NOW was attracting a lot of other women like Bottini, Friedan started lamenting about "the Lavender Menace" in her organization. Lesbians, she feared, would give feminism a bad name.[27]

Friedan's lament was a clarion call to Rita Mae Brown and the lesbians she'd plucked from GLF. They needed to write a manifesto that would explain them to the world, Brown said. They'd start by distributing it to the women who'd be at a conference that NOW was sponsoring that fall.

They gathered at Rita Mae Brown's apartment—Lois Hart, Cynthia Funk, Ellen Bedoz (née Ellen Shumsky), Artemis March (née March Hoffman), and Barbara XX (née Barbara Gladstone)—and they brainstormed. Each one would write out her ideas, they decided, and then they'd hash them over together. They agreed the manifesto must say that lesbians are just like other women, but more so. "A lesbian is the rage of all women condensed to the point of explosion" would be their opening line. They'd say that heterosexual women become feminists when they finally understand that society doesn't allow them to be complete and free human beings—but lesbians had *always* understood that. Feminists are finally realizing that sex roles dehumanize women—but lesbians had *always* understood that; they'd *always* refused to accept the limitations and oppressions imposed by the womanly role.

March Hoffman, who'd just graduated from Vassar College, volunteered to take all their notes and the ideas that came up when they brainstormed, and compose the manifesto in a unified voice.[28] They'd call it "The Woman-Identified Woman." And since it was a group effort, they'd say it was written "by Radicalesbians."[29]

Their fervor was nothing short of evangelical as they tossed around ideas. They'd call for women who'd been heretofore heterosexual to emulate lesbians by ceasing to be "male identified" in their heads. Women must become "woman identified." They'd say that women who had feminist aspirations must stop denying one another the value and love (even sexual love) that they readily accorded to men. "Our energies must flow toward our sisters, not backward toward our oppressors," they'd declare.

Straight radical feminists had been thinking along similar lines. The very heterosexual *Village Voice* writer Vivian Gornick declared in a 1970 article that lesbians "have more to teach Feminists about Feminism than has any other single category of human being."[30] Ti-Grace Atkinson, a onetime southern belle who'd become a leading feminist theoretician, was speaking of lesbians as the "front-line troops" of the women's movement. Lesbianism, she said, was a "political choice" and a "political strategy"[31]—redefining "politics" (with a nod to Kate Millett's 1968 essay "Sexual Politics"[32]) to refer to the manifold conflicts between the sexes. For the first time since the sexologists emerged in the nineteenth century, lesbians were being championed and admired as bold political heroes instead of being deprecated as sickies and criminals. "Can you imagine a Frenchman, serving in the French Army from 9 AM to 5 PM, then trotting 'home' to Germany for supper and overnight? That's called game-playing and collaboration, not political commitment," Ti-Grace Atkinson chided.[33] Lesbians had a full-time commitment to women—which those women who'd been living with men would do well to emulate, radical feminists were now saying. It was exactly what lesbian feminists themselves believed. "Women's Liberation *Is* a Lesbian Plot," Radicalesbians gleefully announced in *Come Out!* "We Are *ALL* Lesbians!"[34]

Betty Friedan had been a star student at Smith College, but she'd gotten married and was fired from a journalism job for being pregnant a second time. Her book *The Feminine Mystique*, published in 1963, was about her own yearning and that of other educated housewives to have a place in what was largely a man's world. The book jarred a nerve. Friedan got tons of mail from women readers, pouring out their sad stories of domestic captivity. "You must start an NAACP for women," one of her readers urged,[35] and Friedan did. The National Organization *for* Women (Friedan chose "for" rather than "of" to make it clear that her organization welcomed male members who were "for women," too) was soon tackling problems such as getting the *New York Times* to stop classifying job ads under "Help Wanted: Male" and "Help Wanted: Female."

Many of the women who became radical feminists, such as Ti-Grace Atkinson, had been awakened to feminism by Friedan's book. But to them, employment inequality was a tiny problem compared with male chauvinist piggery, which they saw everywhere.[36] They soon considered Friedan's organization "hopelessly bourgeois." Friedan considered their embrace of lesbians, whom they welcomed into feminism like long-lost sisters, a horrifying threat to the movement. Lesbians would drive out the "normal" women, "those who wanted equality but also wanted to keep on loving their husbands and children," Friedan said.[37] She told the NOW board that she would not allow the name of Daughters of Bilitis to be included in a list of sponsors for the First Congress to Unite Women. The Lavender Menace was warping the image of the women's movement.[38]

It was impossible for Radicalesbians to be passive in the face of such insults. They congregated for an angry meeting at the East Sixth Street apartment of Ellen Broidy and Linda Rhodes. Rita Mae Brown had heard that NOW was sponsoring another "Congress to Unite Women"—the second one; and, needless to say, not one out lesbian was on the program. "We'll kidnap the Congress," Brown proposed. The boldness of the plan was delicious. They pooled their money to buy forty T-shirts, which they handed over to be "designed" by an artist, Radicalesbian Donna Gottschalk. That evening, Gottschalk took the T-shirts to a graphics studio in Cooper Union; and the next day, with the designed shirts barely dry,[39] she delivered them to Broidy and Rhodes's apartment. Eight other Radicalesbians were there waiting. They poured bottles of lavender dye into the bathtub, threw in the T-shirts, and let them soak.[40]

The last day in April, three dozen Radicalesbians crowded into Barbara

Love's tiny Fifth Avenue digs. They sat on the floor, the radiator, everywhere, and put the finishing touches on the plan.[41]

YOU'RE GOING TO LOVE THE LAVENDER MENACE

The Second Congress to Unite Women was held on May Day 1970, in an auditorium of a junior high school on West Seventeenth Street. Three hundred women sat waiting for the congress to be called to order and the scheduled panel to begin.

Seven fifteen: the lights went out. Women sitting in the dark heard a rebel yell, led by Rita Mae Brown, and then a stampede down the aisles, people running to the front of the auditorium. Then lights again. (One of the Radicalesbians, Michela Griffo, knew where the light switches were.[42]) Rose-colored signs had been plastered on the auditorium walls and in front of the podium. "Superdyke Loves You," "Take A Lesbian To Lunch," "You're Going To Love The Lavender Menace," "Women's Liberation *IS* A Lesbian Plot." Seventeen young women were standing onstage, all looking androgynous, like pretty teenage boys—short haired, clad in bell-bottom blue jeans, smiling happily and defiantly. They wore lavender T-shirts with the words *Lavender Menace* stenciled on their front. (About twenty incognito Lavender Menaces were planted in the audience to help steer a discussion in the right direction.) National Organization for Women officials tried in vain to restore order amid nervous laughter, whooping and hollering, general chaos. "I object to your coming in and taking over this meeting! You're acting like men!" one of the NOW organizers yelled into the microphone.[43]

Rita Mae Brown seized the mic and roared, "This conference won't proceed until we talk about lesbians in the women's movement."[44] A few women got up and stormed out. Most were intrigued by the sauciness of the zap. Karla Jay, one of the Radicalesbians planted in the audience, stood up and yelled, "Yes, yes, sisters! I'm tired of being in the closet because of the women's movement!" Then she ripped off the long-sleeved red blouse she was wearing to reveal a Lavender Menace T-shirt underneath.[45]

The straight women at the Congress listened to what lesbians had to say about how heterosexual women were complicit with the male power structure, how that structure oppressed lesbians, how it oppressed heterosexual women even more. They mostly agreed.[46] The Lavender Menace had put a collective finger on some hard truths. Straight women stood in line at the open mic to pour out their own grievances about the sex roles that limited and dehumanized them, and the rage they felt.[47]

An apoplectic Betty Friedan later speculated that the Lavender Menace T-shirt wearers were CIA-trained operatives, intent on destroying the women's movement.[48]

THE FURY OF THE FURIES

Running consciousness-raising groups and zaps in New York were not enough to hold Rita Mae Brown for long. She was restless. She had grand dreams. Women have to overthrow the present system, she told smitten followers: "The most important thing for the movement is to take over the power of the State. That is the only challenge worth meeting; anything else is a retreat from that responsibility," she proclaimed.[49] She proposed that women organize their own political party.[50] The math said it could be done. Women were a majority in America, and everywhere they were unhappy with male rule. Of course, the work toward overthrow would have to be conducted subtly first, underground. But by 1977—maybe it might take as long as 1979—a woman's party could "break overground."[51]

To begin such serious business, Rita Mae Brown moved to Washington, DC. She would find out how power operated on a large scale, so that when the time came, she'd be ready. Brown haunted the halls of Congress. The only clothes she had to her name, she later wrote, were a pair of white sneakers, a couple pairs of jeans, a few T-shirts, and a peacoat. But she was rich in chutzpah. Her disarming guise got her entrée into the offices of leading government liberals. "What do you think about job security for gay people?" she asked Senator Ted Kennedy. ("He didn't bat an eye.") "I'm an underground reporter, here to see how government works," she told Senator Hubert Humphrey. Caught by the wide-eyed street-urchin charm that Brown cultivated, the Minnesota Democrat let her follow him around for the entire day; he even gave her lunch money because she looked hungry.[52]

But the next step toward Brown's grand goal was unclear. The number of women in Congress in 1970 could be counted on the fingers of one hand.

A few months later, she met Charlotte Bunch, a member of Washington,

DC, Women's Liberation. The twenty-six-year-old Bunch had been born in the mountains of North Carolina and raised in a small town in New Mexico. She was Rita Mae Brown's physical opposite: studious looking, blond, light complected, and soft-spoken; but she was a challenging match in intellectual vigor, a Duke University graduate who was serving as the first woman fellow at the Institute for Policy Studies, a left-wing think tank. She also had a husband, Jim Weeks, a progressive political pundit whom she'd met in her student days through a radical Christian group that held pray-ins at segregated churches. Bunch's four-year-old marriage to Weeks ended six months after Rita Mae Brown's seduction of her over bottles of wine and tantalizing discussions about lesbianism as an ultimate feminist statement.

By the spring of that year the two women had decided to live together—but not in a dyad, which would smack too much of old-fashioned heterosexual marriage. They'd start a collective, they agreed. In the 1960s, Bunch and her husband had been part of a couple of communes that tried to live the principles of sexual equality; and three of Bunch's close friends—Sharon Deevey, Ginny Berson, and Joan Biren—had been in Amazing Grace, a short-lived lesbian collective. Amazing Grace had fallen apart because of squabbles about sharing and privacy, but Deevey, Berson, and Biren were fired up by Bunch and Brown's proposal. They'd rent a couple of houses in DC and invite other lesbians to join them, women who were cutting edge and smart and liked to be a little outrageous.

Twelve women, ages ranging from eighteen to thirty, eventually came into the collective. Most had been movement people—antiwar, abortion rights, civil rights, feminism. Some had been straight before they became radical feminists. All were pledged to living their radical feminism.[53] Two women brought small children along—three of them—who were now to be raised by a dozen mothers.

They'd operate like a Bolshevik cell, they agreed. They rented a third dwelling so that fifteen souls could be more comfortably housed; but they worked together as a single joined-at-the-hip family—with most of the joys and turmoils inherent in such a configuration. All chores shared. All clothes kept in common rooms, belonging to everyone equally. Those in each house sleeping together, on mattresses on the floor. To be independent of men, they'd learn the skills that men had hogged for themselves, like car repair, home repair, and self-defense. Most of the women would have outside jobs to pay the bills (though a few had trust funds or parents who sent checks or ex-husbands who made alimony payments). Their real work would be to find ways to develop a "politics of lesbian-feminism": They'd analyze how heterosexism supports male supremacy. They'd rid the world of patriarchy and remake society to be nonsexist, nonracist, nonimperialist, and socialist. They had no interest in reforming society. It had to be torn down and redone from scratch.

To tell women everywhere who the group was and what they were doing, they put out a newspaper, which they printed in the basement of one of the collective houses.[54] *The Furies*, they called it, after the three Greek goddesses with blood-red eyes and snakes for hair, who took vengeance on Orestes for having killed his mother by driving him crazy. The collective, too, took the name the Furies to honor those goddesses of vengeance who were protectors of womankind. The women of the collective would be inspired by the original Furies to avenge the Chinese women whose feet were bound, the Ibibo women whose clitorises were cut off, and every woman who'd ever been raped physically, economically, or psychologically. They would do it, they promised, by building a movement in America and everywhere that would "effectively stop the violent, sick, oppressive acts of male supremacy."[55]

But that movement they were building must be *lesbian*, the Furies announced. What they meant by "lesbian" was not just a bedroom act but a conscious "political choice." Lesbianism meant escape from male domination; lesbianism undermined the power men exercised over women. "Lesbians are not *born*," the Furies said: Lesbians are women who have *chosen* to refuse to put themselves at the service of men. Women's liberation by itself can't fight male supremacy, the Furies warned in the articles they wrote for their paper: That's because women's liberation alone doesn't grapple with the main problem—which is that heterosexuality feeds male power, which makes patriarchy possible.[56]

On those principles the women of the Furies were in passionate agreement. But there was much on which they disagreed. They rehashed arguments over and over, such as who among them was working class (good), who had class privilege (bad), who was "star-tripping" (vile). Brown and Bunch, as the founders and the most cerebral of the Furies, took on the de facto role of its leaders; but it was impossible to lead a group that detested hierarchy. And familiarity bred contempt. Brown was kicked out for "star-tripping." The Furies collective limped along for about a year. They were torn apart by violent arguments about how best to build utopia. Neverthe-less, the *Furies* newspaper, which was sold at the women's bookstores that were mushrooming across America, inspired thousands of lesbian feminists to form their own collectives in cities, farms, forests, and mountains all over America and in Europe, too.

"LESBIANISM IS WHERE FEMINISM GOES IF IT STAYS ON TRACK"

The *Furies* also inspired scores of other lesbian-feminist newspapers and magazines. Their names proclaimed with in-your-face defiance what they were about: *Dykes and Gorgons, Amazon, Tribad, Pearl Diver, Purple Rage.* Any woman can *choose* to be a lesbian, they all said—and if you're truly com-mitted to feminism, that's the choice you'll make. It became a rallying cry. A popular singer of "womyn's music," Alix Dobkin (one of legions who'd shed their husbands after coming out through the radical feminist move-ment), declared on behalf of all lesbian feminists, "Lesbianism is where feminism goes if it stays on track."[57]

There were probably more lesbians in America in the 1970s than at any time in history. The new lesbians had no connection to old-school lesbians such as the Gab 'n' Java crowd—those who'd thought that if only lesbians would mind their manners, they'd be given a place at the table. The new lesbians didn't want a place at the table—they aimed to trash the whole dining room. They'd fought side by side with leftist men against society's oppression of underdogs; but when they became feminists, they saw that women, too, were underdogs; and men on the Left were as much to blame for it as men on the Right. Refusing to sleep with the oppressor, they be-came newly minted lesbians. The fervor they'd once put into ending racism or the war in Vietnam, they now put into lesbian-feminism.

Thousands of them took their radical lesbian-feminism a giant step further. Men would never change; so instead of spending energy on the impossible task of trying to fix them, why not spend it on making an all-women's world apart from men? They were inspired by the Nation of

Islam's black separatist movement of the 1960s—blacks living in self-sufficiency, cutting the white devil out of their lives altogether. They were also inspired by the back-to-the-land hippie movement and collective living arrangements like the ones in which Charlotte Bunch had lived. They saw nature as "Mother Earth," into whose beautiful bosom they'd escape from the iniquitous struggle to get a bigger piece of the rotten pie in the man-made, patriarchal world. They established communes in California, Oregon, New Mexico, Arizona, upstate New York, Massachusetts, Vermont; also in Michigan, Wisconsin, Minnesota, Missouri; and even in Arkansas, Louisiana, Florida, Tennessee, and Mississippi. "Our feet on the ground. Our heads in the clouds. Our hands on each other," was the motto of lesbian separatists who retreated to women's land.[58]

Lesbian separatists had no interest in the fight for gay and lesbian civil rights.[59] They'd create "Lesbian Nation" instead.[60] They'd avoid interacting in any way with the government, which, they agreed, was nothing but a tool of the patriarchy. They'd settle whatever conflicts might arise among themselves and find ways to circumvent even the "patriarchal legal system."[61] They floated proposals about how to share property and children, and how to be fair to all parties if lovers or a whole commune should split apart. One group of lesbians proposed that Lesbian Nation have its own court, a "Lesbian Fairbody": when lesbians made contracts with one another, they could include a clause saying that in the event of conflict, they'd turn to the Fairbody for a verdict.[62]

The cold reality was different. If they had no civil rights as lesbians, they were powerless when hauled into "the man's" courts. Child custody cases were the most heartbreaking. Even lesbians off in the most remote mountain or forest communes couldn't escape news of the Mary Jo Risher case. The thirty-eight-year-old nurse, described by the media as "a handsome, quietly spoken, former Texas Sunday school teacher"[63] (she'd been PTA president, too), had divorced her husband, Doug Risher, in 1971 because in a drunken rage he'd beat her and broken her nose. He'd also been arrested for drunk driving; and when he got the daughter of a coworker pregnant, he'd procured an illegal abortion for her. Mary Jo Risher had been awarded custody of their three-year-old adopted son at the time of the divorce. Doug Risher hadn't protested.

But when she began living with another woman three years later, he demanded that the child be taken from her and given to him. He'd remarried, he told the Dallas jury of ten men and two women, and he could give the boy a normal family life. "A child shouldn't be used as a guinea pig for someone else's social experiment," his lawyer proclaimed. It worked. The jury members discounted the son's plea to stay with his mother; they ignored evidence that the child was flourishing; and that he was living in a stable, loving family with his mother, her woman partner, and the partner's eleven-year-old daughter. They gave custody of the boy to Doug Risher, despite his history of drunkenness and violence and breaking the law.[64] An appeals court turned down Mary Jo Risher's request for a retrial, and the jury's decision was upheld.[65]

Having no faith in a struggle to procure civil rights, lesbian separatists determined to be creative to avert tragedies such as Mary Jo Risher's. The Wing Family (a separatist commune named after the members' affinity for birds) had settled outside of Northampton, Massachusetts. One Wing Family member was about to give birth. She'd never been married. She'd gone to New York to have sex with an anonymous man because she wanted a baby, but she wouldn't be raising it alone: the Wing Family would share with her the jobs of diapering, reading bedtime stories, putting mercurochrome on scraped knees. The Wings agreed they'd take no chances; they'd keep secret from the hostile "system" what they hoped to do. They were afraid even of a hospital record or a birth certificate. If the patriarchal court could rule that a violent, drunken, philandering lawbreaker was a better parent than law-abiding and conventionally employed Mary Jo Risher, it would certainly not respect the wishes of a bunch of lesbian separatists. The baby would be delivered there on the commune, with the "volunteer mothers" assisting.

They called in a lesbian lawyer, Sue Levinkind, and asked her to witness the woman giving birth and then take signatures from all commune members who were witnesses. In lieu of a birth certificate—which could have alerted the patriarchs that a child had been born out of wedlock, to a lesbian, and was being raised on a separatist commune by a "pretend family"—they asked Levinkind to produce an affidavit that quietly documented the birth, so no one in the future might challenge who the mother was.[66]

·   ·   ·

Many separatists stayed in cities, as the Furies had. The most important thing, they said, was that lesbians cut men out of their lives in every way they could, and that they come home to one another. Urban separatist groups pooled their money and their energy and lived together in a house or adjoining apartments; they struggled to make little lesbian worlds though surrounded by reminders of the patriarchy. Seattle, like other cities of some size, had several lesbian separatist communities. Gorgons were the strict separatists: not even young boys—or lesbians who had anything to do with men or straight women—were allowed to darken their door. The Separatist Gang wasn't as hard-core as Gorgons, but its name alone was a clear don't-mess-with-us threat. So was the Calamity Jane collective, inspired by the cross-dressing, cussing, frontier female gunslinger.[67]

In nearby Olympia, there were another half dozen hard-core separatist houses such as the Emma Goldman collective, Revolting Women, and Raging Women. There were some that were less ferociously militant, too: Nanny Noodles, Millett House, and the Gold Flower Brigade, which got its name from a story of the Chinese Cultural Revolution: a woman complained to her village that her husband had been beating her, the story went. Her comrades seized him with the intent of reeducating him by stoning him to death. But after a few stones hit him on the head, the woman signaled halt. "You scared him enough so he'll never beat me again," she told her comrades. The Gold Flower Brigade liked that story of educating "sexist jerks" to behave. But like most of the other separatist houses, they bought guns and learned how to use them because they were sure the revolution was just around the corner.[68]

The revolution they'd dreamed of never came, and separatist fever broke. Some of the women who'd become lesbians to escape the patriarchy then escaped "lesbian nation"—they returned to heterosexuality. Chirlane McCray, a bright young black woman with deep-set eyes and hair styled in cornrows, had been a junior at Wellesley College in 1974, when the black lesbian-feminist Combahee River Collective was formed. She joined, and along with Audre Lorde, Gloria Hull, Cheryl Clarke, and Barbara Smith—the most salient figures in the black lesbian-feminist movement—helped write the group's manifesto, the "Combahee River Collective Statement." Its sentiments were consistent with most radical lesbian-feminist thought of the era, calling for "the destruction of the political-economic systems of capitalism, imperialism, and patriarchy."[69] In 1979 McCray, a serious writer now, penned an article for *Essence*, a mass circulation magazine for young black women. The article was groundbreaking—the first one ever written for a black magazine by an openly black lesbian. "I Am a Lesbian" the title stated baldly, and in the piece itself, McCray called herself "fortunate because I discovered my preference for women early, before getting locked in traditional marriage and having children."[70]

McCray went on to become a speechwriter for New York's first African American mayor, David Dinkins. In 1991 she fell in love with Dinkins's white aide, who'd been an avid supporter of the Communist Sandinistas of Nicaragua. The aide was Bill de Blasio, and they married three years later. McCray became the "first lady" of New York when de Blasio was elected mayor in 2013. What's left of her radical lesbian-feminist days is that she and her husband are strong supporters of lesbian and gay civil rights and especially of New York's same-sex marriage law.

Other lesbian-feminist stalwarts of the seventies remained lesbians, though not separatists. Corky Culver had lived on North Forty of Florida, outside of Gainesville—forty acres of lesbian land dotted with pine trees and oaks, an Amazon utopia. The lesbian separatists who lived there dug wells, built jerry-rigged houses with renegade plumbing, danced naked in the full moon, and sang lesbian songs to promote harmony. The politics they discussed in their consciousness-raising sessions was sexual politics. Culver had been a new PhD when she came to North Forty, but she had no interest in a regular academic career. She wanted to be a thinker and a writer and "live off the grid and out of the patriarchy." At North Forty she could do all of that. But as she and the other women aged, the Amazon life came to seem less attractive. Culver's anxieties for the future caused her to check on how much money she'd get from Social Security when she was too old to grow sprouts for a living or have a little jam factory on the property. She found she hadn't worked enough quarters at jobs that would qualify her for a monthly check from the government when she was old. None of the women at North Forty had. They all left, "ended up getting jobs, credit cards, health insurance, wanting central heating and air-conditioning."[71]

•   •   •

So, what did it all mean, and how did any of it advance the lot of the les-bian? Some who'd retreated to lesbian-feminist communes later came to regard that time of their life as cocooning in a small, secure hideaway—but only until they were ready to sprout wings. Anna Schlecht arrived in Olympia in 1976, backpack slung over one shoulder and guitar slung over the other—an eighteen-year-old hippie from Madison, Wisconsin. Gold Flower Brigade was her safe haven. She worked off and on as a carpenter, helped out at the Northwest Women's Music Festival, and edited *Matrix*, a radical lesbian newsletter. The charm of a lesbian ghetto for the young Schlecht was that it protected the women from the patriarchy outside—but, as she and others came to realize, it also walled them in. It was a bad gamble, she concluded, living a marginalized existence for the sake of an elusive revolution. But her years at Gold Flower Brigade were only part one of a longer story.

She left Gold Flower Brigade in the 1980s, in pursuit of a piece of the pie. To her that meant a career, a home of her own, and also a claim on America for civil rights as a sexual minority. She got a couple of college degrees and then became the head of the city of Olympia's Housing Pro-gram, through which she instituted affordable LGBT elder housing. She also led victorious fights for city ordinances against hate crimes and job discrimination and for domestic partnership recognition—those civil rights that Frank Kameny had called crucial for "first-class American citizenship."

Charlotte Bunch, thinking of her time as a Fury, has described separat-ism as a necessary step to allow lesbians to build strength and a sense of unity as a people.[72] Ex-Furies were feverishly productive to that end, in the vanguard as creators of what was called "women's culture"—which really meant *lesbian* culture. Ginny Berson and Jennifer Woodul helped found Olivia Records, which popularized a whole new genre of "women's music." The audience Olivia built made possible massive "women's music festivals," women-only retreats that brought thousands of bare-breasted amazons to forests and mountains in unlikely states such as Michigan, Ne-braska, Georgia, and Pennsylvania.[73] Coletta Reid founded Diana Press, one of the first lesbian-feminist publishing houses. Helaine Harris and Lee Schwing started Women in Distribution, the main distributer for all the many "women's book publishers" that were cropping up during the 1970s and 1980s and supplying the many "women's bookstores." Photographer

Joan E. Biren (JEB) captured stunning images of the movement as it grew. Charlotte Bunch, who remained a lesbian though her role as Brown's lover didn't last long, wrote seminal essays of lesbian-feminist theory. She also brought the sexual-politics insights of the Furies into the larger world. Bunch founded UN Women, a United Nations body that promotes gender equality and empowerment of women everywhere—no more "bound feet and cut-off clitorises."

Rita Mae Brown never did manage to launch a women's party that would overthrow the patriarchy. But her autobiographical novel *Rubyfruit Jungle*, which came out soon after she left the Furies, vies with the morbid and depressing *Well of Loneliness* as the most famous lesbian novel ever written. *Rubyfruit Jungle* presents the lesbian as a gorgeous, cheerful, and triumphant hero. It became a cross-over book, selling well over a million copies, to straights as well as lesbians.

PART 5

A PLACE AT THE TABLE

Chapter 15

DRESSING FOR DINNER

THE 1972 DEMOCRATIC NATIONAL CONVENTION

Six feet tall, with a scraggly white-blond beard and ponytail, Bruce Voeller looked at first glance like a radical. He was not. The thirty-eight-year-old had been a PhD evolutionary biologist and a professor at Rockefeller University. When he finally admitted to himself that he was homosexual, Voeller resigned from his prestigious position to work full-time on the gay movement. He'd also had a wife, but after his self-revelation, he asked her for a divorce and was fighting a prolonged and bloody court battle because she wanted to restrict his visits with his three children. He was a bad influence, she claimed: he'd been an early member of the New York Gay Activists Alliance and had taken his children with him to meetings at the Firehouse. Voeller had seen nothing to hide about the Gay Activists Alliance and its fight for gay rights. But by 1972, he was growing increasingly unsure himself about GAA's more radical members who'd begun to overrun the organization, with whose far-left sympathies he had no sympathy at all.

Voeller was at the time the head of GAA's "State and Federal Government Committee." (The following year, in the midst of his domestic strife, he would briefly become GAA's president.) On behalf of his committee he'd written presidential candidate George McGovern, asking about his position on gay rights. To Voeller's astonished pleasure, McGovern responded that "certain assumptions of the majority concerning homosexuals have been used as a rationale for harassment and denial of elemental civil liberties." If he were elected president, McGovern declared, he would put a stop to that. He would pledge "the full moral and legal authority of the presidency for restoring and guaranteeing first-class citizenship rights for homosexually oriented individuals." It was the most promising statement by a politician that Voeller had ever read.[1]

There were about five hundred gay groups around the country by that time. Voeller contacted them all and asked them to send "two of your ablest people" to a "strategy meeting." (He underscored the number, fearing to be overrun by old GLF-types.) They would plan how gays and lesbians could make their needs known at the Democratic National Convention in Miami where, he hoped, George McGovern would get his party's nomination.[2] To assure that activists from the Midwest and other parts of the country understood that the strategy meeting would not be just a "New York thing," Voeller sought the cosponsorship of the Chicago Gay Alliance. The meeting would be held in Chicago, they agreed, on the long weekend of Lincoln's birthday, February 11 through 13. Voeller placed on the agenda those issues that he thought mattered most—such as how to bring attention and power to the gay community by making political candidates know that there's a gay vote and that they could benefit from gay endorsements, and how to get gay people elected to political office.[3]

In the midst of a driving snowstorm, gay and lesbian activists from eighty-five different organizations carpooled to Chicago from the Midwest and east, or they flew in from the west and south. A Chicago Gay Alliance member had arranged for a meeting space at an almost-abandoned church—the Armitage Avenue United Methodist, not far from where twelve thousand antiwar protestors had descended on the Democratic National Convention in 1968. The church had no heating and half its windows were broken. It was so cold that every sentence the participants spoke produced its own little puff of a cartoon bubble. If they got hungry, food had to be brown-bagged in from a little grocery store across the street.[4] But they were too intent on their purpose and their squabbles to complain about the paucity of creature comforts.

There were more radicals than Voeller had hoped to see there (including his old nemesis, Jim Fouratt).[5] They wanted to argue about whether their demands should include an end to all imperialist wars or the abolition of age of consent laws. Somebody proposed a resolution to demand "repeal of all legislative provisions that restrict the sex or number of persons entering into a marriage unit, and the extension of legal benefits to all persons who cohabit regardless of sex or numbers." Nut stuff, Voeller thought; he was relieved that Frank Kameny was there to lead the fight against it. If they could avoid dissipating their energies on foolish or impossible goals, they had the potential to do what Kameny had hoped his short-lived North American Conference of Homophile Organizations might do, before it was taken over and killed by radicals in 1970.[6]

The meeting continued through the following freezing day, the disagreements heating up the icy room. (The sniping was so incendiary that at the next meeting, in DC, the group voted to revise the minutes of the Chicago meeting "to remove character assassinations and other irrelevancies."[7]) Eventually they hammered out a "Gay Rights Platform" that most could agree on. They would drop it on the Democratic National Convention in Miami Beach's July heat, they decided. They'd make it the basis for their demand of a plank in the Democratic Party platform. The plank would say that the party was opposed to discrimination of homosexuals in employment, housing, public accommodations, loans and insurance, armed services, and immigration. It would call for the release of all gays who'd been locked in mental institutions or imprisoned for "sex crimes" where there was no victim. And it would demand repeal of all laws regarding private sex acts.[8] Frank Kameny proposed that to make it clear they were speaking for Americans all over the country, and weren't just a little group of homosexuals from New York, California, and DC, they should call themselves the National Coalition of Gay Organizations.

Steve Hoglund, from the Washington, DC, Gay Activists Alliance, proposed that the National Coalition of Gay Organizations also demand fair representation of gays and lesbians among the delegates to the Democratic National Convention. Fair representation had been written into the rules of the McGovern Commission on the Democratic Party, he said, and he read from the rule book that he'd brought in his jacket pocket: state parties were told to "overcome the effects of past discrimination by affirmative steps to encourage minority group participation in reasonable relationship

to the group's presence in the state." Well, hadn't Kinsey said that 10 percent of America was homosexual? "Let the Kinsey statistics be our guide!"
Hoglund proclaimed.[9] Until the Chicago meeting, few dared think it: of
course out gays and lesbians had a right to be represented among those
who would nominate their party's candidate for president of the United
States.

Jeff Orth, an Ohio State University junior and chair of the school's
GAA chapter, went home and put his name forward at the state caucus.
Caucus participants faithfully followed the rules of the McGovern Commission. Women, ethnic minorities, young people were all voted in as Ohio
delegates. A twenty-one-year-old woman by the name of Mrs. Kathy Wilch
was even elected to be on the party's platform committee. But not one out
homosexual was chosen. Jeff Orth complained to the media. "Homosexuals are the nation's third largest minority—after women and blacks. The
Democratic Party has to comply with its own rules for picking delegates."
His organization would be taking legal action, he threatened. They'd get
ACLU attorneys to help.[10]

Gay agitation didn't get many gays elected as delegates in 1972. But
it did serve to put state caucuses on notice: At the Democratic National
Convention in 1976, Orth and sixty-three other out gays and lesbians were
chosen to be part of their state delegations.

During the days of the 1972 convention in Miami Beach, the radical gays
and lesbians who'd come to protest camped out in Flamingo Park together
with a motley crew that included Yippies, Zippies, Jesus freaks, and Vietnam
Veterans Against the War. They pitched tents, burned flags, smoked pot,
and skinny-dipped in the public pool. Chief of Police Rocky Pomerance
didn't want a repeat of the 1968 Democratic Convention in Chicago,
where there'd been 680 arrests and 1,381 injuries. He told his officers to
be tempered. They were. During the entire Democratic Convention, there
were only two arrests and two injuries in and around Flamingo Park.[11]
But the more remarkable action—certainly as far as gays and lesbians were
concerned—went on inside the Miami Beach Convention Center.

Two weeks before the Democratic National Convention, the Democratic Platform Committee met at DC's Mayflower Hotel to write the
official statement of what the Democratic Party stood for. The platform

committee was not timid. Members told the delegates for George Wallace, a Democratic presidential hopeful and the segregationist governor of Alabama, to shut up. They voted 70 to 27 in favor of a plank declaring that school busing was a "tool to accomplish desegregation." (In doing so, they scoffed at nationwide polls that said that 70 percent of Americans were opposed to "forced busing."[12]) They told the gun lobby to shut up, too, and voted for a plank that would outlaw Saturday night specials. They were utterly intrepid in their vote for a highly controversial plank to abolish capital punishment. But when discussion was called for on the gay rights plank, one delegate voiced the worry of most: "Any apparent outright approval of homosexuality would only be used by the Republicans in the fall," he declared. The plank to prohibit discrimination on the basis of sexual orientation was rejected by a vote of 54 to 34.[13] ·

The Gay Liberation Front announced that unless the platform committee reversed itself, the group would stage a kiss-in, ten thousand gays-strong, right outside Convention Hall on the first night of the convention.[14] The more tempered Frank Kameny informed the media that the National Coalition of Gay Organizations would be meeting "to formulate plans and strategy for the Miami Beach Convention showdown."[15] The kiss-in didn't come off, though the National Coalition of Gay Organizations held a more dignified night-long vigil in front of the Convention Hall—dozens of candles illuming the balmy Miami night, as delegates, lurching back to their hotel rooms at one or two in the morning after an excess of food and beer, peered quizzically at the solemn men and women who held them.[16]

By then, Steve Hoglund, the GAA member from DC who'd urged that gay people demand 10 percent representation on state delegations, had discovered there was a way to challenge a platform committee decision. Convention rules said a rejected plank could be submitted to the whole convention as a minority report if 10 percent of the platform committee would endorse it.[17] About 30 percent of the platform committee had voted for the gay plank. The National Coalition of Gay Organizations had a right to petition for time on the convention floor. An ecstatic Frank Kameny told reporters, "It will be the first time we will have the opportunity to make our case clearly and frankly to the American people. We have nothing to be ashamed of, and we have nothing to hide."[18]

But McGovern's operatives, believing there was something to hide, were livid. The convention was going to be televised. All of America would see that there were homosexuals in the Democratic Party, and that they were taken seriously enough to be permitted to wrangle at the Democrats' most important national meeting. The operatives tried to convince the gays not to do it.[19] But National Coalition of Gay Organizations members were already busy delivering copies of their "minority report" to all 3,016 convention delegates.[20] A dozen New York Gay Activists Alliance members also made themselves into lobbyists, going to the hotel-room meetings of the various state caucuses to plead the cause of the gay rights plank. They didn't have much luck—delegates listened to them stony-faced, at best.

South Dakota was the last delegation on GAA member Ronald Gold's list. But McGovern aides had gotten wind of GAA's peregrinations and were especially worried that the press would show up just when a wild-eyed activist was talking gay rights to the delegates from George McGovern's home state. When Gold arrived at the South Dakota delegation's meeting room, two burly McGovern aides were waiting for him. They lifted him by the elbows and dragged him kicking and screaming down the hall and down the stairs, where they relieved him of his flyers featuring the statement McGovern had written months before, promising that if he were elected president he'd guarantee first-class citizenship to homosexuals.[21]

The man the coalition chose to present the gay rights "minority report" to the convention delegates was Jim Foster. Foster, thirty-eight years old, bald and with a big, dark "gay clone" mustache, had turned to gay activism after being mercilessly witch hunted and discharged from the army.[22] He was the son of Republicans and had graduated from Brown University before his military stint. Unwilling to go home again, he settled in San Francisco in 1959. Foster was canny and confident, and he was bent on making gays a force to be reckoned with by those aspiring to political office in the Bay Area. He'd been credited with getting Dianne Feinstein elected to the board of supervisors in 1969. The year before the Democratic Convention, he teamed up with Del Martin and Phyllis Lyon to turn the Society for Individual Rights's political committee, which he chaired, into the Alice B. Toklas Memorial Democratic Club. Through the Alice club, Foster was showing San Francisco the power of gay political muscle.

Foster's reputation, at least among gays and lesbians, preceded him at the convention. They knew he'd been elected a delegate to the Democratic National Convention because he'd managed to get George McGovern's name at the top of the California primary ballot. Foster had learned that California election law said that the first candidate to file the requisite number of petition signatures with the secretary of state receives the coveted top-of-the-ballot spot. To give his candidate a jump start, Foster enlisted members of both the Alice B. Toklas club and the Society for Individual Rights. Petitions in hands, they descended on all the San Francisco Bay Area gay bars at one minute after midnight on the day the nominating process opened. They obtained thousands of signatures, hours before their opponents got a first signature. It was widely acknowledged that because of McGovern's gay supporters, his name was placed at the top of the California primary ballot—and that it helped him win the state by a comfortable margin.[23] Foster had worked so hard for his man because he'd been thrilled by McGovern's statement that he'd use the "full legal and moral authority" of his presidency to make homosexuals first-class citizens. He let himself dream for a little while that McGovern delegates might help their candidate keep his promise.

McGovern's managers were dismayed that Foster would be allowed to speak in the convention hall, but relieved when he wasn't called up to the podium until five o'clock in the morning on July 12. The plenary session had started ten hours earlier. Three delegates had already passed out from exhaustion, and dozens dozed in the aisles.[24] True, the TV cameras were still rolling, but who was still watching? Walter Cronkite, covering the convention for CBS, said he heard a "groan from the platform" when Minority Report #8, which Cronkite called "the Gay Lib plank," was introduced.[25]

"These are not conservative or radical issues—these are human issues," Jim Foster intoned solemnly over a nattering, muttering drone that didn't cease throughout his speech. Gays and lesbians were not begging for understanding or tolerance, Foster proclaimed. Rather, they'd come to the Democratic National Convention "to affirm our right to participate in the life of this country on an equal basis with every citizen." Democrats, for their own good, had better understand that. Homosexuals vote! The drone kept on, and Foster seemed to be struggling not to let his voice sound tired. "Twenty million gay men and women are looking for a political party that is responsive to their needs," he warned his audience. He must surely have understood that after the decisive defeat of the gay plank at the hands of the platform committee, it wasn't likely that his minority report would sway the delegates. But his purpose was to cheer gay America as much as it was to admonish straight America. "We are here. We will not be still!" he concluded resoundingly. "We will not go away until the ultimate goal of gay liberation is realized: that goal being that all people can live in the peace, the freedom, and the dignity of who they are."[26]

Foster's speech had taken ten minutes. The National Coalition of Gay Organizations had been given twenty minutes to present its minority report. Though only a small fraction of the group's members were lesbian, the coalition gave the rest of its allotted minutes to Madeline Davis, a zaftig earth mother–type with long raven hair. Davis was a founder and vice president of the Mattachine Society in the Buffalo, New York, area. Though she was thirty-two years old and had marched on Albany with the Gay Activists Alliance, and had even lobbied the New York Legislature for gay rights, she'd never registered to vote—until Buffalo gays and lesbians, encouraged by the National Coalition of Gay Organizations to elect lesbian and gay delegates to the Democrat Convention, said they'd campaign for her if she'd register. She did and won.[27] Madeline Davis stepped up to the microphone at 5:10 a.m.

As Foster had, she reminded the delegates that there were twenty million Americans like her out there, and they voted. Homosexuals were demanding an end to their status as "the untouchables in American society," she informed her weary listeners. She appealed to their emotions by telling them that gays and lesbians "suffered the gamut of repression, from being totally ignored to having our heads smashed and our blood spilled in the streets." She appealed to their decency by asking them to reaffirm the American tradition that all citizens have a right to privacy, and that all human beings deserve basic civil rights.[28] Her audience was unmoved. The mental gymnastics required to reconcile the notion of "tradition" with the notion of homosexuality was too great. Exhausted, they just wanted to get back to their hotel rooms and get some shut-eye.

But there was more. Convention rules gave the majority side the last word. The vice chair of the platform committee, an advertising copywriter by profession, got the microphone at 5:20 a.m. It was *Mrs.* (as she wanted to be called) Kathy Wilch from Findlay, Ohio—the twenty-one-year-old woman who'd been elected to the delegation that Jeff Orth, the gay Ohio State student, had vainly hoped to get on. At the Mayflower Hotel meeting, Mrs. Wilch had argued that the gay plank had to go down for the sake of "political expediency." Gays weren't popular, and a president who supported them wouldn't get elected. It was she who was chosen to explain to the delegates the platform committee's rejection of the gay rights plank—but not in her own words. A lawyer on the staff of the committee had written her speech for her. She shouted it out to her convention audience and to whatever night owls were watching on TV. The gay rights plank would be a wedge! Next would come the repeal of all the laws against prostitution, pimping, and pandering, even the repeal of the Mann Act, which prohibits white slavery. Gay rights would destroy the laws that protect the young, the innocent, and the weak. Age of consent laws would be struck down and young boys would be sexually molested by grown men.[29] At this point, the Reverend Troy Perry and seven other gays sitting with him jumped up and raised clenched fists, chanting, "No! No! No!"[30]

"If we approve this plank, we would invite the ridicule of the nation!" Mrs. Wilch concluded with tearful passion.[31]

When a voice vote was called, the exhausted delegates roused themselves. The roar of *no* made it unequivocally clear that as far as the Democratic Party was concerned, gays and lesbians would remain the untouchables of American society.[32]

Gay radicals who'd infiltrated the convention hall had expected nothing different. They'd already made lavish plans for how to respond: three days of "National Shame" protests with picketers "wearing lavender and black armbands of Gay Rage, stationed at all the party headquarters across the county."[33] But now, two gay men in purple T-shirts emblazoned with the logo GAY POWER! were too enraged to wait for the National Shame protests. They ran to an aisle and staged a kissing bout, to demonstrate their contempt for the Democratic National Convention.[34]

Even without the kissing zap, simply that Madeline Davis and Jim Foster had been allowed to speak was—as Mrs. Wilch feared—enough to make the Democratic Party bleed votes. Marvin Griffin, Georgia's former governor who'd been a lifelong Southern Democrat, announced he'd be voting Republican this time around: "I am not a member of the Gay Liberation

movement . . . I am not a hippie or a Yippie . . . The Democratic Party
Convention has something for everybody but me," he complained indig-
nantly.[35] And it wasn't just Southern Democrats who'd been repelled. Since
their inception, labor unions had always endorsed the Democratic candidate for president; but not long after the convention, George Meany, head
of the AFL-CIO, told a group of steelworkers that his powerful federation of trade unions wouldn't be endorsing anyone for the 1972 election.
Because, he said, "The Democratic Party has been taken over by people
named Jack who look like Jills and smell like Johns."[36]

Yet despite the clear rejection of the gay plank, the vituperative rhetoric, and the defections, something important had taken place in the wee
hours of July 12 that made a dent in American consciousness. "I was a bit
shocked about the homosexual giving a speech," Mrs. Theda Brown, delegate from Hutchinson, Kansas, told an Associated Press reporter. "It was a
good speech, but it did shock me. I think it shocked us all," she said, reeling
with confusion and ambivalence.[37] Shocked, perplexed, resentful, or sleepy,
the delegates in the convention hall and those who'd been watching from
their living rooms saw homosexuals on a national political stage. It would
no longer be possible to imagine that such a thing could never happen.

OFF THE STREETS AND INTO THE BOARDROOMS

Bruce Voeller had had a brief romance with the noisy protests and democratic decision-making of the Gay Activists Alliance when he first joined
the organization; but by the time he was elected its president, in 1973,
he was thoroughly disillusioned. He charged GAA with the same chaos,
obstructionism, and silly downward mobility that the GAA founders had
leveled against the Gay Liberation Front three years earlier. He tried, to
no avail, to get GAA to set up a board of directors that would make the
important decisions.[38] He hated the hours of debate devoted to spending
a few dollars on something necessary, like getting the Firehouse cleaned
up. He hated GAA's "blue-denim elitism": "People who come in without
a beard or in slacks or a sport shirt—let alone a tie—are made to feel like
outsiders," he groused.[39] "Homofascist!" one of GAA's most vocal radicals, John O'Brien, called him.[40] "Trolls," he called O'Brien and the other

radical GAA members;[41] and on October 4, after only a few months in office, Voeller resigned. He would start a new organization, he'd decided.

The day before Voeller handed in his resignation, an article had appeared in the *New York Times* about Dr. Howard Brown. Dr. Brown was already well known to the press and the public because he'd been the New York City Health Commissioner. What wasn't known was that in 1967 *New York Times* columnist Drew Pearson had planned to write an exposé on high-placed homosexuals in the Lindsay administration, and he'd intended to begin with Dr. Brown.[42] The only way to avoid disgrace, Brown had thought, was to resign. But six years later, the former health commissioner let himself be outed in the same newspaper. A front-page *New York Times* headline on October 3, 1973, declared, "Ex-City Official Says He's a Homosexual."[43]

Dr. Brown was a friend of Bruce Voeller, and had even testified in court about Voeller's stability and good influence as a parent when Voeller fought for better visitation rights with his children.[44] And now Dr. Brown and his homosexuality were front-page news: Voeller saw that here was a way to get major media attention for the organization he was starting. Brown agreed to help. About two weeks after the *New York Times* announced Brown's homosexuality, he and Voeller called a press conference. As Voeller was sure it would, the *New York Times* published another headline about the doctor—and Voeller's fledgling organization: "Homosexual Civil Rights Group is Announced by Ex-City Aide."[45] The fattest wallets couldn't buy such good publicity.

The group would be called the National Gay Task Force,[46] Brown and Voeller told the *Times* reporter (who made sure to note the doctor's dark blue suit, British-gentry-style tie, and Lambda button on his lapel). The National Gay Task Force would be the coordinator of all the 850 (they exaggerated a bit) gay organizations in the country. They'd be hiring a professional staff of five, Brown and Voeller told the reporter, and they were seeking "suitable office space." (No converted firehouse for this group.) The two men brought along to the interview the "communications director" of the National Gay Task Force, Ronald Gold, the former *Variety* reporter who, like Voeller, had become disillusioned with GAA's street drama. Gold explained that "Gay liberation has become a nine-to-five job." There was no room for amateurs. The National Gay Task Force would be run by professionals who knew how to work within the system.

Nathalie Rockhill, her hair shoulder length, her dark-framed round glasses giving her the look of a bright little owl, was the lone woman at the October 16 press conference. She was introduced as NGTF's national coordinator. The year before, she'd been the vice president of GAA, but she'd been staying away from more and more GAA meetings because she viewed them increasingly as unproductive shouting matches. She felt sorry for Voeller, who had to lead those meetings. But on the night of October 4, Ronald Gold called Rockhill to say, "Nath, Bruce quit! What are we going to do? How are we going to get him to change his mind?" "Forget it!" she said. "Now we can start that national organization Bruce has been talking about."[47]

Voeller and Brown also told reporters that a National Gay Task Force board had already been established, and they introduced one of its members, Reverend Robert Carter, a Jesuit priest and a professor at the Jesuit Theological Seminary, to show the caliber of people who would be making policy for the National Gay Task Force. NGTF would be run by the board of directors, like a corporation, they said. NGTF would represent a new concept in gay organizations: Off the street and into the boardrooms—and courthouses and Congress, too.[48]

Frank Kameny had dreamed of such things in the decade before. But now—thanks to what the radicals had started—"gay" had become a household word and a critical mass of gays and lesbians from "higher" social strata had been exiting the closet. What Kameny had once envisioned had become feasible. When Voeller invited Frank Kameny to be on the NGTF board, he accepted immediately.

Some gays who were just getting into the movement at the time, such as twenty-five-year-old John D'Emilio, who'd eventually become a major gay historian, saw the establishment of the National Gay Task Force as a "sad indicator" that the radicalism and militancy that drew him and many young people to the gay movement was dying.[49] But to other gays and lesbians, who'd been chagrined by rowdy street battles and the antics of zaps, the movement was just beginning.

Voeller's group was called the *National* Gay Task Force because he hoped to get gays and lesbians in Duluth and Durham to feel united with gays and lesbians in New York and Los Angeles, and vice versa. The challenge to the young NGTF was to find a way to show some dramatic and definitive national clout—like getting a congressional bill passed that would protect gay and lesbian rights all over the country.

With her brassy Dolly Levi style and her trademark electric blue or raging red wide-brimmed hats, Bella Abzug could've been mistaken for a drag queen. She was a New York City politician and Greenwich Village resident who'd been elected to the US House of Representatives in 1970. She knew where her votes came from. She'd gotten wild cheers and standing ovations when she campaigned in the gay spots. Her campaign stop at the Continental Baths had become legendary. Her gay and lesbian constituency wrote checks and voted in a bloc for her. She owed them one.

In spring 1974, New York gay activists were again making one of their perennially disappointing attempts to get the city council to approve a gay rights ordinance. Abzug considered the dramatic value of bypassing the local struggle. "It's time to take action on a national level to remove the option from local bigots, in the same way that black civil rights were guaranteed through federal laws," she declared. She got closeted New York congressman Ed Koch (the future mayor) to cosponsor the "Equality Act of 1974." It would be a federal bill that would ban discrimination on the basis of "sexual or affectional preference"—a good phrase to avoid the loaded term "homosexuality."

"Rights Struggle Shifts to Capitol Hill," the national gay newspaper the *Advocate*—which had long been fulminating against what publisher Dick Michaels saw as the childish antics of radical gays—announced deliriously.[50] But while the Equality Act was a brave gesture, it was little more than that. It never even got out of committee. The next year, NGTF pushed Abzug and Koch to try again.

This time twenty-two other Congress members agreed to be their cosponsors on an extended bill, called the "Civil Rights Amendment of 1975." Bruce Voeller took on the job of organizing a press conference on Capitol Hill, in the Gold Room of the Rayburn Office Building. He invited the heavies who supported the bill, such as the American Civil Liberties Union, which had refused to take Dale Jennings's case in the fifties but had transmogrified in the sixties into zealous gay defenders; and the National Organization for Women, which had become avid advocates of lesbian and gay rights, despite the organization's still-recalcitrant founder.[51] Nathalie Rockhill was invited to sit next to Congresswoman Abzug and introduce her while reporters stood at the ready.[52]

Ten percent of Americans are gay, the congresswoman said. Her bill would extend the 1964 and 1968 civil rights acts to protect them in housing, jobs, federally assisted programs, public accommodations, and education. It was a "hate crimes" bill, too, stipulating penalties for anyone who harmed a person because of his or her sexual preference. Into a bank of microphones, Bella Abzug elaborated that the bill was needed to "guarantee that all individuals, regardless of differences, are entitled to share in the fruits of society."[53] (Gay wits later teased her about her Freudian-slip word choice.)

Of course, the bill didn't pass. Not even Nathalie Rockhill, who was so thrilled to be chosen to introduce its author, expected it to.[54] Nineteen seventy-five was too close to the years when gay people had been universally regarded as pariahs. As nationally syndicated Hearst newspaper columnist Marianne Means observed in her column, the present Congress was "reform-minded," but there were limits: few Congress members were "ready to embrace the homosexual cause."[55] More time needed to pass. Abzug and her supporters realized that, too. They introduced the bill knowing it was destined to fail this time around. But, as Means wrote, "For the very first time, twenty-four congressmen and women agreed to openly support equal rights for gays. That indicates that the gays have made considerable progress in their fight for acceptance."[56] It was a message that Americans, homosexual and heterosexual, in big cities and small, couldn't ignore.

Voeller put together a twenty-two-person board of directors, with Dr. Howard Brown at the head and as many professional types as he could find. But to blunt any criticism from the detested radicals in GAA, he made the board "LGBT" before LGBT was a concept. One founding board member, Bebe Scarpi, was a transvestite (she preferred "drag queen") whom Voeller had met in GAA and who'd also been a member of STAR, the Street Transvestite Action Revolutionaries. She was a credible member of the NGTF, though: Scarpi had recently graduated from Queens College, where she'd founded an organization called Gay Community, and she'd started her career as a high school teacher. Scarpi looked very much like a proper middle-class lady. (She would eventually become the first transgender person in America to be a school principal.) Voeller sought out credible lesbians, too. He invited Barbara Gittings to be on the board. He also invited women who'd been outspoken lesbian feminists: Sidney Abbott and Barbara Love, who'd recently coauthored *Sappho Was a Right-On Woman*, one of the first books about lesbians that didn't portray them as odd girls and twilight lovers; Frances Doughty, a young classics scholar who was writing on Sappho; Betty Powell, a black lesbian who taught at Brooklyn College in the school of education and was working on a doctorate; and Meryl Friedman, head of the Gay Teachers Association. It took them no time at all to form a lesbian caucus and demand that the board be 50 percent lesbian; and within six months, it was.[57]

Voeller didn't object. He may have been a genuine feminist; or he may have thought—as Frank Kameny and Jack Nichols had—that a way to short-circuit the image of homosexuality as unnatural sex acts between men was to push a presentable-looking lesbian out front. Whatever the case, Voeller definitely wanted women in prominent places in his organization. He was happy to hire high school English teacher Ginny Vida, who'd been a GAA vice president, to be NGTF media director and lead national protests against homophobic images on TV and in the movies. (On the popular series *Marcus Welby, M.D.*, kindly Dr. Welby, played by Robert Young, had just helped catch a homosexual junior high school science teacher who'd raped a fourteen-year-old boy in an episode called "The Outrage"; an NBC movie, *Born Innocent*, had featured a bunch of reform school girls raping a newbie in the shower with a mop handle; and Angie Dickinson as Sergeant Pepper Anderson on *Police Woman* had collared lesbian murderers.) But when Nathalie Rockhill resigned as national coordinator and legislative director in 1975 to go to law school, Voeller lost an important lesbian staff member.

He thought of Jean O'Leary as her replacement. He'd often been annoyed with O'Leary during the months he was president of GAA. When she'd attacked the performing drag queens at the 1973 Gay Pride Rally, Voeller had responded that he didn't hear her attacking butch dykes who dressed in men's clothes. He didn't like her criticism that GAA spent too much time defending gay men's right to have sex in trucks at the wharves, either. Why wasn't she raising a fuss about heterosexual lovers' lanes instead? "Sauce for the goose!" he'd said.[58] But despite their prickly contretemps, he thought her the most presentable and articulate lesbian committed to the cause of liberation that he'd met in New York. She was just what he needed for his fledgling organization.

She said yes to her old sparring partner because there weren't a lot of paying jobs for full-time lesbian activists. Nor were there a lot of homosexual organizations that could give O'Leary a chance to display her talents on a national stage and extend her reach into mainstream politics. It was a good fit. O'Leary, who'd been a PhD student in Organizational Development at Yeshiva University, had an admiral's shrewdness for strategizing. She planned ways to organize in the electoral districts of New York so that NGTF could promise favored candidates the gay vote. She drew up a five-year plan for NGTF: There'd be seven regions, offices in every state.[59] She knew how NGTF could effectively survey all the 1976 presidential candidates to determine their stands on gay rights. She came up with the idea of a campaign to get delegates who'd be going to the 1976 Democratic Convention to pledge in advance that they'd support planks for gay rights and the repeal of sodomy laws. (Six hundred delegates agreed to take the pledge).[60] Also, she and Voeller managed to coexist in the same small office and bury any impulse to squabble. When she told him she'd like to be named coexecutive director, he thought it a fine idea.

O'Leary seldom had reason to look back on her brief flirtation with lesbian separatism or her time in GAA. It felt like she'd entered the big leagues now. The secretary of the American Bar Association had written NGTF to say that the ABA was urging state legislatures to repeal sodomy laws. The House of Delegates of the American Medical Association wrote to say they, too, were supporting repeal.[61] NBC, which had produced the movie about the lesbian shower rape, and was also home to Angie Dickinson's Sergeant Pepper Anderson, capitulated; the network president and vice presidents met with Voeller and members of the NGTF board and pledged "positive gay images to appear in all areas" of the network's programming:[62] NBC also promised there'd be no discrimination against gay and lesbian employees or in hiring. AT&T had made that promise the year before. Clearly there were more effective ways to win rights than setting off sirens at Democratic fund-raisers or dressing in duck suits to shame the homophobes, O'Leary thought.

·　　·　　·

By now other "big-league" national organizations were cropping up. Lambda Legal Defense and Education Fund, founded by lawyer Bill Thom who wanted it to be a sort of gay and lesbian NAACP, began operations in New York a month after the inception of NGTF. (Nathalie Rockhill was named to its board in 1974. Lambda Legal, too, was anxious to present a cogendered face to the world.) Steve Endean, who'd gotten Minneapolis to adopt a gay rights ordinance when he was still a student at the University of Minnesota, went to Washington, DC, in 1978 to become director of the Gay Rights National Lobby. (Since there were so few lesbians to go around for the boards of these national cogendered organizations, Barbara Gittings was asked to be on GRNL's first board.) The intent of the Gay Rights National Lobby was to "mainstream" gay rights by lobbying members of Congress and raising money for political candidates who could be counted on for support. Thom's and Endean's organizations had not only boards of directors, but also paid staff. They also had dress regulations not too different from those Frank Kameny imposed on his picketers in the sixties. "We will win by capturing the middle," Steve Endean declared. "Fringe" strategies and issues, he said—severing himself and his group completely from the likes of the Gay Liberation Front—"can only be counterproductive."[63]

Gay radicals never stopped hating these "mainstreaming" organizations. (In the next century, they would snidely dub them "Gay Inc.") The animosity between the radicals and the mainstreamers was deemed a war between the "Suits" and the "Streets." But it wasn't truly a class war since many a radical had grown up in an affluent home and had been to college at a time when higher education wasn't for the masses. It was a war of style as much as of political sentiments.

The "mainstreaming" camp held an advantage. It was able to get the word out to more people because it was stridently championed by the *Advocate,* which had become the most widely read gay newspaper in the country.[64] Ironically, the *Advocate* had had its genesis in 1967 as a newsletter for PRIDE, an early radical gay rights organization.[65] But by 1973, its publisher, Richard Mitch (still using the pseudonym "Dick Michaels," which he'd adopted in more dangerous days), left no doubt about what he thought of gay radicals. "Destroyers" he called them. They needed to be muzzled and kept from sabotaging the "mature, responsible, talented experts with widespread financial backing," who knew how to wage an effective fight for reform and justice.[66] Dick Michaels both reflected and influenced what most *Advocate* readers thought (if they thought of the movement at all in between gazing at the magazine's come-on beefcakes).

LOCAL "FAT CATS" AND "PROFESSIONALS"

The middle-brow media was a barometer of Middle America's changing views of homosexuals. For instance, in the forties and fifties, *Newsweek* writers presented homosexuals as "undesirable soldier material,"[67] committers of "the most dastardly and horrifying crimes,"[68] and "disgusting and unnatural."[69] By the sixties and early seventies, *Newsweek* was less melodramatic in its language, but it asked whether homosexuals should be "punished or pitied,"[70] or whether homosexuality was a sickness.[71] By 1976, the National Gay Task Force and Lambda Legal had made a big dent in *Newsweek*'s perceptions. An article titled "Gays and the Law" dismissed the militant homosexuals' tactics of confrontation as alienating to most people—but a new breed of homosexuals has appeared, *Newsweek* marveled, and they've learned "the merits of lobbying and legal stratagems." Bruce Voeller was introduced in the article as a person of some stature, a former biology professor who gave up his academic career to direct the National Gay Task Force, which represented 1,200 organizations(!). "We're using legislation to change society's values," Voeller was respectfully quoted as saying.[72] Such dignified media coverage gave a helping hand to post-Stonewall "mainstream" gays and lesbians in their vault from the closet.

The mainstreamers breathed the open air; then claimed the gay rights movement as their own. In 1972 David Goodstein, a wealthy Wall Street transplant to San Francisco, started the Whitman-Radclyffe Foundation and hired Jim Foster, who'd already made his name in San Francisco gay politics, to run it. Whitman-Radclyffe (named pointedly after both a male and a female homosexual, Walt Whitman and Radclyffe Hall) hoped to dangle the prospect of hefty campaign contributions before the noses of California politicians and to use media advertising to alter perceptions of gay people from radical scruff or "boys who look like girls, and girls who look like boys" to men and women who were and looked more like Middle America. They believed that once that happened, once America was made to see gay men and lesbians who were "virtually normal,"[73] civil rights were sure to follow.

But such an ambitious goal could only be achieved by raising big bucks—or, as Jim Foster confessed in a letter to Frank Kameny soon after the 1972 Democratic National Convention, by "professionally [sic] organizing the community" and "luring out the 'fat-cats,'" instead of "nickel and diming each other to death as we've done since the year one." As Foster knew, Kameny—who'd long endured the frustrating chore of collecting nickels and dimes for the cause—could certainly understand the goal. "It's amazing how politicians respond when you start spending money," Foster underscored.[74] By 1974, he was able to report to Kameny that the Whitman-Radclyffe Foundation had become "proficient in locating affluent Gay people."[75]

Foster took it as glorious proof of his theory about the efficacy of money and expert organizing when 1975 brought a major coup. Homosexual groups had been trying and failing for years to get rid of sodomy laws. It had been a top priority of the homophile movement back in the 1950s; Del Martin and Phyllis Lyon had even pushed the Daughters into the battle.[76] In 1961 one state, Illinois, expunged the law from its books. Connecticut enacted repeal in 1969. The same year, Reverend Troy Perry and Morris Kight, the gay radical activist from Los Angeles, convinced the dapper San Francisco assemblyman Willie Brown to introduce a bill for repeal of the California sodomy law. Brown's own district was already very gay, though "gay political power" was still oxymoronic. The bill failed, but Willie Brown, who was a black liberal committed to righting social inequities and serving his constituency, kept reintroducing it—for five more years.

Serendipitous things happened in 1975. Brown's bill, AB 489, passed the assembly, then went on to the California State Senate. The Democratic majority leader of the Senate was George Moscone, a hard-drinking, rather dashing figure, spotted often speeding up and down the San Francisco hills in his Alfa Romeo. He'd just declared himself a candidate in that city's mayoral race. The size of the San Francisco gay population was by now guesstimated at 100,000 in a city of 715,000. They were organizing. "Gay political power" was no longer an oxymoron. Moscone's Democratic opponent in the primary election, board of supervisors president Dianne Feinstein, had assiduously curried favor among San Francisco gays and lesbians. Eight months before the mayoral primary, she'd even made sure that Jo Daly—a plump, gregarious twenty-nine-year-old lesbian who was vice president of the Alice B. Toklas club and the first avowed lesbian ever on the Democratic State Committee—would be appointed to a paid position on the San Francisco Human Rights Commission. Daly was hired to help correct discrimination against gays and lesbians in jobs, housing, and the criminal justice system. (No more San Francisco vice squad officers harassing gay bar patrons.) Her appointment to the Human Rights Commission was headline making—an out homosexual on a government payroll.[77]

It wouldn't be easy, Senator Moscone knew, to match Dianne Feinstein's good deed for gays. His liberalism and passion for social justice were authentic. As a legislator he pushed through a school lunch program for needy kids, he promoted bilingual education, he strengthened the state's Department of Consumer Affairs. Yet he was also a pragmatic politician. Without gay help he had no hope of winning the San Francisco mayoral race. Willie Brown's bill to repeal sodomy got to the California Senate six months before the mayoral primary. It was now called the Brown-Moscone bill.

The day the bill came to the senate, George Moscone stood beneath a carved Latin motto on the Senate chamber wall, pointed up at it, and translated for his fellow politicians: "Senators must guard the liberty of the Republic." The sodomy law violated the liberty of the Republic because it created opportunities for police abuse and blackmailers, Moscone argued.[78] Heterosexuals, too, would benefit by repeal because the law, a vestige of pervasive puritanism, prohibited anal and oral copulation between opposite-sex couples, too; and it also made "adulterous cohabitation" illegal. (A point that must have unnerved at least a few senators sitting in the chamber.) A long debate followed. Those who rose to speak in support of the bill pointed out it would strengthen the right to privacy for all Californians. Opponents contended it would be fatal for public morality. Finally, a vote was taken. It was 20 to 20.

California law said that the lieutenant governor could break a tie vote in the Senate. But the lieutenant governor, Mervyn Dymally—like Willie Brown, a liberal black politician—was at a political dinner in Denver, where he was to be the evening's speaker. And a proxy vote was not acceptable under the law.

George Moscone had an assistant run out to find a telephone number where Dymally could be reached. The senators were growing restive for their dinner. Moscone, fearing he'd lose his quorum, asked the president pro tem of the Senate, Democrat James Mills, for permission to have the doors locked. It was granted. Dymally was soon boarding a jet for San Francisco. At San Francisco International Airport, a police helicopter waited, its rotor blades spinning. It whisked Dymally to the Senate chamber in Sacramento, where he broke the tie. California's sodomy law was no more.[79]

Jim Foster made sure that gay donors and the members of the Whitman-Radclyffe Foundation, the Society for Individual Rights, and the Alice B. Toklas Democratic Club—all chock-full of gung-ho get-out-the-vote volunteers—knew the story of George Moscone's role in the repeal of the California sodomy law. Moscone defeated Dianne Feinstein in the November primary, and the next month, he won the tight mayoral election against conservative city supervisor John Barbagelata.

Los Angeles had its own version of the Whitman-Radclyffe big-dollar donors' club: MECLA, the Municipal Elections Committee of Los Angeles. (The inoffensive name was chosen with well-heeled closeted homosexuals in mind, so they wouldn't have to write the word *Gay* on their donation checks.[80]) The core group had originally been called Orion and was made up of good-looking men in their early thirties—Harris-tweed-clad lawyers, doctors, psychologists, all products of prestigious universities: "A-Gays," as Armistead Maupin called men like that in *Tales of the City*. Orion was mostly social, until late 1976, when ten or twelve members were snowed out of a weekend party at Lake Arrowhead. Stuck in the dull city of San Bernardino, they began to talk about the need for gay political representation that would counter the image of the "lower-class, street-type people" who'd been representing gays to the world.[81] They agreed to expand their numbers. They'd look for successful and personable men like themselves, invite them to small gatherings at their well-appointed digs, and screen them for membership.[82] The group was all-male at the start, but Peter Scott, the MECLA board's movie-star-handsome president, called himself a feminist, and in 1977 insisted that lesbians be encouraged to join.

Scott dined often at the home of two women friends of his who were life partners and law-firm partners, Diane Abbitt and Roberta Bennett. They were affluent and attractive—lesbian equivalents of the A-Gays. They presented a great public relations image, too—settled in a stable family, raising four children together. And they were founders of NOW's Lesbian Rights Task Force; they helped lesbians fight child custody cases, just as Abbitt had had to do herself when her ex-husband claimed her two sons.[83] Peter Scott thought MECLA needed lots of lesbians of Abbitt and Bennett's caliber. Anita Bryant had just gotten Miami's gay rights law overturned and was beginning her nationwide campaign to instill in voters everywhere disturbing images of homosexuality as nothing but rabbit-promiscuous male-on-male sex. The prominent presence of lesbians on MECLA's board could help deflate that image. Of course, the lesbians had to meet the same qualifications: no lesbian was invited to join the board unless she was classy and had the wherewithal to pledge $1,200 annually to the organization. Bennett and Abbitt went far beyond that monetary obligation, learning how to tap LA's sizeable wealthy lesbian population for hefty donations to MECLA's political coffers.[84] "People who make political contributions are the ones who end up sitting next to the mayor and police chief. That's the way the system works," Peter Scott liked to say.[85]

Scott also wanted in MECLA men like David Mixner, who'd come to Los Angeles in 1976 when he was hired to manage Mayor Tom Bradley's reelection campaign. Brilliant and effervescent, Mixner had been a political animal from his early teens. When he was twenty-one years old, in 1967, he'd been a major organizer of the hundred-thousand-person Vietnam War protest march on the Pentagon. The next year, he'd organized presidential hopeful Eugene McCarthy's successful Minnesota campaign. And the year after that, he'd been the brains behind the mammoth Moratorium to End the War in Vietnam. His boy-wonder smarts had brought him the friendship of liberal politicians such as Ted Kennedy, and Bill and Hillary Clinton. They were the ones who inspired Mixner to get involved in mainstream politics. His address book was fat with the names of political heavies.

Mixner had been closeted; but alone in LA, he ventured out to a meeting of the Stonewall Democratic Club, founded the year before by Morris Kight. Mixner hoped he might meet other gays who were political like himself. But it didn't take long for him to understand that gay politics came in varied forms, and Kight's was radical. Dressed in a suit and a tie, Mixner was shunned. They thought he was an undercover police officer.[86]

To his relief he soon discovered MECLA, where a suit and tie were de rigueur, and everybody had a full wallet that they were willing to open for campaigns to defeat antigay politicians. That was the kind of political group David Mixner could understand, and MECLA members were thrilled to take him in.

In the beginning, mainstream politicians, even those who were liberal in all other areas, wouldn't return MECLA's phone calls. They were afraid they'd be publicly accused of cozying up to homosexuals.[87] David Mixner (by then smitten with MECLA's gorgeous leader) came up with a strategy that helped transform MECLA from a group that even the most progressive politicians thought they had to avoid, to a player perilous to ignore.

Los Angeles had long had a powerful, right-wing city council president, John Gibson. Gibson was proud of his roots as a small-town Kansas boy, proud to describe himself as a religious fundamentalist and follower of Billy Graham, and proud that he never went to a council meeting without first getting down on his knees to pray.[88] But most disturbing to MECLA members was Gibson's unconditional support of the brutal, homosexual-hating chief of the LAPD. For years Chief Ed Davis had carried out a program of entrapment of gay men and routinely sicced his raiders on gay bars. In 1976 the chief famously declared that he'd never celebrate Gay Pride Week but would happily celebrate Gay Conversion Week. So when the police chief's valuable and voluble champion John Gibson ran for re-election in 1977, David Mixner and MECLA had a target.

MECLA threw a black-tie party for the purpose of raising money. If they couldn't defeat Gibson, who'd been president of the city council for sixteen years, they'd at least find a way to seriously weaken him. One of the candidates in the race was a Peace and Freedom Party member, James Stanberry, an inexperienced political science instructor at a local junior college. Nobody had heard of Stanberry, and his lackluster campaign seemed to be dead in the water. Mixner's strategy, worthy of a chess board, was, first, to give Stanberry's campaign serious resuscitation. MECLA would put all the black-tie party money into it and would get volunteers to work their tails off on Stanberry's behalf.[89]

Despite John Gibson's fanaticism, he'd managed to build a public

persona as an easy-going guy with a folksy sense of humor. But the councilman revealed his true colors in the course of the 1977 campaign. He
rabidly attacked his opponent, bellowing that Stanberry belonged to an
extremist left-wing party, and that he accepted money and support from
homosexuals.[90] His temper tantrum, plus MECLA's advertising and leaflet
distributing and helping people get to the polls, was enough to win Stanberry 30 percent of the vote. It was sufficient for MECLA's purpose: Gibson lost his council presidency to the highest vote getter, John Ferraro.[91]
Police Chief Davis retired the next year.

Local politicians sat up and took notice. They courted MECLA's favor
as they never had before. "You bet they're powerful," a politician's aide
whispered to a newspaper reporter as his employer addressed a vetting
group of MECLA members in 1979. "We pay attention, I can tell you
that." "Gay Rights Group Displays Power," the impressed reporter wrote in
the Los Angeles Times.[92]

The doors of not only elegant closets but the closets of Middle America's
gays and lesbians were also swinging open—and in the most unlikely
places. Linda "Pokey" Anderson was a young woman with pretty, long
tresses and a cheerleader's smile that belied her braininess. Anderson left
college in 1972 and went to Houston, following a classmate named Barbara, with whom she was secretly in love. They'd planned to find jobs there
and live together in sisterly harmony forever, but Barbara fell for a man
before Anderson could get around to telling her that she loved her. Stuck
in Houston, Anderson discovered Montrose Gaze, Houston's new gay and
lesbian center in the heart of the Montrose district, which had recently
become a gay magnet. She also joined the Houston chapter of the National
Organization for Women and attended the first National Women's Political
Caucus convention and the lesbian-feminist Great Southeast Lesbian Conference. The twenty-three-year-old Anderson was a political animal. But no
one issue grabbed her attention, until the Texas State Legislature made her
a presumptive criminal.[93]

Though a southern state, Texas had not been totally oblivious to the
sexual revolution that the 1960s ushered in. In 1973 the state decided that
sexual puritanism was outdated, and that it needed to get out of people's
bedrooms. The sodomy law was abolished—for heterosexuals. At a time

when the media was filled with stories about agitation for gay rights in New York, San Francisco, and Los Angeles, Texas legislators vowed, "It will not happen here." To make sure all homosexuals stayed in their closets, they added to the criminal code a new section 21.16—the Texas Homosexual Conduct Law, which not only specified that anal and oral sex between men was illegal, but also—for the first time in Texas law—that oral sex between women was illegal.

Houston voters had just elected a thirty-two-year-old state representative, Craig Washington, a black man who was a criminal defense lawyer and an eloquent speaker on the subject of civil rights. Members of the newly formed Texas Gay Task Force, which Pokey Anderson had joined, met with Washington and asked him to try to get the Homosexual Conduct Law repealed. He was amenable, but he knew he'd better get his bearings before he dived into something so controversial. Washington held off until 1975, when he authored an omnibus bill into which he sneaked a clause that would repeal the sodomy law. His fellow legislators immediately detected the ruse. A congressman from Dallas called out to Washington as he presented his bill to the venerable House of Representatives, "Only a homosexual would make such a proposal!" That set off sniggers and catcalls and preadolescent hijinks. One congressional wit grabbed a purse off the secretary's desk and pranced with it, swishing and twirling, all around the stately chamber. Craig Washington's repeal clause went down with a thundering 117 nays to 14 ayes.[94] News of the Austin debacle infuriated Anderson. It was bad enough to be a second-class citizen, she thought, but it was really outrageous to be laughed at by elected representatives.

At the Montrose gay center, she'd met Hugh Crell, a thirty-three-year-old mainframe computer programmer. Crell, a soft-spoken man with a razor-sharp sense of humor, had helped start Integrity/Houston, a "homophile" group that was more in the vein of pre-Stonewall Mattachine than the Gay Activists Alliance. "I fail to see the value of releasing mice in council chambers or hanging bloodstained effigies outside the home of a council member who does not support us," Crell said of GAA zaps. He pointed out that those stunts hadn't gotten a single gay rights law passed in New York, though GAA had been at it for years.[95] Instead of zapping, Crell and other Integrity members preferred a more dignified approach, like politely requesting an audience with Houston's mayor,

Fred Hofheinz, and asking his help in making life more bearable for the city's gay population.

Mayor Hofheinz was of their generation, thirty-five years old when he took office in 1974. He didn't mind "stepping a bit on old Southern toes," he said. Among the first things Hofheinz did as mayor was to integrate city hall and to force the Houston Police Department to hire and promote black and Hispanic officers. "Civil rights trumps all," he'd declared.[96] So Hugh Crell and his friends had reason to expect sympathy from Mayor Hofheinz. He was sympathetic—as well as pragmatic. "Resistance against gays is greater than against minorities," he said, explaining why if he did anything to help it would have to be secretive.[97]

Pokey Anderson thought she knew a surer way to get politicians to be helpful. She'd heard that in San Francisco gays were organizing voting blocs and winning elections. Weren't there enough gay people in Houston to swing elections, too? What was the average margin of victory? She gathered election statistics and did the math: 5 percent was the number she came up with. It was true even in mayoral elections. In 1971, the first time Fred Hofheinz ran for mayor, he lost to conservative Louis Welch, 141,753 to 126,637—a margin of just about 5 percent of the vote. If Hofheinz had appealed enough to gays and lesbians to make them all get out and vote in 1971, he might have won. It wouldn't even matter that much of Houston's gay population was closeted. As a writer for the Associated Press observed about California gays, "In the privacy of the voting booth, they 'step out of the closet' to help elect the candidate who supports gay rights."[98]

But the women she knew in NOW weren't especially interested in gay and lesbian civil rights; nor were the bar lesbians she'd encountered.[99] Hugh Crell and two other Integrity members, Keith McGee and Bill Buie, were the most political people she knew in Houston. In mid-June 1975, six weeks after the Texas state legislators told Craig Washington and all of Texas what they thought about homosexuals, Pokey Anderson invited the three gay men over to her apartment on Maryland Street in the Montrose district that she now shared with her terrier puppy.

It was time to put together a lesbian and gay voting bloc, she told them. They agreed immediately. They'd call the group the Gay Political Caucus. Their policy statement would say, "Our approach is that we are reasonable people making legitimate complaints. We dress and speak like the people whose help we are seeking."[100] In July they called a press conference at the gay Metropolitan Community Church of the Resurrection. The Houston Gay Political Caucus had been formed, they announced, and gays now expected the media to cover gay issues extensively and fairly. "There are a hundred thousand gay persons in the Houston area," Pokey Anderson told the astonished reporters[101]—and the Gay Political Caucus intended to register every last one of them. Gays would help swing all future Houston elections.[102] Because the typical Houston mayoral election attracted just a bit over 250,000 voters, Anderson's bold statement was big news.

Later that month, Anderson opened the *Houston Chronicle* to a picture of a very presentable fellow in his early thirties—a bit dashing, actually, like Errol Flynn. Gary Van Ooteghem was a Chicagoan who'd been hired seven months earlier, after a nationwide search, to be Houston's assistant county treasurer. "Quite brilliant," his boss, County Treasurer Hartsell Gray, had said in an evaluation of him.[103] But now, the newspaper said, Gray had fired Van Ooteghem. On July 28 Van Ooteghem had told the treasurer he'd be taking time off to go to a meeting of the Harris County Commissioners. He'd be asking them to pass an ordinance that would protect gays and lesbians against job discrimination. Van Ooteghem had been inspired by an article he'd read in the June 1 *New York Times* about an air force sergeant, Leonard Matlovich, who'd done three tours of duty in Vietnam, was decorated for each of them, and then was discharged because (at the urging of Frank Kameny) he tested the military's policy against homosexuals by announcing to his superior and to the world that he was one.[104] Van Ooteghem, a former naval officer, had sent a fan letter to Matlovich, who invited him to come to DC and tag along as Matlovich and Bruce Voeller lobbied congressmen for repeal of the West Virginia sodomy law and on behalf of Bella Abzug's gay rights bill.

As a result of his DC experience, Gary Van Ooteghem, who'd never before dreamed of being a gay activist, became one overnight. But his boss, Hartsell Gray, told him he did not have permission to go to the county commission meeting. Van Ooteghem went anyway; and he alerted the Houston media that he'd be telling the commissioners he was a homosexual and asking them to pass a gay rights ordinance. The press showed up in force,[105] and Gary Van Ooteghem was now Houston's most famous homosexual. When Pokey Anderson called him to ask if she could come to his home and tell him about a gay political organization she'd started that would fight for rights through the ballot box, he was ready to listen.

Gary Van Ooteghem's image was just what most members hoped the Gay Political Caucus would project: well dressed, intelligent, conservative. (In the 1990s, he would found the Houston Log Cabin Republicans.[106]) At the first official meeting of the Gay Political Caucus that September, Van Ooteghem was elected president. Before that month was over, the caucus had registered 3,100 new voters.[107] Its mailing list was soon over 13,000, and then 15,000.[108] "The hottest organization of its kind in the nation," the *Advocate* called it.[109]

They invited candidates to an October 21 rally in Cherryhurst Park in the Montrose district, to be screened for the upcoming November 1975 election. Not all accepted, but quite a few had read the Associated Press article about the new strength of the gay vote, and they happily submitted to the questions the caucus fired at them in front of an audience of five hundred gays and lesbians: "Will you support an ordinance banning discrimination in housing, private employment, and city employment?" "Will you support a police chief who won't harass gay people who are lawfully gathered?" "Will you hire a qualified gay person for your own staff?" The caucus scored the candidates 0 to 100 depending on their responses. Then they printed tens of thousands of little cards and mailed them, had volunteers walk the precincts to distribute them, left them in all the gay places. The cards told Houston's lesbians and gays which candidates deserved their vote and urged them to the polls.

As it turned out, Pokey Anderson had gotten it right: Houston, America's fifth-largest city, had a huge gay and lesbian population, and as the *Houston Post* reported, 95 percent of them were registered to vote, and 86.9 percent of them cared enough about gay causes to contribute money to them. They cared about supporting public officials with whom they resonated, too: 73.9 percent had made a contribution to a political candidate within the preceding two years.[110]

1978: Houston's bluff and hearty new mayor, Jim McConn, who looked as though he might once have played defensive tackle for his alma mater,

Notre Dame,[111] wrote a letter to the Houston Gay Political Caucus. It was in appreciation for its assistance in helping him win the 1977 election, and in the hope they'd do it again in 1979. Mayor McConn congratulated the caucus for "its commitment to the cause of human and equal rights."[112] The letter was particularly remarkable because when McConn, a businessman and president of the Houston Chamber of Commerce, had been a city councilman five years earlier, he'd objected publicly about the growing number of homosexuals in Houston: "What are we doing wrong?" he'd wailed.[113] But by 1978, the caucus had become a force to be kowtowed to by Houston politicians.

Those who didn't know that, or didn't care, eventually got a rude awakening. Councilman Frank Mann, blinded perhaps by Anita Bryant's triumphant antigay campaigns in other cities,[114] had not understood just how powerful the caucus had become. Mann had been a councilman since 1960. In 1974 two brave souls from a short-lived gay group appeared at an open council meeting to say that the police were harassing the gay community. Mann shouted them down, screaming, "You're abnormal! You need to see a psychiatrist instead of the city council!" Five years later, in 1979, Mann was running for his tenth two-year term, and he foolishly compounded the gay community's anger at him. He ranted against his opponent, Eleanor Tinsley—a genteel, pearl-necklace-wearing southern lady (with a backbone of high-carbon steel)[115]—that she was supported by "oddwads and homosexuals." The Gay Political Caucus could not let that pass. This race was the true test of its power. The caucus printed fifty thousand endorsement cards in favor of Tinsley. It produced T-shirts proclaiming, "Oddwads and Homosexuals for Tinsley," which gay people and their friends sported all over the city.[116] It distributed thousands of flyers that presented side by side a statement issued by Eleanor Tinsley saying, "Every Houstonian has a right to expect fair and equal treatment at the hands of city officials, departments, agencies, and commissions, regardless of sexual orientation"; and one by Frank Mann reiterating his "oddwads and homosexuals" wisecrack.[117]

Eleanor Tinsley won with over 54 percent of the vote. Women had never before served on the Houston City Council—nor had an incumbent councilman ever before lost his seat. Steve Shiflett, president of the Gay Political Caucus in 1979, told the cheering members at an election night victory party, "In Houston we have proven that gay power is at the ballot box."[118] The *New York Times* agreed: the caucus had very quickly become "a major political force in a city whose image is so often associated with the Wild West," its writer observed wryly. "Virtually all the major candidates take homosexuals' political power seriously."[119]

Chapter 16

HOW GAYS AND LESBIANS
STOPPED BEING CRAZIES

THE MAY DAY ZAP

On a bright Saturday morning on the first day of May 1971, fifty thousand protestors calling themselves the May Day Tribe converged on Washington, DC. The government would not shut down the war in Vietnam, so they had come to shut down the government by using their bodies, tree limbs, rubbish bins, nails, tires—any barricades they could devise—to foul up traffic and prevent all federal offices from functioning. Of course, government workers would not be going to their jobs on Saturday or Sunday, so the May Day Tribe spread out over the meadows of West Potomac Park, in view of the Washington Monument, set up tents, and partied. Their scheduled rock concert went on all through the night. Early Sunday morning, the US Parks Department canceled their permit to congregate. Because the May Day Tribe did not clear out immediately, the park police donned riot gear, invaded the encampment, and succeeded in dispersing them with billy clubs and tear gas and pepper spray; but the May Day Tribe found refuge on DC college campuses and in sympathetic churches.

At the start of the workweek, they mobilized to shut the city down. The Washington Metropolitan Police Department again descended on them in riot-control phalanxes. For police backup, President Nixon summoned the marines, the army, and the National Guard, which came armed with bayonets. Over twelve thousand people were hauled off to DC jails in the largest mass arrest in American history. The timing of the May Day protest was serendipitous for out-of-town Gay Liberation Front members. They had made the trip to DC to do double duty.

Their second shift was on the evening of May 3, the first day of the annual American Psychiatric Association convention. Euphoric about their May Day exploits, twenty GLF members, male and female, donned "Gay Is Good" or "Gay Revolution" T-shirts; a dozen more GLF males dressed in drag—fabulous wigs; high, high heels; glittering lamé dresses; outrageously bright lipstick and eye shadow; and then they all piled into VW vans or cars and headed up Connecticut Avenue to the Omni Shoreham Hotel in northwest Washington.[1] There, in the Regency Ballroom, two thousand psychiatrists had gathered for a Convocation of Fellows, at which several psychiatrists were to be honored for their lifetime achievements, and US Attorney General Ramsey Clark would deliver a keynote address.

Frank Kameny, Barbara Gittings, and Jack Baker had already grabbed seats in the front row. They'd been given guest passes because they were to be speakers on a panel, "Lifestyles of Non-Patient Homosexuals,"[2] which had been scheduled as a concession to protestors at the APA conference in San Francisco the year before: the San Francisco Gay Liberation Front, outfitted with radical gay uniforms of jeans and T-shirts, or with drag makeup and women's feathered hats, had stormed into a room crowded with staid psychiatrists.[3] Dr. Irving Bieber was speaking. Bieber, the author of the 1962 book, *Homosexuality: A Psychoanalytic Study of Male Homosexuals*, had been the zappers' target because he was a chief propagator of the idea that male homosexuality was a mental disease caused by "close-binding" mothers, and it needed curing by the shrinks. Most APA members agreed with him. A poll of psychiatrists taken that same year showed that 90 percent of them believed that homosexuality was pathological.[4]

"Sadist!" the zappers called to Bieber. "Motherfucker!" "If your book talked about black people the way it talks about homosexuals, you'd be drawn and quartered and you'd deserve it," one yelled. Many of the psychiatrists in the audience fled the room in horror, and the session was shut down. From there the zappers went to an auditorium packed with five hundred psychiatrists listening to a presentation by a young Australian doctor on the use of aversion therapy to cure homosexuality. One of the DC GAA insurgents seized the mic to scream, "Stop talking about us and start talking to us!"[5] The others were not as reasoned in their exhortations. "Vicious!" "Torturer!" "Where did you take your residency, Auschwitz?" they yelled.[6] The psychiatrists yelled back, "Paranoid fool!" "Stupid bitch!"[7]

To ward off a repeat of the 1970 debacle, the APA had agreed to let gays and lesbians have their own panel in 1971, scheduled for nine o'clock on the last evening of the convention. But even if it had been scheduled for prime time, it wouldn't have made a difference to the activists, because they understood by now that as attention getters, outrageous tactics were indispensable.

As the attorney general walked to the podium on the ballroom stage and began his keynote speech, beads of sweat gathered on the foreheads of Kameny, Gittings, and Baker. It was not because of DC's humid weather—they were waiting tensely for what they knew would happen any minute now.[8] What ensued had been set up weeks earlier by Mattachine Society Washington in cooperation with Washington's Gay Activists Alliance and Gay Liberation Front. The three groups all agreed that the American Psychiatric Association must be forced to excise from its *Diagnostic and Statistical Manual of Mental Disorders* section 302.0, which defined homosexuality as pathological.

The night before the convocation, members of the DC Gay Activists Alliance had paid the Shoreham Hotel a furtive visit. They knew that police scrutiny would be heavy around the neighborhood the next day because of the May Day protest. But even if the GLF and GAA people could make it as far as the Shoreham lobby, they'd be spotted by security and kicked out because they didn't look like the conventionally garbed clientele of a four-diamond luxury hotel. So Gay Activists Alliance moles located a path that went directly from the Rock Creek Park woods to the fire doors that led into the Regency Ballroom where the convocation would take place. They sneaked inside and inserted wedges so that the fire doors wouldn't close. Then they advised their fellow infiltrators how to dodge security via the park path and the ballroom fire doors.[9]

Ramsey Clark had gotten midway into his speech. He never finished. The fire doors burst open and the zappers flooded in, chanting "Psychiatry is the enemy!" Mayhem ensued, with psychiatrists physically attacking the invaders, shouting, "Get out!" "You sick faggots!" "We don't want you people in here!" Gays linked arms and plopped on the ballroom floor, resisting attempts to eject them. As more gays tried to force their way in, two psychiatrists, screaming execrations, locked the fire doors, but not before they'd managed to push back out a few of those who'd already squeezed in.

Among those pushed out was Cliff Witt, the Washington GAA leader who'd organized the zap. The plan had been that Witt would seize the microphone and give a speech about the horrors perpetrated on homosexuals by the psychiatric profession. But with Witt locked out, the invaders were at a loss about what to do next. Frank Kameny didn't hesitate. He jumped up and seized the microphone from the moderator, who was trying to restore order. "We are here to denounce your authority to call us sick or mentally disordered," Kameny shouted amidst psychiatric boos and jeers. Someone pulled the microphone's plug, but Kameny only shouted louder. "For us, as homosexuals, your profession is the enemy incarnate. We demand that psychiatrists treat us as human beings, not as patients to be cured! You may take this as a declaration of war against you!"[10] Pandemonium reigned. The convocation was over.

But some doctors in that large ballroom had listened, and after Kameny's tirade, a few of them came to him and Barbara Gittings with a promise: they would get the program managers to give Kameny and Gittings permission to do an exhibition at the 1972 APA conference. "We'll have our own gay booth at next year's conference," he reported with glee to New York gay leader Morty Manford.[11] "Gay, Proud, and Healthy: The Homosexual Community Speaks," it would be called.

"THE MOST IMPORTANT SINGLE ISSUE FACING OUR MOVEMENT TODAY"

The 1971 zap on the American Psychiatric Association was years in the making. It was helped along by the ethos of the sixties, which made authority less sacrosanct and credentials and "experts" less prestigious. Psychiatric wisdom had come under particularly devastating attack. Most notably, Thomas Szasz, in a popular 1961 book, *The Myth of Mental Illness*, presented the "mental health" profession as virtual quackery. Psychiatrists convert moral judgments into medical terms and then give them a misleading scientific aura, Szasz declared. They deem a person "mentally ill" just because he or she doesn't conform to social norms.[12] Szasz's insights and critiques would prove invaluable to the homophile movement.

Frank Kameny's first recruit, in 1961, to Mattachine Society Washington, twenty-three-year-old Jack Nichols, had long brooded on the memory that when he was an adolescent, an aunt had found out he liked boys, and she called him "sick." Her insult threw him into depression and made him suicidal. Nichols came to believe that psychiatrists and other credentialed "experts," the original sources of Aunt Betty's notions about homosexuality, ought to be among gay people's chief targets. In 1963, bolstered by Szasz's work, he wrote the Mattachine board urging battle with the life-warping lie that homosexuals "are not well, that they are less than completely whole," which was promulgated by so-called mental health professionals.[13] Frank Kameny, a scientist who'd always believed that psychiatry's assessment of homosexuality was nothing more than "shabby, shoddy, sloppy, sleazy pseudo-science,"[14] wholeheartedly agreed. Kameny drafted a challenge to psychiatric lore that his DC Mattachine board adopted as a major tenet: "Homosexuality is not a sickness, disturbance, or pathology in any sense. It is merely a preference, on a par with, and not different in kind, from heterosexuality."[15]

Randy Wicker, who'd been pushing and pulling New York Mattachine to more militancy since the 1950s, also went after the psychiatric profession about that time. In 1964 the Cooper Union Forum series had announced its December lecture: "Homosexuality, a Disease," by Dr. Paul Dince, associate in psychiatry at the New York Medical College. Wicker showed up at Cooper Union with two other gay men and a lesbian. They carried a sign that said, "We Request 10 Minutes Rebuttal Time," and they stationed themselves at the entrance to the lecture hall.

The organizers of the Cooper Union Forums had conceived of the forums as edgy and controversial, and when the head was informed that there were protestors in the hall and they wanted to rebut, he came out to meet them. "Okay, one of you can speak for ten minutes during the Q and A," he told the little group.

The instant Dr. Dince's lecture was done, Randy Wicker jumped to his feet and ran to the microphone. "How can you dare pretend that genuine scientific research supports this lie that homosexuality is a disease? What's the evidence?" he demanded angrily. Dince looked dumbfounded. He'd never before heard anyone question the disease theory of homosexuality. "What kind of 'scientific research' is it that looks only at homosexual patients—people who are in therapy because they're so miserable—and then makes statements about the whole population of homosexuals?" Wicker went on with his tongue lashing. "You 'scientists' begin with the premise that homosexuality is a disease, and then you make the conclusion that it's a disease—that's bullshit logic!" he shouted.[16]

Wicker's was the first public challenge to psychiatric wisdom about homosexuality. Other, more polite challenges followed. In 1968—when the National Association of Research and Therapy of Homosexuality (NARTH) was barely a gleam in the eye of Dr. Charles Socarides, its founder—Socarides advocated to an American Medical Association conference that there be established a government-supported "national center for sexual rehabilitation" for homosexuals. The next day, the San Francisco Daughters of Bilitis, together with the homophile group Society for Individual Rights (SIR), and members of the Council on Religion and the Homosexual wearing their clerical collars stood outside the Veterans Memorial Auditorium, where a session of the conference was being held, and they passed out two thousand leaflets to the doctors as they walked through the doors. "We call upon the American Medical Association to undertake to educate the medical profession," the leaflets implored politely, "and to help educate the general public on the subject of homosexuality."[17] Needless to say, the AMA did not change its policies as a result of the leaflets.

Frank Kameny was not so polite. "Psychiatric balderdash" became one of his major talking points. Psychiatrists have been posing as authorities, but they're ignorant about homosexuality, he complained in the Mattachine Society Washington newsletter of spring 1964. They decreed homosexuality to be pathological not because they had scientific evidence that it was, but because they needed to cover up their discomfort with nonconformity.[18] Kameny was quick to seize the political implications of overthrowing that decree. "The entire homophile movement is going to stand or fall upon the question of whether or not homosexuality is a sickness, and upon taking a firm stand on it," he told his New York Freedom House audience the night of the summer 1964 Harlem riot, when he urged homophiles to more militant combat.[19] "THE most important single issue facing our movement today," he wrote the following year, is "the proclamation of homosexual sanity."[20]

Barbara Gittings, who'd flunked out of college because she'd spent most of her freshman year in the library reading what the shrinks had to say about homosexuality, came to believe that the American Psychiatric Association ought to be the major audience for the proclamation: Didn't that organization have the last word on who was crazy and who was sane? She'd go undercover, "be a sheep in wolf's clothing," as she quipped to Kameny, and infiltrate a 1968 APA meeting in Boston, to see what they were saying about homosexuals. Gittings was outraged by the ubiquitous but unexamined assumption of the APA members that homosexuality is something to be gotten rid of, and she was horrified by the aversion therapy movies she watched sitting in an audience of psychiatrists.[21] The movement's top priority needed to be the overturning of the APA's classification of homosexuals as crazies. Unless homosexuals were acknowledged to be as mentally sound as the average heterosexual, she and Kameny would argue with irrefutable logic, they'd never be first-class citizens.

But exactly how could the message of homosexual sanity be disseminated to those who were responsible for creating the myth of homosexual madness? There was only one way to do it. Homosexuals had to get into the "rough-and-tumble," Kameny kept reiterating. It was time "to move from endless talk to firm, vigorous action."[22]

Theirs was not a popular position among homophile groups. "Florence Conrad," a pseudonym for Daughters of Bilitis member Florence Jaffy, represented the reigning view in her debate with Kameny in the pages of *The Ladder*.[23] Conrad, a junior college professor of economics and the research director of DOB, had been a procurer for professional "mental health" researchers who needed lesbian subjects and were happy to get them from the DOB membership. Conrad was outraged that in Kameny's speeches and writing, he took it upon himself to denigrate the duly credentialed "experts" by proclaiming "without evidence" that homosexuals were just as healthy as heterosexuals.

"Where's the evidence that we're not?" Kameny wanted to know.

The wiry, short-haired Conrad, as combative as Kameny and superserious in her professionalism at a time when few women were professionals anywhere, harangued him: "If we put forward these views on our own, no one will listen. It's empty propaganda. We need to be vindicated by the professionals. You can't sell the gay movement like toothpaste!"

"Yes, you can," Kameny answered.[24]

TROJAN HORSES

Homosexuals weren't only patients treated by psychiatrists—some homosexuals *were* psychiatrists, including chairs of some of the most prestigious psychiatric departments in American universities and the head of the Transactional Analysis Association.[25] But most of the homosexual psychiatrists were not happy in 1970, when gays started staging their zaps on the APA. Psychiatrist John Fryer was taught as a student at Vanderbilt University Medical School that homosexuality was a mental disorder, classified as such in the *Diagnostic and Statistical Manual of Mental Disorders* since its first edition in 1952; and though he was himself homosexual, he believed what he was taught. Fryer would eventually play a role in the APA's depathologizing of homosexuality, but when gays started zapping the APA, he was embarrassed by their demands and "wished they'd just shut up." "Nothing would ever change the way psychiatry viewed homosexuality," he thought. "They were on a fool's errand."[26]

Since the 1960s, Fryer had belonged to an underground, unofficial group of gay psychiatrists who drolly dubbed themselves the GayPA. They suffered from the same internalized homophobia as did lay homosexuals of their generation, and they agreed with Fryer that the gay activists should just shut up. The thought to question the definition of homosexuality as pathological never even came up at GayPA get-togethers.[27]

But, cautious as they were, eventually they were not immune to the era's changing spirit. In May 1970, coincidentally the same week of the first APA zap, the United States invaded Cambodia; and at Kent State University, Ohio National Guardsmen fired sixty-seven rounds of bullets to scare off students who were at a rally protesting the invasion. Four students were killed and nine were seriously wounded. A young psychiatrist, Lawrence Hartmann (who, two decades later, would become the American Psychiatric Association's first openly gay president), was appalled that the APA had no comment to make on the disasters, nor on any social issue. Hartmann was closeted in 1970, and did not even dare join the GayPA; but he'd been involved since his student days at Harvard Medical School with social justice campaigns, such as organizing psychiatrists to volunteer to work in prisons and agitating to get female medical students in residency paid as much as male residents. Though barely in his thirties, Hartmann had name recognition in the APA because he was the son of two well-known Viennese psychoanalysts, and his father had even worked with the venerated father of the discipline, Sigmund Freud. Shortly after the Cambodian invasion and the Kent State massacre, Lawrence Hartmann helped start a group called the Committee for Concerned Psychiatrists, whose purpose was to push the APA to develop a social conscience.[28]

The eastern contingent of the committee met often in the kitchen of the Cambridge, Massachusetts, home of Dr. John Spiegel, who would also eventually become a president of the American Psychiatric Association. Spiegel was married with children, and no one—except his wife, whom he'd told two weeks before their wedding—knew that he was homosexual.[29]

Most members of the Committee for Concerned Psychiatrists were straight, but they were all liberal young Turks and, like Hartmann, they all wanted to make the APA more sensitive to the changing world. They decided the only way to do it was to replace the old boys' club—the silver-haired conservatives who'd always run the APA—with people who were in tune with social concerns. Their choice for APA president was Alfred Freedman, chair of the Department of Psychiatry at New York Medical College. Freedman, already well into his fifties, was far from being one of the young Turks, but he was well known for his work that applied psychiatry to social problems. In 1959 he established a treatment center in East Harlem for adult and adolescent drug addicts; he led a delegation of psychiatrists to the Soviet Union to urge change in the government's practice of declaring political dissidents insane and then locking them up in mental hospitals; he campaigned against the use of psychotropic drugs to make psychotic death-row prisoners "mentally competent to be executed." Freedman's liberal activism, coupled with his solid reputation in the profession, made him exactly the candidate that the Committee for Concerned Psychiatrists had in mind when they dreamed that the old order might be overthrown. The committee nominated him in 1972 to run for president for the 1973–74 term. He was not a shoo-in. Half of the eighteen thousand members of the APA voted in that election. Freedman won by a margin of just three votes.

The Committee for Concerned Psychiatrists also managed to get some of its own on the all-powerful APA Board of Trustees and the Nomenclature Committee, which was responsible for deciding what goes into—and what comes out of—the *Diagnostic and Statistical Manual of Mental Disorders*. The APA was gearing up for huge changes.

THE PUSH FROM OUTSIDE AND IN

Nineteen seventy-two: Barbara Gittings received a generous grant from the Pennsylvania-based Falk Foundation, a charitable-giving group interested in promoting liberal social policy and mental health. The money paid the way for several gay activists to make the trip to the APA Convention in Dallas; it also paid for an architect friend of Gittings to make the Gay, Proud, and Healthy booth that would be displayed in the APA exhibit hall. The booth was constructed of Styrofoam so that Gittings could easily transport it from Philadelphia, but it was eye grabbing. "Gay, Proud, and Healthy: The Homosexual Community Speaks," it announced (to the evident discomfort of those who hurried past but couldn't avoid seeing the message anyway). Never in the history of the APA had there been anything remotely like it, with pictures of happy-looking homosexual couples plastered all over. Then there was a whole rack of literature—essays by gays and lesbians on their hurtful experiences with shrinks who tried to cure them; an article by Evelyn Hooker on her 1950s study that showed that psychiatrists could not distinguish between homosexual and heterosexual respondents in blind tests; a study by biologist Frank Beach that concluded that human homosexuality was a reflection of the bisexual character of our mammalian inheritance; an article that had just been published by Judd Marmor, a vice president of the APA, titled "Homosexuality—Mental Illness or Moral Dilemma?," which strongly refuted the sickness theory.

The word LOVE printed in huge white letters on a red background, was the booth's focal point. "The only place at the whole APA Convention where that word appears," Gittings pointed out to any psychiatrist who stopped to look at the booth's displays.[30]

There was no need to zap the 1972 convention. There was the Gay,

Proud, and Healthy booth that was assigned to a prominent corner of the exhibit hall; and there was a panel titled "Psychiatry: Friend or Foe to Homosexuals?—A Dialogue," in which Frank Kameny and Barbara Gittings were invited to participate. They'd be joining heterosexual psychiatrists Judd Marmor and Robert Seidenberg, both of whom rejected the pathologizing theories of colleagues such as Irving Bieber and Charles Socarides. Seidenberg went even further than Marmor did: he'd just written an article in which he asserted baldly that "homosexual culture" is a valuable asset to civilization, and he predicted that in the future homosexuals would be considered "ecological cult heroes" in a world burdened by dangerous overpopulation.[31]

The panel was set at four participants—until Kay Tobin, Gittings's partner, came up with a startling suggestion. "You've got two gays who are not psychiatrists and two psychiatrists who are not gay," she said. "What you need now is a gay psychiatrist."[32] Gittings and Kameny understood good theater. They immediately contacted Dr. Kent Robinson, who was to be the panel's moderator. "If we can find a gay psychiatrist, may we add him to the panel?" they asked. Robinson could hardly say no to such a unique prospect, and Gittings started searching for the fifth panelist.

By now she knew of the existence of the GayPA, and even knew personally several psychiatrists who were members. They liked her. She was close enough to them that she could joke about being their "fairy godmother."[33] But they refused even to think about participating on the panel. "The American Psychoanalytic Association and all its affiliates have policies that bar homosexuals from being analysts," one gay psychiatrist friend informed Gittings. "If my colleagues in the APA knew I was gay, I'd never get their referrals—or their respect," another said. "I could lose my license," another told her. One suggested that she contact Dr. John Fryer.

Fryer had been thrown out of his residency at the University of Pennsylvania when his supervisor learned that he was homosexual, he'd lost another position for the same reason, and now he had only part-time employment at Temple University. He thought fellow psychiatrists needed to hear his story. But he didn't want to invite more trouble into his professional life. "I'd like to do it, but I can't do it as me," he told Gittings.

"Okay, what if we disguise you?" she asked.[34]

When Frank Kameny heard of Gittings's offer to disguise Fryer, he

was irate. "A masked psychiatrist goes against everything we've been fighting for!" he shouted. He'd find a gay psychiatrist for the panel himself—
someone who wouldn't think he had to resort to disguise! But after weeks
of trying, with the 1972 conference looming, Kameny had to concede
there was no such animal as an uncloseted psychiatrist.[35]

Dr. John Fryer was six foot four, weighed about three hundred pounds,
and had bulldog jowls. Disguise seemed impossible. But Fryer's lover, a
drama major in college, was tickled by the challenge. He dressed Fryer in
a tuxedo that was three sizes too large and so made him look smaller, a
rubber mask of Richard Nixon that went over his head and face and was
crimped to look clown-like, and a frizzy fright wig. On the day of the
panel, Gittings spirited Fryer into the packed auditorium through a back
corridor, so no one would get too close a look at him. He was billed as Dr.
H. Anonymous. Kameny had to concede he'd been wrong about not presenting a psychiatrist in disguise. The effect was sensational.[36]

"There are more than a hundred homosexual psychiatrists registered
at this convention," Dr. H. Anonymous informed his APA audience. That
news alone was astounding to most of them; they'd thought of homosexuals as being always *on* the psychiatric couch, not behind it. "Cease
attempting to figure out who I am and listen to what I have to say," he
admonished. Then he told his audience that homosexual psychiatrists were
forced to endure a variety of what he called "nigger syndromes." They were
like black men with light skin who needed to pass. They didn't dare to be
seen with their real friends and family—other homosexuals—"lest our secret be known and our doom sealed." And like those black men who were
driven to be "superhuman," homosexual psychiatrists, too, felt constrained
to overachieve, because if their homosexuality should be found out, their
capabilities would be doubted. He implored the homosexual psychiatrists
in the audience to challenge their fellow psychiatrists and not stand back
when they hear them denigrating "faggots and queers." "Make your homosexual patients know they're all right. Find ways to counter the attitudes
toward homosexuality that your profession has inculcated in both heterosexuals and homosexuals."[37] He was given a standing ovation.

But though Dr. Fryer rocked his audience that day in 1972, homosexuals
still remained crazies in the *DSM*, which confirmed militant gays in their

conviction that it would take more zaps to get a real rise out of the APA. That October at the New York Hilton, New York Gay Activists Alliance members infiltrated the annual conference of the Association for the Advancement of Behavior Therapy. A dozen activists registered for the conference as "students," which permitted them access to the sessions. (Dozens more staged agitprop outside the hotel, farcically acting out the roles of "unhappy heterosexuals" and "shrinks": "You must submit to electroshock convulsions and apomorphine-induced vomiting. This treatment is guaranteed to turn you off even to the most attractive members of the opposite sex. It will convert you into a happy, healthy homosexual!" the "shrinks" promised.)[38]

Inside the Hilton, GAA members descended on a lecture by Dr. James P. Quinn, a psychiatrist from Northern Ireland. He'd been scheduled to present the aversion therapy techniques he'd been using—electroshock and chemically induced vomiting—with which, he claimed, he'd succeeded in turning homosexual men off to members of their own sex. Quinn must have thought he was back in Belfast in the midst of an IRA attack: A few minutes into his talk, GAA members who were scattered around the room shoved their chairs back loudly and jumped up to announce that Quinn had talked long enough; they were taking over. Ronald Gold, then the media director of New York GAA, took on the role of main spokesman.[39]

"We're interrupting you. We can't let you go on doing what you're doing," he said from the front of the room. "But please don't go away. We want to have a dialogue with you." A woman psychologist in the audience came to Dr. Quinn's defense: "These people who come to us for help— they don't want to be homosexuals. We're doing what they ask us to do!"

"If a woman came to you saying, 'Help me be what society says women are supposed to be, shy and retiring,' would you do it?" Gold challenged her. She would not, she confessed.[40]

About a quarter of the psychiatrists got up and left, but the rest stayed to hear GAA's gripes, and some even agreed that the first choice of treatment ought not be therapy to change the homosexual but rather therapy to help him get rid of the anxieties caused by a hostile society.

Dr. Robert Spitzer and his assistant were among those who stayed, but Spitzer was annoyed. He'd come to the conference to hear about behavioral therapy, and the GAA had shut down Quinn's session. "I know Ron

Gold. I actually went to college with him," Spitzer's assistant whispered. "Wanna meet him and tell him what you think?"

In the hallway, as everyone was leaving, she introduced the two men to each other. Spitzer informed Gold that he resented what he saw as GAA's "bullying techniques" to shut down Dr. Quinn. Gold gave him examples of how disastrous practices like Quinn's had been for homosexuals; Spitzer listened. Their altercation changed to conversation. Eventually it came out that Spitzer was a member of the APA's Committee on Nomenclature— the group responsible for determining what went into or out of the *DSM*.

"Gee, could my group talk to your group?" Spitzer later recalled Gold asking. "Gee, that's an interesting idea," Spitzer, who would always enjoy being something of a gadfly, thought. "Maybe we could even have a symposium on the subject."[41]

A short while later, Frank Kameny and several others from DC tried another approach. They'd infiltrate a meeting of the APA assembly in Washington, DC. They'd found out that Dr. Robert Campbell, another member of the Committee on Nomenclature (and a closeted gay), would be at the assembly. They buttonholed him: "We really need your help." He listened. For two hours, they overwhelmed him with data such as the Evelyn Hooker study, which he admitted he'd never seen.[42] Then they asked him to get them invited to appear before the Nomenclature Committee. Campbell agreed—but Robert Spitzer had already beat him to it. He'd gone to Henry Brill, the elderly head of the Nomenclature Committee and director of a large New York state hospital, and told him that gays would like to address the committee. Brill knew, of course, about the disruptions of the last three years and the growing controversy over the pathologizing of homosexuality. "Okay, let's meet with them and see what happens," he told Spitzer jovially.[43]

A small group of activists was invited to the Nomenclature Committee's meeting at Columbia University's Psychiatric Institute on February 8, 1973. Before the meeting, they'd sent the Nomenclature Committee a report about research that challenged psychiatric shibboleths on homosexuality.[44] Like Robert Campbell, most of the committee members seemed never to have heard of Evelyn Hooker's study that showed no perceptible difference in the responses of homosexual and heterosexual men to psychiatric tests such as the Rorschach and the Thematic Apperception

Test—nor of the details of the Kinsey studies that found that big numbers of the sample admitted to having "extensive or more than incidental" homosexual experiences. The members of the Nomenclature Committee listened respectfully to Jean O'Leary—the sharp, articulate former nun—tell them that psychiatry's classification of homosexuality as a mental disorder kept homosexuals from being granted the civil rights due to any American. Ronald Gold gave them a list of the discriminations suffered by gays because society said they were mentally ill. "Being told you're sick makes you sick," he chided them.[45]

Charles Silverstein, a GAA member who was working on his PhD in Psychology because he wanted some credibility in his fight with the shrinks, entertained them to the point of hilarity. Silverstein compared the diagnosis of homosexuality as pathology to the silliness of diagnostic categories of the past: Syphilophobia, Pathological Mendacity, Vagabondage—even Masturbation. It all sounds funny now, Silverstein told them, but it hurt a lot of people. "We have paid the price for your past mistake. Don't make it again," he admonished them.[46]

"Okay, Bob," Brill said good-humoredly to Spitzer when the gay and lesbian contingent left. "You got us into this mess. Now what do we do?"

"Let's have a symposium," Spitzer said.[47]

"A Symposium: Should Homosexuality Be in the APA Nomenclature?" was scheduled for the 1973 APA Convention in Honolulu. Irving Bieber and Charles Socarides, leading proponents of the illness theory, presented the "yes" side. Perhaps GayPA members felt that by 1973 they could be more vocal, or perhaps the APA in general had undergone a cataclysmic change in the last couple of years. Whatever the explanation, Bieber was greeted with loud boos when he declared, "If all discrimination against homosexuals ceased immediately, I do not think their anxieties, conflicts, loneliness, and frequent depressions would be short-circuited."[48]

At one point, Bieber, rehashing his views on how homosexuals are created, said that on Israeli kibbutzim, where children did not live with their parents and hence were not messed up by close-binding mothers, everyone was heterosexual. "Well," Ronald Gold spoke up, "I just got back from Israel, where I had a thing with a man who was raised on a kibbutz."[49] The audience abandoned themselves to laughter.

"If our judgment about the mental health of heterosexuals were based only on those whom we see in our clinical practices, we would have to conclude that all heterosexuals are also mentally ill,"[50] Judd Marmor, vice president of the APA, answered Bieber and Socarides; he was applauded wildly. Ronald Gold concluded his presentation, which he called "Stop It, You're Making Me Sick!" with the rousing demands that the APA take homosexuality out of the nomenclature, work for the repeal of sodomy laws and for civil rights protections for gays, and tell the world that gay is good. He got a standing ovation.[51]

Gold had been such a hit that members of the GayPA discreetly came up to him after the symposium and issued a quiet invitation to their annual party, which was still a very secret affair. Pumped by his success, yet frustrated that section 302.0 of the *Diagnostic and Statistical Manual of Mental Disorders* remained intact, Gold settled on a daring ploy. He knew that Robert Spitzer had been given an assignment by the Nomenclature Committee to research and report back the "scientific findings" about homosexuality.[52] What happened next with 302.0 would hinge on Spitzer—and though Spitzer had held the door to the Nomenclature Committee open so that gays could step in, his own position thus far had not gone beyond "Gee, that's an interesting idea." What's more, he admitted to having been trained by psychoanalysts who "took it for granted that homosexuality was not only an illness, but it was a very severe illness."[53] Spitzer had never knowingly mingled with homosexuals, Gold knew, and he was acquainted with no homosexual colleagues. It was time to educate him.

Gold told Spitzer about the secret group and his invitation to their get-together; then he invited him to come along. Spitzer was curious. "But you can't let on you're not gay," Gold warned him nervously. "Just don't say anything. Just observe." Spitzer agreed. The GayPA party was held in a campy Honolulu gay bar with grass-skirted waitresses; a multipage list of drinks that were colored red, blue, purple, green; and island-themed geegaws and bamboo furniture.[54] But Spitzer saw little of that. He was too busy being flabbergasted at how many faces he recognized among GayPA members: prominent APA officers, heads of APA affiliates, heads of prestigious university psychiatry departments. He kept neither his promise not to stare nor his promise not to speak, and he gave himself away by asking GayPA members what Gold thought were "absolutely dim-witted questions" such as "How long have you known you were a homosexual?" As Spitzer went around talking to one man after another, it was obvious that he wasn't a candidate for GayPA membership. The panicked head of the group pulled Gold aside and told him to get Spitzer out of there. Now. "Get rid of him!"

"No! He's willing to help us," Gold answered, but he went to tell Spitzer to cool it.

Just then a man in an army uniform walked in. He recognized Gold from the symposium earlier that day. Then he looked around and recognized psychiatrists he'd seen in the audience, and he threw himself on Gold and burst into tears. He told Gold that he was an army psychiatrist. This was the first time in his life he'd dared go to a gay bar, and it was Gold's speech that had given him the courage to do it.

"Let's go," Spitzer said to Gold. He'd seen and heard enough.[55]

That night, Spitzer sat at his hotel room desk, Ronald Gold prompting at his elbow, and wrote an APA resolution removing homosexuality per se from the *DSM*. It was Frank Kameny who later helped Spitzer draft the justifying letter to the Nomenclature Committee: "The only way that homosexuality could be considered a psychiatric disorder would be the criterion of failure to function heterosexually, which is considered optimal in our society and by many members of our profession. However," Kameny wrote in Spitzer's voice, reiterating the theories he'd promulgated for years, "if the failure to function optimally in some important area of life as judged by either society or the profession is sufficient to indicate the presence of psychiatric disorder, then we will have to add to our nomenclature the following conditions." The list included celibacy (failure to function optimally sexually), religious fanaticism (dogmatic and rigid adherence to religious doctrine), racism (irrational hatred of other groups), vegetarianism (unnatural avoidance of carnivorous behavior), and male chauvinism (irrational belief in the inferiority of women).[56]

Spitzer's resolution stated specifically that "homosexuality per se implies no impairment in judgment, stability, reliability, or general social or vocational capabilities." But his resolution did not go far enough to satisfy gay activists because section 302.0 was not entirely deleted from the *DSM*:

"Homosexuality" was replaced by "Sexual Orientation Disturbance," a category for those who were "ego-dystonic"—that is, "disturbed by, or in conflict with, or wishing to change their sexual orientation." It was a necessary strategy, Spitzer believed. There was no way the APA would have approved of getting rid of *all* references to homosexuality.[57] Psychiatrists could still "cure" those who wanted "curing"; there was still money to be made by their "services."

The Nomenclature Committee approved the change, and in November 1973 the proposal passed to the APA Reference Committee and the assembly and was endorsed by both bodies. In December, the eighteen-member board of trustees voted: two were absent, three abstained, and thirteen voted aye. The resolution had passed overwhelmingly.[58]

But Spitzer's sop to those of his colleagues who still wished to cure homosexuals did not mollify them. Debate and confusion raged. The press demanded to know from Dr. Alfred Freedman, new president of the APA, "If it's not a mental illness now, why was it on the list of mental illnesses for all those years?" Dr. Freedman, elected through the efforts of APA progressives, was at a loss. Answering such questions required a complicated disquisition about the Zeitgeist's influence on notions of mental illness. "Are you saying that homosexuality is normal?" the reporters continued. "No," Freedman said, "only that it's not abnormal."[59]

The *New York Times* fanned the flames of the controversy. Just days after the board of trustees's vote to declassify, two of the paper's editors arranged for Spitzer and Irving Bieber to spar with each other while reporters took notes. Young Dr. Spitzer argued, "We have to keep step with the times. Psychiatry, which was once regarded as in the vanguard of the movement to liberate people from their troubles is now viewed by many, and with some jutsification, as being an agent of social control. So it makes absolute sense to me not to list as having a mental disorder those individuals who are satisfied and not in conflict with their sexual orientation."

The notion that psychiatrists ought to "keep step with the times" incensed and dismayed the sixty-four-year-old Bieber. That the official line of the APA would be that the "most injured" homosexual, one who doesn't want to change, is fine; and the "least injured," one who has "potential left for restoring his heterosexuality," suffers a disorder "seems wild," Bieber asserted.

"It seems wild to you because you have as your value system that everybody should be heterosexual," Spitzer retorted. A *Times* photographer caught the two men as they punctuated sentences by jabbing angry fingers in the air. "You think it's a value system?" Bieber cried. "[The homosexual's] heterosexuality has been irreparably injured! Injury is not a value. A broken leg is not a value."[60]

Spitzer's arguments in their *New York Times* debate only exacerbated Bieber's indignation, which was shared by more than a few irate APA members. The board had foolishly bent under political pressure from well-organized, militant homosexuals, they complained. Charles Socarides, still seething from the 1973 Honolulu "symposium" at which he'd been booed for making statements about homosexual illness that, until recently, had been widely agreed-upon truths, jumped in to mobilize those who remained on his side. At the next APA convention, he circulated a petition he knew like-minded colleagues would be happy to sign. It demanded that before the APA deleted homosexuality per se from the *DSM*, the entire body of the organization be allowed to vote on it. Under APA regulations, only two hundred signatures were required to force a referendum on any decision made by the board of trustees. The signatures were easily obtained.

The referendum was held in 1974 by mail. Of the 17,905 APA members eligible to cast a vote, only 10,555 bothered to send in a ballot. Fifty-eight percent of them voted to uphold the board of trustees's decision. The seventh printing of the *DSM-II*, which would be published later that year, would not include "homosexuality per se."[61]

Jack Nichols, who'd been the first to say, way back in 1963, that Mattachine must fight the psychiatric stigmatization of homosexuals as sick, was living in Cocoa Beach, Florida, away from the fray. He was working on a book about men's liberation and redefining masculinity. After the APA votes, Frank Kameny wrote to tell him, "All the work that we did through the '60s, with faith and foresight that perhaps someday it might be productive—all that work is now paying off."[62] He knew that Nichols, of all people, would remember how hopeless things had seemed as recently as the preceding decade, and would exult with him about how they seemed to be now.

Chapter 17

THE CULTURE WAR IN EARNEST

A FOOT IN THE WHITE HOUSE DOOR

March 26, 1977: Twelve years earlier, Frank Kameny and his small troop of homosexuals had picketed in front of the White House carrying angry signs: "U.S. Claims No Second Class Citizens: What About Homosexuals?" Now Kameny descended on the White House once again. With him was a small troop of homosexuals—conservatively dressed, just as the picketers had been in April 1965. This time they went through the west gate, walked right up to the door of the West Wing, and entered. They'd been officially invited by Midge Costanza, head of President Jimmy Carter's Office of Public Liaison. Major newspapers were alerted by a National Gay Task Force press release, and their editors sent reporters and photographers to get the extraordinary story. Costanza, playing gracious hostess, zeroed in on Frank Kameny. Her welcome to him relayed to the press what the current event was meant to signify: "I'm sorry it's taken so long for you to be invited to come into a house that belongs to you as much as it belongs to anyone in the country."

Kameny was accompanied through the White House door by six other gay men and six lesbians.[1] It was exhilarating—and eerie, too—to think, as Reverend Troy Perry did, "I am a homosexual, and I am walking through the front door of the White House, where I've been invited for coffee and a chat."[2] "Incredible! We're here! The heartbeat of the country," thought Charlie Brydon, a buttoned-down-looking Seattle businessman serving on the National Gay Task Force board. He'd been invited to the "chat" to talk about the persecution gay people suffered at the hands of the military.[3] A straight woman was with them also: Charlotte Spitzer, mother of a lesbian and leader of a Los Angeles branch of Parents and Friends of Gays. It was Reverend Perry's suggestion that a mother of a homosexual be part of the party, to show America that gays and lesbians weren't those clichéd figures of desolation, wretchedness, and twilight—that they belonged to families who stood up for them and loved them.

The party was told to arrive a little early for a look into the Oval Office, which was just opposite the Roosevelt Room, where the meeting was to take place. The Oval Office was empty. President Carter was nowhere to be seen. It was a Saturday—and he just happened to be at Camp David. How much he knew of the meeting before it took place wasn't clear, even to the invitees. Carter had mandated Midge Costanza to be his "window to the nation" and, she claimed, he'd never expected her to get his okay in advance for what she needed to do in that role. It was her job to meet with special interest groups and then convey to him their gripes and hopes. "I'm not in the position where I need permission to do anything," she said defensively to a scandalized reporter who was covering the homosexuals' White House visit for *Stars and Stripes*, the daily newspaper of the armed forces.[4] Some newspapers referred to her as an "unguided missile."[5]

Margaret "Midge" Costanza, daughter of Sicilian immigrants who owned House of Costanza, a sausage factory in Rochester, New York, was the only female in the upper echelons of Carter's staff. She'd been the highest vote getter when she was elected to the Rochester City Council in 1973. She met Jimmy Carter the following year, when she ran, unsuccessfully, to be representative to the New York State Congress and he was the Democratic National Committee campaign chair for congressional elections. When Carter ran for president, Costanza, still a councilwoman, became the first New York Democrat with an official-sounding title to endorse him. He was grateful because at the time hardly anyone in New York knew who he was.[6] Costanza became his New York State campaign coordinator. On

Christmas Day 1976, president-elect Jimmy Carter called to offer her the public liaison job in his White House. The emotional Costanza burst into tears and accepted.[7]

Carter was charmed by Costanza. She was a character. Her work uniform was a tailored pantsuit and three-inch high heels that masked her elfin stature (five feet, 109 pounds), to which her outsized hexagonal-shaped eyeglasses and pixie haircut called attention. Her puckish look allowed her to carry off a cheeky sense of humor. She'd stride into the White House, calling out, "Tell the president I'm back so he can feel secure again!" Once she placed hand on hip, lowered her voice to husky, and quipped to White House visitors about Carter's guileless admission that, being human, he'd committed adultery in his heart many times:[8] "When you see me, you know what the president meant when he talked about lust in his heart."[9]

Costanza had begun work on the meeting with lesbians and gays almost as soon as she started her job in the White House. The official word for the press was that the meeting had come about because Jean O'Leary and Bruce Voeller, cochairs of the National Gay Task Force, had contacted Midge Costanza to request it. And because her job was to meet with representatives from all sorts of diverse groups—veterans, blacks, Hispanics, Native Americans, senior citizens, the disabled, vegetarians—why would she say no to this one? Costanza and O'Leary left a careful paper trail of correspondence, in which the National Gay Task Force requested a meeting; O'Leary and Bruce Voeller went to the White House for a preliminary discussion; and Costanza confirmed that she and her staff would indeed meet with a group of gay and lesbian representatives, whom she asked O'Leary and Voeller to appoint.[10]

But, in fact, the meeting had come about through pillow talk. Throughout her career in politics, Costanza had cultivated the image of a young woman too committed to her work to have amorous relations.[11] When she took the job at the White House, at the age of forty-four, she told the press she'd lived with her parents all her life.[12] She continued to be secretive about her love life all the time she was Carter's assistant. "I date, but not steadily," she said to a *People* magazine reporter, adding that she was "happily buried in White House work."[13] But the seductive Jean O'Leary (once the heartthrob of a half dozen Sisters of the Holy Humility of Mary) had already made a conquest of Midge Costanza.

They'd met in 1976, when O'Leary and the National Gay Task Force were trying to get the Democrats to add the words *sexual orientation* to an antidiscrimination plank in the party platform. Former congresswoman Bella Abzug had failed to make headway with the gay rights bills she'd introduced in 1974 and 1975. But she knew Midge Costanza and suspected she'd want to be helpful to O'Leary. She was right. Costanza was on the Democratic Platform Committee, and she agreed to do what she could. She couldn't do anything. Democrats remembered all too well the 1972 convention where two homosexuals were allowed to speak, and the colossal defeat of George McGovern that followed. Costanza's motion to add "sexual orientation" to the antidiscrimination plank failed by two-thirds of the vote; but she and O'Leary became lovers. Their affair was carried on all during Midge Costanza's White House tenure. Very secretively, of course.[14] In 1977 there was no way an assistant to the president could have let it be known that she had a same-sex lover—one whose great desire was to take a delegation of lesbians and gays inside the White House.

Costanza was realistic and even somewhat cynical about the extent and meaning of her power. As she once admitted about another official meeting, with a visiting foreign dignitary, "What can I do for him? Probably nothing, but he got to see me. He can go home and say he was heard at the White House, and that's what really matters."[15] Gays and lesbians would be heard at the White House.

The fourteen people at the meeting were handpicked by Jean O'Leary and Bruce Voeller. They were on the NGTF board, or they'd founded a gay or lesbian organization back home. They also filled a particular demographic. There were representatives from the east, west, north, and south. There was a black woman (Betty Powell) and a Hispanic man (George Raya). There were young people (Raya, in his twenties, fit a double demographic; as did Pokey Anderson, the twenty-seven-year-old Houstonian who'd started the Gay Political Caucus two years earlier); and there were much older people (Frank Kameny and Myra Riddell, both in their fifties). There was nobody too wild-looking or too politically radical.

O'Leary and Voeller had asked each of the invitees to give a ten-minute presentation on a particular area in which lesbians and gays were discriminated against.[16] Almost no one was an expert on the topic to which he or she had been assigned; they scurried to libraries before the meeting to do their homework. Myra Riddell, a psychotherapist and founder of Southern California Women for Understanding, a group for lesbian professional women, was asked to talk about how the policies of the Department of Housing and Urban Development (HUD) and the Federal Communications Commission (FCC) affected gay people. Charlie Brydon, who worked in the insurance business and founded a gay organization, the Dorian Group, in Seattle, was asked to talk about gays and the Department of Defense. (He'd been an intelligence officer in Vietnam.) Pokey Anderson, whose paying job was now administrative assistant for an oil exploration company, was asked to talk about the treatment of gay people in federal prisons. George Raya, who'd worked as a lobbyist in Sacramento on a consenting adults bill, was asked to talk about what the Department of Health, Education, and Welfare (HEW) could do to help gays.[17]

Costanza brought along to the meeting her chief assistant, Marilyn Haft, a heterosexual attorney who'd coauthored an ACLU handbook, *The Rights of Gay People*. She also brought in a couple of civil rights specialists with the White House Office of Domestic Policy, and two women from the Democratic National Committee. Not exactly individuals with the clout to fix the ills from which lesbian and gay American citizens suffered. But as Costanza knew from the beginning, the meeting was to be not so much a serious forum that would lead to important policy changes as it was a statement that this "house"—the White House—belongs to homosexuals as much as it belongs to any other American citizen.

There'd be follow-up meetings, she promised at the end of the three hours. On behalf of gays and lesbians, she'd get the ears of the Departments of Defense and Justice, the Civil Rights Commission, the Civil Service Commission, HEW, and HUD. She'd make them hear everything she'd just heard about the sufferings and injustices toward gays and lesbians in America. And she'd talk to President Carter right away about reforming the immigration policy and getting the less-than-honorable military discharges of homosexual men and women—an estimated 75,000 since World War II—upgraded to honorable. In six months, she'd call this same group back to the White House, too, Costanza pledged, and at that meeting she'd make sure President Carter would be present.[18]

There were a few follow-up meetings—with the Federal Bureau of Prisons director, who promised to appoint a staff person to deal directly with homosexual complaints and to cease to call prison rape "homosexual," when it was really an act of violence; and with the Public Health Service director, who pledged to inform officers of the US Immigration and Naturalization Service that PHS had adopted the American Psychiatric Association's position and no longer defined homosexuals as "sex deviates."[19] (The INS paid the PHS no mind; the old definition continued to be used until the US Congress passed the Immigration Act of 1990.) President Carter never did meet with the group. Yet Charlie Brydon, Pokey Anderson, Troy Perry, Elaine Noble, Charlotte Bunch, and other gay and lesbian White House guests felt that even if the meeting yielded few concrete results, it had great symbolic weight. The gay and lesbian community, treated so recently as criminals, crazies, sinners, and subversives, had actually been invited inside the White House. They'd sat across the hall from the Oval Office. They'd been given visibility as legitimate American citizens. O'Leary and the National Gay Task Force exaggerated when they called the meeting "a happy milestone on the road to full equality under the law for gay women and men."[20] Yet it felt, at the least, like a foot in the door.

Soon after Midge Costanza sat with gays and lesbians in the Roosevelt Room, antihomosexual rights campaigns broke out across the country. Homosexual teachers were a particular target. When Carter was asked at a press conference what he thought about homosexuals teaching kids, he weaseled out. "I know there are homosexuals who teach, and children don't suffer," he said. "But this is a subject I don't particularly want to involve myself in. I've got enough problems without taking on another."[21] Yet he was implicated in the "subject" by Midge Costanza's audacity in throwing open White House doors to a troop of homosexuals. At other press conferences, President Carter pointedly expressed his deep concern for "preserving the traditional values of the American family," and he urged federal workers living out of wedlock with a member of the opposite sex to get married.[22] Regardless, right-wingers were enraged not only with Midge Costanza but also with the president who hired her and who, as a born-again Christian, should have been one of them and not an enabler of homosexuals. The White House meeting generated more mail—much of it hate mail—than any other single issue during the Carter administration.[23]

Midge Costanza's aide, Marilyn Haft, who'd sat through the

unconventional meeting of lesbians and gays at the White House, was queried about it in the press. She tried to tap dance around the questions of
what the president knew in advance of the visit and what his attitude was
toward homosexuals. "The point is homosexuals are being discriminated
against; the point is not their sexual views," she said.[24] Presidential press
secretary Jody Powell also attempted to do damage control. On *Face the
Nation*, he explained, uncomfortably, that all Americans have a right to put
their grievances before high officials, and what he or anyone feels about
gay rights "doesn't have a thing in the world to do with it."[25]

But there was nothing anyone on the president's staff could say to placate conservatives. The day after the White House meeting, Anita Bryant,
the Florida orange juice singing icon who'd recently started a Christian
crusade against homosexual rights, issued vigorous tirades to all the newspapers that would listen. Homosexuals were trying to say they were discriminated against in jobs and housing, but the fact is, if they'd just stay in
"the closet" they wouldn't have any problem. What they really wanted was
devious: they wanted "the legal right to propose to our children that being
a homosexual or lesbian is not really wrong or illegal."[26] The Office of the
President of the United States had been duped into blessing their abnormal
lifestyle, "dignifying them with a serious discussion on their alleged 'human
rights,'" Bryant howled to the press. She vowed to "lead such a crusade to
stop homosexuals as this country has not seen before."[27]

The following year, Carter demoted Midge Costanza to special assistant for women's affairs and domestic human rights. He also cut her staff
of more than a dozen down to one and moved her office to the basement.
She resigned in August 1978, out the door after twenty months in office.

"NO MORE HIDING IN THE UPSTAIRS
CLOSET WHEN COMPANY COMES"

The Radicalesbians' zap at the Second Congress to Unite Women in 1970
had been lesbians' first successful skirmish with the National Organization
for Women. Word of the little triumph encouraged lesbians who'd long
been closeted in NOW. Arlie Schertell Scott, a Los Angeles NOW officer, seized the day. Scott's petite five-foot-two stature belied strategy skills
worthy of a war room. (She would go on to become NOW's national vice

president for action, and then an assistant attorney general for the state of Massachusetts.) Her status as "Mrs. Doug Scott"—the name of a man to whom she'd been briefly married when she was a student at UCLA—hid her lesbianism during her first year or two in NOW. By 1971, Mrs. Scott was ready to come out and to pull the secret of NOW's substantial lesbian presence out of the closet with her.

With the encouragement of LA NOW's grande dame founder and president, Toni Carabillo (also closeted at the time), Scott drafted a hard-hitting position paper and resolution to be presented at the national NOW conference which, serendipitously, was to be held in Los Angeles. To pull together armies of lesbians and lesbian-friendly NOW members in chapters from New York to San Francisco, Scott was helped by Del Martin and Phyllis Lyon, as well as by Aileen Hernandez, a black woman who'd been a union organizer and was national president of NOW. They lined up the votes in advance of the conference. In case they missed anyone, Scott made sure that her beautifully argued position paper would be placed in the conference packet that all delegates received.

Scott's paper charged that because NOW had been fearful of what "the public" would think, lesbian members were being "treated as step-sisters of the movement." They did the hard work in the National Organization for Women, yet they were expected to "hide in the upstairs closet when company comes." Scott demanded that NOW openly acknowledge the existence and leadership of lesbians in the women's movement and support lesbian rights.

She wouldn't change a syllable to mitigate the paper's harsh tone, but she orchestrated its presentation with Hollywood flair, asking a very feminine-looking actress with heterosexual credentials and a sultry voice, Eve Norman ("Eve Normal," the lesbians in NOW liked to call her among themselves), to read the paper and the resolution at the plenary session which five hundred delegates would be attending. The resolution declared that NOW recognized the double oppression of women who were lesbians and acknowledged that lesbian rights were a legitimate concern of feminism. An astounding 90 percent of the delegates voted aye.

It was obvious that NOW's members and the founder of their organization, Betty Friedan, were at odds. They continued to be at odds when the membership agreed to establish a national task force on lesbian issues, and when they resolved to support civil rights legislation that would end dis-crimination based on sexual orientation. Friedan was furious. Those "con-tinually trying to push lesbianism" on the organization she founded were "disrupters of the women's movement," she complained in 1973.[28] But the women who succeeded her as NOW's national presidents—first Aileen Hernandez and then Wilma Scott Heide—ignored Friedan's jeremiads. Lesbian rights became official NOW policy.

The women's movement didn't fall apart as Friedan predicted. But NOW's friendliness to lesbians did become a favorite talking point of the right-wingers who aimed to crush women's liberation and everything as-sociated with it.

THE RIGHT TAKES ON THE LESBIAN
THREAT TO AMERICAN WOMANHOOD

The Right had plenty of reason to go wild with worry by the 1960s. Life in America was becoming unrecognizable. At the start of the 1960s, there was the birth control pill, approved by the US Food and Drug Adminis-tration (FDA) for use as a contraceptive. Suddenly heterosexual women could have all the sex they wanted without getting married because they no longer had to fear the disgrace of out-of-wedlock pregnancy. And there was no-fault divorce, which meant that in most states no one had to run off to Reno, Nevada, or prove infidelity or cruelty. If a husband or wife claimed "irreconcilable differences," that was enough to put an end to sacred till-death-do-us-part vows. Newspapers were saying that 50 percent of married couples were doing just that. Then there was the feminist movement, which pushed women out of their roles as homemak-ers and child rearers—and those who didn't want to be pushed out were being made to feel like fossils even in their own living room by popular 1970s TV shows touting female independence and power: *The Mary Tyler Moore Show*, *Rhoda*, *One Day at a Time*, *Charlie's Angels*, *The Bionic Woman*, *Wonder Woman*. Then there was legalized abortion, which not only made it possible to be sexually immoral with impunity but also to murder unborn babies. And to crown these iniquities, there were parades in cities all over the country in which perverts and outlaws flew out of closets and marched down streets proclaiming pride in what should be shame and ignominy.

The old-fashioned American family, right-wingers complained, was in danger of extinction.

Phyllis Schlafly was a slim, trim woman with a prominent, obstinate jaw and the look of a 1950s housewife—though she was a graduate of Harvard, ran twice for an Illinois seat in the US Congress, and held a degree in constitutional law. Despite her busy schedule out in the world, she had six children with her husband, John Fred Schlafly, a wealthy corporate lawyer. In the sixties, she wrote a self-published book that sold millions, *A Choice, Not an Echo: The Inside Story of How American Presidents Are Chosen*, which touted the presidential candidacy of Barry Goldwater and made an impassioned plea for the Right to take back the Republican Party from the liberal eastern establishment that was ruining it.[29] She and her husband, both staunch Roman Catholics, were also alarmed by the ungodliness of the Soviets, so they started a rabidly anticommunist organization. But in the 1970s, Phyllis Schlafly found a new cause.

An Equal Rights Amendment, which said, "Equality of rights under the law shall not be denied or abridged by the United States or by any State on account of sex," had been bumping around Washington with no impact since it was drafted by suffragist leader Alice Paul in the 1920s. In February 1970 Betty Friedan and her National Organization for Women descended on the US Senate for a massive demonstration demanding its passage. Because lawmakers hadn't been responsive, on August 26—the fiftieth anniversary of the passage of the Nineteenth Amendment that gave women the vote—NOW mobilized tens of thousands of women to participate in a Women's Strike for Equality. They also finally got Martha Griffiths, Democratic senator from Michigan who'd been in Congress since 1955, to agree to introduce the ERA as a congressional resolution. Griffiths was a good choice to do it. With a "tongue like a blacksmith's rasp," as the media was fond of saying of her,[30] she reminded her fellow Congress members that women made up 51 percent of the nation's population; two million more women than men had voted in the 1968 election; and estimates were that in the next elections, it would probably be three million.[31] Those were the magic words.

But no sooner had Congress passed the resolution than Phyllis Schlafly began exhorting conservative politicians, fundamentalist ministers, and bread-baking housewives to join her in a campaign she called STOP (Stop Taking Our Privileges) ERA. She urged women to write their legislators and tell them, "I want to remain a woman. I want to remain on the pedestal. I want to remain a homemaker."[32] And the threat to American womanhood was not the only thing to fear, Schlafly warned: if the ERA were passed, homosexuals would be allowed to teach children and infect them with their low morals.[33]

Her early efforts failed. By 1973, the amendment had already been ratified by thirty states. With only eight states left to go before it became law, the ERA seemed unstoppable. But Phyllis Schlafly was unstoppable, too.

She was heartened the next year. The Tennessee Legislature had ratified the ERA right after Congress passed it, but as a result of STOP ERA lobbying, Tennessee rescinded the ratification. And the pace of ratifications was slowing: only three more state legislatures ratified in 1974. Six still left to go. Schlafly redoubled her efforts. In 1975 she founded the "pro-family" Eagle Forum, declaring that the organization was devoted to making sure that America "honors the full-time housewife"—which she herself decidedly was not and never had been. Eagle Forum members became foot soldiers in the STOP ERA battle.

But despite the traction Schlafly was getting in the United States—only one state voted to ratify in 1975, and several states were talking about rescinding their earlier ratification—she seemed to be bucking a worldwide trend. Patricia Hutar, who'd been a Barry Goldwater Republican and an assistant chairwoman to the Republican National Committee, was appointed by President Gerald Ford to serve as the US representative to a Commission on the Status of Women in the United Nations (a body already deeply distrusted by right-wingers). Hutar made a move that discomfited fellow conservatives. She proposed that member nations of the United Nations hold conventions to focus on how their governments might rectify discrimination against women. The idea seemed innocuous enough to most members. Delegates from 138 nations, almost all men, voted that a working group be established, and that 1975 be designated International Women's Year.[34] National conventions on gender discrimination were to be held everywhere.[35]

In America, three feminist congresswomen—Democrats Bella Abzug and Patsy Mink, and Republican Margaret Heckler—made the cause their own and got members of Congress (who couldn't forget the stats of which Martha Griffiths had reminded them) to appropriate $5 million for the task. Republican President Ford approved the appropriation. In every state, there'd be conventions at which an agenda of women's issues would be discussed, and delegates would be elected to take those issues to an International Women's Year National Women's Conference, to be held in Houston in November 1977.

A KNOCK-DOWN, DRAG-OUT FIGHT

Phyllis Schlafly's indignation was roused to rage when it was announced that Bella Abzug had been appointed chair of the IWY National Women's Conference. Abzug was the embodiment of all Schlafly despised: a liberal Jewish New Yorker who had no reverence for anything the Far Right held dear. The most recent proof of that was that Abzug and another liberal Jewish New Yorker, Congressmen Ed Koch, had introduced a sweeping federal bill, the Equality Act, to force employers and landlords to accept homosexuals. They'd also introduced the Civil Rights Amendment of 1975, which would have added "affectional or sexual preference" to the 1964 Civil Rights Act. Though neither piece of legislation got very far, Phyllis Schlafly was disgusted that a congresswoman would sponsor immorality. And now that same person was going to head a taxpayer-supported International Women's Year national conference.

Schlafly and a committee of her followers distributed thousands of copies of an audiotape that informed the faithful about who Bella Abzug was and the horrors she wanted to perpetrate on America. If the bills that Abzug introduced had passed, the audiotape declared, "homosexuals could teach our children in schools and be counsellors in city, state, and federal camps."[36] Schlafly was doubly determined that an IWY National Women's Conference headed by Abzug would not take place. She urged Eagle Forum members to write Congress and the president immediately. Tell them to take back the $5 million!

When that drive proved futile, Schlafly tried another tack. "We represent the majority of American women," she told her Eagle Forum. "We must take over these conferences and make sure they project a pro-family, pro-homemaker, pro-morality, pro-life image." She exhorted Eagle Forum

women to "do your job right" and "make the libbers sorry they ever decided to have state conferences!"[37] To help her Eagles do their job right,
Schlafly formed Citizens Review Committees for the purpose of prevent-
ing libbers (mostly lesbians, she hinted) from being elected as delegates and
controlling what the agenda would be at the national conference. She also
pulled together a Pro-Family Coalition of various right-wing groups to
help.

Schlafly's suspicion of the perverted intent of the IWY National Women's
Conference was confirmed when one of her Review Committee spies in
Vermont reported to her that the state conference adopted a lesbian rights
resolution, and delegates were going to present it at the national conference. Jean O'Leary had sent out alerts to lesbian groups in every state of
the union in the name of the National Gay Task Force, saying it was urgent
that at the state conferences they "outmaneuver the right-wingnuts."[38] She
implored lesbians to show up, make their presence felt, vote.

They did, and they got others to vote, too. In Southern California,
Roberta Bennett and Diane Abbitt of MECLA even convinced the men
of their organization to show up at a state conference to be held at the
University of Southern California. MECLA chartered two school buses to
drive the men across town, from West Hollywood to the campus. Jeanne
Córdova, a leader of LA's grassroots lesbians, corralled radical gay men, too,
as well as hundreds of grassroots lesbians.[39] To get into the auditorium, the
radicals in jeans and sweatshirts and the MECLA men in suits stood in line
for hours, and they voted for every lesbian on the slate.[40] But LA's lesbian
activists didn't stop with that victory. They wanted to make sure the lesbian
delegates would find familiar friendly faces in Houston; so they formed an
ad hoc group, Freedom Ride-IWY, which held "Send a Lesbian to Houston" benefits. With the proceeds, they rented a big bus from Continental
Trailways, christened it "the Spirit of Sappho," and offered free transportation to lesbians who weren't delegates but were willing to go to Houston
to cheer on the lesbians who were.[41]

The Pro-Family Coalition vied to outdo them. In Utah, the Mormon
Church urged members to go to the state conference and make their pro-
family views known.[42] Of the eleven thousand people in attendance at
the Salt Lake City meeting, Mormons outnumbered non-Mormons by

ten to one. They adopted pro-family resolutions to present at the national conference, and they swept the delegates election. In some states, huge contingents of Baptists showed up in chartered buses, hoping to control the agenda and elect their own. In Oklahoma, pro-family groups outnumbered other attendees by five to one.[43] Participants in the Mississippi conference thumbed their collective noses at Public Law 94-167, which funded International Women's Year and stipulated that delegations must include "members of diverse racial, ethnic, and religious groups." The Mississippians voted in a delegation of twenty—all white and all Christian, including five men.[44] Their advisor was George Higgins, the grand dragon of the Mississippi Knights of the Ku Klux Klan.[45]

Right-wingers in Des Moines, Iowa, piled into the state meeting to make sure a young woman who was an active Republican and an avid pro-lifer was elected to the Iowa delegation. They got fooled. At the national conference, the woman did vote against the abortion plank as she was supposed to, but she wasn't reliable about the rest of the pro-family slate. Christine Pattee, the only lesbian on the Iowa delegation, was surprised to see the pro-lifer stand when the aye vote was called for the sexual preference resolution. "Well, I'm a teacher," the young woman later told Pattee when the Iowa delegation gathered for cocktails back at the hotel, "and my best friend is another teacher, a gay man. I voted yes for him."[46]

The "libbers and lesbians" outmaneuvered the Right even in the Texas state conference. The Texas Eagle Forum thought they'd easily dominate the proceedings, but only six of the fifty-eight who were voted in as delegates were Christian conservatives. Working through a group called "Lesborados," Texas lesbians had managed to make a deal with Texas Chicanas to support each other's resolutions and delegate candidates.[47] One Pro-Family Coalition member echoed her mentor, Schlafly, in her bitter complaint to the press, "The militant libbers and lesbians were in control, not the grassroots Texas women. There was no shred of morality from the platform."[48] In Minnesota, when an Eagle Forum woman suggested the opening session begin with a prayer and a pledge to the flag, she was hissed, shouted down, and voted out of order. The same thing happened in Colorado: Eagle Forum spies were shocked at the workshops there on atheism and humanism, and "at least twelve workshops on lesbianism."[49]

"Sexual preference" resolutions were eventually adopted by IWY conferences in thirty states. When it was clear that the Right would be outnumbered at the IWY National Women's Conference, Schlafly decided she'd make her displeasure known in other ways. In September her Eagle Forum and the Pro-Family Coalition circulated a petition to be presented at the Houston conference, voicing their objection to the agenda filled with ERA, abortion, and "The Teaching or Glorification of Homosexuality, Lesbianism, or Prostitution [*sic*]."[50] They also decided to hold a counterrally in Houston's Astrohall, which seated eleven thousand people. Conservative churches and right-wing groups from all over the country chartered buses and even planes. Thirteen thousand men, women, and children showed up,[51] cheering wildly at statements such as Republican congressmen Robert Dornan's description of the National Women's Conference delegates as "sick, anti-God, pro-lesbian, and unpatriotic."[52] It was "a war between God and the Devil," as a Louisiana minister characterized it.[53]

The Pro-Family Coalition also raised money to pay for a half-page ad in the *Houston Post* showing a little girl holding a nosegay, a boldfaced headline above her head: "MOMMY, WHEN I GROW UP CAN I BE A LESBIAN?"[54]

They could have saved their ad money because they got plenty of free opportunities to spread their message. On the first day of the National Women's Conference, the *Houston Chronicle*'s front-page headline read "No Apology for Blasting Women's Meet," followed by an article about attorney Jerry E. Smith, who'd just been elected Harris County Republican chairman. In his acceptance speech, the ambitious Smith, who'd later be appointed to a federal judgeship by President Reagan, said that the funding of the conference—a "lesbian-abortionist gathering"—was an "illegal use of taxpayer money," and that the "gaggle of outcasts, misfits, and rejects" who made up the delegates had better "get out of town." Bella Abzug was so upset by the allegation that she was chairing a lesbian-abortionist gathering that she hastened to assure the press that of the forty-six members of the International Women's Year Commission, which was in charge of the conference, thirty-four were married, four were widowed, one was engaged, and "Among us we have seventy-four children and grandchildren."[55] (She neglected to mention that the commission included the lesbian couple Jean O'Leary and Midge Costanza.)

· · ·

Jean O'Leary, still stoked by her adventures in the White House inner sanc-
tum that spring, counted up the number of delegates who were out-front
lesbians: 130. She'd leave nothing to chance when the sexual preference
resolution came up at the National Women's Conference. She arranged
with Pastor Jeri Ann Harvey for meeting space at Houston's gay and lesbian Metropolitan Community Church of the Resurrection, a converted
print shop on Joe Annie Street;[56] then she contacted the lesbian delegates
and asked them to arrive in Houston a couple of days early. They needed
to caucus, to map out a strategy for getting the lesbian rights plank passed.

Two days before the conference opened, O'Leary and Charlotte Bunch
stood at the church's modest makeshift altar and told the lesbian delegates
seated on the rickety metal chairs in the nave that "right-wing elements"
had already singled out lesbians for ferocious attacks. "We need to put
together a careful strategy," O'Leary said. Planks would be discussed in al-
phabetical order during the conference. The lesbian rights plank was titled
"Sexual Preference." That put it way down on the agenda, probably the last
day of the conference. "That's bad and good," she told them. "We need to
make sure that the agenda keeps moving so our issue can get heard. But
being on the last day gives us time. We have to be visible. The delegates
have to see us as an integral part of the conference."

Bunch, still the lesbian movement's best strategist, told them that as
they lobbied for support, they needed to tell straight delegates, "No one is
free until all women are free" and "The right to choose another woman is
an extension of the right of all women to control their own bodies." The
stakes were high, she admonished. "What happens in Houston can help
eliminate myths and stereotypes about lesbians. It can let everyone know
exactly what kind of discrimination we face in society."[57] On a portable
chalkboard, Bunch drew diagrams of where the microphones would be in
the hall. She assigned people to sit close to a mic, to jump up quickly and
make this or that point if necessary.

The caucus met again the following day. It was not a good sign when
policemen banged on the metal door, demanding entrance. "Complaint
from the neighbors," they said. "There are lots of cars parked on the wrong
side of the street." The cars were moved, but the problems didn't go away.
Pastor Harvey came into the nave from her office to say there'd been a
bomb threat. Not necessarily something to take seriously, she said with a

sad smile. They got threats all the time. Houston's MCC was used to such things. The KKK had recently burned a cross on the vacant lot next door.[58]

November 21, 1977: Almost two thousand delegates and eighteen thousand spectators were gathered in the massive Sam Houston Coliseum. Progressive groups had dramatically outfoxed and outmaneuvered Schlafly and the Pro-Family Coalition. Eighty percent of the delegates elected to the conference were not in her pocket. The four hundred or so who were had been incensed on the first two days of the convention when an overwhelming majority had passed hot-button resolutions in support of abortion rights and the ERA. But they were most incensed by the resolution that supported the elimination of discrimination against lesbians in jobs, housing, and credit, and that declared their right to custody of their children.

Those who were pledged to vote for the sexual preference resolution wore orange armbands, which had come about because at the state conference in Los Angeles, Roberta Bennett, chair of the NOW Lesbian Task Force, had printed on orange paper a slate of lesbian and feminist delegates that the task force was supporting. Any participant pledged to vote for those delegates was given an orange armband. Bennett and Jeanne Córdova imported the idea to the Houston conference,[59] where the swaths of orange among the delegates multiplied each day—so that at the plenary session on the last day, when the lesbian resolution was to come up, it seemed *almost* everyone was wearing an armband. It happened as a result of good strategizing. For example, two black lesbians, Betty Powell of the National Gay Task Force board and Barbara Smith of the Combahee River Collective, attended a conference meeting of the Black Women's Caucus where they gave impassioned speeches supporting that group's stance on problems such as domestic violence and welfare rights. Then they asked the Black Women's Caucus to support the sexual preference resolution. Powell overheard women in the audience whispering, "What did they say? They're lesbians? Well, all right. But look at that! The daughters are preaching!"[60]

The sexual preference resolution was presented by Jean O'Leary, Charlotte Bunch, and Ellie Smeal, the newly elected NOW president. Midge Costanza took the microphone to announce she had a word to say on behalf of her boss: "President Carter has said that he knew people who were taught by homosexuals and they were never negatively affected by that," she told the crowd (omitting his Pontius Pilate statement that followed: "This is a subject I don't particularly want to involve myself in"[61]). Then Costanza added on her own behalf, "I get very emotional about this issue because I feel very strongly that you should have the right to love whomever you want. I do."[62] Cryptic as her personal statement may have been to most people, it was a love-offering to Jean O'Leary, and was as close as Costanza would come to outing herself.

When Betty Friedan walked onto the stage, those who'd been familiar with her "Lavender Menace" pronouncements were uneasy. Pokey Anderson, a Texas delegate, felt her heart sink. What good could come of this?[63] Anderson couldn't know that Ellie Smeal and Aileen Hernandez, the past president of NOW, had made clear to Friedan that if anything was a "disrupter of the women's movement," it was her divisive stand on lesbians. If she hoped to bring women together in a final push to get the ERA passed, they'd cautioned her, she needed to stop dividing them. Even former First Lady Betty Ford, a Republican, had endorsed the lesbian plank, they said. (Betty Ford would tell the media, "It's not lesbians' fault that they happen to be born with different genes, and they shouldn't be discriminated against.")[64] Nor could Pokey Anderson know that Dolores Alexander, who'd once worked closely with Friedan as the executive director of NOW, had cornered her earlier in the conference. "It'll never happen," Barbara Love warned Alexander; NOW's founder was a homophobic harridan. But Alexander, sitting next to Friedan in a half-empty auditorium, waiting for a session to begin, convinced her it was in her power to transform the energy wasted on dissention into an overwhelming push for what was dearest to her heart. All she had to do was stand up onstage and say something good about the sexual preference resolution.[65]

Getting the ERA passed had been Betty Friedan's obsession since 1970. If making nice about lesbians—which even a prominent Republican was now doing—would help garner support for her most important project, how could she hold out? "I'll do it," she told Dolores Alexander, who arranged for her to speak.

"I am known to be violently opposed to the lesbian issue in the women's movement, and, in fact, I have been," Friedan solemnly told the audience. Pokey Anderson held her breath. Friedan talked about growing up provincially in Peoria, Illinois, and about loving men ("too well," she added, and the audience fell into such peals of laughter that the chair had to call out, "Please stay in order!").[66] "I've had trouble with this issue, as have many other women who grew up as I have. We've all made mistakes in our view of the issue, but we have all learned." Pokey Anderson was dumbfounded. Was Friedan reversing herself? The hall erupted in deafening cheers. "Please stay in order! Please stay in order!" the chair yelled frantically.

"And now," Friedan said when the din subsided, "in the historic unity of this day, and because we will need every ounce of all our efforts in the next thirteen months to get the ERA ratified, I suggest that you waste no further time in debating this issue, and join us in voting support of the resolution on sexual preference. There's nothing in the ERA that will help lesbians, so it's the duty of the women's movement to help them win their own civil rights." Then she seconded the resolution.

"Please stay in order!" the chair shouted again above the wild roar.[67]

Barbara Love, wearing a T-shirt that proclaimed "Matriarchy,"[68] was sitting next to a floor mic, and she jumped up to seize it. "I'm a proud lesbian delegate-at-large from New York State," Love shouted into the microphone, "and I move that we call the question." Eleanor Holmes Norton was right behind her, waiting to talk in support of the resolution, but the chair asked all those in favor of the sexual preference resolution to please rise.[69] Almost everyone in the hall leaped to her feet.

The convention hall erupted in pandemonium. "Thank you, sisters!" lesbians shouted. The nondelegate lesbians sitting in the balconies[70] released one thousand blue, red, pink, and yellow balloons (which some volunteers had quietly inflated with a helium tank that Pokey Anderson hid behind the bleachers that morning). "We Are Everywhere" was the logo stamped on them. Women cried, jumped up on their chairs, snake-danced around the convention hall.[71]

"All those opposed, please stand," the chair, forgotten now, shouted above the chaos. Almost no one in the crowd-gone-wild noticed. The twenty Mississippi delegates stood, turned their backs to the podium, bowed their heads in prayer, and raised signs saying "Keep Them in the Closet."[72]

Others from the Pro-Family Coalition got out their address books and scribbled down one another's addresses. Delegate Winkie LeFils, vice president of the National Council of Catholic Women, told media reporters that what had just happened would "strengthen my communication with other pro-family delegates. I'll be corresponding with all of them this month."[73]

To ignite the Right further, particularly the Christian conservatives, who'd always regarded homosexuality as the devil's work, Schlafly spread word through her *Eagle Forum Newsletter* of the "dreadful goings-on," real and imagined, at the conference. She informed her readers that in the Houston Coliseum's exhibit hall, "lesbian forces" had been handing out "materials" touting their lifestyles. (The "materials" were mostly circulars that advertised services, events, and businesses such as lesbian support groups, lesbian music festivals, and lesbian publishers.) Not only were the lesbians "waging war on the American family," Schlafly proclaimed, but also "it will shock you to know that this kind of materials is financed with $5 million of your money." (The "materials" were paid for by the groups and businesses involved.) One of Schlafly's adherents, a western Oklahoma farmwoman, collected every one of the lesbian circulars and pasted them onto sixty poster boards to display at a Farm Bureau Convention, to show what taxpayer dollars were funding in lieu of more generous funding for farm subsidies. Her display was so "eye opening" that it traveled to thirty states and became a recruiting tool for the Far Right.[74]

The original mandate of the International Women's Year Conference had been "to identify the barriers that prevented women from participating fully and equally in all aspects of national life," and to make recommendations for ways to knock down those barriers. But by the time of the conference, conservatives had created gridlock in the Senate. Almost none of the conference recommendations were acted upon. Yet the conference was hugely encouraging for lesbians. For the first time, they were assured on a large scale that they had good friends among heterosexuals. Some of the most surprising groups had supported their resolution, including the Young Women's Christian Association, the American Association of University Women, and the National Federation of Business and Professional Women's Clubs. Perhaps even more important, the lesbians' strategizing at the conference and their learning to think big—on a national stage—would be critical for future battles.

But the conference itself accomplished nothing for their civil rights.

Even worse, it created fodder for the Right. Through what Phyllis Schlafly billed as the "outrages" of the conference, she built an empire of right-wing fanatics who would work to kill the ERA and to push their pro-family and virulently antilesbian and antigay agenda.

Time magazine reported that as a result of the National Women's Conference, the ultraconservatives were "on the march as never before."[75] The culture war, one that was to last for decades, had begun in earnest.

PART 6

HOW ANITA BRYANT ADVANCED GAY
AND LESBIAN CIVIL RIGHTS

Chapter 18

ENTER, ANITA

EARLY WARNING: THE LIMITS OF LIBERAL MIAMI

Bob Basker, a fifty-four-year-old transplant from New York and Chicago, arrived in Miami a couple of years after the Stonewall riots and was appalled that South Florida gays seemed to spend their time lolling under the palms or frolicking on the sand instead of rolling up their sleeves and advancing the cause. Basker's conservative, mild-mannered appearance belied his long history of political activism, which began in 1935, when, at the age of seventeen, he threw himself wholeheartedly into a peace strike. He'd also protested the Vietnam War. He'd worked for black civil rights—his house had been firebombed because he helped a black family move into an all-white neighborhood of Skokie, Illinois. And in Chicago, he'd cofounded Mattachine Midwest, which he led in a successful campaign to fight police roundups of homosexuals ("The Harvest of the Fruits," Basker sardonically called such harassment).[1] In the midst of all this, he'd married a woman because he wanted children. When she divorced him and took the children to live with her and her new husband in Communist Cuba, he followed to be near them. He had to flee Cuba after he protested government persecution of two lesbian teachers.[2] Now he was ready to stir things up again in Miami.

He finally ran into others who'd join with him in a Miami Gay Activists Alliance, and they found a meeting place at St. John's Lutheran Church, which had long been a hub of progressive activity. The pastor of St. John's, Reverend Don Olson, even made the church's Center for Dialogue available to them for open meetings to organize protest demonstrations at the upcoming 1972 Republican and Democratic Conventions.[3] Another member of the Gay Activists Alliance, Steven Wayne Foster, asked Reverend Olson if it would also be possible to have a gay library at St. John's. "Certainly," the reverend said. They could make a library on the second floor of the church building, right next to the Center for Dialogue. Basker and Foster and other Gay Activists Alliance members were soon lugging boxes of gay books and art up to the second floor of St. John's Lutheran Church, and Florida's first gay library was born.

It didn't last long. Less than three weeks later, the reverend passed the open door of the library. From the corridor, anyone could see posters of bare-chested men on the walls, and in prominent display on the shelves, among titles such as *The City and the Pillar* and *The Lord Won't Mind*, other titles like *The Leather Boys*, *Gay Whore*, and *Hollywood Homo*. The reverend was uncomfortable. "Keep the library door closed at all times," he told Foster, who, insulted on behalf of the Gay Activists Alliance, put all the books back into boxes, wrapped up the art, and carried everything down the stairs again.[4] In its rapid rise and fall, the infant gay library at St. John's Lutheran revealed not only the limits of liberal Miami in the early 1970s, it foreshadowed the surprising betrayal of gays and lesbians by liberal Miamians in 1977.

BABY STEPS OUT OF THE 1950S

During World War II, an air force training base was located in Miami, and gay soldiers from colder climes were introduced to the paradise of laid-back sophistication and weather that stayed balmy even at winter's height. After the war, many returned, just as they did to other cities where they'd been stationed or had gone for R & R, and had found to be more copasetic than their hometowns.[5] A gay community burgeoned in Miami, and gay hangouts flourished. Police harassment soon grew, too. When a seven-year-old girl was abducted, raped, and murdered in 1954, one of the first targets of police investigation (under the logic that "sexual perverts" were capable of any perversion) was Miami's "Powder Puff Lane." Police en masse swooped down on the gay bars and hauled everyone off for questioning. Needless to say, the little girl's homicidal rapist was not found among the gay bar patrons; but the homosexual nature of the bars and the names of the arrestees, along with their addresses and places of employment, were printed in the papers—by now a common occurrence in American cities. *Miami Herald* headlines in the summer of 1954 were screaming almost daily about gays: "5,000 Here Perverts, Police Say," "[Homosexuality,] a Disease 'Worse Than Alcohol,'" "Pervert Clean-Up Starts Tonight."[6]

Throughout the 1950s and 1960s, Miami police kept trying to "clean up the perverts." In 1972 the Gay Activists Alliance decided to take them on: "What precisely constitutes an 'indecent, lascivious, or lewd proposal?' Does dancing between two members of the same sex automatically violate the prohibition against 'any indecent or lewd act'? How about rock n' roll dancing where no bodily contact takes place?" they demanded of Police Chief Eugene Gunn.[7] He did not dignify such questions with answers.

The following year, Gay Activists Alliance members filed a class-action suit. They complained to the US District Court that in Miami Beach's gay neighborhood during the previous month four hundred homosexuals had been hauled off to jail for no substantial reason. Police officers who prowled the area hurled verbal abuse at gay people, calling them animals, faggots, fairies. Police cars regularly sat in front of a gay discotheque with their lights turned on high beam while officers videotaped all those who entered or left. One Saturday night in May, a paddy wagon backed up to the door of the disco and patrons, who were doing nothing but talking and drinking or dancing, were pulled out, shoved into the van, and carted off to the police station. Four years past the Stonewall riots, nothing had changed in the Miami area since the 1950s—and nothing came of the class-action suit. It was dismissed.

Having met only frustrations, the Miami Gay Activists Alliance fizzled out, but Bob Basker was not ready to give up. When the Florida Advisory Committee to the US Commission on Civil Rights convened in Miami in 1975, he showed up to testify. Miami police were abusing gay people and violating their civil rights, he complained. He described a raid a few months earlier at a private gay bathhouse, Club Miami. Undercover policemen had bought memberships so they could return night after night to spy on what the patrons were up to. Then they pounced. They seized the club's membership records, and they demanded a pass key from the manager. They barged into private rooms. Even those found simply sleeping were hauled out into the corridor and made to stand there totally nude. When one man asked to be allowed to cover himself, the policemen yelled antigay insults at him. Sixty-four patrons were arrested for "unnatural and lascivious conduct." They were dragged out of the building amid the glare of television lights and cameras and were taken to jail. The "St. Valentine's Day Massacre," gays called it. Eventually all charges against them were dismissed because the judge acknowledged that what they were doing was between consenting adults, without any effect on or interference with the general public. But, Basker testified to the committee, though the men were exonerated under the law, they had suffered trauma and public exposure, for which there was no remedy. The Florida Advisory Committee to the US Commission on Civil Rights did not think there needed to be one.[8]

Basker would not give up. The following February he tried to bring together the various Miami lesbian and gay groups, such as the Lesbian Task Force of the National Organization for Women and the Metropolitan Community Church, and unite them under the banner of the Alliance for Individual Rights. He asked representatives of those groups to come with him to an Issues Convention of the Democratic Party of Dade County, which includes Miami. There Basker testified that dozens of cities all over the country now had inclusive antidiscrimination ordinances. They protected people not only on the basis of race and religion, as a Dade County ordinance already did, but also on the basis of "personal appearance, affectional or sexual preference, family responsibilities, matriculation, political affiliation, or source of income," he told the convention. He added that even Washington, DC, the nation's capital, had such an ordinance, "and Washington, DC, is still in existence!" he quipped.

The convention delegates rejected his resolution, but the vote had been remarkably close: 42 to 38. Basker thought that Miami's lazy and apolitical gays and lesbians were to blame for the loss. He'd gotten delegate status to the convention for several members of the Alliance for Individual Rights, but not one of them showed up for the vote. He was barely able to contain his anger when he wrote them, "I believe that this is a time for some serious self-examination. Had only five delegates from the Alliance for Individual Rights been there, we would have won a great victory. Just their presence would have made the difference . . . I have run out of steam," he concluded. "It's now up to you."[9]

Though Basker was puzzled by gay and lesbian Miami's apathy, it's not hard to surmise the feelings of hopelessness behind it and the cultivated modus vivendi of "keeping one's head down," which had allowed Florida's homosexuals to survive. Miami, Florida's most liberal city, was no New York or Los Angeles or San Francisco. Gays and lesbians had yet to see any reason to believe that hostility toward them would be reversed by fiat of law anywhere in the mid-1970s South. Why should they spin their wheels at a Democratic Party Issues Convention?

But Basker was from New York. He was friends with Frank Kameny, who kept him informed about the progress gays and lesbians were making in Washington, DC. And in Chicago, he'd witnessed how political activism could stop "the Harvest of the Fruits." A few weeks after his peeved declaration that he'd run out of steam, he was again raring to go. Basker convinced Jack Campbell, the proprietor of the recently raided Club Miami, to help him set some fires. Campbell (a putative descendant of Queen Victoria, to whom he bore a slight resemblance) was the wealthy owner of not only Club Miami but also a long string of gay bathhouses all over America. In 1975 he'd run for the Miami City Commission, hoping to unseat J. L. Plummer, a right-wing moralist who'd purportedly pressured the police chief into raiding Club Miami. But running as an out gay man, Campbell received only 20 percent of the vote, for which he, too, angrily blamed apathy within the gay community.[10] The two men agreed: the gay community had to be shaken up.

In the spring of 1976, Campbell and Basker arranged a meeting with Dr. Alan Rockway, a clinical psychologist, and Bob Kunst, an energetic and handsome thirty-four-year-old who'd been fired recently from his job as publicist for the soccer team the Miami Toros after a brochure for a gay retreat was spotted on his desk. Kunst and Rockway were now codirectors of the Transperience Center, a small operation on the second floor of a building above a marine supplies shop. The Transperience Center offered very 1970s "alternative counseling" and encounters in the nude, meant to put people in touch with their sexuality and confirm to straight and gay participants alike that everyone is naturally bisexual. The four men sat in the elegant living room of Campbell's Coconut Grove home and brainstormed. Surely there were others in Miami who might be interested in demanding gay rights. Who were they? What rights should be demanded? How exactly should they go about it?

By early summer, Basker, along with Campbell, Kunst, and Rockway, managed to pull together a few representatives of various lesbian and gay groups, none of them very political: the Theban Motorcycle Club, the Metropolitan Community Church, and the gay and lesbian synagogue, Etz Chaim. They would form a coalition. In anticipation of predictable lesbian-feminist criticism that the group was largely male, Lisa Berry, the assistant pastor of the Metropolitan Community Church, was made a cochair, along with Jack Campbell and Bob Kunst. But after some weeks, Berry dropped out, which confirmed lesbian feminists in their conviction that lesbians couldn't work with gay men. Since there were no more women in the group, the general meetings were now held at the Candlelight Club, a lushly landscaped private club in Coconut Grove that catered primarily to wealthy, white gay men and was owned by Bob Stickney, who headed the Bar Association, an organization formed recently to fight police harassment of gay bars.[11]

In August the group struggled to name itself. Bob Kunst suggested the Sexual Civil Liberties Coalition. Someone else suggested the Dade County Coalition for Gay Rights. Another person suggested the Dade County Humanistic Coalition for Gay Rights. The secretary who took the minutes crossed out one name after another.[12] Jay Pryor of Etz Chaim came up with the pompous but somewhat less threatening Dade County Coalition for the Humanistic Rights of Gays. That was the name they finally agreed on.[13] Then they struggled to define their purpose. They would figure out which local political candidates they should be supporting and then get those candidates to pass legislation that would help the gay community. . . . Their first goal would be to get a bill passed that would ban antigay discrimination in housing, employment, and public accommodations.[14] They would dangle before the politicians the promise of the "gay vote," and they would invite them to be vetted to appear on an "election recommendation flyer."

An important local race was coming up. All the Dade County Commission seats were in contest for that fall's election; and several of the candidates agreed to be vetted. What was there to lose? Despite police prejudice, 1976 Miami was, after all, fairly liberal, with its many transplants from New York and other big eastern cities. And anyway, who but other gays would pay attention to the fact that a politician was being endorsed by a gay group?

As it happened, five of the Dade County Commission's nine seats were won by candidates that the coalition endorsed. "Okay! We did the work, and now it's time to collect our chips," Bob Kunst urged.[15] They decided to invite a heterosexual University of Miami professor of law and psychiatry, Bruce Winick, to help draft a statement. They'd request that the board of county commissioners declare itself "sensitive to the fact that many persons who have homosexual preferences often experience great difficulty in finding suitable employment and housing accommodations," and they'd ask the commissioners to add the words "affectional or sexual preference" to the existing Dade County nondiscrimination ordinance.[16]

The coalition's next step was to decide on the most effective sponsor for the revised ordinance. Of the candidates they vetted, Ruth Shack impressed them most. She was another New York transplant who'd been an activist for all sorts of progressive causes: black civil rights, elder rights, legalized abortion, the ERA. She was forty-five years old, the mother of three grown daughters, and married to a successful theatrical agent with clients such as the Arbors Quartet ("Up in the valley of the Jolly Green Giant!" "When you're out of Schlitz, you're out of beer!"), who pitched jingles for advertising heavyweights. Ruth Shack was straight, but she'd been a rebelliously ambitious daughter of the Depression, and she spoke of her struggles against conforming to gender roles. She understood those who were different. She made it clear she was very sympathetic to gay people.

Basker and Campbell met with her again. Of course she'd be delighted to sponsor an amendment to the county's nondiscrimination ordinance, she told them. But the language they wanted to use in the amendment made her a bit uncomfortable. "Why does *sex* have to be mentioned? Why not substitute a word like *gender* instead?" she suggested.

Jack Campbell said that *gender* was ambiguous in this context. Bob Basker assured her that nearly forty cities in America had nondiscrimination ordinances with a phrase like "affectional or sexual preference." It was the accepted language; it created no problem in other places, he said. Shack finally agreed to sponsor the amendment with the four words intact.[17]

But, as she feared, those words waved a red flag. "You're sponsoring a gay-protection law?" a reporter from the *Miami Herald* asked. "The amendment is about nothing but *human rights*," she insisted. The reporter implied that she was in thrall to the "strength of the gay lobby." Untrue! she answered; she was sponsoring the measure only because she believed in its *appropriateness*. "Wherever there is discrimination, it is *inappropriate*," she kept reiterating.[18] She'd been certain, she said later, that the citizens of Miami shared her conviction that everyone deserves human rights, "because Miami is a very liberal community."[19] But she and the coalition had misjudged. By the seventies, most Americans, not just liberals, would agree heartily that "everyone deserves human rights"—except for homosexuals, the one group it was still "appropriate" to hold in utter contempt.

Ruth Shack presented the bill for a first reading on Pearl Harbor Day, December 7, 1976. The Dade County commissioners were told that many other American cities already had ordinances that prohibited discrimination against people for their affectional or sexual preferences. Commissioner James Redford raised his hand to object: under Florida's antisodomy laws, homosexual sex was illegal. "I'm a landlord myself, and I want to protect other landlords' rights against having illegal acts performed on their premises."

"Of course," Shack agreed. They could insert a provision. Landlords would remain free to impose lease clauses prohibiting "illegal acts."

Stuart Simon, the county attorney whose job it was to advise the commissioners, assured them that the amendment did nothing but ban discrimination in housing and employment. Under the amendment, a person wouldn't be discriminated against if he or she had homosexual *preferences*, but there was nothing in the amendment that legalized *acting* on those preferences.[20] A comparison could be made to President Carter admitting in the pages of *Playboy* that he sometimes experienced "lust in his heart": *acknowledging* his lust was not the same as *acting* on it.[21] That was assurance enough to several commissioners who'd been wrestling with the fact that sodomy was criminal in Florida.

There were no further objections. Perhaps as new commissioners, they didn't want to be responsible for making Miami look more provincial than, for instance, East Lansing, Michigan, which had adopted such an ordinance in 1972.

But Miami media seemed unconcerned about "provincial" and uninterested in fine distinctions between the *status* of being homosexual and the *act* of homosexuality. They were shocked by what the commission had done. The *Miami News* editor wanted to know, "If homosexuals are accepted as a legitimate minority, then why not people with long hair? . . . Why not nail biters?"[22] Steve Daily, radio host at Miami station WINZ, opined with loathing: "To say that county commissions have any obligation to ease the life of homosexuals is to say that the same attention is deserved by drunks, drug addicts, and habitual criminals."[23] The new Dade County commissioners were caving in to the demand of outlaws, it seemed. How might they be brought to their senses?

THE "DIVINE DISTURBANCE" IN
ANITA BRYANT'S HEART

Anita Bryant was an Oklahoman who'd moved to Miami sixteen years earlier when she married Bob Green, a good-looking teen-idol disc jockey rumored at the time to be the choice for Dick Clark's successor on *American Bandstand*. Bryant, who grew up in the tiny town of Velma-Alma, Oklahoma, had been beauty-queen pretty. As an eighteen-year-old, she'd been Miss Oklahoma; and as a nineteen-year-old, she'd been the second runner-up in the Miss America Beauty Pageant. She'd also been a staunch Southern Baptist since childhood and never lost her Old Testament horror of cities as cesspools of depravity. But she'd had ambitions for a theatrical career, and her husband convinced her that they could not be realized if she remained in Velma-Alma.[24] Soon after coming to Miami she'd met agent Richard Shack, who was impressed by her stage presence and pleasant singing voice, and he promoted her career. By the 1970s, she was a familiar face and voice all over America, earning $500,000 a year and living in a twenty-seven-room Spanish stucco mansion on Biscayne Bay.

Bryant taught Sunday school and tithed a bountiful 10 percent of her income to the Northwest Baptist Church in Northern Miami, a Southern

Baptist congregation. In June 1976, six months before the first reading of the Dade County Commission's extension of the antidiscrimination ordinance, the Southern Baptist Convention, concerned about the various recent successes of the gay and lesbian movement across the country, had passed a resolution at the national meeting. It affirmed that homosexuality was a sin, and it urged all Southern Baptist congregations "not to afford the practice of homosexuality any degree of approval." Northwest Baptist Church wholeheartedly supported this resolution.

It was through Anita Bryant's pastor at Northwest Baptist, the Reverend William Chapman—"Brother Bill," as his flock called him—that she learned that the county commissioners were revising the nondiscrimination ordinance to protect homosexuals—and that they must be stopped. "As our pastor spoke," she recalled, "I suddenly started to realize what he was saying. The thought of known homosexuals teaching my children . . . bothered me."[25] The Reverend Chapman was thrilled that she was "bothered," because he couldn't have found a more illustrious spokesperson as figurehead for the battle against the county commissioners. Bryant's recordings of the singles "Till There Was You," "Paper Roses," and "My Little Corner of the World" had each sold over a million copies. She did commercials for Coca-Cola, Tupperware, Kraft Foods, Holiday Inn. She was paid $100,000 yearly by the Florida Citrus Commission to push orange juice with her jingle "Come to the Florida Sunshine Tree." The Republicans had invited her to sing "The Star Spangled Banner" at their national convention. Lyndon Johnson, a fellow southerner, had invited her often to the White House, and she'd sung "The Battle Hymn of the Republic" at his graveside. And she had a contract with Singer Sewing Machines to star in a weekly television program for which she was doing a pilot.

But why would a national figure, a much-in-demand pop icon like Anita Bryant, become involved in so minor a local issue as the addition of four words to an existing county ordinance? Because, she said, she'd learned to sing "Jesus Loves Me" at her grandfather's knee when she was two years old, and she never forgot it. In addition to her singing career, she wrote books that bore titles such as *Bless This Food: The Anita Bryant Family Cookbook—An Inspiring Personal Guide to Christian Family Togetherness Through Home Cooking, Faith, and Love* and *Raising God's Children*. In 1976 she'd toured the country, singing gratis and talking about her Christian beliefs in

Baptist churches large and small. Asked in Blytheville, Arkansas, "Which has priority in your life, your commercial career or your evangelical work?" she answered as quick as an eye blink, "No question!" She chose God.[26]

And now, Bryant lamented, the Dade County amendment to promote homosexuality was at least partly her fault. When Ruth Shack had decided that she would run for a seat on the Dade County Commission, her husband's client the Arbors Quartet presented her with a gift of a singing commercial to promote her campaign. Soon after the ad aired, Anita Bryant found herself on an airplane with her agent. "Richard, why didn't you ask me to do a commercial for Ruth, too?" she said graciously. "I'd be happy to."[27] She was also happy to donate $1,000 to Ruth's campaign.[28] So it was Anita Bryant's good name, talent, and money that had helped Ruth Shack get elected: Christians had voted for Shack because Bryant had vouched for her.

After listening to Brother Bill's sermon against the amendment to protect homosexuals, Bryant went home and called Ruth Shack. For more than an hour, she begged Shack to withdraw sponsorship. Red leather-bound Bible in hand, Bryant even read Leviticus to her. Shack's response was to quote the Constitution.[29]

But Bryant could not drop the issue that had created a "divine disturbance" in her heart because, she claimed, she was "into God's word more deeply than ever before." God, with the help of Brother Bill, dictated to her a letter of protest, replete with biblical quotations that called for the death of sodomites, which she sent to the commissioners: "As a concerned mother of four children—ages 13 to 8 years—I am most definitely against this ordinance amendment [because] you would be discriminating against my children's right to grow up in a healthy, decent community," she wrote.[30]

The letter of protest was only the beginning. God also told her, Bryant proclaimed, to go with others from her church to the commission hearing and make her protest known. As she waited for the day of the requisite second reading of the amendment to approach, she spent agonizing hours walking through the house and crying because she did not want to go to the meeting and have to get up there and speak. But, she said, it was Brother Bill and God who "built up my faith and confidence." In the weeks before the meeting, Bryant agreed to appear on every local radio program that would have her, to alert the public to the dangers of the ordinance that the commission intended to pass.[31]

The average January daytime temperature in Miami is 75 degrees; at night it might dip as low as 60. But on January 18, 1977, the day of the Dade County Commission's second reading of the amendment, the temperature dropped to the low 30s. Busloads of people bundled in heavy coats and scarves, carrying placards that read "Don't Legislate Immorality for Dade County," "Protect Our Children," and "God Says *No!* Who Are You to Say Different?" stormed the county courthouse. The commission chamber was soon clogged with four hundred churchly people who took up most of the seats and stood three and four deep all around the room. Another hundred kept vigil in the lobby.

Mayor Stephen Clark led the meeting. He announced he would limit the debate to forty-five minutes for each side. The revered senior rabbi of the reform Temple Israel, Joseph Narot, who'd been a champion of black civil rights and a strong opponent of the war in Vietnam, spoke in favor of the amendment: "If God is love, then let it be the love for all mankind," he said.[32] Those who'd come to protest the amendment jeered him. Bob Kunst, speaking on behalf of the Dade County Coalition for the Humanistic Rights of Gays, hailed the amendment as "a breath of fresh air." (Ruth Shack remembers being mortified because "The first words out of Kunst's mouth were 'Oral is moral.'"[33]) He was booed loudly. Mayor Clark banged his gavel and threatened to cancel the hearing if the onlookers didn't behave.

The crowd became only slightly subdued. Those speakers who made antihomosexual biblical allusions were greeted by loud calls of "Amen!" A representative of the Archdiocese of Miami said that allowing homosexuals to teach children was like allowing a fox in the chicken coop. Alvin Dark, onetime star major-league baseball player and manager—who famously complained in 1964 that black and Hispanic players on his San Francisco Giants team "are just not able to perform up to the white players when it comes to mental alertness"[34]—waved a Bible at the commissioners and declared homosexuality to be "an abomination to the Lord." Reverend Charles Couey from the South Dade Baptist Church took the podium, opened his Bible, and read from Romans 1:22–32. Joseph Betsey, a member of the Community Affairs Committee of the Glendale Missionary Baptist Church, testified that his church "had prayed about this situation," and he was here to say that "God has wrath against those who disobey him . . . The wages of sin is death [*sic*]."[35]

It was the Scopes Monkey Trial, replayed in Miami fifty-two years later.

Anita Bryant was, of course, the star of the antis. She spoke in a voice choked with emotion. She opposed the amendment because, she said, "Homosexuals will recruit our children. They will use money, drugs, alcohol, any means to get what they want."[36] As an entertainer, she'd worked with homosexuals all her life, she told the crowd. Her attitude had always been "live and let live." But, she proclaimed, eyes shiny with tears, the commissioners had absolutely no right to impose homosexuals on the citizenry. Enough was enough: "Now it is time to realize the rights of the overwhelming number of Dade County constituents."[37]

Finally, after eighteen impassioned testimonies, the commissioners voted: five ayes and three nays: one nay from Neil Adams, an African American Baptist minister; one from the only woman on the commission other than Shack, Clara Oesterle, who covered her face and wept after she voted; and one from Mayor Clark. Commissioner Barry Schreiber, an Orthodox Jew, had claimed illness and avoided the vote. The amendment to add the words "affectional or sexual preference" to the Dade County nondiscrimination ordinance, Mayor Clark announced, had passed.

Those who'd come to city hall to make the recalcitrant commissioners understand the displeasure of the citizenry chanted loudly, "Recall! Recall! Recall!"[38] It was a futile demonstration because the entire commission had been elected the preceding fall, and under Dade County law, no commissioner who had served for less than a full year could be recalled. "Now I'm not only aflame, I'm on fire!" the flushed and furious Bryant told reporters who waylaid her in the corridor. She vowed not to rest till Dade ceased coddling homosexuals.[39]

There in the corridor, attorney Robert Brake, a staunch Catholic who fought against the legalization of abortion and was now a suburban city commissioner from Coral Gables, stepped up to Bryant where she stood with Brother Bill and her husband. Brake had spoken against the amendment at the hearing so they knew he was on their side. If the Dade County Commission would not reverse its decision, Brake told them solemnly, there were other ways to keep the amendment from taking effect. They must form an organization to defeat the amendment by petition and referendum, and Anita Bryant must lend her famous name to it as its "chairman." "Absolutely! I will!" Bryant exclaimed. "Absolutely!" Brother Bill and Bob Green agreed.[40] They would get started immediately. As the angry mob was filing out of the chamber, Brake pulled pads of blank paper from a briefcase. "Listen, everyone. If you're against what just happened, sign and give your phone number!" he called above the din. All who signed would be contacted with petitions to put repeal of the amendment on the ballot. Let the voters of Dade County decide if they want to protect the rights of homosexuals.[41]

That night, during the wee hours, it snowed. As the *Miami Herald* observed later, snow in Miami was "the equivalent of hell freezing over."[42]

Robert Brake's collecting of signatures in the corridor of city hall was the beginning. Next Anita Bryant called a press conference. She was flanked by a small army—Brother Bill, the pastors of the First Spanish Presbyterian Church, the Shenandoah Presbyterian Church, St. Sophia's Greek Orthodox Church, representatives of the Orthodox Rabbinical Council of Greater Miami, the Caribbean Baptist Association; and, close to her side, her strapping blond husband, Bob Green (a lukewarm Lutheran who'd been "born again" at her urging on their wedding night).[43] She was starting an organization called Save Our Children, Bryant announced, and on behalf of "our children," she was fighting to overturn the "homosexual ordinance."[44]

The men of the cloth who'd accompanied Bryant to the press conference were only a fraction of those who were passionately supportive of her cause. Week after week, ministers standing in the pulpit urged their congregants to put their signatures on the petitions and, in the name of scripture, make a stand against homosexuality. Save Our Children volunteers stood on street corners and went door to door distributing leaflets in both English and Spanish about the dangers of homosexuality. Spanish leaflets aimed at the Cuban community declared, "Children are the hope of our future!" (quoting nineteenth-century Cuban patriot José Martí out of context).

The Save Our Children campaign—by now comprising a variety of interfaith and interracial individuals who had little in common except homophobia—was a huge success. Only 10,000 signatures were required to place repeal of the amendment on the ballot; 64,304 signatures were obtained in a mere three weeks.[45] It was a loud, clear message that to a lot of their fellow citizens, gays were loathsome, bogeymen, a blight on humanity. The war was on. Bryant called it a holy war: "a battle of the agnostics, the atheists, and the ungodly on one side, and God's people on the other."[46]

Chapter 19

HOW TO LOSE A BATTLE

AN ANTIGAY HATE FEST

Ruth Shack, the wary sponsor of the amendment, felt the rage right away. She got so many anonymous threats over the phone that the police chief offered her protection. A woman followed her into a private dressing room in Saks Fifth Avenue department store and called her a lesbian. So did a man standing next to her in a crowded elevator. "Your mother must be a dyke," high school classmates taunted her youngest daughter. "I didn't have to be black to support black civil rights," Shack defended herself by saying. But that wasn't enough. She had her picture taken with her husband and three daughters for a full-page ad that she placed in the *Miami Herald*. It thanked Dade County for having helped the Shacks enjoy twenty-five years of married life.[1]

The Dade County Coalition for the Humanistic Rights of Gays had been lulled to confidence because it had believed, as Ruth Shack had, that Miami was "a very liberal community." When told by reporters of the drive to repeal the amendment, Bob Kunst said on behalf of the coalition that he was certain that even if enough petition signatures were gathered to qualify a repeal measure for the ballot, it would "fail miserably" because the people of Dade County favored equality for all.[2] The coalition could surely have made an effective preemptive strike on Save Our Children. It could have disseminated dramatic stories about poster gays and lesbians—innocent, upstanding citizens who'd suffered discrimination in housing and employment and who now would be safe because of the amendment. Evidence of past discrimination wouldn't have been hard to find. But the coalition made no preemptive strike. It took weeks before its members even understood that war was being waged.[3]

The Dade County Coalition for the Humanistic Rights of Gays had, in fact, never really thought out its purpose in getting Commissioner Shack to sponsor the amendment. Its members had hoped primarily to "raise consciousness," as Bob Kunst had testified, in 1970s idiom, at the commission hearing: "We are there now [in Dade County jobs and housing], and what we want to do is tell you where we're at." It was not a goal that could make many gays and lesbians feel, as their enemy did, that they were "not only aflame, but on fire." And so when Bryant and her Save Our Children team began to dominate the media, the coalition was, for a time, dumbstruck and inert.

Save Our Children, however, was in active mode from the beginning and never let up. The organization bought full-page newspaper ads, such as one in the *Miami Herald* that proclaimed, referencing the name "Coalition for the Humanistic Rights of Gays," "There is no 'Human Right' to Corrupt Our Children." Save Our Children ads prominently featured bits of articles from newspapers around the United States: stories of homosexual pornographers who took dirty pictures of young boys, scoutmasters who had sex with the scouts in their charge.[4] Save Our Children ran a Mother's Day ad warning mothers that homosexuals were out to get their kids— even the youngest of them—by scheming to abolish age-of-consent laws.[5] Bryant gave frequent radio and newspaper interviews in which she claimed to have files stuffed with evidence "confirming that children are lured into homosexual activity in schools by homosexual teachers."[6] She emphasized always that the amendment said that no one could be fired from a job because of sexual preference, and so it would protect the "rights" of homosexual teachers to continue to ruin the young.

Bryant dubbed her fight a "Christian Crusade,"[7] and she starred in huge prayer rallies alongside fanatical preachers such as youth evangelist

Jack Wyrtzen—who in 1957 told Billy Graham he was breaking fellowship with him because Graham was not sufficiently strict in his fundamentalism. Wyrtzen flew to Florida from his Word of Life ministries headquarters in upstate New York in order to appear with Bryant at the Miami Beach Convention Center, jammed with ten thousand believers, to share in an antigay hate fest. "If this bill passes in Dade County in favor of the gay crowd," Reverend Wyrtzen told the masses in rhetoric that matched Bryant's for hysteria, "it could be the end of the United States of America."[8]

Jack Wyrtzen's journey from New York for a minor amendment issue in a Florida county, the big crowd that avidly affirmed the evangelist and the singer's homophobia, the wild enthusiasm that greeted their claim that homosexuality endangered not only Dade County but also the entire nation—these fueled Save Our Children's larger but not-yet-articulated goal: Why should their antigay crusade be limited to battling a little non-discrimination amendment in South Florida when hordes of homosexuals were, or might soon be, demanding rights in cities and towns all over the United States of America? While the Dade County referendum campaign still raged, Bryant and her advisors were already dreaming of spreading Save Our Children far beyond Dade County.

To that end, Bryant started writing *The Anita Bryant Story*, which explained to a national audience the urgency of her message: Gay people are dangerous. "Gays can't reproduce, so they have to recruit," her book warned, reminding her readers often that God was most certainly against homosexuality, and that "Hell will be populated [by unrepentant homosexuals] who are proud they are gay."[9] In the spring, before the June special election in which the amendment would be voted on, Bryant was flying all over America to deliver her message to rallies, talk shows, and newspaper reporters. "Do you know how God punishes homosexuality?" she asked reporters. "A Southern California town passed an ordinance for them, and now California is having its worst drought in history."

In pushing beyond Dade County, Bryant and her team understood what it took Dade County gays a dangerously long time to comprehend. As Robert Brake, who dreamed up Save Our Children, observed jeeringly: "If [gays] can't win in Dade County—as liberal a community as this is—then they can't win elsewhere."[10] The referendum to repeal a South Florida amendment was to become no less than a testing ground for the future of gay rights in America.

It was quickly apparent that Bryant's campaign struck a chord not only among fundamentalists and the fringe types who rode around Miami with "Kill a Queer for Christ" bumper stickers on their cars,[11] and not only among the testosterone laden, such as the entire Miami Dolphins football team, which passed the hat for a Save Our Children kitty,[12] but also among those who were politically progressive. "New South" governor Reubin Askew, for example, supported school busing to achieve desegregation and also appointed an African American as his secretary of state (the first black person to hold a Florida cabinet-level position since Reconstruction). He was so liberal that in 1972 George McGovern asked him to be his vice presidential running mate (which he declined), and he was named US Trade Representative in the Carter administration. Yet Askew proclaimed in 1977 that if he could vote in the Dade County election, he would definitely vote to repeal the amendment. "I have never viewed the homosexual lifestyle as something that approached a constitutional right," the governor told the media. "I do not want a homosexual teaching my child."[13]

But it was not just southern governors who felt no compunction to hide their prejudice. Even the most sophisticated and intellectually elite were not ashamed to be homophobes in 1977. *Washington Post* columnist Richard Cohen, for example, admitted that he had tried hard to write a column saying that Anita Bryant "should shut up and stick to pushing orange juice," but he simply couldn't. "In my head, I'm anti–Anita Bryant. In my heart, I'm not so sure," he confessed. Though he decried the "hateful" language that Bryant and her camp employed, nevertheless he championed the "normal" and "healthy" and admitted in his column to repulsion at things homosexuals did, citing as an example "a man who's been going to work at the Smithsonian Institution dressed as a woman." (Thirty-five years later, in a very different social climate, Cohen, who'd "evolved," roundly criticized the Boy Scouts of America for their unfounded fears that gays in the Scouts "will Pied Piper the boys of America into the gay life.")[14] With so much ignorance coming from a left-leaning public intellectual in Washington, DC, in 1977, what could gays of Dade County expect from their run-of-the-mill Florida neighbors?

•   •   •

TAKING AIM—AT ONE ANOTHER

Once they realized the enormity of the attack on them, gay people of Dade County—a few of them, anyway—got in gear. Bob Basker, now executive director of the Coalition for the Humanistic Rights of Gays, understood that the amendment vote would be a do-or-die issue for gay people. "It will send ripples across the country either way. If this is defeated, we're looking at a witch hunt against gays," Basker told the *Miami Herald*.[15] He set himself to directing the pro-gay campaign as though his life depended on it, as did Bob Kunst, who dreamed up an apt and pithy response to "Save Our Children" bumper stickers: "We *Are* Your Children."

For a while, the coalition was attracting an increasing number of gays (almost all men), and because the size of the Tuesday night membership meetings had outgrown Bob Stickney's Candlelight Club, the venue was changed to another Stickney club for gay men, Warehouse VIII, which had a disco downstairs, a cruise bar upstairs, and a Levi's-and-leather back room. The meetings were held at the back of the very noisy disco, and they became at least as much a social event as a political one.[16] The coalition board finally got another lesbian, Edda Cimino, a teacher and one of the organizers of the radicals' protests at the 1972 Republican Convention in Miami. But she didn't stay long: "There'd be guys wandering into the Warehouse VIII meetings from the dance floor so they could cruise. There'd be guys at the meeting who were more interested in getting it on than in what was going on. I didn't let myself be put on the board to go and see that," she objected, and in disgust she stopped coming.[17] That was the end of lesbians on the coalition board.

Lesbian disaffection was far from the coalition's only problem. Bob Basker and Bob Kunst were committed to the same goal, but they could not work together. Their styles clashed. To Basker, Kunst was a loose cannon: he endangered the coalition's campaign by ranting to the media about the opposition's "sexual hang-ups" and spewing pronouncements about "gay rights" and "sexual freedom." Basker was convinced that in order to win, the coalition must be circumspect, even a little duplicitous. He supported a name change that emphasized the new tack. Dade County Coalition for the Humanistic Rights of Gays would become Dade County Coalition for Human Rights (DCCHR), because "Straight people

preferred not to think about homosexuality." Most of the coalition's steering committee agreed and thus erased from their campaign for gay rights
all references to "gay." Kunst, however, was still going about proclaiming
the word everywhere. "There are probably three hundred thousand gays in
Dade County, twenty percent of the population. Gays like the sun," he told
a *National Observer* reporter.[18]

Finally, at a coalition strategy meeting at Jack Campbell's home, Kunst
and Basker sat in deep sofas surrounded by expensive gay erotic art and
political memorabilia (including a silver peanut that Campbell was given
for donating generously to Jimmy Carter's presidential campaign), and they
duked it out. In his usual fervent style, Kunst presented a daring proposal.
Gays need to stand up and show their numbers and power, and it could
be done with drama and great effect if they would boycott orange juice,
which would pressure the Florida Citrus Commission to fire Anita Bryant
as its spokesperson. Just as the 1950s Montgomery, Alabama, bus boycott by
black people turned all eyes to their civil rights struggle, an orange juice
boycott could do the same for gay people.

"No!" Basker jumped in to say. An orange juice boycott would do
nothing to stop repeal—just the opposite. It would hurt the workers
hired to pick the oranges, which would backfire against the campaign.
Jack Campbell, the meeting's host, who was expected to be a top financial
donor in their fight against repeal, agreed. A boycott would hurt the minorities who worked in the groves as much as it would hurt the growers.
Obviously, the coalition couldn't control orange juice boycotts elsewhere,
but it must not call for one in Miami. Everyone but Kunst concurred. And
the coalition must be mum on the subject of gay numbers and gay power
and anything else gay, too, they agreed again. Bob Basker had won the
bout.[19]

Kunst went home angry and defeated. To him it seemed that Basker
and the coalition had become dishonest, timidly conventional, conservative
(an especially annoying insult to Basker, a lifelong Marxist). Kunst resented
that most of the leadership seemed to want to put a Band-Aid over his
mouth: that they thought he was "too radical, too hot to handle."[20] Yet he
had some passionate supporters, such as Jack Nichols, who'd been one of
the most creative thinkers in Mattachine Society Washington and who was
now a Florida resident. Kunst, Nichols said, was a heroic warrior, "a shining

knight on the horse, attacking the enemy."[21] It was true that Bob Kunst had colorful ideas and wasn't afraid to push them. At one point, he purchased a thousand big orange and yellow shopping bags with the logo "Tell Anita You're Against Discrimination!" and he distributed them to shoppers on Washington Avenue, relishing the idea of "a thousand little old ladies walking up and down the street, supporting us!"[22]

But as the opposition gained ground, Kunst and Basker wasted valuable time fighting each other instead of fighting Anita Bryant. Although Kunst ate and slept the cause—devoted his youth and his life to it—he seemed always to be blamed for creating discord. So after the strategy meeting, with less than two months left before the vote, he quit the coalition and started a rival group, the Miami Victory Campaign, which he ran with Alan Rockway out of their Transperience office. This unhappy split was in keeping with a long tradition in gay politics: the virulent schism between "radicals" and "conservatives" that dated back a generation earlier to the clash between Harry Hay and Hal Call. It would continue into the twenty-first century.

Finally, the Dade County Coalition for Human Rights opened a campaign office with a phone bank and a few committed people to run it. Jesse Monteagudo, an earnest young college student and Cuban refugee, was one of them. He'd been an avid member of the coalition since its earliest meetings at the Candlelight Club, and now he began looking high and low for volunteers to man the phones and pass out flyers. At Sears, Roebuck, where he worked part-time, he tried to convince a gay manager to join the campaign. "What for?" the man asked. "We're doing fine without an ordinance. It'll just bring out the screamers and the flamboyant queens, and then there'll be a backlash." Monteagudo tried to enlist other gay coworkers at Sears—he tried to enlist gays anywhere he met them—but the response was almost always negative. He found, as Basker had a few years earlier, that gays just wanted to be left alone "to do their thing": hooking up in Miami's wild gay scene.[23]

With so little political fervor in the gay community, the DCCHR counted it an excellent evening when a few hundred people showed up for a pro-amendment fund-raiser. A rally at Miami Dade Junior College just weeks before voters would go to the polls brought out about a hundred people; but at the same time, ten thousand people were jamming into the Miami Beach Convention Center for an antiamendment prayer rally.[24] Jesse Monteagudo, sapped by what had seemed a hopeless cause, blamed the coalition. The leadership naively believed that a campaign that used tame buzzwords such as *human rights* and *equal opportunity* could defeat an opposition that talked of "the destruction of civilization" and "a war for the nation's soul."[25]

Discord continued in the coalition even after Kunst left. The coalition wanted to run a centralized operation, which meant that volunteers had to be willing to take orders from those on top. Not many were. "It's like a big powwow where all the chiefs come out, but the warriors stay at home," Jack Campbell lamented. "We need the warriors!"[26] But those at the top lacked credibility. They had no experience in managing a major campaign.

The battle of the sexes also continued to rage. Lesbians, particularly lesbian feminists, abhorred the sexist terms that were being used to characterize Anita Bryant: "bitch" and "whore," gay men called her. The lesbian feminists were especially riled by an illustration in the *Advocate* that presented Bryant as a cow with huge udders spewing out hatred: "The Orange Juice Cow," David Goodstein, publisher of the *Advocate*, dubbed Bryant.[27] Lesbian feminists were no friends of Anita Bryant, of course, but neither were they friends of men who flaunted their disdain for womankind. They were also offended when Jack Campbell offered his Club Miami for a major coalition fund-raiser. Club Miami was a men's bathhouse, lesbian feminists protested. They would feel weird and unwelcome there.[28] But the most dramatic split between the gay men and lesbian feminists was at a fund-raiser at the Coconut Grove Playhouse, where a straight woman vocalist entertained the audience by singing "I Enjoy Being a Girl." Edda Cimino led the women in a noisy exodus from the theater.[29]

Class animosity, too, reared its head in the coalition. The nervous and inexperienced strategists of the campaign held the reins very tightly. They scrutinized carefully who could and who could not work on the campaign. Grassroots volunteers from outside Miami were shooed away. John O'Brien, one of the founders of the New York Gay Liberation Front, had fancied that through his left-wing activism he had close ties to African American communities. "Listen, I know people from the South. We worked together on issues," he called Jack Campbell to say. "I can go into the black churches and deliver the black vote for you." Campbell asked the former Gay Liberation Front leader to stay home.[30] But worried about what the eighty-five thousand black voters of Dade County might do, Campbell and others put up money to hire a professional community organizer, Clarence Edwards (who was known to be "not especially favorable" to the gay cause), to bring in the black vote. Edwards was paid about $10,000, even though local black leaders had already warned not to expect support; the black community was too concerned about black jobs and housing to go to the polls and vote for gay rights.[31]

Howard Wallace, a part-time truck driver and longtime labor organizer in San Francisco—who played a big role in organizing the boycott against Coors beer for firing gay employees and giving money to antigay groups—also offered to come to Miami as a volunteer. He promised to deliver the labor vote. But he, too, was discouraged from coming, though a couple of weeks before the election, he showed up anyway. Wallace might as well have stayed home, because the coalition leadership kept him muzzled. If coalition volunteers weren't even allowed to say the *gay* word, Wallace complained, how could they effectively challenge Save Our Children's depiction of the maniacal, child-molesting, homosexual boogeyman?[32]

HOW NOT TO RUN A CAMPAIGN

The jittery coalition leadership was petrified that if grassroots activists and radicals from the outside descended upon Miami, the Right would claim that the coalition was being fueled by a bunch of carpetbaggers; and even worse, the radical carpetbaggers would be sleeping in parks and on beaches and would give Miamians the impression that gays were a scruffy and unsavory lot. Yet the coalition had no confidence in its own ability to run a campaign.[33] And there was so much to lose. By April, David Goodstein, owner and publisher of the *Advocate*, was alarming everyone by writing in the pages of his widely circulated magazine that if Bryant and Save Our Children weren't stopped in Dade County, they'd export their venom to Los Angeles, New York, San Francisco, Chicago—gay people would be safe nowhere. A Holocaust was coming, and it could be averted only if the gays of Dade County did the right thing now.[34] The coalition panicked. They'd have to call in carpetbaggers after all, political consultants to run the campaign. Campbell and Goodstein agreed to bankroll them.[35]

But in 1977 there weren't many gay political consultants to choose from. San Franciscan Jim Foster, Goodstein's fair-haired boy who'd risen to national prominence when he spoke at the 1972 Democratic Convention, was Goodstein's choice. Foster knew a lot about winning local elections, Goodstein pointed out to the coalition. He'd brought out the gay vote that gave Dianne Feinstein her margin for victory when she ran for the San Francisco Board of Supervisors. He did the same for Richard Hongisto when he ran successfully for sheriff. And he was now serving as assistant to Mayor George Moscone. Jack Campbell's choice was New Yorker Ethan Geto, who'd been George McGovern's New York press secretary when McGovern ran for president and had also worked in the New York campaigns of Birch Bayh, Hubert Humphrey, and Jimmy Carter. He'd been married twice, had two children, and was bisexual. (He and Michelle deMilly, his second wife, had married in secret because Geto feared gays would say, "How can you be a gay rights leader if you're married?"[36]) Foster and Geto were imported to Miami. "Together these two guys have had a quarter century of experience in running campaigns," Campbell told the coalition hopefully.

But Foster and Geto were overwhelmed. Foster claimed that in sixteen years in politics, he'd never seen such underhanded tactics and lies as those perpetrated by the Bryant camp. And the opposition forces weren't his sole source of frustration. He and Geto worked assiduously to get liberal politicians such as Ted Kennedy and Hubert Humphrey, and civil rights leaders such as Julian Bond, to issue statements in support of the amendment. Not one of them came through.[37] The coalition did succeed in raising $350,000: $150,000 from readers of the *Advocate* who responded to David Goodstein's panicked appeal; $50,000 from Dade County—a chunk of that sum from the Jack Campbell coffers; and $150,000 from donors all over the country.[38] They bought media ads that emphasized justice and liberty: "Freedom in America begins and ends here," accompanied by a picture of a voting booth; and "Don't let them chip away at the Constitution," with a picture of a hammer cracking the Bill of Rights.[39] But not a word about "gay" or "sexual."

While Foster and Geto skirted the gut terms, Bob Kunst laid them bare. Kunst was a perfect embodiment of the Age of Aquarius, and newspaper and TV reporters loved him. He was striking-looking, with a head of thick black curls and a gorgeous white-toothed smile. He had a mellifluous voice, too, and was given to spouting flower-child aphorisms that the media found very quotable, such as, "The only thing that matters is our human capacity to love and be loved." Kunst had been passionately involved in all sorts of movements. He'd demonstrated for black civil rights; he'd organized for the New Mobilization Against the War; and he'd battled "hang-ups" and "uptightness" as a "human potential" guru in his Transperience Center, which was devoted to exploring "the entire question of human sexuality."[40] Because Kunst was photogenic and colorful, he—and not the coalition—became the public face of the campaign against Anita Bryant.

In their lifestyles, Bob Kunst and Anita Bryant were diametrical opposites. She lived lavishly in her mansion by the bay and drove a Mercedes; he lived in a modest apartment with a succession of roommates to help defray expenses, and because gasoline prices were high, he seldom used the old car he'd inherited from his deceased father. She was usually dressed as though going to church (but never without false eyelashes and peachy-colored foundation makeup); he was usually dressed in Levi's 501s and colorful shirts, bearded and mustachioed in the 1970s "clone" style. Yet in their fervid zeal for their causes and their fiery rhetoric, Bryant and Kunst were mirror images of each other. "Do you know why homosexuals are an abomination to the Lord?" she asked newspaper reporters. "Hold your stomach. It's because they're eating new life. There's nothing reproductive about it."[41] Kunst, shown a piece of Save Our Children propaganda in the *Miami Herald* by a reporter, shouted, "Jesus, what a piece of shit!" He called Bryant "a vicious woman." Bryant called him "a Homosexual," as though the word itself were an abomination.[42] The media had a field day fashioning them into a Punch-and-Judy show.

Despite all the press coverage he received, Kunst was no more able to get local gays and lesbians animated about his Miami Victory Campaign than they were about the coalition. But his call for an orange juice boycott caught fire far beyond Miami. Most gays outside Dade County had not known that the "day-without-orange-juice-is-a-day-without-sunshine" lady was spearheading a movement to repeal gay rights, until Kunst proposed the boycott. He was right about the dramatic value of the ploy. It kindled zealous action. Gay people all over America began to take the struggle against Anita Bryant far more seriously than did gay Miami. Gay bars everywhere—even the only gay bar in Idaho—took screwdrivers off the drink menu and replaced them with concoctions such as vodka and apple juice, called an "Anita Bryant" in her "honor";[43] or for the sake of the cause, they made screwdrivers out of vodka and Tang, a sugary chemical-tasting powder that hinted only vaguely of orange flavor.

T-shirts with sassy boycott messages became fashion statements among gays all over the country: "Anita Sucks Oranges," "Anita Bryant Eats Lemons," "Suck a Fruit for Anita." In New York, they picketed supermarkets, chanting, "Hey, Hey, Ho, Ho, Florida Citrus Got to Go" and "O.J. No Way!"[44] Troy Perry, founder of the Metropolitan Community Church, which by now had scores of congregations across America, was on a plane from Los Angeles to New York when the stewardess placed glasses of fresh-squeezed orange juice in front of all the business-class passengers, including the reverend in his clerical collar. "Take it away. I can't drink it!" Perry shouted. "I'm a homosexual!"[45] Author Barbara Love and her partner, founders and sole members of Gay Guerrillas, invaded New York supermarkets and surreptitiously punctured every carton of Florida orange juice in sight. At the time, Love happened to be an editor for *Supermarketing* magazine, which reached eighty thousand supermarket retailers. She wrote an article for the magazine warning retailers not to stock Florida orange juice in their stores because the product was attracting vandals.[46]

While Kunst got reporters out and ignited people's imaginations, Geto and Foster kept insisting that the only way to victory was to take a careful *human* rights strategy. "A gay rights campaign has no way of winning," Foster kept reiterating. "Most people just don't care about gay rights. They're too removed from it."[47] In the ads they bought, they aimed at convincing voters, as Geto said, that "America is all about the majority respecting the rights of minorities, about the right to be different, and that rights are not rewards to be distributed to people that you like but are the birthright of every American."[48] It wasn't an approach that would capture headlines.

Hoping to capture a few headlines for the coalition, Jack Campbell invited Leonard Matlovich to come to Florida, be his houseguest, and let himself be used as a campaign icon.[49] A couple of years earlier, on September 8, 1975, Sergeant Matlovich, sporting his air force cap and numerous medals, had made the cover of *Time* magazine, the first out gay person ever to appear on a nationally circulated mainstream magazine cover. Sprawled across the picture of an intense-looking air force sergeant were the words "I Am a Homosexual: The Gay Drive for Acceptance." He was now the most famous homosexual in America. But the hope that Matlovich would grab the attention of the media and supplant Bob Kunst didn't materialize, since Kunst continued to offer reporters amusingly outrageous copy, such as when he called Reubin Askew, the homophobic governor of Florida, "a sexually insecure lame duck."[50]

It was Ethan Geto's idea that it might give Matlovich more credibility as spokesperson for the coalition if he had prominence in its hierarchy. So the old executive committee was reconstituted into a steering committee that included him. Jack Campbell remained the committee's president, and Bob Basker remained executive director of the coalition, though he seemed to have diminishing say once Geto and Foster took over. Matlovich was made vice president. The second vice president was Alexias Ramón Muniz. (Jesse Monteagudo, who was by now very disillusioned with the coalition, thought Muniz's was a "token position to placate the Hispanics."[51]) Bob Stickney, owner of the Candlelight Club and Warehouse VIII, was treasurer; and the lone woman on the steering committee, Carolyn Sarnoff, a heterosexual, became secretary. No one seemed to notice that there was no lesbian presence on the steering committee of the Dade County Coalition for Human Rights—except the Dade County lesbians.

Among the coalition's many problems was the widespread perception (which the makeup of the steering committee did little to correct) that its members were primarily spoiled white men who already had all the rights anyone could possibly use and didn't need any more. *Newsweek* magazine said as much in a long cover article on the Dade County referendum. The article featured prominently Bob Stickney's exclusive Candlelight Club, where gay professional men dined on rack of lamb and Châteauneuf-du-Pape; and Jack Campbell's mansion, where he kept a gorgeous young lover and a boy who did nothing but tend his oversized swimming pool. Though the *Newsweek* article wasn't flattering to Anita Bryant and her fulminations against homosexuals, the ordinary reader must have come away thinking that fat-cat gays certainly had no cause to bellyache about jobs and housing: they were already doing immeasurably better than most Americans.[52]

"ARE WE GOING TO PROTECT PEOPLE
WHO MIGHT HURT CHILDREN?"

In the weeks before the election, a Lou Harris poll found that 62 percent of registered voters of Dade County claimed they supported "antidiscrimination laws."[53] But it was clearly not *this* antidiscrimination law they supported. Few key institutions or organizations spoke out in favor of the amendment. The United Teachers of Dade, an affiliate of the American Federation of Teachers, did finally declare support—but seventy-five teachers quit the organization in protest.[54] Even more worrisome, though, and a harbinger of what was to come on election day, was the viciousness with which the opposition expressed itself. "Listen you S.O.B.," one listener wrote local radio talk-show host Neil Rogers, who'd supported the amendment on his program. "If you and your 'lover' have to corn hole for your kicks, then by God keep it to yourselves, go crawl in a hole some where and quit trying to brain wash people via radio to your sordid way of life, because if you don't quit you had better lock your doors tight and get yourself a bodygard [sic] because me and my buddies are going to get you some dark night then you will really find out what corn holeing means— with an iron spike [sic]."[55]

When the handful of Cuban volunteers for the Dade County Coalition for Human Rights decided to form Latinos pro Derechos Humanos (Latinos for Human Rights), hoping to address the Cuban community, they were invited to appear on a Spanish-language radio show and face off against Cuban supporters of Save Our Children. The two sides were supposed to debate the pros and cons of the amendment, but the Save Our Children contingent refused to sit in the same room with the gays.[56] So, instead of a debate, each group stated its position, and then the telephone lines were opened to listeners. Homosexuals, one after another said, should be thrown in concentration camps (as they were in Communist Cuba, from which the callers had escaped[57]), or kicked out of the country, or killed.

The PR person for Latinos pro Derechos Humanos, Manolo Gomez, who'd arranged the radio "debate," was beaten and left for dead in an alley.

His car was firebombed. He was also fired from his job as an editor for the Spanish-language edition of *Cosmopolitan* magazine because he'd made public declarations about his homosexuality. Ovidio Heriberto Ramos, a twenty-eight-year-old Cuban immigrant who went by the American-ized name Herb, was another member of Latinos pro Derechos Humanos who'd been on the radio program. Ramos had long suffered from severe bouts of depression and drug use,[58] and the hostility of the callers may have been enough to push him over the edge. After the broadcast, he went home and put a bullet through his head. Gay newspapers and even straight liberal journals were soon calling Ramos the "first victim of the Bryant crusade," renaming him *Ovidio* Ramos, and emphasizing his immigrant background, to counter the image of gays as rich, complacent white guys.[59]

But the martyrdom of Ovidio Ramos did nothing to change the con-servative Cuban community's antipathy. Maybe some of their hatred can be explained by their anxiety that they'd fled Communism to end up in a morally lax land to which their kids were assimilating. Anita Bryant also spurred them to panic by playing on their worst fears: "It would break my heart," she told the Cuban community, "if Miami would become another Sodom and Gomorrah, and you would have to leave again."[60]

Still reeling from the horror of the radio program but unwilling to give up, Jesse Monteagudo, who'd been coaxed back to the coalition to help with Latinos pro Derechos Humanos, proposed going door to door in the Cuban community: Maybe if Cubans actually saw gay Cuban faces, their minds would be changed. But Geto and Foster thought that to alert Cu-bans even further about the issue was a terrible idea. With the sad evidence of the disastrous radio program, Geto and Foster concluded that their best hope was to keep Cubans away from the polls.[61] It was a false hope. In every Catholic church with a Cuban congregation, the devout were bom-barded by antiamendment propaganda and ordered to go vote.[62]

In Protestant churches, too, the Sunday before the election, ministers were urging congregations to do the right thing: vote *against* nondiscrimi-nation of gays. But devout Protestants already knew to "do the right thing." Two weeks earlier, the most famous Protestant minister in America, Jerry Falwell, had come to Miami to inform a crowd of thousands about homo-sexuals and their scheme to get a nondiscrimination law passed.

"I want to tell you we are dealing with a vile and vicious and vulgar gang. They'd kill you as quick as look at you," Falwell told his audience.[63] And the faithful weren't the only ones who got the word. In the days before the election, Save Our Children took out full-page ads in Miami newspapers warning voters that if they didn't repeal the amendment, there would soon be an "epidemic of child pornography." Save Our Children blitzed TV channels with ads showing all-American types at the Orange Bowl juxtaposed with drag queens, leather men, and bare-bosomed Dykes on Bikes at the San Francisco Pride Parade. If the amendment was not repealed, the wholesomeness of the Orange Bowl would be replaced by pride in decadence.[64]

The same Lou Harris poll that said 62 percent of eligible voters were opposed to discrimination also said that only 15 percent would show up to vote on June 7. But voters flocked to the polls: seasoned precinct workers at one Coconut Grove polling place said they'd never seen such long lines. Some voters, such as Cuban émigré millionaire Charles "Bebe" Rebozo, had self-satisfied expressions on their faces as they waited to cast their votes. Rebozo had been involved in serious money scandals with Richard Nixon and had been investigated for bank fraud the year before. Now he drove up to the polling place at Key Biscayne Elementary School in his white Lincoln Continental, shook hands and grinned broadly at his neighbors, did his duty at the ballot box, and announced he'd voted for repeal. "Why?" someone asked. "Because I felt that way!" he answered.[65]

Bob Kunst, in his usual brash optimism, told the newspapers there'd be a landslide in the amendment's favor: a 60 percent to 40 percent win. The week before, the Dade County Democratic Party had belatedly endorsed the amendment, and Kunst and others had hailed that endorsement as a last-minute push toward victory. Robert Brake, spokesman for Save Our Children, was happy to rain on their parade. "This is not the kind of issue where a political party is going to have that much influence," he said, meaning that the subject of homosexuality transcended politics—it disgusted Republicans and Democrats alike.[66]

Brake was right. Of Miami's 446 precincts, 385 voted for repeal. The amendment was rejected by a margin of over 2 to 1: 89,562 citizens of Dade County had cast their ballots to retain the addition of the words "affectional or sexual preference" in the existing ordinance, which already prohibited discrimination against almost every other minority group. But 202,319 voted to ban those words. Ruth Shack, the county commissioner who'd sponsored the amendment, was flabbergasted. Impossible that all those negative votes should have come out of liberal Miami![67]

But Shack shouldn't have been so astonished. An avalanche of propaganda had equated gays with child molesters, and neither the coalition nor the Miami Victory Campaign had been able to create new images in people's minds, not even in the minds of educated and liberal people. As the chairman of the Politics and Public Affairs Department at the University of Miami told the press, "If you put a moral issue like this one to a vote [in any city, no matter how liberal], the basic question for a lot of people would be, 'Are we going to protect people who might hurt our children? Such an ordinance might even be defeated in San Francisco."[68]

On top of that "basic question," Catholics had been virtually ordered to vote for repeal by no less an authority than their archbishop. And blacks had been warned by their leaders, too, that homosexuals were trying to "confuse" the black community by comparing the gay "struggle" to the black struggle, attaching themselves to the civil rights movement, and "trying to take it over to the point of equating civil rights with homosexual rights."[69] There were economic reasons also that made black Miamians unhappy about the amendment. They'd had enough to contend with in the huge influx of Cubans who competed with them for jobs; why would they want to help legitimize another group who claimed discrimination—and who weren't even a true minority? With all due respect to heroic Ruth Shack: what was more astonishing than the fact that over 200,000 Miamians voted against her amendment was that almost 90,000 voted for it.

The Coalition for Human Rights had rented the Fontaine Room, the grand ballroom at Miami's premier hotel, the Fontainebleau, for a victory party. It had also paid for a separate room to be set up as a working area for the press, and a two-bedroom suite to function as offices where the poll watchers could call in the early results for tabulation. It had hired a six-piece combo to play disco and oldies for forty minutes out of each hour between eighty thirty and half past midnight. And the coalition had arranged to equip the grand ballroom with three three-foot-wide television screens, so everyone could keep track of the election returns and news coverage all evening.[70] It took no more than one hour after the polls closed for those watching the TVs to understand they'd been trounced.[71] A thousand gays—many of them more willing to come out for a party than they'd been to come out for campaign work—dressed formally in suits and ties despite the South Florida weather, now stood stunned and tearful, looking up at the screens that told them that most of their neighbors loathed them.

Leonard Matlovich, the good soldier who'd been a recipient of a bronze medal and a purple heart in Vietnam, wouldn't permit mawkishness. "When you walk out of here tonight," he took the mic and told them in a strong voice, "you go out of here with your heads high and your shoulders back, and you be proud you're gay and don't let anyone put you down." Matlovich began singing a hymn, and the crowd responded by joining hands and loudly singing with him, verse after verse of "We Shall Overcome," the anthem of the 1960s civil rights movement."[72] They understood that what they'd been through was the gay Alamo, and that they must find ways to transform it into the gay Selma. Many of them who'd been in the closet up to that minute, came out right there on the floor, for all the world to see, kissing their same-sex partners in front of live TV cameras.[73] But the most striking image appeared the next morning on the front page of the *Miami Herald*. Gays in the grand ballroom of the Fontainebleau Hotel holding up the American flag.

Anita Bryant was said to have "danced a jig" when she learned the election results. She and her husband, Bob Green, posed for the media in a lip-lock. "This is what heterosexuals do, fellows," Green told the newsmen jovially.[74] The Save Our Children victory party was held at the Holiday Inn, a hotel just down the street from one of Miami's most popular gay beaches. With her husband and four children by her side, Bryant, decked out in a powder-blue dress, her auburn hair coiffed in stiff, midcentury proper-lady style, stood before a crowd delirious with its victory. The bulbs of news cameras popped incessantly. "Tonight the laws of God and the cultural values of man have been vindicated!" Bryant shouted. "The people of Dade County—the normal majority—have said "Enough! Enough! Enough!"

She then announced that she was carrying her campaign to Washington, Minneapolis, all over California, wherever ordinances kowtowed to homosexuals. "All America and all the world will hear what the people have said, and with God's continued help, we will prevail in our fight to repeal similar laws throughout the nation which attempt to legitimize a lifestyle which is both perverse and dangerous to the sanctity of the family, dangerous to our children, dangerous to our freedom of religion and freedom of choice, dangerous to our survival as 'one nation under God'!" The crowd went wild.[75]

Chapter 20

GRAPPLING WITH DEFEAT

"WE'RE TIRED OF YOU"

Anita Bryant was an inspiration. In May 1977, a few weeks before Dade County citizens voted to repeal the "sexual or affectional preference" amendment, State Senator Curtis Peterson from Lakeland, Florida (headquarters of the Florida Citrus Commission, for which Bryant sang her "day-without-orange-juice-is-a-day-without-sunshine" TV commercials), sponsored two Senate bills. One prohibited homosexuals from adopting children; the other outlawed "single-sex marriage."[1] "The problem in Florida," Senator Peterson declared in his down-home idiom, "has been that homosexuals are surfacing to such an extent that they're beginning to aggravate the ordinary folks who have a few rights of their own. They're trying to flaunt it. We're trying to send a message telling them, 'We're tired of you. We wish you'd go back into the closet.'"[2]

The lone dissenting voice on the Senate floor was that of Senator Don Chamberlain, who spoke against Peterson's adoption bill by comparing the antigay discrimination at its heart to the anti-Jewish discrimination of Nazi Germany: "To kill the human spirit was their first step toward killing the human," Chamberlain admonished, and he implored his fellow legislators not to stigmatize, not to deny anyone "the joy of being a family. Vote for love and tolerance and dignity for all human beings," he exhorted them.[3] They answered his impassioned pleas with stony faces. The bill banning homosexuals from adopting children passed 31 to 3. The bill outlawing "single-sex marriage" passed 37 to 0. (Democratic senator Jack Gordon got belly laughs from his colleagues when he observed that the next thing you know, homosexuals will want to change the traditional wedding march song to "Here Comes the Bride in Drag." Not even Don Chamberlain dared to support so outrageous a notion as marriage equality.)[4] Governor Askew signed both bills into law. When Chamberlain ran for reelection in 1980, his opponent reminded voters that he'd voted for the right of homosexuals to adopt. He became a one-term senator.

Gay activists around the country laid the blame for the reawakening of hostility toward homosexuals squarely on Anita Bryant. But they were at a loss about how to fight back. The continued national boycott of Florida orange juice—"gaycott," it came to be called—was making some dent in sales, but the Florida Citrus Commission stood by Bryant. A Citrus Commission spokesman admitted that his group had received substantial amounts of mail, "mostly from California," that threatened an orange juice boycott; but, he insisted, there was no objective evidence that the boycott was working, and the Florida Citrus Commission had no intention of canceling Bryant's contract.[5] "She's doing a great job for us," he declared.[6]

In fact, the commission had reason to worry. A national consumer survey showed that the impact of its advertising program was lower than it had been in years.[7] Yet if the commission canceled her contract, its management knew, it would be inundated by protests from the religious right; and the Dade County vote had shown there were more of them than there were activist homosexuals. In November 1977 the Florida Citrus Commission announced not only that it was renewing Anita Bryant's $100,000 a year contract, but also that it was "affirming our support of Anita Bryant for her courageous leadership on a moral issue."[8]

Gay activists also targeted Singer Sewing Machine because Bryant had a contract to shoot a pilot as hostess of a syndicated television variety show, "The Singer Sewing Machine Hour." Singer was soon bombarded by enough letters of protest from gay activists to cause the vice president Edward Trevorrow to announce that Singer would be looking for another

hostess: "We want this to be a pleasant show. We'd like to have as little difficulty as possible in any direction,"[9] he told the press. Bryant called a news
conference at her Biscayne Bay mansion. Looking tragic and besieged,
she bitterly complained to reporters, "The blacklisting of Anita Bryant has
begun. Because I dared to speak out for straight and normal America I have
had my career threatened."[10] Her followers waged a massive letter-writing
campaign, some picketed Singer stores, and one town held a Singer sewing
machine bonfire.[11]

Like the Florida Citrus Commission's management, Singer's chief
executive officer, Joseph Flavin, anxiously concluded that it made more
economic sense to appease the masses on the Right than to worry about
a few gay activists. He responded personally to each of the pro-Bryant letter writers, claiming that the Singer board had actually not heard about
the controversy until they read of it in the newspapers. "The following
day," Flavin assured Bryant fans, "we contacted Ms. Bryant by telephone
and informed her that the decision to cancel her participation in the pilot
program had not been cleared with the top management of the company."
Singer was in the midst of negotiating a contract with her, he said, and
would be strong in affirming her "right of free speech."[12]

AN INVITATION FROM GOD

Despite Anita Bryant's post-victory declaration, she modestly told the
media that she would not be bringing her campaign to other cities "unless
invited by God."[13] The divine call came soon. Richard Angwin, an ambitious thirty-three-year-old fundamentalist preacher at the Temple Baptist
Church in Saint Paul, Minnesota, prevailed upon Anita Bryant to help
him do in Saint Paul what she'd done in Dade County. The city council of
Saint Paul had passed a nondiscrimination ordinance in 1974 that included
precisely those four words—"sexual or affectional preference"—that had
horrified Bryant into founding Save Our Children. The words had gone
unnoticed and unchallenged in Saint Paul since their passage,[14] but now
Reverend Angwin wanted them removed. Like Bryant, he believed that
"homosexuality is a murderous, horrendous, twisted act . . . It is a sin and
a powerful, addictive lust,"[15] and that "grassroots Americans don't want to
be thrust into contact with immoral people."[16] (Angwin made no mention

of the fact that in his youth in Kansas, he had been sentenced to jail for the immorality of car theft.)[17]

Bryant, with the aid of Brother Bill, advised Reverend Angwin on how to manage a repeal campaign; she also donated $10,000 to get him started. With the seed money, Angwin formed Citizens Alert for Morality—a name as frenzied as "Save Our Children"—whose main propaganda message was modeled on that of the Bryant group: laws that protect homosexuals, who are inveterate child molesters and sinners, endanger and corrupt our children. Through Citizens Alert for Morality, Angwin organized a petition drive in churches; volunteers knocked on doors; they buttonholed people on street corners—even though it was by now the dead of winter and Saint Paul temperatures had dropped below freezing. In a mere three weeks, Angwin had obtained well over the required number of signatures needed to place repeal on the April 1978 ballot.[18]

Reverend Angwin replicated almost step-by-step the strategy that Save Our Children had developed in Dade County. For the next months, he and his group bombarded Saint Paul with media messages about homosexual child molesters. Billboard ads proclaiming "Preserve the Family!" all but dominated the landscape. A week before the election, Citizens Alert for Morality rented the St. Paul Civic Center Auditorium and staged a massive three-hour prayer rally, advertising Anita Bryant singing and the Reverend Jerry Falwell preaching on the evils of homosexuality.[19] By the time the vote was held, on April 25, most citizens of Saint Paul were convinced that homosexuals wore horns and were a dire threat to all that was good in the world.

As in Dade County, Saint Paul turned out in force to vote 2 to 1 to remove the words "sexual or affectional preference" from the city's nondiscrimination ordinance.[20] Richard Angwin, like Anita Bryant, "danced a jig": "We whopped them," he gloated. "It's a warning that you can't flaunt your perversions."[21]

Flush with his success, Reverend Angwin flew immediately to Wichita, Kansas. He would teach the techniques he'd learned from Bryant and Brother Bill to his old friend and fellow Baptist preacher Ron Adrian, the head of Concerned Citizens for Community Standards. Adrian's group was leading the campaign to strike gay rights from Wichita's nondiscrimination ordinance.[22] Wichita, which had added the four controversial words to the city ordinance only the summer before, had already been well primed by Anita Bryant. She'd visited the city that winter to sing in a revival concert and tell voters that the Wichita homosexual rights amendment was a danger not only in itself but also because it set a terrible precedent: "Next you will have thieves, prostitutes, and people who have relations with Saint Bernards asking for the same rights," she warned.[23] Bryant's message, bolstered by Angwin and by Reverend Adrian's Concerned Citizens for Community Standards, met with stunning success: 57,251 Wichita voters went to the polls on May 9; 47,246 of them, a ratio of almost 5 to 1, voted to repeal any reference to gay people from the law protecting minorities from discrimination.

The momentum Bryant had created seemed unstoppable. Two weeks later, voters in Eugene, Oregon, a university town with a liberal reputation despite its share of lumberjacks and born-agains, cast their ballots 13,838 to 7,685 to remove those four controversial words from its nondiscrimination ordinance. While Anita Bryant had little to do directly with the Eugene campaign, the repeal drive would surely not have happened then and there had her homophobic rhetoric not captured headlines everywhere for the previous year and a half.

Before Bryant's victories, gays and lesbians in cities all over America had been working for passage of nondiscrimination ordinances; but by 1978, it was clear that the times were not propitious. In Cincinnati, a proposed ordinance to extend "human rights" protections to the elderly and the physically handicapped almost failed because it included protections for homosexuals as well. Council members threatened to vote against the entire ordinance unless references to homosexuals were excised.[24] They were. But taking no chances that some homosexual zealots might yet find a way to convince the council that homosexuals deserved rights, Protect America's Children—Anita Bryant's renamed Miami organization—announced to Cincinnatians that the group "would be glad" to make "anti-homosexual pamphlets available for distribution" in Cincinnati immediately.[25]

The inchoate movement for gay and lesbian civil rights was on a precipitous downhill slide, and gays were unable to figure out how to apply the brakes. There'd been some valiant efforts in gay communities to fight,[26] but there weren't enough activist gays and lesbians, there wasn't enough political savvy, and there weren't enough straight allies to counter the propaganda campaigns that appealed to blind bigotry.

THE USES OF A DEVIL

It's ironic that it was Anita Bryant who pumped vital energy into a renewed battle for gay and lesbian civil rights. She created fervent activists
out of those who'd previously been content simply to enjoy their newfound freedoms—which now, they realized, could easily be taken away.
She made them fighting mad. They were ready to do what Bob Basker had
once hoped in vain Miami gays would do: wage war against an enemy that
denied them first-class citizenship. Eric Hoffer famously observed in the
1950s that a mass movement can get along fine without a god, but it won't
get along at all without a devil.[27] For gay people all over the country, Anita
Bryant became that devil.

In the gay pride parades of 1977 and 1978, Bryant figured prominently.
Marchers, carrying placards that displayed her image side by side with images of Hitler, Idi Amin, and Joseph McCarthy, shouted denunciations of
her until they were hoarse. As parade sponsors told the *New York Times*, the
parades in New York, San Francisco, Los Angeles, Chicago, Kansas City,
Atlanta, and Seattle were far bigger than they'd ever been because of the
"spreading resentment caused by the efforts of Anita Bryant."[28] The San
Francisco parade attracted two hundred thousand—more people even than
had participated in the anti–Vietnam War march of the sixties, which to
that date had been San Francisco's largest demonstration.[29]

Gay and lesbian fury toward Bryant was raging even higher in San
Francisco than in other cities because they'd just witnessed a horrifying
result of the hatred she'd provoked. As participants in the 1977 parade
marched past the San Francisco City Hall, they bowed their heads before
flags flying at half-staff. Mayor George Moscone had ordered the flags to
be lowered in memory of Robert Hillsborough, a gardener who tended
the lawns and flowers in a playground near city hall.[30] The children called
him "Mr. Greenjeans."[31] He'd been killed, San Francisco gays believed,
because Anita Bryant had "unleashed a bloodbath" through her hate campaign.[32] A few days earlier, on a warm evening at the start of summer, the
thirty-three-year-old Hillsborough had gone dancing at a disco with his
boyfriend Jerry Taylor. The two left the nightclub about midnight and
stopped for a snack at a drive-in restaurant. There they were spotted as
gays by four young men who taunted them and then followed their car to

the Mission District apartment building where Hillsborough lived. Just as Hillsborough and Taylor were about to enter the building, the four men pulled up, jumped from their car yelling "Faggots! Faggots! Faggots!" and attacked them. Nineteen-year-old John Cordova, an auto mechanic, had a fishing knife in his pocket. He pulled it out and began slashing at Hillsborough, screaming, "This is for Anita!" Jerry Taylor broke from the grip of one of the assailants and ran, but Hillsborough was pinned by the other two and then thrown to the ground while Cordova stabbed him fifteen times in the face and chest.

The slain man's mother, Helen Hillsborough, also knew the name of the devil to blame. The seventy-eight-year-old widow sued Anita Bryant, Bryant's husband, Bob Green, and Save Our Children[33] for $5 million, charging that Bryant had "incited violence and riot" against gay people. "My son's blood is on Anita Bryant's hands," Helen Hillsborough said.[34]

It took awhile before the expanding community of gay and lesbian activists discovered the most effective ways to fight. Initial battles were primarily against their devil rather than for their cause: they were set on destroying Anita Bryant's career. When Bryant was sent by the Florida Citrus Commission to Minneapolis to dedicate a new fruit warehouse, two hundred demonstrators lay in wait for her and staged a picket outside the warehouse.[35] Gay people were soon waiting for Anita Bryant everywhere. Three days after the Dade County vote, she performed at a Tidewater Religious Crusade in Norfolk, West Virginia. Five hundred gays and lesbians were scattered among the crusade crowd of two thousand. They sat quietly, as though they were part of the faithful, until Bryant read her favorite anti-sodomy passage from Leviticus. Then chanting "Two! Four! Six! Eight! Gay is just as good as straight!" they rose as a group, hoisted placards with messages such as "Save Our Children: Defend Lesbian Mothers," and stormed out as noisily as they could; they joined a picket with four hundred more protestors, some in drag, who were marching outside the arena. Onstage Bryant burst into tears.[36]

A few days later in New Orleans, she was performing with a Summer Pops Orchestra at the Municipal Auditorium, which bordered the French Quarter. Activists hung huge banners from French Quarter buildings that spelled out in big black block letters: "A DAY WITHOUT RIGHTS IS

LIKE A DAY WITHOUT SUNSHINE." Inside the auditorium, Bryant received a standing ovation for her performance; but outside the auditorium, hundreds of protestors kept vigil with flaming candles in their hands. The following day they rallied in Jackson Square and marched through the French Quarter streets. The police were on hand, videotaping marchers in order to intimidate them. But gays were not in the mood to be intimidated. Frank Kameny, who'd flown in from Washington, DC, told the press, "This is only a preliminary. We intend to stage protests all over the country, wherever she's performing."[37]

And that is what they did. In Atlanta, when Bryant was invited to speak and sing at a Southern Baptist Convention, 1,800 gays picketed.[38] In Washington, DC, when she was invited by the National Association of Religious Broadcasters to help launch a campaign to rid TV of sex, violence, and homosexuality, 2,000 gays held a service in a nearby church, accusing Bryant of "perverting the Christian message of love to one of hate." Then, as Bryant sang hymns to the broadcasters, gays marched in a candlelight protest around the Washington Hilton Hotel.[39] The Shriners invited Bryant to Chicago, to star in a Flag Day program, and 2,000 gays were waiting for her there, too.[40] In Houston, she was invited to entertain the Texas Bar Convention at the Hyatt Regency. More than 3,000 protestors, organized by the Texas Gay Political Caucus, paraded around the hotel carrying signs comparing her to Hitler.[41]

When *The Anita Bryant Story: The Survival of Our Nation's Families and the Threat of Militant Homosexuality* was published, Bryant and Bob Green called a news conference at the New York Hilton to publicize the book, but the hotel management was informed that 5,000 to 10,000 gays were planning to march on the Hilton in protest. Gays had already burned her in effigy in a bonfire big enough to cause the NYPD to rush over and stomp out the flames.[42] Claiming fear for her life, Bryant and Green canceled the news conference, dropped all plans to publicize *The Anita Bryant Story* in New York, and scurried back to Florida.[43] "Why don't they just kill us and get it over with!" an exhausted Bob Green lamented as they hurriedly departed the hotel.[44]

Activists staged zaps against Bryant, too. Most famously, as she sat at a televised press conference in Des Moines, Iowa, Bob Green at her side, gay activist Thom Higgins ran onto the set and smashed a banana cream pie in her face. The cameras kept rolling. Bryant burst into tears, and then she and her husband bowed their heads and prayed for the assailant, "God forgive him for his deviant lifestyle"—but not before she indulged in a catty quip: "At least it was a fruit pie."

Gays and lesbians didn't protest alone. In the fifties, sixties, and through much of the seventies, gay and lesbian activists attracted few straights to their cause. Though the Sexual Revolution made hip, young heterosexuals neutral about homosexuality, homophobia was not their battle, and they usually stayed on the sidelines. But Anita Bryant's Bible-thumping took away their neutrality. The sexual sanctimoniousness of Bryant and her ilk were a threat to heterosexual freedoms, too, and straight hip culture began reflecting antipathy. A country-rock band, Gravel, produced a 45 record, "(Lord Knows) I Don't Need Anita," ridiculing Bryant: "She was Miss Oklahoma, 1958 / Now she's usin' God and Country to make everybody straight." She was mocked, too, by the punk band Dead Kennedys in their song "The Moral Majority": "God must be dead if you're alive . . . Pissed at your neighbor? Don't bother to nag / Pick up your phone and turn in a fag." The humor magazine *National Lampoon* spoofed her with a parody of the Charles Atlas muscleman advertisements: "Anita Bryant's Homo No-Mo Macho-Building Course," illustrated by a saccharine picture of the singer saying, "Hi, I'm Anita Bryant. And I can cure your homosexuality in just 10 days!"[45] She was a regular target of disdain on *Saturday Night Live*, too, where actress Jane Curtin satirized her as prissy, silly, and clueless.

The protests of gay and lesbian activists and their friends had their desired effect: Bryant's career was decimated. She recorded a single that referenced her antigay crusade in its title, "There's Nothing Like the Love Between a Woman and a Man," but she could get no record company to distribute it. Bob Green was at his wits' end about his wife's failing career. Her show business earnings dropped 70 percent in the first months after her Dade County campaign. "Conventions have been totally inhibited from booking us," Green lamented. "We just want to get back to leading normal lives. This is no fun and games. The homosexuals are haunting us wherever we go."[46]

Bryant was reduced to performing almost entirely at revivals, where she was paid only whatever was dropped in the cardboard buckets that were passed around. At evangelist Cecil Todd's Revival Fire held at the Blossom Athletic Center on the outskirts of San Antonio, she sang hymns and helped preach Reverend Todd's message of bringing prayer into public schools and keeping homosexual teachers out of them. "The first step toward that goal," Todd announced to the faithful, who were mostly factory workers and farmhands, "is to help Anita by dropping ten dollars or a hundred dollars into the bucket."[47]

Incredibly, Bryant claimed to be astonished by the gay fury that had hurled her from bookings that paid upward of $8,500 a performance to bucket passing at a revival meeting. After her Revival Fire appearance, a *New York Times* reporter came to interview Bryant as she sat in the Blossom Athletic Center cement-block locker room that smelled of basketball players. In what can only be seen as a psychotic disconnect, Bryant wailed to the reporter, "Nobody had ever said a bad thing about me in my life. It's hard to understand this viciousness."[48]

Her $100,000-a-year gig inviting people to "come to the Florida sunshine tree" came to an end, too. The Florida Citrus Commission had been airing her commercials less and less because it could no longer ignore the fact that the gaycott was having an effect on sales. In addition, the venues that Bob Green once could depend on to publicize Anita Bryant's work had dried up. "The talk shows won't take her," he complained. "We've got books to plug, albums to plug, and they won't take her. The rule is, 'Yeah, we'll have Anita Bryant, but [for political balance] a gay must sit next to her.'"[49]

To raise money, she and Green established Anita Bryant Ministries, the purpose of which, they claimed, was to "seek help and change for homosexuals, whose sick values belie the word *gay*, which they pathetically use to cover their unhappy lives." Fund-raising letters from Bryant requested that recipients who want her to pursue that goal send their "gift of love to me in the reply envelope I am enclosing."[50] But Anita Bryant Ministries was not a moneymaker. Bryant and Green realized they could no longer afford their twenty-seven-room home. The shock of penury, Bryant's failing career, the constant emotional strain she was under (reduced often to tears by gay protests)—all of it together overwhelmed the marriage. In 1980 she divorced Green and announced that she was returning to Oklahoma.[51] Many of her fundamentalist fans shunned her because their church did not believe in divorce. "Rotten apples have gotten into the American pie," they complained.[52] Gays beat the devil.

But beating the devil is not the same as achieving civil rights. That was a trick gay and lesbian activists had not yet mastered, as the sweeping defeats in Saint Paul, Wichita, and Eugene amply illustrated. Despite their victory over Anita Bryant, the blitzkrieg against gays and lesbians continued. The very liberal city of Seattle and the entire state of California were next.

Chapter 21

LEARNING HOW TO WIN

RED ALERT IN CALIFORNIA

Morris Kight, by now the white-haired éminence grise of gay Los Angeles, kept close tabs on the Dade County massacre. Two days after the landslide vote, Kight sprang into action. He called a meeting of local gay leaders at his home on McCadden Place. Sixty men and a handful of women packed his living room as Kight stood in the center and told them, "We need to get the grassroots together, right now. No time to waste. We need a broad coalition that's ready for the fight: gays, feminists, ethnic minorities, straights. We need to be ready for the Orange Juice Lady when she comes. And she will come." Kight had already picked a name for the group he wanted to form: the Coalition for Human Rights.[1] He'd already decided on its first action, too: a march down Hollywood Boulevard.

The march that summer of 1977 was 9,500 strong, including a contingent of middle-aged straight men and women who, influenced by Jeanne Manford's founding of a group of mothers and fathers of lesbians and gays,[2] addressed Anita Bryant's ploy to save children from homosexuals with placards exhorting "Parents of Gays—Join in the Fight for Your Children's Rights" and "We Love Our Gay Children."[3] It was a tactic that would become essential in the rights fight for the next decades: take the rhetoric the enemy uses against you ("Homosexuals are a threat to our children") and make it your own ("These gays and lesbians *are our children!*").

It was just about the time of the march that California state senator John Briggs, from ultraconservative Orange County, sprang into action, too. During Anita Bryant's campaign, Briggs, son of a minister and a self-proclaimed born-again Christian, paused in his work on a measure to broaden the number of offenses punishable by the death penalty and flew to Miami with his Spanish-speaking wife. They were there to help Save Our Children win the Cuban vote. Briggs saw for himself the fanatical fervor with which the evangelical Right fought the gay amendment and the ease with which they achieved victory over liberal Miami, and he believed he'd discovered his main chance, a way to the governorship of California. His first step was to go before the California Senate Rules Committee to propose a laudatory resolution like one that had passed in Arkansas, commending Anita Bryant for her "courageous stand to protect American children from exposure to blatant homosexuality with resultant pornographic exploitation."[4]

The California Legislature, however, was not as gung-ho about putting homosexuals in their place as their Florida and Arkansas counterparts had been. "The legislature has enough business to conduct without debating topics beyond its responsibility," the Rules Committee chair, James Mills, told Briggs curtly. Briggs, whose short fuse was notorious, exploded: "This committee routinely approves laudatory resolutions. I'm the victim of a double standard!" He took his resolution directly to the Senate floor. "The members of the rules committee are shallow people, interested in protecting special interests," Briggs railed at the senators. One of them rose to object. "Shut up," Briggs told him and continued his tirade, at the end of which he moved for the resolution's adoption. He was seconded by Republican senator H. L. "Wild Bill" Richardson,[5] who'd voted against the bill to repeal the California sodomy law in 1975 with the argument that in Leviticus 20:13, God declared that sodomy should be punishable by death.[6] Richardson was ignored this time around, too. The resolution was defeated by a vote of 36 to 2.[7]

Briggs could not believe that most voters in the state shared the legislature's tolerance. Soon after being crushed in the Senate, he announced he would introduce a bill that would require all prospective teachers to swear they never engaged in homosexual behavior. The bill would also allow any school board to suspend employees charged with homosexual acts, and those found guilty at an administrative hearing would be dismissed within thirty days. If the legislature wouldn't pass the bill, Briggs vowed, he would lead a petition drive to bring the issue to the voters.[8]

Briggs was an unabashed opportunist, so it's hard to know what he really thought of homosexuals.[9] But he had no compunction about sacrificing them to his ambitions. "It's the hottest social issue since Reconstruction," he declared of the movement against gay rights,[10] and he announced he would run for the Republican gubernatorial nomination at the same time that he announced he was sponsoring two bills, one to expand the death penalty, and another to get rid of homosexual teachers.

Briggs hired a campaign consultant, Don Sizemore, who told the press that the senator received letters and phone calls every day from religious groups, "Mormons, Jews, Roman Catholics, Baptists, Presbyterians—you name it," who agreed with him that "taking homosexual influence out of the classroom is just one step to eliminating moral decay." Sizemore hoped to help his man profit from the notoriety of the woman who had started it all. He boasted of Briggs's "fairly good contact with Anita Bryant and Bob Green in Miami" and promised that both of them would come to California "after they rest up from their Miami campaign."[11]

Bryant and Green, busy with their own worries by then, stayed in Miami, and Briggs dropped out of the race when early polls showed that his chances were slim. But he still believed he'd hit on the hottest issue since Reconstruction, and he wasn't giving it up. If it wouldn't help him to the governorship, he'd use it in a run for the US Senate. To that end, he announced that the California Legislature had been derelict in refusing to prevent homosexual teachers from endangering children, and he was leading a petition drive that would let citizens decide for themselves at the ballot box if homosexuals ought to have such easy access to innocent youth. Oblivious to Anita Bryant's diminished prestige, he continued to use her name, printing petition-drive ads showing him with sleeves rolled up, sitting side by side with the singer as they talked on telephones in the service of the Save Our Children campaign.[12]

Briggs's focus on teachers was shrewd. Why would most people in liberal California care about what the other guy did, as long as it didn't hurt anyone else? So what if gay men moved in next door? So what if lesbians worked behind a desk or counter? A Gallup poll taken in summer 1977 had even shown that the majority of Americans approved of equal job rights for homosexuals in general—but 65 percent of them said they were opposed to homosexuals being allowed to teach children.[13] Briggs had cherry-picked the most explosive issue of all regarding gays and lesbians.

He needed 312,404 signatures in order to qualify his initiative for the ballot. He had no trouble getting that number and almost 50,000 signatures more. Proposition 6, the Briggs initiative, as it came to be called, was validated by the secretary of state for the November 7, 1978 ballot.[14] It said that any teacher, administrator, counselor, or teacher's aide would be discharged for "advocating, soliciting, imposing, encouraging, or promoting private or public sexual acts defined in the penal code between persons of the same sex in a manner likely to come to the attention of other employees or students, or publicly and indiscreetly engaging in such actions."

As had the Reverends Angwin and Adrian in Saint Paul and Wichita, Briggs replicated Anita Bryant's campaign in California, replete with her outlandish accusations and hysterical rhetoric. "One-third of San Francisco teachers are homosexuals. I assume most of them are seducing young boys in toilets," Briggs told one reporter.[15] He told another why Governor Jerry Brown would not support Proposition 6: "Let's face it, homosexuals have a tremendous amount of money. Jerry Brown knows that, wants it, and respects it."[16] Money poured into Proposition 6 coffers not only from fundamentalist churches, but also from groups as diverse as the California Farm Bureau, the San Diego Board of Realtors, and the Los Angeles Deputy Sheriffs Association. It paid for panic-inducing advertising like a widely distributed flyer that was illustrated by a Norman Rockwell–style picture of little children, school books under their arms, bidding their parents good-bye. In large, bold type, the ad read: "Preserve Parents' Rights to Protect Their Children from Teachers Who Are Immoral and Who Promote a Perverted Lifestyle. Vote 'Yes' on 6!"[17]

Briggs's rhetoric seemed well pitched to a surefire issue. Polls showed that 61 percent of the electorate would vote for the initiative. Only 31 percent opposed it. California voters, like those in the other states where antigay initiatives and referenda had passed, seemed set to send the message that to them, too, homosexuals were outcasts, outlaws, and disgusting.

California gays and lesbians had to find ways to fight better than had their counterparts in the four locales that had already fallen. But they were as wildly disparate as gays and lesbians everywhere else. Never in their entire history—as homophiles, gays, lesbian feminists—had the various factions put aside their differences and pulled together. They'd distrusted and disdained each other, though their enemies didn't distinguish among them: gay, lesbian, radical, liberal, conservative, working class, middle class, wealthy, black, brown, yellow, white, or purple—they were all child molesters, lawbreakers, and sick sinners.

Now, though, the threat was enormous. After almost a decade of progress, they could be set back to the dark ages of the midcentury or worse. They had to cooperate, if only like fingers of a hand, separate yet working together. Everything depended on it.

FRIENDLY FIRE AND SHARPSHOOTERS:
THE CAMPAIGN IN THE NORTH

Advocate publisher David Goodstein had nervously predicted in early 1977 that if Anita Bryant won in Dade County she would take her campaign everywhere. Events were proving Goodstein right. She was now on his doorstep in the guise of Senator John Briggs. Goodstein knew that a big gay loss in the liberal state of California would be far more disastrous than all the losses thus far. It would topple every domino of gay progress all over America. He feared, as he readily admitted, that Briggs was unstoppable, just as Bryant had been; but he believed that as owner of the biggest gay magazine in America he had responsibility for assuring that at the least the California defeat wouldn't come in a mortifying 5 to 1 landslide as it had in Wichita.

Goodstein was the man to whom Jack Campbell had turned for advice about how to defeat Anita Bryant in Dade County. Goodstein had recommended that the grassroots types and the gays who were too gay be kept out of the Miami battle; and he thought they needed to be made invisible in California, too. He was furious when, hours after the loss in Dade County, thousands of angry gay radicals in San Francisco assembled on

Castro Street and marched through the city threatening to riot, screaming, "Civil Rights or Civil War!"[18] The radicals were "their own worst enemy," Goodstein proclaimed. He cautioned in the editorials he wrote for his magazine that a huge loss would be guaranteed "if gay activists or hedonists choose to be outrageously visible." If they take any role at all, it should be only to register other gay voters or to stuff envelopes at headquarters.[19] Goodstein's attempts to muzzle radical gays were exactly what they expected of him. They disdained him as much as he disdained them. They disdained his magazine, too—a *People* for gays, they called it.

During the Bryant battle, Goodstein had bankrolled Jim Foster—the best gay political maven he knew—to go to Dade County and help lead the fight. That had failed miserably, of course, but now, panicked by the threat of the Briggs initiative, Goodstein went back to Foster, and together they formed Concerned Voters of California. They were sufficiently unnerved by the threat, though, to agree that for a statewide issue as hugely important as this one, they needed help from someone with broader professional experience than Foster's. Someone who'd know how to procure endorsements from the famous and powerful—a heterosexual who'd be able to communicate the message that straights, too, opposed Briggs. Don Bradley, who'd headed the winning California campaigns of presidents John Kennedy and Lyndon Johnson, agreed to take the job. Goodstein and Foster were thrilled: in 1977 there weren't many heterosexual professionals who would have said yes.

The only out elected gay politician in San Francisco, Supervisor Harvey Milk, distrusted Goodstein and his role as a power broker as much as the radicals did. "Aunt Mary," Milk called him.[20] At a Concerned Voters of California meeting to which San Francisco notables were invited, Milk showed up and heard Congressman Phil Burton earnestly read aloud from a brochure that CVC had paid for. It talked about human rights and why gays deserved them just as much as any citizen, and it sounded very much like the failed rhetoric of the Dade County Coalition for Human Rights. "Masturbation!" Harvey Milk cried. "It's tepid!"[21] And he went off to form his own group, San Franciscans Against Prop 6.

Into leadership positions in San Franciscans Against Prop 6, Milk put his trusted followers—such as former Methodist minister Harry Britt, president of the San Francisco Gay Democratic Club, which had been formed in 1976 to get Milk elected to the board of supervisors. Though Milk had his detractors—Jim Foster considered him "a fast-talking, long-haired political novice"[22]—he did know how to build coalitions, and he never underestimated the vital role of grassroots volunteers. The campaign needed people to stand on street corners and do voter registration, to ring doorbells and talk with voters face-to-face, to get them to the polls. Milk hired a young graduate student from Berkeley, Bill Kraus, and a black lesbian activist, Gwenn Craig, as campaign directors; and their job was to find people like them—young, minority, female—who would go out and make sure sympathizers from those demographics didn't only nod in agreement but actually cast their ballots. He also put his new protégé, a smart, spirited, boyish twenty-three-year-old by the name of Cleve Jones, to work: Jones, who was then an undergraduate poli-sci major at San Francisco State University, was assigned the job of locating all the gay college student groups in the state and mobilizing them for the battle.[23]

Milk knew, too, that San Francisco's big lesbian-feminist community was resentful that Concerned Voters of California was oblivious of them. To defuse lesbian-feminist suspicions and make them fight the real enemy, he needed to have a prominent lesbian-feminist sidekick. Cleve Jones found him the perfect one—a Speech and Women's Studies professor at San Francisco State University, Sally Gearhart, who, Jones told Milk, "exuded dignity."[24] Gearhart, a tall and handsome Virginian with a slight southern accent, became Milk's partner in a high-profile public-television debate against John Briggs and crusading minister Ray Batema. As a radical lesbian feminist, Gearhart usually dressed in relaxed, androgynous fashion; but she and Milk agreed that she would match his newly cultivated well-turned-out conservative appearance, so that together they'd present themselves to the straight voter as "Mom and Pop of Middle America." Parodying their efforts even as he embraced them, Milk called Gearhart just as she was leaving her home to go to the TV studio for the debate. "I've lost my earrings, dear! Whatever shall I do?" he cried.[25]

They were a good team. In their TV debate, they overwhelmed John Briggs's hysterical rhetoric with facts, pointing out, for instance, that studies showed heterosexual men were far more likely than homosexuals to be child molesters. They appeared together, too, at San Franciscans Against

Prop 6 rallies where Milk habitually raised Gearhart's arm and called her "San Francisco's next Supervisor!" tacitly promising that he'd help bring a lesbian feminist into mainstream politics.[26] Lesbian-feminist devotion to San Franciscans Against Prop 6 was clinched.[27]

But not that of the most radical gays and lesbian feminists, who distrusted Milk almost as much as they distrusted Goodstein. "He's promoting himself," they complained. "This is another Harvey Milk power grab."[28]

San Francisco radicals formed their own groups, such as the Bay Area Committee Against the Briggs Initiative (BACABI), in order to do what Goodstein was uninterested in doing and what they believed Milk could not do as well as they.[29] They were far more skillful than Goodstein gave them credit for being. For instance, they put together a "Third World Outreach Committee" that sent lesbians and gays of color out to do public speaking to straight people of color and to distribute brochures that hammered home points tailored to such audiences. Senator John Briggs has one of the worst records in the State Senate on issues concerning minorities, they said, and pointed to his support of the death penalty, which affected third world people disproportionately. "This Is What Third World Leaders Are Saying About Proposition 6," their brochures announced and quoted black militant heroine Angela Davis, board of supervisors member Gordon Lau, community activist Jim Gonzales, even Native American and Filipino leaders who opposed the Briggs initiative.[30] BACABI tailored messages to unions, too: "The Briggs initiative endangers the job security of *all* public school workers; destroys the right of unions to protect workers from discrimination; threatens to erode collective bargaining and the right to organize for public employees."[31]

When BACABI speakers addressed these groups they emphasized that Briggs was bad for all sorts of people, but they understood that sometimes the gay issue must be addressed directly. One of the most prominent outreach speakers was Amber Hollibaugh, a very blond young woman who billed herself as a working-class high-femme dyke. Hollibaugh was sent to rural areas of California where many people never knew they'd met a gay person before. Her job was to make them see her humanity and, by extension, the humanity of all gay people. Speaking to a teamsters local in rural California, she told them not only that Briggs was antilabor but also that his initiative would push people into denying an essential part of their lives: "There are gay people in this room, in your union, that you will never know are gay," she told them, and then pulled empathy out of them, asking: "What does it mean not to be able to acknowledge the primary things in your life? What would it mean to you not to be able to acknowledge your children, your primary relationships, your parents?"[32]

In Redding, California, Hollibaugh was invited to debate Pastor Royal Blue, founder of Shasta Bible College and a local Christian radio station. A buddy of Jerry Falwell, Pastor Blue took credit for prodding Falwell to establish the Moral Majority. He himself was active in Californians for Biblical Morality, through which he lobbied the legislature in Sacramento on issues such as school prayer, abortion, and homosexuality. A few days before the debate he'd conducted a rally attended by twenty-five hundred people. It had been a patriotic, homophobic spectacle—fifty children on stage waving little American flags in front of Statues of Liberty whose eyes blinked green lights as the pastor preached hellfire. The debate with Hollibaugh was held at Pastor Blue's North Valley Baptist Church, and much of it was devoted to his spouting the biblical condemnations of homosexuality. During the question-and-answer session, a member of the audience asked the pastor, "Do you think homosexuals should be imprisoned if they're that unsafe?"

"Well, let me put it this way," he answered, smiling all the while. "I think Hitler was right about the homosexuals. I think we should find a humane way to kill them."

Hollibaugh sized up the audience and saw that many there were over fifty, and she realized how she could isolate the pastor. "Well, you know, Reverend Blue," she said, "my guess would be that most of the people in this audience fought against someone who had that position in World War II, and my guess is that the audience does not support genocide. I may be wrong, but I suspect that most people don't feel that mass murder is an answer to a sexual question." She'd made the audience chagrined by Blue's horrifying "final solution," and a small crowd came up to her to apologize for their pastor.[33] Neither Goodstein with his expensive ad campaigns nor Milk with his army of volunteers stood a chance of getting these fundamentalist Christian voters on their side. Hollibaugh reached at least some of them.

A GLITTER CAMPAIGN IN SOUTHERN CALIFORNIA

David Mixner, MECLA's well-connected strategist, had been operating behind the scenes, lest his coming out interfere with his day job as campaign manager for Tom Bradley's reelection bid. But in June 1977 Mayor Bradley was reelected in Los Angeles, and gays lost their rights in Miami. When John Briggs began to threaten California by channeling Anita Bryant, Mixner decided he could no longer work from the closet. He came out to everyone. He wrote all his good friends in politics, and in the entertainment industry, too, to tell them first that he was gay and then that he intended to wage war on Briggs and that he was asking for their support. Most of them, including his old friend Bill Clinton, said yes. Clinton called as soon as he received Mixner's letter to assure him, "Hillary and I will always be your friends and you can count on us . . .You're doing the right thing."[34]

With Peter Scott and the two founding women of MECLA, attorneys Diane Abbitt and Roberta Bennett, Mixner called a press conference to announce that "Los Angeles will be ready for Bryant or her friends," and that they were forming New Alliance for Gay Equality—New AGE—to lead the battle.[35] To pull in lesbians, they knew, a lesbian needed to be prominent in the leadership of the group. Roberta Bennett agreed to be cochair. They opened an office, and Scott and Mixner were hired by New AGE at $2,000 a month to devote all their energies to organizing the diverse lesbian and gay communities to fight against Proposition 6.

They scrambled to find big money to kick off the kind of anti-Briggs campaign they hoped to run. Reverend Troy Perry was the first to come to their rescue. In 1970 the reverend had used dramatic means to challenge the abuse of gay people by the Los Angeles Police Department. He'd sat himself down in front of the LA Federal Building and commenced a fast and prayer vigil, taking no sustenance but water for over a week, until he got commitments from city attorney Bert Pines, and city councilmen Bob Stevenson and Tom Bradley (the future mayor) to pressure the LAPD to clean up its act.[36] Now, seven years later, when David Mixner came to Perry to say that the anti-Briggs campaign needed money to begin its operations in Southern California, the reverend promised to raise $100,000 by reprising his successful 1970 performance.

Perry called a press conference to announce that he'd go on a hunger strike in order to raise the money and simultaneously to educate the American public about "the harm done by bigots like Senator Briggs and Anita Bryant": "I am preparing to fast to death if necessary," he declared.[37] Then he sat on the steps of the Federal Building and fasted and prayed once again. He subsisted on water and vitamin capsules. The LA police drove their patrol cars by to be annoying; they kept sounding their sirens late at night to deprive him of sleep. But Reverend Perry would not budge. Throngs came to keep him company, and money came pouring in like the abundant loaves and fishes. A couple of weeks into the fast, a Metropolitan Community Church parishioner in Kansas City telephoned Perry's office to ask how he was doing. When told the reverend was very weak, the parishioner sold two thousand shares of stock in her business and sent him $20,000, which put the total Perry had raised to $107,000. On the sixteenth day of fasting, the reverend, twenty pounds lighter, packed up his water bottles and vitamin vials and went home.[38]

Mixner and Scott found fancier ways to bring in money, too. Mixner had been friendly with Senator George McGovern since 1969 when he invited the senator to be the keynote speaker at the Moratorium to End the War in Vietnam. Now Mixner and Peter Scott flew to DC, paid McGovern a visit in his office, and asked him to do what no US senator had ever done before: speak at a big openly gay fund-raiser. Much to Mixner's surprise, McGovern needed no convincing. "I'd be delighted to do it," he said.[39]

Affluent gay people packed the grand ballroom of the Beverly Wilshire Hotel, whose management had absolutely not wanted to host a gay event—but wanted even less to insult a US senator.[40] Over foie gras and champagne, six hundred gay people listened to George McGovern talk about the battle against Briggs as a fight for human dignity. For many of them it was a coming-out party, the first public gay event they'd ever attended. The anti-Briggs campaign—supported by a US senator speaking to gay people in the ballroom of a world-class luxury hotel—had suddenly made it respectable to be gay, and safer to come out.

But the polls were still favoring Briggs two to one. Mixner worried that if gays lost, their victimhood would know no end.[41] More money was needed to counter Briggs's barrages such as the lurid antigay billboards and

flyers in which the old nemesis of Los Angeles gays, former police chief
Ed Davis, proclaimed, "There is no question that homosexuals are a threat
to children."[42] In the past, when MECLA supported the campaigns of the
politicians they favored, it was largely "the boys north of Franklin"—as
grassroots gays wryly referred to wealthy gay men who lived in the Hollywood Hills, north of Franklin Avenue—who supplied the money. But New
AGE had to find ways to expand the donor base.

Gayle Wilson, a lesbian Realtor, was a familiar and glamorous image in
West Hollywood, driving around town in her Corniche Rolls-Royce convertible, wind blowing through her stylishly bobbed blond hair. "The pioneer of the lipstick lesbians," David Mixner dubbed her. The closest she'd
gotten to gay politics had been to join the West Hollywood Community
Guild—a sort of gay Chamber of Commerce—because it was good for
business.[43] But now Mixner and Scott came to her to say that if Briggs succeeded, all lesbians and gays would be victims of the fanatical Right, and
she had to use whatever clout she had to help defeat him. Wilson tapped
her client list, which included wealthy Hollywood heterosexuals as well
as gays; and then she tapped her wealthy lesbian acquaintances, most of
whom had never before given even a dollar to a lesbian or gay cause. Then
Wilson organized a luncheon at the Beverly Hilton Hotel in Beverly Hills.
She invited her entertainer friends Cher and Donna Summer to sing, and
Midge Costanza, who'd just left her White House post, to speak about the
snowballing threat that would eventually hit all lesbians if California should
fail to stop Briggs.

Probably for the first time in the history of the world, hundreds of
lesbians, dressed to the nines, drove up to a posh hotel in their Mercedes
and BMWs and Cadillacs, asked the doorman the way to the dining room
where a lesbian luncheon was being held, and there joined an overflowing
crowd of other affluent lesbians for a public lesbian event whose purpose
was to raise money for a gay and lesbian cause.[44] They donated about
$50,000 that day, which was used to help run the New AGE campaign of-
fice and to pay for anti-Briggs ads.

The appearance of hundreds of lesbians of means at a public event was
not the only first that day of the Beverly Hills luncheon. It was also the first
time that Hollywood celebrities had let themselves be seen at a fund-raiser

whose express purpose was to support a lesbian and gay cause; and it was the start of a series of such celebrity events in LA. At the next glittering fund-raiser for the anti-Briggs campaign—a black-tie and chic-pantsuit dinner attended by one thousand gays and lesbians—Burt Lancaster, John Travolta, and Lily Tomlin appeared. They raised $150,000 for the war chest.[45] When more money was needed, leading cosmetologists all over the state held a "hair-a-thon," donating all their proceeds from fancy haircuts to the anti-Briggs campaign.[46]

By then, Mixner and Scott were working with David Goodstein and Harvey Milk in Northern California in an unprecedented cooperative north-south effort. There would be a statewide "No on 6" umbrella entity, they agreed. Don Bradley, Goodstein's handpicked campaign manager, would be the statewide campaign consultant, working out of No on 6 headquarters on LA's fashionable Wilshire Boulevard.[47] Harvey Milk would coordinate the Northern California campaign. David Mixner and Peter Scott would coordinate the Southern California campaign.

HOW TO COVER ALL BASES

Not all factions let themselves be coordinated. Groups kept proliferating along the usual divides: "Suits" (as New AGE types were called) versus "Streets" (as grassroots types were called); grassroots gay men versus grass-roots lesbian feminists. Streets were unwilling to work with Suits, and lesbian feminists were unwilling to work with gay men. Jeanne Córdova, the young firebrand who'd organized a first-ever national lesbian conference at UCLA in 1973, had been one of the five or six lesbians among the sixty men who were invited to the grassroots organizing meeting in Morris Kight's living room soon after the Dade County victory. Córdova looked around her that night at the artwork on the walls—ephebes and musclemen—and the overwhelming male presence in the room, and she knew that lesbian feminists would scoff at the idea of cooperating with a group so dominated by testosterone. She went home, pulled out of her desk her list of lesbian-feminist contacts, and got to work. A few weeks later they met in a separate all-women's group, the Ad Hoc Committee for Lesbian Rights. But the splits continued. When Diane Abbitt of New AGE saw Córdova's knack for organizing, she tried to draw her into New AGE, saying, "Jeanne, you've got the gift as a leader, and we have the power to get things done. Join us." Then she glimpsed the black boots with chains on the heels that Córdova was wearing—definitely grassroots. "But we'd have to make changes in how you present yourself," Abbitt added. Córdova told her she was sticking with the Ad Hoc Committee for Lesbian Rights.[48]

David Mixner did eventually succeed in attaining some cooperation among the factions. Ivy Bottini, another leader of grassroots lesbians, had also been one of the few women invited to Kight's organizing meeting. The fifty-one-year-old Bottini, who'd come from blue-collar roots, was the woman who as president of the New York chapter of NOW had pushed the lesbian issue which triggered Betty Friedan's Lavender Menace tirades.[49] Bottini had moved to Los Angeles in 1971, in shock after Friedan got her booted out of NOW's leadership. At the time that Kight invited Bottini to the organizing meeting, she was calling herself a lesbian separatist.

Bottini arrived at Kight's McCadden Place home, looked around as Jeanne Córdova did, and thought, "I'm in enemy territory."[50] She thought of leaving. But Kight, always politically astute, knowing he needed all the hands he could get for his new group and he wouldn't have lesbian support without lesbian leaders, maneuvered the election of Ivy Bottini as his cochair.

David Mixner was even two steps ahead of Kight. Ivy Bottini could not only bring many more lesbians into the campaign; she also had grassroots appeal and street cred. She knew exactly how to present the Briggs's problem in a way that would get the attention of the working class. This is a labor issue, and organized labor needs to take it seriously, Bottini emphasized: "This jerk Briggs is talking about firing thousands of workers because of who they sleep with."[51] Mixner offered Bottini—who was struggling to make a living as an artist—a paid position as deputy director of Southern California's No on 6 campaign. She would be able to attract the volunteers to knock on doors and hand out leaflets, to post No on 6 signs, to register voters and drive them to the polls—and those were not the jobs the Suits did happily or well. "If you come in, the grass roots will come in," Mixner told Bottini. He sent over Gayle Wilson in her Corniche convertible to convince her, too.[52]

• • •

Sallie Fiske, who'd been one of the first women in television broadcast journalism in Los Angeles, was another lesbian Mixner hired to be a magnet. She'd been hosting her own afternoon television talk show, *Strictly for Women*, when Anita Bryant and Save Our Children grabbed the country's attention. Fiske had always been mum in front of the camera about being a lesbian and was closeted even in her personal life. But now her anger about Bryant pushed her to come out before the eyes of all her *Strictly for Women* viewers. That was the end of her broadcast career; but as a result she became the best known and most admired lesbian in the city. Mixner made her the public relations director of No on 6, hoping Fiske's presence would draw in more lesbian volunteers. His ploy succeeded. Eventually even the Ad Hoc Committee for Lesbian Rights worked the phone banks in the No on 6 office. "For this one, we've got to let go of our feelings and join the guys," Jeanne Córdova told her group.[53] Before the campaign was done, Suits and Streets and gay men and lesbians were working together in the movement for civil rights—for the first time ever on a large scale.

Only the far-left radicals held out. They conducted their own campaign in groups such as the Action Coalition to Defeat the Briggs Initiative, a sister group to Oakland's East Bay Action Coalition Against the Briggs Initiative. Shop steward and trade union organizer Robin Podolsky, a cerebral young woman who wrote for local progressive papers, became an Action Coalition strategist. A "doctrinaire Marxist," she'd been very interested in questions such as, How does race predetermine class? But she hadn't thought at all about gay and lesbian rights—until the Briggs initiative qualified for the ballot. With other Action Coalition people, black and white, she walked the precincts in Watts, the major black area of Los Angeles, where they handed out flyers, signed people up to vote, and talked the talk many of them had learned as Marxist activists—but now with a twist: the Action Coalition's slogan was "Discrimination: Who's Next?" and their message in Watts was that gays were merely first on Briggs the Bigot's hit list. After he finished with gays, black people could expect to be next.[54]

THE CAMPAIGN'S STRANGEST BEDFELLOW

Taken together, No on 6 and the radical campaigns against the Briggs initiative covered every important demographic and technique—men, women, north, south, the Suits, the Streets (grassroots and radicals), big-buck ads, a fortune spent on shoe leather, eloquent speeches in big halls, face-to-face entreaties at the thresholds of front doors. Every group doing its share and doing what the other groups could not have done, or could not have done as well. At the start of Briggs's campaign, polls had shown that Proposition 6 would win two to one, exactly as the other antigay measures had in presumably liberal places. In the months that followed, the various anti-Briggs groups did an amazing job whittling away at Briggs's lead. Every poll showed them closer and closer.

But *close* is not enough if you need to win. In September, with a little over two months left before the election, polls indicated that 55 percent of the electorate still intended to vote in favor of Proposition 6.[55] Gays and lesbians had already done everything they could possibly do. Something like a miracle would be needed to get another 6 percent of the voters on their side. The miracle came in the very unlikely form of the most prominent Republican politician in California, the former governor and future president of the United States.

Ronald Reagan was a pure political conservative. The government's primary goal, he believed, should be to keep law and order, and it ought to stay out of people's personal lives. David Mixner understood this. If only he could get Reagan's ear, he thought, he would know exactly what to say to bring him to the side of No on 6. He would not bother to tell the former governor that Prop 6 would violate people's human rights; Reagan was too hard-nosed to care about that. He would tell him instead that the Briggs initiative would violate the tenets that Reagan held most sacred.

Mixner called his friend David Jones, an upscale LA florist who counted Nancy Reagan among his regular customers. "How do you think the Reagans feel about gays?" Mixner asked Jones. "Well, they like me . . . And they socialize with gay people," Jones told him.

Then Mixner called his friend Don Livingston, a closeted gay man who'd been on Governor Reagan's administrative staff. "Do you think that if Reagan were approached in the right way, he might be willing to make a statement opposing Proposition 6?" Mixner asked. Livingston was pretty sure Reagan was in favor of the Briggs initiative, but he agreed to put Mixner in touch with a top Reagan aide.

The aide agreed to meet Mixner—but not in West Hollywood or Beverly Hills or anywhere anyone could possibly recognize them. Feeling as though he'd stepped into a spy movie, Mixner suggested a place where they'd be anonymous, Denny's in East LA. East Los Angeles was a poor Mexican American area. "The likelihood of a Republican showing up there was minimal," Mixner thought ironically.

"You're wasting your time," Don Bradley, the statewide campaign consultant, told David Mixner when he heard of the plan. "Look, Reagan wants to run for president. There's no way he's not supporting the initiative." When Mixner called Harvey Milk in San Francisco to tell him he hoped to get Reagan's ear, Milk shouted, "That's crazy! We shouldn't be meeting with a criminal!"[56]

Peter Scott accompanied Mixner to the clandestine rendezvous at Denny's. The aide, another closeted gay man, had a wife and passed as straight. He'd have to remain anonymous, he told Mixner and Scott over coffee, but he'd try to help. Nancy Reagan might be helpful, too. She had many gay friends. (She even had a lesbian godmother—the silent screen star, Alla Nazimova.) But if the aide set up a meeting, Mixner and Scott had to give their word they wouldn't badger Reagan.

They promised. Even a brief fifteen-minute meeting would do. They'd merely point out to Reagan how the initiative violated important conservative principles.[57]

Months earlier, Mixner had decided to get in shape, and he'd lost so much weight that now nothing in his closet fit. In thanks for the work he was doing to fight Briggs, his movement friends took up a collection and bought him a whole new wardrobe for his birthday on August 16.[58] About a week later, Mixner dressed up in his brand-new dark blue suit, and together with Peter Scott, he went to meet Ronald Reagan. The meeting took place in Reagan's sunlit office overlooking West Los Angeles. The future president offered Mixner and Scott jelly beans from a jar on his desk and made good-humored small talk before he said, "I understand you boys have a case you want to make to me."

"The boys'" opening salvo, tailored to Reagan's sentiments, was sage: "Governor, you know about Proposition 6 that would allow any school child to file a complaint against any teacher that he thought was homosexual," Mixner began. Reagan was familiar with the proposition, he said. He'd spent time studying it; he thought he'd probably endorse it. "Well, this proposition would create anarchy in the classroom," Mixner plowed ahead, though he was quaking. "Imagine a kid getting a failing grade or being disciplined by a teacher or facing expulsion. To get even, all he'd have to do is accuse the teacher of being a homosexual. Teachers will be afraid of giving a low grade. They won't be able to maintain order in the classroom."

"Governor, if Briggs passes, the kids are going to run the schools," Peter Scott chimed in. "Teachers will be terrified of their students. It'll be chaos."

Reagan seemed surprised. "Hmm, I never thought about that," he said. "That's not what we want for California schools." Before their fifteen minutes were up, Reagan told them, "This might be a good day for you boys."[59]

A few weeks after the meeting, Reagan echoed Mixner and Scott's statements almost exactly to the press: "What if an overwrought youngster, disappointed by bad grades, imagined it was the teacher's fault and struck out by accusing the teacher of advocating homosexuality?" He pointed out that the Briggs initiative was not needed to protect children because current laws already protected them from molestation, and that Proposition 6 "has the potential for real mischief."[60]

It turned the tide. The Briggs initiative's 10-percentage-point lead evaporated soon after Reagan declared himself to be against it. On November 7, 1978, Proposition 6 was defeated by a margin of over a million votes—58.4 percent to 41.6 percent. Even Orange County, John Briggs's hometown and the area he represented in the State Senate, voted against his initiative.

In the main ballroom of the Beverly Hilton Hotel in Los Angeles, a Statue of Liberty was draped in a "No on 6" banner. Three thousand gays and lesbians who'd worked for No on 6 had shown up to celebrate. Jeanne Córdova was there in her black boots with the chains across the heels. Ivy Bottini took the microphone to declare, "I loved working with those men! Let me tell you, I will never again be a separatist."[61]

On the other side of town, in a large rented room at the American Bulgarian Culture Hall, one thousand gays and lesbians who'd worked with the Action Coalition and other radical groups were also gathered together to celebrate. No fancy dress here. They wore their usual uniforms of jeans and flannel plaid or sweatshirts. A few weeks earlier, the polls had shown that 63 percent of black voters would vote against the Briggs initiative.[62] The radicals knew that blacks had been won over because of their strategy of making minority voters a linchpin of their campaign; it was because of them that the anti-Briggs campaign enjoyed a comfortable margin of safety. In the midst of jubilation, they took time to scoff that the Suits had run "an old fashioned election campaign, raising a million dollars and wasting it, telling the activists who did the real work, 'We're in charge, we have the money.'"[63] Not even a glorious victory could heal the rifts between Suits and Streets. But they'd each done what had to be done to make the victory possible.

THE EL ALAMEIN OF GAY RIGHTS
CITY ORDINANCE BATTLES

David Estes, a thirty-two-year-old Mormon with two young children, was a Seattle police officer. He claimed that as a normal concerned parent he was horrified at the city's acceptance of homosexuality because the inevitable "side effects" of such tolerance were "increased child prostitution, crimes of violence, strange behavior, and so on."[64] Estes organized a petition drive together with another police officer, Dennis Falk, who, along with being a leader in the local John Birch Society, had gotten in a bit of trouble a few years earlier for using brass knuckles on University of Washington students who were protesting the war.[65] With 17,626 signatures, Estes and Falk could place an initiative on the November 1978 ballot. It would repeal a 1973 ordinance that promised gays and lesbians they wouldn't be discriminated against in city employment and a 1975 ordinance that promised they wouldn't be discriminated against in housing. The two policemen easily got the required number of signatures—plus ten thousand to spare.

Seattle was to be the El Alamein of the gay rights city ordinance battles. If gays could mount a successful campaign to defeat Initiative 13, the juggernaut of losses—Dade County, Saint Paul, Wichita, Eugene—might be halted, and the thirty-five or so remaining gay rights city ordinances around America might be safe. But if Initiative 13 passed in liberal Seattle, there would surely be no stopping repeal drives everywhere.

Estes and Falk called their antigay rights campaign Save Our Moral Ethics (SOME), and they patterned it on Save Our Children's well-tested strategy. Though Anita Bryant was still too busy with her own problems to attend a prayer rally that Estes and Falk hoped to stage in order to fire up voters,[66] Save Our Children contributed several thousand dollars to the SOME campaign. With the money, Estes and Falk could run radio ads, such as one informing the public that because of Seattle's gay rights laws, normal people and their children risked being "exposed to homosexual behavior in parks, neighborhood theaters, your favorite restaurant, and shopping malls."[67] They also created a "fact sheet" to distribute to reporters and anyone who would take it. The "facts" were that homosexuals were unstable, unable to keep a job, child molesters—and they accounted for half the murders and suicides in American cities and half the nation's syphilis cases.[68] Early polls of likely voters showed Initiative 13 at a 30-point lead.

As soon as Charlie Brydon got word of Estes and Falk's plan to repeal the city's gay rights laws, he and members of Seattle's Dorian Group—an "organization of mainstream gays," Brydon called it—started Citizens to Retain Fair Employment. Charlie Brydon had come to Seattle in 1974. He'd found that the most visible gay organization at that time was the Union of Sexual Minorities, a radical group headed by zappers Faygele Singer and Paul Barwick. Brydon, who has been described as seeming "always to be wearing a conservative sport jacket, even when he was not,"[69] was decidedly not a radical. He'd been an intelligence officer in Vietnam, the recipient of two bronze stars, and then a successful business executive in San Francisco. In Seattle, he was chief of the branch office of an insurance company. He'd started the Dorian Group for people like him.[70]

When Initiative 13 qualified for the ballot, Brydon studied the repeal fights from Miami to Eugene and decided that gays lost in all those places because their approaches were always wrong. They had argued that gay people shouldn't be discriminated against because everyone deserved human rights, or that gay is good and deserves respect, or that heterosexuals should like gays because they were nice people. But why would those arguments

make most heterosexuals in the 1970s get themselves to the polls to endorse
gay rights? Brydon chose a more nuanced approach. Initiative 13 wasn't just
about depriving gays of their rights, he argued; it would usher in a new era
in which *all* citizens could be deprived of their rights. The Citizens to Retain
Fair Employment logo was a keyhole with a spying eye looking through
it. Television ads showed a family seated around a table—vulnerable to the
world because their house was made of glass. Under Charlie Brydon's top-
down direction, the battle that CRFE waged was simply about the right to
privacy. If the government can spy on the private behavior of anyone, it can
spy on the private behavior of everyone.[71]

FRIENDLY FIRE AND SHARP
SHOOTERS, SEATTLE STYLE

Charlie Brydon masterminded a steering committee for Citizens to Retain Fair Employment that was made up of local politicians, state legislators, clergy, University of Washington professors—almost no one who was
openly gay. The day-to-day work of the campaign was done primarily by
gay people, but they kept a low profile. Brydon's approach earned him
predictable animosity from Seattle's various radical lesbian and gay groups.
A newly formed Washington Coalition for Sexual Minority Rights, a leftist organization that billed itself as "dedicated to building a united front
of gays, women, minorities, and workers," announced it would sponsor
a gay pride parade the summer before the election. Brydon tried to get
the group to cancel it. He feared media coverage would focus on the drag
queens and the leather men in chaps and bare bottoms, and those would be
the images that would stick in voters' minds when they went to the polls
in the fall.

For their part, the Washington Coalition for Sexual Minority Rights
mocked Brydon as classist and antediluvian. They went on with the parade,
three thousand people—Radical Women, the Stonewall Committee, Freedom Socialists—marching through downtown Seattle.[72] One speaker at
the parade rally called Charlie Brydon "Seattle's Gay Uncle Tom." Another
jeeringly referred to "Anita Brydon."[73]

As in California, warring anti-initiative groups proliferated. Some
of the marchers in that summer's parade went on to establish the

Seattle Committee Against Thirteen. They chose their name for its acronym, which said "SCAT" not only to SOME but also to CRFE, and announced that they refused to be civil and unSCATological in their fight against Initiative 13. Another group, Women Against Thirteen, was formed because lesbian feminists refused to work with gay men, whether conservative or radical. The acronym WAT (cf. twat) was chosen purposely as an in-your-face reminder that not only did WAT eschew middle-class mealy-mouthed gentility, but also that WAT was resolutely female.

Charlie Brydon and Citizens to Retain Fair Employment had a lot to worry about in addition to Initiative 13, such as SCAT holding signs over Seattle's freeways that proclaimed, "Someone You Know Is Gay," a message that Brydon and CRFE believed was as pointless as a prank. But the most irritating action to them was WAT's "Blood on SOME" caper. On the night of June 13, WAT members Betty Johanna and Jane Meyerding were apprehended by the Seattle Police for breaking into the offices of SOME and "perpetrating mischief."[74] Meyerding had been arrested several times before: in 1967, when she was seventeen years old and took part in a march on the Pentagon; the following year when she was charged with felony for her disruptions at the 1968 Democratic Convention in Chicago; and in 1971, when she was charged with felony again for her participation in a Vietnam War protest with an angry pacifist group that broke into the Federal Building in Rochester, New York, and tried to destroy draft records and FBI files. For that action she was sent to prison for a year.[75]

Jane Meyerding was the architect of the SOME office invasion. She and Betty Johanna broke into SOME headquarters with several vials of blood—their own and that of other women—which they poured all over SOME's initiative petitions and financial records. They left behind not only bloody stacks of paper but also a signed "open letter to the staff, volunteers, and supporters of SOME," in which they identified themselves as lesbians and declared, "We have brought our blood here to you today for three reasons: to share our lives, our human-ness with you in the clearest, strongest way we can; to challenge your human-ness by showing you that the work you do here imperils our lives and our human-ness; & to disrupt with our lives, with our blood and our human-ness, the anti-life Initiative 13 campaign."[76] They dubbed what they did "an unpatriarchal and pacifist, nonviolent direct action."[77]

The two women were picked up in a police car later that night and taken down to the station. Both were booked, tried, and sentenced to eighteen days in the Seattle City Jail for "property destruction." The metaphorical intent of their action went far over the heads of the likes of David Estes and Dennis Falk, but it captured the imagination of the Left. Meyerding and Johanna became legends and brought other radicals into the battle.[78]

Charlie Brydon and his coworkers at Citizens to Retain Fair Employment had to reconcile themselves to the fact that there was no way they could stop SCAT and WAT from doing as they liked; but eventually the three groups figured out how to complement one another.

Brydon's organization took the initiative. Citizens to Retain Fair Employment hired a young college student, Randy Henson, to serve as liaison to the two radical groups. "We can each go after a different demographic," he convinced them. They met regularly in the months before the election to share what their groups were doing and brainstorm about what else needed to be done. SCAT and WAT leafleted at workplaces; they focused on getting-out-the-vote drives among "nontraditional voters"—minorities, feminists, the Left, union members, especially like-minded gays and lesbians. CRFE connected with middle-class voters, got support from politicians, appealed to big donors to raise the hundreds of thousands of dollars needed to conduct the campaign.[79] It worked.

But fate was on their side, too. The anti-SOME campaign was clinched a few weeks before the election by a single fortuitous, though—unlike the Reagan coup in LA—tragic event. One evening, ten weeks before the election, John Alfred Rodney, a twenty-six-year-old black man who'd spent five years in a state institution for the retarded, went on a harmless jaunt in the crime-ridden Rainier Valley neighborhood of Seattle. Rodney, whose IQ was measured at 61, wandered around backyards, and if residents saw him, he offered to mow their lawns; then he ran off. One of the homeowners called the police, and Patrolman Dennis Falk, SOME's cochair, was sent to investigate. Falk spotted Rodney and chased him by foot for six blocks. As Rodney tried to climb a fence, Falk—keeping his brass knuckles in his pocket this time—shot him, first in the heel and then in the back. Rodney died instantly.[80]

An investigation showed that he hadn't stolen anything and that he'd been unarmed. When Falk was acquitted of his murder by a police department inquest panel, hundreds of people from Seattle's black community marched in protest to the office of the chief of police and stood chanting out their fury. They were joined by members of the Church Council of Greater Seattle. The anger against Dennis Falk was so strong that David Estes asked him to recede into the background in the Initiative 13 campaign.

In Falk's place, Estes hired a black man, Wayne Perryman, hoping that would calm the black community. Perryman's idea was to pit black suffering against gay pretensions. Homosexuals didn't know what they were talking about when they complained about discrimination, Perryman told black church congregations and newspapers. Homosexuals were just copycatting the black civil rights battle. But the outraged black community wouldn't be distracted from the real issue: Perryman was consorting with racists who shot an unarmed black man. After only a few weeks, he resigned from SOME under pressure.[81]

On the night of the election, SCAT and WAT and other grassroots and radical lesbians and gays joined together in a candlelight vigil at the Pike Place Market. Citizens to Retain Fair Employment congregated at the Olympic Hotel, which had the biggest and fanciest ballroom in Seattle. They all waited in their places to see whether Initiative 13 would cast them into the same second-class status as the gays and lesbians of Dade County, Saint Paul, Wichita, and Eugene. As soon as the votes began to come in, it was clear what the results would be. Finally, almost 63 percent of the voters rejected the initiative. The candlelight vigil at the Pike Place Market turned into a victory party. Then, chanting "Two! Four! Six! Eight! Seattle stopped this wave of hate!" two thousand of the celebrants marched from the market to the Olympic Hotel to share victory space with Citizens to Retain Fair Employment, on whose side they'd fought.[82]

PART 7

ASHES AND PHOENIXES

Chapter 22

OF MARTYRS AND MARCHES

MURDER

Harvey Milk wasn't the first out gay politician to be elected in America, but his martyrdom made him the most famous. In 1974, three years before Milk's election, Kathy Kozachenko, an out lesbian student at the University of Michigan, won a seat on the Ann Arbor city council. Kozachenko, round-faced and with an eager smile, perpetually sporting a worker's cap like her immigrant Ukrainian forebears might have worn, ran for election in Ann Arbor's Second Ward. Kozachenko's party had originally been called the Radical Independent Party, but when members decided to put up candidates for the city council, they renamed themselves with the less confrontational moniker, "Human Rights Party." They probably needn't have bothered. Kozachenko's major constituency was student radicals at the height of radical chic. They loved her platform: no fine over $5 for possession of small amounts of marijuana (which effectively made pot smoking legal), and a rent control law that placed a ceiling on the amount of profit a landlord could make from rents on a building.[1]

City councilman Clyde William Colburn lost his reelection bid that same year. Colburn, an incumbent with mayoral ambitions, had been called a "Republican superstar."[2] But he'd led the charge the previous winter in bringing McDonald's and Burger King to Ann Arbor—to the fury of thousands of residents who signed petitions to keep the "plastic food business" out of the university town.[3] When he lost his seat that spring, it was homosexuals and their ilk whom he scapegoated. Colburn claimed to be outraged not only by Kozachenko but also by two other council members, Jerry DeGrieck and Nancy Wechsler, who came out after they were elected the preceding term. Colburn accused them of mischief, such as convincing the majority of the council to issue a "Lesbian-Gay Pride Week Proclamation" when no city government had ever before cheered homosexuals on. Then, the following December, DeGrieck and Wechsler got the council to add "sexual orientation" to the city's antidiscrimination ordinance. And to crown it all, now, in 1974, an out lesbian ran for office, and she won—and Colburn lost. Ex-councilman Colburn grumbled angrily to the media after his defeat, "This city is being taken over by hippies and faggots!"[4]

The same year that Kozachenko was elected, Colburn's Boston counterparts who loathed "hippies and faggots" suffered an even greater affront: Elaine Noble, an out lesbian, won a seat in the Massachusetts House of Representatives.[5] An energetic young speech professor with an open Irish face (she'd kept her half-Jewish parentage secret),[6] Noble had wanted to get involved in gay issues after reading about the Stonewall riots. She briefly joined the Homophile Union of Boston, an organization mostly of gay men, who told lesbians they could work with the group but couldn't vote. She then joined Boston's Daughters of Bilitis; but when they ejected a male-to-female transsexual from an open meeting, she rebuked them, just as her father—who'd helped organize the NAACP in Pennsylvania—would have: "No one is free until everyone is free!" Then she quit in disgust. She quit NOW, also, after Betty Friedan made her pronouncement about the "lesbian menace" in the women's movement.

But finally Noble found an organizational home in the Boston branch of the National Women's Political Caucus, a feminist group begun in 1971 to recruit and train women to run for political office. Noble became fast friends with one of NWPC's founders, Ann Lewis, who had just started her career as a political advisor.[7] Eventually Lewis would work for Jesse Jackson, Barbara Mikulski, and Bill and Hillary Clinton, but now she was working on the state campaign of her younger brother, Barney Frank. Ann

Lewis recognized political talent when she saw it, and she saw it in the young Elaine Noble.

Noble was passionately interested in gay issues, but she could also speak eloquently about rent control, street lighting, the problems of the elderly, and the importance of ending de facto school segregation; and she campaigned tirelessly for Barney Frank's 1972 run for the Massachusetts House of Representatives. Frank was closeted (and wouldn't come out for another fifteen years), but Elaine Noble managed to deliver the lesbian and gay vote to him. With her exuberant handshake and toothy smile, and a "Hi, how are you?" that seemed genuine every time she said it,[8] she lit up the room.

In 1974 Boston's Fenway and Back Bay became part of a new congressional district, Suffolk 6, and had to elect a representative to the state legislature. Fenway was where Noble lived. Her neighbors were low-income immigrants, the elderly, and students. Ann Lewis invited Noble out for breakfast. "You could win this, Elaine," Lewis urged her. "You've got to run."

She did. Her rival, who ran as an Independent, was Joseph Cimino, a suave young assistant district attorney. Cimino also owned two upmarket Boston saloons—Gatsby's and Daisy Buchanan's—but he wasn't beyond gutter tactics. Just a few days before the election, Cimino sent all registered voters in the district a "Dear Voter" letter: "I urge that no one vote against my opponent because of her homosexuality,"[9] it said—which, of course, very pointedly called attention to the fact that Noble was a homosexual. But Cimino's tactic fizzled. Noble had announced from the beginning that she was a lesbian, and that homosexuality was not the only issue with which she was concerned. The little old ladies who dominated her district loved her. She was gifted in convincing her listeners of her utter sincerity—and she promised that as their representative she'd fix streetlights and potholes, improve mass transit, and make sure their rent didn't keep going up. Noble won the election by a vote of 1,730 to 1,201.

Her campaign headquarters was inundated by thousands of congratulatory letters and telegrams from elated gays and lesbians all over America, all over the world. But as an out lesbian politician—at a time when almost all gay politicians hid their gayness deep in a dark closet—Noble wore a bull's-eye on her back. The thirty-year-old woman was hardly a threatening personage. The first subject she brought up in an interview with a reporter for the *Advocate* was not gay rights but revenue sharing.[10] A few months later, she told the same gay periodical that her biggest concern was "the educational crisis in Boston."[11] But newspapers around the country manufactured a more sensational story. Elaine Noble, a "self-proclaimed lesbian," they said, "won on a gay liberation ticket."[12]

Noble did eventually author legislation to prohibit discrimination against gay people in public employment. She earnestly introduced her bill on the House floor and spoke about it at length. Then she returned to her desk, sat down, opened the drawer to reach for a pen, and found a little pile of human feces.[13] She was still looking for help to get the mess cleaned up when a fellow Democrat, William Connell of Weymouth, took the podium. He implored his colleagues not to vote for Noble's bill. "These lesbians, these faggots and queers, are after your sons and daughters," he railed. Then Democrat Thomas Lopes jumped up. Lopes represented New Bedford, a town whose liberalism went back to the nineteenth century, when it had sheltered many a runaway slave, including Frederick Douglass. "These people are like the emotionally disturbed and mentally retarded!" Lopes cried out. "They should not be given such rights! This bill would water down civil rights for all of us," Lopes concluded, without bothering to explain how.[14] No matter that the bill's opponents made little sense—it failed. The Massachusetts Legislature would not pass a gay rights bill until 1989. By then, Noble was long out of politics.

She'd started receiving death threats and bomb threats as soon as she declared her candidacy. They didn't let up all during the time she was in office. The plateglass window of her small storefront campaign headquarters was shattered by bullets in the middle of the night. "LESBEAN" was spray painted on the trunk of her Chevy Vega. Sugar was poured into its gas tank.[15] She was in a relationship at the time with the ubiquitous Rita Mae Brown. Brown was trying to finish her novel *Six of One*, but an incessantly jangling telephone interrupted her concentration—hate callers with obscene messages. She tried to convince Noble to move, or at least to get an unlisted telephone number, but Noble refused. She wanted her constituents to be able to reach her whenever they needed something. The coup de grace to their relationship came when the living room window was shot out with a pellet gun one day, and Brown's Audi was riddled with bullet holes the next. Noble wouldn't heed Brown's pleas to get out of Boston.

She was needed by the little old ladies in her district, she said. Brown called a moving company and announced to her politician-lover, "I'm out of here, honey."[16]

Elaine Noble believed for the first time that someone was seriously trying to murder her when she discovered that the lug nuts of one of the wheels on her car had been loosened and the hubcap replaced to hide what had been done. She heard a racket as she was driving three nuns to a meeting and pulled off to the side of the road, just before the wheel separated from the axle. That was the start of her premonitions that something horrendous would happen to her in office.[17] Noble's second and last term ended in 1978. Something horrendous did happen before that year was over, but it was to another openly gay politician.

Though Elaine Noble was out when she ran for election, she didn't campaign as a gay person. Harvey Milk did. Milk, a businessman, was finally elected to the San Francisco Board of Supervisors in 1977, after failed runs in 1973 and 1975 (and another defeat in 1976, when he ran for the state assembly). He won in 1977 because that year San Francisco replaced citywide elections with district elections. The strong gay voting bloc of the newly created District 5, which included the Castro and the hippie Haight-Ashbury area, chose Milk as an out, proud, and very voluble gay who could be trusted to push gay interests. He was not the only new supervisor demographically representative of his or her district. For the first time, the board included a black woman, Ella Hill Hutch; a Chinese American man, Gordon Lau; and from the progressive South of Market area, an unwed mother who was an outspoken feminist and former Freedom Rider, Carol Ruth Silver. Dan White, a fireman, was elected that year in a white working-class district. The San Francisco Board of Supervisors, made up historically of well-to-do or well-known politicos, was changed dramatically.

The following January, Harvey Milk walked arm in arm with his lover Jack Lira, from the Castro to San Francisco's city hall, where he was sworn into office. Then he asked Anne Kronenberg, his twenty-two-year-old leather-clad lesbian campaign coordinator, to take him on her motorcycle from city hall to the victory party back home.[18] To be a politician, Milk had cut his hippie ponytail and traded in his jeans and sneakers for conservative business suits and wing-tipped shoes; but he still eschewed the A–Gay image. He'd kept the vocabulary, vision, and fire of gay liberation but married it to a tradition of politics and political organizing that would have been recognized by folks in Tammany Hall.[19] And it had worked. In front of his whistling, cheering well-wishers that night of the victory party, Harvey Milk, a teetotaler, lifted high a bottle of champagne, jubilantly drenched his head and shoulders with celebratory bubbly,[20] and told the ecstatic crowd what his victory meant for them all: "Don't ever let anyone tell you that you can't make it, that you don't have power because you're gay . . . We've shown that you *can* do it."[21]

Milk received death threats right away. They came as no surprise. As he told his young friend Cleve Jones, he saw himself as "a born shit-stirrer and rabble-rouser."[22] He knew those were dangerous traits, made even more dangerous by his prominent new position; but he couldn't tone down what made him Harvey Milk. Ten days after his election victory, Milk locked the door at Castro Camera, the shop he still ran, and went into the back room with its dilapidated old couches where he sometimes held neighborhood political meetings. There he tape-recorded a will. He named Harry Britt— chair of the San Francisco Gay Democratic Club that had been formed to help Milk win the election—as the man he wished to be his successor on the board of supervisors.[23] The next day, he gave copies of the tape to three of his friends. "Play it for Mayor Moscone," he told them, "in the event that I'm assassinated." Cleve Jones, one of the friends, thought Milk was being melodramatic. "Hey, you're not Martin Luther King! You're not important enough," Jones joshed him.[24]

"Let the bullets that rip through my brain smash through every closet door in the nation," Harvey Milk had intoned into the tape recorder.

Dan White, who was also elected to the city council that year, was thirty-one years old. He had clean-cut, youthful good looks, but he seldom smiled, and in his three-piece suits and slicked and glossy hair he looked a bit like a kid dressed up to act the part of a serious adult. The second of nine children in a devout Irish Catholic family, White had an erratic history. In high school he'd been a star baseball player, until the coach kicked him off the team for not taking directions. He never went to college. At nineteen, he enlisted in the army, became a sergeant, and served as a paratrooper in Vietnam. He left the military after six years of service with an honorable discharge; but he was at a loss about what to do next. He had vague ideas about becoming a writer. He went to Alaska, where he found a job as a school security guard. Then he quit and went back to San Francisco, where he got accepted at the police academy. He became a policeman, but he quit that, too. Then he became a fireman, like his father had been. He'd married and his wife was expecting a baby when he was elected supervisor; but he quit his job at the fire department, though the salary for a supervisor (supposedly a half-time position) was only $9,600 a year. The median annual household income in the United States at that time was $13,570; so to supplement his salary, White got a Hot Potato franchise and set up a stand at Pier 39. His wife had to find a babysitter for their infant son or take him along with her when she worked the stand.

The voters of Dan White's district, finally getting to vote for someone from the neighborhood, had chosen him though he'd never before held office. He'd gone door to door, visiting seven thousand houses and five thousand businesses in the area, shaking hands and personally asking for people's vote.[25] "Danny boy," many of his constituents called him. They were smitten with his nice appearance, his boyish sincerity, his "old-fashioned values." If elected, he promised, he'd fight against San Francisco's "radicals, social deviates, and incorrigibles." The San Francisco policemen's union, to which he'd once belonged, gave him an enthusiastic endorsement. But White knew little about politics aside from what he'd learned in high school civics class.[26] At board of supervisors meetings, he sometimes exploded when he felt wronged—jumping to his feet, flailing, glaring fiercely.[27]

He'd hoped finally to prove that he knew what he was doing as a politician when some of his Portola constituency asked him to halt the building of a home for disturbed and delinquent juveniles in a residential neighborhood by blocking its rezoning. White invited them to come to city hall and sit in on the meeting. He was confident of victory because he was sure he'd lined up six votes on the eleven-person board, including Harvey Milk's. But White was humiliated and livid when his motion, which he'd argued for with all the debating-class skills he could muster, went down in defeat. Harvey Milk had decided that a home for troubled adolescents was, after all, more important than pleasing residents who opposed it, and he cast the deciding vote in favor of rezoning.[28] Whatever quiet antipathy White had felt for Milk stopped being quiet.

April 1978: Press cameras captured a grinning Harvey Milk handing Mayor George Moscone a lavender-blue pen to sign a sweeping San Francisco gay rights bill. A few weeks earlier the bill, cosponsored by Milk and Carol Silver, had been endorsed by ten of the supervisors on the board.[29] "This will be the strongest gay rights law in the country," Milk declared in triumph over Bryant, Briggs, and their henchmen. "This one has teeth. A person can go to court if his rights are violated."[30] The lone vote against it came from Dan White. "This bill lets a man in a dress be a teacher," White said to the media. "People are getting angry!"[31]

By then, White had repledged himself in earnest to his campaign promise: Hadn't he been elected to fight against the blight of "social deviates"? He complained to an interviewer about the San Francisco Gay Pride Parade that June (in which Milk, in his element, rode joyously in an open car): "It's not proper, all those naked men and women." The parade should be stopped, he said.[32] Nor did White and his constituency approve that Harvey Milk got the board of supervisors to officially honor Del Martin and Phyllis Lyon for "twenty-five years of living together, of working together, of collaborating together; twenty-five years as leaders and pioneers against bigotry."[33] White was disgusted, too, by all the transvestites in San Francisco—and that Milk insulted the dignity of his office by accepting endorsements from them. He even let himself be photographed with people such as Jose Sarria and the full-drag female impersonators of Sarria's Imperial Court.[34]

There were, in fact, board of supervisors issues on which Milk and White could have been allies. Harvey Milk was interested in a lot more than gay rights. From the start of his political ambitions, he'd liked to cast himself in the role of "little guy fighting the big political machine"[35]; and as a supervisor he worked on many "little guy" issues—such as an ordinance to hinder real-estate speculators from pricing the working-class out of San Francisco. Dan White, who represented a populist, working-class district, might have appreciated such efforts—had not his hatred of Milk, as bitter and bizarre as Iago's toward Othello, trumped all for him.

Twelve months after both men were elected to the board of supervisors, a series of events finally sent Dan White over the edge. The first event may have been triggered by the resounding defeat of the Briggs initiative, for which Harvey Milk could claim much credit. Of the more than nine hundred San Francisco precincts, only four had voted in favor of booting out of public school jobs anyone who was homosexual or said anything nice about homosexuals. All four of those precincts were in Dan White's District 8. Three days after the vote, White went to Mayor Moscone's office and turned in his resignation from the board of supervisors.

He said he was leaving the board because the $800-a-month salary a supervisor received wasn't enough to feed his wife and kid. But he was uncertain, tormented—he'd campaigned so hard to get his seat on the board. A couple of days later, he showed up again in Mayor Moscone's office. He wanted to retract his resignation, he said. Those who'd supported him were disappointed that he'd resigned. He looked anguished and confused, and Moscone felt sorry for him. "A man has a right to change his mind," the mayor said,[36] and he promised he would figure out the legal steps he needed to follow in order to reinstate White. "Will you let me know as soon as you know anything?" White asked anxiously. Moscone said he would.

But when Harvey Milk, who'd been delighted at the news of White's departure, heard that Moscone had promised he'd try to give White's seat back to him, he called the mayor, incredulous. "George, what are you thinking?" Milk asked. Gays would never again vote for Moscone if he reappointed the rabid homophobe who was totally out of sync with the sentiments of most of the city. Moscone remembered how he got to be mayor—and that he had to run again the following year.

Sunday evening, November 26: Dan White's wife, Mary Ann, had put Charlie, the baby, to bed and was trying to cheer her sullen husband. He'd been on tenterhooks waiting for the mayor to call and tell him he was reinstated. He'd hardly slept for nights; he was nervous, and fuming, too, that Moscone seemed to be taking his own sweet time about it. It had been two weeks already since he'd told George Moscone he wanted to retract his resignation.

At ten thirty, the phone rang. It was a reporter, Barbara Taylor, who worked for KCBS, a local radio station. She'd just gotten a scoop on

Moscone's decision. She wanted to know what White thought about it. The mayor was giving White's old position on the board of supervisors to Don Horanzy, a former federal housing official. Horanzy was a neighborhood activist working with some progressive group called the All People's Coalition. He lived in Visitacion Valley, a run-down corner of White's District 8.

Monday, November 27, ten thirty in the morning: Moscone had invited his friend Assemblyman Willie Brown, who'd be in city hall for a trial that day, to come witness the swearing in of Don Horanzy. The press would also be there, due at eleven thirty; but the trial judge had called a recess and Brown decided to go down to the mayor's office early. On his way, he passed the mayor's reception room. A beaming Don Horanzy was waiting there with his family, all of them decked out in the traditional Hungarian and Filipino ceremonial garb of their ancestors. Willie Brown went on to Moscone's inner office, where he and the mayor sipped coffee and talked about sports for twenty or so minutes. But a little before eleven o'clock, Brown received a call from his assistant saying that the judge had ended the recess. Brown had to return to the fourth-floor courtroom. On his way out of Moscone's office, Willie Brown ran into Dan White, who was on his way in.[37]

White had entered the building through a basement window and climbed up to the second floor by the back staircase. He'd first gone to the main entrance on Polk Street, but the policeman assigned to the metal detector at the entrance that morning wasn't someone he knew. That meant White wouldn't be waved on—he'd have to pass through the detector. Before leaving home, he'd oiled his .38 Smith & Wesson service revolver and filled it with five cartridges. He'd taken ten more cartridges out of their Styrofoam slots, wrapped them in a handkerchief, and put them in his pants pocket. The gun he put in a holster, which he strapped to his belt and hid under his vest.

Moscone, awkward as he must have felt to have Dan White standing in his office at that moment, tried to mollify him, offered him something to drink, expressed interest in his plans for the future. White pulled the gun from its holster and fired five bullets into George Moscone. The last two he shot directly into the back of the mayor's head as he straddled his fallen body.

Then he put the gun back in its holster, buttoned his vest to hide it, and walked quickly west, down the block-long marble corridors of city hall, to the other side of the second floor, where the supervisors' chambers were. Milk was outside his office, talking to aides. White went into his old office and reloaded the gun. Then he went out again. "I need to speak to you," he said to Harvey Milk. Milk looked surprised, but he followed White into his office. Again, this time at 11:10, White fired five shots, three into Milk's chest and two into his brain.

Then the ex-supervisor ran from city hall. He called his wife from a pay phone and told her to meet him at the Cathedral of St. Mary of the Assumption on Gough Street. They huddled together in the empty church before Mary Ann White went with her husband to the Northern Station of the SFPD, where White knew he'd find his old friend, Officer Paul Chignell, vice president of the Police Officers Association.[38] In a dramatic gesture that White seemed to think would explain all, he pulled something from his jacket pocket and threw it down on Chignell's desk. It was a book cover that had been ripped from the Leon Uris novel *Trinity*, which had recently come out in paperback. *Trinity* was about the struggle of Irish Catholics against the British who'd taken over their country—just as "deviates," in White's mind, had taken over San Francisco.

After White was booked, he gave his weeping confession to Police Inspector Frank Falzon (who'd been White's baseball coach when he was a boy and a buddy when White was on the police force), saying he'd murdered Milk and Moscone because "I saw the city going kind of downhill."[39]

MAYHEM

In 1974 Harvey Milk and the teamster truck driver and gay activist Howard Wallace had visited all the gay and lesbian bars in the Bay Area, about one hundred of them. They asked the bar owners and customers to boycott Coors beer. The teamsters union wanted the boycott because Coors was refusing to let the workers unionize. Not only was Milk sympathetic to the union—he'd also found out that prospective employees of Coors had to take lie detector tests that nosed into their sexual orientation. Soon after the Harvey Milk and Howard Wallace visits to the gay bars, Coors's market share in California dropped precipitously, from 43 percent to 14 percent.[40] The grateful local head of the union presented Harvey Milk with a bullhorn that had history—scarred by the billy clubs of antiunion policemen. Milk had made good use of the bullhorn during anti–Anita Bryant rallies; but he finally handed it over to Cleve Jones. "We'll play bad cop/good cop," Milk had said in his mischievous style. "You go out in the streets, make the demands, be the radical; I'm gonna stay inside and fix things."[41]

On the morning of November 27, Cleve Jones had been working in Harvey Milk's city hall office when Milk remembered he'd left some papers at home that he'd need that day. He sent Jones to his apartment to fetch them. To save time, Jones took a bus back. A woman on the bus recognized him. "Cleve," she called out, "have you heard that Mayor Moscone's been shot?" The instant the bus stopped, Jones jumped off and sped to the west side of city hall, looking for Harvey Milk, remembering the tape Milk had recorded ten days after his election: "Let the bullets that rip through my brain . . ." Jones tore down the hall to the supervisors' chambers. The first thing he saw was Milk's beat-up wingtip shoes, soles up, sticking out of Dan White's office door. He felt sick. Twenty-four-year-old Cleve Jones had never seen a dead body before.[42]

Jones had already used the bullhorn that Harvey Milk gave him to lead thousands of gays and lesbians up and down the streets of San Francisco, protesting the Briggs's imitation of Anita Bryant. Jones had rallied gays and lesbians by repeatedly screaming into the bullhorn, "Civil Rights or Civil War!" But on the night of November 27, Jones didn't need the bullhorn. Around seven o'clock, gay people, and straight people too, spontaneously began to gather at Castro and Market Streets. Most brought candles. They marched silently toward city hall, thousands of candles, as far as the eye could see, illuminating the dark streets. The only sounds that night were those of people crying.[43] Future supervisor and state assemblyman Tom Ammiano held his candle aloft along with the other marchers as he passed a black man standing on a corner watching, incredulous because the only emotion people showed was grief. "Where is your anger?" the man yelled at Ammiano and all of them. "Where is your anger? Where is your anger?" But the marchers were too overwhelmed by sadness.[44] Anger would come six months later.

•   •   •

In 1977 the California Legislature passed a statute that reinstated the death penalty, which had been suspended since 1972. Execution again became a possible punishment for first degree murder under "special circumstances," which included murder of multiple victims and assassination of a public official.[45] Dan White had confessed to just those crimes.

District Attorney Joe Freitas pulled out as prosecutor on the trial because he'd known Moscone, Milk, and White personally. He assigned the job to Assistant District Attorney Thomas Norman. Norman, who'd argue that White be given the death penalty, inquired of all potential jury members whether they were opposed to capital punishment. He dismissed outright anyone who said yes, unwittingly getting rid of all the liberals—who would have been most troubled about the murder of a gay man and a man who supported gays.

Defense attorneys Douglas Schmidt and Steve Scherr were also picky about who they would permit on the jury. They were far better chessplayers than Norman. One promising potential juror, who came from a family of policemen (which might have made him sympathetic to White, the former cop), was asked by Douglas Schmidt where he lived. "With my lover," the young man said.

"A woman?" the thirty-two-year-old Schmidt pursued.

"No, a man."

Attorney Schmidt dismissed him summarily.[46]

The jury that was thus seated was comprised largely of conservative, working-class people—seven women and five men—who were very much like Dan White and his family:[47] housewives, clerical workers, a saleswoman, a retired beauty supply businesswoman, a security officer, a couple of printers, a mechanic. Several were Irish Catholic. The most educated person, a construction engineer, was chosen foreman. There was not one person of color and, needless to say, not one gay person among them.

All through the eleven-day trial, White sat in the courtroom looking catatonic—a pathetic shell of a once handsome and vibrant young man was what the jury saw. It was what White's skillful defense attorneys wanted them to see. Prosecuting attorney Norman, intending to establish that White was without a doubt guilty of the two murders, played the twenty-four-minute tape of his confession to Police Inspector Falzon. It was another wrong move. Dan White, weeping audibly on the tape as he "confessed," talked a lot about the money worries he'd had, how it had been so hard to support his wife and little baby. They had no time to be a family together. He hadn't intended to kill the mayor and the supervisor; he'd just gone to city hall to talk to them. And then, "I got kind of fuzzy; my head didn't feel right," he said with ingenuous Huck Finn diction. Yes, he'd brought a loaded gun with him, but many supervisors, even Dianne Feinstein, carried loaded guns around—for self-protection. (Never mind that White stored ten extra cartridges in his pants pocket or that he walked to the other side of city hall and went into his old office to reload before he asked Milk to come in there with him.) He'd been an idealist, fighting political corruption, trying to keep the city from deteriorating, the jury heard White weeping into the tape recorder. And Milk had smirked at him when he was already feeling so bad about himself. He loved his wife; he loved his little son; he'd just wanted to provide for them and take care of them, and take care of the city he loved . . .[48] By the time the taped "confession" was finished, there wasn't a dry eye in the jury box.

The defense also outwitted the prosecution in the witnesses they called. Four psychiatrists and a psychologist testified that the financial and emotional pressure Dan White had been under had been too great for him, and that when Harvey Milk defeated and humiliated White, he cracked. He'd been so emotionally ill, psychiatrist Martin Blinder testified, that he'd abandoned his lifelong practice of exercise and healthy eating. He was gorging himself on junk foods, the doctor said: Coca-Cola. Twinkies.[49] Defense attorney Schmidt jumped on Blinder's theory. That's exactly what pushed White over the edge, he explained—depression that led to sugar poisoning. "Good people, fine people with fine backgrounds, simply don't kill people in cold blood."

The jury deliberated for six days. The verdict came down on May 21, 1979, a day before Harvey Milk's birthday—had he lived he would have been forty-nine. In a packed and emotion-charged courtroom, the jury foreman handed the written verdict to Anne Barrett, the court clerk. Several jurors wept as she read aloud: the jury found Dan White guilty on two counts of voluntary manslaughter.[50] For shooting George Moscone five times and then shooting Harvey Milk five times, Dan White was given the maximum penalty for manslaughter: seven years and eight months in prison.[51]

"Well, no one could come up with any evidence that indicated premeditation," the foreman later told the press.[52]

Most gay liberals and radicals were categorically opposed to capital punishment. But the grieving community had been vehement that Dan White should be sentenced to life in prison, without parole. "We're gonna raise hell!" some said from the beginning of the trial, certain that the all-straight jury wouldn't make the punishment fit the crime.[53] And when it turned out they'd been right, the slap on the wrist the jury gave Dan White felt like a slap in their collective gay faces.

The verdict was announced a little before five in the afternoon. Cleve Jones called Del Martin and Phyllis Lyon, still San Francisco's most famous lesbians, to come down to the Castro and help him talk to the swarms of reporters that had already descended. As the three stood in the street being interviewed, gays began congregating around them. Eric Garber, the young writer with whom Jones shared an apartment a few doors away from what had been Castro Camera, came running breathlessly. Throngs of gays were congregating at their apartment, too, "ready to kill," he told Cleve Jones. Jones ran back to the apartment, tried to calm them, got the bullhorn, and rushed back to Castro Street. They'd have another candlelight march, he thought as he shouted over and over into the bullhorn, "Out of the bars and into the streets! Out of the bars and into the streets!" A crowd of about five hundred appeared almost immediately. As they marched, the numbers swelled to thousands. By the time they got to Civic Center Plaza, it was almost eight o'clock, and darkness was falling. This would be no candlelight vigil. A mob was massed in front of the Polk Street entrance to city hall. Those standing closest to the building, looking up to the second floor where Milk and Moscone had been murdered, suddenly couldn't contain their fury. They started ripping apart the building's ornate grill work, using the pieces as makeshift battering rams, smashing the glass doors.

Then others picked up chunks of pavement or broke rocks off the new aggregate trash containers that lined the streets and hurled them at city hall windows. In minutes, the sidewalks were covered with glass. "We want justice!" the rioters screamed. "He got away with murder!" "Avenge Harvey Milk!" Gay rage, lulled for ten years after the Stonewall riots, was spreading through the huge mass. They uprooted parking meters and newspaper vending racks and used them as javelins to shatter ground-floor windows. They broke the windows on parked police cars and hurled burning shrubs and newspapers looted from the vending racks into them. The sirens of the torched cars shrieked into the night, till meltdown shut them up.[54] A radical lesbian activist yelled to Cleve Jones, "Hey, I think we ought to do this more often!" She and three or four other lesbians ran around to the basement window into which Dan White had crawled six months earlier, pushed through as he had, and used looted newspapers to set fires inside.[55]

Sally Gearhart, who'd played "Mom" to Harvey Milk's "Pop" in the fight against Briggs, was rushed to the steps of city hall by a small contingent of peacemakers. She had to calm the crowd down, they said. Someone gave her a bullhorn. "There's nobody in the city angrier than I am tonight. But Harvey Milk would not be here tearing down the doors of this building," Gearhart shouted above the deafening roar of the horde. "Harvey Milk would say, 'I don't want my death avenged by violence. There are other ways to deal with our rage!'"[56] But the mob was in no mood to be calmed. Her peace speech was a snowball thrown into a fiery pit.

Civic Center Plaza turned into a battlefield. Hundreds of rioters broke limbs from the plaza's trees and used them to smash every car window in sight. Squads of police cars arrived, officers suited up in riot regalia. The crowd was too big and unruly to control. They needed more men. Dianne Feinstein, mayor since Moscone's murder, peeped at the throng gone wild from behind her office curtains in city hall. She called in every off-duty San Francisco police officer. That wasn't enough. She called for police backup from Marin, San Mateo, Santa Clara, Oakland. Scores of policemen massed in wedges, Roman style, holding big shields on which they pounded with their batons, advancing on the mob, trying to drive them away from city hall and out of the plaza.

"Don't run! Slow down! Turn around! Fight back!" Cleve Jones and others shouted. And the crowd did. "Skinny little queens in tank tops and blue jeans hurling themselves against the police!" Jones marveled and exulted. Bottles and rocks bounced off riot shields and helmets. The police fired tear gas till the plaza was hazy with it.[57]

Hundreds of rioters moved north up to Larkin Street, setting fires in trash cans, making burning pyres of looted tires, smashing all the plate-glass in sight, looting clothing stores, pharmacies, liquor stores. "Political trashing," they named their looting for a *San Francisco Chronicle* reporter. "Make sure to put in the paper that I ate too many Twinkies!" one rioter screamed as he helped torch another police car.[58]

By one in the morning, fifty-nine police officers had been injured, most cut by flying bottles and rocks. Seventy demonstrators had to be treated for injuries from police billy clubs. Twenty rioters were arrested. The cost of the damage was over $1 million. Harry Britt—the man Harvey Milk had chosen to succeed him as supervisor "in the event" that he was assassinated—told the media the morning after the riot, "Now the society is going to have to deal with us not as nice little fairies who have their hair dressing salons, but as people capable of violence. This was gay anger you saw. There better be an understanding of where this violence was coming from."[59]

MARCHING ON WASHINGTON

A week before Harvey Milk's death, he'd issued a press release. He was calling for a massive gay march on Washington in summer 1979, to commemorate the tenth anniversary of Stonewall. It would be a spectacular sign of gay unity and expression of gay demands, like Martin Luther King's 1963 March for Jobs and Freedom was for black people.[60]

A gay march on Washington was an idea that had been kicking around for a while. In 1973, a year before Kathy Kozachenko was elected to the Ann Arbor City Council, twenty-one-year-old Jeff Graubart, an openly gay undergraduate at the University of Illinois, ran for mayor of Urbana. He lost; but he also announced that it was time for gays and lesbians to meet in Washington and have their own march against job discrimination and for freedom. The ambitious plan fizzled when leaders such as Frank Kameny (who'd dreamed for years about just such a march) warned that if only a small number of people showed up, it would make the gay movement look ridiculous.[61]

But in spring 1978, when Anita Bryant exported her antigay campaign around the country, the idea for a march came up again. Four days before voters in Saint Paul, Minnesota, were to go to the polls to vote on whether to repeal that city's gay rights ordinance, University of Minnesota's lesbian and feminist groups staged a rally for St. Paul's Citizens for Human Rights, the group fighting repeal. It featured Robin Tyler, the first out lesbian standup comic, suited up in an army shirt as though ready for battle. After her bows, Tyler took the microphone again and solemnly roused her audience to fight with all their might. "Forget about being nice. How long will lesbians and gay men tolerate not having rights in this country? We must organize for a national march on Washington, DC!" Tyler shouted into the mic.[62]

Her call caught fire. On April 25 voters repealed the Saint Paul gay rights ordinance by a margin of almost two to one. But by then, lesbian feminists had joined with gay men to form a Twin Cities committee to organize a National March on Washington for Lesbian and Gay Rights. They drew up a seven-page appeal—"An Idea Whose Time Has Come . . . A March on the Nation's Capital," they titled it. The Dade County and Saint Paul disasters would make gay people hide in the closet again or perpetrate "mindless violence," they wrote, unless a march made them unify nationally and gave them a constructive way to focus their anger.[63] They invited prominent gay and lesbian leaders to serve on the steering committee. Harvey Milk was one of them; but he initially had serious reservations. "Marches make no difference. We need to put the resources into getting more out gay politicians elected," he called Robin Tyler to say.[64]

After Wichita, Kansas, and Eugene, Oregon, joined Dade County and Saint Paul in telling gays and lesbians they had no rights, Milk changed his mind: something really dramatic needed to happen—to show America that there were millions of gay citizens, and they were united and ready to fight back. At the Los Angeles Gay Pride rally that June, Harvey Milk announced that the time had indeed come. Gays and lesbians must march on Washington for an end to job discrimination and for freedom, just as black people had done in 1963.

Only weeks before the Minnesota planning group was to hold its first national meeting, it imploded. The lesbian feminists couldn't trust the gay men. The radicals complained that "low income" gays and lesbians were being snubbed. Unauthorized people were speaking to the press on behalf of the committee. All the usual gender, class, and power feuds.[65] But San Francisco took over. Milk gave the nitty-gritty job of organizing to Harry Britt, who formed a National Outreach Committee and reached out to the National Gay Task Force. Its cochairs, Bruce Voeller and Jean O'Leary, were hesitant for the same reason Frank Kameny had discouraged the Illinois college students in 1973: it was too risky. Some gays and lesbians, still in the closet, had been pushed in even further by Anita Bryant's campaigns; and if a puny number of marchers showed up, that would be a humiliating setback. Harvey Britt got more interest from the New York Coalition for Gay and Lesbian Rights, a group that had formed in the wake of the Dade County defeat and was taking over the perennial fight for a New York gay rights ordinance. But progress on march planning was sluggish.

The drama of Harvey Milk's death sped it up. On the afternoon of November 27, the Coalition for Lesbian and Gay Rights had just opened a meeting to talk about the feasibility of a march when a call came from San Francisco: Milk had been killed. Joyce Hunter, a black Jewish woman who was a leader in the group, broke through the stunned silence to say, "Now we have to do it. For Harvey."[66] Days later, in San Francisco, Milk's assistant Anne Kronenberg told a large grief-stricken crowd who'd gathered to mourn Harvey Milk that a march on Washington had been "Harvey's dream." They must make it come true. "The time is now," she urged them. The crowd rose to its feet and cheered.[67] Milk's death had to have purpose. The city supervisor, who'd been in elected office less than eleven months, would become a much-needed national icon. A martyr. The gay movement's Martin Luther King. What could be more appropriate than a march on Washington to honor his dream?

At the first national planning meeting, held in the Friends Meeting House in Philadelphia on President Washington's birthday weekend, Steve Ault, the high-energy head of the New York Coalition for Lesbian and Gay Rights, was elected coordinator. Ault came from an upper-middle-class family, but he'd worked as a cab driver and a typesetter until his father died and left him enough money to devote his life to causes such as the peace movement and the lavender left. He'd helped found the Committee of Lesbian and Gay Male Socialists. He'd been in massive antiwar marches in Washington, too, and had made himself a student of how to organize huge demonstrations. Soon after the Dade County loss, he'd helped mobilize a hundred thousand gays and lesbians to march up Fifth Avenue in New York's 1977 Gay Pride Parade. Ault had no doubt that what had been done in New York could be done in DC.[68] He rebuked the naysayers who feared puny numbers. The march would be held on October 14, 1979.

Conflicts developed again in the planning stage. Lesbians were upset by the white male leadership, so Joyce Hunter was chosen as cocoordinator. But that wasn't the last of the tensions. Discussions about the march platform were so bellicose that the original founders of the Friends Meeting House would have trembled. On the first four points of the platform there was general agreement: All antigay laws must be repealed. Congress must pass a comprehensive gay rights bill. The president must sign an executive order banning discrimination against gays and lesbians in federal government, the military, and federally contracted private employment. Discrimination against lesbian mothers and gay fathers must be prohibited. But it was the fifth demand that was the sticking point. Members of NAMBLA, the North American Man/Boy Love Association, proposed that the marchers demand the repeal of all age-of-consent laws.[69] Joyce Hunter called it disgusting and exploitative. Lesbian Feminist Liberation leader Eleanor Cooper (who ran an extermination company called "Lady Killers") protested that it was exactly what Anita Bryant was saying gays wanted: to have sex with children. Another Lesbian Feminist Liberation leader, Betty Santoro, was ready to stage a walkout.[70] The NAMBLA proposal was finally replaced by the innocuous demand that lesbian and gay youth be protected from harassment.

A "Gay Freedom Train," starting in the Northwest and traveling to the Southeast, picked up masses of gays and lesbians and brought them to the doorstep of the march. The Reverend Troy Perry and Robin Tyler, Angelenos and consummate show people, stole an idea from Franklin and Eleanor Roosevelt. Surely there'd be crowds of gays and lesbians who couldn't go to DC but who would come out to meet them and cheer them on whenever the train stopped at a station. Perry and Tyler would address them from the caboose. Robin Tyler alerted the local media in every place the train would be making a scheduled stop.

Of course, she and Perry couldn't be *certain* there'd be huge gay and lesbian crowds waiting for them at the stations—and the publicity value of the idea would flop without crowds. So for insurance, the minute the train stopped, dozens of Perry and Tyler's gay and lesbian traveling companions jumped off, then doubled back. They stood listening and cheering on the platform as Tyler and Perry stood in the caboose and declaimed about the march for gay rights. "Hundreds of Homosexuals Meet Train," local papers reported.[71]

But even without hijinks, the media paid attention. Cosmopolitan newspapers such as the *New York Times* informed millions that gays and lesbians were marching on Washington;[72] small-town papers picked up stories through the Associated Press and United Press International: "Homosexuals to March," people read in Cedar Rapids, Iowa.[73] "Gay Rights Supporters March on Washington," people in Odessa, Texas, learned.[74] In Clearfield, Pennsylvania, they learned that the marchers represented every state in the union and twenty-three foreign countries.[75] Harvey Milk had talked often in his speeches about an apocryphal "suicidal sixteen-year-old gay boy from Altoona, Pennsylvania" who'd called him and begged for a reason to have hope.[76] Now that boy could open the Altoona newspaper and find a reason.

Over a hundred thousand marchers streamed for several hours down ten blocks of Pennsylvania Avenue. They carried signs that made proclamations to America such as, "We Are Everywhere" and "Lesbians and Gay Men of Tidewater, Virginia." (About thirty men and women marched behind that one.) They carried banners memorializing Harvey Milk as martyr and hero; and telling their archenemy: "Eat Your Heart Out, Anita!" They carried individual signs, too, such as "I Served My Country as a Gay American USN1969-1973 / I Demand My Rights." Elderly women held signs that said, "My Son Is Gay, And That's Okay" and "I Am Not A Closet Mother." The speakers at the rally on the Washington Monument grounds told their elated listeners (and even more to the point, Washington) that there were twenty million lesbians and gays in the country, and they were moving "from gay pride to gay politics."[77]

It was years before the federal government took their "move to gay politics" seriously enough to pay attention to the marchers' list of demands for civil rights. To anyone who'd expected quick results, the march must have seemed a failure. But, in fact, it served as a crucial building block. It was the occasion for gay people to formulate what they needed to ask for from their government. It brought out into the daylight gays and lesbians from the boonies and hinterlands of Tennessee, Idaho, Oklahoma; and it alerted many more gays and lesbians in those places to the knowledge that they weren't alone. It dramatized the idea that there was a national movement. It encouraged gay people to think in terms of a national consciousness. It was a catharsis, too, uniting them in claiming emotional victory over the woman who'd become an iconic enemy and mourning the death of the man they'd made an iconic hero.

Chapter 23

THE PLAGUE

PARIAHS

The disease appeared out of nowhere. In June 1981 a thirty-three-year-old physician and assistant professor of medicine at UCLA, Michael Gottlieb, reported in the Centers for Disease Control's *Morbidity and Mortality Weekly Report* that between October 1980 and May 1981, there'd been five cases in Los Angeles hospitals of previously healthy young men whose biopsies had confirmed a rare illness, pneumocystis carinii pneumonia, which, he wrote, had been seen before only in severely immunosuppressed patients. All the young men were active homosexuals. By the time Dr. Gottlieb wrote the report, two had already died.[1]

The following month, the Centers for Disease Control reported that twenty-six homosexual men had been diagnosed with Kaposi's sarcoma, a rare cancer that shows up as skin lesions. Twenty of those men were in New York, and six in Los Angeles and San Francisco—three cities that had led the gay revolution of the preceding decade. Eight of the men were already dead.[2] The *New York Times* article that announced the sudden appearance of this "gay cancer" emphasized that in most cases the men had been promiscuous, having "as many as ten sexual encounters each night, up to four times a week."[3] The *Times* revised the figures upward a year or so later. Many of the infected had had "sex with fifteen to twenty deliberately anonymous men" per night on a typical visit to a gay bathhouse, the country's most widely read newspaper reported.[4]

The Far Right did not waste the shock value. Paleoconservative Patrick Buchanan gloated in his syndicated column that AIDS was a sign that "Nature is exacting retribution"; but now, he wrote, not only were these homosexuals a "moral menace," they were a "public health menace," too. Buchanan reported that policemen were so worried about getting AIDS and bringing it home to their families that they had to don masks and gloves when dealing with homosexual lawbreakers; landlords were so worried about the spread of AIDS on their premises that they had to evict infected homosexuals from their property. Because of homosexuals' morally irresponsible and unhealthy sex practices, they were the spreaders of a host of other diseases, too, that could affect innocent heterosexuals, such as hepatitis. Therefore, Buchanan ranted, they must not be allowed to work in restaurants or any job in which they handled food.[5] "Gay rights"— homosexuals' demands to live and work wherever they wanted—were dangerous to heterosexuals.

In his column, Buchanan called for the total undoing of the bits of progress that gays and lesbians had been slowly making toward civil rights, and the undoing of the Democratic Party along with them. At the last Democratic National Convention, in 1980, seventy-seven of the seated delegates had been openly gay or lesbian and had agitated for the adoption of a gay plank. To get a hearing on the convention floor, they nominated for vice president Melvin Boozer, a young African American PhD from Yale who was then a sociology professor at the University of Maryland. Boozer was also the head of the DC Gay Activists Alliance, and in that role he won a court battle with the Washington Transit Authority for the right to place an ad on buses proclaiming "Someone you love is gay." He also won a battle with the US Army for the right to place a wreath on the Tomb of the Unknown Soldier in honor of gays and lesbians who died in military service. In his stirring speech at the Democratic National Convention in New York's Madison Square Garden, Boozer said he wouldn't accept the vice presidential nomination, but he pleaded for the adoption of a gay rights plank to help the "twenty million Americans who love this country and long to serve it in the same freedom that others take for granted." He dared compare the struggle for black civil rights to the struggle for gay civil rights: "I know what it means to be called a 'nigger' and I know what it means to be called a 'faggot,'" Boozer's voice rang out in the huge auditorium that August night. "And I understand the difference in the marrow of my bones. I can sum up that difference in one word: *none*."[6]

The delegates were a lot more receptive to his speech than they'd been to the speeches of Foster and Davis eight years earlier. The Democratic National Committee started making sympathetic noises about adding gay rights to the next platform. The three leading contenders for the 1984 Democratic presidential nomination, Walter Mondale, Alan Cranston, and Gary Hart, all promised to support such a plank.

Buchanan used their pledges to jibe at both Dems and gays. In light of the threat homosexuals now presented to the health of the whole nation, Buchanan asked incredulously in his column, "Does the Democratic Party still maintain its solemn commitment to federally protected civil rights for active homosexuals—equal access to jobs, housing, and public accommodations?"[7]

Despite his decisive role in defeating the Briggs initiative in 1978, Ronald Reagan, who'd win almost 59 percent of the popular vote over Walter Mondale, had cultivated ignorance or worse about AIDS. His press secretary, Larry Speakes, represented the president's attitude in an October 1982 press conference. "Larry, does the president have any reaction to the announcement from the Centers for Disease Control that AIDS is now an epidemic and there have been over six hundred cases?" a reporter wanted to know.

"What's AIDS?" Speakes asked.

"Over a third of them have died. It's known as 'gay plague.'" Speakes and others laughed.

"No, it is. I mean it's a pretty serious thing that one in every three people that get this has died. And I wonder if the president is aware."

"I don't have it," Speakes, a Mississippian, drawled jocularly. "Do you?" More laughter.

"In other words, the White House looks on this as a great joke?" the reporter asked.

"I don't know anything about it," Speakes answered, impatient now, and he called for other questions.[8]

Reagan himself wouldn't even utter the word *AIDS* until his good friend from Hollywood days, Rock Hudson, died of it in 1985. The year before, however, when three hundred thousand Americans had already been diagnosed with the disease and Ronald Reagan was running for reelection, he told a group that kept tally of a "presidential Biblical score-board" that his administration would continue to resist all attempts to "obtain any government endorsement of homosexuality."[9] That seemed to include any effort to help save homosexual lives.

AIDS could easily have meant the end of the movement for gay civil rights—not just because extremists were calling for its end, but also because gay people were paralyzed by confusion and fear. "Gay power" and especially "gay pride" had come to seem oxymoronic. Even the more so-phisticated newspapers were reporting gay "contrition" in Moral Majority language: "As they waste away, many AIDS patients begin to reflect on their lives, sometimes feeling they are being punished for their reckless, hedonis-tic ways," a journalist for the *New York Times Magazine* announced.[10]

Around Christopher Street—where the gay revolution had started and its celebrants had marched victoriously every June for more than a decade—young men were looking skeletal. A lot of them had already been given their death sentence; many more suspected it was coming. Larry Kramer found himself spending his days visiting dying friends in hospitals or going to their funerals or memorial services. Kramer was famous around the Village as a successful screenwriter and movie producer (his 1969 adaptation of D. H. Lawrence's *Women in Love* was nominated for four Academy Awards). But he'd always been an irascible man, given to bombastic anger; and he'd been controversial since 1978, when he published *Faggots*—a novel so sear-ingly denunciatory of the "hedonism" of New York's gay culture that Craig Rodwell refused to sell it in his Oscar Wilde Memorial Bookstore. But in the midst of the plague, Kramer turned his rage on those who attacked gays. The number of sex partners that people had is irrelevant, he angrily wrote. You could get infected by the virus with a single contact. "All it takes is one wrong fuck. That's not promiscuity—That's bad luck."[11]

In January 1982, as the epidemic galloped on, Kramer summoned prominent New York A-Gays—including medical doctor Lawrence Mass, attorney Paul Rapoport, and acclaimed writer Edmund White—to his spacious Greenwich Village apartment whose walls were decorated with glamorous pictures of his good friend, Glenda Jackson, star of *Women in Love*.[12] The stories of death and disaster which Kramer's guests exchanged that evening were in stark contrast to the pleasant surroundings in which they were sitting. Scores of young gay men, seemingly healthy one day, were being laid low by a host of horrors the next. Family and friends were deserting those with the disease. In the hospitals, people with AIDS were pariahs. They often sat for days in emergency rooms. If they were finally admitted, terrified orderlies would let them lie in their own excrement and urine, refusing out of fear even to enter their room. They left the patients' food trays piled up in the hallways. When a patient with AIDS died, he'd be put in a black trash bag. Many funeral parlors were refusing to handle the dead.[13] Kramer had called his influential friends together, he told them, because they needed to do something to help. They agreed. They'd start a group called the Gay Men's Health Crisis, which would do everything for people with AIDS that the rest of New York was refusing to do.

Gay Men's Health Crisis advertised in the gay papers for "buddies" to pay visits to people with AIDS and hold their hand, clean their apartments, walk their dogs, shop for groceries, cut up their food and feed them, take them to doctors, read to them in hospitals. Five hundred volunteer buddies—gay men, lesbians (many who'd been lesbian separatists in the 1970s but found their grudge against males to be irrelevant in the face of such devastation), straight women—all flocked to give succor to the sick. Gay Men's Health Crisis also established a twenty-four-hour hotline so that people all over the country who were panicking could call in for moral support and solid information. GMHC volunteers ran therapy groups for people with AIDS and their partners. They got lawyers to work gratis to help the sick make wills or fight landlords who wanted to evict them. The old Chelsea brownstone on Twenty-Second Street that GMHC rented for its headquarters was soon cluttered with volunteers' desks and bulging file cabinets. Telephones rang continuously; computers and typewriters were always in use. To keep it all going, GMHC held benefits and parties in gay bars. Within the first year, the group raised $600,000. The state and the city gave GMHC $200,000 more.[14]

In Los Angeles, where the first cases had been observed, AIDS Project LA was started in 1982 by a small group with the same charitable goals.[15] Their proximity to Hollywood made it possible to raise substantial sums to buy food and shelter for the ill and dying. Star-studded banquets featured celebrities such as Barbra Streisand, Elizabeth Taylor, Burt Lancaster. At one APLA fund-raiser, Hollywood mogul Barry Diller announced at the end of the night, "My money-grubbing, money-raising friends and co-chairs have just delivered $3.2 million dollars!"[16]

The San Francisco Bay Area, too, had its versions of GMHC and APLA that would make whatever little life they had left easier for people with AIDS. Dr. Marcus Conant, a gay dermatologist who'd worked on some of the first Kaposi's sarcoma cases, teamed up with Cleve Jones, San Francisco's most famous gay leader since Harvey Milk's assassination, to start a volunteer-staffed hotline and referral service for San Francisco's panicked gay population.[17] There was also the Shanti Project, which began in Berkeley in 1974 to help people with terminal cancer live out their last weeks or months in peace. By 1982, Shanti volunteers were mostly visiting those with "gay cancer" or GRID (Gay-Related Immune Deficiency, as AIDS was being called in 1982), helping them to cope and die.[18]

But for all their good work, groups like GMHC, APLA, the San Francisco KS Research and Education Foundation, and Shanti could do nothing to halt the epidemic. Whole gay communities and their organizations—some which had only recently gotten started—were being decimated. All through the seventies, Latinos had been barely visible in LA's many gay and lesbian organizations. But in the early eighties, things changed. Jose Ramirez had been an activist in the Puerto Rican National Liberation movement. After graduating from NYU, he came to Los Angeles to work at the Gay Community Services Center, helping young gays who'd been street kids find jobs. Roland Palencia was born in Guatemala and came to Los Angeles as an eighteen-year-old after his father, a small businessman, was assassinated for protesting Guatemala's military dictatorship; the son had learned to fight for causes from the father. In the summer of 1981, Ramirez and Palencia were part of a group of gay Latinos who decided it was time to get political. They invited Latina lesbians to join them, and they formed Gay and Lesbian Latinos Unidos. They'd be a bridge to represent Latinos to the mainstream gay and lesbian world, and gays and lesbians to the Latino world.

One of GLLU's members, Mexican American Frank Mendiola, had been a farm worker as a child and was still active in the United Farm Workers, America's most powerful Latino political group. Mendiola, a short, slight young man, was a dynamo of energy with remarkable political know-how. Though only twenty-three, he'd led a fight to unionize the LA Gay Community Services Center, which was a flourishing institution by the early eighties. Soon after Mendiola joined GLLU, he went to the United Farm Workers' president, Cesar Chavez, and asked him to make a public statement in support of Latino gays and lesbians. Chavez agreed to do that and more. In 1983 Assembly Bill-1, which would ban job discrimination against gays and lesbians, was pending in the California Legislature. Chavez paid visits on GLLU's behalf to Democratic assemblymen and even the president pro tempore of the Senate, David Roberti, to tell them that he and the United Farm Workers were urging passage of the bill.[19] That June, Chavez and United Farm Workers cofounder Dolores Huerta marched beside Gay and Lesbian Latinos Unidos in the Los Angeles pride parade. The strong Catholicism of the Latino community had always encouraged its members to see homosexuals as sinners, but Chavez told them, "You can't demand equality for yourself while tolerating discrimination against anyone else." Frank Mendiola and his friends were euphoric.

But many of the men in Gay and Lesbian Latinos Unidos, including Frank Mendiola and Jose Ramirez, were by now beginning to show symptoms of the virus. In a few years, the group was decimated by death. GLLU's lesbians, the group's Mexican American president Oscar de la O, Roland Palencia, and the few other GLLU men who were still healthy thought it crucial to form an AIDS Education Committee. The old ambitions of Gay and Lesbian Latinos Unidos were put on a back burner. GLLU morphed completely into Bienestar, a service organization for gay Latinos with AIDS.[20] This was the story of gay rights groups around the country: no matter their initial goals, the biggest enemy in the 1980s was AIDS, and before they could fight any other war, they had to fight that one.

1983: Doctors were still grasping at straws. No drug was effective. In New York, Larry Kramer was battling the board of the organization he'd helped found. The catastrophe that had struck the gay community needed something far more radical than service organizations that fed the sick and held their hands while they died. Gay Men's Health Crisis was applying Band-Aids, Kramer told the board in his usual blunt manner. The AIDS calamity required dramatic action—something powerful. The board reminded Kramer of all the good that GMHC had been doing and asked him to please stop yelling. He told them to go to hell.

He would form a new group, he decided, the AIDS Network. It would tackle the problem at its base. America needed to be convinced to stop blaming the victim and start pushing for a cure. The government must cut loose more funding for AIDS research. The protocol on drug testing must change: people with AIDS couldn't wait years and years for new drugs to be approved. They didn't *have* years and years. Kramer called a meeting at New York's gay synagogue, Beth Simchat Torah. Ginny Apuzzo, now the coordinator of the National Gay Task Force, ran it with him. They invited to the meeting an African American man who'd worked with Martin Luther King. He would teach the gay community the tricks of civil disobedience, to show them how they could send the message to the powers that be that more resources must be provided immediately to fight the plague's devastation. But for civil disobedience to be effective, the man told them, a lot more bodies were needed than those that showed up at Beth Simchat Torah.[21]

Kramer set out to get them. In March 1983, he published a heated, hard-hitting piece in a leading gay paper, the *New York Native*. Maybe it would serve as a slap in the face to somnambulists who still didn't realize the Apocalypse was almost upon them. "If this article doesn't scare the shit out of you, we're in real trouble," Kramer declared. "If this article doesn't rouse you to anger, fury, rage, and action, gay men have no future on this earth." The hospitals were so packed with AIDS patients, Larry Kramer told his readers, that even after diagnosis, it could take up to a month for a sick person to get a bed. He reminded them that during the first two weeks of the 1982 Tylenol scare (seven people were killed by Tylenol that had been laced with cyanide), the government had put $10 million into finding out what was happening. But over a thousand people had already been killed by AIDS, and the National Institutes of Health (NIH) hadn't yet funded a single grant to study the epidemic. If the devastation AIDS had wrought over the last two years had happened to any other community, Kramer wrote, "there would have been long ago such an outcry . . . that the governments of this city and this country wouldn't know what hit them." But because the disease affected gay men, nobody gave a damn.

But gay men paid taxes just like everyone else, Larry Kramer argued, and the NIH should be paying for research into a gay illness just like it pays for research into everyone else's illnesses. "We desperately need something from our government to save our lives, and we're not getting it," Kramer raged. He begged his readers to join him in the AIDS Network. The network needed three thousand people who would participate in sit-ins and traffic tie-ups, and who would let themselves be arrested for their civil disobedience.[22]

Kramer's impassioned essay drew the grand sum of fifty people to the next meeting of the AIDS Network.[23] He was Jeremiah in the wilderness, screaming about AIDS when everyone else just wanted to get on with his own life.[24] Kramer kept trying to rouse the community. "Where is your rage?" he demanded to know. He went all over New York speaking to gay groups, hoping to shock them into action. He'd point to an imaginary demarcation in the room—"This two-thirds of you, please stand up," he'd ask them. Then he'd tell them, "You're going to be dead in four years."[25] But he could get few takers for his plans for massive civil disobedience.

It wasn't that gay people were inured in 1983. Their misery was palpable. AIDS was the leprosy of the times; and gay men, whether infected or not, were the lepers. The largest festive gathering of gays and lesbians in big American cities had been the pride parades; but the parades these days were led by contingents of gay men with AIDS, some already so weak they had to be pushed in their wheelchairs. Instead of their usual carnival-like hilarity, the parades became funereal. As Phil Miller, a San Francisco man who'd never missed a parade since they started, mourned, "People are dying, dying, dying. We're lucky we're still alive, but there's nothing anymore to celebrate."[26] If gays didn't already know they were pariahs—even in a city like San Francisco where they'd recently seemed to have genuine clout—they were reminded at the 1983 Gay Freedom Day Parade by the policemen wearing rubber gloves as they diverted traffic around the marchers. And the city crew assigned to sweep up the trash after the parade was issued surgical masks and disposable paper suits. Who could be sure that you couldn't catch AIDS through street litter?[27] Gay depression made action impossible.

WAKE-UP SLAPS

Three years later: Some alarmist estimates claimed that a million Americans had already been infected. Homosexuals weren't just the victims of the plague, people were saying—they were also the spreaders of the plague. In June the US Justice Department declared that businesses had the right to discriminate against people with AIDS if they believed such discrimination would prevent the spread of the disease; employers could fire those with AIDS, merely on the grounds that their presence might make other employees feel discontent or emotional distress. Brutal attacks on gay men were up everywhere. That same month, June 1986, in what used to be gay-friendly San Francisco, there were sixty beatings of gay men horrific enough to be reported to the police.[28]

It seemed that society was again agreeing it was all right to hate gay people. Conservative pundit William F. Buckley proposed in his syndicated column that to prevent the spread of AIDS, infected gay men should be tattooed on the buttocks, so potential sex partners would know and stay away.[29] In California, a multimillionaire demagogue, Lyndon LaRouche, took a pause from advocating war with Russia to form the Prevent AIDS Now Initiative Committee (PANIC); he paid for a petition drive that gathered seven hundred thousand signatures. His initiative qualified for the November 1986 ballot: California voters would go to the polls and decide whether to put people with AIDS in quarantine.[30] Camps? Such things had happened before—homosexuals been had put in camps in Nazi Germany; even in America, during World War II, American citizens of Japanese descent had been sent off to camps. It had been terrifying enough that the lives of gay men were threatened by AIDS; but now it seemed their liberty was also being threatened.

Marty Robinson, who'd perfected the zap for the Gay Activists Alliance back in the early seventies, was still zapping. In 1985 he'd been a founding member of the Gay and Lesbian Alliance Against Defamation (GLAAD), a group modeled on the Jewish Anti-Defamation League. GLAAD's first protest was against a spate of sensationalistic articles about AIDS in the *New York Post*. One article focused on AIDS patients, on the verge of death, who were still lasciviously getting it on with one another in hospitals. The dismayed nurses were unable to stop them, the *Post* writer announced. Another article focused on the "animal" orgies that had been carried on at the Mine Shaft, a notorious S&M leather bar in the Meatpacking District, until the Department of Health padlocked the place because it was such a dire threat to public well-being. Another attacked the mayor for not closing down all the gay bathhouses.[31] For a year, Marty Robinson directed zaps with a GLAAD group he called, with characteristic grim humor, the Swift and Terrible Retribution Committee.[32]

But in the fall of 1986, he set out on his own, founding a group that he christened the Lavender Hill Mob. (The name was a gay gloss on a classic British comedy.) The group's few members, such as twenty-six-year-old Michael Petrelis, were furious with mainstream AIDS groups like the Gay Men's Health Crisis. Petrelis had gone to a dermatologist in 1985 because he had a little purple bump on his arm. The doctor told him it was Kaposi's sarcoma. When he showed up at the GMHC office shortly after the diagnosis, he was told by a volunteer, "I can help you make out a will, Mike."

"I'm not gonna die!" Petrelis screamed at the well-meaning man. "Listen, GMHC needs to be fighting for drugs to get people well instead of helping them give up!"[33] A few days later, Petrelis interrupted a GMHC board meeting to scream the same message. The executive director called the police and had him ejected. The Lavender Hill Mob was just the kind of group that Michael Petrelis was seeking.

Marty Robinson's Mobsters began by taking on New York's Catholics. Pope John Paul II had just issued an encyclical reaffirming the Church's condemnation of homosexuality. On the first Sunday of November 1986, the Lavender Hill Mob showed up at St. Patrick's Cathedral, with two of the Mobsters dressed up like priests. Just as Cardinal John O'Connor began his sermon, the Mobsters unfurled a banner that announced they were homosexuals and would not be silenced. A few weeks later, Robinson wrote a check for $3,200 so that eight Mobsters could get into an event for New York City's Catholic elite, a $400-a-plate dinner. They delivered the same message there. And the day after the zap, Robinson went to the bank and stopped the check.

But before November was over, the Mobsters had turned their attentions to AIDS. They visited Senator Alfonse D'Amato's New York office and plastered "arrest warrants" all over his walls, charging him with

personal responsibility for killing 15,354 people because he'd done nothing
as senator to help fight the AIDS epidemic. (If Marty Robinson knew already that he was himself harboring the AIDS virus, he kept it to himself.)
The following February, the Mobsters flew to Atlanta, to attend a Centers
for Disease Control conference in which mandatory testing for AIDS was
to be discussed. They were irate. People would be forced to take the test,
though there was no cure for the disease. What would be done with those
who tested positive?

Before the Mobsters left New York, Michael Petrelis bought gray shirts,
pants, and caps at a Good Will store. He and another HIV-positive Mobster, "Esquizito," the Puerto Rican jazz musician Eric Perez, drew prisoner
stripes on the garments with black shoe polish. They stenciled numbers on
the left side of the shirts. They also sewed on inverted pink triangles[34]—the
insignia the Nazis had forced male homosexuals to wear. Marty Robinson was Jewish and couldn't bring himself to wear a concentration camp
uniform; but remembering the attention-grabbing duck-suit zap of Fidelifacts fifteen years earlier—and knowing that Atlanta was a media hub that
would provide terrific opportunities for publicity—he didn't stop Petrelis
and Perez.

They invaded the Atlanta Marriott Marquis ballroom in time for the
preconference cocktail party. Though conference-goers had their hands
full with glasses of wine and little plates of hors d'oeuvres, several of the
Mobsters went around foisting flyers on them. "What does CDC stand
for? Center for Detention Camps!" the flyers read. The huge party came
to a shocked halt. If the conferees were too busy to absorb the written
message, they couldn't miss the two stalking concentration camp inmates.
But that wasn't the end of it. During the three days of meetings, Mobsters
passed out bright yellow leaflets that demanded, "Test drugs, not people!"
At the final plenary session, Marty Robinson and Eric Perez ran up to the
front of the auditorium with their big unfurled Lavender Hill Mob banner, blocking the dais, yelling, "When are you going to get to the issue of
AIDS education?" and "Why are you talking about testing instead of about
saving people's lives?" Michael Petrelis stood on a chair shouting, "Drugs
into bodies now! This conference is a sham!" The chairman called for early
adjournment.

The Lavender Hill Mob's Atlanta zaps made the *New York Times*.[35] CNN

Headline News presented a clip of the "angry homosexuals" every thirty minutes for most of a day. When a Mobster was also invited to appear on CNN's *Crossfire*, Bill Bahlman, a sometime-journalist and disc jockey in the New York club scene, volunteered. Hundreds of thousands watched as Bahlman tussled verbally with William Dannemeyer, a fear-mongering and rabidly antigay congressman from Orange County, California, who'd been a proponent of the Lyndon LaRouche quarantine initiative. The media hubbub didn't go unnoticed by Larry Kramer. He'd spent years in the Hollywood movie industry and understood the value of lively publicity. A week later, Kramer tracked down Michael Petrelis in New York, showed up at his place with a bagful of gourmet cheeses and breads from Balducci's, and picked his brain about the CDC zap.[36]

The next month, March, popular journalist and screenwriter Nora Ephron, an outspoken heterosexual advocate for gay and lesbian rights, was scheduled to be part of a lecture series for New York's Lesbian and Gay Community Services Center on West Thirteenth Street. When Ephron caught a cold and had to cancel, Larry Kramer, who'd never given up trying to rouse the gay community to anger, was invited to fill the spot. Since Kramer wasn't Nora Ephron, only about seventy people showed up. A lot of his talk was cribbed from his 1983 article. But perhaps now, after AIDS deaths had multiplied thirtyfold, gays were ready to listen. "If my speech tonight doesn't scare the shit out of you, we're in real trouble," he began. He upbraided his listeners, accused them of having a death wish. They were "literally being knocked off man by man and not fighting back," he told them. "It's your fault, boys and girls!"[37] He smiled only when he mentioned the Lavender Hill Mob's colorful zap on the CDC. "But they can't do it all by themselves!"

The Mobsters who'd been in Atlanta were all in his audience that night. They were flattered by the shout-out and came up to thank Kramer after his talk. "Come on over to my apartment and see all the media stuff we have," Bill Bahlman suggested, and the next day Kramer did.[38] Kramer was already thinking that the Mob's flare for getting attention through flamboyant zaps was just what was needed for the militant action group he'd wanted to found since 1983. Zaps were a million times more effective than mere civil disobedience. And now the time for militant action was riper than ever: AIDS deaths astronomical, no end in sight, and kooks proposing tattooing and incarceration for the plague's unlucky victims.

Kramer put out a call again to start a group. At the third or fourth meeting, which still hadn't attracted huge numbers, a male nurse suggested a name—the AIDS Coalition to Unleash Power: ACT UP.[39] That's exactly what they'd be doing: *acting up* until the government put money into research to find a cure.

At the New York Gay Pride Parade that June, an ACT UP truck float reified the nightmare of all gay men—barbed wire surrounding prisoners decked out in concentration camp uniforms with pink triangle badges. "Concentration camp guards" in military garb handed out ACT UP flyers. That bit of startling theatrics was a mighty wake-up slap. The next day, at the regular Monday ACT UP meeting, there were three hundred people.[40] Soon the number doubled, tripled—every seat was filled. Crowds standing at the walls were three and four deep. The Lesbian and Gay Community Services Center couldn't hold them all. Monday night meetings were moved to the Great Hall at Cooper Union, where Abraham Lincoln and Frederick Douglass had once spoken. It seated almost a thousand.

In 1986 gay graphic artist Avram Finkelstein, mindful of another Holocaust, had designed a poster: "Silence = Death" it said under a pink triangle pointing upward, to proclaim hope—the opposite of the downward-pointing triangle of the Nazi badge. Finkelstein's graphic became the symbol of ACT UP. Members wore T-shirts emblazoned with it to all zaps and demonstrations.

ACTING UP

Sunday, October 11, 1987: Six hundred thousand gays and lesbians from all over America gathered in the nation's capital for a second March on Washington.[41] There were six times as many marchers as there'd been in 1979 because there was so much more now to be mad about and to mourn. The year before, the *Bowers v. Hardwick* case had gone to the Supreme Court. In the privacy of his own home, Michael Hardwick had been caught by a policeman having oral sex with another man, and in Georgia, where Hardwick lived, oral sex was considered "sodomy" and was against the law. The majority of the Supreme Court justices, confirmed in their prejudices

26. Elaine Noble, elected to the Massachusetts House of Representatives in 1974, the first "out" politician to hold a statewide office, offers her hand to a constituent. He refuses to touch a lesbian.

27. Harvey Milk at San Francisco's Gay Freedom Day rally in June 1977. That November he would be elected to the San Francisco Board of Supervisors. The following year he would be killed by a fellow supervisor.

28. Barbara Gittings, Frank Kameny, and Dr. H. Anonymous on the panel "Psychiatry: Friend or Foe to Homosexuals?—A Dialogue" at the 1972 American Psychiatric Association Convention.

29. Midge Costanza, head of President Jimmy Carter's Office of Public Liaison (and the lover of activist Jean O'Leary) invited gay and lesbian leaders to the White House in 1977. Front, left to right: Charlie Brydon, Jean O'Leary, Bruce Voeller, George Raya.

30. San Francisco's 1977 Gay Freedom Day Parade: singer Anita Bryant, who led the charge to repeal gay rights in Miami, is held up to disdain along with other villains.

31. The AIDS Memorial Quilt on display at the Washington Mall. The quilt was conceived by Cleve Jones to convey the message that those who died of AIDS "belonged to the American family and had been loved."

LEFT: 32. Hate crime victim Brandon Teena (née Teena Brandon) with his girlfriend, Lana Tisdel, in 1993, a few weeks before he was raped and murdered.

RIGHT: 33. David Mixner (right) arranged for his old friend Bill Clinton, 1992 presidential candidate, to speak at a gay and lesbian fund-raiser at the Hollywood Palace. "I have a vision for the future, and you are a part of it," Clinton told the crowd.

34. Karen Thompson (right) fought for eight years for custody of her partner, Sharon Kowalski, rendered a paraplegic after a car accident. In 1991, a Minnesota judge declared them "a family of affinity."

35. John Lawrence (right) and Tyron Garner, with lawyer Suzanne Goldberg. "When sexuality finds overt expression in intimate conduct with another person, the conduct can be but one element in a personal bond that is more enduring," Supreme Court Justice Anthony Kennedy declared in *Lawrence v. Texas*.

36. Sergeant Leonard Matlovich reading *Time* magazine's 1975 cover article about himself: Matlovich's discharge from the air force was "the opening skirmish in a battle over the definition of good soldier."

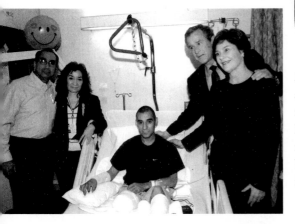

37. President George W. Bush and the First Lady thanking marine staff sergeant Eric Alva for his service: Alva, who'd been terrified he would be discharged for being gay, became the first American casualty in the Iraq War.

38. Major Margaret Witt, air force nurse and poster girl, discharged under Don't Ask, Don't Tell: the judge who ordered her reinstated declared, "There is no evidence that wounded troops care about the sexual orientation of the flight nurse or medical technicians tending to their wounds."

A Good Life Choice... The Air Force Nurse Corps

Choices we make in life determine which roads we'll travel. Many choose the easy way that is routine or uninspired—while others choose to Cross Into The Blue on a path that takes them new challenges and opportunities.

If you choose to Cross Into The Blue, you can experience what it takes to make a real difference in your career, professionalism, self-esteem and lifest

39. Colonel Margarethe Cammermeyer, discharged in 1991 after admitting she was a lesbian, speaking in 2013 at the twentieth anniversary of the dedication of the Vietnam Women's Memorial: General Colin Powell (to her left) is among her appreciative listeners.

40. Robin McGehee, cofounder of Get Equal, is arrested at a Don't Ask, Don't Tell protest at the White House. "Gays and lesbians have lobbied for years and years," McGehee said. "Now it's time to rumble."

41. Lieutenant Dan Choi, who was discharged from the army in 2009 because he "told," removes a Don't Ask, Don't Tell tape from his lips.

42. Kylar Broadus, a transman, testifying in the US Senate chamber for the Employment Non-Discrimination Act. His supervisor was contemptuous of "women who looked like men."

43. Frank Kameny shaking hands with President Barack Obama, who signed a memorandum in 2009 extending benefits to partners of federal employees. Vice President Joseph Biden, US Representative Barney Frank, US Senator Joe Lieberman, and US Representative Tammy Baldwin are witnesses.

44. Robin Tyler (left) and Diane Olson, the first same-sex couple permitted to wed in Los Angeles, in 2008, lawyer Gloria Allred behind them: every Valentine's Day since 2004, the couple and their lawyer had appeared at the Beverly Hills Courthouse to request a marriage license.

about gays by the AIDS epidemic, upheld the right of states to continue to outlaw homosexual sex. Chief Justice Warren Burger (citing the eighteenth-century British jurist William Blackstone) even deemed sodomy "a crime not fit to be named . . . the infamous crime against nature."

But the time was past when public officials could make such statements with impunity. Thousands of gays and lesbians who'd come for the march on Sunday remained in Washington till the following week so they could descend on the Supreme Court and let the justices know what they thought of their decision. The protestors were greeted by three hundred policemen holding batons at the ready and wearing Darth Vader visors and yellow latex gloves—to keep them safe from AIDS. ("Your gloves don't match your shoes! They'll see it in the news!" gay wits chanted; a flicker of a smile appeared on the faces of some of the officers.) For six hours, demonstrators scattered pink paper triangles like confetti. They sang "America, the Beautiful" and "We Are a Gentle, Angry People," emphasizing the lines "and we are singing, singing for our *lives*." They chanted "Equal justice under the law, that's what it says on the wall!" pointing to the words carved above the entrance to the court. Wooden barricades blocked off the steps that led up to the Supreme Court building, and signs on the barricades warned the protestors not to go any farther. But wave after wave of the protestors did anyway, holding hands, pushing through the barricades, running up to the building's plaza, where it's illegal to hold a protest. "Shame! Shame! Shame!" they shouted at the marble edifice and the austere justices inside. Six hundred protestors were arrested, the largest mass arrest in Washington since the Vietnam War protests.[42]

But it was anger and grief about the AIDS epidemic that drew most of the huge crowd to the March on Washington. More than forty-one thousand people had already died of the disease. There was no cure in sight, and the government wasn't spending much money to find one. At sunrise on the day of the march, an AIDS quilt was unfurled at the Washington Mall—thousands of rectangular three-foot-by-six-foot handmade panels, each in memory of a person who'd died of AIDS. The quilt was the brainchild of Cleve Jones, whose grandmother in Indiana had been a quilter. Jones conceived of the quilt as a political statement that would sidestep the issue of gay male sexuality to focus on the larger message that these people who died of AIDS belonged to the American family and had been loved.[43] Each panel was embroidered with a message, such as "Our Son, Our Brother, Our Uncle, Our Friend"; "I pray that mothers and fathers will stand by their gay children," signed "A mother who's glad she did"; "James, you silly boy, you weren't supposed to leave yet. Love ya, Douglas"; and "Dear God, I pray that soon this plague, too, shall pass. Be with us and those departed. Amen." The names of the dead were read by volunteers, as a sea of gay people and those who loved them walked along the fabric borders, wiping tears from their cheeks and clinging to one another.

The other powerful message about AIDS at the 1987 march came through the colorful and dead-serious outrage of the ACT UP-ers. Most of them were young men in their twenties and thirties, clad in jeans, black leather, macho gold-stud earrings—their tough-guy style a challenge to the stereotype of weak, womanized "fairies." "You Say Don't Fuck. We Say Fuck You!" their signs proclaimed to the hostile world. The ACT UP-ers' energy and impudence were reminiscent of the first days of the old Gay Liberation Front. Their insouciance was like thumbing one's nose at the grim reaper. It was exciting, seductive; it was an adrenaline rush to a people who'd been beaten down for six years.

After the 1987 March on Washington, autonomous ACT UP groups sprang up everywhere—just as Gay Liberation Front groups had after Stonewall: immediately in Los Angeles, San Francisco, Chicago, Boston; soon in Philadelphia, Houston, Miami, Atlanta, Seattle, Milwaukee; eventually in places such as Shreveport, Louisiana; Louisville, Kentucky; Kansas City, Kansas; Portland, Maine; and thirty other cities as well.

Jean O'Leary left NGTF in others' hands at the end of the 1970s and went west. In Los Angeles, she was hired to head a new organization, National Gay Rights Advocates. It had been founded in 1978 as a public interest law firm to promote gay and lesbian civil liberties; but in the mid-1980s the organization turned its attention to fighting for the rights of people with AIDS. O'Leary also joined the powerful Municipal Elections Committee of Los Angeles, where she became close friends with psychologist and rabbi's son Rob Eichberg, who'd masterminded some of MECLA's best schemes to exert gay political influence in LA. Eichberg had recently discovered he was HIV positive. He and O'Leary came up with an idea that would take Avram Finkelstein's "Silence = Death" slogan a step further: all gays and lesbians must exit the closet and let the straight world see their familiar faces, huge numbers, and collective power. O'Leary and Eichberg proposed that October 11, 1988 (the near-anniversary of the 1987 March on Washington), be the first "National Coming Out Day."

ACT UP-ers loved the idea. They agreed that the most effective way to celebrate the day would be to congregate in Rockville, Maryland, at the headquarters of the Food and Drug Administration. ACT UP's beef with the FDA was that to test AIDS drugs the FDA used the same inflexible protocols—including trials that lasted for five to ten years—that it used to test nasal sprays. No one was dying because of the withholding of nasal sprays, ACT UP-ers complained, but people who could perhaps be saved by certain drugs were dying because the FDA was still "testing" them. The way the tests were conducted was also unconscionable in the urgency of a plague. A control group of 50 percent of test participants was always given placebos. That meant that even if you were included in experimental AIDS drug testing, chances were only half that you'd actually be getting the drug.

At seven thirty in the morning on that first National Coming Out Day, a thousand ACT UP-ers from twenty different states descended on the FDA. On the manicured lawns in front of the sprawling seventeen-story building, hundreds of ACT UP protestors lay down beside the cardboard tombstones they'd brought with them—tombstones with bloody handprints and epitaphs that said, "Killed by the FDA" and "Killed by the System." Others wore their message on their backs. "If I Die Of Aids, Forget Burial. Just Drop My Body On The Steps Of The FDA," one young man's leather jacket proclaimed. Protestors plastered the FDA building with banners and posters: "We Die and They Do Nothing!" "One AIDS Death Every Half Hour." "Forty-two Thousand Dead of AIDS! Where was the FDA?" They screamed angry chants at the bureaucratic government administrators who were just arriving for their workday: "We need the drugs now!" "Drugs into bodies!" "Act up! Fight back! Fight AIDS!" They blocked the doors so that FDA workers couldn't enter the building. "Seize control! Seize control! Seize control!" some ACT UP-ers yelled.[44] Two glass doors were broken. New York ACT UP member Peter Staley, a former Wall Street bond trader (who'd quit his job when his boss, who'd also been his mentor, remarked that people with AIDS deserved to die), set off colored smoke bombs.[45] Other ACT UP-ers hung a sign identifying the place as the "Federal Death Administration."

ACT UP had choreographed much of it beforehand. Marty Robinson, who'd had plenty of experience being arrested from the old GAA days, and Amy Bauer, a lesbian who'd perfected direct-action techniques through her work in radical peace organizations,[46] had trained ACT UP-ers about what to do when the cops came. The entire Rockville, Maryland, police force and every police bus they could commandeer showed up. They padlocked the doors of the building so ACT UP-ers couldn't storm inside—which meant that ACT UP succeeded in shutting the FDA down for the whole day since the workers couldn't get in either. For six hours the Rockville police, wearing clear plastic surgical gloves, tried to keep the peace. They dragged protestors off to waiting police buses and to jail. One hundred seventy-six were arrested, though the Rockville police had been told to be restrained and arrest as few as possible, so the protest wouldn't be turned into a media circus.

But it was. ACT UP's media committee made sure that every major newspaper and TV station was alerted that there'd be mayhem at the FDA. The protest got international coverage. United Press International and Associated Press articles appeared with exactly the headlines ACT UP had hoped for, such as "Demonstrators Demand Easier Access to AIDS Drugs." HIV-positive writer and film historian Vito Russo was quoted in newspapers around the country saying that there were drugs out there that could help people like him, but the FDA wouldn't let those drugs get to market. In Europe it takes nine months to make sure a drug doesn't have "bad side effects"—why does it take the FDA five to ten years to do the same thing? Russo wanted to know. "The side effect of AIDS is death!" he declared.[47]

The major media attention that ACT UP was getting had not happened by chance. ACT UP had a media committee, headed by a young fireball, Michelangelo Signorile, who would go on to become a leading gay journalist. It also had Ann Northrop—Upper West Side resident, grandchild of a bona fide Daughters of the American Revolution member—as a media advisor. The group couldn't have found a more knowledgeable one. Northrop was a smart-looking blonde who'd spent seventeen years in an impressive career as a writer and producer for network news programs such as ABC's *Good Morning America* and the *CBS Morning News*. At Vassar

College, she'd broken with her family's conservative sympathies and had become a strong feminist and an antiwar activist—she wore a peace sign on her mortar board at graduation. By the time she was hired at CBS in 1982, she was out as a lesbian (but her male boss asked anyway, "So when are we sleeping together?").[48] She finally quit network news because, she thought, "it was getting stupider and stupider"; she was craving for something more meaningful in her life. The Hetrick-Martin Institute had been established in 1979 by a gay couple, Dr. Emery Hetrick and Dr. Damien Martin, to advocate for poor gay and lesbian teens—most of them from Harlem, where Dr. Hetrick worked as chief of Psychiatric Emergency at Harlem Hospital Center. By 1987, a lot of Hetrick-Martin's services were related to AIDS. To Ann Northrop, AIDS seemed like the war in Vietnam all over again—again the powerful didn't care about the powerless, who were dying. She took a 75 percent pay cut to go to work for Hetrick-Martin as an AIDS educator—which in February 1988 led her to ACT UP.

Ann Northrop felt in her element again, taking to the streets to protest injustice. Now she could also teach those with whom she protested valuable things: How to work the media to get maximum coverage. How to dangle an event in front of reporters so that they'd think it irresistible, and imperative that they be there. How to do a five-second sound bite so that if a microphone is pushed in front of an ACT UP-er's face, he or she will say something that will make the six o'clock news. "Talk in brief spurts that are usable as quotes," Northrop instructed them. "Remember, you're not speaking *to* the media but *through* the media. You're using them to get to the general public."[49] It was urgent to get to the general public. If people were allowed to forget about AIDS, the government could forget to put money into helping to end it.

It was urgent, too, that ACT UP fight the rhetoric and attitudes that were hurtful to people with AIDS. Marty Robinson's Lavender Hill Mob had zapped Cardinal O'Connor three years earlier, but a lot of ACT UP-ers thought that the most influential Catholic in New York deserved it again. Sunday, December 10, 1989: Hundreds of ACT UP-ers, men and women sedately dressed in go-to-church clothes, went to church at St. Patrick's Cathedral. There'd been a meeting of the Roman Catholic bishops under Cardinal O'Connor, at which the ecclesiastics agreed to make public declarations reiterating to the faithful that Catholic doctrine deemed the use of condoms uncatholic. "Good morality is good medicine," the cardinal declared. It didn't make a difference that the New York Health Commission said that the Church's continued prohibition would bring on a worse public health disaster. To the Church, it was irrelevant even that condoms could prevent the spread of AIDS to women through infected bisexual men. Abstinence was the only AIDS preventive that the Catholic leadership would condone. "Cardinal O'Condom," some ACT UP-ers rechristened him. The cardinal, for his part, reiterated that "to the end of time," the Church would be teaching that homosexual activity is sin.

Before the ten o'clock morning mass, ACT UP infiltrators, smiling like church ushers, handed out "church programs" to the faithful as they entered St. Patrick's. The "programs" were flyers that told why ACT UP would be disrupting the service. Cardinal O'Connor had been apprised that ACT UP-ers would be in his church. "Pay no attention to them," he announced from the pulpit and began a homily. Despite the bitter cold outside and inside the church (worshippers kept their heavy coats on and held their hymnals in gloved hands),[50] scores of infiltrators lay down on the marble floor of the main aisle of St. Patrick's and staged a die-in. Parishioners glared at the prone bodies. Two gay leather men who were an ACT UP couple chained themselves side by side to a pew. Ann Northrop chanted to the faithful, "We're fighting for your lives too!" The cardinal kept on with the mass while several ACT UP-ers stood and read a statement about how Church policies were making the AIDS epidemic worse. Michael Petrelis, who'd worn the concentration camp uniform at the Lavender Hill Mob's CDC zap, was by now suffering from herpes, gastrointestinal amoebas, and a host of other opportunistic infections; he hadn't been up to wearing a suit and tie to get into St. Patrick's, but he sneaked in through a side door. Petrelis thought the activists weren't being heard over the cardinal's amplified homily; so he stood on a pew and blew a whistle over and over. Then he shrieked as loud as the whistle, "O'Connor, you're killing us! Murderer! We will fight O'Connor's bigotry!"[51] The policemen who'd managed to squeeze through the huge crowd out front pulled Petrelis down off the pew, handcuffed him, and marched him out to the waiting paddy wagon as he kept up a banshee screech.

At the call to take communion, ACT UP-er Tom Keane, who'd been an altar boy and whose mother still taught catechism classes, went to the front of the church and knelt with the rest of the worshippers. By now the cardinal had stepped down from the altar and was sitting dramatically on his gilded throne, head cradled in hands,[52] an image of despair. A dark-skinned priest was giving communion. Keane, dressed in a dark blue suit, looking like a young Republican stockbroker,[53] held his mouth open as the priest intoned with a Spanish accent, "the body of Christ," and then placed the wafer on Keane's tongue. In a gesture large enough for all to see, Tom Keane spit the host out, crumbled it, and dropped the crumbs to the ground. That's what started a near riot. The police had their hands full.

They had their hands full outside, too, with over four thousand protestors. The ranks of ACT UP had been swelled by abortion activists from Women's Health Action and Mobilization, WHAM. Some ACT UP demonstrators lay "dead" in the middle of the street; others blocked the sidewalk and the entrance to the cathedral. Many carried signs: "Public Health Menace: Cardinal O'Connor," "Condoms Save Lives," "Papal Bull," and the most popular one: beneath the word *SCUMBAGS*, a picture of the chubby Cardinal O'Connor side by side with a big condom, and underneath the condom the message, "This one prevents AIDS." The police came out of the church carrying the "dead" on stretchers because they wouldn't walk. All told, 111 protestors were arrested.[54] Ann Northrop was ecstatic. The zap "made headlines all over the world for weeks."[55] ACT UP chapters were started in Moscow, Cape Town, and big cities all over Europe.

There was no letup into the next decade. On January 17, 1991, President George H. W. Bush ordered air and missile strikes against Iraq. ACT UP-ers were agitated because billions of dollars would be spent on war instead of on finding a cure for AIDS. Ann Northrop had kept her old CBS identification card, which one of New York ACT UP's many artists used as a template to make phony ID cards for a half dozen ACT UP-ers. Northrop instructed them to dress up in business suits. "If anyone asks who you are—some of you are salesmen from CBS headquarters and some of you are potential advertising clients who want a peek behind the scenes." She told them the exact location of the room in which the *CBS Evening News* was shot and which security desk to go to and how to flash their ID cards quickly.[56]

Just as Dan Rather was greeting *Evening News* viewers, the activists tore off their jackets, ties, and white business shirts—like Superman—to reveal their Silence = Death T-shirts beneath. In a flash, they ran in front of the TV cameras and into the homes of millions, chanting their sound bite, "Fight AIDS, not Arabs!" A flustered Dan Rather called for an immediate commercial break. No commercial was available, so the station went off the air for several seconds. "There were some rude people here, and they've been ejected from the studio," Rather explained when the program resumed. The protestors were carted off to jail, but America was reminded, not only through the zap but also through the huge newspaper attention in big cities and small,[57] that the anguish and anger of AIDS activists would not go away.

Those ACT UP-ers who invaded churches and television stations and tied up traffic were the bad cops, doing the job of getting the culprits of indifference to sit up and take notice. The nicer cops were a handful of ACT UP-ers who got together to learn everything they could about AIDS treatment. The group included the film historian, Vito Russo; Mark Harrington, a Harvard graduate who'd wanted to be a writer but became a full-time AIDS activist instead; Spencer Cox, a theater arts major at Bennington who dropped out for AIDS activism; Peter Staley, the ex–Wall Street bond trader; and one person with a science background: a middle-aged straight woman, Dr. Iris Long, a retired organic chemist who'd studied the major AIDS drug AZT when it was being tried on cancer patients. (It didn't work.) Long had never been any sort of activist before. She'd never even had openly gay friends; but she was intrigued by the baffling mystery of AIDS. She met with the group regularly in a four-thousand-square-foot loft in downtown Manhattan that belonged to Herb Spiers, who'd been one of the founders of Canada's first important gay magazine, *The Body Politic*. Now Spiers was trying to make a living by publishing graphic novels out of his loft. But mostly he and the others of the group were being instructed in the science of AIDS by Dr. Long. Pretty soon they were all instructing each other. They called themselves the Treatment and Data Committee of ACT UP.

They became much more knowledgeable about AIDS than most doctors, who'd had neither the time nor the inclination to study the disease. To share what they'd learned, they published a comprehensive *Glossary of AIDS, Drug Trials, Testing, and Treatment*.[58] They also put together a National

AIDS Treatment Research Agenda that discussed, clearly and knowledge-
ably, past problems with AIDS drugs and treatments. They included a list
of thirty promising drugs whose studies needed to be speeded up. They
demanded to know why the FDA, the agency that regulated drugs, wasn't
moving on those drugs; and why it wasn't making drug companies pay
attention to research that showed that the recommended dose of AZT
caused severe anemia and that lower doses had proven to be more effective.
The Treatment and Data Committee furnished copies of their AIDS Treatment Research Agenda to the FDA and the National Institutes of Health.
They told the scientists what they needed to be studying about AIDS and
how they should go about it.

When they didn't get responses, or when they were crossed by an
antigay politician, they called out the bad cops. Sometimes they were
themselves the bad cops—as in the Jesse Helms escapade. The conservative Republican senator from North Carolina had turned all the venom
he'd once had for integrationists onto gay people and especially those with
AIDS. "We've got to call a spade a spade and a perverted human being a
perverted human being," Helms had told the Senate when he proposed
an amendment adding "sexual abstinence only" to a $300 million appro-
priation bill for AIDS education. (The Senate supported him, 94 to 2.[59])
Later, Helms also tried to block a $600 million AIDS bill, telling his fel-
low senators that the government should not spend money on "a disease
spread through immorality."[60] Peter Staley and six other members of the
Treatment and Data Committee, calling themselves the "Treatment Action
Guerrillas," answered Helms with a zap worthy of Marty Robinson.

Staley's lover was a close friend of gay Hollywood producer David Geffen, who'd heard that Staley was planning an action on Helms. Geffen gave
the former bond trader a wad of cash, $3,000, with which to do the zap.
Staley commissioned a company that produced giant inflatables for advertising purposes, and out of parachute material the company made a thirty-
five-foot yellow-beige condom. Staley and the other merry pranksters then
rented a truck. In its bed they put two blowers, a portable generator, a tall
ladder, and the deflated condom; and they drove to Arlington, Virginia, a
suburb of DC. That was where Jesse Helms lived when the Senate was in
session. They stayed overnight at a cheap motel; then early the next morning they alerted the local and national media, and they went off to Helms's

two-story redbrick colonial house. There, with clockwork precision (they'd practiced), they scurried up the ladder to the roof, draped the parachute material to cover the roof and front of Helms's house, and inflated it.

If anyone missed the meaning of the oblong object that covered the house, the message printed on it informed them what it was: "A Condom to Stop Unsafe Politics: Helms Is Deadlier Than a Virus." "What does this mean?" an Associated Press reporter superfluously asked Peter Staley. The newspapers quoted him faithfully: "We're saying if you mess with us, you're going to wake up one morning to find a condom on your roof."[61]

But ACT UP's most serious use of bad cops and good cops was on May 21, 1990, when ACT UP-ers from all over the country paid a visit en masse to the campus of the National Institutes of Health in Bethesda, Maryland. The name the activists knew best at the NIH, because he'd published a lot about AIDS, was Dr. Anthony Fauci, head of NIH's Institute of Allergy and Infectious Diseases. Fauci had read Michael Gottlieb's June 1981 article about the five mysterious pneumonia cases of gay men in Los Angeles. The following month, he'd read that twenty-six gay men had been diagnosed with Kaposi's sarcoma. As an infectious-disease specialist, he'd always been something of a detective, and the stories intrigued him. He dropped his old research interests and turned his full attention to the new disease.

Fauci, as chief officer of the Institute that studies infectious disease, had a significant influence over what drugs would be tested and what protocols would be followed. Now the ACT UP activists were targeting him, yelling beneath the window of his office, "Fauci, you're killing us!" "The whole world is watching, Fauci!" When they set off smoke bombs, the National Institutes of Health police showed up right away. They were about to summon a Black Maria and have the obviously homosexual protestors dragged off. But Anthony Fauci wouldn't let them. He wanted to hear what ACT UP had to say. He told the police to ask five or six of the protest leaders to come in, to meet with him in a conference room.

Peter Staley, Mark Harrington, and the other Treatment and Data experts who met with Fauci lectured him on the inappropriateness of lengthy drug testing trials in the midst of a plague. Some of those at the meeting, like Peter Staley, knew they were HIV positive. "We don't have the years to wait while new drugs are tested," they said. They talked about the ethics of using placebos in tests instead of real drugs, which might save people who were dying. The amount of information they had was astonishing to Fauci. Everything they said made great sense, as he told his NIH colleagues: "These guys are extremely valuable. They can give us input into how to design the trials and the kinds of needs they see in their community. We have to listen to them. How can we work in partnership with them?"[62]

The "partnership" started a revolution in the way things were done at the National Institutes of Health. It brought about major changes in how the federal government tests and distributes experimental drugs, beginning with the Accelerated Approval process that the Treatment and Data Committee demanded.[63] As a result of that "partnership" NIH advisory committees and counsels always include activists from communities that are directly affected by NIH's policy decisions. ACT UP changed America's "scientific culture" to profit everyone.[64]

Big Pharma, also shamed by the activists, eventually listened, too. When Burroughs Wellcome first put a drug on the market that sounded promising, AZT, the cost to the user was between $8,000 and $10,000 a year. ACT UP zappers embarrassed the company by infiltrating its headquarters and inviting the media to come take pictures of a sign they hung from a second-floor window that accused the company of having blood on its hands. Burroughs Wellcome still wouldn't lower the price of AZT, so ACT UP infiltrated the New York Stock Exchange, sneaking up to the VIP balcony and unfurling a "Sell Wellcome!" banner. They also staged a "die-in" in the street in front of the exchange. Five days after the Wall Street zap, the company cut the price of the drug to $6,400 a year.[65]

ACT UP's more cerebral Treatment and Data Committee also worked its magic to persuade Bristol-Meyers-Squibb to put its promising drug DDI on accelerated approval. Even more important, Treatment and Data (which broke away from ACT UP in 1992 and became the independent Treatment Action Group) guided Roche, Merck, and other companies in developing the most potent protease inhibitors and designing and speeding along the trial process for them.

Protease inhibitors were made widely available in 1996. In that first year, deaths from AIDS in the big cities dropped about 50 percent. Kaposi's sarcoma lesions melted away. Michael Petrelis, who'd screamed at the CDC conference in 1987, "Drugs into bodies now!" began taking protease inhibitors when his T-cell count dropped below 100.[66] Like so many who'd been inches from the end, he went into remission.

Before the plague was controlled, it killed millions worldwide and decimated gay America. AIDS took some of the community's best leaders: Marty Robinson, Jim Owles, Morty Manford, Bruce Voeller, Steve Endean, Peter Scott, Rob Eichberg, Vito Russo, Dr. Emery Hetrick, Dr. Damien Martin, Jim Foster, Melvin Boozer, Leonard Matlovich, Eric Garber . . . the list goes on and on. Gay organizations such as the National Gay and Lesbian Task Force and Jean O'Leary's National Gay Rights Advocates turned much of their efforts away from fighting for gay civil rights and focused mostly on fighting for the rights of people with the disease. Yet the plague also brought some unexpected dividends to the gay community, if such a tragedy can be thought to have wrought anything good. Gay men stared their mortality in the face, concluded they had little to lose, that silence equaled death, and they made a giant collective leap out of the closet. Many who didn't leap were shoved out by the terrible telltale signs of the disease. The coming out of so many meant that millions of heterosexuals who might have mocked gays before as "those weirdos" were forced to acknowledge that sons, brothers, friends, even idols they'd revered, were gay.

Gay men also achieved an incredible victory over enemies who wanted to brand and banish them during the plague years. Gays remembered their history—that not too long ago, the law, the medical experts, and the Church were determining the dialogue about them and controlling their fate; they knew that all the progress that had been made in the 1970s could be reversed and history could easily repeat itself. So they fought with all their might against that happening, and they won. They took control of the public discussions about AIDS; they made their own voices heard. They even determined what their sick would be called: not passive and powerless "AIDS patients" or "AIDS victims," but "people with AIDS" who could fight for what they needed.

It's an irony that despite the horrors of the plague, the late eighties and early nineties was also a period of some collective healing in the gay community. Gay people learned to work together a little better than they had before because their overwhelming purpose didn't permit a plethora of petty arguments.[67] The times were "full of deaths, but one of the most beautiful moments the gay community ever experienced,"[68] Peter Staley later said of those years. "To be that threatened with extinction and not lay down. To stand up and fight back. The way we did it. The way we took care of ourselves and each other. The goodness we shared. The humanity we shared."[69] It was excellent preparation to bring to the renewed struggle for civil rights, which had been on hold while tens of thousands were dying. Those who survived were ready to resume the war and win it.

Chapter 24

FAMILY VALUES

SAVE *OUR* CHILDREN

Members of the New York Gay Activists Alliance had just been dropped off at the old Firehouse on Wooster Street by the bus they'd chartered to and from Albany. It was after ten at night. They'd spent that Saturday, April 15, 1972, marching at a rally with eight hundred other gays, agitating yet again for a statewide gay rights law. The Firehouse telephone rang soon after Jim Owles opened the meeting house door. It was Ethan Geto, the semiclos-eted politico who'd later direct the failed campaign against Anita Bryant in Dade County. He was calling from the lobby of the New York Hilton Hotel. He was at a banquet of the Inner Circle, an organization of political writers who every year hosted an evening of lampoon entertainment to which they invited civic and business leaders. This night's banquet was es-pecially gala—the governor, the mayor, and two senators were there to help celebrate the Inner Circle's fiftieth anniversary. Geto was sure that the Gay Activists Alliance would like to know that the sixteen hundred movers and shakers at the banquet had just been laughing uproariously at a lampoon that presented gay men as limp-wristed lady-wannabes screeching at the city council in falsetto to give them their civil rights.[1]

Most of the GAA members had already expended all their fight for the day in Albany; they just wanted to get home. But several of them found their second wind, grabbed handfuls of GAA leaflets that protested media treatment of gays, and hopped the Midtown train to the Hilton Hotel.

As the guests, now sipping their brandies, chortled at a new round of lampoons, the GAA men wandered from table to table passing out leaflets. It was obvious they weren't getting the movers and shakers' attention. Allen Roskoff, still carrying the megaphone he'd used that day in Albany, jumped up on the stage and boomed into it, "Listen! This dinner is now over. We will not tolerate homophobia in this city!"[2]

In seconds, the gays were bum-rushed by a tuxedoed pack. Its leader was president of the Uniformed Firefighters Association, Michael "Mickey" Maye—a forty-one-year-old, six-foot-two, 215-pound former Golden Gloves heavyweight boxing champ.[3] Maye prided himself on his John Wayne directness. "What the fuck are you doing here, you fucking bastard! If you don't get out, I'll kill you!"[4] he shouted as he lifted Roskoff by his shirt collar and dragged him out of the ballroom. Jim Owles ran after them, yelling, "You're violating his civil rights! Get your hands off him!" Maye did—so he could smash Owles's face and toss him onto the Hilton's down escalator, headfirst.[5] Fire battalion chief David McCormack, Maye's beefy, bald-headed VP in the Uniformed Firefighters Association, wasn't far behind;[6] according to witnesses, he'd already jumped Morty Manford, socked him, dragged him to the down escalator, and now shoved him onto it, too. Mickey Maye, like a scrappy movie cowboy in a barroom brawl, wasn't finished. He sprang onto the escalator, hopping over the prone and semiconscious Manford to bang some more on Owles. Then he turned to grind his heel repeatedly into the groin of twenty-one-year-old Manford as the escalator made its way to the ground floor.[7] Jim Owles and Morty Manford were both hospitalized.[8]

Charles Manford had committed suicide in 1966 because it was too hard, he thought, to live his life as a homosexual. Morty, Charles's younger brother, was an outstanding student at Columbia University, a handsome and personable young man with a brilliant future ahead of him. (He would become an assistant attorney general for the state of New York.) But in 1969, after he discovered that he, too, was gay, he tried to do the same thing his brother did: he went up to his room in his parents' Flushing home and swallowed a bottleful of tranquilizers. His dentist father and his mother, an elementary school teacher, found him in time to save him. It wasn't homosexuality that killed their first son and almost killed their second, Jeanne and Jules Manford told each other; it was society's hostility toward homosexuals.

After Michael Maye's brutish beating of Morty Manford, an outraged Jeanne Manford wrote a letter to the editor of the *New York Post* excoriating "the hoodlums who work for our city"—the policemen who were at the Hilton and did nothing while young gay men were being beaten. "I am proud of my homosexual son," she declared, praising him for leading the fight against "bigots and sick people who take advantage of gays."[9]

Had any parent ever before dared tell the world, "I am proud of my homosexual son"?

That June, Morty Manford asked his mother to walk alongside him in the Christopher Street Liberation Day March. They agreed they had to convey to spectators why she was there. On a piece of the same stock of poster paper that she handed out to her fourth-grade students for their art projects, Jeanne Manford wrote the message she'd carry in the gay pride parade. "PARENTS of Gays: UNITE in SUPPORT for Our CHILDREN," her handwritten sign said.

Medium-tall Morty Manford, towering by a head above his diminutive and naturally shy mother, thought at first that the wild cheering of the crowds was for Dr. Benjamin Spock, the famous pediatrician and antiwar activist who was marching right behind them in a contingent of Homosexual Veterans Against the War.[10] But—as Morty Manford learned from the many young gays and lesbians who ran up to his mother, showering her with hugs and tears and begging her to talk to their parents who'd disowned them or piled guilt and sadness on them because they were homosexual[11]—the cheering was for Jeanne Manford. Morty, moved to tears himself, told his mother as they marched, "You and dad have got to start an organization for parents of gays."

The first meeting was held on March 11, 1973, at New York's Metropolitan Duane Methodist Church on Thirteenth Street. Jeanne and Jules Manford told the twenty or so parents who showed up, all of them in anguish over the homosexuality of their son or daughter, "You need to understand: there's nothing wrong with our homosexual children. They're okay. It's society that isn't okay."

A peevish father, who'd been dragged to the meeting by his despairing wife, protested, "Why should we brag about our son's homosexuality? I don't tell people the details of my sex life."

Soft-spoken Jeanne Manford told him, "I loved my child as a child. I love him now. I want to see society give him a fair chance." Cast beyond the pale, their gay children would have no fair chance, she said.[12] It was up to parents of gays and lesbians to show family values by acknowledging their gay kids as family—"*our children*," she and Jules Manford kept emphasizing the words. They needed to make public proclamations that "these are *our children*; we love *our children* as they are; and we fight for their right to equal treatment in jobs, housing, and privacy."[13] They needed to remind politicians that "there are twenty-five million homosexuals in this country and fifty million parents of homosexuals"[14]—that made a lot of votes.

Jeanne Manford's ballot-box math was surely helpful to the gay and lesbian civil rights struggle. But *crucial* was her group's transformation of the outcast homosexual into somebody's child, a member of a family. It opened a whole new rhetoric.

THE "FAMILY VALUES" WAR

One afternoon in 1974, a nervous Philip Starr sat his mother and father down in the living room of their middle-class Brentwood home. "I'm a homosexual. I can't change, and I won't," he told them. In their Los Angeles suburban circles, "homosexual" still meant "sick." Mr. and Mrs. Starr were visibly shaken. Philip had read about the Manfords, and he told his parents about their group. As it happened, Jeanne and Jules Manford were already traveling around the country to talk about Parents of Gays. When they came to Los Angeles, they inspired Adele Starr, a housewife, and Larry Starr, an accountant, to start a group like theirs. Within a few years, such groups were cropping up all over. They evolved from support groups, in which despairing parents offered one another solace, to groups in which they fought at the side of their gay and lesbian children in their struggle for civil rights.

The logo on the stationery of the national group, Parents and Friends of Lesbians and Gays (PFLAG), of which Adele Starr became president, announced, "I refuse to be a closet parent."[15] PFLAG grabbed headlines in

1979 when members descended en masse on Washington, DC, to participate in the March for Lesbian and Gay Rights. Even in small Midwestern
cities such as Hutchinson, Kansas, newspaper readers were informed in
bold letters that "**Parents of Gays March**," and that they were urging
all mothers and fathers of gays everywhere to "come out of the closet and
support your gay children."[16] PFLAG rebuked antigay groups such as the
Traditional Values Coalition, the Institute for American Values, and the
Moral Majority. "You have no monopoly on morality," Adele Starr, mama
lion to all gays and lesbians, scolded the right-wingers. "The American way
means respect for diversity and the right to life, liberty, and the pursuit of
happiness."[17] By 1981, there were literally hundreds of PFLAG chapters.

That same year, James Dobson, head of Focus on the Family—an
evangelical Christian group—started the Family Research Council, whose
purpose was to lobby Capitol Hill in order to "advance a family-centered
philosophy of public life." James Dobson had been a child psychologist.
He was catapulted to fame a few years earlier because two million readers
bought his book *Dare to Discipline*, about the virtues of walloping disobedi-
ent kids, and he became a leading conservative spokesman. What Focus on
the Family and the Family Research Council meant by "family" excluded
precisely the family members championed by PFLAG.

President Reagan regularly invited Dobson to the White House to consult with the presidential staff on issues related to families. One of the biggest issues, as Dobson saw it, was fighting the "homosexual agenda" which,
he said into the presidential ear, was a deadly threat to family. Dobson said
the same thing on his *Focus on the Family* daily half-hour radio program,
which was played on fifteen hundred stations and attracted five million
listeners.[18] He was more powerful in the evangelical Right than even Jerry
Falwell or Pat Robertson. In 2004 the media dubbed Dobson "kingmaker"
because through his influence on "pro-family values voters," he guaranteed
the reelection of George W. Bush by delivering Ohio and Florida to him.[19]

Emulators of James Dobson—all claiming a Christian-Right monopoly
on family values—sprang up like poisonous mushrooms. Donald Wildmon,
an ordained minister, started the National Federation for Decency in 1977,
the same year Dobson founded Focus on the Family. But when Dobson's
family focus garnered so much attention, Wildmon rechristened his own
group the American Family Association, through which he sponsored One

Million Moms. The Moms (more like a few thousand) engaged in pro-family activities such as trying to pressure J. C. Penney to break its contract with lesbian TV celebrity Ellen DeGeneres, who'd been hired to show her wholesome face on Penney's advertising. (The Moms failed.)

Psychologist Paul Cameron was another right-winger learning from Dobson. Cameron called the group he founded in 1982 the Institute for the Scientific Investigation of Sexuality; but he rechristened it the Family Research Institute. Though not a religious figure, Cameron (who was expelled from the American Psychological Association because of his dishonest interpretation of research on homosexuality) liked biblical stories of whippings, stonings, and worse. "The death penalty for homosexuals is not an unreasonable thing," he proposed. "I am open to it."[20] Putting homosexuals to death would be one way to "restore a world where homosexuality is not taught and accepted but is discouraged and rejected at every level," which was the chief mission of the Family Research Institute.[21]

A tragic event in 1983 involving a lesbian couple became a cause célèbre in the "family values" war. Sharon Kowalski was a champion athlete from her high school days through college: five foot eight inches tall, she ran track, threw discus, and played softball, basketball, volleyball, golf. She was a free spirit who rode a motorcycle and would pitch a tent anywhere that suited her. In 1975, at Minnesota's St. Cloud State University, she fell in love with one of her health and physical education professors, Karen Thompson; the following year, Kowalski was an assistant coach in women's track under Professor Thompson. When Thompson left St. Cloud to work on a PhD at Ohio State, Kowalski hopped on her motorcycle and went to visit her. They became lovers, and in 1979, after Thompson returned, Kowalski moved into her house in Clearwater, a little village near Saint Cloud in south-central Minnesota. The two women had a secret commitment ceremony, exchanged rings, and made each other beneficiaries on their insurance policies—the closest things to marriage in the days when same-sex couples couldn't even form legal domestic partnerships.[22]

They'd always been closeted, and when Sharon Kowalski became a high school PE teacher, they felt even more urgency to pretend they were roommates: Saint Cloud, after all, wasn't New York, LA, or San Francisco—and Sharon Kowalski also suspected that her Catholic parents, who still lived on the provincial Iron Range in northeastern Minnesota, wouldn't understand. "Being gay on the Iron Range is a hanging offense," Sharon always quipped. But in the fall of 1983, the lesbian singer Meg Christian came to Minneapolis, and Kowalski got tickets for herself and Thompson. She was tired of hiding. After the concert, she wanted to go to a lesbian bar, too.[23]

A week later, on the afternoon of November 13, 1983, Sharon Kowalski was bringing her four-year-old niece and seven-year-old nephew home from a Sunday outing when a drunk driver crashed his pickup truck into her car. The little girl was killed instantly; the boy was slightly banged up. Sharon Kowalski was badly injured. Karen Thompson rushed to the hospital. For two hours, Thompson tried to find out if Kowalski was dead or alive, but because they weren't legally related, no one would tell her anything. Finally, a priest came by and said he'd find out. "They're still working on her," he reported. When Kowalski's parents arrived hours later, Thompson learned that her lover was in a coma, had suffered a serious brain-stem injury, and would be a quadriplegic, if she survived.

As far as Kowalski's parents knew, Karen Thompson was nothing but Sharon's landlady and friend. In a state of grief and confusion, Thompson didn't correct their illusion. She would have had to tell them what their daughter hadn't wanted them to know. But she petitioned for legal guardianship of Sharon. She'd have her house modified with ramps for Kowalski's wheelchair; she'd get a Hoyer lift, which would help move Kowalski from wheelchair to bed; she'd do anything else that was necessary, Thompson said. She'd been trained in physical and occupational therapy. She'd work with Sharon, she promised. She'd already been working with her at the facility where Sharon Kowalski was staying, and Sharon was now able to type simple sentences. One said, "Karen, make love to me."[24]

Donald Kowalski, a rough-hewed man, a retired iron miner, also petitioned for guardianship. "No one can love Sharon like family," he said.[25] Thompson's attorney advised her to let the father have guardianship. As long as she could see Sharon regularly, as she'd been doing, and work with her and take her for outings, there was no point in fighting him. Mr. Kowalski wouldn't be able to understand why she'd want to be named his daughter's guardian: in the petition Thompson had filed originally, she'd described herself only as "a friend and housemate of four years." But she'd been so anguished about the tragedy that she'd gone to a psychologist. "You've got to tell the parents the truth about your relationship with Sharon," was the psychologist's simple advice.

Thompson was apprehensive, but in a carefully worded letter to Donald Kowalski, she did what the psychologist advised. When Donald Kowalski next saw Thompson at the hospital, he was red faced and shaking. "My daughter is not a lesbian!" he shrieked at her. Right there in Sharon's room, her mother, Della Kowalski, lunged at Thompson, fingernails in claw position, and then pinioned her to the wall as Thompson struggled to hold her off. Sharon saw the skirmish, and a tear rolled down her cheek.

At a loss for how to deal with Sharon's parents, Thompson contacted a Minneapolis PFLAG and begged them to intercede. "We understand your pain," they wrote Mr. and Mrs. Kowalski on Thompson's behalf. "Could we please sit down and talk to you?"

It was Donald Kowalski's lawyer who responded to PFLAG's request: "I merely ask you to mind your own business. Quit harassing my client, or we will take legal action."[26] Karen Thompson decided she had to challenge Sharon's father for guardianship lest she never see Sharon again.

In court, Donald Kowalski told the trial judge that Thompson was a lesbian and a bad influence on his daughter. He'd fight Thompson "till they cover me up in the ground," he said.[27] He'd brought his son with him to the trial. The burly young man glared at Thompson, then couldn't control himself. He leapt across chairs and grabbed her by the neck; he wouldn't let go until he was pulled off.

In the judge's decision, he opined that when Karen Thompson revealed to Sharon's family that she was a lesbian, it created a "schism," and it caused Sharon "emotional harm." Donald Kowalski was Sharon's family, the judge declared, and Karen Thompson was not. "This disabled girl needs the unconditional love of her family." On July 23, 1985, the judge awarded guardianship to Donald Kowalski.[28]

Within forty-eight hours, Donald Kowalski took his daughter back to the Iron Range and put her in Leisure Hills Nursing Home in Hibbing, Minnesota, a small city about two hundred miles away from Saint Cloud. It was a place that warehoused the very elderly and those near death. At Leisure Hills there'd be no attempt to give Sharon Kowalski rehabilitation therapy. She was there to vegetate out of sight until she died. She spent most of her days curled into a fetal position. Thompson could visit, but she was told she must come at times the Kowalski family wouldn't be there. She made the six-hour round-trip from Saint Cloud several times a week. That arrangement lasted for about a year, until Donald Kowalski got a doctor at the facility to write a letter to the court saying that Thompson was a lesbian and there was reason to fear she'd molest Sharon. Karen Thompson wasn't allowed to see her for more than three years.[29]

During that time Thompson hired a team of lawyers. She was ready to fight, to sue: Sharon wasn't getting appropriate care. She hadn't been evaluated for years to determine whether she could benefit from rehabilitation treatment; she wasn't allowed to see those she loved. Thompson had been so closeted before that she'd even feared to tell her colleagues how often she was going to Hibbing lest they suspect that she and Sharon Kowalski were more than just friends. But now she gave interviews to newspapers all over the country. She would break the case open. She traveled everywhere, speaking to lesbian and gay groups about what had happened, warning those in couples to get durable power of attorney for each other. She wrote a book, *Why Can't Sharon Kowalski Come Home?*

Her tragedy struck a chord. Its dark drama stood for the harm suffered by legions of gay and lesbian couples because society refused to recognize their same-sex families. "Free Sharon Kowalski" bumper stickers began appearing on their cars; "Bring Sharon Home" sweatshirts were sold in women's and gay bookstores. Lesbian and gay groups organized vigils in twenty-one cities on August 7, 1988—"Free Sharon Kowalski Day."[30] "Bring Sharon Home" committees raised money to help pay the $300,000 in legal fees Thompson was incurring.

By then, Donald Kowalski had had two heart attacks, and Della was suffering from severe depression. They were ready to relinquish guardianship of Sharon—but not to Karen Thompson. When Sharon was in high school, she'd had a track and discus coach, Karen Tomberlin, a married woman with four children who'd kept up with her athletically talented student. Though Tomberlin had her own family responsibilities and couldn't promise to do more than visit Sharon Kowalski on occasion, she had the great virtue of being heterosexual. Donald asked her to request to be appointed as Sharon's guardian. Tomberlin—who was as averse to Thompson's lesbian "influence" over Sharon as was her family—agreed to do it.

Karen Thompson complained again in court: Sharon Kowalski hadn't been evaluated in five years and Minnesota law required evaluation of someone in Sharon's position every six to twelve months. She petitioned to order a thorough evaluation, and it was granted. Sharon was moved to Miller-Dwan Medical Center in Duluth, Minnesota, where a medical team found that she was capable of understanding and communicating. They also found that she wasn't getting the rehabilitation care from which she could profit; and they recommended she be allowed to see visitors of her choosing, especially Karen Thompson: for Sharon's mental health, the evaluators concluded, she should even be permitted to go on outings with Karen Thompson.

When Thompson brought her guardianship request to court again, sixteen medical experts who'd worked with Sharon Kowalski—occupational therapists, speech therapists, rehabilitation medicine specialists—were called to testify. They agreed that while she had permanent short-term memory loss, she was competent to communicate her desires and preferences. "When Karen comes into the room, Sharon is a different person." "She glows when she's with Karen." "Karen is Sharon's world, and Sharon chooses not to interact unless Karen is with her." "Sharon wants to live with the woman whom she chose to be her lesbian partner," they testified. The court-appointed social worker agreed.

But Sharon Kowalski's sister Debra, who sat through all the testimony looking grim, told the judge that the whole Kowalski family hated Karen Thompson, who, they claimed, was using Sharon for her own lesbian "political agenda." The family would never visit Sharon if they had to step foot in Karen Thompson's home.[31]

Robert Campbell, the district court judge hearing the case, concluded in April 1991 that it was true that Thompson had long "demonstrated commitment and devotion to the welfare of Sharon Kowalski." And it was true that she knew Sharon's "medical, material and social needs." Nevertheless, Judge Campbell declared in a section of his opinion that he labeled "Outing," Thompson had acted contrary to Sharon's best interest by making public their lesbian relationship; she'd "disclosed Sharon's sexual orientation to Sharon's parents and the world, without Sharon's consent."[32] For those reasons, he ordered that Sharon Kowalski remain institutionalized, under the guardianship of Tomberlin—who announced she would return

Sharon to the Leisure Hills Nursing Home because she was sure Sharon "would want to be back up in the Iron Range, where she spent her childhood."[33]

Thompson, tireless and unrelenting, brought her case to the Minnesota Court of Appeals. There her lawyers argued eloquently that it was "astonishing" that a judge would issue an order that would "have the effect of limiting Sharon Kowalski's contact with Thompson and the love Karen feels for her." The lawyers demanded to know, "In what moral framework, in what system of justice, could such an order conceivably be in Sharon's best interest?"[34] The obvious answer was, only in a "moral framework" that narrowly defines *loving family* in the service of bigotry.

The judges of the Minnesota Court of Appeals deemed such a "moral framework" unjust. They concurred with Karen Thompson's lawyers. Judge Jack Davies, writing the opinion for the court of appeals on December 17, 1991, declared that the lower court judge had "abused his discretion" by appointing Karen Tomberlin guardian. Tomberlin hadn't visited Sharon Kowalski more than three or four times a year since the accident. Judge Campbell hadn't even demanded proof of Tomberlin's qualifications as a guardian. Even more serious, sixteen medical experts had testified that Sharon Kowalski wanted to live with Karen Thompson, and that Thompson had the skills, resources, and emotional commitment to help her; and not one medical expert was brought in by the Kowalski family to say the contrary. But most serious of all, Judge Davies wrote, was that "Thompson and Sharon are a family of affinity, which ought to be accorded respect."[35] The court of appeals reversed the lower court's ruling, and Sharon Kowalski came home. It was a landmark decision: one of the first times that a same-sex couple had been called "a family" in a court of law.

Throughout the 1980s, gay and lesbian families tried mostly in vain to get the law to recognize them as families. In San Francisco they had a nibble of success in 1982 when Supervisor Harry Britt, Harvey Milk's chosen successor, introduced a bill to the board of supervisors that would give health insurance benefits to the live-in partners of city employees. It passed—only to be vetoed by Mayor George Moscone's successor, Dianne Feinstein, who caved to pressure from San Francisco's Roman Catholic churches. "To reduce the sacred covenant of marriage and family by analogy to a 'domestic partnership' is offensive to reasonable persons and injurious to our legal, cultural, moral and societal heritage," Archbishop John Quinn advised Mayor Feinstein.[36]

That same year, a San Francisco gay man who was a railroad clerk for Southern Pacific Transportation lost his partner of eleven years to suicide. The clerk's union, AFL-CIO, had negotiated that after a death in the family, an employee was entitled to a three-day paid bereavement leave. But because the deceased wasn't related to the clerk by marriage, blood, or adoption, his leave request was denied. The union refused to fight for him: bereavement leave was intended for real family members, the union rep said. The clerk sued, but the judge found for Southern Pacific Transportation. The California Court of Appeals agreed: the relationship couldn't be verified—there was no legal record of it—and so the clerk had no claim.[37]

A few domestic-partner laws did eventually get passed. The hippie-dominated Berkeley City Council was first, in December 1984. That same year, West Hollywood—fondly dubbed "Boys' Town" by its predominantly gay male population—was incorporated as a city; and in early 1985 one of the first official acts of the West Hollywood City Council, headed by lesbian mayor Valerie Terrigno, was to vote in domestic-partnership benefits for same-sex couples. These were modest victories—hospital and prison visitation rights, health insurance for the partners of city employees.[38] But they set a precedent. In 1999 a domestic-partnership registry was established for the entire state of California (which led hostile opponents to dub the state "land of fruits and nuts").[39] In the years that followed, a handful of other states established domestic-partner registries or civil unions. But most lesbian and gay struggles for recognition as families took place case by case.

One important victory came at the end of the eighties: Miguel Braschi, a Puerto Rican, had come to the mainland on an Ohio State University tennis scholarship. In 1975 he met Leslie Blanchard. The two men became lovers; and Braschi gave up his scholarship, moved into Blanchard's rent-controlled apartment on Fifty-Fourth Street in Manhattan,[40] and worked as the manager of Blanchard's exclusive hair salon on East Sixty-Second Street. (Their clientele included Meryl Streep, Mary Tyler Moore, Robert De Niro, and Donald Sutherland.) Leslie Blanchard also owned Yellow Iris Farm, a farmhouse in northern New Jersey that he'd restored so elegantly that it was featured in *Architectural Digest*. Blanchard and Braschi used the place as a weekend retreat.[41] In 1977 the two men exchanged "Cartier love bracelets"—it was to them like exchanging wedding rings.[42] They paid their bills from a joint checking account and had joint credit cards. They attended each other's family functions, and their families knew and accepted them as a couple. Blanchard's young niece even called Braschi "uncle."

But in 1986 Blanchard died of AIDS. His was the only name on the lease. Two months after Blanchard's death, the landlord sent Miguel Braschi an eviction letter, telling him he had one month to pack up and vacate the premises. Miguel Braschi said that he and Blanchard had been a family, and under New York's rent-control laws a member of the leasee's family couldn't be evicted. He sued to stay. His motive wasn't financial—he was the primary heir to Blanchard's $5 million estate. But he'd agreed to serve as a test case.

By now the American Civil Liberties Union had made a 180-degree turn from the days when it declared that the government was justified in firing homosexuals because they were a threat to the nation's security. William Rubenstein, a brilliant young lawyer fresh out of Harvard Law School, was working for the ACLU's Lesbian and Gay Rights Project, specializing in fighting for the rights of people affected by the AIDS epidemic. Rubenstein was assigned the Braschi case. A lower court had already decreed that the landlord had a right to evict Miguel Braschi because "family" meant only people related by "blood, marriage, or adoption."[43] William Rubenstein took the case to the New York Court of Appeals, where he argued that "family" begged for a new definition because over the last decades families had become remarkably diverse. The Ozzie and Harriet family was rare, a minority.

The appeals court agreed with Rubenstein. By a vote of 4 to 2, the judges overturned the decision of the lower court. The majority opinion, written by Judge Vito Titone, established new criteria—along the lines Rubenstein suggested—for determining what a family is. The exclusivity and longevity of a relationship were central, as was the level of emotional and financial commitment. How a couple conducted their everyday lives and held themselves out to society were also relevant in the court's definition; and so was the reliance the couple placed on each other for daily family services.[44] In the court's definition of family, there was not one reference to biological sex or a marriage license. "New York Court Defines Family to Include Homosexual Couples," the stunned editors of the *New York Times* announced when the case was settled in 1989.[45]

Gary Bauer, who'd been undersecretary of education in the Reagan administration and had become president of James Dobson's Family Research Council in 1988, blasted the 1989 Braschi decision. "The ruling by the Court of Appeals is a dangerous landmark. The fight is about whether or not the heterosexual family will continue to be the central and favored form of family life, or whether we are going to use such a broad definition of family that it will no longer have any significance."[46] He was right: the court's decision on the Braschi case did serve as a "landmark" to help redefine "family" under the law.[47]

THE MOTHER OF ANTIGAY BATTLES

Mounting gay and lesbian legal victories triggered mounting reactionary frenzy and political opportunism, too. Far-right leaders waged all-out war for the sake of "family" (and fund-raising). Beverly LaHaye, wife of evangelical minister and author of the *Left Behind* books, Timothy LaHaye, had started Concerned Women for America in 1979 to stop women's rights and abortion supporters from "threatening the family." But the feminine mystique and abortion weren't great fund-raising issues: most Americans were pro–women's rights and pro-choice. Concerned Women for America enlarged its sights. "The homosexuals' agenda is destructive to the family," Beverly LaHaye wrote in a 1993 fund-raising letter. Homosexuals "want to have the same marital rights as you and your spouse," she told potential donors. "They want to be able to adopt any child. They want young children to be taught there's nothing wrong with homosexual behavior."[48]

In the name of organizations such as the American Family Political Committee, much of the money that right-wingers raised in the 1990s went to fight gays and lesbians at the ballot box: in Idaho, Washington, California, Oregon, Michigan, Arizona, Florida, Ohio. The language of those campaigns reprised Save Our Children in the 1970s: homosexuality was "wrong, unnatural, and perverse"; homosexuals "condoned adult males pursuing sexual relations with young boys"; the diabolical gay agenda was aimed at obliterating the "traditional family structure."[49] The mother of all such antigay battles was waged by Colorado for Family Values. But it ended in a US Supreme Court decision that for gays and lesbians was comparable to *Brown v. Board of Education* for African Americans.

Sixty-three-year-old Wilfred Perkins—Will, he liked to be called—was the owner of Perkins Motor Company, a new-and-used-car dealership, which he'd inherited from his father in 1959. He was a born-again, as was at least a third of Colorado Springs's population of 350,000. The city was home to the army's Fort Carson, the US Air Force Academy, and eighty different evangelical groups, including Focus on the Family and the Family Research Institute. "The Vatican of the Evangelicals," Colorado Springs was called.[50]

Will Perkins was famous in Colorado Springs for his amiable and sincere-sounding TV ads through which he hawked his cars. His two passions were selling cars and proselytizing for his religion. At holiday times, the avuncular Perkins brought both together, injecting Christian family messages into his Chrysler commercials.[51] "He sells Jesus like he sells cars," one friend said of him.[52] So when Will Perkins got word that the Colorado Springs Human Relations Committee was trying to convince the city council to pass a gay rights ordinance like the ones that had been passed in Boulder, Aspen, and Denver,[53] he feared for the future of the traditional Christian family.

Perkins hurried to the city council's public hearings to protest. The council chamber was so mobbed that he couldn't get in. But a few days later, he was able to get into a gathering at a church meeting hall—born-agains like him who were furious about the proposal to bring gay rights to Colorado Springs. The group had been called together by Kevin Tebedo, son of State Senator MaryAnne Tebedo, who'd recently outraged African Americans by proclaiming on TV that their culture "encouraged sexual promiscuity for girls."[54] Young Tebedo's own outrageous statements to the media were all about homosexuality: "Don't even put it in my face! Don't even make me think about it!" Kevin Tebedo roared with junior high school gusto.[55]

Tebedo's group would name themselves Colorado for Family Values, those in the packed church meeting hall decided in a flurry of righteous energy. They'd fight the local proposal for a gay rights ordinance—but that's not all they'd do. They'd also work to get rid of the gay ordinances in other Colorado cities. They'd overturn an executive order signed by Democratic governor Roy Romer that said gays couldn't be discriminated against in jobs that were funded by the state. They'd make sure to nip in the bud a Colorado Civil Rights Commission recommendation that a statewide gay rights law be passed—and they'd end all future bids for gay rights, too. To do all that, they'd get the state of Colorado to amend its constitution. MaryAnne Tebedo advised them how it could be done through a voter initiative.[56]

Because of his TV ads, Will Perkins was the best-known face in the room. He believed so much in what Colorado for Family Values would be doing that he was willing to commit a chunk of his car dealership profits to the fight, too. Perkins was elected hands down as executive board chairman.[57] The group members agreed they'd found a perfect spokesman, "an excellent salesman, in the best sense of the word," with rhetorical skills like Ronald Reagan's, they said.[58] His critics said that "his primary skill was to make hatred palatable to the general public."[59] He could sound imminently reasonable, even temperate and civil, when he talked about how homosexuals were destroying Colorado families.

Will Perkins's job was clear: he needed to sell voters a law that would forever prevent Colorado's gays and lesbians from claiming civil rights. He liked to say in a well-modulated voice that "people don't have a bad feeling toward the homosexual community," but the problem was that homosexuals—who are richer and have more education and better jobs than the average Joe (he produced statistics to prove it)—already have equal rights. It was "special rights" that homosexuals were demanding, and that was unfair to everyone else.[60] "No special rights!" became the rallying cry of the campaign.

But Perkins also got at the voters more viscerally. He worked to foment as much "bad feeling toward the homosexual community" as he could. He warned that gay rights laws could qualify homosexuals for affirmative action quotas and employers would be forced to hire them. He repeatedly declared that homosexuals were promiscuous and obsessed with sex. He somehow got hold of the radical resolutions that had been hotly rejected at the 1972 Chicago meeting of the National Coalition of Gay Organizations,[61] and he presented them as what the gay rights movement was all about: what homosexuals really wanted, he said, was to repeal all age-of-consent laws and all laws restricting the sex or number of persons entering into a marriage unit. "The drive for homosexual rights undermines the family," Perkins reiterated incessantly to op-ed readers, reporters, radio and TV hosts, and church groups up and down the state.[62]

Colorado for Family Values needed only 49,279 petition signatures to get an initiative on the ballot. Over 85,500 signatures were collected. As chairman of the executive board, Will Perkins was taking no chances. He and Kevin Tebedo drove to Denver's Capitol Hill in a Loomis armored truck with the seventeen big boxes of signed petitions locked in bulletproof steel; he hand delivered them to the secretary of state. A showman always, Perkins alerted reporters of his arrival time. When they questioned him about the over-the-top histrionics of his delivering the petitions in an armored car, Perkins responded, "We consider these documents to be among the most important signed pieces of paper in the entire United States."[63]

Amendment 2, as the Colorado for Family Values initiative came to be called, would change the state constitution to prohibit Colorado and all its municipalities and school districts—now and in the future, into perpetuity—from adopting any laws or regulations permitting the right to claim discrimination on the basis of "homosexual, lesbian or bisexual orientation, conduct, practices or relationships." In all of Colorado, only gays, lesbians, and bisexuals, singled out in a constitutional amendment, would never have the right to complain to their government of grievances and demand rectification. Amendment 2 would create a class of untouchables.

Will Perkins's sales tactics were propped up by propaganda literature from Colorado for Family Values. A headline of one CFV leaflet announced with ostensible fairness, "Equal Rights—Not Special Rights." The same leaflet told parents to imagine that their child was a student at CU–Boulder (which had gay rights protections), and his roommate was living an objectionable "gay lifestyle" right under his nose. "What can you or your child do about it?" the leaflet asked. "According to the 'law' in Boulder, nothing!"[64] Another leaflet with an "Equal Rights—Not Special Rights" headline propagated panic by attributing to the North American Man/Boy Love Association (NAMBLA) the motto, "Sex by eight, or it's too late" and citing reports that 73 percent of homosexuals had had sex with minors. "Vote yes on Amendment 2 for the future of our children," the leaflet beseeched hysterically.[65] CFV placed eight hundred thousand of such leaflets on voters' doorsteps.[66]

Eva McGeehan, a Colorado Springs resident whose son Patrick was gay, had founded a PFLAG chapter a couple of years earlier, right there in the heart of "the Vatican of the Evangelicals." Because of Amendment 2, her little PFLAG chapter grew practically overnight from twelve to one hundred members. McGeehan told the media that Amendment 2 was the best thing that ever happened to the gay and lesbian movement in her town: the Right had shown its nasty hand, and parents of gays and lesbians saw clearly what those they loved were up against.[67] They wouldn't be closet parents. Amendment 2 also brought many more gay and lesbian Coloradans out of the closet. There'd been activist gay groups in Colorado since the Gay Coalition of Denver was formed in 1972 to fight police harassment.[68] Now, in response to an even greater threat, new groups cropped up ready to fight.

Months before the November 3 election, two young lawyers, Mary Celeste, a lesbian (who'd eventually become the first openly gay judge in Colorado), and Pat Steadman, a gay man (who'd become a state senator and author of Colorado's civil unions bill), started the Colorado Legal Initiatives Project (CLIP)—to figure out what to do just in case the vote didn't turn out well. They agreed they needed to get a seasoned lawyer on board, the most high-profile Colorado lawyer possible. Among the members of CLIP was Wayne Buchanan, a policy wonk for Governor Romer. He knew just the lawyer. His parents, PFLAG members and long active in supporting gay rights, were neighbors of Jean Dubofsky, who'd been a justice on the Colorado Supreme Court.

Soon after Will Perkins submitted the 85,500 petition signatures to the Colorado secretary of state, Jim and Jan Buchanan paid their neighbor a visit. Jean Dubofsky was a Harvard Law graduate who'd fought for fair housing for blacks and legal services for migrant farm workers. In 1979, when liberal governor Richard Lamm appointed her to the Colorado Supreme Court, she'd been Colorado's deputy attorney general. Thirty-seven years old, she became the court's youngest judge; its first female, too, though she left in 1987 and opened her own law practice because it gave her flextime to spend with her lawyer husband and their two young sons. There was no one as well acquainted with Colorado's legal system and as reliably progressive on all social issues as Jean Dubofsky. The Buchanans asked their neighbor whether she'd be willing to lead the legal battle against Amendment 2, if voters should pass it.[69] "Sure," Dubofsky blithely said, but she was confident Amendment 2 would fizzle in liberal Colorado. Early polls confirmed her certainty: it was trailing.

"Even so, we'd better build our case now, because if we're not ready it'll certainly pass," the superstitious Pat Steadman said.[70] Dubofsky and the young lawyers in Colorado Legal Initiatives Project met all that summer to work out legal theories and line up gays and lesbians who'd act as plaintiffs, just in case. Jean Dubofsky's idea was that if Amendment 2 passed in November, CLIP would file a preliminary injunction right away, to keep it from going into effect in January when the secretary of state would be signing it into law: if it did become law, Dubofsky told CLIP, it would take a mammoth struggle to revoke it.

On November 3, 1992, Coloradans went to the polls. They gave Democratic presidential candidate Bill Clinton all eight of the state's electoral votes; 53.4 percent of them also ticked *yes* on Amendment 2, agreeing to deny gays and lesbians any and all legal protection by the government of their state, forever.

While the gay community in Colorado despaired, gay communities outside of Colorado had reason to despair, too. Colorado for Family Values' easy victory reenergized the religious right all over the country. Copycat campaigns were immediately under way. "Our campaign stands as a guidepost for others," cofounder of Colorado for Family Values, Kevin Tebedo, gloated about the influence of his group's success. CFV's media star, Will Perkins—now seen as the religious right's Anita Bryant of the nineties—promised that Colorado for Family Values would happily "share our experience with people who need help getting an organization going."[71]

When the devastating results on the Amendment 2 vote were in, Governor Roy Romer, who'd been cochair of the group that led the fight against the amendment, met with gays and lesbians at a Denver Convention Center rally. They were all stunned. How had pollsters been so wrong? "It is not you who are gay and lesbian who have lost tonight," Governor Romer told the crowd. "It is all of Colorado who has lost tonight."[72] He was genuinely affected by the loss. But, ironically, the battle to overturn Amendment 2 would carry his name, on the wrong side. *Evans v. Romer* the court fight in Colorado would be called.[73]

Amendment 2 violates federal Amendment 14's equal protection clause and is unconstitutional, Jean Dubofsky complained to the district court when she filed for an immediate injunction. Judge Jeffrey Bayless, to whom the case was assigned, had been a tough prosecutor with the district attorney's office until he was appointed as a Denver District Court judge. Forty-seven years old, pink faced and bland looking, he had a reputation as a political conservative. On January 11, 1993, Judge Bayless began hearings on the amendment. The setting was his polished-oak courtroom that was decorated with gray marble pillars and two big beaux-arts chandeliers. It was so perfect a Hollywood image of a courtroom that it had been rented by Viacom in the mid-1980s to shoot episodes of the new Perry Mason series, though the chandeliers gave so little light that Bayless always complained he had to squint to see the witnesses.[74]

Will Perkins, looking dapper and affable, was the first to testify in support of Amendment 2. He knew better than to cite bogus statistics about homosexual child molesters in court. "How you have sex isn't an appropriate criterion for civil rights," he told Judge Bayless with sweet reasonability.[75]

Jean Dubofsky argued that Amendment 2 had no rational basis and was motivated by impermissible bias. The plaintiffs she and her team[76] called to testify were a contrast to Perkins's Reaganesque calm. They couldn't hold back emotions. Paul Brown, a gay man who worked in a Colorado government job, told about one of his coworkers painting "Paul Is A Fag" in large letters on the wall facing the employees' parking lot. He'd been so harassed at work that he'd considered suicide. "There has to be a clear message from someone in authority that this is not okay," he told Judge Bayless. Angela Romero, a forty-two-year-old police officer, wept as she told the judge about how she'd finally gotten to fulfill her lifelong dream of serving as a school resource officer, a job in which she could be a role model for Latino children; but after someone reported to her supervisor that she'd been seen in a lesbian bookstore, she was transferred to the domestic violence detail. Now she worried that some of her hostile fellow officers might jeopardize her life—she couldn't depend on them to give her backup.

The solicitor general of Colorado argued on behalf of the state that Amendment 2 was meant mostly to send a message to gays saying "Enough!" It wouldn't, and wasn't supposed to, have any "real impact." But dark as the courtroom was, Judge Bayless saw, as he said, that Amendment 2 had the potential to "cause real, immediate, and irreparable damage." He issued the injunction Jean Dubofsky requested.[77]

Attorney General Gale Norton appealed to the Colorado State Supreme Court to get the injunction lifted. (The issue was so heated that the proceedings were broadcast live on Court TV.)[78] That august body backed Judge Bayless: Amendment 2 was dubious, the judges said. "Fundamental rights may not be submitted to a vote," one judge argued. Amendment 2 "fenced out" homosexuals from the political process; it singled out one group that could not get legal protection," another judge argued. "That was contrary to the notion of "We the People," another said in an eloquent recognition that gays and lesbians were indeed part of the American family. The Colorado Supreme Court agreed that the state simply hadn't demonstrated a "compelling interest": it would have to show why such an amendment was needed before Amendment 2 could go into effect. The court upheld Judge Bayless's injunction.[79] *Evans v. Romer* was sent back to him for trial.

Gale Norton was thirty-nine years old, a conservative who hailed from Wichita, Kansas, though she'd lived in Colorado since her undergraduate days at the University of Denver. She'd been elected three years earlier, the youngest person and the first woman to be made the Colorado attorney general.[80] It was now her duty to answer the Colorado Supreme Court's claim that the state had no "compelling interest" in Amendment 2.

Amendment 2 would support the family and the well-being of children and keep at bay "militant gay aggression"—that was the "compelling interest" Attorney General Norton provided on behalf of the state.

It did not fly with Judge Bayless. "If one wished to promote family values," he declared, "action would be taken that is pro-family and not anti some other group." And to Norton's argument that Amendment 2 served "the physical and psychological well-being of children," Bayless responded that all the evidence suggested that heterosexuals are more likely than homosexuals to be pedophiles. The judge ruled Amendment 2 to be unconstitutional.[81]

Attorney General Norton appealed the case again to the Colorado Supreme Court—who again, by a vote of 6 to 1, showed little sympathy. Chief Justice Luis Rovira wrote the majority opinion: "The measure denies homosexuals equal participation in the political process by saying they can have no redress if they feel discriminated against." It was the first decision by the highest court in any state to rule that the denial of rights to homosexuals was unconstitutional.[82] But the best was yet to come.

Attorney General Gale Norton and her solicitor general, Timothy Tymkovich—as reliably conservative (antiabortion, anti–gun control, pro–"religious liberty") as his boss—appealed to the Supreme Court of the United States. Though Roy Romer had been opposed from the start to Amendment 2, as governor he was obliged to support the state's laws. But he was surely chagrined when his name led in the Supreme Court appeal: *Romer v. Evans.*[83]

If the US Supreme Court refused to hear *Romer v. Evans*, the state court's edict would stand, and Amendment 2 would be dead. But the justices didn't refuse. They put it on the SCOTUS calendar for October 10, 1995. Will Perkins and Colorado for Family Values were jubilant: SCOTUS had apparently found something troubling in the state court's decisions. Jean Dubofsky's heart sank.[84]

Whatever big guns could be gotten out needed to be gotten out now. Matthew Coles of ACLU's Lesbian and Gay Rights Project in New York and Clyde Wadsworth, an attorney with Lambda Legal Defense in California, came on board to assist in preparation of the case; New York Lambda Legal Defense also sent Suzanne Goldberg, a young staff lawyer two years out of Harvard Law, to line up *amicus curiae* briefs from liberal constitutional law scholars.[85] The briefs came pouring in. Goldberg's Harvard professor, Laurence Tribe, who'd represented Michael Hardwick against Georgia's sodomy law in the Supreme Court, wrote "There's never been a law as bad as Amendment 2."[86]

It had been agreed that Jean Dubofsky would take the lead in representing the plaintiffs, all the way to the Supreme Court if necessary. Hoping for hints about arguing the case before the Supreme Court, Dubofsky contacted the best appellate lawyer in Washington, DC. It was John Roberts, who a decade later would be made the chief justice of

SCOTUS. "Sure, let's have lunch," he affably told her. She flew to DC. John Roberts offered a major piece of advice: "You just have to be able to count to five."[87]

But the makeup of the court gave Dubofsky reason to worry. It seemed impossible to count to five. William Rehnquist and Sandra Day O'Connor, two of the judges who'd voted in 1986 in favor of upholding Georgia's sodomy law in *Bowers v. Hardwick*, were still on the court. Clarence Thomas, a George H. W. Bush appointee, could always be relied on to silently cast his vote way off to the Right; as could Reagan appointee Antonin Scalia (though never silently). Anthony Kennedy, another Reagan appointee, seemed not much better than those four, at least with regard to homosexuality. When he'd been on the Ninth Circuit Court of Appeals, he held that the navy's policy of discharging homosexuals didn't violate any constitutional provision; he refused to issue an order requiring reinstatement and back pay for government employees who lost their jobs because they were homosexual; he upheld the Civil Service Commission's position that someone could be fired for "open and public flaunting or advocacy of homosexual conduct"—Anthony Kennedy's antihomosexual judicial decisions seemed endless. News of his apparent hostility to gays and lesbians spread during his 1987 Senate confirmation hearings when a detailed list of Kennedy's hurtful decisions was published in the popular gay newspaper *New York Native*.[88]

Who was reliable on the court when it came to gay rights? David Souter had been moving to the Left since George H. W. Bush appointed him to the Supreme Court in 1990, but he'd had a suspicious past. In 1987, when he was a member of the New Hampshire Supreme Court, Souter voted with the majority (6 to 1) to advise the New Hampshire legislators that they wouldn't be violating the state constitution if they stopped gays and lesbians from adopting or fostering children. "The provision of appropriate role models is a legitimate government purpose," Souter and the other justices affirmed—in other words, homosexuals would be bad parents because they'd model homosexuality and turn their kids gay.[89] (The ban against gays and lesbians adopting or fostering wasn't lifted in New Hampshire until 1999.)

Only Stephen Breyer, Ruth Bader Ginsburg, and John Paul Stevens could be counted on to uphold the overturning of Amendment 2. But even if David Souter continued his veer left, that would only give four votes. And four was no better than zero in Supreme Court decisions.

October 10, 1995: Antonin Scalia was predictably on the attack. The Colorado for Family Values's rationale in initiating Amendment 2 was just fine, Scalia thought: homosexuals were asking for "special rights," and they shouldn't have them any more than "bigamists or those with poorly combed hair." He reminded the court that the justices had said in *Bowers v. Hardwick* that states were free to make homosexual behavior a crime. That being the case, he asked Jean Dubofsky in a tone combative, smug, and witty all at once, wasn't it a matter of simple logic that now the states could take the milder step of deciding not to encourage homosexuals by offering them protection against discrimination?[90]

Scalia was undeniably right—it was simple logic: If homosexuality was criminal, why would the court forbid a law that discouraged it? But what Scalia's logical equation didn't take into account was that in the years since the court had judged *Bowers*, gays and lesbians of all stripes had come out of the closet—which had forced a lot of Americans to discover that "the homosexual" wasn't a grotesque stranger lurking in the shadows but someone who'd been near and dear to them all along. The cultural climate had begun to undergo a sea change.

Every one of the four hundred seats was occupied—lawyers, journalists, gays and lesbians and their friends. Those rooting on their side breathed a little easier almost right away. Solicitor General Timothy Tymkovich, a tall man with a twitching brush mustache that gave him a Neville Chamberlain look,[91] had barely begun his oral arguments when Justice Kennedy jumped in. "I've never seen a case like this," Kennedy remarked disapprovingly, echoing almost exactly Laurence Tribe's sentiment in his *amicus curiae* brief. Jean Dubofsky couldn't believe what she was hearing. Anthony Kennedy had just revealed his feelings about Amendment 2.[92] A few minutes later, Justice Ginsburg jumped in to second Kennedy's disapproval: "I would like to know whether in all of US history there has been any legislation like this that earmarks a group and says, 'You will not be able to appeal to your state legislature to improve your status'?"

"So, a public library could refuse to allow books to be borrowed by homosexuals, and there would be no relief from that?" Sandra Day O'Connor wanted to know (to the incredulous relief of all who were there to oppose Amendment 2). Tymkovich fumbled and couldn't make sense. "Would a homosexual have a right to be served in a restaurant?" Justice Stevens wanted to know.

The sea change had clearly affected judicial thought.

"Think of a public hospital that has a kidney machine," Justice Ginsburg jumped in again, sharp sword at the ready. "And the hospital says, 'We have to limit this. We're not going to have any gay or lesbian use this facility'—under the amendment that's okay, right?"

"We don't know," the ruffled Tymkovich had to admit.[93]

The Supreme Court's decision came down on May 20, 1996. It was a breathtaking 6–3. Predictably, Scalia, Rehnquist, and Thomas voted to uphold Amendment 2. Kennedy and O'Connor both voted with the four more liberal judges.

Gary Bauer of the Family Research Council dubbed May 20 "a very dark day for the liberty rights of the American people."[94] Will Perkins called a press conference on behalf of Colorado for Family Values. Gays bent on forcing a deviant lifestyle down the throats of the American family had succeeded in making the government "their pet bully," Perkins announced. But, he threatened, "there'll soon be a drive to impeach the justices who voted against Amendment 2!" It was an idle threat.[95]

Justice Anthony Kennedy, writing the majority opinion on *Romer v. Evans*, declared that the amendment was inexplicable of anything but animosity to a class of people. It was both too narrow and too broad. It identified a person by a single trait, and then it denied that person protection across the board. "Amendment 2 classifies homosexuals not to further a proper legislative end, but to make them unequal to everyone else. This Colorado cannot do. A state cannot deem a class of persons a stranger to its laws," Kennedy resoundingly concluded.

Such pronouncements from the highest court in the land would have been the stuff of opium dreams in the fifties and sixties, when tens of thousands of people were fired from jobs, kicked out of the military, committed to state mental hospitals, and otherwise made miserable precisely because the state identified them by a single trait and then denied them protection. Hadn't the Supreme Court condoned just such state actions even in the 1980s, when it decreed in *Bowers v. Hardwick* that states had all the right they wanted to criminalize homosexual behavior? But in the decade between *Bowers* and *Romer*, gays and lesbians, with a little help from their friends, had been transforming the rhetoric about who they were—rescuing their image from that of unsavory criminal to another member of the family, who must be treated as part of the American family, too. Maybe the Right wouldn't countenance the transformation, but as the *Romer v. Evans* decision showed, reasonable people did.

PART 8

DEMANDING TO SERVE

Chapter 25

NEW GAYS AND LESBIANS VERSUS THE OLD MILITARY

THE GOOD SOLDIER

As a boy growing up in the 1950s on Charleston Air Force Base in South Carolina, redheaded and beanpole skinny Leonard Matlovich had a recurring reverie. He was a Civil War soldier in the battle of Gettysburg—on the side of the Confederacy. Matlovich didn't question the racism around him, not even during the years when blacks began fighting for their civil rights. If black people showed up in the white housing area where he lived with his sergeant father and the rest of his family, the teenage Matlovich joined the kids who grabbed rocks and Confederate flags and chased the intruders out. On Saturday nights, he and other white teens from Charleston Air Force Base would ride a bus through the "Negro" parts of town, shouting out the windows: "Two! Four! Six! Eight! We don't want to integrate! Yea, Little Rock!"[1]

At nineteen, Leonard Matlovich followed his father's footsteps and enlisted in the air force. Twelve years later, in 1975, now a sergeant himself, he appeared on the cover of *Time* magazine. He was wearing a blue air force cap and a crisp white shirt on which were pinned his many military decorations. Superimposed on the picture was the declaration, "I Am a Homosexual."[2] He was the first openly gay person to be on the cover of

Time.[3] How he got there had to do first of all with his transformation from stone-throwing young bigot to supporter of black civil rights as he came to know black people in the air force. After three tours of duty in Vietnam, Matlovich volunteered to teach courses in the air force race relations program. It had been created in 1971 after a three-day race riot at Travis Air Force Base, instigated by people who were like he'd once been. For four years, as Matlovich talked in the classroom about equality and justice, it began to dawn on him that gays needed to fight for rights just as other minorities were doing.[4]

One day he asked his class, "Which do you think is the most oppressed minority group in America?" His students guessed blacks, Hispanics, Native Americans. Matlovich wrote on the board, "Homosexuals."[5]

It had taken Leonard Matlovich a long time to arrive at that point. Just a few years earlier, he'd joined the Church of the Latter Day Saints, hoping Mormonism would somehow help him exorcise the homosexual feelings which had troubled him since he was twelve years old.[6] His fears about those feelings had been reinforced by his political sentiments, which had always tilted right. He'd once described his father's politics as being "so conservative he makes Genghis Khan look like Jesse Jackson."[7] The apple didn't fall far from the tree. Leonard Matlovich had even toyed with joining the far-right John Birch society, though he settled for registering as a Republican and voting in 1964 for Barry Goldwater, an adamant opponent of the welfare state, the Soviet Union, and labor unions. Matlovich's patriotism assumed a disdain for what he called "the looney left" and its criticism of the United States. He liked to say of America, "We're truly better than the average bear."[8]

Because he grew up as a military brat, and knew well the military's attitude toward "queers," he'd never even hugged or put his arms around anyone other than family until he was thirty. But in 1973 he chanced to hear about a Pensacola, Florida, gay nightclub from one of his students in his race relations class, a straight captain who said he'd wandered in not knowing it was a homosexual hangout. Matlovich—sweating and shaking—dared go look. Once inside, he acknowledged to himself what he'd long suppressed. "A million pounds just left my shoulders," he thought.[9] His first homosexual experience followed.

The next year, he read an article in the March 27 issue of the *Air Force*

Times that startled and thrilled him. "Homosexuals in Uniform" it was called,[10] and it mentioned Dr. Frank Kameny as the founder, way back in 1961, of an organization that was fighting for gay rights in Washington, DC. Matlovich had never heard of such an organization. (He'd never even heard of the Stonewall riots.) He wanted to talk to Kameny. He called the long-distance operator, asking for the number of a Frank Kameny in DC, expecting her to say there was no listing. But there was: "Dr. Franklin Kameny." Matlovich wasn't sure what to say . . . he'd say he was teaching a race relations class . . . he'd ask Kameny if he knew of materials he might use in his classes to show that homosexuals, too, suffered prejudice . . .[11] It took him almost two weeks to muster the courage to make the call.

They talked for an hour. Kameny mentioned that he was working with ACLU military lawyers. They were helping gay men and lesbians who'd been thrown out of the military get their dishonorable discharges upgraded to honorable. But he and the ACLU would like to do more. They were looking for an ideal case: someone who had a perfect military record, wanted to stay in the service, was willing to publicly declare "I am a homosexual," and was ready to fight in court when the military discharged him for it. Matlovich didn't exactly tell Kameny he was gay during the phone conversation, but before they hung up, he did nervously say, "Well, I think I know an individual who might fit the bill."

But he'd been a lifer in the air force, and he really believed in service to his country. What would he do with himself if he were kicked out? But he'd been teaching about justice and equality for so long that he believed in that, too. And he believed in heroic gestures. It took four months of weighing before Matlovich called Frank Kameny to say, "I'm the guy I was talking about. I'm ready."

Frank Kameny, by now an old hand at fighting the military on behalf of gays and lesbians, pored over Leonard Matlovich's record. When other young men were running off to Canada to avoid getting drafted and sent to Vietnam, Matlovich enlisted—and he asked to be sent there, three times, "because that's where my nation needed me," he said,[12] and he'd hoped to play a modest role in "spreading democracy."[13] Matlovich was wounded by a land mine in Da Nang as he was preparing to assemble a frontline radar system; after he recovered he asked to be sent to the front again. He got a Purple Heart for his wounds, a Bronze Star for braving Vietcong sniper fire in order to fix crucial air force equipment,[14] and a slew of other decorations. He'd been in the service for twelve years, and there'd been not one complaint of any kind against him. Leonard Matlovich's credentials were impeccable.

Frank Kameny invited him to his home in DC, where they could talk. "I'd like you to meet someone," he said. Matlovich was on assignment at the time at Langley Air Force Base, near Hampton, Virginia. It was a six-hour drive round-trip, but Matlovich said he'd be there. The person Kameny wanted him to meet was a married heterosexual, David Addlestone, an ACLU attorney. Addlestone had been a judge advocate in the air force, defending people who were being kicked out of the military. Now he was devoting himself to helping Vietnam vets get upgrades on less-than-honorable discharges which not only robbed them of veterans' benefits but also saddled them with a lifetime stigma. Addlestone thought it was high time to tackle the homosexual issue.

Long before they finished the first pot of coffee, Addlestone agreed with Kameny: Matlovich would be an ideal test case to challenge the air force prohibition on homosexual airmen. The sergeant not only had a sterling record; he was also a straight-looking squeaky-clean guy who'd blindside the military's prejudices by coming at them not with a "left-wing militant gay activist approach," but with a "very all-American apple pie approach."[15]

They'd challenge Air Force Manual 39-12, chapter 2, section H, Addlestone explained. The regulation said, "Homosexuality is not tolerated in the Air Force," and it affirmed the air force policy to discharge those who engaged or tried to engage in homosexual acts, or had homosexual tendencies, or associated habitually with persons known to be homosexual.[16] He'd help Matlovich take the challenge all the way to the Supreme Court if necessary; he'd be chief counsel. But Matlovich would need a military lawyer, too, who'd serve as assistant counsel. Twenty-eight-year-old Captain Jon Larson Jaenicke was recommended as someone not hostile to homosexuality—a rare attribute among military lawyers.

Captain Jaenicke advised Matlovich to begin his challenge by writing a straightforward statement to his commander, declaring himself to be a homosexual.

March 6, 1975: Sergeant Matlovich went to the office of his superior,

Captain Dennis Collins, and handed him a letter addressed to the secretary of the air force, to be forwarded up the line. "Maybe you better sit down before you read it," Matlovich told him. The letter announced, as Captain Jaenicke had suggested, that Sergeant Matlovich was homosexual, that his sexual preference in no way interfered with his air force duties, and that he was requesting that "those provisions in AFM 39-12 relating to the discharge of homosexuals be waived in my case." Those provisions were anyway "unconstitutional," Matlovich had added.[17]

Captain Collins remained standing as he read it. Matlovich saw the captain's eyes grow "big as baseballs."[18] Then the captain sat down. "What the hell does this mean?" he asked.

"It means *Brown v. Board of Education*," Matlovich answered, because Captain Collins, a black man, would immediately understand.[19] The captain forwarded Matlovich's confession to Lieutenant Colonel Charles Ritchie, commander at Langley.[20]

It wasn't long before two men from the Office of Special Investigations came to see Matlovich. "We don't believe it," they told him. "You can't have a Bronze Star and a Purple Heart and suck cock."[21] To aver that you can, on April 25, 1975, Matlovich gave the OSI a written statement detailing that he'd engaged in homosexual acts of fellatio, as well as mutual masturbation and anal intercourse—in Florida, Louisiana, Virginia, and Washington, DC. To emphasize that he couldn't be blackmailed into giving away military secrets, he added that he was "perfectly open about my homosexuality," and that "my family, friends, and coworkers are now aware of my sexual preference."[22] Three weeks later, Lieutenant Colonel Ritchie informed Matlovich that he was initiating action to have him discharged from the air force.[23]

That was exactly what the Matlovich team expected. They blew the story open to the media. Frank Kameny was right that an "ideal case" would get major attention. He'd worked with scores of discharged service members, but no one like Leonard Matlovich. Even in the heat of his battle with the air force, Matlovich never stopped emphasizing, every chance he got, his "great pride to be an American, to know I'm oppressed but to be able to stand up there and say so."[24] How could anyone continue to maintain that homosexuals were "unfit for military service" once they heard the story of this super-patriot sergeant?

The novelty of Matlovich was irresistible. The *New York Times* was clearly on his side, describing him as "a decorated [air force] career man" who'd done three tours of duty in Vietnam and came back with a medal each time. Commander Ritchie's move to have Matlovich discharged was "only the opening skirmish in a battle over the definition of good soldier," the *Times* reporter observed presciently.[25] At the height of the media frenzy, CBS flew Matlovich to New York in a chartered plane for an interview; he was flown to Chicago to appear on the *Phil Donahue Show*; NBC made a movie, *Sergeant Matlovich Vs. the U.S. Air Force*. He was front-page news in major newspapers all over the country. Matlovich was deluged with fan mail, too; his Middle America appeal cut across demographics, as was exemplified by a woman who identified herself as a very heterosexual North Dakota housewife: "You are an attractive man who is honest and explained your beliefs and stands behind them, obviously happy. You could teach my kids in school anyday [*sic*]. Don't let the ignorance of others get you down. Right on!" the woman wrote.[26]

September 16, 1975, Matlovich's hearing before an administrative discharge board: His attorneys called air force psychiatrist Dr. Douglas Chessen, who said he examined Matlovich four times and believed he was "fully capable of performing his military duties." They called psychologists John Money, a sexual-identity specialist, and Wardell Pomeroy, who'd worked with Alfred Kinsey on the landmark *Sexual Behavior* books. Both said that the sergeant in no way threatened the heterosexuality of his fellow service members. Homosexuality was not "catching," Money said, because sexuality is determined in early childhood. "Sergeant Matlovich is extraordinarily stable," Dr. Money testified. "He has a history of having stood up under pressure. He's just an unusually stable person."[27] Matlovich's military associates testified, too. They said they knew of his homosexuality and it didn't make any difference in their friendship.[28] They called him, "the best there is."[29] They praised his "superior leadership and innovative qualities . . . an excellent team worker, performs superbly . . . has unlimited potential as a career NCO."[30] His unblemished record was presented to the administrative discharge board for its members to contemplate in detail.

Even the government's attorney, Lieutenant Colonel James Applegate, couldn't help but be impressed by that record. It was no small thing for the military to lose a serviceman of Matlovich's qualities. Applegate asked him, "Would you contract to be celibate, not practice your homosexuality?" The air force regulation said that if "the most unusual circumstances exist," and "the airman's ability to perform military service has not been compromised" exceptions to the discharge policy could be made. Applegate seemed to be steering Matlovich to give the panel a reason to do so.[31]

But to foreswear homosexuality would have defeated Matlovich's main purpose. He answered that he was a practicing homosexual and intended to remain so.[32]

The administrative discharge board deliberated for four hours before they returned, after seven o'clock, to the crowded hearing room. They declared that the hearing had revealed that Sergeant Matlovich "could not be considered a candidate for rehabilitation." Thus he was unfit for military service.[33] The board recommended he be given a less-than-honorable discharge.[34]

America was celebrating its bicentennial that year. Matlovich, who had a natural instinct for memorable gestures, stepped outside the hearing room to flashing news cameras and a crowd of forty uniformed airmen who were there to support him. He held up a bicentennial fifty-cent piece. "It says two hundred years of freedom," Matlovich read from the inscription. "Maybe not in my lifetime," he proclaimed, "but we're going to win in the end!"[35]

Attorney Addlestone filed an appeal. It went to the court of Federal Judge Gerhard Gesell, a Lyndon Johnson appointee who in 1969 had made one of the first federal court rulings to uphold a woman's constitutional right to have an abortion. On July 16, 1976, after recognizing all that Matlovich had done for his country, the judge made several astounding pronouncements. It was "impossible to escape the feeling that the time has arrived or may be imminent" when branches of the armed forces would need to reappraise their views of homosexuals in the military service, the judge declared. He pointed out that psychologists, doctors, church leaders, educators were now saying that there's no "standard, stereotypical homosexual." He criticized the air force's "knee-jerk reaction," and recommended that "in the light of increasing public awareness and more open acceptance of what is in many respects essentially a matter of private sexual conduct," the military would do well to have a more discriminating and informed approach in the matter. Strong words. They made his conclusion a non sequitur: the judge upheld the right of the air force to dismiss Sergeant Matlovich because the air force regulation under which he was discharged was "not unconstitutional nor arbitrary and capricious."[36]

At that point, the ACLU officially dropped the case. The US Supreme Court had just upheld the decision of a Virginia court to retain its sodomy law,[37] and the ACLU saw it as a sign that a further appeal of Leonard Matlovich's case would be useless. But Matlovich couldn't walk away from a fight. Frank Kameny assisted him in finding a former Gay Activists Alliance member, E. Carrington Boggan, who'd become a lawyer and had recently helped start the Lambda Legal Defense and Education Fund. Lambda, still financially wobbly, couldn't take on the case, but Matlovich agreed that he'd raise money for out-of-pocket costs, and Boggan would bring his suit to the US Court of Appeals for the District of Columbia.[38]

That court too couldn't fail to be impressed with Matlovich's military record; the judges wanted to know why the air force couldn't somehow fit him into its "exception" for "unusual circumstances." On December 6, 1978, they sent the case back to Judge Gesell to find out why.

But rather than explain why, the air force actually excised the "exception" rule from the Air Force Manual.[39] Disgusted with air force intransigence, the exasperated Judge Gesell ordered Sergeant Leonard Matlovich reinstated immediately.

Rather than take Matlovich back, the air force offered him a settlement. In return for his resignation, they'd give him $62,000 in back pay plus $98,000 in "compensation": $160,000. It was a lot of money—the equivalent of about $600,000 in today's dollars. Not only was so sweet a bundle hard to refuse, Matlovich was afraid that if he accepted reinstatement, the air force would trump up other reasons to get rid of him. He'd be left with nothing. And while a settlement wasn't as dramatic a victory as forcing the military to take an admitted homosexual back into the service, he'd already accomplished a lot. His impeccable record of service had opened a serious dialogue about the ability and the right of gay people to serve in the military. And the air force had been shown up for its mistreatment of a homosexual service member. And all America had learned that gays came in super-patriot flavor, too.

Frank Kameny, never one to compromise, was livid at Matlovich's waf-fling. If Matlovich wouldn't see it through till the end, his case would do nothing to enlighten the military higher-ups. They'd remain "Neander-thals," Kameny admonished. But Matlovich took the money.

MATLOVICH'S MILITARY CHILDREN

Ensign Vernon "Copy" Berg III couldn't take his eyes off the September 8, 1975, cover of *Time* magazine with its picture of a highly decorated air force sergeant behind the bold-lettered declaration, "I Am a Homosexual." It crystalized everything for the sandy-haired, blue-eyed officer. He'd soon be calling himself "the navy's Matlovich."[40]

Berg had graduated from the Annapolis Naval Academy the year before and had joined "the family business." His grandfather, Vernon Berg I, had been a naval officer; his father, Vernon Berg II—of whom he was said to be an exact copy, hence his nickname—was still a commander in the Chaplain Corps. (Vernon II had earned a Bronze Star doing battlefield minister-ing to wounded and dying US Marines during the 1968 Tet offensive.) Twenty-three-year-old Copy Berg made his family proud by graduating from Annapolis and getting picked as assistant chief of staff to a vice admi-ral of the Sixth Fleet in Gaeta, Italy. From the beginning, though, he and the navy weren't a good fit. He'd been a star of the Masqueraders, an An-napolis drama club, and a lead tenor in the Annapolis chorus and glee club, extracurricular activities that had kept him so busy he failed the course in weaponry and had to repeat it.[41] Aboard ship, Copy Berg didn't hide his disdain for the plebeian mentality of navy men and ship life.[42]

But his disdain didn't make it any less traumatic when a superior called him into an office where two men from the Naval Investigative Service awaited him. They told him without preliminaries, "We're here to talk about your homosexuality." The startled Berg, who'd had sex with females all through high school and college and thought of himself as bisexual, cried, "What homosexuality?" "Come on now, Mr. Berg, we're not naïve," one investigator told him and produced a detailed list of supposed male partners: professors at Annapolis, midshipmen, other naval officers. It was a fishing expedition; Berg hadn't been intimate with any of them.[43] But the NIS investigators knew he'd had homosexual affairs because they'd just finished grilling Lawrence Gibson, the man with whom Berg had been in a relationship for the past year.

Berg was scared. He denied ever having sex with anyone who was a member of the armed forces,[44] though he admitted he'd been with Gibson, a civilian who was employed on ship as a teacher of English to the Filipino stewards.[45] The NIS men wanted to know Berg's entire sexual history—or rather, only the homosexual parts—all the way back to his high school years. Head spinning, pulse racing, he told them everything. Then they made him sign a statement of what he'd confessed.

Two weeks later, Berg was notified that the navy was starting discharge proceedings against him. He decided to resign and put an end to his misery. "Finally I will be able to pursue my own interests," he wrote a friend right after handing his superior his resignation.[46] But instead of letting him go, the navy gave Berg a three-week active duty assignment in the Mediterranean. Then they sent him back to the United States, to the Norfolk Naval Base, to await his trial—even though he'd already resigned. Ensign Berg soon realized that the NIS was tailing him and had bugged his phone, looking for evidence they could use to prosecute him criminally. He concluded that the navy was seeking to destroy him.

It was just at that time, his panic at its height, that he saw the picture of Leonard Matlovich on the cover of *Time* magazine. It was an epiphany. He wouldn't let the NIS send him into a tailspin, he told Lawrence Gibson; he'd fight like Matlovich was fighting. Gibson, bald and bearded, fifteen years older than Berg, had made his living as a teacher but fancied himself a writer. He cheered his young lover on: Berg would defend his professional record and right to remain on active duty, and Gibson would write a book about it. They'd tell the world.[47]

Copy Berg set about developing a political rhetoric; he tested it on friends: "My own battle is one for civil rights. No matter what my position, I'm entitled to fair and equal treatment in the eyes of the law," he wrote them.[48] Yes, *I am a homosexual*, he informed his superiors on November 4, 1975, "but I feel strongly that I bring to the Navy talents which are versatile and unique." He had submitted his letter of resignation, he said, "while under duress," and he was hereby withdrawing it.[49] Though he sometimes professed, "I am a homosexual only by the definitions of the US Navy, and I do not rule out the possibility of heterosexual marriage or fathering children in the future,"[50] he also glommed on to the political position that "sexual persuasions are determined hormonally in the prenatal stages of human development" and the navy was openly discriminating "against a minority who have no more choice as to their preferences than they do over their actual sex and skin color."[51]

While Copy Berg awaited his hearing, he and Lawrence Gibson moved to New York, looking for a gay community. Serendipitously, in a Greenwich Village coffee shop, Berg saw a flyer announcing that on Thanksgiving weekend the Gay Academic Union would be holding a third annual conference at Columbia University. Gays and lesbians who'd been discharged from the military would be conducting a panel. Berg showed up, and during the Q&A, he told his own story. Bill Thom—the lawyer who'd formed the Lambda Legal Defense and Education Fund three years earlier—happened to be there, and he came up to Berg as soon as the ensign was finished speaking. Thom handed him a card. "Come see me right away," he said.

Lambda Legal hadn't yet had a big case, the kind that would bring the organization national attention; but Thom had a hunch that Berg's case would do it. Though Lambda's Carrington Boggan had been litigating for Matlovich privately, now the Lambda board agreed that the organization would take on and pay the costs for Boggan's defense of Vernon Copy Berg.

January 19, 1976: Berg's two-week-long naval administrative hearing began on a miserably cold day. The big, fluorescent-lit hearing room on the Norfolk Naval Base was packed with reporters waiting to hear the story of the first commissioned naval officer who not only admitted he was homosexual, but also wanted to stay in the service and would argue that it was unconstitutional for the navy to toss him out. Major TV network crews were there, too, setting up lights and cameras. They'd been warned that once the hearing began, no shooting would be permitted. But the case was big news: at least the cameramen could get footage of Berg and his lawyer standing and talking near the defense table, and the five uniformed members of the hearing board parading in and taking their places on a raised platform that was flanked by an American flag to the right and a navy flag to the left.[52]

The expert witnesses that Carrington Boggan called to take the stand on Berg's behalf told the officers of the administrative hearing board what they didn't want to hear. Vice Admiral William Mack, who'd been superintendent at Annapolis Naval Academy when Berg was a student there, said Ensign Berg had the makings of a fine naval officer—but even more important, the vice admiral shared his view that popular opinion about homosexuality had started to evolve. "The country is changing; the navy is not," he admonished the hearing board. Dr. John Money, who'd been an expert witness for Leonard Matlovich, was called by Carrington Boggan to testify in the Berg case, too. Money said he'd given Ensign Berg a battery of tests and found him to be perfectly well adjusted and suited for a naval career; and then he criticized the navy for its deficit of "broad-mindedness." Berg ought not be "stigmatized because of his avowed sexuality," the doctor told the stony-faced board.

Nor were board members any more responsive to the witness calculated to rouse their emotions, Commander Vernon Berg II. Copy's father took the stand decked out in all his navy regalia (and already showing signs of the cancer he'd gotten from exposure to Agent Orange, the defoliant used to clear the jungles of Vietnam). Copy Berg had had no idea whether his father would even show up, or what he might say. "Get out of the service immediately," he'd advised Copy when he first heard about what had happened.[53] But now he was there to help his son in his "battle for civil rights." He too told the hearing board what it certainly didn't want to hear. Many of the marines he'd ministered to in Vietnam were gay, Commander Berg declared. Some of them gave their lives for their country; and as a chaplain, he'd met homosexuals from admirals on down. Their homosexuality in no way interfered with their service.

One of the five hearing board members, Lieutenant Herbert Artis, a black man, interrupted to say that from his experience, "homosexuals aren't accepted by their comrades. They're outcasts." Commander Berg fought him emotionally: "Once servicemen know a man, live with him, fight with him, watch friends die with him, what do they care about what he does in his bedroom? It becomes unimportant. Like *color*," he pointedly told the lieutenant—who cut him off with a snarl this time: "The regulations say that the secretary of the navy is to dismiss homosexuals. They say, 'Prompt separation is essential.'" And before Berg senior could answer, the board president, Captain Robert Gibson, told him he was excused.[54]

The commander's moving testimony did not move the recalcitrant hearing board. (It did have an effect on his own career that was most unfortunate: because he'd dared say that he knew of homosexual admirals, he was passed over for an expected promotion and virtually drummed out of the military.[55]) Expert witnesses and tearful father be damned, the administrative discharge board, as icy as the weather, recommended that Ensign Berg be given a less-than-honorable discharge, no back pay, and no benefits.[56]

Before his trouble with the navy, the ensign hadn't given a thought to the gay and lesbian struggle for civil rights. But his less-than-honorable discharge, and the example of Leonard Matlovich, turned him into an impassioned activist.

He appealed to a civilian court on the grounds that his constitutional rights of freedom of association, privacy, and due process had been violated. The case landed again in the district court of Judge Gerhard Gesell, who'd judged the Matlovich case. Again Judge Gesell wouldn't grant that constitutional rights had been violated, but he did tell the navy, in terms that echoed Vice Admiral Mack, that it had better update its personnel policy to reflect "changing scientific knowledge and social standards."[57] Berg and his lawyers thought that promising enough to take their case to the federal appeals court, which was even more critical of navy policy. "Broad allegations such as 'Homosexuality is incompatible with military service' or 'a person with homosexual tendencies seriously impairs order, good discipline and morale,' would no longer suffice," Judge Oscar Davis wrote for the three-man court. The navy must clarify its standards.[58]

Stung by the negative PR, navy officials adopted a new regulation, declaring that service members who committed homosexual acts in the past but showed no proclivity to repeat them could be considered for retention.[59] Ensign Berg could easily have gotten his position back if he were willing to say he'd never do it again. He wasn't.

But the judgments of the district court and the federal appeals court seemed to signal the coming of a new day. Navy officials couldn't help but understand that there were loaded cannons aimed at old policies long taken for granted. Rather than try to *prove* that Ensign Berg's homosexuality would seriously impair order, and so on—as the appeals court said it must if it hoped to discharge Berg—the navy offered him a financial settlement.[60] The money enabled him to pay tuition bills for his MA degree from Pratt Institute of the Arts and begin his career as a graphic artist.

Another of Matlovich's offspring who was offered a monetary settlement by the military didn't take the money. And her decade-and-a-half war with the army produced judicial decrees such as Kameny had long sought.

Miriam Ben-Shalom grew up as a tomboy in rural Wisconsin.[61] In 1974 she was twenty-six years old, twice divorced, and the mother of a little girl. She called herself a lesbian feminist, though she didn't share lesbian feminism's view of the military as a stronghold of male-chauvinist piggery; and she joined the US Army Reserve looking for a career. The colorful Ben-Shalom worked at cultivating a salty manner: she joked that in the past she used to say things such as "Up against the wall, redneck asshole," but she'd "mellowed" and was now more apt to say, "Up against the wall, you redneck."[62] She was a plausible choice to be named one of the two first women drill sergeants in the Eighty-Fourth Training Division of the army reserve. She could also bench-press 175 pounds and deadlift 400 pounds,[63] so when she was given an all-male squad to drill, the men didn't spend a lot of time questioning her ability. Her evaluations as a drill sergeant were superlative.

Ben-Shalom was a larger-than-life character, attracted to bold gestures. She'd converted from Roman Catholicism to Judaism, spent several years in Israel and became an Israeli soldier and citizen, and envisioned herself someday joining the US military chaplaincy as a rabbi. When she applied to the army reserve, she was asked the routine question about whether she had "homosexual tendencies." She claimed to have answered, "No, no tendencies. I am one." The recruiting officer ignored Ben-Shalom's quip and signed her up.[64] (America's role in the Vietnam War was over, but there weren't legions of people clamoring to enlist so soon after soldiers had been called "baby killers.") The next year, in September 1975, Ben-Shalom picked up a copy of *Time* magazine and read about Leonard Matlovich. It was then that she resolved she'd soon let the world know there were lesbians in the military, too.[65]

So when a reporter for her division newspaper interviewed Ben-Shalom about her novel position as a woman drill sergeant,[66] she didn't hold back. She was a lesbian, she told him. It was the first volley in her war with the military. Her commander, who, she claimed later, had always known she was a lesbian and didn't think it important before, was furious. "Well, I couldn't lie," she told him.

"You should've said 'No comment'!" he yelled at her, and he started discharge proceedings.[67] For Ben-Shalom, it was the beginning of a drawn-out, tenacious struggle to get back her job and, even more important, convince the world that homosexuality wasn't incompatible with military service.

After she exhausted all possibilities of military appeal, Ben-Shalom took her case to the US District Court. She was lucky in her judge, Terence Evans, who didn't keep it a secret that he'd been raised by a single mother whose humble circumstances[68] were like those of Ben-Shalom, who was raising her young daughter alone. Judge Evans was sympathetic to Miriam Ben-Shalom from the beginning. Yes, she admitted she was a homosexual, he said in his remarkable May 20, 1980, judgment, but the army had no proof of her homosexual *behavior*. The judge proclaimed that his court "will not defer to the army's attempt to control a soldier's sexual preference, absent a showing of actual deviant conduct."[69] But even had the army been able to prove her "deviant conduct"—Judge Evans continued his rebuke in words that showed he'd been listening to what gay activists were saying—that wouldn't have been sufficient grounds to dismiss Ben-Shalom. The army had to change with the times, he lectured. Black soldiers were once segregated because racial tensions were feared; women were once limited in the military roles they could play because sexual tensions were feared. Just as the army had "managed to withstand" the integration of blacks and women, it should be able to withstand the integration of open homosexuals.

But the major declaration in Judge Evans's decision was right out of the Frank Kameny playbook—exactly what Kameny had argued after he was discharged from the Army Map Service in 1957: "The army has not even tried to show a *nexus* between [Ben-Shalom's] sexual preference and [her] military capabilities," Judge Evans scolded. He ordered Miriam Ben-Shalom reinstated "with all duties, responsibilities, and privileges earned by her prior to her discharge."[70]

His order went into one proverbial army ear and out the other. When Ben-Shalom was still not reinstated by 1983, she filed a motion for contempt of court. But in lieu of reinstating her, the army (like the air force in Matlovich's case and the navy in Berg's case) offered Ben-Shalom a bit of money. She refused.

In 1986 she took her case back to district court, and again it was ordered that she be reinstated for the remaining eleven months of her three-year enlistment. The recalcitrant army wouldn't budge. It brought the case to the US Court of Appeals. Again Ben-Shalom was lucky in her judge. Walter Cummings's liberal record was solid throughout his career. He opposed his fellow judges who upheld a Boy Scouts regulation that anyone who didn't swear to carry out his "duty to God" could be excluded from the organization. He ordered steel companies to stop polluting Lake Michigan. And he didn't disappoint in Ben-Shalom's case. "We are baffled by the secretary of the army's confusion over the word *reinstatement*," Judge Cummings declared with irony in August 1987. The army had been ordered to reinstate Miriam Ben-Shalom with all her duties, responsibilities, and privileges, he reminded John Marsh, the army secretary. "The order could hardly be clearer." Judge Cummings also reminded Secretary Marsh that Ben-Shalom "has a First Amendment right to claim she is a lesbian." And he admonished the secretary to make sure "no member of the army retaliates against Ben-Shalom in any way because she was successful in her attempt to gain reinstatement."[71] The next month, Ben-Shalom returned to the army reserve to finish out the eleven months of the three-year hitch she'd begun thirteen years earlier.

That was not the end of it as far as Ben-Shalom was concerned. She still had points to make. When her eleven months were up, she tried to enlist again. The army would not have her. To make sure she'd go away, the army actually changed its regulations, which now excluded not just those who *behaved* homosexually but also anyone who was "an admitted homosexual but as to whom there is no evidence they have engaged in homosexual acts, either before or during military service." That is, *saying* that you were a homosexual was as much a "nonwaivable moral and administrative disqualification" as *behaving* homosexually.[72]

She would not let "those baggy-assed old men in the Pentagon" (as she dubbed the military brass in an interview with a gay paper[73]) get away with it. She took her case again to the US District Court—and for the third time she lucked out in her judge. Myron Gordon, a Lyndon Johnson appointee, had braved angry popular sentiment a few years earlier by dismissing the case of the Milwaukee Fourteen, who'd been accused of treason because they'd broken into a Selective Service office and destroyed draft records. He was clearly not afraid of standing up to the military. This time a judge was actually willing to say that the army's regulation was *unconstitutional*: it violated Miriam Ben-Shalom's Fifth Amendment right to due process and her Fourteenth Amendment right to equal protection. And, just as troubling, it wasn't "rationally related to the advancement of any compelling government interest." Judge Gordon ordered that Ben-Shalom be allowed to reenlist.[74] By 1989, after decades of gay and lesbian activism aimed at expunging old prejudices, attitudes were indeed changing in some areas. The more liberal judges, at least, had been won over.

But the army had not. As far as the military was concerned, homosexuals were still subversive sicko sinners, just as they'd been in the 1950s. They broke the law and would weaken military morale and fighting readiness. Secretary of the Army John Marsh appealed Judge Gordon's order to reenlist Sergeant Ben-Shalom.

This time the army lucked out. The three-judge panel of the US Court of Appeals consisted of two Reagan appointees: one would pave the way for the enactment of an Illinois law mandating that parents of girls seventeen or younger seeking an abortion be notified, while the other jurist's consistently low ratings by the American Bar Association would cause the Bush administration to cease consulting the ABA about federal judgeships.[75] The third judge, Harlington Wood, a Gerald Ford appointee, penned the appeals court's defiantly diehard opinion in the Ben-Shalom case: the military should not be required to "assume the risk" of accepting admitted homosexuals because they "might imperil morale, discipline, and the effectiveness of our fighting forces." The three judges refused to buy the idea that Ben-Shalom's rights of free speech, association, or equal protection were being interfered with by the army. She's "free to say anything she pleases about homosexuality and about the Army's policy toward homosexuality," Judge Wood wrote, wiseacre style; but "what Ben-Shalom cannot do, and remain in the Army, is to declare herself to be a homosexual."[76]

Miriam Ben-Shalom appealed to the US Supreme Court. "I do not believe America will let me down," she told the *New York Times* and all the other media that would listen. "I refuse to give up the privilege to serve my country."[77] SCOTUS refused to hear her case and the court of appeals decision stood. Ben-Shalom couldn't throw the "baggy-assed old men in the Pentagon" up against the wall by reenlisting.

Yet for lesbian and gay service members, the remarkable opinions of the lower courts—that the military had failed to prove a nexus between homosexuality and impaired military performance, and that it had violated homosexuals' constitutional rights—brought a silhouette of the future into eyeshot.

"HIGHEST-RANKING OFFICER EVER TO CHALLENGE THE ARMED FORCES OVER SEXUAL ORIENTATION"[78]

Margarethe Cammermeyer had never heard of Leonard Matlovich. In 1975 and 1976, when the air force sergeant's case was making headlines, she was Mrs. Harvey Hawken, serving in the army reserve and living with her husband and four young sons on a working farm in Maple Valley, twenty miles outside of Seattle. Since the Hawkens didn't have a television or radio, and they didn't subscribe to magazines or newspapers, she hadn't heard that homosexuals were demanding rights, that they were even making demands of the military. She couldn't have guessed she'd someday be at the center of the struggle.[79]

She'd been head nurse at an army neurosurgical intensive care unit in Long Binh, Vietnam, during the sixties and had reenlisted in the army reserve in 1972. Despite her husband's belief that she belonged at home, she performed so well at work that her supervisors couldn't help but notice. In short order, she was promoted to lieutenant colonel, and then made assistant chief of the Fiftieth General Army Reserve Hospital at Fort Lawton in Seattle. But the thirty-seven-year-old Mrs. Hawken found herself in a deep depression. She had to battle a consuming desire to crash her car into a telephone pole.

Six feet tall, square jawed, and with a tousled Amelia Earhart hairdo, the fantasy image she'd always had of herself, formed in her native Norway (she'd come to America as a nine-year-old), was that of a Viking Brunhilde with sword in hand.[80] She needed heroic challenges. Her husband, a state patrolman who at six foot six towered over her, needed her to be cooking and cleaning. Her dreams of someday becoming a colonel and even a general confounded him and made him more and more domineering and explosive.

Instead of ending her life, she started divorce proceedings and took back her own name. The judge, who'd recently lost his two sons in a mountain-climbing accident,[81] felt more sympathy for a father than for the Amazonian female who stood before him with natural stoic-soldier bearing. To Margarethe Cammermeyer's anguish, he awarded custody of her four children to her ex-husband. (The judge did grant her visitation rights, but whenever she came for her sons, Hawken, chronically enraged, hurled at her the two most insulting epithets he could think of: "dyke" and "queer"—though she'd never had a sexual relationship with a woman.)[82]

Cammermeyer tamped down emotions and carried on, becoming chief nurse of an Army Reserve Evacuation Hospital; writing research papers for the journal *Military Medicine*; setting up a major training hospital for field operations; receiving the Veterans Administration's first Nurse of the Year Award in 1985. Two years later she was promoted to colonel, and in 1988 she became chief nurse of the Washington National Guard and was halfway through her PhD program in nursing at the University of Washington. She was too busy for much of a personal life. But when friends introduced her to Diane Divelbess, a lesbian artist and art professor, Cammermeyer was smitten as she'd never been with a man. For the first time, at the age of forty-six, she saw herself as a lesbian.

Romantic bliss with Divelbess didn't obviate professional ambition, of course. The prize on which Colonel Cammermeyer had her eye, and for which she was eminently qualified, was the position of National Chief Nurse of the Army Nurse Corps. To get that job, the colonel needed to attend the War College. That meant she'd have to upgrade her security clearance to "Top Secret." It seemed a mere detail. She put in her application for an upgrade. A Defense Investigative Service special agent, Brent Troutman, called her in a few weeks to say he could schedule the routine interview. "It'll only take about forty-five minutes," he told Colonel Cammermeyer.

Military women who'd long lived as lesbians knew what and how to camouflage; but Margarethe Cammermeyer, a lesbian naïf, didn't quite understand that now there was a part of her life she must hide. Later, she'd vaguely remember that when she went through basic training in 1963, her group was told something about homosexuality being incompatible with military service. But that had had nothing to do with her. If she'd ever had a lesbian thought herself, she'd pushed it aside, until she met Diane Divelbess.[83]

Cammermeyer jotted down the appointment with Special Agent Troutman in her agenda book: April 28, 1989, forty-five minutes, starting at eleven o'clock. Before the interview she could see patients and run her clinic on epilepsy seizure; after, on her lunch hour, she could meet with a real estate agent to sign final papers for the larger house she'd just purchased so her elderly widowed father could join the household.

The tight space, bare walls, and high windows that gave the basement office in the VA hospital the feel of a dungeon—none of it registered with Cammermeyer for the first half hour of her interview. Agent Troutman, a pleasant man in a dark business suit, sat across from her at a long table and asked her routine questions that he read from a list, nodding amiably and checking boxes as she answered. In the same disinterested voice he'd been using, he asked the next question, his pen poised to check the *no* box: "Did you ever engage in homosexual acts?"

She'd had no occasion to track the military's variable policy on homosexuality. When she served in Long Bình during the Vietnam War, she was pretty sure there'd been lesbian nurses in her hospital, and no one had moved to kick them out of the nursing corps. She'd assumed—if she thought of it at all—that what mattered still was the homosexual individual's usefulness to the military. "Yes, I'm a lesbian," she told Agent Troutman with her usual directness. It was a top secret clearance and she didn't want to lie.[84] She didn't know that in 1981—soon after the Pentagon lost its battle with Leonard Matlovich (and with no war going on that made it essential to keep trained service members serving)—the Defense Department had passed a new directive, 1332.14. It called for total exclusion from the armed forces of all homosexuals, no exceptions.

Troutman stopped reading from his list of questions. Cammermeyer's breath caught at the change in his look. It was like somebody had just given him a piece of pie, she thought. "How many women have you had sex with?" he asked. "Who are the other lesbians you know?" Even his voice had changed. He craved details, specifics. His probing went on and on—for the next five hours. "Is this for your own curiosity, your own pleasure?" she wondered. She considered herself "traditionally Norwegian"—talk of sex was repugnant to her. She kept emphasizing to Troutman her *emotional* connection to her partner.[85]

Agent Troutman finally let her leave at five o'clock, after he'd typed up a "Statement of Subject" in which Colonel Cammermeyer "disclosed" her lesbianism; he demanded she sign it. She insisted he include in her "disclosure" the statement "I want the government to see me as a human being, not a woman who has sex with other women." She also handwrote on it: "Lesbianism is an orientation I have, emotional in nature, toward women. It does not imply sexual activity."[86] In retrospect, the colonel couldn't pinpoint the exact moment at which she knew she was in trouble.

For the next months she waited. Nothing happened. She felt like she was sitting on a powder keg and couldn't see whether someone was hovering with an open flame. In October her commander, State Surgeon Colonel George Koss—who'd championed her promotions, encouraged her national-chief-nurse ambition, and knew her to be the best of soldiers—called her into his office and regretfully informed her he'd been ordered by the Department of the Army to start the procedure for discharging her. "Are you sure you didn't make that statement under duress?" he asked hopefully. "Maybe you were just having a bad day?" "No," she answered. "I'm a lesbian." She wouldn't disavow her newfound understanding of who she was.

Dr. Koss delayed his discharge report. He selected her to be the Washington State representative to a National Guard conference in Arkansas. She continued working closely with him on plans for recruiting and training personnel for a new Washington National Guard hospital. But finally, Koss's commander completed the investigation of Cammermeyer and turned in the report. In March 1991 she was informed that the army was withdrawing its "federal recognition," which was tantamount to discharge. It was as though all her years of service, even the Bronze Star she'd gotten for heroism in Vietnam—all of it had been negated. And she'd not only be stripped of her rank: she'd lose her salary, life insurance, medical coverage, everything.

She never doubted what she needed to do. She'd take on the military, the "huge monster" to whom she'd paid loving fealty her whole adult life. It might kill her, she explained to Diane Divelbess, with whom she now lived, but she wouldn't drop her sword.[87]

Lambda Legal Defense and Education Fund happily took Colonel Cammermeyer's case and put together a team of a half dozen attorneys, led by a young military law expert, Mary Newcombe. They demanded an administrative hearing. It was scheduled for July 14, 1991, the thirtieth anniversary—to the day—of when, as a nineteen-year-old, Margarethe Cammermeyer was sworn into the military.

The hearing room at Camp Murray, headquarters for the Washington National Guard, was in a building that looked like a World War II bunker, with dingy walls and scant light. The administrative hearing board of five colonels heard expert witnesses testify that homosexuality wasn't catching; that hundreds of thousands of homosexuals, undetected, had served well in the military. The board received into the record a copy of a letter that the governor of Washington State, Booth Gardner, wrote to Defense Secretary Dick Cheney, protesting "a senseless end to a career by a distinguished longtime member of the armed services."[88] Dr. Koss and others from Cammermeyer's unit testified that her work was exemplary and crucial, and that the unit's morale had been in no way affected by the knowledge that she was a lesbian. Her oldest son, now married, and her daughter-in-law, both Mormons, testified that they knew of her homosexuality and that she was a loved member of their family. Cammermeyer, dressed in her most formal uniform, with all her medals on display, testified that her professional career, her abilities, her contributions "have nothing to do with my sexual orientation."[89]

The five colonels deliberated for only an hour before they called Margarethe Cammermeyer back into the hearing room. It was the job of board president Colonel Patsy Thompson, who'd been chief nurse of the National Guard Bureau, to read the verdict. "I truly believe you are one of the great Americans, Margarethe," Thompson began and talked about her great admiration for all Cammermeyer had done for the Army National Guard, and how proud they were of her and her accomplishments. Thompson then read testimonies that young nurses had submitted to the hearing board—about what a fine role model Cammermeyer had been, and how well she led and inspired others, and how she was "one of the few members of the unit who knew anything about being an officer."

Before Colonel Thompson finally read the board's verdict, she choked up. It was her "sad duty," she said in a quavering voice, to announce that though Cammermeyer had been "a great asset" to the military and to the medical profession, and though she'd "consistently provided superb leadership and has many outstanding accomplishments to her credit," she was an admitted homosexual—and therefore army regulations demanded that the board recommend she be discharged.[90]

Margarethe Cammermeyer had dreamed throughout the two-day hearing, when so much praise was heaped on her, that the board would be swayed to make an exception to military policy. But lawyer Mary Newcombe—who'd studied the administrative board hearings of Matlovich, Berg, Ben-Shalom, Perry Watkins, Dusty Pruitt, Keith Meinhold[91]—never believed the five colonels capable of leaping over hidebound regulations. She didn't wait for the verdict to ready an appeal to the civilian court.

District court judge Thomas Zilly rendered his decision in 1994. He observed what was obvious: all the evidence showed that Colonel Cammermeyer was an outstanding officer and army nurse, and the government policy that mandated her discharge was based "solely on prejudice." There was no rational relationship, no *nexus*, between the military's regulations against homosexuality and a legitimate government purpose. The claim that because of her homosexuality the decorated and dedicated Colonel Cammermeyer somehow interfered with the military's "ability to maintain readiness and combat effectiveness" was clearly preposterous. Moreover, Judge Zilly declared, there wasn't and must never be, a "military exemption" to the Constitution—the military had violated Colonel Cammermeyer's constitutional rights to equal protection and due process. He ordered that she be reinstated to her former position and that the military expunge all record of her sexual orientation.[92]

The Department of Defense did what it had done in all the cases in which district court judges found military policy on homosexuals to be irrational: it appealed. It asked that the district court's decision be struck from the books. But the Ninth District Court of Appeals that heard the case in 1995 refused to do that.[93] Margarethe Cammermeyer, already back at the National Guard hospital, continued to serve until she retired in 1997.

For two decades, since Leonard Matlovich first declared that he was a homosexual and wished to keep serving in the military, civilian courts had been reiterating the same point: Exclusion of homosexuals from the armed forces was based on nothing but prejudice. It had nothing to do with pre-serving fighting readiness or unit cohesion or anything else with which the military needed to be concerned. Stereotypes about homosexuals as secu-rity threats and moral weaklings had lost their currency, the civilian court judges were saying. It was a powerful affirmation of the gay and lesbian movement's tremendous progress in challenging bigotry. The judges were comparing the military's bias against homosexuals to its earlier bias against blacks. In language sometimes respectful and sometimes rebuking, the judges were telling the military it had no right to violate the constitutional rights of American citizens. The country was changing, the judges said, and it was time the military changed along with it.

The man elected president in 1992, in the midst of the Colonel Cam-mermeyer case, believed that the military was finally ready to listen. He was wrong.

Chapter 26

DON'T ASK, DON'T
TELL, DON'T SERVE

"THE MOST PRO-LESBIAN AND
PRO-GAY TICKET IN HISTORY"

May 18, 1992: The event at the Palace, a showy Hollywood venue that jumped with rock concerts on the weekends, took place on a workday evening; but it was as celebratory as the Fourth of July—flashing red, white, and blue neon lights framing the stage and lighting up the six-foot-tall letters of the name CLINTON, "76 Trombones" and "Stars and Stripes Forever" loudly blaring, the throng wildly cheering.[1] David Mixner, who'd been a friend of Bill Clinton since 1969 when Mixner organized the Moratorium to End the War in Vietnam, had been appointed to the National Executive Committee of the Clinton for President Campaign—the first openly gay person ever to serve on such a high-profile committee. It was he who'd invited his old friend and introduced him to the audience of six hundred gays and lesbians who could afford to pay $180 apiece for a ticket to the Clinton-for-president fund-raiser. This was the biggest presidential rally yet in the gay and lesbian community. "It's because of Bill Clinton," Mixner announced with feeling, "that I'm allowing myself to dream again." When Clinton became president, he'd do for gay and lesbian civil rights what Harry Truman, John Kennedy, and

Lyndon Johnson had done for the civil rights of other minorities, David Mixner solemnly promised.

That the governor of Arkansas and candidate for the presidency of the United States had agreed to attend a gay and lesbian fund-raiser was wondrous enough. Just four years earlier, another Democratic candidate for president, Michael Dukakis, had turned down a gay group's offer to raise a cool $1 million for his campaign because the group wanted Dukakis to publicly acknowledge its support.[2] But what Bill Clinton would tell his entranced gay and lesbian audience made this event even more wondrous. It was breathtaking. "I have a vision for the future, and you are a part of it," he said. "You represent a community of our nation's gifted people that we've been willing to squander. But we can't afford to waste the capacities, the contributions, the hearts and souls and minds of the lesbian and gay community."[3] If he were elected president, he vowed, not only would he make war on AIDS with an effort so extensive it would "vie with the Manhattan Project"—big research budget, AIDS education for all of America, appointment of an "AIDS czar" who'd oversee it all—but he'd also make sure that gays and lesbians got federal civil rights protections. And, he swore to the applauding, whistling crowd, he'd end the ban on gays and lesbians serving in the military. Thousands of red, white, and blue balloons descended from the ceiling as people cheered till they were hoarse.[4]

They weren't the first to whom Clinton said he'd end the gay and lesbian ban. In 1991, after Clinton decided to run for the presidency, he'd approached gay congressman Barney Frank for an endorsement. "Okay," Frank said, and then asked Clinton if he'd pledge to let gays and lesbians serve openly. "That sounds like a good idea," Clinton had answered.[5] In October of that year, Clinton spoke at Harvard's Kennedy School of Government, where he promised that if elected he'd eliminate the military's discriminatory policies against gays with a stroke of the pen: he'd sign an executive order, just as Harry Truman did in 1948 when he banned military discrimination against black service members.

The Republicans pounced on Clinton's promise. At the Republican National Convention in August of 1992, Patrick Buchanan, keynote speaker, told the delegates who convened in the Houston Astrodome that homosexuals were touting Clinton and his running mate Al Gore as "the most pro-lesbian and pro-gay ticket in history." Clinton and Gore were creating "a battle for the soul of America," he bemoaned as Republican delegates punctuated his remarks by waving signs proclaiming, "Thank God for AIDS" and "Family Rights Forever / Gay Rights Never." "This is a culture war," Buchanan persisted, "as critical to the kind of nation we will one day be as was the Cold War."[6] He spoke for the entire party, or at least for those who had sway over it. The Republican platform that year opposed all laws that would give gay people any kind of civil rights, including even the right to adopt children.

The lines had been drawn. At the Democratic Convention in Madison Square Garden, Clinton wasn't hesitant to broadcast his support of gays and lesbians, even his intention to end the military ban. He arranged spots on the program for his environmental advisor, Bob Hattoy, an openly gay man with AIDS, and Roberta Achtenberg, cofounder of the National Center for Lesbian Rights and a mover and shaker in Clinton's California campaign. Hattoy and Achtenberg addressed the convention not at five in the morning, as Jim Foster and Madeline Davis had done in 1972, but during prime time. TV cameras panned the sea of rainbow flags and bold-lettered signs demanding "Lesbian and Gay Rights Now!" as Hattoy told America that lesbians and gays were part of the American family, and "Bill Clinton sees the value of each and every member of the American family." Achtenberg told America that the time had come for equal treatment in civilian employment and in the military, also.[7] She'd been on the Democratic Party's platform-drafting committee, too, where she spearheaded the party's adoption of a gay rights plank that included "an end to Defense Department discrimination."[8]

Bill Clinton—no George McGovern, who made secret promises to gays and canceled them in the light of day—openly embraced the plank, including its call for the military to treat gays and lesbians fairly. Clinton had done his research, of course, and it seemed practically certain that the Pentagon itself was or soon would be concluding that the armed services needed to stop discriminating against homosexuals. He'd learned of a 1988 report that had been ordered by the Office of the Secretary of Defense and conducted by a distinguished research psychologist and a military psychiatrist for the Personnel Security Research and Education Center (PERSEREC), an arm of the Pentagon.[9] The report left no doubt about what the military ought to do with regard to gays and lesbians in the armed forces.

The authors of the report reminded the secretary of defense that in recent years the federal courts had been ruling that the military's discrimination against homosexuals was unconstitutional; the justices had been comparing discrimination against gay and lesbian service members to discrimination against black service members before President Truman integrated the military; the justices had also been making the military pay out big money to settle homosexual discrimination suits. Moreover, the writers of the report admonished the secretary of defense, the Civil Service Commission had declared more than fifteen years earlier that no person would be denied federal employment on the basis of sexual orientation; and in 1988 the Veterans Administration had been forced to give full benefits to those who'd been discharged on the grounds of homosexuality. Any discrimination against gays and lesbians that was still going on in the military flouted not only the courts and the Constitution, but the government's policies as well.

The authors also cited earlier studies such as the 1957 Crittenden Report, which concluded that homosexuals were less a security risk than alcoholics, promiscuous heterosexuals, and "people with marked feelings of inferiority who must brag of their knowledge of secret information";[10] they cited the 1971 Colin J. Williams and Martin S. Weinberg study that concluded that having a same-gender or opposite-gender orientation is as unrelated to job performance as is being left-handed or right-handed;[11] and they cited a study that was ordered by PERSEREC and would be published the following year, which found that homosexuals' military "suitability-related adjustment is as good or better than that of the average heterosexual."[12] Finally, the report's authors reminded the secretary of defense, "in the recent past, we've learned how to integrate racial and other minority groups into nearly every aspect of political and social life," and that could and should be done with regard to homosexuals, too. Social attitudes toward homosexuality had been shifting, the authors emphasized. The decades-long struggles of gay and lesbian rights movements had made a dent. "Homosexuals" were no longer the pariahs they once were.

It would be impossible to read this report and not conclude that it was high time the military got with the program and ceased witch hunting and discharging homosexual service members. Bill Clinton certainly came to such a conclusion. And because the report had been ordered by the

Department of Defense, and conducted by one of its arms, he'd assumed that military leaders would be receptive to its recommendations. They weren't.

There's no question that Clinton made his promise to gays and lesbians in good faith. As soon as he took office, he was ready to grab the pen and sign the executive order. At his first press conference, he told the media what he intended to do.[13] But he'd never served (during the Vietnam years, when males his age were being drafted, he received deferment as a Rhodes scholar), and he knew little about military culture. He hadn't imagined the opposition he'd get from the Joint Chiefs of Staff when he told them that recruiters should no longer ask about an applicant's sexual preference, and that discharges of homosexual service members should be suspended.[14] Led by General Colin Powell, the first African American chairman, the Joint Chiefs threatened to resign en masse if Clinton "forced the gay issue" upon them.

General Powell had expressed disapproval of Clinton's plan even before Clinton won the election. Pat Schroeder, a Democratic representative from Colorado, read about the general's opposition in the summer of 1992: "I am sure you are aware that your reasoning would have kept you from the mess hall a few decades ago," she wrote to chastise him. But Powell insisted there was no parallel between homosexuals and blacks: "Skin color is a benign, nonbehavioral characteristic," he'd answered Congresswoman Schroeder; "homosexuality is a *behavioral* issue." *Homosexual* referred not to people but *acts*.[15] The chief of naval operations, the marine corps commandant, and the army chief of staff all agreed with General Powell that those acts couldn't be kept off of military bases if the people who indulged in them were tolerated. They'd be distracting and would destroy fighting readiness; they'd be divisive and would destroy unit cohesion and morale.

The Far Right rallied over the issue, as it had been doing for decades whenever it seemed that gays would be given a civil right. As soon as word got out about the president's intention, the Christian right began orchestrating massive church campaigns to inform him and all of Washington about their displeasure. They flooded congressional offices with tens of thousands of letters pleading that the ban not be lifted lest the nation's fighting forces be destroyed by perverts. Most of the objectors preferred to deliver their message via telephone. During eight days in early February, soon after Clinton announced his intention to keep his promise to lesbians and gays, the Capitol switchboard logged 1,650,143 calls, mostly from people saying that his plan endangered the country.[16] To emphasize their horror at the prospect of open homosexuals in the service, the Family Research Council made sure that every US congressman got a copy of its video *The Gay Agenda*—which included such gems as defrocked psychologist Paul Cameron declaring that 80 percent of homosexual men ingest human feces.[17]

But it wasn't only the Christian right that urged eternal banning of homosexuals from the military. Senate minority leader Bob Dole threatened that if Clinton signed an executive order ending the ban, the Republicans would offer its reinstatement as an amendment to the Family and Medical Leave Act, a high-priority bill for labor and women, two of Clinton's largest constituencies.[18] Maine senator George Mitchell—the Senate majority leader from Clinton's own party—warned the new president that a nonbinding resolution that upheld the homosexual ban would pass the Senate 70 to 30. It would be a huge embarrassment to his new presidency.[19] The head of the Senate Armed Services Committee, Georgia Democrat Sam Nunn, also admonished Bill Clinton about his bad judgment: "To keep homosexuals out of the military is not prejudice—it's *prudence*," Nunn declared.[20]

Clinton's advisors panicked. They'd thought from the start that the issue was dangerous and regretted Clinton's commitment.[21] A high-profile defeat in the early days of his administration would be disastrous, they told him; and this issue was hardly central to his program for the nation. He must slow down, they said. But Clinton publicly restated his determination to end the ban. Before his first week in office was over, he asked his secretary of defense, Les Aspin, to draft the executive order. His worried secretary pleaded with him not to be precipitous. The executive order could be postponed for six months. Aspin would hold extensive consultations with all branches of the services; then he'd draft an order incorporating their requirements. Clinton gave Secretary Aspin permission to consult with the chiefs.

Secretary Aspin had become a US representative from Wisconsin in 1971; from 1985 until he accepted the position as Clinton's secretary of defense, he'd served as chair of the House Committee on Armed Services. For eight years, he'd worked closely with the Joint Chiefs of Staff, so he could guess their response to Clinton's extraordinary notion. He held the meeting with the chiefs in "the tank," a soundproof chamber on the second floor of the Pentagon. It was good that the chamber was soundproof because the two-hour meeting was stormy. (Maybe not coincidentally, Aspin was hospitalized soon after with a cardiac problem.) There was no way the Joint Chiefs of Staff would agree to support a change in the section of the Uniform Code of Military Justice that made sodomy a crime, they told the secretary.[22] Clinton, they believed, was an elitist civilian official, totally out of touch with the realities of military life.[23]

"AN HONORABLE COMPROMISE"

Finally, the chiefs, the secretary, and the president did agree they'd listen to the hearings that the Senate Armed Services Committee would hold on the advisability of letting homosexuals serve.[24] March 23, 1993, six days before the Senate hearings were scheduled to begin, Clinton and his advisors had a bright idea. There could be certain restrictions on homosexual service members. They wouldn't be allowed to go to combat; they'd be restricted from some other jobs, too. They could serve in separate units (pre-1948 all over again), even have separate barracks.[25]

As can be easily imagined, that proposal was as infuriating to all sides as it deserved to be. Those opposed to homosexuals in the military complained that such a scheme condoned sodomy by allowing homosexuals to serve; and just as bad, homosexuals would be taking noncombatant jobs away from heterosexuals, thus giving heterosexuals a bigger chance of ending up in risky combat. Gay groups objected that banning lesbians and gays from combat and other important military jobs would doom them to an unequal career path. Tom Stoddard, a Manhattan lawyer and cocoordinator of the newly formed Campaign for Military Service, funded by gay Hollywood mogul David Geffen, complained, "This is no compromise. This is capitulation to the other side!"[26] The segregation plan was scuttled.

Congressman Barney Frank came up with a more plausible proposal— "on base, off base," he called it. "On base, while you're on duty, you don't talk about your homosexuality and you don't let it show. Off base, you live your life," he proposed to General Powell.

"I could accept that," Powell said, "but I wouldn't want to be the only member of the Joint Chiefs in favor of it." Powell took the idea to the other chiefs, who couldn't be budged.[27] The Senate Armed Services Committee hearings were held as scheduled.

They began on March 29, 1993. Those who liked the ban stole the show. The media made a minorities war out of the testimonies of service members they identified as being from groups that had been discriminated against in the past, quoting them as avowing the importance of keeping discrimination in place—against homosexuals. A black sailor said he "resented equating homosexuality with civil rights"; a Hispanic sailor said he'd "mutiny if the ban were lifted"; a female naval instructor said "there are lots of reasons to keep people out of the service, including flat feet."[28] The hearings also featured testimonies such as that of retired army lieutenant general C. A. H. Waller, who'd been deputy commander of the US Forces in the Persian Gulf War. Waller told the committee that "allowing homosexuals to serve in the military would make America's armed services second rate." Why? Because "openly avowed homosexuals want to foist their lifestyles upon soldiers, sailors, airmen, and marines."[29] Herbert Hart, spokesman for the Reserve Officers Association, declared that his organization wanted it known that "the mission of the military isn't social experimentation. It's to go to war and fight and die if necessary. If you have an individual who has a different type of lifestyle like this, it's going to affect cohesion of that unit."[30]

Representatives from various gay organizations (and Margarethe Cammermeyer, the only lesbian invited to testify about her experiences) argued that homosexual service members are military people first; they're in the military to do their jobs, not to force their sexuality on their straight comrades. Their testimony made no dent. It was clear where Senator Nunn stood halfway through the hearings when he pointed out that if someone admitted to being homosexual, he or she was "stating a basic tendency, at least, to breach the sodomy statute,"[31] which the Supreme Court had upheld seven years earlier in *Bowers v. Hardwick*. Nunn was making sure everyone understood that the president was asking the military to let criminals serve.

As though more were needed, the leading American military sociologist, Charles Moskos, a professor at Northwestern, came up with facts and figures about why homosexuals should be banned from the service. Moskos testified that he and his PhD student Laura Miller had surveyed 946 military men and women: 78 percent of the men and 47 percent of the women opposed ending the ban; 90 percent of the men would feel uncomfortable sharing a room with a gay; 45 percent of noncommissioned officers said they'd leave the service if the ban were lifted.[32]

A few years earlier, Senator Nunn had worked with Professor Moskos to draw up a "Citizenship and National Service Act."[33] The legislation would have mandated that no one could receive a federal grant or loan for education before serving the country either in the military or through some sort of "national service" job, such as street cleaner, hospital orderly, policeman, or tutor. (Wags compared it to the *Hitler Jugend*, in which male adolescents were forced into service for the Fatherland.) The proposal couldn't pass Congress in the stringent form that Dr. Moskos designed, but he and Nunn remained friends. The barrel-chested, plainspoken Moskos—he called himself "a short, fat, bald Greek"—had made his name by interviewing soldiers in the field in Vietnam and writing articles about how racial integration had benefited the army. Never one to modulate his pronouncements, Moskos often gave out such wild generalizations as "In the volunteer army, you're recruiting the best of the blacks and the worst of the whites."[34] Nunn had hired his professor friend to get "empirical data" on the matter of homosexuals in the military; hence Moskos's survey. Now Moskos offered to use his expertise as a military sociologist to write a proposal about homosexuality and military service that military leaders could live with.

The fervent champion of a racially integrated army was no champion of integration when it came to gays and lesbians. It would be hard for "morale" if homosexuals served openly, Moskos believed. "Heterosexual soldiers have a right not to be inescapably confronted with intimate gay behavior," the professor reported to Sam Nunn. "To me, the issue comes down to privacy. Prudes have rights too," Moskos quipped to newspaper reporters with his usual flippant good humor.[35] Nevertheless, he opined, all young people were obliged to serve their country, and gays and lesbians were no exception. They ought to serve, but they must keep who they are a secret; and they must never be caught doing, or even hoping to do, what makes them homosexual. He dubbed the policy he proposed "Don't Ask, Don't Tell, Don't Seek, Don't Flaunt." "Sure, it's a bit of hypocrisy," Moskos admitted to the media. "But hypocrisy is necessary now and then in a civil society."[36]

President Clinton—having suffered the disaster of the Senate Armed Services Committee hearings, and being worn out by the struggle over gays that kept him from turning his attention to the mounting budget deficit and the growing welfare rolls—wanted the astounding flap to be over, even at the cost of making a compromise with bigotry. He accepted Moskos's proposed policy. The Pentagon in turn accepted a change in the Uniform Code of Military Justice. Service members with a homosexual identity wouldn't be kicked out—as long as they didn't talk about it or get caught acting (or seeking to act) on it, on or off base.

The Don't Ask, Don't Tell policy went into effect on July 19, 1993. Clinton declared it to be "an honorable compromise." The consummate politician, he touted his failed effort as though it were a triumph, announcing, "This is an end to witch hunts that spend millions of taxpayer dollars to ferret out individuals who have served their country well." That particular sop was for gays and lesbians and their supporters. Speaking about the new policy to high-ranking officers at the National Defense University in DC, he adopted the military leaders' usual rhetoric about the dangers of open homosexuality, which he said Don't Ask, Don't Tell would prevent. "We must and will protect unit cohesion and troop morale," President Clinton emphasized.[37]

Fourteen months earlier, David Mixner had listened, with happy tears in his eyes, as the presidential candidate told the gays and lesbians gathered at the Hollywood Palace, "I have a vision for the future, and you're a part of it." Now, soon after Don't Ask, Don't Tell became official policy, Mixner and about twenty other people who'd been at the Clinton fund-raiser chained themselves to the White House fence in protest. They were carted off to jail by the DC Park Police.[38]

DON'T ASK, DON'T TELL IN ACTION

Don't Ask, Don't Tell might have seemed a polite and innocuous accommodation to both sides: gay and lesbian service members would be discreet, and the military would be restrained and not inquire into private lives. But in practice, it didn't work that way. The mere existence of the policy was repugnant to all gays and lesbians, in the military or out of it. It confirmed the stigma against which the movement had been fighting for decades. It made explicit that homosexuality, to the military at least, was still so disgraceful that it remained, despite all the hard-won advances, "the love that dared not speak its name."

In the beginning of the Don't Ask, Don't Tell years, the military made an effort to show that the policy worked. Bridget Wilson, a lesbian lawyer and a vice president of Dignity, a national Catholic LGBT organization, migrated from Omaha to San Diego in the early seventies; and in that navy town, she found herself with a large clientele of gay and lesbian sailors. They were being discharged, often en masse, and wanted a civilian lawyer to help them in their battle. She was soon specializing in military law. Before Don't Ask, Don't Tell, Wilson did a lot of "witch-hunt fighting" against the Naval Investigative Service. When Don't Ask, Don't Tell was first adopted, it seemed to Wilson, for a little while, that the military really might become more reasonable.

In early 1994, a few months after the policy went into effect, a navy officer came to Bridget Wilson asking for help. A classic "manly man," he was a Naval Academy graduate and had served for more than ten years without arousing a single suspicion that he was gay. He was perfectly willing to honor the new policy, too. So when he was told by a San Diego hospice doctor that his partner, who had AIDS-related pneumonia, "won't get through the weekend," he went to the ship's captain to request a two-day leave. "My aunt is dying," he said, because he wasn't supposed to "tell."

"We don't give time off for aunts," the captain informed him. That was when the distraught officer said, "You don't have to give me a leave, but I'm going. I have no choice." And he "told."

He was soon called up before the Navy Board of Inquiry, which voted to discharge him under the Don't Ask, Don't Tell policy. Bridget Wilson pleaded his case in a military appeals court. Though DADT had been in effect for only a little over six months, lawyers arguing for gay and lesbian service members had already been saying that it was unconstitutional because there was no way to fight a discharge under it, regardless of the circumstances. Anxious to show that DADT was a reasonable policy and could work, the navy appeals court rescinded the officer's discharge.[39]

But as Wilson learned, military anxiety soon diminished. The "tell" part of Don't Ask, Don't Tell came to mean "anyone, anywhere, anytime," regardless of circumstances. Later in 1994 Bridget Wilson took the case of a woman sailor who'd left her military husband for another woman. The husband had shown up at the other woman's house with a gun, screaming he'd kill them both; the woman sailor called the police and pressed charges. Before the case came to trial, the man informed her superiors that she was living as a lesbian. Two NIS men were sent to sit at the back of the gallery during the man's trial and take notes—not about his waving a gun at the two women and threatening a double murder, but about his ex-wife admitting on the stand that she was in a relationship with another woman. She'd "told." That was enough to get her thrown out of the navy; no recourse.[40]

Most gays and lesbians in the military were able to serve without incident under Don't Ask, Don't Tell. They didn't get caught. They weren't booted out. They didn't endure disgrace. But they suffered anyway. The policy was a Sword of Damocles, hanging always over their heads. They didn't have to "tell" to make the sword come crashing down. They could be exposed in all sorts of ways that would be considered tantamount to telling.

Lieutenant Commander Judy "J. P." Persall had been a boat engineer and an engineering instructor in the Coast Guard. She'd earned ribbons in all the colors of the rainbow and a chestful of silver and brass medals (commendation, achievement, meritorious service). She took her work so seriously that her fellow officers used to say she was "married to the Coast Guard." She wasn't, but she couldn't tell them to whom she really was "married"—another woman, also in the Coast Guard. Though Persall was pretty sure to make commander, she retired before that happened because she feared they'd be found out, even though they did everything they could to prevent it.

To her and her younger partner, Coast Guard chief of waterways management Diana Wickman, the things they had to do not to "tell" kept chipping away, every single day, at the essence of who they were. They felt the grief of it strongly when Wickman was in a car wreck, a head-on collision at forty-five miles an hour. Sitting in the middle of the street in her banged-up automobile, with a banged-up and bloody head, she fought to keep consciousness. She managed to call Persall on her cell phone. Then, good soldier that she always was, she realized she had to report the accident to her commanding officer. She called him next.

In her mixed-up state, Wickman had forgotten to do what she'd always done—take care that no one could possibly see that she and Persall were a couple. In the past, she'd managed not to "tell" by keeping Persall away from unit parties, being careful about whom they invited to their home, making sure that in restaurants she never said anything like, "Hey, honey, what are you getting?"—because you never knew who was at the next table. But now Wickman saw her partner approaching from one direction and her commanding officer approaching from the other. She panicked. "Don't hug me, don't show too much worry," she tried to mentally telegraph Persall, even as blood dripped down from her head and she felt she might faint. Persall, still running toward the car, slowed down because she got the telegraph. She couldn't comfort Wickman or show too much concern. "I'm her roommate," she told Wickman's commanding officer, trying to sound uninvolved, like someone who shared the rent and nothing more. "You okay?" she asked Wickman without touching her, thinking, "That's the rule of the game. Step back. Don't give him any idea that I love her."

"Yeah, you can go now. Thanks for coming," Wickman said, though she was suffering neck pain and bleeding badly and wanted Persall to hold her and take her to the hospital. But she was terrified that if the commanding officer saw them together too long, he'd guess. She had to send her partner away—get her out of the scene immediately, and she did.

Diana Wickman remained in the Coast Guard until 2009, but she, too, retired early, before she was eligible for her full pension—because, like J. P. Persall, she feared constantly that she'd be kicked out of the military that she loved ("my military family," she called her unit), and she'd lose the pension she'd already earned and all the benefits she'd worked for during her twenty-two-year career. All it would take was one misstep.[41]

•　　•　　•

In fact, it didn't even take a "misstep" to lose everything. Under Don't Ask, Don't Tell, caution and discretion guaranteed nothing. You didn't have to "tell" by word or deed to get in trouble. Someone else might tell for you. And that could end your career, regardless of how many medals or years of exemplary service you'd racked up. Women service members seem to have been particularly vulnerable. They made up only 14 percent of the army, but they accounted for 46 percent of its discharges under the Don't Ask, Don't Tell policy. They made up only 20 percent of the air force, but they accounted for 49 percent of its DADT discharges.[42]

Margaret Witt joined the air force at the rank of second lieutenant in 1987, after graduating from college with a nursing degree. She was deployed to Iraq as a flight nurse on cargo aircraft that had been converted into flying "intensive care units" in which to medevac the wounded. She became a legend in her unit for having saved the life of an airman who'd been given up for dead. Witt's comrades and subordinates loved her because she was gregarious and funny and, as they'd later testify, the calmness of her look under pressure and her knack for making them all feel important to the team were inspiring.[43] In 1999 she was promoted to major. In 2004, her eighteenth year of service, she was in the Air Force Reserve, and because she'd been highly decorated and had always received outstanding performance reviews, she expected that a promotion to lieutenant colonel was imminent. She was stationed at Joint Base Lewis-McChord outside of Tacoma, Washington, working as the chief of standards and evaluations, when one July day her commanding officer, Colonel Mary Walker, showed up at her office door and said, "Come with me." There was "some kind of investigation going on, about something on base," the colonel told Witt. "They just want to ask you a few questions."[44]

Witt assumed the questions had to do with standards or evaluations; she followed her commander down the hall and into a conference room. There she was introduced to a lone man, a Major Adam Torem, who was sitting at a table. "Nice to meet you," Witt said. "What's your relationship with Tiffany Jensen?" Major Torem answered.

Margaret Witt had done everything during her time in the air force never to be asked such a question. She'd lived discreetly with Tiffany Jensen, 250 miles away from the base where she did her Reserve duties. They'd been together for six years; but when Jensen said she wanted to have a baby and wanted Witt to legally adopt the child, Witt knew she couldn't do it. She couldn't put her name on adoption papers because that would be "telling." She and Jensen broke up over it. A year or so later, Witt began a relationship with a woman who'd been married, Laurie Johnson McChesney. Laurie's estranged husband, Pat McChesney, stalked the two women, stole Margaret Witt's address book, and called everyone in it—her priest, her favorite high school teacher, her parents—to complain that she'd stolen his wife. The one person he called who said she'd testify against Witt was Tiffany Jensen.

Pat McChesney sent Witt's superiors an email accusing her of being a lesbian and messing with his wife. He followed it up by sending them a copy of the Ten Commandments. Witt's superiors discounted his complaint as coming from a kook. But when Tiffany Jensen called to inform them of Witt's lesbianism, they listened.

That November, Colonel Walker showed up again at Witt's office door, this time to say, "Margie, this is the hardest thing I've ever had to do. I have to ask you to pack your things and leave the base. You can no longer serve." Witt wasn't formally discharged yet, but she was suspended with no pay. It wasn't until March 2006 that she was finally informed that the air force was starting discharge proceedings against her.

Witt had heard of Colonel Margarethe Cammermeyer. (Probably most gay and lesbian service members had heard of the colonel's victory over the Department of Defense.) Cammermeyer, too, lived in Washington State. She'd been Witt's hero, though Witt had never imagined she'd be in a situation like Cammermeyer's. Now she called the colonel and told her her story: how she'd had a long and perfect service record, how she'd followed the rules and kept her personal life hidden, how she wanted to stop the military from doing to other gays and lesbians what they were doing to her.

"This is what you're going to do," Cammermeyer told her. "Drive to my house, Major. Your mission has changed. You're going to make a difference." She put Witt in touch with an army of lawyers looking for a case just like hers that would help give DADT its coup de grace.[45] In April, they filed suit in a federal district court, saying that Don't Ask, Don't Tell violated Margaret Witt's constitutional rights to equal protection and due process.

But in judicial deference to the military, the district court judge,

Ronald Leighton, a George W. Bush appointee, declared that "the prohibition against homosexual conduct is a longstanding element of military law that continues to be necessary in the unique circumstances of military service." He dismissed Margaret Witt's suit.[46] She appealed.

In 2003, after hearing *Lawrence v. Texas*, the US Supreme Court had reversed itself on the subject of sodomy. The justices threw out the 1986 *Bowers v. Hardwick* decision that said states had a right to make sodomy illegal, and they declared that sodomy laws violated a citizen's constitutional right to privacy. Now, in 2008, a three-judge appeals court that heard Witt's case ruled that under *Lawrence*, Don't Ask, Don't Tell intruded on the personal and private lives of homosexuals—and if the military wanted to intrude, at the least it had to show there was a reason for it. "What's the *nexus*?" the appeals court judges asked—just as judges had been asking since the mid-1960s.

The Washington State Appeals Court tossed Margaret Witt's case back to Judge Leighton. Conduct a trial, the appeals court judges ordered—and let the air force try to prove that Major Witt was bad for military morale.[47]

The trial in Judge Leighton's Tacoma courtroom lasted six days and was packed every day with Major Witt's military friends, including Margarethe Cammermeyer. "When Major Witt left, it was like losing a member of our family," one airman testified. "It was a dishonorable act on the part of the air force to discharge her. It should not be about what you are, but who you are," a master sergeant said. "It was her being fired that actually hurt morale in our unit," another airman said. "We were at war when she was discharged. It was the loss of an able flight nurse," a lieutenant colonel complained.[48] Several said they'd always suspected that Margaret Witt might be a lesbian but it never made a bit of difference. And, some added, they'd known or suspected other members of their unit were also lesbian or gay—it had no effect whatsoever on unit morale and cohesion.[49]

The best the government lawyers could offer to counter the walk-on-water testimony for Margaret Witt was that she might be deployed someplace where "primitive facilities and forced intimacy would be the norm"—and what then? they wanted to know. There was no question about which side was more persuasive.

Judge Leighton did an about-face on his 2006 judgment. "Good flight nurses are hard to find," he said. The evidence produced at the trial not only showed that her discharge didn't advance the military's purpose; her leaving "resulted in a *diminution* of her unit's ability to carry out its mission." The judge went even further in repudiating DADT by offering an eloquent defense of all the gays and lesbians that the witnesses had said were in the unit: "These people train together, fly together, care for patients together, deploy together," Leighton emotionally declared. "There is nothing in the record before this court suggesting that sexual orientation has negatively impacted their performance, dedication or enthusiasm. There is no evidence that wounded troops care about the sexual orientation of the flight nurse or medical technicians tending to their wounds." President George W. Bush's appointee ordered that Major Witt be restored to her position as a flight nurse as soon as possible.[50]

It's ironic that Don't Ask, Don't Tell had its genesis in Bill Clinton's good intentions to get rid of military witch hunts and to include gays and lesbians in his vision of a just America. Under the policy that he accepted as a compromise to his initial brave impulse, well over 14,000 service members were discharged—most of them not because they "told" but because the military found out, in one way or another. Taxpayers spent more than $1.3 billion for investigations to help the military find out and to justify the discharges.[51] Despite the gains the gay and lesbian movement had made in shifting public opinion, even into the twenty-first century, military leaders, hardly the most progressive thinkers, continued to regard gays and lesbians as disruptive to their mission, just as their predecessors had in the 1950s when, without a shred of evidence, they accused homosexuals of being a threat to the nation's security. The discharges peaked in 2001, when 1,273 service members were booted out that year through the policy.[52] The shibboleth was "unit cohesion threat" instead of "security threat"—but Don't Ask, Don't Tell was applied as viciously as the old regulations had been.

However, not even the military could hold out indefinitely against court decisions and the social change effected by years of gay and lesbian activism. The Gallup News Service announced in spring 2007 that its latest poll had found that "tolerance for gay rights" was "at a high-water mark."[53] That same year, twenty-eight retired generals and admirals signed a letter urging Congress to repeal Don't Ask, Don't Tell. There were over a million gay and lesbian veterans, the generals and admirals pointed out; 65,000 gays and lesbians were presently serving honorably; and the "current genera-tion" of young people entering the military were much more accepting of gays and lesbians than earlier generations had been.[54] The next year, 104 re-tired admirals and generals came forward to say the same thing.[55] (Perhaps not so coincidentally, the military was being stretched thin by continued deployments in the Middle East and, as General John Shalikashvili, who'd been a chair of the Joint Chiefs of Staff pointed out, "We must welcome the service of any American who is willing and able to do the job."[56]) The year after that, in 2009—after a *Washington Post* poll announced that 75 percent of those polled agreed that gay people should be allowed to serve openly[57]—Colin Powell, who'd headed the Joint Chiefs of Staff when DADT was adopted, declared to the media, "Sixteen years have now gone by, and I think a lot has changed with respect to attitudes within our coun-try." It was time to reconsider the old policy, General Powell said.[58]

Chapter 27

"GET 'DON'T ASK,
DON'T TELL' DONE!"

JUSTICE AT TORTOISE SPEED

As a senator from Illinois, Barack Obama abhorred Don't Ask, Don't Tell. Gays and lesbians had a *right* to serve their country, he resolutely declared in 2007. Just as black people had been integrated into the military, gays and lesbians should be, too, he said.[1] He won gay and lesbian hearts, this young, eloquent, forthright champion of justice, who belonged to a persecuted minority and was in tune with other persecuted minorities.

As a candidate for the 2008 Democratic presidential nomination, Obama was more slippery. His major rival, Hillary Clinton, had opened herself from the start to the LGBT media, giving interviews to LGBT newspapers, appearing on the LGBT television channel Logo, telling the community in person how strong a champion for their rights she'd be. The Obama campaign placed ads in LGBT papers, but Obama wouldn't talk to anyone from the gay media.[2] Finally, two weeks before the April 27 Pennsylvania primary, he did a careful interview for the *Advocate* with a carefully vetted interviewer: female, young, no radical baggage.

Obama's answers to Kerry Eleveld's Don't Ask, Don't Tell questions were oddly cautious, as though he were speaking not to gays and lesbians who comprised the *Advocate*'s readership, but to spies peering over their shoulder. He'd never make the repeal of Don't Ask, Don't Tell "a litmus test for the Joint Chiefs of Staff," he firmly told Eleveld, almost scolding in his tone. There were "so many issues that a member of the Joint Chiefs has to deal with, and my paramount obligation would be to get the best possible people to keep America safe." He did grant that it was counterproductive for the military to be spending large sums of money to kick out highly qualified personnel. But he immediately followed that point by going back to his first: "What I'd want are members of the Joint Chiefs of Staff who are making decisions based on what strengthens our military and what is going to make us safe, not *ideology*."[3]

After such disappointing wariness, it was pleasantly surprising for gays and lesbians that during Obama's first week as president, he called a meeting with Secretary of Defense Robert Gates and chairman of the Joint Chiefs of Staff, Admiral Michael Mullen, both Republican appointees, and told them, as he later recalled, "I think Don't Ask, Don't Tell is wrong. So I want you guys to understand that I want to work with the Pentagon, I want to figure out how to do this right, but I intend to repeal this policy."[4] The secretary of defense was taken aback. Like Bill Clinton, Obama had never even served in the armed forces; and yet he, too, was jumping headlong into a military issue even before all his suits were hanging up in the presidential suite closet. Gates would later claim resentfully, "The only military matter, apart from leaks, about which I ever sensed deep passion on [Obama's] part was 'Don't Ask, Don't Tell'."[5]

Despite Obama's putative passion, as Kerry Eleveld observed in August 2009, seven months had already passed in his presidency, and nothing was happening. The issue of repeal, she complained, "seemed to get dropped like a hot potato."[6]

It wasn't precisely that Obama had dropped the issue; but he'd been unready, just as Clinton had been, for the blowback. He slowed to a crawl on repeal. Lesbian and gay leaders, frustrated yet again by a president whom they'd supported with gusto, tried to prod him. The times had changed, they insisted.[7] In 1993, when Clinton backpedaled, only 40 percent of Americans had said *yes* to the question, "Should gay men and lesbians be allowed to serve openly in the military?" It might be understandable that Clinton retreated in the 1990s, but in the next decade and a half, mainstream gay and lesbian groups—the Human Rights Campaign, the

National Gay and Lesbian Task Force, Lambda Legal, the Servicemembers Legal Defense Network—had grown huge membership lists and could boast impressive financial resources. Thanks to their incessant work, the shift in public opinion was more and more dazzling. A spring 2009 Gallup poll showed that 69 percent of Americans were now saying *yes* to the question of whether gay men and lesbians should be allowed to serve openly in the military.[8] And the Democrats had big majorities in Congress, too. Obama had no reason not to go forward. The circumstances couldn't be better. He needed to act now, LGBT leaders said.

But a memo from Admiral Mullen's legal advisor said the opposite: "Now is not the time to lift the ban," the memo warned. America was in the midst of two wars. It was crucial not to do anything that might interfere with winning in Iraq and Afghanistan—and there was no way of predicting what would happen if homosexuals who weren't willing to keep quiet about their sexuality were suddenly allowed to serve.[9] An "open letter" to President Obama from the Center for Military Readiness, a far-right organization that claimed to represent over a thousand retired military officers, said the same thing, replete with old chestnuts about how open homosexuality would damage military morale, unit cohesion, and readiness. The thousand-plus retired officers even warned that the presence of homosexuals would destroy the All-Volunteer Force because "it would have adverse effects on the willingness of parents who lend their sons and daughters to military service."[10] Secretary Gates also chimed in to remind Obama that it was Congress that had passed Don't Ask, Don't Tell. If the policy were to be gotten rid of, it shouldn't be by presidential executive order. It should be Congress that repealed it. In April, Gates proposed that he appoint a task force to study what the best way might be to implement a change, and what impact could be expected as a result of the change.[11]

President Obama feared repeating President Clinton's early misstep; and he was stretched thin managing two wars and a financial crisis; and he wanted to follow through on his biggest ambition, to reform America's health care system. He agreed to Gates's proposal.

Gates was in no rush. He made an informal study first. He sat with ten junior enlisted soldiers over lunch and queried them about Don't Ask, Don't Tell. They told him, "If gays are allowed to serve, there'll be violence." They asked him whether combat arms units, at least, could be exempted from having gay soldiers foisted upon them.[12] Soon after doing his "study," Gates, speaking for himself and the president, opined on television in comically mixed metaphors: "The president and I feel like we've got a lot on our plates right now, and let's push that one down the road a little bit."[13] During that first year of the Obama administration, 169 more women and 259 more men were discharged under Don't Ask, Don't Tell[14]—including fifty-nine Arabic linguists whose services were desperately needed while the United States was advising and training Iraqi security forces in preparation for the American pull-out.

Members of Congress who thought such a senseless discharge policy needed to be stopped had a tough battle ahead. In June 2008 the only out-lesbian congresswoman, Tammy Baldwin, proposed to Barney Frank that they start an LGBT Equality Caucus, which would include any Congress member who supported full equality for LGBT citizens. It would facilitate "counting the votes" to see how much support could be relied on if Don't Ask, Don't Tell were brought to the House floor. It would be a whip operation, too: members would work to get votes from those in their circle of influence. About 100 of the 435 members of Congress joined the Equality Caucus.[15]

In June 2009 Patrick Murphy, congressman from Philadelphia, went around the House of Representatives gathering signatures for the bill he'd sponsored to get rid of Don't Ask, Don't Tell. The pro-repeal contingent in the House couldn't have had a better standard-bearer. He'd been a paratrooper in Bosnia and Baghdad and had received a Bronze Star for bravery. He was the first Iraqi War vet elected to Congress. He wasn't a liberal—Blue Dog Democrats claimed him as one of their own when he was elected in 2006—but on the repeal of Don't Ask, Don't Tell, Murphy was passionate. "Why is a straight, Irish Catholic, former altar boy of the year in 1987 at St. Anthony's fighting for this?" he asked jocularly. "It's because I took an oath as a congressman to support the Constitution and what the Constitution stands for—and that's equality," he answered solemnly.[16] He persuaded 170 of his fellow representatives to sign on as cosponsors of a repeal bill.

But that was no guarantee of success, and there were early signs that the battle would be a long one. Murphy, who was a member of the House

Armed Services Committee, tried to get the committee's chairman, Ike Skelton, to hold hearings on repeal. Skelton was a socially conservative Democrat from Missouri: pro-gun, antiabortion, and as rabidly antigay as his fellow Missourians had been in the days of Professor E. K. Johnston. He'd been in the House since the 1970s and had helped craft Don't Ask, Don't Tell in the 1990s. He declared flatly, "I am personally not for changing the law."[17] Why? He feared that having a national debate on the issue would dump the subject of homosexuality onto America's breakfast tables. "What do mommies and daddies say to their seven-year-old child?" he asked in all seriousness.[18]

But opposition wasn't only from the boors, as Florida congressman Alcee Hastings found out when he tried to nudge the repeal issue. Hastings, an African American, had been elected to the House of Representatives in 1992, part of the first significant wave of black politicians to be sent to Congress since Reconstruction. He was committed to fighting not only for the rights of African Americans but for the rights of sexual minorities as well. In May 2009, he and seventy-six other Democratic members of Congress, many of them from the Congressional Black Caucus, sent Obama a letter asking him to "take leadership on the issue of Don't Ask, Don't Tell right away." No answer.[19] When the president didn't respond, Hastings proposed a simple amendment to the Defense Appropriations Bill on the House floor: the military may not spend money to investigate gay and lesbian personnel or to discharge them. He was forced to withdraw it the next day under pressure from the White House.[20]

There's no doubt that Barack Obama genuinely wanted a military that was open to anyone willing and able to serve; yet he feared weakening his presidency. His frustration was palpable. In October 2009 he accepted an invitation to speak at a dinner for three thousand members of the one-and-a-half-million-member-strong Human Rights Campaign, the gay civil rights advocacy organization that had grown out of Steve Endean's tiny Gay Rights National Lobby. The president of the Human Rights Campaign, Joe Solmonese, introduced the president of the United States by saying, "We have never had a stronger ally in the White House. Never." But Obama knew, and his audience knew, that thus far his track record did not bear that out.

In his speech, stirring as always, Obama said all the things about repeal that he'd always believed, such as, "We should not be punishing patriotic Americans who have stepped forward to serve the country. We should be celebrating their willingness to show such courage." He acknowledged sadly, "It's no secret that our progress may be taking longer than we like," but he pledged yet again, "I will end Don't Ask, Don't Tell!" He got a standing ovation—but many among his three thousand listeners had reached the breaking point in their patience. "It was a brilliant speech," Cleve Jones, the Harvey Milk assistant who'd created the AIDS quilt, observed with cynicism, "but it lacked the answer to our most pressing question, which is *when*?"[21]

January 27, 2010, President Obama's first State of the Union address: In front of all America, he repeated the promise, "This year, I will work with Congress and the military to finally repeal the law that denies gay Americans the right to serve the country they love because of who they are. It's the right thing to do!"

Secretary of Defense Gates later claimed that he was "blindsided" by the announcement,[22] though it had been a solid year since Obama's first week in office, when he'd told Gates and Admiral Mullen emphatically, "I intend to repeal this policy." But Gates offered again, as he had during Obama's first year, to direct the Department of Defense to do a study of all the issues associated with repeal. It would be thorough, a "top-to-bottom review," done by a Comprehensive Review Working Group. Of course, it would take until the end of the year to complete such a wide-ranging inquiry. Again President Obama agreed.

Even before the Comprehensive Review Working Group could start its work, the opposition to it was fierce. In February, the Senate Armed Services Committee listened to the testimony of officers such as four-star Marine Corps general James Conway, who told the senators that the important question wasn't whether a policy was "fair to homosexuals," but whether it would "enhance the war-fighting capabilities" of the military. Never mind waiting for a Pentagon survey; Conway had done his own, he claimed—and that survey indicated it wasn't age or rank dependent, and it didn't matter where a service member was from, all of them were against repeal. "My best military advice to this committee, to the secretary of defense, to the president, would be to keep the law as it is," General Conway declared.[23]

Democrats in Congress who wanted repeal guessed they didn't have a lot of time. They couldn't count on keeping their comfortable majority much longer because the party in power usually loses seats at midterm elections, which were coming up in November 2010. House Speaker Nancy Pelosi, who'd been gay friendly since her early days in Democratic politics in San Francisco, made a proposal for an immediate measure. While the Department of Defense was conducting its extensive review, the president could at least place a moratorium on dismissing gay and lesbian service members.

Bad idea, Secretary Gates said. Nothing at all should be done until the study was completed.[24]

Heated hearings began in May 2010. "The military is not a social experiment," a Republican representative from Texas harangued. "We should at least wait to hear from the military before taking action. If we don't we're saying, 'We're shoving this down your throat. We don't care!'"[25]

"Twenty-six countries already allow homosexuals to serve openly," Barney Frank fairly growled at congressmen. "Those who tell me that the presence of gay and lesbian members in the military undermine the effectiveness of a fighting force and undermine unit cohesion have never heard of Israel!"[26] Arguments like Frank's seemed to prevail on May 27, 2010, when the House voted 234 to 194 to pass the Murphy amendment. But the vote didn't mean that gays and lesbians could start serving openly. No changes were to take effect until the Pentagon completed its study.[27]

In the meantime, Obama's Justice Department kept filing briefs defending the constitutionality of Don't Ask, Don't Tell.[28] Even in September, four months after the House vote—nineteen months after President Obama told the chairman of the Joint Chiefs of Staff and the secretary of defense that he wanted to lift the ban—Obama's Justice Department was still defending Don't Ask, Don't Tell in court, appealing the decision of a federal judge in California who ruled that Don't Ask, Don't Tell encroached on service members' right to free speech, and that the government had failed to come up with any evidence that the law was necessary to protect governmental interest.[29]

What was going on that the Justice Department was fighting in favor of Don't Ask, Don't Tell? the confused media wanted to know. Hadn't the president said he thought it was a bad policy? Hadn't the House voted to get rid of it? Why was the Justice Department acting as though the administration favored the policy? Furious gays and lesbians and their supporters protested that the president of the United States could have—should have—told the Justice Department not to appeal.[30] Presidential press secretary Robert Gibbs found himself in the awkward position of having to defend his boss's defending a law he'd said made no sense.[31]

One of the highest-ranking service members ever to suffer under DADT was Lieutenant Colonel Victor Fehrenbach, who'd served in the air force for nineteen years, flying eighty-eight combat missions over Iraq, Afghanistan, and Kosovo. He'd often been handpicked for missions that required the sort of exceptional abilities that he had in abundance—his hit rate was 98.4 percent.

The macho-looking Fehrenbach claimed that everyone on base knew he was gay; he'd had "absolutely zero negative reactions" from his comrades. But because Don't Ask, Don't Tell was still policy when Fehrenbach's homosexuality came to the attention of the commander of the Idaho Mountain Home Air Force Base, where he'd last been stationed, a military board recommended discharge.[32]

While Fehrenbach fought his discharge, formidable enemies fought to keep service members like him out of the military.[33] One of the most formidable, Senator John McCain, had been an aviator, just as Fehrenbach had. He'd been shot down on a 1967 bombing mission in Vietnam, had suffered almost six years of imprisonment and torture in Hanoi, and had turned down early release, proclaiming that he wouldn't leave until all the men who'd been captured before him were permitted to leave.[34] His military heroism gave him tremendous authority on the Senate Armed Services Committee—and he believed homosexuals would ruin the military. The Pentagon was doing the wrong sort of study, John McCain complained to his committee. The question shouldn't be how repeal could be implemented; it should be how repeal would affect battle readiness and morale. The present study ought to be scratched. The Pentagon ought to start again. Anyway, regardless of what the Pentagon report might say, there needed to be a lot more congressional hearings, McCain insisted.[35]

"A COWARD, A BIGOT, AND A PATHOLOGICAL LIAR"

In April 2010, as President Obama was about to make his final defense budget recommendations to the House and Senate Armed Services Committees, Aubrey Sarvis, head of the Servicemembers Legal Defense Network, wrote to him. Sarvis, representing the organization that had been formed by gay lawyers soon after DADT became law, reminded Obama of his promise in his State of the Union address three months earlier: "I will work with Congress and the military to finally repeal the law that denies gay Americans the right to serve the country they love because of who they are," the president had righteously declaimed. Now Sarvis pleaded with him to "reaffirm your strong commitment to repeal" before signing off on the defense budget; at the least, say something about cutting out of the budget the funds used to investigate people's private lives in order to axe them.[36]

The commander in chief never deigned to respond. "There was no 'profile in courage' at the White House," Sarvis said, sarcasm uncontained.[37] Rumors were also flying that Obama's congressional liaison team was urging Democrats in Congress to block a vote on repeal because it was a midterm election year.[38]

By now, a total of 14,346 service members had been discharged since the start of Don't Ask, Don't Tell.[39] If Obama was really sincere about getting rid of the policy, why didn't he just issue an executive order? Even if he had to wait on implementing the "how-to" of repeal until the Pentagon submitted its study, why didn't he at least put a halt to the discharges? "He's a coward, a bigot, and a pathological liar," former army captain and JAG lawyer James Pietrangelo complained to the press. Pietrangelo had been in both the first and second Iraq Wars. He was booted out of the army just before his third tour of duty because he admitted he was gay. He'd tried to take his case to the Supreme Court, but the move was blocked by Obama's solicitor general, Elena Kagan (future Supreme Court justice). As solicitor general, Kagan's role was to represent the federal government's position before the Supreme Court. She argued that the ban on gays in the military was indeed "rationally related to the government's interest in military discipline and cohesion."[40]

Captain Pietrangelo was furious. He was ready for some old-fashioned gay militant action, as were other discharged service members, such as Dan Choi, a first lieutenant who'd served as an infantry officer at the height of the Iraqi surge. Choi, son of a Korean-immigrant Southern Baptist minister, had been a founding member of Knights Out, a group of gay West Point alums formed to protest the Don't Ask, Don't Tell policy. In March 2009 he was invited to be interviewed about Knights Out on the *Rachel Maddow Show*. In his television interview, he "told." Choi's skills as an Arabic linguist had been vital to the military, but he was discharged anyway. The army sent him a letter giving him a choice. He could take an honorable discharge and walk away with full benefits such as medical care and pension, or he could fight his discharge and maybe end up with nothing.

For him, it was a no-brainer. He'd fight.[41]

PUTTING A FACE ON IT

Since 1993, the Servicemembers Legal Defense Network had offered legal aid to gays and lesbians kicked out of the military under Don't Ask, Don't Tell. It had also been a watchdog, tracking the discharges and issuing annual reports that were wryly titled (like Randy Shilts's famous 1993 book about gays in the military) *Conduct Unbecoming*. The reports showed that under Don't Ask, Don't Tell, investigations of lesbian and gay service members were "as bad, if not worse" than before. Persecution too had gotten worse, because the policy had "stirred up a hornets' nest" of homophobia, which culminated in the brutal 1999 murder at Fort Campbell of Army PFC Barry Winchell, bludgeoned with a baseball bat by another soldier who learned that Winchell was dating a transgender showgirl.

Dr. Alan Steinman had known about the Servicemembers Legal Defense Network for a long time, but it took a few years after he left the service before he dared send a fax to SLDN's Washington, DC, office: "I am a retired gay admiral, living near Seattle. How can I help?" Dixon Osburn (cofounder of the group and Aubrey Sarvis's predecessor as executive director) faxed back immediately, imploring Dr. Steinman to come to SLDN headquarters.[42]

Rear Admiral Steinman had been in the Coast Guard since 1972, when he was commissioned by the Public Health Service as a lieutenant. For a while, he'd been a flight surgeon, tending to air crewmen; he'd sometimes had to stop one of his patients who seemed on the verge of coming out to him, because it would have been Steinman's duty to report him as a homosexual. All through his twenty-five years of service, Steinman knew he himself was gay, but he told no one, not even his family. "There's really nothing to tell," he always thought, because for all twenty-five years he was celibate, afraid to be caught and thrown out of the job to which he'd dedicated his life. Steinman was promoted to admiral in June 1993, shortly before Don't Ask, Don't Tell went into effect; he became the Coast Guard's surgeon general. But his wonderful promotion exacerbated his fears and complicated his life. He was obliged to attend formal functions to which admirals always took their ladies.[43]

By the 1990s, the fib of the "beard" had stopped being necessary for gay men and lesbians unless, of course, they were in the military. The admiral had to find a female "beard"—just like gays in the 1950s and 1960s did when they were obliged to pass for straight; he also had to figure out how to do it safely. The *Washingtonian*, a sophisticated upscale magazine, had an "In Search of . . ." section. He placed an ad: "Gay male executive seeks female companion to assist with social obligations," it read. In about a week, he got a beautifully written letter from a woman who said she'd been married to a bisexual man whose gay friends had become like family to them; she'd volunteered at AIDS clinics, too, and she would be delighted to assist with the "executive's" social obligations.

When they met, at the Ritz Carlton in Pentagon City, Steinman could see that Mireille Key would be perfect: intelligent, well dressed, presentable looking. They hit it off immediately and would become great friends. Key had been a costume designer and loved high theater, which is what she and the admiral would play in lavish settings such as military balls, where they'd make an entrance and be introduced in extravagant 1930s-Hollywood style: "The admiral Alan Steinman and his lady, Mireille Key," the spotlight shining on them as they descended the circular staircase, the admiral in his uniform, his lady in her elegant evening gown, the Drum and Bugle Corps and the commandant's own band playing in the background. That, in lieu of a home life and the comfort of intimacy with a loving partner, was how top-ranked gay officers survived in the military under Don't Ask, Don't Tell.

December 2003, the tenth anniversary of the issuance of the

Department of Defense Directive 1304.26, Don't Ask, Don't Tell: The Servicemembers Legal Defense Network orchestrated a grand coming out for Admiral Steinman together with Virgil Richard and Keith Kerr, two brigadier generals who'd retired from the army. The *New York Times* opened its pages to the three most senior military officers ever willing to slip off their heterosexual masquerade masks. They'd been forced to lie to their friends, family, and colleagues, to "evade and deceive others about a natural part of [our] identity," in order to serve their country, the admiral and two generals said.[44] But Americans needed to know the people that the policy threatened and often destroyed. Now the admiral and generals would "put a face on it."

Americans needed to know not just about the highly decorated officers but also about the youngsters who'd joined the military with sincere love of country. Admiral Steinman also became advisor to the Call to Duty Tour, which brought together young gay and lesbian vets and sent them out, especially to the red states, to tell their stories about how they'd served with devotion and faultless records and had been discharged only because they were gay, or had left before being kicked out because the stresses and strains of hiding were intolerable.

By design—to "destroy the stereotypes that were driving a lot of the antipathy"—the Call to Duty vets were mostly strapping, straight-arrow-looking young men. (Call to Duty was criticized by some in the gay community for not selecting a more representative spectrum of gays and lesbians.) The admiral felt assured they were making dents in places like Knoxville, Tennessee, where he watched as a man in a uniform walked in and sat down in the back of the auditorium while the Call to Duty speakers told their stories. During the Q&A, somebody asked the usual "showers" question. The man in the back raised his hand and introduced himself as an active duty Special Forces soldier in his eighteenth year of service. Early in his military career he'd had a gay roommate, "a damn fine soldier," he grunted, "but still I didn't agree with his lifestyle." But, he said, he'd just listened to the five young vets tell their stories about being good members of the military family and being cast out by DADT, and he was deeply moved. He pointed to each of the speakers on the dais, saying, "I'd be *honored, honored, honored, honored, honored*, to serve with any of you guys."[45]

Call to Duty soon had emulators, such as the Human Rights Campaign's Voices of Honor, which featured Eric Alva, a feisty five-foot-one marine. Alva, a third-generation military man from a Latino family, had a compelling story. He'd joined the marines in 1990, served in Somalia and Japan, and was promoted to staff sergeant—but he left the service in 2003, when his right leg was blown off in Iraq. Alva had been in charge of an eleven-man logistical unit. One morning at the start of the war, his convoy departed Kuwait and drove to Basra on what had been called, during the first Iraq War in the 1990s, the "Highway of Death." The convoy reached its destination, and Staff Sergeant Alva got out of his Humvee, ready to take charge, when he stepped on a landmine buried in the sand. He had the sad distinction of being the first American casualty of Operation Iraqi Freedom.

As Alva lay recovering in a Bethesda military hospital, George and Laura Bush, Dick Cheney, and Donald Rumsfeld all paid their respects, with shoals of photographers in tow. President Bush pinned a Purple Heart on him. Staff Sergeant Alva liked to tell his Voices of Honor audiences that each time he was praised for his courage by these VIPS who had pictures taken of themselves beaming down on him in his hospital bed, he remembered how scared he'd been all through his years in the service that his superiors would find out he was gay and he'd be kicked out.[46]

But, stirring as such stories may have been, the polite panels that groups such as the Human Rights Campaign sent out on the road didn't convey the raw rage of discharged gays like James Pietrangelo or Dan Choi, who disdained well-funded, well-mannered gay organizations; they labeled them with the sneering moniker "Gay, Inc." Radicals would have heartily approved their angry rhetoric (even while finding their goals to get back in the military execrable). "Jesus up on the cross did not have a party with all his major donors and raise money for his cause," Choi mocked HRC. "Gandhi did not need three-course dinners and a cocktail party to get his message out."[47]

The organization that Choi and Pietrangelo wanted was started in early 2010. Robin McGehee, an effervescent young lesbian, was a Mississippi transplant to Central California and an unlikely radical activist. McGehee had been PTA president at her five-year-old son Sebastian's Catholic elementary school in Fresno. She'd never hidden the fact at the school that she was a lesbian and had married her partner in June 2008 as soon as it became legal, and that both of them were "Mom" to her two children. It seemed no one at the school cared, and she didn't make an issue of it when she led the PTA. She'd raised more money for St. Helen's than had any PTA president before her: silent auctions, walkathons, cheerleading for school spirit. But the parish priest in charge of St. Helen's, Father Salvador Gonzales, asked her to resign four days after the November 2008 election. She'd given an interview to the local paper about a candlelight vigil she organized against Proposition 8—the proposition that reversed the six-month-old California Supreme Court ruling that had allowed her and her partner and eighteen thousand other same-sex couples to marry. The Catholic Church had been a major supporter of Prop 8.

That same Election Day the proposition was passed, McGehee had lifted Sebastian up in the polling booth and had him pull the lever for Obama. "This man will protect our family," she told him with unquestioning faith in the candidate's goodwill. But in quick succession, California voters denied gay people the right to marry and she got "fired" from the PTA. It was clear, McGehee thought, that "trying to change hearts and minds"—the "we've-got-to-get-America-to-like-us-more" approach of groups such as the Human Rights Campaign and the Servicemembers Legal Defense Network, and her own approach, too—hadn't made an impression on the American psyche. What the movement really needed was the loud confrontational tactics of the Gay Activists Alliance, ACT UP, all the other angry gay groups that had popped up through the years and then receded, muffled by "Gay, Inc." "Gays and lesbians have lobbied for years and years," McGehee complained to her wife and everyone else who'd listen; "We've manned thousands of phone banks. We've walked the precincts for politicians who've promised to support us and didn't. Now it's time to rumble!"[48]

The following year, McGehee threw her considerable energy into co-directing a grassroots National Equality March on Washington, where she was "discovered" by the gay heir to the Progressive Insurance fortune, Jonathan Lewis. He'd been a major donor to the Human Rights Campaign, but he was disillusioned. "I've fallen in love with your call for aggressive action. I'm tired of us playing nice. I want trash cans turned over, cars on fire," he told McGehee. He'd give her and a young gay male activist, Kip Williams,

$440,000 in seed money to start a gloves-off organization that would fight the foes with "the biggest actions that your group can pull off."[49] Violence wasn't what McGehee had in mind, but civil disobedience was. She and Williams accepted Lewis's offer and founded Get Equal. They put out a call to gays and lesbians everywhere: "Are you willing to take arrestable action?" Dan Choi and James Pietrangelo were among her first recruits. She explained to them that her group was funded by "a billionaire who wants to die equal."[50]

Get Equal's first action, on March 18, 2010—planned out by Choi like he would plan a military mission in the army[51]—was a Don't Ask, Don't Tell protest. McGehee alerted the news media; then she, Choi, and Pietrangelo went down to Pennsylvania Avenue. "Will you do the honors?" Choi asked McGehee. "Yes, I'd be honored," she replied, and as cameramen clicked away, McGehee chained the two discharged servicemen to the White House fence.

"I shouldn't have to be doing this. I should be at home with my kids, watching them grow up!" McGehee shouted to the press. She was a Middle America PTA mom, she informed the media. (That would be her persona throughout her activism.) She was different from other PTA moms only because her spouse was a woman, and she was engaging in dramatic civil disobedience only because the government hadn't listened to less histrionic pleas to honor families like hers. Twenty Secret Service agents quickly descended with guns pointed.[52] The police had to use bolt cutters to remove the handcuffs from the fence. McGehee, Choi, and Pietrangelo were arrested by the US Park Police. McGehee spent six hours in jail and was fined $35 for disturbing the peace. Choi and Pietrangelo both refused to pay the $100 fines levied on them. They were brought to court in leg shackles and cuffs. When the judge asked, "How do you plead?" Dan Choi shouted so the press and everyone in earshot might hear, "Not guilty, not ashamed, and not finished!"[53]

As soon as McGehee was released, she got on a plane back to California and her family. But she was in DC again in April and in May to repeat the chained-to-the-White-House-fence zap. She did it again in November, joined this time by a slew of ex-service members who did the chaining honors for one another. Miriam Ben-Shalom, the drill sergeant who fought the army and won in the 1980s, was among them. Sixty-two years old by now, dressed in army fatigues and combat boots, Ben-Shalom announced to the media before she and the other protestors were unfastened from the fence and dragged off to jail that, though seventeen years had passed, she was still forced to protest the "injustice and hypocrisy of a failed law."[54] Dan Choi, also in military fatigues, shouted at the TV cameras, "We have served our country valiantly to defend our freedom and justice, and now it is time for our leaders to do the same." He called the president a "silent homophobe."[55]

Such anxieties about whether Don't Ask, Don't Tell would get repealed reinvigorated the old internecine wars in the gay and lesbian movement. "Queers" (the true spiritual descendants of the radicals of the seventies) couldn't understand why any gay person would give a damn about being discharged from the military, or why he or she would sign up in the first place. Queers were disgusted at the distance the movement had traveled from the "culture of resistance" that had started everything. It had been freaks, outsiders, troublemakers, queers said, that had kick-started the movement as far back as 1950, when Communist Harry Hay dreamed up the radical Mattachine; it had been freaks, outsiders, and troublemakers who'd triggered the Stonewall riots. "Genderqueer" activist Mattilda Bernstein Sycamore had been an ACT UP-er; she'd founded the in-your-face Fed UP Queers (FUQ). Now, she complained on behalf of a collective that dubbed itself "Against Equality," the movement's freaks, outsiders, and troublemakers had been replaced by "white gays in white T-shirts," applying for Community Spirit credit cards and fighting to be included in "the most blatant institution of U.S. imperialism."[56]

Queers derided gay service members who were in a tizzy not about "the atrocities of war and killing innocent civilians" but about whether they could list their boyfriend as next of kin should they get killed fighting an imperialist war.[57] Queers despised both the mainstream groups such as Servicemembers Legal Defense Network and the militant groups that filched the protest techniques of the radicals.

Under McGehee's direction, Get Equal dogged congressional leaders. Dan Choi, a media darling because of his striking story—a gay Asian American Arab-linguist West Point grad—starred in many of Get Equal's zaps, wearing his army uniform and all his medals. Three months before the 2010 midterm elections, Harry Reid, Senate majority head and the senator from Nevada, was the invited speaker at an annual convention of Netroots Nation—thousands of liberal bloggers and activists who'd be convening at the Rio Hotel and Casino in Las Vegas. In a dramatic gesture calculated to win headlines, Choi, who'd just gotten his official discharge letter from the army, wrote an angry note to Senator Reid which he gave to the event moderator, along with his West Point ring. He asked her to hand the ring to Senator Reid during the Q&A and read out Choi's message: "This ring means nothing to me if you don't repeal 'Don't Ask, Don't Tell.'" An embarrassed Reid (his majority party had still made next to no progress on the issue) tried to return the ring. "You earned it!" he called out to Choi. But many in the audience were yelling, "Keep it till Don't Ask, Don't Tell is repealed!" "Repeal Don't Ask, Don't Tell!"

A poll of Nevada voters taken the month before had shown that Tea Party star Sharron Angle had a very worrisome lead over Harry Reid, 50 percent to 39 percent.[58] He'd come to Netroots Nation hoping to spur liberals and progressives to get themselves to the voting booths in November and help him beat her. The senator knew what he must do next. He invited Dan Choi up to the stage, where he gave the ex-lieutenant a warm public hug. "I'll get this ring back to you soon," the head of the Senate solemnly promised Choi in front of the audience that had already shouted out where its sympathies lay.[59]

"THIS IS DONE!"

Meanwhile, the Comprehensive Review Working Group's study that Secretary of Defense Robert Gates had ordered was under way. Surveys were sent to 400,000 active duty and reserve troops. Separate surveys were sent to 150,000 military spouses (asking, for instance, about their level of comfort with openly gay people being around their kids in military-base housing). Military personnel were encouraged to send anonymous comments to an online drop box. Focus groups were formed and their responses were recorded. Results were tabulated and analyzed. More than 70 percent of respondents said the effect of repealing Don't Ask, Don't Tell would be "positive, mixed, or nonexistent." They knew there were already regulations in place that said anyone who disrupted the military mission by any sort of inappropriate sexual behavior would be in trouble, and they didn't have a lot of anxiety that gays and lesbians would disrupt the mission of the armed forces by making passes at them. Most troops said they were already serving with someone they believed to be gay or lesbian, and 92 percent said the effect on unit cohesion was very good, good, or neutral. The Comprehensive Review Working Group reported that their study also affirmed that any objections to openly gay colleagues "would drop once troops were able to live and serve alongside them." Even though America was still at war, the group concluded, there'd be few problems if the ban were lifted now.[60]

The report of the study was scheduled to be in the president's hands on December 1. But it was leaked to the press three weeks early. A *New York Times* headline announced on November 11, "Pentagon Group Finds There Is Minimal Risk in Lifting Gay Ban During War."[61]

General James Amos, the Marine Corps commandant, didn't believe it. He continued to argue—as he had at the Joint Chiefs of Staff meetings back in 2009, when Obama first raised the issue—that it was "risky" to let homosexuals serve openly. "There is nothing more intimate than young men and young women (when you talk of infantry we're talking about young men) lying out, sleeping alongside one another, and sharing death, fear, and loss of brothers," he declaimed emotionally; and he reiterated that, study or no study, nobody could be sure "what the effect will be on cohesion and combat readiness" if gays were part of that "sleeping alongside one another."[62]

Senator John McCain wasn't convinced by the study's findings either. First of all, it was the wrong study, he complained again. The questions shouldn't have been about how the armed forces can implement a repeal of the law but whether the law should be repealed at all. And anyway, only about a quarter of the four hundred thousand servicemen responded to the study group's questionnaires. The others didn't respond because they believed repeal was a done deal, it was being foisted on them, and no matter how much they complained it wouldn't matter. But they'll let their feelings be known with their feet, McCain warned his fellow senators: "Most military personnel will change their career plans if the policy is changed." He wanted to start the discussion all over again. He wanted a referendum. The boys in the service should be allowed to vote on whether to repeal Don't Ask, Don't Tell, he insisted.[63]

In May, the House had passed an amendment to the Defense budget that would repeal Don't Ask, Don't Tell contingent on the Pentagon's report; on December 15, the representatives voted again, this time on the Don't Ask, Don't Tell Repeal Act, a stand-alone bill. After the ayes and nays were tallied by the clerk, Speaker Nancy Pelosi called Barney Frank up to the Speaker's chair, gave him her gavel, and asked him to announce the vote.[64] It was a fitting gesture for the gay congressman who'd tried to prevent Clinton's disastrous "honorable compromise" eighteen years earlier. Barney Frank called out in his gravelly voice, "250 to 175," and on the Speaker's podium, he gavelled DADT to perdition—in the House.

In the Senate, the fate of Don't Ask, Don't Tell wasn't so clear, despite repeal's stalwart supporters. Senator Joe Lieberman had once been a top Democrat, even selected by Al Gore to be his presidential running mate in the 2000 election. Lieberman had left the party six years later, after losing a primary race to an antiwar candidate. To win his reelection bid, he became an independent. His liberal political credentials were not reliable. He also practiced Orthodox Judaism, which, like most religious orthodoxy, wasn't very sympathetic to gay and lesbian issues. But, in fact, Joe Lieberman was the Senate's most zealous standard-bearer for the right of gays and lesbians to serve openly in the military. He'd sponsored the Senate's repeal bill and had fought vigorously for its passage.

But at the December 9 Senate session, chances for repeal were looking poor. Republican foes had imposed on Lieberman's bill so many procedural hurdles that the New York Times declared it to be at death's door. Senator Susan Collins of Maine, the only Republican who'd seemed to favor an end to Don't Ask, Don't Tell, told the Times reporter, "I'm sad to say, the chances are very slim for getting it through."[65] The vote in the Senate was scheduled for December 18, 2010.

J. P. Persall and Diana Wickman were watching in their living room as the Senate proceedings were broadcast on C-Span. Persall and Wickman were the two Coast Guard women who'd feared to hug after Wickman's bloody car accident because her superior was on the scene. Now, before J. P. Persall and Diana Wickman tuned in to C-Span, they hung an American flag to one side of their TV set and a Coast Guard flag to the other. The two retired officers still had their Coast Guard caps from their service days. They held them on their laps as they watched. Soon after the roll call vote began, it was pretty clear how it would go. Persall and Wickman put the caps on their heads and stood up, at attention. Senate leader Harry Reid announced that the vote was 65 to 31 in favor of repealing Don't Ask, Don't Tell. Eight Republicans had joined the Democrats. In their private little ceremony, the two women brushed away tears in between saluting the flags. As Wickman would recall, each of them had given twenty-some years in service to their country, and now "it finally felt like our country was validating us, like we were part of America. It was healing."[66]

At the signing ceremony for repeal of Don't Ask, Don't Tell, the president told a story about his visit a few weeks earlier to troops stationed in Afghanistan. He was "working the rope line," shaking hands with soldiers who'd lined up to greet him. A uniformed young woman in the line shook his hand, and then she hugged him. "Get 'Don't Ask, Don't Tell' done," she whispered into his ear. President Obama told her, "I promise you, I will."

After his speech at the December 22 ceremony, he sat at a table onstage and—encircled by Patrick Murphy, Harry Reid, Nancy Pelosi, Joe Lieberman, Eric Alva (the gay marine who'd been the first American casualty in Iraq), and a half dozen others who'd pushed for an end to Don't Ask, Don't Tell—he bent his head and signed the bill that repealed the policy. Then he looked up and grinned. "This is done!" he said.[67]

Needless to say, not everyone in the LGBT movement was thrilled. The dustup over the right to serve in the military was the culmination of the sixty-year battle between the radicals and those they called the "assimilationists."

New York public advocate and civil libertarian William Dobbs, a distinguished-looking, stentorian-voiced gay man, bore an uncanny physical resemblance to Admiral Michael Mullen, even to the round, wire-rimmed glasses they both wore. Dobbs's appearance seriously belied his impassioned radicalism. Wrongheaded ambitions, he thought, have distracted the LGBT movement from momentous aims such as those dreamed by the Gay Liberation Front decades earlier—bringing economic justice to the

indigent, social justice to minorities whether straight or gay, sexual liberation to everyone. He'd been an antiwar crusader (both Vietnam and Iraq), a
gay liberationist, an ACT UP-er. Those were his kind of movements: calling the government out for its wrongdoings, demanding the right to be
free, battling dramatically for underdogs' lives. He believed that the LGBT
movement had gotten hijacked by assimilationists who shifted its resources
and energies to all things conventional—such as the right to marry, which
"feeds into the drive for a homogeneous, orthodox American culture";
and even worse, the "equal right" to serve in the armed forces, to wear a
uniform and march in lockstep and salute some clowns who outrank you.
What could be more inimical to "liberation"?[68]

Dobbs was especially disgusted by the tactics of DADT repeal groups
that "trundled around the country gay veterans who'd been in Iraq, pulling
them out as 'patriots,' never looking at the bigger issues connected with
the military"—for instance, its role in defending the failures of US foreign
policy. He believed that gays and lesbians' desire for "equality" ("a low
and paltry ambition compared to *liberation*, which is as big as space") had
blinded them to the lunacy of militarism.

But Dobbs's radical rhetoric was gibberish to gays and lesbians who'd
been in the armed forces and had wanted to serve, and now finally felt, as
Diana Wickman said, "like we were part of America."

July 22, 2012, San Diego—the navy town where, fifty-five years earlier,
retired Rear Admiral Selden Hooper had been called back to active duty
only to be court-martialed and stripped of his rank and his pension because of his homosexuality; the navy town where, eighteen years earlier,
lawyer Bridget Wilson had defended a naval officer who was being discharged because he'd "told" when he asked for a two-day leave to be with
his partner who was dying of AIDS. It's the day of the Gay Pride Parade.
The lineup begins as usual: a contingent of Dykes on Bikes motorcyclists,
the LGBT American Indian Nations of the Four Directions, the parade's
board of directors. And then a sight never before seen.

Marine sergeant Bris Holland, back from two tours of duty in Iraq, is
dressed in her marine blue-white dress uniform, carrying the American
flag, looking very solemn, as though fully aware of the dignity of her role
and the long history that preceded it. She's followed by lesbian and gay

service members from the army, navy, air force, marines, and coast guard. Many are in full-dress uniform, though it's a sweltering Southern California day; others wear fatigues or T-shirts that identify their branch of service. Two elderly retired colonels—Vietnam vets, one army and one marines— are wearing all their medals. There's also a forty-six-year-old commander who'll retire in a few months after twenty-six years in the navy. An army truck—displaying a Servicemembers Legal Defense Network "Freedom To Serve" banner and flying a dozen rainbow flags—moves slowly alongside the marchers.

A crowd of over two hundred thousand onlookers line the streets for blocks and blocks and cheer them on. Those in the throng not busy taking pictures are waving little American flags. Bris Holland's seven-year-old son is holding her partner's hand; when his mother marches by he, too, waves a little flag. A middle-aged woman who's wearing a rainbow-colored lei around her neck holds up a sign that says, "My Gay Son Is A Naval Officer." She's saluted by the young military people as they pass.[69]

PART 9

LGBT AMERICAN CITIZENS

Chapter 28

HOW LESBIANS AND GAYS STOPPED BEING SEX CRIMINALS

LOOKING FOR "THE PERFECT CASE"

Frank Kameny, still one of the movement's brainiest strategists in the early 1970s, knew that until the Supreme Court repealed all sodomy laws the Department of Defense would keep using them as an excuse to refuse gays and lesbians security clearances. Judges would keep denying gays and lesbians custody of their children and the right to adopt. Public and private employers, and landlords, too, would keep treating lesbians and gays shabbily. Though people were seldom thrown in jail for sodomy after the mid-century, the laws that remained on the books made any homosexual, ipso facto, a presumptive criminal.[1]

By 1972, a handful of states had joined Illinois, which repealed its sodomy law a decade earlier in a general overhaul of the criminal code.[2] Hoping to hurry the day when the Supreme Court might hear a test case and abolish all the remaining laws by a single decree, Kameny, in his usual spirited style, sent letters to the three top law-enforcement officials in DC. He invited them to engage in sodomy with him—and he demanded they arrest him for his invitation. "If you do not arrest me, that would be setting a precedent," he wrote, "since if I could with impunity solicit you, then anyone could solicit anyone." Two of the officials never answered. The DC chief of police responded with a note saying, "Sorry, I can't accept your invitation because my wife would never stand for it."[3]

Dallas, February 4, 1969: A stocky, dark-eyed Texan, Alvin Buchanan, was letting himself be fellated by another man in an open toilet stall of the men's room of Reverchon Park. Two vice squad officers burst in—they'd been spying from a hidden perch—and arrested them. Buchanan contacted a twenty-six-year-old gay lawyer, Henry McCluskey, who promised he'd help him make a federal case out of it, all the way to the Supreme Court. They'd challenge Article 524 of the Texas Penal Code, which criminalized all sexual acts except heterosexual intercourse.[4]

McCluskey filed suit for *Buchanan v. State* on May 26, 1969, but he'd decided that a case involving restroom sex might be a hard sell at the Supreme Court; so he expanded the complainants to Craig and Jannet Gibson, a married couple, and Travis Strickland, another gay man. Strickland declared that he engaged in sodomy, but only in the privacy of his own home.

The district attorney who represented Dallas County in the federal district court was Henry Wade, enemy of all that wasn't straight and narrow—the same man, cigar-chewing and with a slow and heavy Texas drawl,[5] who, a few years later, would become enshrined in history as the Wade of *Roe v. Wade*. Wade's opinion of Travis Strickland was that he was as much a criminal for engaging in sodomy in the privacy of his own home as Alvin Buchanan was for doing it in an open stall of a public toilet. But, the DA declared, Mr. and Mrs. Gibson had nothing to fear from the law. True, Article 524 stipulated that *anyone* who copulated into anything other than "sexual parts" was "guilty of sodomy"; but heterosexuals were never arrested.

Nevertheless, the federal district court's three-judge panel declared that the law as written was "overbroad."[6] In 1971 the Texas sodomy law was repealed.

The repeal did Alvin Buchanan no good. Judge Ed Gossett of the criminal district court in Dallas had sentenced him by now to two simultaneous terms of five years in prison. (Out on bail for the park incident, he'd gotten himself arrested again for the same reason in a Sears,

Roebuck restroom.) Judge Gossett announced he had no intention of letting Buchanan off just because Article 524 was defunct. "Liberal decisions in the federal courts are aiding and abetting the crime wave from which we suffer," the judge snarled. "This court is not going to release a confessed and convicted homosexual until and unless compelled to do so."[7] Members of the Texas Legislature, too, thought that homosexuals needed to be controlled. In 1973 they replaced the old sodomy law with section 21.06. This one targeted gays and lesbians only, whether they were caught having sex in public or in private, whether orally or anally, whether with mouth, penis, or dildo.

It was just as well that the Buchanan case didn't get to the Supreme Court, Kameny thought. He penned a script for the perfect test case. First, the actors: two respectable same-sex volunteers. Then, the setting: a respectable private home. Then, the action: "Notify the appropriate authorities and the media. Let them arrive and find the volunteers engaged in private, consensual, adult flagrante delicto, and proceed from there." If that seemed too risky, Kameny thought, a good effect might also be gotten by having the volunteers formally attest to the authorities that they'd just broken the law by indulging in forbidden sex acts.[8]

Activists in Los Angeles borrowed the script. Albert Gordon, a straight attorney whose gay son had been entrapped and prosecuted under the sodomy law, told Morris Kight, LA's gay éminence grise, that he'd defend a case pro bono if Kight would produce and direct it. The actors they enlisted were the Reverend Troy Perry and his partner, the well-known lesbian grassroots leader Jeanne Córdova and her partner, and a conventional-looking heterosexual man and woman. Each couple signed declarations "confessing" that "on or about May 8, 1974, in the County of Los Angeles, State of California," they broke the law by having sex of the prohibited sort. Attorney Gordon hand delivered the confessions to the Ramparts Division police station. He informed the police that the criminals would be available for arrest on June 13 at the Los Angeles Press Club. The "Felons 6," they called themselves hopefully. The press showed up, but the police didn't.

Act 2 of Gordon's little play: Because the police didn't come to arrest the felons, Morris Kight made a "citizen's arrest." All six of the lawbreakers, accompanied by Albert Gordon, piled into Kight's car and, media people caravanning behind, he drove them right up to the door of the Ramparts station. But the police commander refused to book them. "I didn't see you committing any crime," he said.[9]

Gay activists in Virginia also tried to challenge the sodomy law. But rather than presenting a pair of über-sympathetic actors to put a human face on it, and staging a scene in a private home to point up how egregious police were to burst in on people making love, they mounted a colorless class-action suit. *John Doe v. Commonwealth's Attorney for the City of Richmond* simply threw half the Bill of Rights at the US District Court. The suit claimed that Virginia's "crimes against nature" statute, 18.1-212, violated the First Amendment guarantee of freedom of speech, the First and Ninth Amendments' guarantees of privacy, the Fourth and Fifth Amendments' guarantees of due process, and the Eighth Amendment guarantee against cruel and unusual punishment.[10]

The judges rejected outright the sweeping suit of "all Richmond homosexuals" against "all officers who might prosecute plaintiffs and their class." They questioned whether "John Doe" even had a right to sue. "John Doe" had never shown that "they" experienced prosecution for consensual sodomy in private; and if they'd never been directly affected by the law, they had no "standing." Anyway, two of the judges said, sodomy laws have "ancestry going back to Judaic and Christian law." Such laws had a legitimate purpose, to discourage "the conduct that is likely to end in a contribution to moral delinquency."[11]

"John Doe's" attorneys appealed to the US Supreme Court, which issued a summary judgment on March 29, 1976, upholding the Virginia District Court.[12] The ripple effects of the loss of *Doe v. Commonwealth's Attorney* were felt in Virginia for a long time.[13] All a vengeful ex had to do to assure child custody was claim that the former husband or wife was homosexual. Virginia courts regularly took children from gay or lesbian parents, who were ipso facto "lawbreakers" under Virginia's sodomy statute. In the most egregious case, a trial judge in 1997 declared that Sharon Bottoms's homosexuality was a felony under the commonwealth's sodomy laws; and he gave custody of Bottoms's two-year-old child to its grandmother— who'd lived for seventeen years out of wedlock with a man who, Sharon told the judge, had sexually assaulted her at least twice a week, from the time she was twelve to the time she was seventeen.[14]

"THE PERFECT CASE" FOUND

Dallas, again: Donald Baker, a well-spoken, personable young man whose story would have touched anyone capable of empathy, was vice president of the Dallas Gay Political Caucus. His grandfather had been an Assembly of God minister, and Baker had grown up in an ultraconservative household. He'd been a Boy Scout. He'd sung in the church choir. He'd been taught not only in church but also at the dinner table that homosexuals would be cast out of families and jobs in this world, and would burn in hell in the next. But his homosexual feelings started about the same time his adolescent acne did. He was so troubled by them that at the age of twenty, in 1970, he dropped out of college in his junior year. He needed to run away from what he was.[15] He went off to serve in Vietnam, where he was celibate, and suicidal.

But when he left the military four years later and reenrolled in college, he saw an announcement for a gay student group meeting. He went, and for the first time, he met young gays who didn't hang their heads in shame. Baker became a gay activist; he also remained "an active and devout Christian." He graduated and took a job as an elementary school teacher of language arts. His evaluations were stellar. Students, colleagues, everyone loved him. He was school principal material. He enrolled at Southern Methodist University to get a graduate degree in education.[16]

Mort Schwab, a lawyer who'd started the Texas Human Rights Foundation in 1977, knew Don Baker through the Dallas Gay Political Caucus. Schwab's foundation was planning to raise money to mount a sodomy suit. Who could be a more perfect "face" for the suit than Don Baker?[17] They filed in November 1979. Again, Dallas gays would sue District Attorney Henry Wade, this time in *Baker v. Wade*.[18]

Yes, he'd had sex with men in the privacy of his own home, and he intended to continue to do so, Don Baker—clean-cut, honest, hardworking—told the Texas court. It didn't matter that statute 21.06 wasn't enforced when a homosexual carried on his sex life in private; he was still affected by it, Baker said. The law made all homosexuals de facto criminals.

Expert witnesses were called to bolster his argument. Judd Marmor, past president of the American Psychiatric Association, testified that the mere existence of the law created "stigma and stress" in gays and lesbians. Don Baker's parents—Middle America personified, but passionately supportive of their gay son despite their Pentecostal history—sat in the courtroom. Baker's lawyers had placed them directly in the sightline of Federal District Judge Jerry Buckmeyer.

The best the state could do was forensic psychiatrist James Grigson, famously called "Dr. Death." Grigson had earned his moniker because he'd testified in dozens of capital trials. Almost always, according to him, the accused was "sociopathic" and "would definitely kill again if he were set free." He thus sealed numerous defendants' sentences of death by lethal injection.[19] At the *Baker v. Wade* trial, Grigson testified that homosexuality was a sickness. He knew that because he evaluated many homosexuals who'd been arrested. Homosexuals had to get treatment for their malady, Grigson said, but they wouldn't do it if the state didn't make homosexuality criminal.

Judge Buckmeyer was unimpressed. He asked District Attorney Wade how the sodomy law, which didn't forbid heterosexuals from having oral and anal sex, advanced the state's interest in procreation. Wade's honest answer was, "I don't know." "What kind of societal welfare is furthered by a law that intrudes into the bedroom of consenting adults?" the judge pressed on. Again, Wade didn't know.[20]

Judge Buckmeyer declared in his written opinion on *Baker v. Wade* that "every individual has the right to be free from undue interference from the State in important and intimate personal matters." The sodomy law promoted no state interest. And it violated the constitutional right to equal protection of Don Baker and all Texas homosexuals.[21]

But it was 1982; the AIDS epidemic was just becoming daily news. Danny Hill, a newly elected, go-getting district attorney for Potter County, called together a small group, Dallas Doctors Against AIDS, who were willing to testify that homosexuals were dangerous to public health and safety. Homosexuals had always been "a reservoir of serious transmissible diseases," they said, and now, by their "sodomitic acts," they were spreading AIDS. Judge Buckmeyer's decision, District Attorney Hill argued, warranted judicial review.

The sixteen judges of the entire Fifth Circuit Court of Appeals met in New Orleans to hear the appeals case *en banc*.[22] Nine of them agreed with the DA. For seven centuries, Western culture had had strong moral objections to homosexual conduct, they said. "Implementing morality is a permissible state goal." On October 23, 1985, they reversed Judge Buckmeyer's decision. Statute 21.06 was again in full force in Texas.[23]

That was exactly what Don Baker and his team had hoped. Now they could turn to the US Supreme Court. They got Laurence Tribe, a Harvard law professor and top constitutional law expert, on board; and in January 1986, they filed an appeal.

SCOTUS rejected it. The justices had already decided to hear another sodomy suit, *Bowers v. Hardwick*. Laurence Tribe had agreed to argue that one, too. It was far from "the perfect case" that activists had hoped for.

SODOMY AND SCOTUS, PART I

Twenty-eight-year-old Michael Hardwick had nothing of Don Baker's squeaky-clean-American-boy history. He came from a broken home. He'd been a heroin addict, though he kicked the habit through a rehab program. His enthusiasms for Buddhism, "personal growth," and vegetarianism were outside the mainstream. He had a sketchy employment record. And his long curly blond hair accentuated his surfer-dude panache.

In 1982 Hardwick was working as a bartender at the Cove, an Atlanta gay bar, when his trouble with the law started. At seven in the morning on July 5, police officer Keith Torick drove by the Cove and saw Hardwick out on the street with a bottle of beer in his hand. "I was just throwing it in the trash bin," Hardwick said. The twenty-three-year-old policeman didn't like Hardwick's looks. He ticketed him for imbibing in public and warned him he'd be arrested if he didn't show up in court.[24]

Hardwick missed his court date. But when he learned that while he was out Torick had come to his apartment with an arrest warrant, Hardwick hurried down to the courthouse to pay the $50 fine. He assumed that was the end of the weird teapot tempest. But on August 3, Officer Torick (oddly obsessive about nailing Hardwick for his misdemeanor) came to Hardwick's apartment again, at 8:30 a.m. He had another arrest warrant for failure to appear in court. The front door was open. The officer stepped inside and found a drunken houseguest snoozing on the sofa. "I don't know if Mike is here," the man said when Torick awoke him. The police officer proceeded down the hallway. He found a door that was open just a crack. He pushed it farther—and saw Michael Hardwick, naked on a bed, sixty-nining with another man.

Officer Torick told the two they were under arrest. He ordered them to get dressed. (He peeked around the bedroom as they did and found Hardwick's marijuana stash, for which he ticketed him another $50). Then he handcuffed the two men together and drove them to the police station, not sparing invectives such as "cocksuckers" as he waited to book them.

Under Georgia's sodomy laws both oral and anal sex acts were felonies, punishable, if the state chose to prosecute, by one to twenty years in the penitentiary. Attorneys of the Lesbian and Gay Rights project of Georgia's ACLU had been looking for years for a test case to challenge the draconian law; they'd been reading daily police dockets of arrests, hoping to find a good case. Michael Hardwick may not have been the ideal plaintiff Frank Kameny had dreamed of, but he had the virtue of having chosen an adult sex partner; their coupling had been consensual; and it'd been in the presumed privacy of Hardwick's own home. ACLU lawyers called him.

Hardwick agreed to be their test case. The lawyers felt obliged to warn him he could be sentenced to up to twenty years in the pen if things went wrong. "I get it. But I'd feel pretty bad about myself if I just walked away from this," he said. The Atlanta district attorney, however, aware that Officer Torick's odd behavior couldn't stand up under legal scrutiny, squelched the plan. He dismissed all charges against Hardwick outright.

If the disappointed ACLU attorneys still wanted to challenge Georgia's sodomy law, they'd have to take the initiative. They sued Georgia attorney general Michael Bowers; the DA, Lewis Slaton; and the Atlanta chief of police, George Napper. In the suit, they described Hardwick as "a practicing homosexual, who regularly engages in private homosexual acts and will do so in the future." His arrest, they said, had violated his constitutional rights to free expression, free association, and privacy.

Despite his forbidding ice-blue eyes, Judge Frank Johnson had been a vocal champion of minority rights in the heart of Dixie since 1965, when he'd issued a controversial ruling against Governor George Wallace and in support of the Selma marchers' right to demonstrate on the highways and streets of Alabama.[25] Johnson didn't disappoint in Michael Hardwick's case. Representing the US Court of Appeals, Eleventh Circuit, three-judge panel, he wrote the majority opinion on *Bowers v. Hardwick*. The Georgia sodomy statute infringes upon Michael Hardwick's fundamental constitutional rights, Judge Johnson declared; and he demanded that the state prove its "compelling interest" in regulating sodomy.[26] Attorney General Bowers straightaway turned to SCOTUS.

The other sodomy cases that had been appealed to the Supreme Court, such as *Doe v. Commonwealth's Attorney for the City of Richmond,* had aimed to overthrow a ruling that upheld the law. But *Bowers v. Hardwick* was different: the Georgia attorney general wanted to overthrow a ruling that repealed Georgia's sodomy law. The conservative Warren Burger court agreed to hear it.

Laurence Tribe, for all his shrewdness and savvy, got it wrong when he thought the *Bowers v. Hardwick* battle would be "very sharply uphill but not a sure loser."[27] The times were as bad as they could be. The AIDS epidemic was fully under way; the general public had fear and loathing for homosexuals almost as intense as it did in the dark old days; and Hardwick wasn't the poster boy who could sway a court that included only three reliably liberal justices.[28] Why would SCOTUS in 1986 declare that homosexuals should be free to do as they like?

Laurence Tribe argued that the real question "wasn't what Michael was doing in his bedroom but what the police were doing there."[29] And he argued that the law must respect "intimacies of private life in the sanctity of the home." But to the majority of the court, "sanctity" and "homosexual" were simply oxymoronic. Justice Byron White baldly proclaimed that the Constitution didn't confer a fundamental right to engage in sodomy. To claim that it did was outrageous—"at best, facetious." Chief Justice Burger harangued that Judeo-Christian morality and all of Western civilization, even the Romans, found homosexual acts repugnant. He quoted from the eighteenth-century Tory jurist, William Blackstone: sodomy was "a deeper malignity than rape, a heinous act . . . a crime not fit to be named." It was the "infamous crime against nature." It couldn't be legalized without "casting aside millennia of moral teaching."[30]

After Laurence Tribe presented his arguments about liberty and justice and human rights, Chief Justice Burger asked, "Well, Professor Tribe, didn't we used to put people to death for this?"[31]

SODOMY AND SCOTUS, PART 2

As the 1990s progressed, the AIDS panic died down; organizations such as Lambda Legal and Gay and Lesbian Advocates and Defenders grew in resources and know-how;[32] more and more families and friends began standing up for gays and lesbians who were coming out to them; and even if some Americans knew no lesbian or gay people personally, they met them weekly in their own living rooms through endearing TV characters such as Ellen DeGeneres's "Ellen," and "Will Truman" of *Will and Grace*. Things were clearly changing. Sensitive to the change, the states, one by one, did what the Supreme Court wouldn't do in a single sweeping decision. They recognized that their sodomy laws were an invasion of privacy and violated a host of other constitutional rights, and they repealed them. By 2003, only thirteen states had sodomy laws. Texas was one of them.

This time, Houston: About eleven o'clock on the night of September 17, 1998, a Harris County sheriff's dispatcher received an emergency call. "A black man is going crazy with a gun!" the man on the other end of the line shouted. Four sheriff's deputies were sent out immediately to a run-down apartment complex in East Houston. The deputies broke down the door. They saw no one in the front room. They moved to the bedroom, their guns drawn. There they found John Lawrence, a balding white fifty-five-year-old navy vet, and (maybe) Tyron Garner, a thirty-one-year-old African American man.

What the two were doing—or even whether they were in the same room—no one who wasn't there will ever know. For a time, John Lawrence would claim that he was alone in the bedroom. After the case was settled, he'd claim that he and Garner were in the bedroom together but seated about fifteen feet apart. One of the deputies would testify that when he entered the bedroom he saw the two men engaged in anal sex. Another would testify they were having oral sex. Two of the deputies said they saw the two men on the bed but didn't see them doing anything sexual. What all the deputies did see was a pencil drawing hanging on the wall: actor James Dean, nude, sporting a giant-sized penis. Obviously, this was the bedroom of a homosexual. Lawrence and Garner were handcuffed; dragged, almost naked, down the stairs; and taken off to jail. They were held in custody overnight and charged by a justice of the peace with violating Statute 21.06.[33]

John Lawrence and Tyron Garner were hardly the picture-perfect homosexual pair that Kameny and other activists believed indispensable to a Supreme Court win. There was a twenty-four-year age difference between the two men. John Lawrence worked at a hospital as a medical technician, but in 1967 he'd been convicted for killing someone with his car while under the influence. He'd been given a five-year parole but had racked up two more convictions on drunk-driving charges. Tyron Garner, who supported himself when he could by cleaning houses or washing dishes in local restaurants, had no fixed address. He also had a drunk-driving record, and he'd been convicted in 1995 for assault.[34]

The circumstances around their case were unsavory, too. The man who'd made the phone call that brought the deputy sheriffs to Lawrence's apartment that September night was Robert Eubanks, aka Roger Nance, Tyron Garner's on-again, off-again lover. Eubanks, a sporadically employed alcoholic, had known John Lawrence for several years. The three men had gotten drunk together that evening, and Eubanks, imagining that Lawrence was coming on to Garner, announced he was going downstairs to buy a soda. Once outside, he found a pay phone and, in a fit of outlandish mischief, called the sheriff's department, screaming about a black man going crazy with a gun. When the deputies arrived, Eubanks directed them upstairs. "He's in there!" he told them, pointing the way.

Just two years earlier, in 1996, the four liberals and two swing voters on the US Supreme Court had recognized in *Romer v. Evans* that homosexuals really were American citizens. To what better court than that one could gays and lesbians hope to bring a challenge to sodomy laws? But a case hadn't been easy to find. In the thirteen states that still had laws in 1998, almost no one was being arrested, though the existence of the laws continued to stigmatize gays and lesbians everywhere as "moral criminals."[35] Yet a case that would get rid of the laws once and for all couldn't be brought to the Supreme Court without a plaintiff who had provable "standing"—and if gays and lesbians weren't being thrown in jail for sodomy, it wasn't easy to prove standing. Activists were desperate for a solid case. They had feelers out everywhere. Lawrence and Garner came to their attention when a gay file clerk in the sheriff's office saw a report of their arrest and told Houston activist Lane Lewis about it.

Neither Lawrence nor Garner had ever cared about gay politics. When Lane Lewis called John Lawrence and introduced himself as a "gay activist," Lawrence asked him, "What's a gay activist?" But he and Garner were hopping mad: they'd been roughed up, paraded in the street in their underwear, thrown in jail; they'd be fined $125 apiece for violating statute 21.06 and $141.25 for court costs.[36]

"Let Mitchell Katine sue on your behalf, for free," Lewis said. Lawrence and Garner said okay. Katine, a Houston gay lawyer who'd been doing mostly HIV discrimination cases, quickly got on the phone to Suzanne Goldberg at the Lambda Legal headquarters in New York. She'd been co-counsel on *Romer v. Evans* when she was fresh out of Harvard Law School, and she was now a senior staff attorney. Katine had met her at conferences. He knew she'd been trying to develop sodomy-law challenges in Tennessee, Arkansas, Montana—but she'd been frustrated in finding anyone who'd actually been arrested under the law.

"Yes!" Goldberg said, of course she was interested, but it had to be a tentative yes. She hurried down the hall to the office of Ruth Harlow, Lambda's legal director, who made the case assignments. "I just got this call from Texas," Goldberg told her. In no way did the Lawrence and Garner case fit the ideal scenario—yet, the two women agreed, it was the best Lambda Legal might ever have. It presented everything the lawyers needed: two consenting adults arrested in a private home and willing to say before the court that they'd committed sodomy. If handled right, it could be the case to take down *Bowers v. Hardwick*.[37]

Goldberg would be the lead attorney. She'd work with Katine and a couple of other Lambda lawyers to develop a strategy. In the court of the justice of the peace, Lawrence and Garner would plead "no contest." But they'd demand a trial. They'd be found guilty of sodomy, and they'd sue in the court of appeals. They'd complain that their rights to equal protection, privacy, and liberty had been violated.

The brilliantly plotted chess moves couldn't have gone better, from beginning to end. In 2000 a three-judge panel of a Texas appeals court overturned the trial court conviction. Chuck Rosenthal, Harris County's law-and-order DA, brought the case to the Fourteenth Circuit's full nine-judge court of appeals. The judges voted 7 to 2 to reverse the earlier decision and uphold the trial court. They quoted the Supreme Court's 1986 decision calling sodomy "the infamous crime against nature."[38] Suzanne Goldberg appealed to the Texas Supreme Court, which refused to hear the case. Perfect. There was only one place to appeal now. She and the other lawyers were ecstatic. They filed a writ of certiorari with the US Supreme Court.

Out of flawed plaintiffs they made a flawless case—though maybe it was simply a case whose time had come. At any rate, the lawyers got Lawrence to stop claiming he and Garner had never done the deed. Then they kept the two men away from media interviews as much as possible. The media noticed: "The two men at the heart of the case have retreated from view," an Associated Press article announced.[39] "They're on the quiet side, passive type individuals," Mitchell Katine nervously explained when asked why Lawrence and Garner weren't being brought out much.[40] The Lambda lawyers barely referred to them, except to use their names and the fact and circumstances of their arrest for sodomy. What the lawyers wanted to emphasize was that sodomy laws empowered the state to invade the privacy of people's homes and to punish them for consensual adult intimacy.[41]

March 26, 2003: The case wouldn't be heard until eleven o'clock, but droves of would-be spectators had started lining up in the cold wee hours. Those who'd been tracking the struggle for gay and lesbian rights knew the magnitude of what would be going on that day in the white-marble-and-red-velvet courtroom. They wanted in. Most would be disappointed because there were seats for only a fraction of them. Members of the Supreme Court Bar stood in a separate line. Seats in the center of the courtroom were reserved for them; but by six thirty, every one of those seats had been claimed, mostly by gay men and lesbians from among the core of elite DC lawyers. Just seeing how many of them there now were was a "transformative moment" for them.[42]

Lawrence sat in the courtroom, but only his lawyers knew who he was. Garner wasn't there.

Those gays and lesbians who got in must have felt jubilant very soon after the oral arguments started. Paul Smith, the Lambda Legal lawyer who would present the oral arguments for Lawrence, had been a Supreme Court clerk. Supreme Court doings were nothing new to him, and to many of the justices he was a familiar face. He appeared assured and elegant.[43] Chuck Rosenthal, the Harris County district attorney, would argue for Texas. Rosenthal, sporting a white "horseshoe" mustache a la 1880s Wild West, was out of his element in more ways than fashion. It was soon clear that his arguments were befuddled, illogical. Maybe he already suffered from the substance abuse issues that would drive him out of office a few years later.[44] Several spectators in the court that day agreed that he delivered "the worst oral argument in years."[45]

Justice Scalia, as passionately opposed to repealing sodomy laws as he'd been in 1986, tried to help Chuck Rosenthal along, even arguing his case for him. The public has not altered its opinion since the court decided *Bowers v. Hardwick*, Scalia declared. There was no reason in 2003 to reconsider their earlier decision. Americans still found homosexuality morally unacceptable—wasn't that right?

Everything hinged on that very point: Had the last seventeen years of activism and struggle changed society's collective mind about homosexuals, or had they not?

Instead of grasping Scalia's helping hand and agreeing that Americans looked down on homosexuality no less now than they had then, the flummoxed Rosenthal declared, as though desperate to show he'd done a little homework, that "since 1986, many state legislatures have changed their position on sodomy."[46]

Paul Smith's point exactly. The Supreme Court's 1986 decision had been based on "faulty assumptions about gay lives and gay relationships." But things had changed since then, Smith said. "It has to be apparent to the court that there are gay families, that family relationships are established, that there are hundreds of thousands of people registered in the 2000 Census who have formed gay families." And because gay people form families, Smith eloquently argued, their right to privacy in their own homes "performs much of the same function that it does in the marital context."[47]

Of course, Lawrence and Garner had not formed a family, had not been in a home they shared together, had not even had a relationship. But it didn't matter.

Justice Anthony Kennedy wrote the majority decision for himself and the five justices who had voted with him. They declared all sodomy laws throughout America to be unconstitutional. Kennedy waxed eloquent about how the laws dishonored deep relationships: "When sexuality finds overt expression in intimate conduct with another person, the conduct can be but one element in a personal bond that is more enduring." The states had no right to interfere with that bond, six justices agreed.

Justice Antonin Scalia wrote a prickly dissent. He read it to the court in a voice tinged with sarcasm for Justice Kennedy's arguments.[48] The majority decision to repeal all sodomy laws was a slippery slope, Scalia declared. If sodomy laws were no more, he demanded to know, "what justification could there possibly be for denying homosexuals the benefits of marriage?"[49]

"THE FIRST LAW IN AMERICAN HISTORY THAT BEGINS THE JOB OF PROTECTING LGBT PEOPLE"

HATE

Twenty-one-year-old Brandon Teena (née Teena Brandon, and called a tomboy from the time he could walk) moved from a trailer park outside of Lincoln, Nebraska—where he'd grown up and where too many people thought of him as a girl—to Falls City, a hundred miles away. Falls City was a dusty town of about 4,700 inhabitants, "a close-knit God-fearing community," one reporter later said of it, the Land of the Pickup Truck, where gun-toting men spent their leisure at the Demolition Derby.[1] Brandon Teena had hoped that there, where he was a stranger, he could live as a man.

He bound his breasts, and though only five foot four, he quickly charmed a bevy of young and pretty Falls City women with his dazzling smile and courtly manner. They'd refer to him later, with varying degrees of bemusement, as "a perfect lover" who "really knew how to treat a woman the way she wants to be treated."[2] In November 1993 he started dating Lana Tisdel, a nineteen-year-old, long-haired strawberry blonde. He also met and palled around with two of Tisdel's bad-boy friends—her hard-drinking, explosive ex-boyfriend, John Lotter, who was still enamored of her; and Marvin "Tom" Nissen, Lotter's buddy, a sly, wolfish-looking fellow with shoulder-length yellow curls. Nissen and Lotter had both spent years of their youth in state correctional institutions.[3]

Trouble began when Brandon Teena forged a check, was caught, and the local police discovered he was already on probation after an arrest in Lincoln the previous year for second-degree forgery—a crime usually punished by one to five years behind bars. On December 15, a Falls City judge sent him to jail. A week later, Lana Tisdel, already devoted to Teena though they'd been together for only a month, bailed him out. Her father had given her a blank check to get a hair perm, and she'd written it for $250 and cashed it for the bail money. But when Tisdel sent Nissen to spring Teena from the Richardson County Jail, he was directed to the women's section. Then the sheriff, Charles Laux, called Teena an "it."[4] Then an article in the local paper about Brandon Teena's arrest referred to him as Teena Brandon. His secret was out in Falls City.

Teena explained to the perplexed Lana Tisdel that he'd had a sex change operation though it wasn't yet complete. He intended to have more done, he said. Tisdel was upset, confused; she couldn't think of giving up a romance that for weeks had been exquisite. But Lotter and his sidekick took Brandon Teena's "deception" of Lana Tisdel as a grave affront.

Christmas Eve, 1993: Teena and Tisdel went together to a Christmas party at Tom Nissen's home. John Lotter was there, too; he and Nissen had been guzzling beers since ten in the morning. "I wanna have sex with you," the very drunk Lotter told the slightly drunk Teena in front of Lana Tisdel.

"You'll have to get over it," Teena answered.

Lotter jumped him, and Nissen helped pinion him. They pulled down his pants. "You better look," Lotter ordered Lana Tisdel, who'd covered her eyes. "We'll hold him like this until you do."[5]

A short while later, Tisdel, also a little drunk, said she had to leave to do an errand for her mother. She asked Teena to come with her. Inexplicably, Teena said he'd stay. "Just come back quick. Don't leave me here long," he told her.

Soon after Tisdel left, Lotter and Nissen knocked Teena down, kicked him in the ribs, stepped on his back, and pulled him by his coat into Lotter's car. They drove him to the parking lot of a deserted factory and made him get into the backseat, where they raped him. After, Nissen beat him again, splitting his lip. They warned him not to tell anyone about what they'd done.

It was dawn, Christmas day, when they got back to Nissen's house.

Nissen demanded that Teena, who was bloody and soiled, take a shower. Alone in the bathroom, Teena escaped through a window and ran barefoot down the freezing streets to the house where Lana Tisdel lived with her mother, Linda Gutierres. Mrs. Gutierres had no fondness for Teena because he'd deceived her daughter,[6] but she called an ambulance. At the local hospital, a rape exam showed Teena had been penetrated vaginally and anally. The case was turned over to the sheriff's department.[7] It wasn't an entirely unusual incident. In that year alone, the Federal Bureau of Investigation had documented over a thousand reported hate crimes based on the "sexual orientation" of the victim,[8] though the federal government had no law that addressed the problem.

Deputy Sheriff Tom Olberding began the questioning of Teena about the rape, but his boss, Charles Laux, who recognized Teena from his week in jail, said he'd take over. Laux was a burly, mean-eyed law-and-order man who'd been elected sheriff four times by the voters of Richardson County. His interrogation of Teena in 1993 was as brutal and lascivious as the grilling of gays and lesbians by Johns Committee goons had been in the 1950s. The sheriff was clearly less interested in the kidnap and rape than in mortifying the victim and exciting himself. "After he pulled your pants down and seen you was a girl, what did he do? Did he fondle you any?" he demanded. "You were all half-ass drunk. I can't believe that he pulled your pants down and you are a female and that he didn't stick his hand in you or his finger in you," the sheriff kept on. "Did he have a hard-on or what? Did you work it up for him?" Deputy Olberding was uncomfortable with his boss's questions. He left the room. But he came back in time to hear Sheriff Laux ask Teena, "Why do you run around with girls instead of guys, seeing as you're a girl yourself? Why do you make girls think you're a guy?"

"What does that have to do with what happened last night?" Teena dared to say.[9] Deputy Olberding told Teena he didn't have to answer any question he chose not to answer.[10]

Teena had informed the sheriff and his deputy that Lotter and Nissen threatened to kill him if he talked. He feared for his life, he'd said. "We need to find Lotter and Nissen and arrest them," Olberding told Laux after the interrogation.[11] But Olberding was only a deputy—Laux made the decisions about who got arrested. "No, I don't have any evidence yet against them," he said. He'd first send the rape kit from the hospital to the Nebraska State Patrol Crime Laboratory in Lincoln, and then he'd see.

Sheriff Laux called Dr. Reena Roy, a supervisor in the crime laboratory, to say, "I need to process this fast because they threatened to kill her. She's a dyke." Dr. Roy, a Bengali immigrant, had never heard the term. "A what?" she asked. He explained what it meant; Dr. Roy couldn't figure out how that was relevant.[12] Her lab report confirmed there'd been a rape. But Laux made no move to arrest Lotter and Nissen.

Afraid of what the two men might do next, Teena left Falls City and went to Humboldt, a town thirty miles away, to stay with a friend, Lisa Lambert, a nurse's aide and single mother of an eight-month-old baby. There, in a rented farmhouse, Teena hoped he might hide. Lambert had another houseguest, a twenty-two-year-old African American man, Phillip DeVine, an amputee with one leg. He was the out-of-town boyfriend of Lana Tisdel's sister, Leslie; they'd had a fight, and Lambert was letting him, too, stay in her home, until he and Leslie could patch things up.

On December 31, Lotter and Nissen tracked Brandon Teena down at the farmhouse. Because the dead can't testify in court, Nissen later confessed, Lotter shot Brandon Teena, execution style, with a stolen .38; Teena was still twitching, so Nissen stabbed him.[13] They killed Lisa Lambert and Phillip DeVine, too, so there'd be no witnesses. Only the baby survived.[14]

Brandon Teena's story, which became the subject of the Academy Award–winning 1999 film *Boys Don't Cry*,[15] brought the murderous violence perpetrated on LGBT people to wide national attention. (It also brought back into America's mass consciousness the subject of transgender people, which had lain virtually dormant since the "sex change" operation of ex-GI Christine Jorgensen had made sensational headlines in 1951.) But it was Matthew Shepard—a gay, "cisgendered"[16] male, a student at the University of Wyoming—whose murder finally rallied the masses. Reported hate crimes based on the "sexual orientation" of the victim had risen in 1998 to 1,488; several had been murdered.[17] But statistics don't appeal to mass emotions: the hauntingly innocent face of a young martyr does. LGBT groups had been intensifying the battle to get the federal government to pass a law against hate crimes based on sexual orientation. Matthew Shepard would become the face that made their case.

On the night of October 6, 1998, Shepard, who was blond and soft-spoken and looked like a winsome sixteen-year-old though he was twenty-one, was driven out to a Wyoming field of prairie grass and sagebrush, and was beaten on the head twenty times with the butt of a seven-inch gun. His skull was fractured and his brainstem crushed. Then his assailants trussed his limp five-foot-two, 105-pound body, tied him to a split-rail fence, took his wallet, ring, and shoes, and left him there, in near-freezing temperatures. Eighteen hours later, he was discovered by a passing bicyclist who first thought the crumpled form was a Halloween scarecrow. Shepard never regained consciousness; he died in a Fort Collins hospital on October 12.[18]

His assailants, Russell Henderson and Aaron McKinney (whom Henderson accused of masterminding the assault), were caught the next day. McKinney told the officers who took his confession that he and Henderson had met Shepard at the Fireside Bar and Lounge in Laramie, and Shepard had told them he was gay. They said they were, too, and offered him a lift home. Shepard sat in the front seat, between the two of them, McKinney declared; and as Henderson drove his pickup truck through Laramie, Shepard placed his hand on McKinney's leg. "When are we going to get to where you live?" Shepard asked.

McKinney would claim that at that point he told Shepard, "Guess what?—we're not gay. You're going to get jacked."[19] McKinney's lawyer would argue in his client's defense that McKinney killed Matthew Shepard out of "gay panic."

National gay organizations banded together immediately to organize a vigil on the Capitol steps and demand that a federal hate crimes law be passed in Matthew Shepard's name to protect all LGBT people. Vigils and protests were held from Denver to the University of Maryland. The giant rainbow flag that flew in San Francisco's Castro district was lowered to half-mast. NGLTF's political director likened Matthew Shepard tied to the fence to the crucifixion. That image was emblazoned on the American imagination and conscience: a childlike, sweet-looking, boy-next-door-type tortured and killed, crucified, only because he was gay. "The Crucifixion of Matthew Shepard," a *Vanity Fair* article was titled. President Clinton urged Congress to pass a federal hate crimes protection act. A Gallup poll showed that 75 percent of Americans had been so moved to compassion by the horrific murder that they were now in favor of hate crime laws that would protect gays.[20]

Fifteen years after Shepard's death, Stephen Jimenez, who'd been an ABC News *20/20* writer and producer, published *The Book of Matt: Hidden Truths about the Murder of Matthew Shepard.* Jimenez, a gay man, had originally intended to write a screenplay about the iconic gay hate crime.[21] In the course of more than a decade, Jimenez said, he interviewed about a hundred people in Laramie who'd known Shepard and his murderers. He claimed they told him that McKinney was bisexual; that he'd had sexual relations with Shepard before that fatal night of October 6; that Shepard, McKinney, and Henderson were all crystal meth dealers. And that the gruesome murder of Matthew Shepard was not about gay hatred or gay panic: rather, the meth-crazed McKinney, who'd been on a five-day drug binge, had hoped to rob Shepard because he erroneously thought Shepard had on him $10,000 worth of crystal meth, which he was going to deliver that night to Denver.[22]

But if it were true that the murder was about drugs, why didn't McKinney (who'd already copped to being the killer) say so in court? Why did he claim "gay panic" instead?

Because it seemed in 1998 that history had proven—beginning with the famous wrist-slap of Dan White for the murder of Harvey Milk—that juries hated homosexuals and were soft on those who murdered them. If McKinney had said he'd made plans to rob and kill Shepard for drugs he'd be more likely to be convicted of premeditated first-degree murder than if he said that when Shepard came on to him he suddenly snapped because of "gay panic."

For his "Judas take down" of a gay martyr, Stephen Jimenez was lambasted in the gay community, accused of giving "aid and comfort" to homophobes who wanted to "turn a blind eye to anti-LGBT violence and bigotry."[23] Yet whether or not Matthew Shepard was killed because he was gay is in a sense irrelevant to laws against hate crimes, no less than it was irrelevant to sodomy repeal whether or not Lawrence and Garner really were lovers. Lawrence and Garner were stand-ins for the many thousands of gay and lesbian couples who really were lovers and had suffered because of the sodomy laws. At the least, Matthew Shepard was a crucial stand-in for the many thousands of LGBT people who'd been brutally assaulted or murdered by people who hated them simply for what they were. According to FBI hate crime statistics, the third most frequent hate crime motivation, after race and religion, was the victim's "sexual orientation." That statistic alone should have been ample justification for a federal bill to protect LGBT people; but the limits of human imagination required a "face" to justify such a bill.

MAKING HATE UNLAWFUL

The mounting number of violent attacks in the nineties jogged national LGBT rights groups—the Human Rights Campaign, PFLAG, National Gay and Lesbian Task Force, Gay and Lesbian Alliance against Defamation—to push the federal government to take a stand. In 1997 they banded together to lobby Senator Ted Kennedy to introduce in the Senate a Hate Crimes Prevention Act. It would say that violence motivated by race, religion, national origin, disability, gender, and sexual orientation "posed a serious national problem" and that existing federal laws didn't address it sufficiently. The bill would propose "enhanced sentencing" for those committing hate crimes. It would also permit the federal government to help state and local governments prosecute such crimes; and the feds would be authorized to act if state or local governments didn't.[24]

But the bill failed to get out of committee. It failed again in 1998, shortly before the murder not only of Matthew Shepard but also of James Byrd Jr., a black man who'd been killed in Jasper, Texas, by three white supremacists who offered him a ride on a country road, and then beat him, stripped him naked, chained him to the bumper of their pickup truck, and dragged him for two miles, until he was dismembered and decapitated. They ditched his torso in a black cemetery.

The next year, 1999, Judy Shepard, Matthew's mother, appeared before the US Senate Judiciary Committee to urge passage of the reintroduced hate crimes bill. If there'd been such a law in 1998 when her son was killed, she told the senators, "perhaps these murderers would have gotten the message that this country does not tolerate hate-motivated violence."[25] After her impassioned speech, the bill did pass the Senate, but it couldn't get traction in the House.

October 2000, the televised presidential debate: Candidate Al Gore said that if elected, he'd sign a federal hate crimes bill. He referred to Matthew Shepard having been "crucified on a split-rail fence by bigots" and said that "Hate crimes don't aim just at a single victim; they're intended to stigmatize and dehumanize a whole group of people." His opponent George W. Bush, then governor of Texas, had let a state hate crimes bill die that year, despite the pleas from James Byrd's family that he support it. In the debate, Bush insisted at first that his state did indeed have a hate crimes law. When Gore assured him it did not, Bush backpedaled to say that all crimes are hate crimes, and Texas was already plenty tough on criminals so no special hate crimes legislation was needed.[26] He was elected president the following month.

During the years of the Bush administration, Focus on the Family's founder James Dobson, widely considered "America's most influential evangelical leader,"[27] had the ear of the president in part because Dobson had the ear of seven million evangelicals who tuned in weekly to his *Focus on the Family* radio program, broadcast on more than a thousand stations. Pundits called him the "kingmaker" after he helped Bush to a second-term victory.[28] On twenty-four different occasions, Dobson was invited to visit the White House, to talk to Bush or to suggest policy to his aides.[29] He urged the president to promote a "Christian social agenda," which opposed all "special rights for homosexuals."

The hate crimes bill had passed the Senate again in 2000 and died in the House; it passed another time, in 2004—at which point Focus on the Family's soul sister, Concerned Women for America, complained, "Under a hate crimes law, someone who mugs your grandmother will not be prosecuted as vigorously as someone who commits the same crime against a homosexual. This says to criminals, 'Mug Grandma; it's less risky.'"[30] The bill failed in the Republican-dominated House once again.

In 2005 it was reintroduced in the House for a fourth time by its lead sponsor, the congressman from Michigan, John Conyers. A seasoned politician who'd been in Congress since 1965, Conyers was a founding member of the Congressional Black Caucus and one of the most liberal members of the House of Representatives. Knowing that his bill would never pass by itself in a Republican-controlled Congress, he inserted it as an amendment to the Children's Safety Act, which strengthened sex-offender registration programs and established federal mandatory minimum sentences for child molesters. The entire Children's Safety Act/Hate Crimes bill passed with a vote of 223 to 199.[31] But now the Senate didn't take it up.

Even the bill's most ardent supporters had known it hadn't a prayer of becoming law in a Republican administration.[32] Yet each time the bill was reintroduced, it garnered more support. Barney Frank pointed out to cosponsors that it was necessary to keep introducing the bill to get their fellow Congress members acclimated to the idea that gay and lesbian people were citizens, too.[33] In the world outside Congress, thanks to more than a half century of gay and lesbian pickets, zaps, and mainstream activism, attitudes had changed among large swaths of Americans. But Congress members were still backward when it came to the subject; Frank's theory was that they needed to be reminded over and over from the floor of Congress.

When the 2006 midterm elections put the House of Representatives and Senate back into Democratic hands, the House again considered a hate crimes bill. By now, it had been about a decade since "gay and lesbian"— which used to include in its definition a spectrum of gender identities and same-sex orientation—had morphed into the more precise "lesbian, gay, bisexual, transgender," or "LGBT." Representatives of groups such as the National Center for Transgender Equality, founded in 2003 by Mara Keisling, a Harvard-educated, conventional-looking middle-class lady who'd come out as a woman in 1999 at the age of forty, had begun showing up at board meetings of big advocacy groups such as the Human Rights Campaign, to say they must fight for a trans-inclusive hate crimes bill.[34] Their arguments were compelling. Transgender people were more likely than anyone else in the LGBT community to suffer violent hate crimes. There'd been a spate of high-profile murders of young transgender people of color in recent years—such as that of sixteen-year-old Native American Fred Martinez, killed in 2001, and seventeen-year-old Latina Gwen Araujo, killed in 2002. Congresswoman Baldwin spearheaded the move to add "gender identity" to the hate crimes bill and made converts of other leaders such as Barney Frank.[35]

The vote was taken on May 3, 2007. Speaker Nancy Pelosi asked Congressman Frank, who along with Baldwin had worked on multiple versions of the bill for years, to preside over the chamber. When the tally was complete, Frank called out, "237 ayes and 180 nays," banged the gavel, and solemnly said over great applause, "The bill is passed."[36]

James Dobson wasted no time in spreading his outrage to his radio listeners. Protecting homosexuals was bad enough; protecting people who wanted to change their God-given sex was horrifying. The hate crimes bill would "muzzle people of faith who dare to express their moral and biblical values against homosexuality." It would usher in an Orwellian era: "If you read the Bible in a certain way, you may be guilty of committing a thought crime," Dobson proclaimed about the dangers of the hate crimes bill.[37]

In the Senate, Ted Kennedy attached the bill as an amendment to the Defense Authorization Bill. It was moved forward by a vote of 60 to 39. For the first time, both houses of Congress agreed on the need for hate crimes legislation with a bill that included gender identity as well as sexual orientation.

But the presidency hadn't changed. The White House spokesman announced that George W. Bush would veto the bill because "there was no persuasive demonstration of any need to federalize such a potentially large range of violent crime enforcement"; then he added (oblivious to his illogic) that the bill "leaves other classes of people, such as the elderly, the military and police officers, without similar status."[38] In view of the threatened presidential veto, the hate crimes bill was withdrawn.

It was introduced yet again in the 2009 Congress as an amendment to the National Defense Authorization Act. To answer the religious Right's objections that a hate crimes bill would inhibit pastors from speaking about homosexuality as a biblical sin, the bill's sponsors were careful to emphasize that it was about punishing violent acts and in no way affected freedom of speech, even hate speech. Barney Frank quipped to conservative Iowa congressman Steve King, who'd fought on the floor against the bill, "If hate crime legislation passes tomorrow, you'll still be free to call me a fag." (That wasn't assurance enough for King, who appeared on *Focus on the Family* and another ultraright radio program, *The Sean Hannity Show*, to complain that the hate crimes bill was really a "Pedophile Protection Act.")

But almost all Democrats and a few Republicans in the House and the Senate had come to support federal hate crime legislation. In the 2009 Democrat-dominated House, the hate crimes bill passed with a 74-point margin—249 to 175. In the Democrat-dominated Senate, it was again introduced by Ted Kennedy, who was in his forty-seventh, and final, year as a senator. The bill passed in August, with a vote of 63 to 28.

President Obama had promised since taking office that he'd sign a hate crimes bill if it came to his desk. On October 28, 2009, with the families of Matthew Shepard and James Byrd Jr. at his side, and representatives from the national LGBT groups that had waged a long fight for the bill looking on, Obama declared, "No one in America should ever be afraid to walk down the street holding the hands of the person they love. No one in America should be forced to look over their shoulder because of who they are," and he signed the Matthew Shepard and James Byrd Jr. Hate Crimes Prevention Act.

Barney Frank called it a "bittersweet day." It was the first law in American history, he said, "that begins the job of protecting LGBT people against prejudice," but, he added, it came "too late to save countless victims."[39]

The hate crimes bill was yet another issue that divided the community between "LGBTQ" radicals (the acronym was expanded with the new century to include "queer") and "Gay, Inc."—their hostile name for the mainstream groups. Radicals insisted from the start that the energy spent on getting hate crime legislation passed was wasted or worse. They said that hate crime laws do nothing but lengthen prison sentences, and the longer people stay in prison the more hardened they get. They argued that the LGBTQ community must be in the business of seeking justice, not vengeance. Queers for Economic Justice claimed that hate crime laws most often hurt people of color or poor people. It's useless to focus on single acts of violence, radicals said; the various social forces that lead to those acts have to be dismantled. People need to be educated. Men's hearts need to be changed.[40]

Indeed, a government can't outlaw hate. The number of reported hate crimes based on the victim's "sexual orientation" went up slightly right after the hate crimes bill was passed (though perhaps that was because the existence of the law, which implied someone would listen, encouraged more victims to report an attack). But while laws can't do much to control the wild-eyed, for the vast majority of the population, laws help shape attitudes, and attitudes influence behavior.[41] When the laws said that homosexuals were criminals, most Americans—even liberals and radicals—regarded them as criminals and treated them that way. In the 1950s, for instance, even the ACLU, devoted to protecting the civil rights of the oppressed, refused to help homosexuals who were witch-hunted out of government jobs because it found "nothing unconstitutional" in the government's desire to get rid of them. Laws also warn the mean guys that someone more powerful than they are is watching. Would Richardson County, Nebraska, sheriff Charles Laux have conducted such a brutal interrogation of Brandon Teena—would he have dared to refer to him as "a dyke" to another public official; would he have done nothing to arrest the men who threatened to kill him—if there'd been a federal law in 1993 that specifically protected transgender people like Teena?

More recently, rookie law officers in Nebraska have had to view and discuss the documentary *The Brandon Teena Story* as part of their training, which also includes instructions in dealing with sexual assaults on gay as well as straight victims. Today there are mechanisms in place in Richardson County, Nebraska, to assure that someone like Brandon Teena would be put in a safe house if he complained that his life was being threatened. He'd even be given a cell phone that has a direct line to the sheriff's office. Randy Houser, the man who was elected sheriff of Richardson County the same year the federal hate crimes bill was passed, arranged for his sheriff's department, as well as the local police and a neighboring sheriff, to attend LGBT sensitivity training sessions given by Nebraska PFLAG.

Houser recalled that one of his deputies asked him, "What is the definition of a transgender person?" "A transgender person is whatever he or she says they are," the Richardson County sheriff told him.[42]

In 2009 Frank Kameny—who'd often used the phrase the "Homosexual American Citizen" to remind the government of its neglected responsibilities—was invited to the White House to witness the signing of the Matthew Shepard and James Byrd, Jr. Hate Crimes Prevention Act. (For this occasion he'd traded his now-usual polo shirt and slacks for a dark suit and tie like he used to wear on his picket lines.) President Obama told those present that the new law was "a step forward" in a "journey to a more perfect union." Kameny remarked, "It's a start in a long list of things to come from President Obama. It's just the start."[43] It was.

Chapter 30

A FORTY-YEAR WAR:
THE STRUGGLE FOR
WORKPLACE PROTECTION

"FEW AMERICAN PEOPLE THOUGHT
WE'D COME THIS FAR, THIS FAST"

Congressman Barney Frank and Congresswoman Tammy Baldwin agreed on almost every issue that came before the House of Representatives, though they were an odd couple. Barney Frank had come to Congress from Boston in 1980. A caustic wit (about Ronald Reagan's propensity to fall asleep at cabinet meetings, for instance, he quipped in 1984: "I don't begrudge him an occasional nap. We must understand it's not the dozing off of Ronald Reagan that causes us problems. It's what he does in those moments when he's awake."[1]), Frank became known as Congress's wise man/wise guy. He was a familiar figure on the national news, dressed almost always in a rumpled suit and lopsidedly knotted tie, chewing a cigar, holding forth brilliantly, though in mumbles and at breakneck speed. In 1986, after learning he'd soon be outed by a former congressman's tell-all memoir,[2] and preferring to tell his own story, he came out—first to his colleagues and then to the country.[3] He'd worked for gay rights even while in the closet, but once out, he redoubled his efforts.

Tammy Baldwin—a soft-spoken, well-groomed Midwesterner with a big, pleasant smile—was a whole generation younger than Frank. In her public life, she'd never known the closet. In 1986, when she was twenty-four years old and still in law school at the University of Wisconsin, she won a county board of supervisors race. Then she got elected to the state assembly three times. In 1998 she won a seat in the US House. Ron Greer, an evangelical minister who'd run for the same seat, was endorsed by James Dobson of Focus on the Family. Greer had sent out fundraising letters that not only attacked Baldwin's stands on affirmative action, welfare, "partial-birth" abortions, and taxes, but also implored voters not to send a "left-wing lesbian" to Congress.[4] Voters in Wisconsin's Second Congressional District, which included students and professors from the University of Wisconsin, ignored his warning with zeal. In some parts of the district, the turnout for Baldwin was so huge that polling places ran out of ballots.[5]

In 2007, with Democrats finally holding the majority in Congress after twelve years of Republican rule, Barney Frank and Tammy Baldwin thought it was time to reintroduce the Employment Non-Discrimination Act, legislation that would protect lesbians and gays in the workplace. But their generational differences made them see the issue differently.

Federal bills to protect gays and lesbians had had a long and frustrating history by then. In 1974 New York's "Battling Bella" Abzug had teamed up with her closeted gay colleague Ed Koch to propose an omnibus gay and lesbian Equality Act to the Ninety-third Congress. It went nowhere.[6] Twenty years later, after the devastating passage of Don't Ask, Don't Tell, the National Gay and Lesbian Task Force and the Human Rights Campaign lobbied Senator Ted Kennedy and gay congressman Gerry Studds to do something for gays and lesbians.[7] Studds and Kennedy authored a bicameral Employment Non-Discrimination Act, ENDA. Judging from polls, the time actually seemed ripe for such a bill. In 1994 only 27 percent of Americans told pollsters they favored "gay marriage,"[8] and only 46 percent said that homosexuality "should be accepted"[9]—but 77 percent said they favored equal rights in employment for homosexuals.[10] Even Republican Mitt Romney, running in 1994 for a seat in the US Senate, thought it safe to pledge to the gay and lesbian Log Cabin Republicans that if elected he'd cosponsor ENDA.

In the House, the Subcommittee on the Constitution squelched the bill immediately. In the Senate, Ted Kennedy introduced it with eloquence. It wasn't about "granting special rights," he said, but about "righting sense-less wrongs." He told stories about gays and lesbians who'd suffered in the workplace: a waitress who'd worked for years at a Cracker Barrel restaurant in Tennessee but was fired when her manager found out she was a lesbian; a postal worker in Ohio who'd been beaten unconscious by his coworkers because he was gay. When the postal worker brought his case to court, it was rejected, Senator Kennedy said, "because discrimination based on sex-ual orientation is not covered under federal law."[11] The Senate referred the ENDA bill to the Labor and Human Relations Committee, where it died.

Senator Kennedy introduced the bill again in 1996. This time it made it to the Senate floor—on the same day the senators were to vote on the Defense of Marriage Act. (The Human Rights Campaign, hoping to out-maneuver the homophobes, convinced Kennedy to present it as an amend-ment to DOMA. Senate Majority Leader Trent Lott blocked the move, declaring that ENDA "would amount to the federal government endorsing the homosexual lifestyle."[12]) The Defense of Marriage resolution passed 85 to 14 and sent a brutal message to gays and lesbians about the disesteem in which their elected officials held them. Had some senators had pangs of conscience about the harshness of the message? Whatever the reason, the Employment Non-Discrimination Act almost squeaked through: the vote was 49 to 50. Senator David Pryor, a Democrat from Arkansas, had been expected to vote in favor of the bill, but he was absent that day because his son was having cancer surgery.[13] Had there been a tie, Vice President Al Gore, as president of the Senate, would have voted in favor of ENDA.

Senator Kennedy was actually astonished that his bill had done as well as it had: "Few American people thought we could come this far, this fast," he marveled to the press.[14] Surely the next time he introduced ENDA it would pass. Kennedy presented the bill again in 2001; it was placed on the Senate's legislative calendar but never came up for a vote. He introduced it again in 2003. It died in the Senate Committee on Health, Education, Labor, and Pensions.

"WHAT IF SOME MALE PERVERT WANTS TO BRING HIS DICK INTO THE WOMEN'S SHOWER, AND SAYS, 'I JUST DECIDED I'M TRANSGENDER'?"

Barney Frank had witnessed it all. Knowing the hard time ENDA had had getting traction, he was nervous. He'd been proud to be the first person to talk about transgender people before the House, when he argued for their inclusion in the hate crimes bill. But that didn't demand of his colleagues so great a leap in understanding as the idea that people who expressed their gender in ways that didn't match their biological sex deserved protection in the workplace. He worried that Congress members were as ignorant about transgender people as was most of America. Nevertheless, in April 2007 he introduced HR 2015, a workplace protections bill that included gender identity.[15] He could get only a handful of cosponsors. His worries were confirmed when the bill fizzled in subcommittee hearings on September 5, 2007.[16]

The transgender issue was too new, Frank said. Hardly anyone had spoken of "transgender" before the 1990s.[17] Transgender people used to be lumped together with "homosexuals" or hidden in "gays and lesbians." Congress needed more time to be educated, he insisted. He infuriated the organized transgender community by telling them that they needed to work harder at lobbying, that they seemed to think that the lesbian and gay movement was a train, and they were "a car on the train," waiting to be pulled along by the lesbian and gay engine.[18]

Frank was certain that ENDA had to be done in increments. First get Congress to vote on employment protections for gays and lesbians. Then, after trans people did their job—lobbied, told their stories, educated the legislators so that trans wouldn't seem weird to them—go back and ask Congress to vote for protections for them, too.[19] Congresswoman Baldwin, young enough that the relatively new term "LGBT" could roll easily off her tongue, disagreed. The movement had built up such strong support for ENDA that even if "gender identity" were attached to the bill, it would pass. "But if it's not attached," she argued, "it'll take decades before a bill that protects the rights of transgender people can make it through Congress on its own."[20]

"What it really boils down to," she told Barney Frank, "is, 'Do we have the votes for a trans-inclusive bill?'" She was convinced they had. Maybe colleagues would agonize over it, but in the end, most Democrats and even a few Republicans would do the right thing. (Florida Republican Congresswoman Ileana Ros-Lehtinen, for instance, had a transgender son.) They'd win with a few votes to spare.[21]

Frank didn't believe it. "We'll never get the votes," he argued, "because they'll think about people who haven't had a physical change and at work there are communal showers—they'll think, What if some male pervert wants to bring his dick into the women's shower, and says, 'Well, I just decided—I'm transgender.'"[22] He introduced a "sexual-orientation"-only ENDA on September 27, 2007.[23] Joe Solmonese, president of the Human Rights Campaign, the largest lesbian and gay lobbying group, and a politico since his college days in the eighties, applauded his approach. Transgender people must not be abandoned, but lawmakers had to be educated, and that takes time. Progress would have to be incremental.[24]

But as Frank was stunned to discover, all the other big gay and lesbian rights groups were furious that he wanted to "drop the T." Organizations such as the National Gay and Lesbian Task Force (later changed to the National LGBTQ Task Force) and ACLU's Lesbian and Gay Rights Project (later changed to the ACLU LGBT Rights Project) knew that trans people were the ones who suffered the most from job insecurity because of who they were.[25] And anyway, as Jenny Pizer of Lambda Legal pointed out, gender presentation was a continuum. Under a transgender-exclusive ENDA, butch lesbians and effeminate gay men might also be fired with impunity.[26]

"You go forward on a bill based on the reality of the situation," Frank tried to explain to disgruntled LGBT groups. Reality always boiled down to *Are the votes there?*[27] The groups weren't having it. Matt Foreman, executive director of the National Gay and Lesbian Task Force, declared, "We are one community, and we demand protections for all of us, and nothing else will suffice."[28] On Coming Out Day, October 11, 2007, a coalition of three hundred LGBT organizations—legal, political, grassroots—announced they'd come together in a United ENDA Coalition. Spearheaded by the National Gay and Lesbian Task Force, they'd organized almost overnight, using Listservs, web pages, conference calls. They were launching a "vigorous and vocal lobbying campaign" for a fully inclusive ENDA, they announced. They'd already informed Congress of their strenuous objection to "a diminished bill that abandoned transgender people."[29] It was one for all and all for one. No compromise. It was the first time mainstream organizations raised united voices for transgender rights.[30] A week later, Tammy Baldwin offered an amendment to the ENDA bill adding the words *gender identity*.

But the House Committee on Education and Labor voted to approve a "sexual orientation"-only ENDA and send it to the House floor for a vote. Frank had guessed right about the support for gays and lesbians. The bill passed, 235 to 184. Though twenty-five Democrats voted against it, thirty-five Republicans voted for it. However, the Senate never got around to an ENDA vote that year. President Bush had vowed he'd veto the bill if it came to his desk.

For excluding transgender people from ENDA, Barney Frank, who'd been rightly revered for decades as a champion of LGBT rights, was vilified among LGBT radicals and mainstreamers alike.

"THESE ARE OUR FELLOW HUMAN BEINGS"

When Barack Obama was running for president in 2008, he was sent a questionnaire by the Houston GLBT Political Caucus. One of the questions was, "Would you support a formal written policy of nondiscrimination that includes 'sexual orientation' and 'gender identity or expression' for all federal contractors?" Obama's answer was yes. In fact, he told the caucus, his campaign had a "written nondiscrimination policy that includes sexual orientation and gender identity," and he emphasized that "an Obama White House will implement a similar nondiscrimination policy."[31] Barack Obama was swept into office that fall; the Democrats got a solid majority in both the House and the Senate, too. The times couldn't have been better for passing an Employment Non-Discrimination Act.

Barney Frank was in a quandary. He believed still that Congress members were ignorant about transgender people, and the trans community wasn't lobbying enough to educate them. But LGBT organizations didn't let up on their pressure to include transgender people in the ENDA bill. They accused him of throwing transgender people "under the civil rights bus." Perplexed and frustrated that the trans community seemed deaf to his good advice, he put in a call to fifty-one-year-old Diego Sanchez, who for years had helped fund-raise in Massachusetts for Frank's election campaigns. Sanchez was now the director of the AIDS Action Committee's transgender health program. "I need you to give notice today on your job," Frank told him. "Whatever your salary is, I'll beat it."[32]

Always conservatively dressed (dark blazers and ties), sporting close-cropped silver hair and a neatly trimmed goatee, Sanchez was a transman who was well known even outside the LGBT community. He'd been named by *Hispanic Business* magazine as one of the "100 Most Powerful Latinos in Corporate America." He'd been the point man for media relations and diversity management in the Coca-Cola Company. In February 2008, Howard Dean, chair of the Democratic National Committee, had named him to the DNC Platform Committee, where he'd worked on immigration and AIDS issues. As Barney Frank's legislative assistant, he became the first transsexual staff member in Congress.

Just by his being on Capitol Hill, Sanchez would show the legislators what nondiscrimination in hiring looked like. But his biggest job was to encourage the trans community to do the legwork, as Frank had been admonishing—to knock on their congressmen's doors, let them see transgender people on a human level, tell the legislators from their own experiences why it was important that transgender people as well as lesbians and gays have employment protections. Sanchez got Mara Keisling of the National Center for Transgender Equality to begin holding transgender lobbying days on the Hill.[33]

Sanchez also helped find trans people with employment discrimination stories to tell; and Frank convinced the chairman of the House Education and Labor Committee, California Democrat George Miller, to let them testify before his committee. On the day of the testimony, Frank introduced the subject with apprehension: "Let me just say to my colleagues, there's nothing to be afraid of. These are our fellow human beings. They aren't asking you for anything in this bill other than the right to earn a living. Can't you give them that?"[34]

The first person to testify was Vandy Beth Glenn. Young, sincere sounding, neatly dressed, with shoulder-length brunette hair, Glenn was a good choice to make the Congress members see a "fellow human being." She had a degree in journalism from the University of Georgia; for a couple of years she'd been an editor and proofreader of legislative bills for the Georgia General Assembly. On Halloween 2006, some of her fellow workers

showed up at the office dressed in costume. Glenn came in women's business attire—a knee-length black skirt and a red turtleneck sweater. It wasn't
a costume, it was an expression of who she was; and it was her announcement to her fellow workers that she'd be transitioning from the Glenn
Morrison they knew to Vandy Beth Glenn, whom she'd always been inside.[35]

Someone must have sent for her big boss, Georgia legislative counsel
Sewell Brumby, who came flying up the stairs from his office on the lower
floor. A heavy smoker who took the stairs with great difficulty, Brumby
had never appeared in the editors' workroom before. He took one look at
Vandy Beth Glenn and felt discombobulated, as he later testified in court.
"It's unsettling to think of someone dressed in women's clothing with male
sexual organs inside that clothing." "You're dressed inappropriately!" he
boomed, and sent her home to change clothes.[36]

When Brumby was informed sometime later that Vandy Beth Glenn
intended to stop "cross-dressing" by completing her transition, he called
her into his office to say she was fired and needed to clear out that very
day.[37] He was afraid to upset the Georgia Legislature by having a "female
impersonator" on the payroll, Brumby would testify. They'd consider cross-
dressing in a government office to be "perhaps immoral, perhaps unnatural,
and perhaps, if you will, liberal, ultraliberal."[38]

"My skills hadn't changed, my work ethic hadn't changed," Glenn
recounted to the House committee. She'd worked twelve hours a day or
more to get the legislative reports she was editing perfect. Her abilities
were never in question. The only thing that had changed was her gender.
"And because of that, the legislature I'd worked so hard for, no longer had
any use for my skills." She was asking the government for just one thing:
"To be given my job back. I love that job. I can do it well," she said with
quiet dignity.[39]

Attorney Tico Almeida, who was serving as Congressman Miller's
committee aide and had helped select Vandy Beth Glenn from a roster of
possible trans witnesses, was sitting in the counsel's chair on the dais as she
testified. He watched several members of the committee "quietly tear up
and shake their heads" while she spoke.[40] If they'd seen and heard "transgenders" before, it was no doubt in popular films such as La Cage aux Folles.
The committee hearing marked the first time most of them had sat in a

room with a trans person and been made to think of her as "our fellow human being."

The LGBT Equality Caucus that Tammy Baldwin and Barney Frank had started in the House[41] managed, in concert with the LGBT lobbyists, to get 203 representatives to sponsor a transgender-inclusive ENDA.[42] But in the Senate, things were trickier. In 2008 Ted Kennedy, who'd always carried the ENDA ball, had been diagnosed with a malignant brain tumor. Only weeks before his death on August 25, 2009, still working on Senate matters from his home in Hyannis Port, Kennedy issued a statement: "The promise of America will never be fulfilled as long as justice is denied to even one among us." ENDA, he said, was needed "to fulfill that promise for gay, lesbian, bisexual, and transgender citizens."[43] Jeff Merkley, a progressive Democrat who'd just been elected to the US Senate from Oregon, had sponsored a state trans-inclusive employment nondiscrimination bill, which had been passed in 2007. Kennedy asked him to take over sponsorship of ENDA in the US Senate.

Merkley did get forty-four cosponsors; and on August 5, Kennedy already on his deathbed, Merkley introduced a trans-inclusive ENDA. It never made it to discussions on the floor.

As of March 2010, ENDA still hadn't been taken up on the House floor either. Tammy Baldwin told reporters that there'd been no action before because the Democrats had had their hands full all year with health care reform. But she and the LGBT Equality Caucus had been lining up votes. It was looking good. Barney Frank, always cautious, thought there were still too many "undecideds." He called again on LGBT activists: "Get out there"—help get the votes by lobbying lawmakers.[44]

Activists were getting out there in various ways. On Friday, March 19, Get Equal, the group that fought in seventies-radical style for the unradical right to be soldiers and to get married, invaded the San Francisco and Washington, DC, offices of the House Speaker. "We're not leaving until we get confirmation from Nancy Pelosi that she's going to have this bill up for a vote before the end of the month," they announced. In DC, Congresswoman Pelosi's office staff told the protestors, who'd been there all day, that the office would close at seven o'clock; the protestors didn't budge. At seven thirty, ten policemen showed up and marched them into a van. In

San Francisco, the police arrived, wrote the protestors tickets for loitering, and told them if they didn't disperse, they'd spend the weekend in jail.[45] Nancy Pelosi was nowhere to be seen in either office.

Midterm elections, November 2010: Democrats lost the House. The window to get LGBT rights legislation passed had been sealed over, and chances for the passage of a trans-inclusive ENDA would now be nil for at least two years.

Nancy Pelosi, no longer the Speaker but the House Minority Leader, declared her support for President Obama issuing an executive order.[46] It couldn't be as far-reaching as ENDA, but at the least it could protect the jobs of lesbians, gays, bisexuals, and transgender people who worked for federal contractors. Those contractors employed twenty-six million workers—22 percent of the American workforce. The Labor Department, which oversees federal contract compliance, also urged the president to sign such an executive order. So did the Justice Department. Even the editorial board of the *Washington Post* joined in, suggesting to Obama that the executive order signed by Lyndon Johnson that protected workers based on race, religion, and national origin could be extended to protect LGBT people.[47] Most voters wouldn't have objected: an April 2011 poll showed that 81 percent of Democrats, 74 percent of Independents, and 66 percent of Republicans supported workplace protections not only for gays and lesbians but also for transgender people.[48] LGBT activists showered the White House with the data.

President Obama could hardly have been accused of being unsympathetic to LGBT concerns. In fall 2009, he'd signed into law the hate crimes bill, trans-inclusive. By fall of 2010, less than halfway through his first term as president, he'd smashed all presidential records by appointing 150 openly gay officials, from agency heads to senior staffers. (Bill Clinton had appointed only 140 during his entire eight years as president.[49]) At the end of that year, President Obama had signed the bill repealing Don't Ask, Don't Tell. In winter 2011, Obama's press secretary Jay Carney had told the media that "the president regards DOMA as unfair," and Attorney General Eric Holder announced he was "following President Obama's lead," and would no longer defend the Defense of Marriage Act in court.[50]

However, in 2012 Obama was up for reelection. He'd been pilloried again and again for passing regulations that "hurt business."[51] Regulations against employment discrimination were aimed at business.

But as long as Republicans controlled the House of Representatives, LGBT activists had no hope but the White House.[52] They had to convince the president. In April 2012—after petitions and phone-call and letter-writing brigades and lobbyists who wouldn't quit—representatives of LGBT advocacy groups were finally granted a closed-door meeting with senior Obama aide Valerie Jarrett, head of the White House Office of Public Engagement. Twenty years earlier, Jarrett had been deputy chief of staff to Chicago's mayor, Richard Daley. In that capacity she'd hired a young lawyer, Michelle Robinson, who introduced Jarrett to her fiancé, Barack Obama. In 2009 Jarrett made the trip to the White House along with the Obamas. She could be relied on to deliver the president's views with accuracy. She assured the LGBT advocacy representatives that President Obama was very supportive of ENDA. He believed that just as Congress had led the way in the repeal of Don't Ask, Don't Tell, so should it lead the way in ending employment discrimination. It was up to Congress. He would not sign an executive order.[53]

It set off a rift between the White House and the LGBT community. "They want zero new obligations on business before Election Day," gay rights activists complained bitterly of the Obama administration. "This is an artful way of kicking the can down the sidewalk."[54]

The Far Right—for the first time ever—broadcast its praise for Obama: "This decision recognizes that sexual orientation nondiscrimination policies are not necessary and would be used to silence the speech of people of faith," a Focus on the Family spokeswoman declared.[55]

Obama triumphed in the 2012 election. So did Republicans, who maintained control of the House, 242 to 193—again making ENDA a lost cause in that body for the duration.

But a spate of new LGBT rights groups, such as Freedom to Work; Americans for Workplace Opportunity; and the Trans People of Color Coalition, had formed and were revved up to keep the fight going. They concentrated first on the Senate because Democrats were still in control there. Now trans activists "pounded shoe leather," as Kylar Broadus, founder of the Trans People of Color Coalition, described their going from the Dirksen to the Russell to the Hart Senate office buildings, lobbying senators for an ENDA that would include gender identity as well as sexual orientation.[56] Tammy Baldwin, who'd won her bid in the 2012 election to be a senator from Wisconsin, also kept up the fight. She sat face-to-face with the recalcitrant among her new colleagues and told them her personal story as a lesbian and why she felt the bill was crucial.[57] Jeff Merkley, still determined to keep the promise he'd made to Ted Kennedy, sponsored ENDA once again.

A dozen of Merkley's Republican colleagues in the Senate told him they'd vote for the bill—if he'd get rid of its protection for transgenders. As Arizona senator Jeff Flake, a Mormon—who like Tammy Baldwin had just graduated from the House to the Senate—flatly declared: if Merkley didn't ditch the trans protection, "I'm a no."[58]

On June 12, 2012, the Senate's twenty-two-member Health, Education, Labor, and Pensions Committee held hearings on the bill. Conservatives enlisted testimony from Craig Parshall, author of Christian suspense novels such as *The Last Judgment* and *Edge of the Apocalypse* and senior vice president of the National Association of Religious Broadcasters: ENDA threatened to "infringe on the constitutionally protected autonomy of religious organizations"; it threatened to be a "burden" to Christian employers, he said.[59]

Parshall, with his theoretical arguments, was nowhere near as affecting as Kylar Broadus, who shared his life story. No Senate committee had ever before heard from a transgender. Echoing Frank Kameny's striking twentieth-century refrain, "I am a homosexual American citizen," Broadus—a diminutive, forty-nine-year-old, light-skinned African American transman—declared solemnly to the committee, "I am a transgender American." He recounted how people had always related to him as a man: "That is my essence and my soul," he explained. He told how he used to go to work in a dress, which felt to him like wearing drag; how he was valued in his job for his "workaholic work-ethic"; how, when he finally decided to start wearing men's clothes to work, his male colleagues taught him how to properly tie a tie. And how a new supervisor, contemptuous of "women who looked like men," harassed him out of his job. The supervisor questioned him about his sex life, accused him of hitting on a white woman in the office, told him that his "man's haircut" was unacceptable and said, "the next time you want to do anything with your hair, call me first." He also gave Broadus impossible, irrelevant tasks, intending to make him fail. "It was devastating, demoralizing, dehumanizing," Broadus attested to the Senate committee. The harassment caused him panic attacks and depression—and he had no legal recourse, because Missouri, where he worked, had no laws protecting transgender workers.[60]

After hearing such testimony, the committee, in a 15-to-7 bipartisan vote, sent a gender-identity-inclusive ENDA bill to the full Senate. To placate the Senate's conservative Democrats and moderate Republicans, the bill also included a religious exemption: religious entities that didn't want to hire gays, lesbians, bisexuals, or transgender people didn't have to.

November 7, 2013: The bill came to the Senate floor. Republican Pat Toomey, junior senator from Pennsylvania, offered an amendment. He wanted to expand the kinds of businesses that could claim "religious exemption": a gym run by Mormons, for instance, or a Presbyterian-run retirement home. Such an amendment, Toomey said, would "relieve tension between two vitally important American values: equality and religious liberty." It was voted down, 55 to 43.[61] The vote was called for a trans-inclusive ENDA with the limited religious exemption.

Senator John McCain, who'd been so vociferously opposed to gays in the military two years earlier, had long declared he'd vote no. He'd complained that ENDA could be like busing, breeding worse problems than it solved—it could lead to quotas or even reverse discrimination.[62] But one day in October, a couple of weeks before ENDA came to the Senate floor, a Human Rights Campaign canvasser was standing in front of a Staples store in Phoenix, handing out postcards that were to be signed and mailed to Senate offices: "No One Should Be Fired Because of Who They Are," the postcards read. The canvasser spotted Cindy McCain, wife of the senator, coming out of the store. He gave her a card, and asked her to sign it and send it to her husband. She did. She even had a picture taken of herself together with the canvasser, holding up the signed postcard with its clearly legible message.[63]

A few days after the Senate voted on ENDA, John McCain announced to his constituency, "I have always believed that workplace discrimination, whether based on religion, gender, race, national origin, or sexual orientation, is inconsistent with the basic values Americans hold dear." Assuring Arizonans that he'd made sure "religious protections" were in place, he informed them he'd voted for ENDA.[64]

Senator Tammy Baldwin got a conservative Republican lawmaker, parent of a young transgender child, to convince Jeff Flake to vote aye. Another Mormon, Utah senator Orrin Hatch—"reassured" by the "religious exemption" that fellow Mormons wouldn't be forced to violate Latter-Day Saints' policies that cut LGBT people out of church and religious-school hiring—also voted aye. ENDA passed the Senate, 64 to 32. Ten Republicans had finally acquiesced.

Another of the sixty-four aye votes was cast by Senator Mark Pryor, Democrat from Arkansas and son of David Pryor—the senator who would've been the fiftieth aye vote on Ted Kennedy's ENDA bill seventeen years earlier, had David not had to go back to Arkansas to be with young Mark, who was having cancer surgery.

But the problem of the recalcitrant House, in which Republicans outnumbered Democrats, 234 to 201, remained.

GAME CHANGER

June 30, 2014: The Supreme Court finally issued its ruling on the infamous Hobby Lobby case. Hobby Lobby was a family-owned national chain of six hundred arts and crafts stores, founded by billionaire David Green, son of a Pentecostal minister. Under the direction of Green and his family, Hobby Lobby was committed to "honor the Lord in all we do by operating the company in a manner consistent with biblical principles." From their headquarters in Oklahoma City, they had music piped into all Hobby Lobbys via Signature Channel satellite. For the pleasure and edification of all within earshot, hymns such as "Amazing Grace" and "Praise the Lord, the Almighty" played constantly while shoppers loaded their shopping carts with soap-making supplies or doormats that declared, "We will serve the Lord." The stores were closed on Sundays so people could go to church instead of roaming shopping malls. All the Hobby Lobbys carried a huge line of holiday items, but nothing as unchristian as Hanukkah menorahs or dreidels.[65] When, under the Affordable Care Act, Hobby Lobby was obliged to provide its workers with health insurance, Green and family objected.

Their religious principles, they asserted, would be violated if they had to pay for their workers' birth control pills or abortifacients.

In a 5-to-4 decision, SCOTUS, referencing the Religious Freedom Restoration Act of 1993, which prohibited the government from "burdening" a person's exercise of religion, affirmed that "closely held" corporations—that is, those in which five or fewer people owned at least 50 percent of the company—were exempt from laws that violated their owners' religious principles.[66]

More than 90 percent of American corporations are "closely held." About 52 percent of the American workforce is employed by these "closely helds."[67] LGBT activists understood it was time to worry—not just because Hobby Lobby didn't have to pay for contraceptives or that the Green family was putting tens of millions of their Hobby Lobby dollars into right-wing causes to fight same-sex marriage and aid businesses that didn't want to serve LGBT people.[68] Even more troublesome was the implication of the Supreme Court decision. As Justice Ruth Bader Ginsburg observed, it was "a decision of startling breadth." It could mean that any "closely held" company might find individuals (such as "homosexuals") "antagonistic to the Bible," and so refuse to hire or even serve them.[69] Justice Samuel Alito, dependable foe of anything that smacked of gay rights, had authored the majority opinion. He answered Ginsburg's concerns by assuring her and America that the ruling "would certainly not permit discrimination based on race"—pointedly keeping mum about discrimination based on "sexual orientation" or "gender identity."

The writing was on the wall. The Hobby Lobby decision made any "religious" compromise dangerous. "Religious exemption" might mean that church-affiliated universities, schools, hospitals, nursing homes, and even for-profit businesses, could claim a religious "right" to discriminate against LGBT people, who'd be recast as pariahs.[70]

LGBT advocacy groups had worked for years to get ENDA as far as it had finally gotten; but now leaders of the ACLU, the National Center for Lesbian Rights, Gay and Lesbian Advocates and Defenders, the Transgender Law Center, and Lambda Legal joined together to issue a painful statement: because of ENDA's religious exemption—"limited" as it may have been—they were pulling their support from the version of the bill that the Senate had passed the year before. The National Gay and Lesbian Task

Force implored President Obama to veto ENDA if it should ever get to his desk with the religious exemption intact.[71] (The divide between Barney Frank's generation and younger activists was again apparent when Frank complained to the press about the move, "There's an element in my community that insists on being cutting edge. They are determined never to be for anything that could pass because that means they are stodgy.")[72]

AMERICA BECOMES "JUST A LITTLE BIT FAIRER"

Monday, July 21, 2014, the White House: The crowd seated in the East Room wouldn't stop cheering and peppering the president's remarks with "Amen!"—"an amen corner," Obama dubbed them and laughed. Large LCD screens, lit with the message "Opportunity for All," hung on either side of the stage. Senators Tammy Baldwin and Jeff Merkley were in the audience; as were representatives from the Human Rights Campaign, the National Gay and Lesbian Task Force, Get Equal, Lambda Legal, the Gay and Lesbian Alliance Against Defamation, Freedom to Work, Freedom to Marry, Parents and Friends of Lesbians and Gays, the Family Equality Council. General Tammy Smith, whose wife had pinned the general's star on her epaulet in a public ceremony in 2012, was there, too. They'd come to see President Obama sign two executive orders. "I hope as everybody looks around this room, you are reminded of the extraordinary progress we have made," he told them. "Not just in our lifetimes, but in the last five years. In the last two years. In the last year. We are on the right side of history."

Onstage, the president was flanked by several government officials, as well as Kylar Broadus, the transman who'd testified in front of the Senate committee; Anne Vonhof, a transwoman who was the LGBT diversity program manager in the US Office of Personnel Management (successor to Frank Kameny's old nemesis, the Civil Service Commission); Faith Cheltenham, president of BiNet U.S.A., a bisexual legal-advocacy organization; and Michael Carney, a gay police officer in full uniform, who'd testified before a House committee in 2007 and a Senate committee in 2009 about his struggles to get his job back on the Springfield, Massachusetts, police force after being fired because the department found out he was gay.

A minister and a rabbi were onstage, too. Together with a hundred other clergy—Catholic nuns, Episcopal bishops, the imam of the Light of

Reform Mosque in DC—they'd implored the president not to include in his executive orders a "religious exemption" because "public dollars should not be used to sanction discrimination."[73] Obama didn't—despite a threatening missive from over 150 right-wing religious groups and leaders that stated, "Any executive order that does not fully protect religious freedom will face widespread opposition and will further fragment our nation."[74]

One of the executive orders that President Obama would sign amended Bill Clinton's 1998 Executive Order 11478, which had protected those directly employed by the federal government from discrimination based on their "sexual orientation." Now protection based on "gender identity" would be added. The other one amended Lyndon Johnson's 1965 Executive Order 11246. It had banned discrimination by federal contractors based on race, creed, color, and national origin; and it had already been amended—in 1967—to say that women couldn't be discriminated against.[75] Now it was amended once again, to say LGBT people couldn't be discriminated against. Amending the earlier orders sent a plain message to the Far Right: just as it would be outrageous to permit a "religious exemption" concerning race or national origin, it would be equally outrageous to permit one concerning sexual orientation or gender identity.

This day had finally happened, the president told his East Room audience, because of the years of work of most of those present. "You organized, you spoke up, you sent petitions, you sent letters—I know, because I got a lot of them," he joked.

Of course, the orders he was about to sign wouldn't solve the bulk of the employment discrimination that the community suffered; only ENDA would do that, he reminded the activists. They had to finish the unfinished business, to "keep putting pressure on Congress to pass federal legislation that would solve this problem once and for all." But their passion and advocacy and the irrefutable rightness of their cause, the president acknowledged, had brought them all there that day to see "our government become just a little bit fairer."

PART 10

"WHAT JUSTIFICATION COULD THERE POSSIBLY BE FOR DENYING HOMOSEXUALS THE BENEFITS OF MARRIAGE?"

Chapter 31

"THE STATUS THAT EVERYONE UNDERSTANDS AS THE ULTIMATE EXPRESSION OF LOVE AND COMMITMENT"

A SEISMIC WIN

Honolulu, winter 1989: The city's most energetic activist, Bill Woods, working the help line at the Gay and Lesbian Community Center which he'd cofounded, fielded a phone call from a thirty-year-old lesbian, Ninia Baehr. She had a part-time job at the University of Hawaii Women's Center, and no health insurance, she said. She'd been sick with an ear infection, and she wanted to know whether the health insurance of her partner, an engineer for Hawaii Public Television, would help pay her doctor bills.[1] Of course it wouldn't, Woods had to tell her, because she and Genora Dancel weren't married. The incident made him research what else the two women lost out on because they couldn't get married: over a thousand federal rights and responsibilities.

Woods, a member of a committee that was planning the first Honolulu Gay Pride Parade and Rally, brought a proposal to the next meeting. They'd find thirty same-sex couples who wanted to get married; they'd get one of the major rights organizations—maybe Lambda Legal or the ACLU's Lesbian and Gay Rights Project or the National Gay and Lesbian Task Force—to fight to get marriage licenses for the couples; but with or without licenses, they'd hold a mass wedding at the Gay Pride Rally. The planning committee thought it a fine idea. If nothing else, it would bring out the press and spread the word that Honolulu was finally having a gay pride parade.[2]

Woods found thirty couples easily. Then he contacted a dozen of the major gay and lesbian rights organizations to help with step two: suing for marriage licenses. He was reminded by some organizations' lawyers that people with AIDS were being fired from their jobs, denied insurance coverage, thrown out of their homes. Obviously those cases had to take priority. Other groups that Bill Woods contacted told him that same-sex marriage was a pipe dream; they were fighting for domestic partnership instead. Lambda Legal's legal director, Paula Ettelbrick, a fiery activist who'd been a lesbian feminist since her college days in the 1970s, reminded lesbians that they shouldn't want to be "Mrs. Attached-to-Somebody-Else." No gay or lesbian should have to assimilate in order to get rights, she argued. "Being queer isn't setting up house and seeking state approval for doing so."[3]

The couples who'd promised Woods they'd be part of his marriage production figured that if none of the gay and lesbian rights groups wanted to help get marriage licenses, it must be hopeless. They all pulled out, except for the original pair, Ninia Baehr and Genora Dancel. The city's first gay pride parade and rally went on without a mass wedding.[4] But months after the parade, Woods managed to find two more couples who were willing to challenge Hawaii's marriage law.

December 17, 1990: Baehr and Dancel, along with Patrick Lagon and Joseph Melillo, who'd been together fifteen years; and Tammy Rodriguez and Antoinette Pregil, who'd raised a daughter together who was now nineteen, marched down Beretania Street. They were preceded by a TV cameraman scurrying backward, trying to get good angles for frontal shots of six homosexuals walking determinedly, on their way to the State Health Department, which issued marriage licenses.[5] The befuddled clerk at the marriage desk informed the couples they'd have to wait until John Lewin, director of the Health Department, consulted with Rick Eichor, the state's deputy attorney general. Eichor would later claim he had "no strong opinions" about same-sex marriage. Nevertheless, he did his job to uphold the prejudices of the state. The marriage law was intended to promote a good environment for children, who thrive best when reared by biological parents, he declared. And on top of that, Eichor said, same-sex marriage would "open the door to demands that the state also license bigamy, polygamy, and consensual incestuous relationships."[6]

That might have been the end of the story if Dan Foley, a heterosexual with a wife and two children, hadn't heard about it. Foley was a forty-four-year-old San Francisco transplant and Peace Corps veteran who was on his way to becoming Hawaii's most prominent civil rights attorney. A few years earlier, when city officials refused to grant a permit for the Miss Gay Molokai drag pageant because "the participants might spread AIDS," Foley sued on behalf of the pageant and won. He also sued Hawaii nursing homes that refused to take in people with AIDS. Now he offered to sue the state on behalf of the three same-sex couples. The case, *Baehr v. Lewin*, was heard in the circuit court of the First Circuit, where Judge Robert Klein, declaring that only opposite-sex marriages "promote the welfare of the community," dismissed the same-sex marriage suit with prejudice.[7] Foley appealed to the Hawaii Supreme Court.

As Lambda's legal director, Paula Ettelbrick didn't want the organization's lawyers spinning their wheels on marriage, but in 1989 Executive Director Tom Stoddard had hired a thirty-two-year-old Brooklyn-born visionary, Evan Wolfson. Six years earlier, Wolfson had written a 140-page Harvard Law School thesis on how keeping marriage from gays and lesbians was a violation of both human rights and constitutional rights.[8] It was serendipitous that a friend of one of the plaintiffs in the Hawaii case knew Wolfson and knew of his thesis. The plaintiff contacted him. Wolfson thought his chance had finally come to plead his dearest convictions in court.[9]

But Ettelbrick, who assigned Lambda's cases, needed him to work on legal issues related to AIDS. And he was needed to argue in the Supreme Court Lambda's case on behalf of a young assistant Boy Scout master who'd been dismissed after it was discovered he was president of the Lesbian, Gay, Bisexual Alliance at Rutgers. (The Rehnquist court's 5-to-4 opinion was that a gay troop leader would "send a message, both to the young members and the world, that the Boy Scouts accept homosexual conduct as a legitimate form of behavior.")[10] However, he was permitted to write a friend-of-the-court brief for the Hawaii case.

May 7, 1993: The Hawaii Supreme Court announced its opinion. It was written by forty-six-year-old Associate Justice Steven Levinson, the court's most liberal member, who'd come of age during the turbulent period of the black civil rights movement and called himself "a child of the sixties."[11] Levinson declared that the ban on same-sex marriage was probably in violation of the state's prohibition against sex discrimination, and that "freedom to marry is one of the basic civil rights." He bounced *Baehr v. Lewin* back to the circuit court, saying it had failed to make its case: it had to show how the ban on same-sex marriage "furthers compelling state interest."[12]

Evan Wolfson called it "a seismic win." Same-sex marriage didn't seem such a pipe dream anymore. Gay and lesbian organizations were forced to rethink their indifference: "If a court is going to stand with us, shouldn't we be standing up for our own community?"[13] they started asking among themselves. Lambda agreed to send Evan Wolfson to be cocounsel with Dan Foley and to argue the case before Circuit Court Judge Kevin Chang, to whom it had been reassigned. The ACLU jumped in, too.

One of the claims the state had made was that a ban on same-sex marriage was "in the best interests of children." But during the nine-day, Court TV–televised trial,[14] Foley and his now substantial crew were able to call expert witnesses—psychiatrists, psychologists, sociologists—who testified that gay people could be as competent at parenting as were straight people, and it would help children of same-sex couples if their parents could wed. The state of Hawaii had failed to show "sufficient reason" to prohibit same-sex marriage, Judge Chang said and declared the ban on such marriages unconstitutional.[15]

It was looking like a sure thing. Hawaii was set to make same-sex marriage legal. But the State announced it would appeal to the Hawaii Supreme Court. Judge Chang granted a temporary stay on his judgment.

DREAM DEFERRED

South Dakota, whose state motto is "Under God, the People Rule," panicked. There were only seven hundred thousand South Dakotans; but what if some of them were homosexuals, and they'd go off to Hawaii to get married—and they'd come back to South Dakota and say that Article IV of the US Constitution, the "Full Faith and Credit" Clause, meant that South

Dakota had to recognize their marriage? On February 2, 1995, the South Dakota House of Representatives made a preemptive strike. Bill 1184, which declared that "any marriage between persons of the same gender is null and void," passed 54 to 13.

South Dakotan homosexuals had been mostly closeted. Now they leaped from the closet and formed the state's first activist group, the South Dakota Gay, Lesbian, and Bisexual Federation. Evan Wolfson advised them on lobbying senators and testifying in the Senate.[16] They seemed to be succeeding—the first time around the bill failed to get enough votes.[17] But conservatives politicked, sent it through again, and it passed.

An avalanche followed. Utah passed a similar bill in March 1995; then Alaska. By early 1996, thirty-seven states were considering bills to "defend marriage."

In Hawaii where it all started, 74 percent of those polled in 1996 on what they thought of gay marriage said they disapproved.[18] The state legislators, obedient to their constituents' wishes, amended the state constitution in 1997 to say, "The legislature shall have the power to reserve marriage to opposite sex couples." In 1998, 69 percent of the voters ratified the amendment. That trumped the Hawaii Supreme Court declaration that "freedom to marry is one of the basic civil rights."

Senator Bob Dole, who'd hoped to snatch the presidential election from Bill Clinton, saw an irresistible wedge issue. He got Georgia Republican Bob Barr (thrice married) to introduce a "Defense of Marriage Act" in the US House. Barr declaimed it like a fire-and-brimstone sermon: "The very foundations of our society are in danger of being burned. The flames of hedonism, the flames of narcissism, the flames of self-centered morality are licking at the very foundation of our society: the family unit."[19] Barney Frank demanded to know how "two people loving each other somehow threatens heterosexual marriage?" His question was never answered.[20] Barr's bill said that no state had to recognize a same-sex marriage performed in another state; that the federal government's definition of marriage was "a legal union between one man and one woman"; and that that definition would determine the meaning of any federal law or regulation related to marriage.[21] It passed the House in July, 342 to 67. The House *Report* explained that the Defense of Marriage Act was needed "to reflect and honor a collective moral judgment about human sexuality [which] entails moral disapproval of homosexuality."[22] In September DOMA passed the Senate, 85 to 14.

When Bill Clinton told his gay and lesbian supporters at the Hollywood Palace, "I have a vision for the future, and you are a part of it," he was sincere; but he was naïve about Washington's virulent homosexual hatred. Not only did he have the gays-in-the-military debacle on his hands almost as soon as he took office; he also had a battle over his nomination for Assistant Secretary for Housing and Urban Development. His choice was a San Francisco Supervisor, who'd also been the cofounder of the National Center for Lesbian Rights. No out lesbian or gay man had ever held so high a government position as second-in-command to a presidential cabinet member. Conservatives in the Senate were determined that none ever would.

During the two days of Roberta Achtenberg's confirmation hearings, Senate conservatives waged character assassination, led by Senator Jesse Helms. The North Carolina senator distributed to the entire Senate a video of Achtenberg, together with her partner, Judge Mary Morgan, and their seven-year-old son, perched on a Gay Pride Parade float, surrounded by bare-breasted lesbians, drag queens, and leather men. Helms called her "a damn lesbian." The real reason why the Achtenberg nomination is before the Senate, he told his fellow congressmen, was because the homosexual lobby had put $5 million into Clinton's presidential race, and the homosexual Human Rights Campaign had deployed ten thousand gays and lesbians to canvas for Clinton.[23]

To his credit, President Clinton never wavered in his support of Achtenberg, and she was confirmed.[24] That same year, too, he hired Richard Socarides—the openly gay son of the infamous antigay psychiatrist Charles Socarides—to be a White House advisor. Clinton also put a lesbian, Marsha Scott, into a groundbreaking role as the White House liaison to the gay and lesbian community.[25] But his advisors told him he could only go so far if he hoped to be reelected for a second term. The Senate had passed the Defense of Marriage Act in September, two months before voters were to go to the polls; the bill came to Clinton's desk to sign or veto. After weighing the possible cost of not signing DOMA—almost three-fourths of Americans said they were opposed to same-sex marriage—he signed.[26] Bill

Clinton, avowed champion of gay people, had virtually killed the same-sex marriage movement.

Not all gays and lesbians were heartbroken. One of the Gay Liberation Front's first declarations after it had formed in the summer of 1969 was that it would "expose the institution of marriage as one of the most insidious and basic sustainers of the system."[27] Radical thinkers never changed their minds on the issue. Michael Warner argued that marriage "represents a widespread loss of vision" in the gay movement;[28] Michael Bronski argued that all the money and energy that would have to be lavished on fighting for marriage should be spent instead on helping queer youth;[29] "Let's not talk about marriage. There are funerals we have to worry about first—young people killing themselves because of all the hate they have to deal with in schools," transgender leader and Empress of the Imperial Court Nicole Murray-Ramirez argued.[30] Rather than being "a cheerleading squad for sameness" and yearning for the "undisturbed private life" of marriage, gays and lesbians should be "celebrating queer sexualities" and fighting for larger social issues—LGBT job security, for instance, or fixing racism and economic disparities—Urvashi Vaid, former executive director of the National Gay and Lesbian Task Force, said.[31] True, married people got advantages, such as benefiting from a spouse's health insurance—but free health insurance should be available to everybody, even the unmarried, activist lawyer William Dobbs argued.[32]

"Genderqueer" activist Mattilde Bernstein Sycamore compared the "marriage boat" to the *Titanic*, "doomed to crash into an iceberg and take the rest of us down."[33]

SCALIA, THE SEER

In 1978 lawyer John Ward established a small public-interest law firm, Gay and Lesbian Advocates and Defenders, to fight the Boston Police who were still up to old tricks, entrapping gay men in the toilets of the Boston Public Library. A dozen years later, Gay and Lesbian Advocates and Defenders, much expanded, hired Mary Bonauto, a slight, five-foot-tall young lesbian from a working-class "highly Catholic family," as she described it.[34] She was only four years out of law school, and her job was to be the watchdog over a new Massachusetts state law that banned discrimination based on sexual orientation in housing, employment, and public accommodations.

Her attention was pulled in other directions. It was still the height of the AIDS epidemic. She'd get desperate phone calls from partners of men who'd died—the survivor had been kicked out of the home they'd shared together. "His family is here, and he was never out to them," the survivor would tell her from a telephone booth. "They're taking everything from our apartment. What can I do?" Often the person with AIDS had died intestate; there was nothing to be done. Or sometimes she'd get calls from AIDS support groups, imploring her to go to the hospital and help someone on the verge of death do a will. She'd have to rush to his bedside to determine that he was mentally competent, then have him dictate a will, then go back to her office and type it up, struggling to get it right, then hurry back to the hospital—hoping all the while he hadn't yet died. She got calls from lesbians also, asking questions like, "Isn't there anything we can do so that when Sheryl picks our daughter up at day care they'll acknowledge that she's our daughter's mother, too, that I'm 'Mama' and Sheryl's 'Matka'?"[35] Bonauto had to answer no, there was nothing to be done.[36]

Her mind was changed when she went with the rest of the GLAD staff to a semiannual, national gathering—called "The Roundtable"—with lawyers from all the LGBT legal organizations. There she met Evan Wolfson. He convinced her that marriage would be the surest shield against society's contemptuous abuse of those in same-sex relationships.

Bonauto was so animated by his exhilarating vision that Wolfson found himself in the unaccustomed position of tamping down another lawyer's hurry to sue for marriage. He'd been sure after the 1993 Hawaii Supreme Court ruling that victory was imminent. He told Bonauto they mustn't muddy the legal waters.[37] But it was three years before Judge Chang issued his decision. And then the judge agreed to a stay while the state prepared its case for an appeal. And then President Clinton signed DOMA, and state legislatures were ganging up on gays. Something needed to be done to reverse the bad run, Mary Bonauto thought. She reasoned from what the Hawaii Supreme Court had said about same-sex marriage that if there was a good suit, with the right plaintiffs, and a strong constitutional argument, and a sympathetic high court—miracles could happen.

She and Wolfson agreed it was time for a second front. GLAD had grown to represent all six New England states; Bonauto thought Vermont seemed a good choice for a marriage case because in 1994 Vermont's Supreme Court had approved second-parent adoptions for same-sex couples.[38] In July 1997, she and Vermont lawyers Beth Robinson and Susan Murray sued on behalf of two lesbian couples and a gay male couple for the right to marry. In trial court, they lost for the usual reason. Marriage was for making babies and rearing them, the judge declared. That two of the couples were rearing children, or that their families were suffering without the protections of marriage, was irrelevant.

As she'd hoped to do from the start, Bonauto appealed to the Vermont Supreme Court; and as she predicted it would, that court, like Hawaii's Supreme Court, found that the plaintiffs had been treated unfairly and the state owed them remedy. However, instead of declaring that now same-sex couples must be allowed to marry, the Vermont Supreme Court justices left it up to the General Assembly to figure out how to fix the wrong.[39] Vermont's state senators and representatives decided that the remedy was to allow gay and lesbian couples "civil unions." The state would give them all the rights of marriage—except the name.

It was a booby prize. "Separate is not equal!" Bonauto insisted. Next time, she vowed, she'd forestall such a second-class remedy.[40]

In 2001 Bonauto and her longtime partner, law professor Jennifer Wriggins, decided to start a family. Wriggins was already in her forties; Bonauto, who was thirty-nine, would carry the baby (twin girls, it turned out). In fighting for marriage, she'd be fighting not just for abstract lesbians and gays but also for her own family. Massachusetts was the next state she'd take on. This time she'd battle for nothing less than the golden ring.

Bonauto and Gay and Lesbian Advocates and Defenders looked for plaintiffs who could stand up under scrutiny. In court, Bonauto would shine a light on them as real people who'd been harmed by the ban on same-sex marriage; she'd get them to tell gut-wrenching tales. "What kind of problems have you had because you can't get married?" "Why did you want to make a commitment to each other?"[41] she asked in her search for plaintiffs. "Tell me now if there's anything in your background that would be embarrassing if it became known," she demanded. She and her team chose four lesbian and three gay male couples: black and white, young and

old (from thirty-five to sixty), affluent to lower-middle class (business executives, a computer engineer, therapists, teachers, nurses). Spotless. Four of
the couples were raising young children.

For the lead plaintiffs she sought a couple who presented well, could
speak to the media, had an especially compelling story. She chose Julie and
Hillary Goodridge (an investment banker and a development officer for
the Unitarian Church). They'd taken the last name of Hillary's maternal
grandmother in 1996, when their daughter Annie was born. Julie gave
birth by C-section, and Annie had had to spend time in neonatal intensive
care. Hillary wasn't allowed to see the baby because she wasn't "the parent."
She couldn't get into Julie's room in recovery to see her either, until in des-
peration she told the nurses, "I'm her sister." The Goodridges again felt the
deprivation of not being able to marry when Annie was five years old and
remarked that her parents didn't love each other, "because if you did, you'd
be married."[42] "Talk from your hearts," Mary Bonauto coached them and
all the couples. "Explain again and again why you put yourself forward and
want to challenge the government's discrimination against your relationship."[43]

Escorted by Bonauto (and the police for protection because word had
gotten out to the media), they applied for marriage licenses and were, of
course, turned down. They sued. A lower court judge dismissed their case,
declaring that "procreation is marriage's central purpose."[44] On March 4,
2003, Bonauto appealed *Goodridge et al. v. Department of Public Health* to the
highest court in the state, the Massachusetts Supreme Judicial Court.[45] At
the John Adams Courthouse in Boston, where she pled the case, she made
it clear to the judges that her clients were demanding marriage, not civil
unions. "There really is no such thing as separating the word 'marriage'
from the protections it provides," she told the court. "The word is what
conveys the status that everyone understands as the ultimate expression
of love and commitment." To create a separate system, as in civil unions,
"merely perpetuates the stigma of exclusion," she argued. It says that gay
people and their love relationships are unworthy of the civil institution of
marriage.

It was a lucky coincidence that in June, three months after the Supreme
Judicial Court of Massachusetts listened to Bonauto's pleading in the
Goodridge case, the US Supreme Court handed down its *Lawrence v. Texas*

decision. There was no longer anything criminal about being gay. *Lawrence* had a profound effect on the Massachusetts Supreme Judicial Court decision in the *Goodridge* case, which was announced the following November. The court's chief justice, South African–born Margaret Marshall, appointed to the Supreme Judicial Court by one Republican governor and named chief justice by another, wrote the 4-to-3 majority opinion.[46] Marshall quoted *Lawrence v. Texas* liberally. The government may not intrude "into the deeply personal realms of consensual adult expressions of intimacy and of one's choice of intimate partner," SCOTUS had affirmed in *Lawrence.* "Our obligation is to define the liberty of all, not to mandate our own moral code." Same-sex couples, Justice Margaret Marshall declared for the Massachusetts Court, had the same right as had opposite-sex couples to marry.[47]

Antonin Scalia, the Supreme Court's arch antigay justice, had posed a sarcastic question in his dissenting opinion in *Lawrence v. Texas*: If sodomy laws are overturned, "what justification could there possibly be for denying homosexuals the benefit of marriage?"[48] *None,* was the implication. He'd been prescient.

Chapter 32

GETTING IT RIGHT, AND
WRONG, IN THE WEST

THE GAY AGENDA: WASHINGTON

In the state of Washington, the success of the struggle that culminated in
the right to marry ("the gay agenda," the right wing disdainfully called the
struggle) began with a tragedy. Seattle, where Charlene Strong and Kate
Fleming lived as a couple, had had incessant rains and powerful windstorms
in December 2006. On December 14, as Strong was about to leave the
downtown Seattle dentist office where she worked, she called Fleming to
say that before coming home to dinner, she'd stop at the nearby apartment
of her brother. Her mother, who'd just moved to Seattle from Louisiana,
was staying there. Fifteen minutes later, Fleming called Strong back on her
cell phone. There was a flash flood in their Madison Valley neighborhood.
The rains had overwhelmed the area's stormwater system. The rising waters
had become a turbulent river that was running down the hill toward Fleming and Strong's small house. Water was coming through the back door,
pouring into the basement where Fleming, an award-winning actor and
producer of audiobooks, had a studio. She kept her expensive recording
equipment there.[1]

"Please don't go down there! I'll be right home," Strong yelled as a
twelve-foot supporting wall in their home began caving. Fleming ran

down the basement stairs to retrieve her equipment. The basement door slammed shut behind her with the force of the rushing water. She couldn't open it; the water kept rising. With the cell phone she'd had in her pocket, she called Strong again. "Charlene, hurry." She was crying. "Be my hero, darling," she implored. Then she called 911. (Her last words on the 911 tape were "Tell my family I love them. Charlene, I love you.") Charlene Strong, running through streets in which water was rushing like rapids, arrived before the rescue crew. She struggled to take the pins off the basement door, but she couldn't. She had to swim as the water rose around her. Finally, the rescue workers arrived and cut a hole through the upstairs floor. One of the men jumped into the water and pulled Kate Fleming out. She was unconscious.[2]

They wouldn't let Strong ride with her partner in the ambulance. "We need room to work on her," they said. Strong's brother arrived and driving on the sidewalks, through the flood, the distraught Strong shrieking as loud as the siren, they followed the ambulance. At Harborview Medical Center, a social worker stopped her as she ran after the gurney that carried Fleming. "I'm her partner. We've been together ten years. I have to be with her," she told the woman. "Only family are allowed in. You need to find her next of kin," was the answer. Strong and Fleming had had a commitment ceremony, officiated by Fleming's progressive aunt, who'd been a nun for sixteen years. But a commitment ceremony had no legal standing.

Strong finally called Fleming's sister in Alexandria, Virginia, who told the social worker to let Strong into the room where Fleming lay. Strong found oil to anoint her lover's hands and feet; then Fleming died in her arms. Later, at the mortuary, the director told Strong that though she was paying for the funeral, she had no right to make decisions, "a family member must do it." Fleming's death certificate stated she was unmarried.[3] Charlene Strong, who hadn't been a gay rights activist before, became one.

Out gay senator Ed Murray had been in the Washington State Legislature since 1995. He'd chaired the Senate's budget and transportation committees, and he knew how to work well even with Republicans and conservative Democrats. But for years, he'd been frustrated about the gay rights legislation he kept introducing. It went nowhere—until finally in 2006 he got a bill passed adding LGBT people to the state's Civil Rights Act, protecting them from discrimination in housing, employment, and lending. The next year, Murray introduced a bill that mandated the creation of a state domestic partnership registry. It would provide mostly "death and dying rights" for domestic partners: hospital visitation, the ability to authorize autopsies and organ donations, and inheritance rights where there was no will.[4] Despite his 2006 success, Murray knew not to be overly confident about the new bill; right-wingers were already calling it a "slippery slope."

On January 27, 2007, six weeks after Fleming's death, the bill was scheduled to undergo a public hearing before the Senate voted on it. The death of Kate Fleming, who'd recorded over 250 audio books and was something of an audiobook star, was widely reported in the Washington media, as was Charlene Strong's horrific ordeal with authorities who'd kept her from her lover. Their story left no doubt about the need for Ed Murray's bill; and Murray understood right away that Charlotte Strong was crucial to the bill's presentation. She'd put a face on "gay and lesbian" for the straight world; her story would make legislators see the reality of gay and lesbian families and the injustices perpetrated on their lives.[5] Charlene Strong was asked to come to Olympia to testify at the bill's hearing. As she spoke in the Senate chamber, Strong held up a large photograph of Kate Fleming for everyone to see. Unitarian Minister Carol McKinley, who'd come to the hearing to represent the progressive faith community that supported gay rights, looked around at the audience while Strong was telling her story. The minister couldn't see a dry eye in the house.[6]

The bill passed in the Democratic-dominated Senate by a vote of 28 to 19. It passed the House by 55 to 43. On April 21, 2007, Washington's liberal governor, Christine Gregoire, signed it into law. The governor, a Catholic, had been a Sunday morning greeter at St. Michael's, her parish church in the Seattle suburb of Snohomish. After signing the bill, she was disinvited. She stopped going to St. Martin's, the largest parish in the state, because she knew the priest would deny her communion.[7]

Senator Murray had known Jamie Pedersen since 1996, when they both joined the Washington Marriage Alliance to fight against DOMA. Eleven years later, Pedersen was elected to the Washington State House of Representatives. He and Murray immediately began to plot a careful road map to the eventual passage of a same-sex marriage law. Pedersen's commitment to the fight had started in 1994 when, still a student at Yale Law School, a friend had taken him to dinner at the home of Evan Wolfson, whose passion on the subject was infectious.[8] In 2003 Wolfson founded Freedom to Marry, to promote the right of same-sex couples to marry by driving a national strategy—litigation, the ballot, direct action, legislation—fighting state by state, leading finally to SCOTUS after most Americans were living in a marriage state and saw "the realities of families helped and no one hurt."[9] But Washington was a referendum state: it meant that even if gay people won marriage in the legislature, they could lose it in the voting booths. Murray and Pedersen knew they had to start small, make incremental steps, get their colleagues and the voters used to the idea that gays and lesbians were citizens who deserved all the rights of citizenship.

The fundamentalist preacher of Kirkland, Washington's mega Antioch Bible Church, Ken Hutcherson—an ex-NFL football player and the most prominent African American on the Billy Graham Crusade team—understood Murray and Pedersen's "gay political agenda," as he called it.[10] Hutcherson and his followers showed up in Olympia to protest every gay rights bill, claiming each one brought the state a step closer to "gay marriage." They were right.

Governor Gregoire had had to struggle with her religious upbringing over gay issues. But when she'd been attorney general and was expected to defend the state's DOMA, she thought arguments such as "marriage is for bringing children into the world" didn't make sense unless the state was willing to say that childless straight couples shouldn't be married either. That much she could see. Senator Murray hoped to make the governor see more. Murray, who was also a practicing Catholic, dined often with the governor and her husband; Murray's longtime partner, Michael Shiosaki, made their dinners a foursome. They talked a lot about their faith; they agreed that the Church had no business being in the state's business. But the governor didn't want to make proclamations in favor of same-sex marriage yet. She was sure Washington wasn't ready. When Murray revealed his patient, years-long, incremental strategy to her, she gave it her imprimatur. She and Washington needed time to evolve.[11]

After the passage of the 2007 "death and dying" bill, Murray and Pedersen's next step was a 2008 bill that gave Washington's domestic partners

160 of the more than 400 rights and responsibilities enjoyed by the state's heterosexual married couples. Governor Gregoire signed it into law on March 12, 2008. Senator Murray didn't disguise his "agenda" at the signing, where he proclaimed, "Today is a beginning, not an end, a sign of hope that one day we'll receive full recognition for our relationships, the day we are finally able to marry."

Next, in early 2009, came the "everything but marriage bill" which Pedersen introduced in the House and Murray introduced in the Senate. The 110-page bill gave domestic partners all the rest of the 400 rights enjoyed by Washington's married heterosexual couples, including tax benefits and survivor's rights in pensions. It passed the House by a vote of 62 to 35 and the Senate by 30 to 18. Legislators such as conservative Democrat Mary Margaret Haugen, whose vote had helped pass Washington's Defense of Marriage Act back in 1996, voted *yes* on the 2009 bill—a testament to the effectiveness of Murray and Pedersen's incremental strategy and to the importance of gays and lesbians everywhere coming out. Haugen told Pedersen, who every "Children's Day" had brought his partner and four little kids to Congress, "Getting to know you and your family, I saw it differently."[12] On May 18, 2009, Governor Gregoire signed the "everything but marriage" bill into law. Her two young adult daughters, who had many gay friends, the governor said, reminded her that just as race was the civil rights issue of her generation, so was sexual orientation the civil rights issue of theirs.[13]

The biggest test of Murray and Pedersen's incremental approach came when a group called Protect Marriage gathered 137,881 petition signatures, more than enough to force a referendum on the "everything but marriage" bill. That November, it would be up to Washington voters to say whether they finally believed that gay and lesbian relationships deserved serious protections. By 53 percent to 47 percent, voters said they did. With the passage of Referendum 71, Washington became the first state in which domestic partnerships were ratified by the electorate.

Yet a 2010 poll showed that while 80 percent of Washingtonians believed that gays and lesbians should have legal recognition of their relationships, only 40 percent were in favor of calling those relationships "marriage."

Two years later, January 23, 2012: Senator Craig Pridemore, chair of the Senate Government Operations Committee, led the hearing. The crowd, packed with Christian fundamentalists and gay activists, overflowed the small wood-paneled room. Tensions were palpable. "I won't tolerate any disruptions, neither applause nor jeering," Pridemore announced sternly at the outset. Senator Murray, as the marriage bill's sponsor, spoke first. He talked about how for everyone present in that room there was nothing more important than family. "It touches what each of us holds most dear," and that was true, too, he said, for him and his partner Michael Shiosaki, Seattle's Parks and Recreation Director, with whom he'd had a loving, committed relationship since 1991. Then he handed the microphone to Shiosaki, who spoke of his parents' fifty-six-year marriage, and how his commitment to Ed Murray was no different from his parents' commitment to each other. He compared with great feeling the Japanese American struggle for inclusion into the mainstream with the struggle he and Murray had for inclusion as a gay couple. He asked the senators to let him and Murray be married "like my mother and father are married."

The conservatives who'd come to testify mocked the two men's emotional speeches. "Humanity is a gendered species," one man pontificated. Reverend Hutcherson complained on the floor, "Since you think God is not smart enough to make it fair, you are saying you are smart enough to make it fair!" A nun read from the Bible and lectured about Sodom and Gomorrah. Another nun proclaimed, "The Bible doesn't mention Eve and Susan." Buttons declaring "Marriage. One Man. One Woman" were everywhere.[14]

February 1, 2012: "Regardless of how you vote on this bill, an invitation will be in the mail," Senator Murray told his fellow senators jocularly, announcing that he and Shiosaki hoped to marry as soon as possible. A wedding at St. Mark's, atop Capitol Hill, an Episcopal church whose dean had already established that St. Mark's ministers would conduct the same marriage ritual for same-sex couples that they conducted for opposite-sex couples.[15]

Ed Murray's Senate colleagues didn't disappoint him in their vote. It was 28 to 21 in favor of same-sex marriage.[16]

A few days later a vote was taken on the House version of the bill. One of its cosponsors was Laurie Jinkins, an out lesbian elected to Washington's Congress the year before. Whenever Jinkins spoke on the House floor she tried to squeeze in some pertinent reference to her partner and their son,

Wulf. (A Republican colleague, who admitted to her that she was "getting" him, nicknamed her "Two Mommies.")[17] Now she brought her partner of twenty-three years and eleven-year-old Wulf to the Senate chamber, so her fellow representatives would have a living image before them when they voted on whether same-sex families should be legitimized by the right to marry.

But it was a third-term Republican representative from conservative Walla Walla who did for the 2012 marriage bill what Charlene Strong had done for the 2007 domestic partnership bill. Maureen Walsh was Pedersen's first House cosponsor on his marriage bill, though she "cried almost every night" after agreeing to do it, afraid it might cost her the next election.[18] (It didn't.) On February 8, 2012, an impromptu "from the heart"[19] House speech by the stocky, gray-haired legislator went viral, scoring millions of hits on YouTube. The fifty-one-year-old Walsh, a bit of a stand-up comic, guilelessly announced she'd been widowed for six years and was looking for a boyfriend. "Not having much luck with that," she sighed and shrugged, and then launched into a story about how she and her husband had had twenty-three wonderful years together, he'd been the love of her life, and it wasn't the sex she missed—"Well, I certainly miss it," she added parenthetically, "but that's not what it boils down to." What it boiled down to, Walsh said, very serious now, "is that incredible bond I had with that human being that I really, really genuinely wish I still had. And so I think to myself, how can I deny anyone the right to have that incredible bond with another individual in life?"

Then Walsh talked about her oldest daughter Shauna, "a fabulous girl who was the light of her father's eyes," and whose sense of social justice even as a kid in elementary school made her stand up for a child who was bullied, though she knew it wasn't the popular thing to do. "It is incumbent on us as legislators of the state to do that," to do what's right though it's not popular, Walsh told her fellow representatives before announcing that Shauna is a lesbian living with a person she loves very much. "Someday, by God, I want to throw a wedding for that kid. I hope that's exactly what I can do," she concluded.

Governor Gregoire and Senator Murray stood together in the wings of the chamber, watching the House vote: it was 55 to 43 in favor of same-sex marriage.[20]

• • •

February 13, 2012, a signing ceremony at the Legislative Building: Representative Jamie Pedersen, Huck Finn–looking despite his proper suit and tie and his forty-four years, thanked his partner and future husband Eric Pedersen, who'd left his job as a high school administrator so he could take care of their four kids while Pedersen served Washington in the legislature. Senator Ed Murray, who the following fall would be elected mayor of Seattle, introduced Governor Gregoire. She wore a red jacket in honor of Valentine's eve and the occasion. Her brief speech was about family values: about "children who will no longer have to wonder why their loving parents are considered different from other loving parents," and "the six-year-old boy who came to me with his two moms and gave me a handwritten note in block letters that said 'PLEASE CHANGE THE LAW SO WE CAN WED.'" There'd probably be a referendum on the bill, the governor predicted, but "voters will say *yes*, because a family is a family . . . and because it's time to stand up for our daughters, our brothers, our sisters."

The Right did bring a referendum to the ballot. On November 7, 2012, a record turnout of 81 percent of eligible Washington voters showed up at polling places. By a vote of 54 percent to 46 percent, they agreed with Governor Gregoire that "a family is a family."

"PROTECTING MARRIAGE" IN THE GOLDEN STATE

William "Pete" Knight—nicknamed the "Fastest Man Alive" after he'd set a speed record flying X-15 rocket planes in Vietnam—had served in the California State Assembly since 1992, representing the ultraconservative desert community of Palmdale. In 1996 Knight decided to make a run for the State Senate. His opponent in the Republican primary, former assemblyman Phil Wyman, was every bit as right-wing as was Knight; the race was tight, and the ex-fighter pilot sought ways to "outconservative" Wyman. A member of Knight's assembly staff had been following the progress of same-sex marriage in Hawaii. He suggested that Knight speak out strong and clear "in defense of marriage."[21] Knight, a devoted Baptist, thought it a fine idea. He won the primary; then he beat his Democratic challenger, 172,000 to 84,000.

That same year, Knight's gay brother was dying of complications from

AIDS. The family-values politician cut ties with him. That same year, too, Knight's son David—who'd made his father proud when he'd followed in his footsteps, graduating from the Air Force Academy and flying fighter planes in the Gulf War[22]—came out to his father as gay. Knight senior threw David out of the family.[23] When a San Francisco paper spilled the son's story two months before the 1996 election, Pete Knight countered by coolly telling the press, "As far as I'm concerned, it's his business. His sexual preference has no consequence to my work as a state legislator."[24]

Knight kept his promise to his constituents by introducing a "California Defense of Marriage Act" into the legislature. But the same election that had brought him to the Senate also brought in a Democratic majority. The bill didn't have a chance there. Nor could it win in the Assembly, whose popular speaker pro tem was an out lesbian, Sheila Kuehl, once the boyish Zelda on *The Many Loves of Dobie Gillis*. In 2000, up for reelection, still not having succeeded in getting his bill passed in the legislature, Senator Knight took the issue directly to California voters as Proposition 22. It said that "Only marriage between a man and a woman is valid or recognized in California." Not only could lesbian and gay couples not marry in California; the state wouldn't recognize their marriage even if they tied the knot in Hawaii or anywhere else same-sex marriage might become legal. Knight would "stop marriage at the Golden Gate."[25] From the distance of Washington, DC, President Bush and Senator McCain endorsed the measure. Signs in neighborhoods all over California proclaimed "Protect Marriage" and "Yes on Knight." His initiative passed overwhelmingly: 61 percent to 39 percent. To make sure California's liberal Democratic governor Gray Davis didn't try to subvert the intent of Prop 22 by sneaking in "civil unions" or giving gay relationships some other advantage, Senator Knight established the Proposition 22 Legal Defense and Education Fund to be a watchdog.

A VALENTINE'S DAY RITUAL

Beverly Hills, the courthouse: Robin Tyler, standing in line at the clerk's office with Diane Olson at her side, holding a pink bakery box that contained a miniature wedding cake. It was to be eaten—regardless of whether there'd be a wedding to celebrate—by the members of the Metropolitan

Community Church who waited on the courthouse steps, waving "Gay Marriage Now!" signs. Tyler was the activist who'd called for the first March on Washington for Lesbian and Gay Rights in 1979; Olson, her partner of more than a decade, had grown up in Beverly Hills. She was the granddaughter of Culbert Olson, California's progressive governor who was so militant about the separation of church and state that at his swearing-in ceremony in 1939 he refused to utter "so help me God." (Instead, he said "I do affirm.") The governor's granddaughter was equally fierce. It was religious bigotry, she declared, that denied same-sex couples the right to marry. Reverend Troy Perry, looking ministerial and distinguished with his silvery goatee and white-collared purple shirt, and Phillip DeBlieck, Perry's partner of twenty years, stood in the line behind Tyler and Olson. Celebrity attorney Gloria Allred hovered close by.

The routine in Beverly Hills had been the same every Valentine's Day since 2004, after same-sex couples had begun marrying in Massachusetts.[26] Each couple walked up to the clerk's window and said why they were there. The clerk was friendly, but Prop 22 left no leeway.[27] He handed them a form, printed in anticipation of their annual visit. It said, "California State law permits the county clerk to issue a marriage license only to an unmarried male and an unmarried female. Changes to this law can only be approved by the State Legislature and the Governor."[28]

Attorney Allred, in her signature red pantsuit and vivid red lipstick, made sure the press was alerted each time, and they showed up with cameras at the ready.[29] In 2004 she announced from the steps of the Beverly Hills Courthouse that she was preparing a lawsuit on behalf of the two couples. She argued that Proposition 22 violated the Constitution's Equal Protection Clause. Allred compared her clients to the interracial couple of the *Perez v. Sharp* case, who'd challenged and overthrown California's miscegenation law in 1948. Like the Perez couple, Allred said, her gay and lesbian clients were asking for marriage licenses.[30]

Gavin Newsom, mayor of San Francisco, also thought it was time same-sex couples could do in his state what they were doing in Massachusetts. A few hours after Gloria Allred had announced that her clients would be suing for the right to marry in Los Angeles, Newsom issued a marriage license to a same-sex couple in San Francisco. The California Constitution's Equal

Protection Clause, he said, gave them the right to be married. Newsom—heterosexual, married, Irish Catholic, and a political centrist except when it came to social issues—had made the decision to act after having been in office only twelve days: He'd heard President George W. Bush say in his State of the Union address on January 20 that he wanted to amend the US Constitution to "protect marriage." The thirty-seven-year-old mayor was "disgusted and outraged";[31] he had his chief of staff Steve Kawa call Kate Kendall, executive director of the San Francisco–based National Center for Lesbian Rights: "Tell me, who should be the first same-sex couple to get a marriage license?" Kawa asked.

"Del Martin and Phyllis Lyon, of course," Kendell said.[32] Martin was eighty-three; Lyon was seventy-nine; that Valentine's Day, they'd be celebrating fifty-one years together. It was a fitting tribute to San Francisco's pioneering lesbian-activist couple. Mayor Newsom officiated over the ceremony himself. He also ordered that the marriage license application form be revised to eliminate all gendered language; 4,035 more same-sex couples were married in San Francisco that month.

Among them were Senator Knight's son David, and David's partner of ten years, Joe Lazzaro, who flew into San Francisco from their home in Baltimore. Wearing dark suits and matching red boutonnieres, a gift from Lazzaro's mother,[33] the two men were married in a ceremony atop the grand staircase of the city hall's ornate, soaring rotunda.

As soon as same-sex marriages started in San Francisco, the Proposition 22 Legal Defense and Education Fund filed in Superior Court to halt them. Senator Knight, who was suffering from an undisclosed illness, didn't pause a moment in his fight to "protect marriage" from his son and other gays. On April 1, 2004, three weeks after David Knight's wedding, the senator was still railing on TV that "there is no civil right that says you should be allowed to marry a man and a man."[34] Five weeks later, Knight Sr. was dead of leukemia. But that was far from the end of the story, or the family drama.

Gail Knight, Pete's devoted widow and David's estranged stepmother, carried on in her husband's name. She helped found California's Protect Marriage organization, which hoped to get a state constitutional amendment passed that would take from gay and lesbian couples even the domestic partnership rights they'd had in California since 1999.

Austrian-born Arnold Schwarzenegger, California's movie-star governor, had already announced about same-sex marriage, "I don't care one way or the other."[35] But he was inundated by letters and phone calls prompted by Knight's group. They reminded Schwarzenegger that he owed his election to a Republican constituency, and they were its loudest voice. Governor Schwarzenegger had been in office only a year. He had visions of a long political career, maybe even overturning the federal law that said only a native-born American could be president. He ordered California's attorney general, Bill Lockyer, to "take immediate steps"—get a ruling from the state Supreme Court—to stop Mayor Newsom from issuing marriage licenses to gays and lesbians.[36] Lockyer, a liberal Democrat, had already made his own public statement: he didn't support policies that gave lesser legal rights and responsibilities to committed same-sex couples. But he did his job and filed a petition in the California Supreme Court to halt the marriages. On August 12, 2004, the state's justices officially put asunder all 8,072 whom Mayor Newsom had joined together.[37]

December 2004: The San Francisco–based National Center for Lesbian Rights spearheaded the consolidation of six same-sex marriage cases from Southern and Northern California, and they sued. Their case was heard in the San Francisco Superior Court of Judge Richard Kramer. The judge, who was known to be "on the conservative side,"[38] had been appointed to the Superior Court in 1996 by antigay Republican governor Pete Wilson.[39] Gail Knight and her group were confident Richard Kramer would protect marriage. But the judge declared in his March 2005 decision that Proposition 22 was unconstitutional. It violated the ban on sex discrimination by making gender a primary requisite for marriage; it also violated the state constitution's equal protection clause. Moreover, the judge said, the old marriage-is-for-bringing-kids-into-the-world saw flew in the face of facts. A lot of unmarried people were bringing kids into the world by the twenty-first century, and a lot of married people weren't. To the argument that lesbians and gays had domestic-partnership rights in California that were equal to marriage, Kramer responded that "marriage-like rights" smacked of a concept that the courts had rejected in 1954, "separate but equal." The state hadn't come up with any legitimate reason to deny same-sex couples the right to marry, Kramer said, so they must be permitted to do so.[40]

For his bold judicial opinion he received bushels of letters threatening to kill him and telling him he'd burn in hell for eternity. Kramer had to live with twenty-four-hour police protection and wear a bulletproof vest under his judicial robes. He also strapped on a gun.[41]

Those bent on stopping same-sex marriage at the Golden Gate accused Attorney General Lockyer of not "defending the marriage laws with vigor,"[42] and they took their case to the California Appeals Court, where they got a decision more to their liking. The appeals court judges opined that Judge Kramer had treated the Constitution as though it were "some kind of 'origami project,' twisting and reconfiguring it to accomplish ends better left to the democratic process." The electorate had voted overwhelmingly for Proposition 22, and it had to stay in place, the Appellate Court ordered.[43]

By then, Bill Lockyer had been elected State Treasurer; but as one of his last acts as attorney general he asked the California Supreme Court to review the Appellate Court's decision.[44] He complained that the Protect Marriage forces didn't even have "standing" to pursue the case. "The attorney general has made it plain that he wishes to put the victory for the State at risk in further litigation," Protect Marriage answered. They had "standing" they argued because they were "sponsors, organizers, financial supporters and volunteers" in the Proposition 22 struggle. But not trusting the California Supreme Court would rule the right way, they organized a petition drive to put a proposition on the ballot for a state constitutional amendment—the "Eliminates Right of Same-Sex Couples to Marry Act." Twelve Catholic dioceses and the Mormon Church supported them with money and volunteers. If passed by the voters, the proposition would override any pro-marriage decision the California Supreme Court might issue.

Just as Protect Marriage feared, the Supreme Court declared in a 5-to-4 decision that marriage was a basic civil right, the state had "no compelling interest" in denying same-sex couples the respect and dignity of marriage, and it was unconstitutional to do so.[45] Starting June 17, 2008, all counties had to issue marriage licenses to same-sex applicants.

June 16, 5:01 p.m.: Robin Tyler and Diane Olson, in honor of their years-long Valentine's Day battle, were permitted to be the first to marry in the county of Los Angeles. The wedding was held on the steps of the Beverly Hills Courthouse, Gloria Allred by their side, and TV crews from around the world memorializing the event. At the same moment, Phyllis Lyon and Del Martin were again married at San Francisco City Hall, Mayor Gavin Newsom again officiating.

The Protect Marriage/Proposition 22 Legal Defense and Education Fund needed 694,354 petition signatures to qualify their anti-same-sex-marriage initiative for the ballot. They got almost twice that number, and the initiative was put on the ballot as Proposition 8. The overwhelming success of the petition drive should have been a wake-up call to California gays and lesbians, as the Anita Bryant–John Briggs threat had been thirty years earlier. California gays and lesbians should have gotten together to organize a hard-hitting "suits and streets" campaign—tens of thousands of volunteers of all stripes, plus the most savvy professional campaigners, all working day and night—just as they'd done against Senator Briggs's Proposition 6.[46] But their guard was down. They already had all those rights that Ed Murray and Jamie Pedersen had labored for years to get in Washington State before asking for marriage. California lawmakers had led the country in passing pro-gay legislation: protections against employment discrimination and hate crimes, laws permitting adoption by same-sex parents, domestic partnership laws that gave same-sex couples all the rights of married couples. And Public Policy Institute surveys and Field Polls, from May 2008 all the way to the end of October seemed to say there was nothing to worry about: Proposition 8 was going to lose—by as much as 7 or 8 percent of the vote. So instead of waging war against the Protect Marriage forces, most California gays and lesbians went to the movies or the beach.

The feeble organized effort led by Equality for All/No on 8 was replete with bad choices. They grappled for a while with whether to tell honest stories about gay and lesbian lives, or to de-gay the campaign. The de-gaying side won. The effort to stop Prop 8 became a "1977 Dade County Coalition for Human Rights" all over again. Instead of showing gay couples in homes they made together, doing the laundry and gardening just as straight people do, talking about their love and commitment and the responsibility they take for each other, No on 8 lavished millions of dollars, donated by gays and lesbians all over the country, on TV and print ads about high-flown abstractions—"human rights," "equality," "inclusiveness"—with hardly a mention of "gay and lesbian." One of No on 8's worst decisions was to keep kids out of the campaign. No children of same-sex couples talking about how the right to marry would help their families. Not even a response to TV ads about how same-sex marriage would harm children. Yes on 8—taking a page from Anita Bryant's Save Our Children campaign—made that their favorite tactic: an ad in which the camera focuses on upset and baffled first graders, who'd been taken to San Francisco's city hall where they were forced to watch their teacher's lesbian wedding; another in which a little girl tells her distraught mother that at school that day she learned that "a prince could marry a prince, and I can marry a princess"; an appeal to California's Latino community by using *telenovelas* star Eduardo Verástegui to tell viewers to "protect marriage and children by voting yes on 8."

The architect of the Yes on 8 campaign, Frank Schubert, a Sacramento political consultant, was chosen by the religious Right to run the campaign because he was one of them: He'd end every Yes on 8 meeting with bowed-head prayers. He masterminded the TV ads about protecting kids. He also masterminded the "ground game." Under his direction, tens of thousands of Yes on 8 volunteers who'd signed up at their churches' "Marriage Sunday" campaigns addressed envelopes, canvassed in the streets, knocked on doors, manned phone banks, and wrote "letters to the editor" about the homosexual threat to marriage.

George Niederauer, the Catholic Archbishop of San Francisco, waged the Yes on 8 war on another front. Before being sent to San Francisco in 2005 by Pope Benedict XVI,[47] Niederauer had been the bishop of Salt Lake City, where during his eleven-year tenure in Mormon territory, he'd made great inroads to improve Catholic-Mormon relations. With the Proposition 8 campaign under way, the archbishop approached his friends in the Mormon hierarchy to form a critical coalition. It didn't take much convincing. The Mormon Church had been behind the "Hawaii's Future Today" campaign, the main champions of Hawaii's constitutional amendment against same-sex marriage.[48] In the California campaign, Mormons, working with Catholics, became the backbone of Yes on 8 fund-raising. Seventy thousand churchgoers contributed $40 million, half of it coming from members of the Church of the Latter-Day Saints. "Get your checkbooks out," Thomas Monson, president of the Mormon Church, exhorted the faithful. "You are a mighty army. You'll be responsible for holding to the doctrines of the Church." The zealous Mormons also made up most of the volunteers who walked door to door, distributing literature and getting out votes in the election precincts. According to exit polls, 84 percent of those who attended church weekly voted yes on Proposition 8.[49]

November 4, 2008, election day: Californians elected Barack Obama, America's first black president by 61 percent of the vote. They approved Proposition 8 by 52 percent, a 700,000-vote margin. There were to be no more same-sex marriages in the state.

But in the five months since the California Supreme Court had upheld the right of gay and lesbian couples to marry, eighteen thousand of them had done so. Arnold Schwarzenegger, now in his second term as governor, couldn't run again because of term limits. With nothing to lose, he urged the California Supreme Court to permit the eighteen thousand to stay married.[50] He also gave a pep talk to the gay and lesbian community. In his twenties, he'd won the Mr. Olympia title as the world's greatest bodybuilder, six years in a row. He urged gay and lesbian couples to follow the lesson he'd learned as a teenager trying to lift weights that seemed too heavy: "Never give up. Be on it and on it, until you get it done."[51]

Chapter 33

THE EVOLUTION OF A
PRESIDENT AND THE COUNTRY

"HOW COULD *I* BE AGAINST GAY MARRIAGE?"

In 2006 a junior senator from Illinois had been invited to the Miami Book Fair International, a major literary event, to speak about his new book *The Audacity of Hope*. The title was a phrase in an eloquent speech he'd given at the Democratic National Convention in July 2004, four months before he was elected to the US Senate. The charisma and charm of the young African American legislator was so overwhelming that during the Q&A for his book, somebody addressed him as "Mr. President" and the audience of two thousand people broke out in spontaneous fervent applause. He had ready answers to difficult questions, too. Another audience member asked what he thought of "gay marriage." Barack Obama responded that he was "a strong believer that there has to be a strong sense of full citizenship enjoyed by all"; and that when his African father and white mother married in 1961, there were eighteen states where they could not have married because of miscegenation laws. "So how could *I* be against gay marriage?" he asked; then added, "though if I were running the movement, I wouldn't start with gay marriage."[1]

"The movement" had, of course, begun a decade before Barack Obama was born, and "gay marriage" had come to it quite late—but his answer to the question foretold how he'd respond to the issue when he did become "Mr. President." His sympathies were with those who wanted same-sex marriage because he had a gut-level understanding of what it was to be an outsider and of how discrimination hurt; yet politics was a game of prudence and expediency, and you wouldn't get anywhere if you didn't play the game.

As a candidate for president, Obama made his genuine sympathy for the LGBT community known—on occasion, and mostly to LGBT people. Early in his campaign, in February 2008, he wrote an "Open Letter from Barack Obama to the LGBT Community," to be published on LGBT websites and in LGBT magazines, promising that when he became president he'd "use the bully pulpit" for LGBT people and he'd support "the complete repeal of the Defense of Marriage Act."[2] Invited to the San Francisco Alice B. Toklas Democratic Club's Pride Breakfast, he didn't come, but he did send a one-page letter to be read aloud there, assuring the LGBT democrats that he was opposed to "the divisive and discriminatory efforts to amend the California Constitution" through Proposition 8. Some club members were put off by a candidate who wouldn't come to their Pride Breakfast, but they forgot about it by the end of the letter, where he congratulated "all of you who have shown your love for each other by getting married these last few weeks."[3]

But candidate Obama's political prudence kicked in often. A month after his letter was read at the Pride Breakfast, he was interviewed by Rick Warren, evangelical pastor of the twenty-two-thousand-member Saddleback Church in Lake Forest, California. The pastor, who'd supported Prop 8 from the start, would urge his followers shortly before the election to vote *yes* on the proposition because same-sex marriage "wasn't a political issue but a moral issue that God has spoken clearly about."[4] In Warren's interview with Obama, he asked the presidential candidate to "define marriage." Obama responded pat and without hesitation, as though having memorized the answer to a question for which he'd studied, "I believe marriage is the union between a man and a woman. For me as a Christian, it's a sacred union." His pronouncement was followed by the cheers of thousands in his audience. But, he added— looking uncomfortable yet unwilling to turn his back completely on a group that had suffered injustice because of who they were—he was "in favor of civil unions." That wasn't a politically expedient statement to make before a multitude of Baptist evangelicals. He hastened to defuse it by saying that civil unions would allow "gay partners to visit each other in the hospital."[5] Surely even the religious Right couldn't be against decency to the dead and dying, sinners though they may have been.

The innate sympathy Barack Obama had for the LGBT community was hugely returned. Polls showed that voters identifying as "gay, lesbian, or bisexual" made up 4 percent of the electorate in the 2008 election, and 70 percent of them had given Obama their vote.[6] In states where the race was tight, such as North Carolina and Virginia, the LGBT vote put him over the top.[7] The community expected a lot of the new president they'd helped elect.

In the beginning, they didn't get much. When Obama invited Rick Warren to give the invocation at his inauguration, LGBT people were outraged. Andrew Sullivan, the pioneering advocate for same-sex marriage,[8] groused, "If anyone is under the illusion that Obama is interested in advancing gay equality, they should probably sober up now."[9] Another big disappointment came that spring. In California, Arthur Smelt and Christopher Hammer, who'd been among the 18,000 couples that had married and were still married under California law, challenged DOMA in a federal court. Their suit referenced Article IV of the US Constitution: "Full faith and credit shall be given in each state to the public acts, records, and judicial proceedings in every other state." That should mean that when Smelt and Hammer traveled to Idaho or Mississippi or anywhere in the country, that state had to recognize that they were married. Moreover, they said, they should be entitled to all the federal benefits that heterosexual married couples get.[10]

President Obama let the Department of Justice file a brief in response to the suit of the two men. It defended the constitutionality of DOMA, argued that the federal government must not violate the rights of the states that had banned same-sex marriage, and moved that Smelt and Hammer's suit be "dismissed with prejudice."[11] Obama's response to LGBT groups who felt betrayed was that if they wanted the law repealed they should be knocking on the doors of their legislators. Congress had passed DOMA, and it was up to Congress, not the executive branch of government, to undo what it had done.[12]

. . .

But before Obama's first term as president was finished, something miraculous had happened that made it possible for him to follow his gut-level feelings for the LGBT community without sacrificing political prudence. In May 2008, when he was running for president, only 40 percent of Americans said *yes* when asked if same-sex couples should be allowed to marry. By May 2011, the change in public opinion was colossal: 53 percent of Americans said *yes* to the question—and a whopping 70 percent of the youngest demographic of voters said *yes*.[13] Young voters had turned out in force in the 2008 presidential election, and 66 percent of them had voted for Obama.[14] And now that important constituency was overwhelmingly in favor of same-sex marriage.

Older people, too, had shifted their opinion. For many of them it was because they now *knew* that they knew someone gay. A generation earlier, in 1993, only 22 percent of Americans claimed to have a close friend or family member who was gay or lesbian. By 2011, the number had practically tripled because gays and lesbians were exiting the closet en masse.[15] Harvey Milk was right in 1978 to urge them to *come out, come out, where ever you are*.[16] While some people, like Senator Pete Knight, become more homophobic when they learn someone close to them is gay, most become less.

However, the biggest reason behind the shift in public opinion was that the sixty-year civil rights struggle of homophiles, gays and lesbians, and the LGBT community had not been for naught. On May 6, 2012, Vice President Joe Biden, stumping for President Obama's reelection bid, appeared on NBC's *Meet the Press*. Sixteen years earlier, when Biden was a senator, he'd voted for DOMA. But now, when David Gregory, the Sunday morning TV host, asked the vice president what he thought of same-sex marriage, Biden answered without a pause, "I am absolutely comfortable [with] men marrying men, women marrying women." For him, he said, it comes down to "who you love." His academic explanation for why he'd changed his mind in the last years was that "things begin to change when social culture changes"—*Will and Grace* was his example. That sitcom, Biden proclaimed, "probably did more to educate the American public [about gay people] than almost anything anybody's done so far."

What the vice president didn't know, or didn't acknowledge, was that

Will and Grace would never have been possible without the long war that gay rights organizations had been waging on multiple fronts—including a battle with the networks that began in 1974, when the National Gay Task Force media committee made its anger known to ABC executives about the episode of *Marcus Welby, M.D.* that equated homosexuality with pederasty.[17] Stop showing gays as villains, rights groups such as the Gay and Lesbian Alliance against Defamation (a full-time media watchdog since 1985) had demanded; start showing gay people who have the human dimension of their straight counterparts. Their phenomenal success in educating the networks was evident by 1997 when fresh-faced Ellen DeGeneres was allowed to admit she was gay on her *Ellen* sitcom and even to lock lips with Laura Dern. The next year, lovable and gay "Will Thurman" began appearing weekly in America's living rooms. The country was clearly opening up. By 2012, even the wife of Mitt Romney was saying that her favorite TV show was *Modern Family*,[18] whose major characters included Cameron and Mitchell, a longtime gay couple raising a little girl they adopted from Vietnam, and getting married in front of a dozen million television viewers. A 2012 poll by *The Hollywood Reporter*, one of the TV industry's main insider publications, found that TV series such as *Modern Family, Glee*, and *The New Normal* were driving voters to favor same-sex marriage—"even Republican voters," the article reported.[19]

Obama himself also had much to do with the shifting climate. As the polls inched upward to indicate that more people supported same-sex marriage, he felt free to say he was "evolving" on the issue. But the polls had been inching upward in part because of the sympathy he'd already shown for LGBT people: signing the hate crimes bill in 2009; announcing in his State of the Union Address in 2010 that Don't Ask, Don't Tell must be repealed; finally letting it be known in 2011 that the Justice Department would no longer defend DOMA. The president's sympathy made the country more sympathetic.

April 2011, DC's St. Regis Hotel: At a classy LGBT fund-raising dinner for Barack Obama's reelection bid, he is asked by a tuxedoed Chad Griffin, the thirty-seven-year-old head of the Human Rights Campaign, "Mr. President, how can we help you 'evolve' more quickly?"

Obama answers, "I think you can tell from what I've done so far the direction that I'm headed."[20]

• • •

May 9, 2012: Obama had fully "evolved." His gut-level sympathies for the LGBT community had ceased to be in a tough tug-of-war with his political prudence. On the issue of marriage equality, he could safely distinguish himself from his opponent Mitt Romney, who'd announced that as president he'd pass a federal constitutional amendment banning homosexual marriage. (Romney seemed oblivious to Gallup, CNN, and *Washington Post* polls that all showed the majority of Americans now supported same-sex marriage.)[21] Same-sex marriage had been a wedge issue in 2004, bringing voters who disapproved of it to the ballot box to vote Republican. It could be a wedge issue in the 2012 election, too, Obama's strategists advised; it could bring more young people and women to the ballot box to vote Democratic. Obama could come out of the closet as who he'd been all along: a same-sex-marriage supporter.

Safe as his coming out was, presidential advisors orchestrated it meticulously,[22] even to the coffee cups sitting on the two little tables at the side of the president and the TV interviewer, to suggest they were having a cozy chat and not that Obama was making a dramatic proclamation. The interviewer, Robin Roberts—handsome, tailored, African American, a coanchor on ABC's *Good Morning America*[23]—was chosen with careful consideration to reaching a recalcitrant demographic: a Pew Research Center poll in 2011 said that only 36 percent of blacks approved of same-sex marriage. (The ploy—two smart, good-looking black people rationally discussing same-sex marriage as just and fair—worked. After the May 9 interview, a Pew Research Center poll found that 51 percent of African Americans favored same-sex marriage.)[24]

"Mr. President, are you still opposed to same-sex marriage?" was the scripted question Robin Roberts asked at the start. The talking points—family, patriotism, American decency and fairness—were scripted, too. "I've been going through an evolution on this issue," Obama began. He reminded America that he'd always been in favor of civil unions because it would give same-sex couples the rights others take for granted—"hospital visitations," was again his cautious example. But at the dinner table, he said, his daughters Sasha and Melia would sometimes talk about their friends who had same-sex parents; his daughters couldn't understand why the friends' parents were discriminated against. "That's the kind of thing that prompts a change of perspective . . . not wanting to explain to your child why somebody should be treated differently when it comes to the eyes of the law."

His mind had also been changed, he told Roberts and the country, by members on his own staff "who are in incredibly committed, monogamous, same-sex relationships, and who are raising kids together." He'd been troubled, too, that there were "soldiers, marines, sailors out there, who are fighting on my behalf," and despite their sacrifice, if they're gay, they aren't permitted to marry the one they love. But, he concluded, "I think the whole country is evolving and changing," because "America is about fairness and treating everybody as equals."[25]

Behind the carefully scripted words, however, was the man who'd declared himself years before to be a "strong believer [that] full citizenship should be enjoyed by all." Earlier that day, as he was leaving the presidential suite to go to the White House Cabinet Room where the interview would be held, Michelle Obama—who knew how her husband had struggled between his deep convictions and what had long seemed politically sensible—called to him, "Enjoy the day. You are free!"[26]

MARRIAGE EQUALITY, HOLLYWOOD, AND THE US SUPREME COURT: A SEMI-HAPPY ENDING

Same-sex marriages stopped in California the day after Proposition 8 was passed, and the real fight began. Gloria Allred joined the *Tyler* case to Northern California same-sex marriage cases and, with the National Center for Lesbian Rights and a dozen other rights groups, tried to figure out what their next move should be. The lawyers all cautiously agreed they shouldn't attempt a federal suit. A loss in federal court could set the movement back decades. They'd petition the California Supreme Court—they'd fight on a technicality: Proposition 8 is illegal, they'd argue, because it isn't an "amendment," as it pretends to be, but rather a "revision" of the state constitution. In stripping an entire group of a fundamental freedom, Prop 8 alters the constitution's guarantee of equality; and a vote to revise the constitution can't be put on the California ballot until two-thirds of both houses of the legislature give their approval. It was at best a timid argument.

And it was soon clear that the lawyers had chosen the wrong strategy.

The justices of the State Supreme Court responded that Proposition 8 did *not* revise the constitution; in fact, it did hardly anything at all. True, it took away from gays and lesbians "the label of marriage," but they still had domestic partnerships, which in California give them all the rights enjoyed by opposite-sex married couples. Marriage would give them nothing more.[27] Same-sex marriage supporters objected that the court's claim that the word "marriage" is merely symbolic is like telling black people that sitting in the back of the bus isn't important, as long as the back and front of the bus arrive at the same time.[28] But the fight was lost, at least in the state court.

"Marriage equality" was the term civil rights professionals came to prefer, to make the point that a marriage between two men or two women should be equal to a marriage between opposite-sex couples. The first marriage-equality case to be heard by the US Supreme Court was as skillfully produced as a Hollywood movie. Its director actually was a movie director, Rob Reiner, best known for the classic *When Harry Met Sally*. The producer was Reiner's friend, Chad Griffin, a PR expert. Griffin first proved his skills in 1992, when he'd been a nineteen-year-old wunderkind from Bill Clinton's hometown, Hope, Arkansas. He helped produce Clinton's first White House run so expertly that after the election, Griffin was hired to be part of the West Wing communications team, the youngest White House staffer ever.

The superstars of the case were not the plaintiffs, but the two lawyers that Reiner and Griffin signed on with multimillion-dollar contracts: first Ted Olson, a political conservative who in 2000 had argued *Bush v. Gore* in the US Supreme Court and won, handing George W. Bush—nemesis of all that was liberal—victory in a disputed election. Olson had been George W. Bush's solicitor general, too. But director Reiner knew that casting against type could bring major attention to a project. It was Olson who recommended the costar: David Boies—the Gore lawyer who'd argued opposite him in the Supreme Court.[29] Director Reiner guessed right about how the drama quotient would soar when word got out that the *Bush v. Gore* adversaries were starring together, on the same side, in the marriage-equality case. News of the odd duo's collaboration made headlines for months.

To hype a marriage case, Chad Griffin formed a new "production company"—literally in the heart of Hollywood—the American Foundation for Equal Rights. He and Reiner also found the perfect faces for supporting roles. Kristin Perry was executive director of the First Five Years Fund, an advocacy group started by Reiner to promote early childhood education for disadvantaged kids. Perry and her partner, Sandy Stier, had been a devoted couple since 1996 and were raising four sons. Reiner and Griffin agreed they couldn't do better than Perry for lead plaintiff. The coplaintiffs, too, were carefully cast. Paul Katami and Jeff Zarrillo were a clean-cut looking couple, notable for their middle-class averageness—together since 1998, living in a quiet Burbank neighborhood, hoping to marry and raise a family together. A top reporter, Jo Becker, was embedded in the production and would bring every step of the behind-the-scenes drama to the public in magazine articles and a full-length book.

Olson and Boies first took the *Perry v. Schwarzenegger* case to the federal district court, where it was heard by Chief Judge Vaughn Walker, a George H. W. Bush nominee. Archconservatives in the US Senate such as South Carolina's Strom Thurmond had supported Walker's nomination to a federal judgeship with great gusto. When Walker was a lawyer, he'd represented the US Olympic Committee in a suit to force a San Francisco–based group that wanted to call their national athletic competition "Gay Olympics" to delete the word "Olympics." But this apparent villain turned out to be the real hero in the California marriage saga.

In a two-and-a-half-week courtroom drama, ProtectMarriage.com (Pete Knight's widow Gail still served as figurehead) reiterated that amending the constitution to forbid same-sex marriage protected families and children. They called as their main witness David Blankenhorn, president of the Institute for American Values, who argued that children suffer if they're not raised by two opposite-sex parents. Lawyers Olson and Boies showed he didn't know what he was talking about. Blankenhorn's "qualifications" were a master's degree from Warwick University in England, where he'd written a thesis on two nineteenth-century cabinet makers unions; none of his published work had been subjected to peer-review by experts; and his opinions came secondhand from right-wing authors whom he quoted with blind credulity.[30] The witnesses Olson and Boies called—psychologists, sociologists, anthropologists—had pertinent academic credentials. They testified emphatically that children in same-sex families were as well-adjusted and happy as those in opposite-sex families—and that legalized same-sex marriage would be great for them.

The denouement came on August 4, 2010, when Judge Walker rendered his verdict. Dismissing Blankenhorn's testimony as "inadmissible opinion," he declared that a private moral view concerning homosexuals "is not a proper basis for legislation," and that Proposition 8 had done "nothing more than enshrine in the California constitution the notion that opposite-sex couples are superior to same-sex couples." Judge Walker ruled that Proposition 8 violated same-sex couples' due process and equal protection rights, and was unconstitutional.[31]

Arnold Schwarzenegger was serving his last year as governor and had long since given up all pretense of wanting to "protect marriage." When he got word of Judge Walker's ruling, Schwarzenegger tweeted his followers: "This decision affirms the full legal protection and safeguards I believe everyone deserves."[32]

But this climax was not the end. A small twist in the plot came in April 2011. Two months after the white-haired, white-goateed Judge Walker retired, he announced he'd been partnered for the last ten years with a physician, who was a man. He let it be known that since he was fourteen years old, he'd had homosexual feelings, which his parents had discovered through an adolescent diary. He'd been made by them to undergo Christian "conversion therapy" and continued to be "treated" on and off even into his thirties, but he never got "cured." When ProtectMarriage.com leaders learned that the judge who'd ruled against them was a practicing homosexual, they tried to get his decision overturned. But as a judicial panel recognized, black judges were permitted to rule on civil rights cases, women judges were permitted to rule on abortion rights cases, and there was no evidence that Judge Walker had been biased. His decision would stand.

ProtectMarriage.com urged the state to appeal the case. Jerry Brown, a progressive who'd succeeded Schwarzenegger as governor, refused. Gail Knight and the others went back to the ProtectMarriage.com donor base for more money. They'd carry on by themselves.

The first sequel, played out in the Ninth Circuit Court of Appeals, was called *Perry v. Brown* (though Brown, of course, was on the side of Perry). The appellate judges, citing the US Supreme Court's 1996 decision in

Romer v. Evans,[33] ruled that voters can't decide to "single out a disfavored group for unequal treatment." Proposition 8 served no purpose other than to "lessen the status and human dignity of gays and lesbians." In a 2-to-1 decision, they upheld Walker's finding that Prop 8's amendment to ban same-sex marriage was unconstitutional.[34]

The final sequel, called *Hollingsworth v. Perry,*[35] was set in the US Supreme Court. On March 26, 2013, a cold and cloudy day in DC, lawyer Charles Cooper, a sixty-one-year-old Alabama native with a genteel southern drawl, argued in front of SCOTUS for the ProtectMarriage.com side. Cooper had had important roles regarding gay issues. In 1986 he'd written the policy memo for the Reagan administration, which declared that the law protecting handicapped people from being fired for their jobs didn't apply to those with AIDS. In the nineties, he'd argued against same-sex marriage in the Hawaii State Supreme Court.[36] In *Hollingsworth v. Perry*, he didn't put homosexuals or same-sex marriage on trial; he merely argued that citizens had the right to decide at the ballot box what they wanted their state's laws to be.

Ted Olson, who'd played before the Supreme Court more than a dozen times, reiterated that Prop 8 was unconstitutional because it denied same-sex couples due process and equal protection. Judge Antonin Scalia (consummate character actor) interrupted Olson with his usual curmudgeonly wit: Scalia wanted to know when the exclusion of same-sex couples from marriage had become "unconstitutional": Was it when the Bill of Rights was adopted in 1791? he asked. Or maybe it was when the Fourteenth Amendment went into effect in 1868?

Olson, not one to be cowed by Scalia's bullying, answered (alluding to the court's 1954 *Brown v. Board of Education* decision), "When did public-school segregation become unconstitutional?"

But it wasn't going well. Chief Justice Roberts kept interrupting the drama of the arguments by asking about "standing": What right does ProtectMarriage.com—which is not a government entity and not a citizen who'd be harmed by same-sex marriage—have to be a plaintiff in this case?[37]

Though Roberts's question seemed to be an attack on the opposition, for Olson and Boies and the American Foundation for Equal Rights, to win marriage for California's gays and lesbians on the unsexy issue of standing would be anticlimactic. Worse yet, a ruling based on standing would be limited; it would dash their hopes of getting rid of DOMA. But Justice Anthony Kennedy—who'd spoken so eloquently on the side of gay people in *Lawrence v. Texas*—was making it clear through his comments that he couldn't be relied on to vote the right way in *Hollingsworth v. Perry*. "The problem with the case," Kennedy declared, "is that you're really asking for us to go into uncharted waters." He got laughs but produced white knuckles in the audience too when he went on, "You can play on that metaphor. There's a wonderful destination. It's the cliffs!" Ted Olson also feared that Justice Ginsburg, who should've been a reliable vote for same-sex marriage, wasn't. She'd been warning since 1992 that courts mustn't get too far ahead of public opinion: SCOTUS did that in *Roe v. Wade*, she'd said, and it had triggered a backlash.[38] Judge Sotomayor, who also should've been a reliable vote, gave Olson pause when she asked, "Is there any way to decide this case in a principled manner that is limited only to California?"[39]

Olson took the meatless bone that Sotomayor threw him. "You can decide the standing case that limits it to the decision of the District Court."

That was just what SCOTUS did, with an odd-bedfellows vote— Justices Ginsburg, Scalia, Kagan, Roberts, Breyer on one side; Justices Sotomayor, Thomas, Kennedy, and Alito on the other. Chief Justice Roberts, writing the majority opinion in a decision issued June 26, 2013, said that to have "standing" it wasn't enough to be "concerned bystanders" or to claim a "keen interest" in a case; the petitioner "must have suffered a concrete and particularized injury."[40] ProtectMarriage.com had no standing and therefore no claim in the Supreme Court. They shouldn't have been granted a hearing in the federal appeals court either, Roberts declared and rendered that decision void. The decision SCOTUS upheld was that of Judge Vaughn Walker of the district court, who'd said that Proposition 8 was unconstitutional and same-sex couples in California must be allowed to marry.

It was a happy enough ending: at a quarter after four on June 28, 2013, Kamala Harris, California's attorney general, rushed to San Francisco's city hall, where Kristin Perry and Sandy Stier were waiting for her. As the attorney general was walking up the grand staircase to the baroque rotunda to meet them, she tweeted her followers: "About to marry the Prop 8 plaintiffs, Kristin Perry and Sandy Stier. Wedding bells are ringing."[41]

But the federal Defense of Marriage Act still said that lesbian and gay couples, even if married in their state, were single as far as the US government was concerned.

SCOTUS HEARS A LOVE STORY—AND GETS IT

In the early 1960s, Portofino, a smoky Italian restaurant/club near Bleecker Street in Greenwich Village, was where upscale lesbians went for dinner on Friday nights.[42] When Thea Spyer came over to say hello to a friend at the table where Edie Schlain Windsor sat, they were introduced. They had a lot in common—both smart dressers, silver-screen glamorous (Spyer, like the butchy Garbo in *Queen Christina*; Windsor, a Liz Scott: platinum blonde, high breasted, fuchsia-polished nails); both were also Jewish, quick witted, ambitious. Windsor had been married to a man for less than a year before she realized she preferred women and parted with her husband on friendly terms. In 1955 she went back to school at NYU, where she got an MA in applied mathematics. She became a pioneer in the new computer industry, working for IBM as one of its rare women program developers. Thea Spyer, who'd escaped from Amsterdam with her affluent family when Hitler's invasion of the Netherlands was imminent, had been kicked out of Sarah Lawrence as an undergraduate, caught kissing a woman; but now she was getting a PhD in Psychology from Adelphi University.

Spyer and Windsor also had in common that they loved to dance. "We immediately just fit, our bodies fit," Spyer liked to say when she remembered their first meeting and how they danced so long and hard the first night that Windsor wore a hole in her stocking.[43] They were each involved with someone else at the time, so after that meeting at Portofino, for a couple of years they saw each other only at occasional parties. Their partners would be buttoning coats, ready to go home, but Spyer and Windsor would seek each other out for one last irresistible dance together.

In 1965 both happened to be single again. When Windsor heard that Spyer (who never quite left Windsor's mind) would be spending the weekend at the Hamptons, she got herself invited to the home of friends whom she knew Spyer would visit. Spyer came by when the friends were out. "Is your dance card full?" Windsor quipped. "It is now," Spyer answered, and all that afternoon they made love.

Two years later, Spyer, always a romantic, got down on her knees and proposed to Windsor (Windsor said yes before Spyer could finish the poetic speech she'd composed). Same-sex couples couldn't get married anywhere in 1967, but Spyer wanted to buy Windsor a diamond engagement ring. "How can I wear it at IBM?" Windsor asked. She got along fine with her coworkers but always turned down their invitations, such as going to weekend wine tastings, because she didn't dare bring Spyer.[44] An engagement ring would have prompted questions she knew she couldn't answer honestly in an era when people lost jobs if they were found to be gay or lesbian. So instead of a ring, Spyer gave her a diamond brooch, which Windsor wore on her lapel—even forty-five years later, when her picture was appearing in newspapers and magazines all over the globe.

Thea Spyer was diagnosed with multiple sclerosis in 1977; she was forty-five years old. The disease was progressive. First she needed a cane to walk, then two canes; then she was confined to a wheelchair; finally she became quadriplegic. Through it all, she continued to work as a psychotherapist, seeing clients in the eighth-floor apartment on lower Fifth Avenue where she and Windsor lived. In the last years of her life, Spyer required oxygen to breathe and Hoyer lifts and slings to get in and out of bed. Though she and Windsor couldn't make the "in sickness and in health" vow legally, they'd made it anyway to each other. When it became mostly "in sickness," Windsor took early retirement at IBM to be able to minister full-time to her lover.

But even in sickness, they didn't stop dancing—Windsor on Spyer's lap, the two of them twirling in the motorized wheelchair. Windsor liked to remember that they were never on the dance floor together when they didn't scream out to each other above the music, "I love you!"[45]

Spyer's multiple sclerosis became complicated by heart disease; in 2007 she was told by her doctor she probably had less than a year to live. She was seventy-five years old, but what she'd wanted in 1967 she still wanted. When the doctor left the examination room after breaking the news, Spyer turned to Windsor and asked, "Do you still want to get married?"

Windsor did, very much. She'd attended a meeting of the Human Rights Campaign at New York's LGBT Center, and during the Q&A she'd asked when the organization would seriously start pushing for marriage.

The speaker told her that it was on the agenda for the future. "I'm seventy-seven years old!" Windsor shouted, "I can't wait."[46]

Same-sex marriage was legal in Massachusetts, but that didn't do Spyer and Windsor much good because Massachusetts had a residency requirement.[47] To move their household, and all the equipment Spyer needed to stay alive, to another state when she was facing imminent death—it would have been impossible. But marriage was also legal in Canada; all that was required there before you could get a license was a one-day visa. Spyer and Windsor knew what they must do. Six friends—two "best men" and four "best women"—agreed to do it with them. On May 22, 2007, they flew to Toronto lugging duffel bags with tools to dismantle and put together again Spyer's motorized wheelchair, which couldn't be driven onto the small plane. The two men carried her to her seat in the plane, and, once landed, carried her off the plane, to her reassembled wheelchair.

Spyer, still a handsome woman, sitting tall in her wheelchair; and Windsor perched on the arm of the chair, decked out in pearls, her beautifully coifed hair still platinum blonde (thanks to Clairol now), were married by Canada's first openly gay judge, Harvey Brownstone. Windsor and Spyer had agreed they wanted to make the ceremony as traditional as possible. They wanted to say, "With this ring, I thee wed." When Spyer was to say it, her arm had to be lifted by two of the best women so she could hold up the ring. Windsor slipped her finger through it. When they got back to New York, Spyer said happily, "I can die now because it's completed."[48]

She died in their home on February 5, 2009. A week later, Edie Windsor had a heart attack. "Stress cardiomyopathy," the doctor called it. Windsor called it "a broken heart."[49]

Though she recovered, her problems were far from over. New York still didn't allow same-sex marriages, though in 2008 the state had started recognizing those performed elsewhere. But the federal government did not. Not long after Spyer's death, Windsor received an estate-tax bill from the IRS. As far as the federal law was concerned, she'd "inherited" from Spyer half the value of the apartment and the little cottage that the two women had bought in the Hamptons. To the federal government, she and Thea Spyer, despite their forty-plus-year history, despite their legal marriage, were no more than strangers to each other. The estate-tax bill was for $363,053.

Windsor had no choice but to pay it. To do that she had to sell investment bonds that she'd counted on to see her through for the rest of her life. After paying, she figured she had enough left to live on for no more than four years. If she'd been married to a Theo instead of a Thea, she knew, she'd have had to pay no estate taxes whatsoever—not even if she'd met and married "Theo" the month before he died.[50] Windsor called Lambda Legal.

"Sorry, it's the wrong time in the movement to bring up a case like this," a Lambda lawyer told her.[51] None of the rights groups was interested in her case. Mary Bonauto, deservedly revered for her pioneering successes in Vermont and Massachusetts and dubbed the "Thurgood Marshall of the same-sex marriage movement," had warned LGBT lawyers back in 2004 that they mustn't rush into federal court to challenge DOMA with a case about some "wealthy individual" who had to pay a tax bill because the federal government wouldn't recognize his or her same-sex marriage. "I can't think of a less sympathetic prospect," Bonauto had said.[52]

Robbie Kaplan was a partner in the litigation department of Paul, Weiss, Rifkind, Wharton, and Garrison. Her cases involved high-powered corporate clients such as JPMorgan Chase & Co. and Fitch Ratings, a Hearst Corporation subsidiary. But one day in 2009, she got a phone call from a woman who said she was eighty-one years old, a lesbian (as was Kaplan), and when her spouse died, the IRS hit her with an estate-tax bill for hundreds of thousands of dollars. No LGBT rights organization would help. Was Kaplan willing? A friend had given Windsor her name.

The one same-sex marriage case Kaplan had taken, thirteen couples suing New York for the right to marry, she'd lost in 2006.[53] She had some doubts about taking another one. But she lived four blocks away from the elderly woman. She said she'd drop by to see her on her way home.

When Robbie Kaplan learned to whom Edie Windsor had been married, she recognized the name at once, because, she later recalled, "If you were a New York lesbian and you were looking for a psychologist, everyone said, 'Go to Dr. Thea Spyer.'"[54] Then talking to Edie Windsor—hearing from the lips of an octogenarian the story of her forty-four-year love affair with someone who'd been paralyzed for thirty of those years, the diamond brooch, the wheelchair dancing, the 24/7 ministrations, the passion that didn't stop almost to the day Thea died, and seeing Windsor's charisma and charm and intelligence—Kaplan knew this was a case she wanted to take. She'd take it pro bono. She wanted to help Windsor get her money back, so Windsor wouldn't be homeless after four years.[55] Only as she started work-ing on the case did Kaplan realize it could and should go far beyond Edie Windsor's money.

It was section 3 of the 1996 Defense of Marriage Act that had caused the trouble for Windsor: it said that as far as all US agencies were con-cerned, "marriage" meant only heterosexual unions, and "spouse" meant only a person of the opposite sex who is a husband or wife. So even if a same-sex couple had gotten married in a state where same-sex marriage was legal, the federal government wouldn't recognize the marriage. Rob-bie Kaplan filed Windsor's suit in the US District Court for the Southern District of New York. On June 6, 2012, Judge Barbara Jones declared in her decision that section 3 of DOMA violated the plaintiff's rights of equal protection under the Fifth Amendment. The judge ordered the IRS to give Edie Windsor all her money back—plus interest for the time that the IRS had kept it.

Sixteen months earlier, in February 2011, President Obama had announced that he and the Justice Department had determined that DOMA violated the Constitution. His administration would no longer be defending it. The president's declaration was a red flag to the Republicans in Congress, who'd been constantly seeing red since Barack Obama settled into the White House. Urged by the Republican majority in the House, Speaker John Boehner convened a standing body of the House of Representatives, the Bipartisan Legal Advisory Group. If the Justice Department wouldn't defend a federal act, he said, BLAG must.

To head the defense, BLAG hired Paul Clement, an appeals lawyer who'd clerked for Justice Scalia, had followed Ted Olson as George W. Bush's solicitor general, and had fought dozens of cases in the US Supreme Court. In July 2012 Clement asked the Second Circuit Court of Appeals to reverse the lower court's decision on the Windsor case.

Judge Dennis Jacobs, writing the majority opinion for the three-judge court of appeals panel, declared that it's true that same-sex marriage is "unknown to history and tradition" if one is looking at "holy matrimony."

But the state's business wasn't to concern itself with "holy matrimony" but rather with civil law. And under civil law, Windsor and Spyer had been married. The appeals court upheld the lower court's decision.[56] Paul Clement, on behalf of the Bipartisan Legal Advisory Group, then brought *United States v. Edith Schlain Windsor* to SCOTUS—pulling Robbie Kaplan and Edie Windsor there with him.

In some LGBT rights suits that had big implications for the community, if the plaintiffs weren't near-paragons, lawyers kept them muzzled in the background, as they did in *Lawrence v. Texas*. Robbie Kaplan knew Edie Windsor belonged in the foreground. There couldn't be a better plaintiff to challenge DOMA. Not only did she have a deeply compelling story of love and incredible commitment, and she looked good and talked well, but also she was female, postmenopausal, in her eighties, and her partner was dead. Judges who might have a hard time if forced to contemplate homosexual sex acts didn't have to in her case. (Kaplan told Windsor, "Just one thing. Until we've won, you have to stop talking about you and Thea as passionate butch-femme lovers." Scalia wouldn't like it.)[57] Kaplan also guessed that Mary Bonauto missed the mark in 2004 when she said it would be a mistake to fight DOMA with a case about some "wealthy individual" who had to pay a tax bill because the federal government wouldn't recognize her same-sex marriage. Nobody liked taxes, Kaplan knew, and judges were "wealthy [enough] individuals" to identify with Windsor's plight.[58]

As soon as SCOTUS agreed to hear *U.S. v. Windsor*, there was pressure on Robbie Kaplan from LGBT rights groups to let a "professional" who'd argued in the Supreme Court before, who could match Paul Clement in experience, take the case. She thought about it for a while. She'd written herself a Post-it note that she looked at whenever she felt she was getting too ego involved or scared. It said, "It's all about Edie, Stupid!"[59] The case meant too much to her to step back.

Kaplan's arguments in front of the justices were clear and cogent. The Defense of Marriage Act, she emphasized, had been passed by Congress in 1996 because the legislators, looking at what the Supreme Court had said in *Bowers v. Hardwick*, thought it permissible to express "moral disapproval of homosexuals." But the Supreme Court had since apologized for

Bowers. It had said in 2003, in the *Lawrence* decision, that it understood it had been wrong in thinking that same-sex relationships were fundamentally different from heterosexual relationships. DOMA was inconsistent with the Supreme Court's present understanding; and just as the Supreme Court had changed its views about same-sex relationships, so had much of America.

Paul Clement was often less than logical in his arguments. It's fair for the federal government to say, "We want to treat the same-sex couple in New York [where same-sex marriage is legal] the same way as the committed same-sex couple in Oklahoma [where it's not]," Clement argued.

"But that's begging the question because you're treating *married* couples differently," Justice Sotomayor jumped in.

Same-sex couples may be married under state law, Clement argued at another point, but under federal law, "It's a different matter."

"So there are two kinds of marriages, the full marriage and then this sort of skim milk marriage," Justice Ginsburg said.

But it was the remarks of the swing voter Anthony Kennedy that held the clue to who would win. Justice Kennedy kept going back to the point that deciding who is married is up to the states. If same-sex marriage is legal in a particular state, an agency of the federal government (like the IRS) has no right to say that it doesn't recognize the marriage.[60] He'd all but announced how he would vote. "Justices Cast Doubt on Benefits Ban in U.S. Marriage Law," the *New York Times* announced the next day.[61]

On June 26, 2013, Justice Kennedy delivered the majority opinion. "DOMA writes inequality into the entire U.S. Code," he declared. It singles out a subset of people and makes them unequal. "It disparages and injures those whom the state, by its marriage laws, sought to protect in personhood and dignity. . . . It humiliates tens of thousands of children now being raised by same-sex couples."[62]

What the decision meant was that not only would married same-sex couples be treated by the IRS as their heterosexual counterparts were treated, but also that they could get social security and veteran's survivor benefits, they could hold on to their homes when widowed, they could get green cards for an alien spouse, they were eligible for over a thousand other benefits that only straight couples had enjoyed before.

•   •   •

Robbie Kaplan had known the decision would be announced sometime in June. On the days that the court was in session she asked Edie Windsor to come to her apartment and sit and wait—because that might be *the* day. On June 26, ten years to the day when the Supreme Court handed down its decision on *Lawrence v. Texas*, Windsor was sitting and waiting in Kaplan's apartment. Minutes after news of the decision came, the phone rang. Kaplan answered it and handed it to Windsor. "Hello? Who am I talking to?" Windsor asked. "Oh, Barack Obama?"

He was calling from Air Force One, on his way to Senegal. He said he wanted to congratulate her on the victory of her historic case and to thank her for her fight to make America better. Edie Windsor answered, "I want to thank *you*. I think you coming out for us made such a difference throughout the country." She was right.

EPILOGUE

Jim Kepner, the homophile journalist who drove cabs and worked in a milk-carton factory in the 1950s so he could give quality brain-time to the embryonic movement, died in the fall of 1997. His memorial service was held in the Samuel Goldwyn Theater of the Motion Picture Academy in Beverly Hills. Hundreds of leading gay and lesbian activists from all over the country came to pay their respects to a pioneer.[1] Frank Kameny flew in from Washington, DC, to give a eulogy. Kameny marveled at the miracle of the preceding forty years: "We started with nothing, and look what we have wrought!" he declared, recalling the dark decades when "the government was our enemy, and was out to get us—and they did"; then reveling that in the nineties almost a million lesbians and gays filled the Washington Mall; lesbian and gay federal employees came out at work and weren't fired because there were laws protecting them; and the president and vice president of the United States sent congratulatory letters or showed up in person at major lesbian and gay events.[2]

In the years that followed, things got even better. Kameny lived to see the Supreme Court strike down all sodomy laws and same-sex marriage legalized in seven states. In 2009, after Obama took office, Kameny was practically a regular at the White House, invited on June 17 to see the president sign an executive order that would give benefits to partners of federal employees; invited again on June 29, a guest of the president and First Lady, to an East Room celebration for the fortieth anniversary of the Stonewall riots. At that event, the head of the Office of Personnel Management (successor to the Civil Service Commission, which had kicked Kameny out of his job in 1957) presented him with the Theodore Roosevelt Award, "for defending our nation's Merit Principles." He was invited again to the White House that October to witness the signing of the hate crimes bill. Before he died, he even saw the demise of all regulations that interfered with gays and lesbians serving openly in the military.

His November 16, 2011, memorial service was held on Capitol Hill in the Cannon House of Representatives Office Building—in the Cannon Caucus Room, where Communists and homosexuals had been targeted fifty years earlier by the House Un-American Activities Committee. Three members of Congress spoke at the memorial service. Each in turn proclaimed Kameny a great American who had made the country a better place.[3] A street in Dupont Circle was named after him, too. Frank Kameny's most fevered early dreams had actually come true.

Yet he missed some even more remarkable advances that even he, visionary that he was, couldn't have imagined. Kameny would have loved it that in the summer of 2014, a federal appeals court judge, nominated by President Reagan, overturned Wisconsin's and Indiana's bans on same-sex marriage, declaring on behalf of his three-judge panel: "Imagine if in the 1960s, the states that forbade interracial marriage had said to interracial couples, 'You can have domestic partnerships that create the identical rights and obligations of marriage, but you can call them only "civil unions" or "domestic partnerships." The term "marriage" is reserved for same-race unions.'"[4] Kameny would have been deeply moved, too, to open the *New York Times* that same summer of 2014 and see an announcement of the marriage of two women: one who served as legal counsel to the Senate Select Committee on Intelligence; the other an attorney for the National Security Council.[5]

To be sure, in the years after Frank Kameny's death the advance in rights hasn't been without setback and confrontation. For instance, the continued failure of Congress to pass a no-exemption Employment Non-Discrimination Act wreaked mischief, as in the case of a much-loved fifty-seven-year-old physical education teacher at a Catholic school in a suburb of Columbus, Ohio. Carla Hale had taught at Bishop Watterson High School for nineteen years. It was widely understood among the students that she was gay, but she never brought her private life to school.[6] In February 2013 Hale's mother, Jeanne Roe, died. The local newspaper, the *Columbus Dispatch*, ran an obituary, mentioning those in the family "who preceded Mrs. Roe in death," including her toy poodle Molly; and those who survived her, including her son (his wife was named in parenthesis) and her daughter, "Carla Hale (Julie)."[7] Julie was Hale's partner of ten years, who'd been loved and taken up as one of the family by Hale's mother; it would have been odd to leave her name out of the obituary, Carla Hale thought.

On learning of the death of her favorite teacher's mother, one of Hale's young students asked her own mother to pray for Mrs. Roe's soul. The woman looked in the local paper for the obituary. What she found made her rush to write a letter (signed only "A Concerned Parent"), complaining to Bishop Frederick Campbell, diocese head: "I was shocked by what I saw. The obituary had my daughter's teacher's name and that of her 'spouse' listed. It was 2 females!" The parent didn't want a lesbian to be teaching Catholic children.[8] Neither did the diocese.

The state of Ohio has a law protecting workers from discrimination on the basis of sexual orientation; the city of Columbus does as well. Students also rallied on Carla Hale's behalf, marching with posters that declared "God Doesn't Discriminate," and that quoted Galatians 3:26: "We Are All God's Children." Her supporters circulated a petition asking that she be reinstated. It got 8,000 signatures.[9] When they put the petition on the net, it got 130,000 signatures. (A petition in support of the diocese's firing of Hale got 700 signatures.)[10] Nevertheless, the diocese remained firm: it gave Hale a cash settlement but refused to reinstate her because she'd violated the Church's "moral teaching" by having a "quasi-spousal relationship" with a woman.[11]

The diocese was also determined to guard against further homosexual infiltration. In 2011 the Supreme Court had ruled that churches must be free to choose and dismiss ministers without government interference: a "ministerial exemption," the justices said, was "grounded in the Religion Clauses of the First Amendment."[12] The diocese lawyers advised Bishop Campbell to "update" teacher contracts by classifying all teachers—even those who taught Physical Education, Algebra, Drama, Home Economics—as "ministers." That maneuver would let the diocese refuse employment to any homosexual applicant and fire those teachers who might already have sneaked in.[13]

Nor was the news on the marriage front invariably good. Even after the Supreme Court's *Windsor* decision; even after voters in Maine, Maryland, Minnesota, and Washington went to the ballot box to show their overwhelming support for same-sex marriage; even after numerous consecutive rulings in federal courts that said that bans against same-sex marriage were unconstitutional, pockets of powerful and impassioned resistance continued.

Jonathan Robicheaux and Derek Penton-Robicheaux, two Louisiana natives, had married in Iowa in 2012. As they testified two years later when they were trying to get their home state to recognize their marriage, they'd been in a committed relationship since 2005, raising a child together, "commingling funds, and holding themselves out as monogamous partners that are living together as one union." But the same summer in which the wedding of the two high-security-clearance-holders was announced in the pages of the *New York Times*, a US District Court judge in Louisiana, Martin Feldman, another Reagan nominee, made the old "slippery slope" argument against marriage equality: If same-sex marriages were allowed, "must the state permit or recognize a marriage between an aunt and niece? Aunt and nephew, brother/brother, father and child?" In a decision that bucked the trend of wins, Judge Feldman ruled that Louisiana didn't have to recognize the Robicheauxs as being anything other than legal strangers to each other.[14]

The following fall, Republican victories in the midterm elections gave the historically antigay party a majority in both houses of Congress.[15] Two days after the elections, the Federal Appeals Court for the Sixth Circuit, which includes Kentucky, Tennessee, Ohio, and Michigan, voted 2 to 1 to uphold those states' same-sex marriage bans, affirming "the people's" power to decide who gets a fundamental right of American citizenship and who doesn't.[16] It was a startling setback after a long succession of same-sex marriage triumphs in federal courts. However, it pushed the US Supreme Court to announce that it would hear the Sixth Circuit cases and finally consider two questions: whether the Constitution should be interpreted as mandating all states to issue same-sex marriage licenses; and whether what remains of DOMA—section 2, which says no state is obliged to recognize a same-sex marriage performed in another state—should be done away with.

By the time the Supreme Court agreed to hear those Sixth Circuit cases, seventy percent of Americans were living in states in which same-sex marriage was lawful. But in fourteen states, gay or lesbian couples were still legal strangers to each other. In eleven states they could marry on Saturday afternoon and be legally fired because of their sexual orientation on Monday morning.[17] And the Right was becoming more and more creative in devising tricky tactics.

But in early spring of 2015, something astonishing happened. On March 25, Indiana legislators passed a "Religious Freedom Restoration Act" (RFRA). Such an act was suddenly necessary, the Republican-dominated

Indiana Legislature decided, because the US Court of Appeals for the Seventh Circuit had recently made same-sex marriage legal in the Hoosier State. Indiana gay and lesbian couples couldn't be stopped from getting married, but under RFRA, florists, wedding-cake bakers, and gown- and tuxedo-makers wouldn't have to serve them; they could claim their religion didn't allow it. On March 26, Indiana governor Mike Pence signed the bill into law.

He and the Legislature were caught off guard by the immediate firestorm of protests. Marc Benioff, CEO of Salesforce.com, which had recently spent $2.5 billion in Indianapolis buying a software company, set off the conflagration by declaring he would "dramatically reduce" investment in Indiana because of his "employees' and customers' outrage over the Religious Freedom Bill."[18] Then Angie's List, headquartered in Indianapolis, threatened to halt a big expansion project. Then the National Collegiate Athletic Association, also headquartered in Indianapolis, protested that the legislation would have a bad effect on "our student-athletes and employees." Gen Con, the gaming convention that drew 60,000 people annually to Indianapolis, threatened to relocate. City and state governments threatened to prohibit official business travel to Indiana. The *Indianapolis Star*, the state's biggest and most influential newspaper, demanded of Governor Pence, in a massive front-page black-boxed headline, "FIX THIS NOW."[19]

Meanwhile, the Arkansas Legislature, afraid that same-sex marriage would soon be the law of the land, passed a copycat RFRA. Governor Asa Hutchinson, who'd announced his certain intention to sign the bill into law, was as surprised as his Indiana counterpart had been by the thunderous uproar of protest. It was led by the top Fortune 500 company, Arkansas's largest private employer—Walmart.

Big business, reliably Republican, had spoken. On April 2, 2015, both governors "fixed" their "religious freedom" bills by removing the possibility of discrimination, the sole raison d'être for the bills. Fortune 500 companies were, in fact, following the lead of most Americans, who by now were firmly opposed to discrimination against LGBT people. Polls taken in April 2015 showed that 61 percent of Americans approved of same-sex marriage.[20]

A few weeks after the Indiana/Arkansas debacle, on April 28, 2015, SCOTUS heard oral arguments for the Sixth Circuit same-sex marriage cases, consolidated under the name *Obergefell v. Hodges*. The lead plaintiff, James Obergefell, was an Ohioan whose partner of twenty years, John Arthur, had been dying of Lou Gehrig's disease when the couple chartered a private plane, flew to Maryland—a same-sex marriage state—and were married on the plane as it sat on the tarmac of the Baltimore-Washington International Airport. But despite the couple's dramatic efforts, after John Arthur died, the Sixth Circuit Court of Appeals upheld Ohio's right to refuse to list him as "married" on his death certificate.

June 26, 2015, the twelfth anniversary, to the day, of the *Lawrence v. Texas* decision and the second anniversary of the *United States v. Windsor* decision: Again Justice Kennedy wrote for the majority in the 5–4 vote. He did not disappoint. The plaintiffs, he declared, "ask for equal dignity in the eyes of the law. The Constitution grants them that right." And with these momentous words, marriage equality was made the law of the land.

The Right's blowback was immediate. Republican presidential candidate Mike Huckabee announced, "The fight is not over!" Candidates Scott Walker and Ted Cruz called for a Constitutional amendment that would let states bring back their same-sex marriage bans. Groups such as the Family Research Council called for stronger religious freedom laws to protect those who have biblical aversions to same-sex marriage.

Yet despite the virulent prejudice that remains; despite Congress's failure to pass an Equality Act, such as Bella Abzug and Ed Koch had proposed more than forty years earlier, that would in one fell swoop give LGBT people complete, first-class citizenship; despite occasional setbacks, it's undeniable: the arc of the moral universe has been bending toward justice. Frank Kameny's observation bears repeating: "We started with nothing, and look what we have wrought!"

                                                                    June 2015

ACKNOWLEDGMENTS

It's impossible to convey the depth of my gratitude to all those who gave me so much of their time, encouragement, wisdom, knowledge, hospitality, and practical assistance. For helping me birth this book I thank Sandy Dijkstra, my friend and agent since 1978; my editors at Simon & Schuster, Thomas LeBien and Alice Mayhew; and assistant editor Stuart Roberts.

I was truly blessed in the archivists and librarians that I encountered at the ONE National Gay and Lesbian Archives at USC and the June Mazer Lesbian Collection at UCLA; the Library of Congress, the Archives Center at the National Museum of American History, the Smithsonian Institution, and the Rainbow History Project in Washington, DC; the New York Public Library Manuscripts and Archives Division; Special Collections and Archives at SUNY Albany; the Rare and Manuscript Division at Cornell University Library; the Gay and Lesbian Historical Society of Northern California Collection at the San Francisco Public Library and the San Francisco GLBT Historical Society; Special Collections at the Shields Library at UC Davis; California State Archives, Sacramento; Lambda Archives of San Diego; the Map and Government Library at California State University, Fresno; the Botts Collection in Houston; the Washington State Historical Society Research Center in Tacoma and the Northwest Lesbian and Gay History Museum; the Florida State Archives in Tallahassee, Special Collections at the University of South Florida in Tampa, Department of

Special and Area Studies Collections at George A. Smathers Libraries at the University of Florida, and the Stonewall Library in Ft. Lauderdale. My very special thanks to Michael Oliveiras, Kyle Morgan, Marjorie Bryer, Angela Brinskele, Ruth Pettis, Philip Clark, Florence Turcotte, Larry Criscione, Carol Doyle, Diane Germain, Thomas Lannon, Brian Keough, Jennifer Brathovde, Andy Huse, Wendy Shay, and Tim Wilson. Their amazing knowledge helped guide my research.

I received great kindness from many historians, activists, and friends, who generously shared material with me, set me on the right path to discover new materials, or introduced me to individuals whose stories were invaluable to this book. My special thanks to Randy Wicker, Stephanie Donald, Becky Smith, Charles Francis, Charles Silverstein, Robin Cohen, Bonnie Morris, Jerry Gerash, Michael Bedwell, Pokey Anderson, Arden Eversmeyer, Gloria Stancich, Mary Ann Cherry, Susan Stryker, Lisa Hardaway, Elizabeth Owen, Margaret Purcell, Anna Curren, Robin Tyler, Ronni Sanlo, Sally Gearhart, Jon Davidson, Jill Kelly, Jenny Pizer, Bill Dobbs, Jeanne Córdova, Carolyn Weathers, Kay (Tobin) Lahusen, Martin Meeker, Paul D. Cain, Jesse Monteagudo, Gary Atkins, John Howard, Ronald Gold, Ethan Geto, Jim Gaylord, Alec and Gabi Clayton, JoAnne Passet, Mary Zarba, Linda Garber, Gloria Allred, and Diego Sanchez.

I'm blessed with good friends who opened their homes to me when I traveled to do interviews or archival research, read drafts of this book, and gave me invaluable feedback, help, and encouragment. I thank Anne du Pontavice, Katherine Gabel and Eunice Shatz, Gloria Stancich and Donna Douglass, Robin Tyler and Diane Olson, Margaret Purcell and Mary Henry, Marcia Perlstein and Nyla Dart, Llyn De Danaan, Sue Weinheimer, Linda and Val Roosna, Steve and Ewa Yarbrough, Kay (Tobin) Lahusen, Mary Meriam, Ann Birnbaum, Rosalind Ravasio, Kathy Hall, Oliva Espin, Janice Steinberg, Anne Marie Walsh, Sheryl Tempchin, Carolyn Marsden, Sharon Young, and David Carter. I'm awed by the organizing and scheduling talents of Gloria Stancich and my newfound sister Linda Federman Roosna. Thank you for being so extraordinary.

I'm grateful to all who agreed to be interviewed for this book and so generously gave me hours of their time, sharing with me their personal histories and their perspectives on the LGBT movement. I have learned from all of them, and that knowledge has deeply informed what I've written in this book. I thank Captain Alice Martinson, Natalie Lando, Marty Selnick, Judy Grahn, Roberta Achtenberg, Ray Hill, Elana (Nachman) Dykewomon, Susan Levinkind, Kilulu von Prince, Robin McGehee, Sally Duplaix, Washington representative Maureen Walsh, Shan Ottey, Washington representative Jamie Pedersen, Washington senator Ed Murray, Charlene Strong, Catherine Swadley, Karen Bolesky, Jeannie Darnielle, Jack Johnson, Admiral Alan Steinman, Washington representative Laurie Jinkins, Kris Schrantz, Lieutenant Colonel Margaret Witt, Captain Midge Loser, Llyn De Danaan, Alec and Gabi Clayton, Anna Schlecht, Judge Richard Hicks, Carol McKinley, Zula Johnston, Jim Gaylord, Diana Wickman, J. P. Persall, Pokey Anderson, Colonel Margarethe Cammermeyer, Earnestine Blue, Carrie Washburn, Jean Huskamp, Kathy Presbindowski, Lynn Grotsky, Lisa Brodoff, Reverend Troy Perry, Robin Tyler, Washington governor Christine Gregoire, Nicole Murray Ramirez, Kay Ostberg, Charlie Brydon, Karen Thompson, Jeri Dilno, Gloria Johnson, Captain Sue Young, Captain Beth Coye, Betty DeGeneres, John O'Brien, Bridget Wilson, Carlita Durand, Carol Stech, Donna Alioto, Frank Buttino, Gloria Allred, Missy Dominguez, Charli Gross, Bamby Salcedo, Steve Schleier, Jake (Ron) Jacobson, Roland Palencia, Dana Hopkins, Morgan Ahearn, Abby Jonson, Lisa Gates, Caroline Hoag, Ronni Sanlo, Michael Vita, Elizabeth Schwartz, Martin Gill, Jesse Monteagudo, Edda Cimino, Patricia Ireland, Stratton Pollitzer, Ruth Shack, Leslie Cohen, Beth Suskind, Julian Earl Farris, Vicki Wengrow, Tom Serwatka, Frieda Saraga, David Andress, Jeff "Chico" Driggers, Rainbow Williams, Corky Culver, Phyllis Plotnick, Shewolf, Kim Emery, Ruthie Berman, Connie Kurtz, Richard Milstein, Bob Kunst, Kathryn Lehman, Brigadier General Tammy Smith, Tracey Hepner, Florida representative Alcee Hastings, Christian Sy, Massachusetts representative Barney Frank, Wisconsin senator Tammy Baldwin, Sister Jeannine Gramick, Bishop John Shelby Spong, Jeanne Córdova, Sally Gearhart, David Mixner, Kenneth Pitchford, Steve Ault, Andy Humm, Perry Brass, Marc Solomon, Evan Wolfson, Williams Dobbs, Ada Bello, Julia Sawabini, Mark Segal, Kay (Tobin) Lahusen, Joyce Hunter, Randy Wicker, Ann Northrop, Rich Wandel, Arlene Isaacson, Joseph Barri, Marty Rouse, Michael Bronski, Cleve Jones, Frank Galassi, Wayne Sunday, Flavia Rando, Fran Winant, Dick Leitsch, Nathalie Rockhill, Renée Cafiero, L. Craig Schoonmaker, Allen Roskoff, Carolyn Weathers, Del Whan, Michelle Crone, Leo E. Laurence,

Ellen Broidy, Ellen Shumsky, Arlene Kisner, Jim Fouratt, Nikos Diaman, Shirley Vaias, Charlotte Bunch, Michael Petrelis, Ethan Geto, Ron Gold, Urvashi Vaid, Roberta "Robbie" Kaplan, Suzanne Goldberg, Mary Bonauto, Jean Dubofsky, Houston mayor Annise Parker, Dr. Reena Roy, Edie Windsor, Kylar Broadus, Jenny Pizer, Diego Sanchez, Jon Davidson, Barbara Love, Dan Choi, Vandy Beth Glenn, Carole (Meyers) Smith, Marge McCann, Eva Freund, Donna Gottschalk, Dr. Helen Cooksey, Dr. Susan Love, Katherine Triantafillou, Elaine Noble, and Rita Mae Brown.

NOTES

PROLOGUE

1. Hal Call (who'd been a student of Johnston), in James T. Sears, *Behind the Mask of Mattachine: The Hal Call Chronicles and the Early Movement for Homosexual Emancipation* (Binghamton, NY: Harrington Park Press, 2006), p. 38.

2. Sarah Lockwood Williams, *Twenty Years of Education for Journalism: A History of the School of Journalism of the University of Missouri* (Columbia, MO: E. W. Stephens, 1929), p. 306.

3. "Professor at M.U. Held on Morals Charge," *Moberly (MO) Monitor-Index*, May 27, 1948, p. 6.

4. "Missouri University Professor Held on Charges of Sodomy," *Alton (IL) Evening Telegraph*, May 28, 1948, p. 1.

5. "Hold Missouri University Man on Sodomy," *News and Tribune* (Jefferson City, MO), July 25, 1948, p. 2.

6. "Professor at M.U. Held on Morals Charge."

7. Associated Press, "Sodomy Charges Filed Against M.U. Professor," *Northwest Arkansas Times* (Fayetteville), May 28, 1948, p. 7.

8. "Jailed Professor Released on Bond: E. K. Johnston Charged with Sodomy, Relieved of Teaching Duties at Missouri University," *Joplin (MO) Globe*, May 29, 1948, p. 3.

9. "Missouri Professor Held for Sodomy: Termed Principal in Homosexual Ring," *Pottstown (PA) Mercury*, May 28, 1948, p. 2.

10. "Homosexual," *Hope (AR) Star*, May 28, 1948, p. 2.

11. Associated Press, "Journalism Professor Held on Charges of Sex Orgies," *Indiana (PA) Evening Gazette*, May 28, 1948, p. 1. Dean Mott, whom Johnston had replaced that year as acting dean, could express only bafflement: "Professor Johnston has been an excellent teacher . . . This whole thing is a terrific shock."

12. Associated Press, "Three Held for Sodomy," *Evening Independent* (Massillon, OH), May 28, 1948, p. 14.

13. "Curators Plan Definite Action at University," *News and Tribune* (Jefferson City, MO), May 28, 1948, p. 1.

14. "Mad Parties Result in Dismissal of Professor," *Indiana (PA) Evening Gazette*, May 29, 1948, p. 2.

15. Associated Press, "Prof Gets Probation," *Abilene (TX) Reporter-News*, November 17, 1948, p. 38.

16. "Homosexual," p. 11. The conclusion of the story about E. K. Johnston is not entirely dismal. He eventually moved to Detroit, where he worked for an advertising agency that handled automotive accounts, and where, Hal Call says, Johnston "earned twice the money he made at the university" (Sears, *Behind the Mask of Mattachine*, p. 40). Johnston died in 1990 at the age of ninety-two.

17. In addition to my interviews with Brigadier General Tammy Smith and Tracey Hepner in Washington, DC, on November 17, 2012, I consulted the following sources: "Promotion Ceremony for Brigadier General Tammy Smith," Army Television, August 10, 2012; Leo Shane, "Smith Becomes First Gay General to Serve Openly," *Stars and Stripes*, August 10, 2012; Laura J. Nelson, "With Promotion, U.S. Army Welcomes First Openly Gay General," *Los Angeles Times*, August 11, 2012; Matthew L. Wald, "Woman Becomes First Openly Gay General," *New York Times*, August 12, 2012; Dorian de Wild, "Tammy Smith: The U.S. Military's First Openly Gay General," *Huffington Post*, August 13, 2012; Bonnie Goldstein, "New Gay General: A Salute Is in Order," *Washington Post*, August 14, 2012; Brigadier General Tammy Smith, interview with Lynn Niery, *Talk of the Nation*, NPR, August 14, 2012.

18. General Tammy Smith, interview with author.

CHAPTER 1: LAWBREAKERS AND LOONIES

1. "A Great Hebrew Charity . . . Brilliant Reception Last Night at Carnegie Hall," *New York Times*, February 28, 1895; "Surf Casting the Sport of the Week—Prize for the Biggest Fish," *New York Times*, June 26, 1910; "Dorothy James to Wed G. G. Haven," *New York Times*, February 2, 1925.

2. Reported in Mark Liebert, MD, "Faces of Criminals," *New York Times*, May 30, 1933; also "Facial Indications of Personality" (presented before the New York State Association of Chiefs of Police in Rochester, New York, 1950), Carleton Simon Papers, box 1, folder 31, Special Collections and Archives, SUNY Albany. I am grateful to Brian Keough for making this material available to me.

3. "Police and Fire Visitors Address Local Rotarians," *Evening Independent* (Saint Petersburg, FL), October 9, 1931; and lecture for the New England Association of Chiefs of Police, reprinted in Carleton Simon, "A Study of the Negro Criminal," *Police Journal* (January 1934): pp. 6–7, 14.

4. Carleton Simon, "Homosexualists and Sex Crimes" (presented before the International Association of Chiefs of Police, Duluth, MN, September 21–25, 1947), Carleton Simon Papers, box 1, folder 34, Special Collections and Archives, SUNY Albany. I am grateful to Brian Keough for making this material available to me.

   Illinois's treatment of homosexuals wasn't unique. In Ohio, a twenty-one-year-old man and two men in their early thirties were charged with being part of a "sodomy ring" and convicted as "psychopathic offenders." They were sent by the judge to Luna State Hospital and after "treatment" were transferred to the penitentiary for "two to forty years." When the men applied for parole after two years, prosecuting attorney Paul Landis testified to the Ohio Pardon and Parole Commission that his office and the community were "unalterably opposed" to their release because the "condition" of the men had "left a trail of evil consequences in this community": "Landis Opposes Parole of Sodomists from Pen," *Lima (OH) News*, February 15, 1948.

5. Arthur Lewis Miller quoted in Hally S. Heatley, "Commies and Queers: Narratives That Supported the Lavender Scare" (master's thesis, University of Texas, Arlington, 2007), p. 108. As influential as Simon and Miller was psychiatrist Paul DeRiver, who established the Sexual Offenses Bureau of the Los Angeles Police Department. His notions about the menace of homosexuals were disseminated to California legislators in 1949 by Richard Keatinge, California's special assistant attorney general, who warned: "The sex pervert, in his more innocuous form, is too frequently regarded as merely a 'queer' individual who never hurts anyone but himself. All too often we lose sight of the fact that the homosexual is an inveterate seducer of the young of both sexes and is ever seeking for younger victims." Quoted in George Chauncey, "The Post-War Sex Crime Panic," in *True Stories from the American Past*, ed. William Graebner (New York: McGraw Hill, 1993), pp. 170–71. Keatinge supported legislation, passed in 1950, that added sodomy and oral copulation to the habitual offender law and imposed a mandatory sentence of life in prison for a third offense. See William N. Eskridge, *Dishonorable Passions: Sodomy Laws in America, 1861–2003* (New York: Viking, 2008), p. 432. See also the discussion of DeRiver in Lillian Faderman and Stuart Timmons, *Gay L.A.: A History of Sexual Outlaws, Power Politics, and Lipstick Lesbians* (New York: Basic Books, 2006); and Paul DeRiver, *The Sexual Criminal: A Psychoanalytic Study* (1949; second edition: Springfield, IL: Charles C. Thomas, 1956).

6. The District of Columbia was at the time under the jurisdiction of the US Congress.

7. HR 6071, 80th Congress, 2nd Session, 1948, in Congressional Record, vol. 94, p. 3884. "Providing for the Treatment of Sexual Psychopaths in the District of Columbia, Senate Report 1377, 2nd Session, May 21, 1948.

8. Alfred Kinsey et al., *Sexual Behavior in the Human Male* (Philadelphia: W. B. Saunders, 1948).

9. Historian Estelle Freedman points out that in the psychiatric and legal literature of the 1940s and 1950s, the terms *sex criminal, pervert, psychopath,* and *homosexual*

frequently overlapped, and she suggests that *psychopath* even "served as a code for 'homosexual'": "Uncontrolled Desires: The Response to the Sexual Psychopath, 1920–1960," *Journal of American History* 74, no. 1 (June 1987): pp. 83–106.

10. Testimony and cross-examination of Thomas L. Ferry, Hollywood Vice Detail, LAPD, in Alcoholic Beverage Control Appeals Board Case File 1960–61, California State Archives, Sacramento.

11. Testimony and cross-examination of Thomas L. Ferry.

12. Memorandum from Deputy Attorney General Warren Deering to Principal Counsel for the Department of Alcoholic Beverage Control, Bion W. Gregory, September 2, 1960, Alcoholic Beverage Control Appeals Board Case File, 1960–61, California State Archives, Sacramento.

13. That same year, the Alcoholic Beverage Commission had recommended suspending a liquor license that had been granted to Sol Stoumen, owner of San Francisco's famous Black Cat Café, on the grounds that Stoumen had let homosexuals hang out in his establishment. The liberal California Supreme Court decided that the commission and the state's Board of Equalization had been too zealous in their crusade against homosexuals. The court restored Stoumen's license, declaring that as long as there was no evidence of activity injurious to "public welfare or morals," even homosexuals had the right to freedom of association: *Sol Stoumen v. George R. Reilly*, 37 Cal., 2d 713, S.F. no. 18310, August 28, 1951. The case started a war between the California Supreme Court and the California State Legislature.

14. California Business and Professions Code (1955), section 24200(e), p. 2230, chap. 1217.

15. Hearing Transcript, April 20, 1960, "In the Matter of the Accusation Against the Criterion Lounge," ABC Appeals Board Case file 1960–61, California State Archives, Sacramento.

16. There were fewer lesbian establishments than those that catered to gay men in the 1950s and 1960s. But police harassment of lesbians and raids of their bars were common across the country. See, for example: (Memphis) Daneel Buring, "Softball and Alcohol: The Limits of Lesbian Community in Memphis from the 1940s Through the 1960s," in *Carryin' On in the Old South*, ed. John Howard (New York: New York University Press, 1997); (New Orleans) Elly Bulkin, "An Old Dyke's Tale: An Interview with Doris Lunden," in *The Persistent Desire: A Femme-Butch Reader* (Boston: Alyson Books, 1992); (Washington, DC) Eva Freund, interview with Mark Meinke, Rainbow History Project, Washington, DC, November 3, 2002 (I am grateful to Philip Clark of the Rainbow History Project for sharing a transcript of this interview with me); (Buffalo) Elizabeth Lapovsky Kennedy and Madeline D. Davis, *Boots of Leather, Slippers of Gold: The History of a Lesbian Community* (New York: Routledge, 1993); (Worchester, MA) Bob Skiba, "Pansies, Perverts, and Pegged Pants," in *Gay and Lesbian Community Guide to New England* (1982); (Philadelphia) chap. 7, here, a discussion of the raid at Rusty's; (Seattle) Ruth Pettis and Lisa Cohen interview with Rosa Bohanan, March 28, 1998, Northwest Lesbian and Gay History Museum Project (I am

grateful to Ruth Pettis for sharing this transcript with me); (Los Angeles) Faderman and Timmons, *Gay L.A.*

17. Kershaw tried unsuccessfully to appeal the revocation of her liquor license: *Pearl Kershaw, Appellant v. Department of Alcoholic Beverage Control*, 318 P. 2d, no. 17693. See also Joan W. Howarth, "First and Last Chance: Looking for Lesbians in Fifties Bar Cases," *Southern California Review of Law and Women's Studies* 5, no. 1 (Fall 1995): 153–72. Howarth discusses undercover surveillance in four lesbian bars, including Pearl's. Officers Gwinn and Davis were also a team in the raid of another Oakland bar, Mary's First and Last Chance. The owners fought successfully against revocation of their license: *Albert Vallerga and Mary Azar v. Department of Alcoholic Beverage Control*, 1 Civil No. 18, 184, January 27, 1959, p. 10, California State Archives, Sacramento; and *Albert Vallerga and Mary Azar v. Department of Alcoholic Beverage Control*, in the Supreme Court of the State of California, S.F. 20285, pp. 12, 14, December 23, 1959, California State Archives.

18. Sten Russell, "A Look at the Lesbian: DOB Convention Report," *Ladder*, July 1960, p. 16.

19. Reported in Del Martin, "The Gay Bar—Whose Problem Is It?," *Ladder*, December 1959, pp. 4–13ff.

20. There were a few early instances of resistance. The largest raid in Baltimore history was at the Pepper Hill Club. It was carried out by Baltimore police because, they claimed, they had "evidence of homosexuality" among the patrons: 139 gay men and lesbians were taken to the police station. All but five were released without being charged, but the convicted included a lesbian who fought the policemen who tried to lead her into a paddy wagon and a man who insisted on testifying in court, though the charges against him were about to be dropped: Associated Press, "Police Raid Leader Plans to Take Case to Grand Jury," *Cumberland (MD) Evening Times*, October 3, 1955.

21. James Mills, "The Detective," *Life*, December 3, 1965.

22. Effeminate men and masculine women (identified usually as "homosexual" or "gay" in the mid-twentieth century but often as "transgender" in later years) were particular targets of police on the streets because they were the most identifiable "sexual deviates." See, for example, Seattle drag queen Kim Drake in Don Paulson and Roger Simpson, *An Evening at the Garden of Allah: A Gay Cabaret in Seattle* (New York: Columbia University Press, 1996), p. 105; Leslie Feinberg's autobiographical novel *Stone Butch Blues* (Ithaca, NY: Firebrand Books, 1993); and Frankie Hucklenbroich's autobiographical novel *A Crystal Diary* (Ithaca, NY: Firebrand Books, 1997). Big-city police targeted transgender people of color especially. See, for example, Piri, a black female "stud" from Buffalo and her drag queen brother, in Kennedy and Davis, *Boots of Leather*, p. 69; and the stories of Meko, a black butch, and Nancy Valverde, a Latina butch, in Faderman and Timmons, *Gay L.A.*, pp. 93–96.

    Police surveillance of the activities of homosexual men in parks and restrooms was indiscriminate with regard to color. In Atlanta, for example, police conducted an eight-day stakeout of the restroom at the Carnegie Library and arrested twenty white men for "sodomy," which was a felony in Georgia. All twenty were indicted, and their names and addresses printed repeatedly in the *Atlanta Constitution* (September 5, 1953, p. 11; September 10, 1953, p. 7; September 15, 1953, p. 32; September 16, 1953, p. 17). The paper called it "the Atlanta Public Library perversion case" and presented lurid headlines such as "Youth Leader [Jack Macaulay, a twenty-four-year-old Boy Scout official] Given 10 Yr. Morals Term." The case is discussed at greater length in John Howard, "The Library, the Park and the Pervert: Public Space and Homosexual Encounter in Post–World War II Atlanta," *Radical History Review* 62 (Spring 1995): pp. 166–87. The Atlanta Association of Baptist Churches, which was made up of 128 Atlanta congregations, also informed the faithful of "1,500 sex perverts pursuing their devious designs" in the city's Piedmont Park: quoted in Arnold Fleischman and Jason Hardman, "Hitting Below the Bible Belt: The Development of the Gay Rights Movement in Atlanta," *Journal of Urban Affairs* 26, no. 4 (2004): pp. 407–26. Similar stakeouts and harassment across the country are discussed in William N. Eskridge Jr., "Privacy Jurisprudence and the Apartheid of the Closet, 1946–1961," *Florida State University Law Review* 24, no. 4 (Summer 1997), especially section 2, "Flushing Out the Homosexual: Spies, Decoy Cops, Raids."

23. *People v. Earl* 31 Cal. Rptr. 76, Dist. Ct. App. 1963.

24. See John LaStala, "Atascadero: Dachau for Queers?," *Advocate*, April 26, 1972. LaStala had been sent to Atascadero a year after the facility was built. See also "Atascadero: Life, Liberty, and the Pursuit of Treatment," *Advocate*, October 11, 1972; and Wayne Sage, "Crime and the Clockwork Lemon," *Human Behavior* 3, no. 9 (September 1974): pp. 16–25.

25. Statutes and Amendments to the Codes of California, 1952, First Ex. Sess., chap. 23, p. 380, enacted April 17, 1952.

26. *People v. Earl* 216 Cal. App. 2d 607.

27. Sally Taft was married only briefly, in the 1950s, but she used her married name, Duplaix, until her death on July 19, 2012.

28. Sally Duplaix, interview with author, Chatham, MA (telephone), May 2, 2012.

29. Howard Whitman, "The Biggest Taboo," *Collier's*, February 15, 1947, pp. 24–27.

30. Duplaix, interview with author; and transcript of Duplaix, interview with Arden Eversmeyer, 2001. I am grateful to Arden Eversmeyer for sharing this transcript with me.

31. The documentary *Changing Our Minds: The Story of Dr. Evelyn Hooker* (directed by Richard Schmiechen, 1992) includes film clips of a young homosexual male being lobotomized in 1949 through the "ice pick" technique that was brought to the United States by neurologist Dr. Walter Freeman. Prefrontal lobotomies were performed on forty thousand mental institution inmates in the mid-twentieth century. Many of them were homosexual. The documentary also shows a 1950s film clip of another young homosexual being given a shock treatment to "cure" him of his homosexuality.

32. Duplaix, interview with author.

CHAPTER 2: AMERICA HUNTS FOR WITCHES

1. Harold B. Hinton, "Welles: Our Man of the Hour in Cuba," *New York Times*, August 20, 1933.

2. Hinton, "Welles: Our Man of the Hour in Cuba"; James B. Reston, "Acting Secretary," *New York Times*, August 4, 1941; Benjamin Welles, *Sumner Welles: FDR's Global Strategist* (Boston: Houghton Mifflin, 1997).

3. Michael Fullilove, *How Franklin Delano Roosevelt and Five Extraordinary Men Took America into the War and into the World* (New York: Penguin, 2013), p. 111. There had been gossip when Welles was in Cuba too that he engaged in homosexual relations: Irwin F. Gellman, *Secret Affairs: Franklin Roosevelt, Cordell Hull and Sumner Welles* (Baltimore: Johns Hopkins University Press, 1995), p. 83.

4. Orville H. Bullitt, ed., *For the President, Personal and Secret: Correspondence Between Franklin D. Roosevelt and William C. Bullitt* (Boston: Houghton Mifflin, 1972), pp. 512–16.

5. Mary V. Dearborn, *Queen of Bohemia: The Life of Louise Bryant* (Boston: Houghton Mifflin, 1996).

6. By 1964, presidents could no longer rely on the discretion of the press. President Lyndon Johnson's top aide and longtime trusted friend, Walter Jenkins, a husband and father of six, was arrested by two undercover agents in the restroom of a Washington, DC, YMCA, only weeks before the November presidential election. The UPI article about Jenkins's arrest ran in newspapers everywhere. The media speculated that the arrest of his aide would hurt Johnson's chances in the election. The president immediately asked for Jenkins's resignation. See, for example, United Press International, "Johnson Is Stung Hard by Arrest of Top Aide," *Great Bend (KS) Tribune*, October 15, 1964; United Press International, "T-Men Knew of Jenkins Since 1959," *Scottsdale (AZ) Daily News*, October 17, 1964. Johnson maintained that he'd had no idea about Jenkins's homosexuality: "I couldn't have been more shocked about Walter Jenkins than if I'd heard Lady Bird had tried to kill the Pope," he is quoted as saying in Robert Dallek, *Flawed Giant: Lyndon Johnson and His Times* (New York: Oxford University Press, 1998), p. 180.

7. Athan Theoharis, *J. Edgar Hoover, Sex, and Crime: An Historical Antidote* (Chicago: Ivan Dee, 1995), p. 32.

8. Bullitt, ed., *For the President*, pp. xi–xiii and 512–14. FDR's tolerance of Welles's homosexual behavior is somewhat surprising considering that, as assistant secretary of the navy in 1919, he conducted the first massive homosexual witch hunt in America. See p. 31.

9. The railway porter incident did not come to public attention until it was reported in the scandal magazine *Confidential*: Truxton Decatur, "We Accuse . . . Sumner Welles," *Confidential*, March 1956.

10. Welles's resignation did not mark the end of his involvement in matters of state: for example, he was a passionate supporter of the creation of Israel, as he wrote about in *We Need Not Fail* (Boston: Houghton Mifflin, 1948).

11. Reported in Drew Pearson, "Merry-Go-Round," syndicated column, November 16, 1943. Pearson, who was no friend of homosexuals (see p. 259), admired Sumner Welles and did not know of what Bullitt had accused him.

12. Benjamin Welles, *Sumner Welles*, p. 350.

13. "Peurifoy's First-Name Diplomacy Succeeded in Hard Assignments," *New York Times*, August 13, 1955.

14. Hugh Morrow, "The Man Who Runs the State Department," *Saturday Evening Post*, reprinted in the *Milwaukee (WI) Journal*, September 6, 1949.

15. Carlisle H. Humelsine, senior State Department official, to James E. Webb, undersecretary of state, confidential memo, June 23, 1950, "Information on Homosexuals" ("declassified 4/12"), ARC Identifier 2666952, National Archives and Records Administration, Washington, DC.

16. Confidential memo from Humelsine, National Archives.

17. Morrow, "The Man Who Runs the State Department."

18. Ibid.

19. Hiss had worked for the State Department and had presided over the United Nations Charter Conference. He was convicted in 1950 after having been accused of being a Soviet spy by Whittaker Chambers, who'd been a Communist and a bisexual (and who claimed to have given up both Communism and homosexuality in 1938).

20. The number of Communists McCarthy specified has been reported variously as 57, 205, and 250.

21. William S. White, "'Never Condoned Disloyalty,' Says Acheson of Hiss Stand," *New York Times*, March 1, 1950.

22. Hill quoted in Max Lerner, "Panic on the Potomac," part 1, *New York Post*, July 10, 1950.

23. Kenneth Wherry, *Report of the Investigations of the Junior Senator of Nebraska . . . on the Infiltration of Subversives and Moral Perverts into the Executive Branch of the United States Government*, May 17, 1950. Lister Hill filed a separate report because he and Wherry disagreed over what the report should cover.

24. "New Shocker," *Newsweek*, May 29, 1950, p. 18. *Newsweek* accepted without questioning Blick's statement, which it called a "real shocker," that 3,750 homosexuals were employed by the federal government.

25. William S. White, "Inquiry by Senate on Perverts Asked," *New York Times*, May 20, 1950.

26. Wherry, *Report of the Investigations of the Junior Senator of Nebraska*.

27. Jack Lait and Lee Mortimer, *Washington Confidential* (New York: Crown, 1951), p. 116.

28. Max Lerner, "Panic on the Potomac," part 3, *New York Post*, July 12, 1950.

29. Wherry, *Report of the Investigations of the Junior Senator of Nebraska*.

30. White, "Inquiry by Senate on Perverts Asked."

31. "Pervert Inquiry Ordered," *New York Times*, June 15, 1950.

32. Congressional Record, House, 81st Congress, 2d Session, April 19, 1950, 96:5403. See also Congressional Record, House, March 31, 1950, 4591.

33. Incidents reported in Joseph and Stewart Alsop, "Why Has Washington Gone Crazy?" *Saturday Evening Post*, July 29, 1950, pp. 20–21, 59–61.

34. David K. Johnson, "'Homosexual Citizens': Washington's Gay Community Confronts the Civil Service," *Washington History* 6, no. 2 (Fall/Winter 1994/95): pp. 44–63.

35. *Employment of Homosexuals and Other Sex Perverts in Government*, report made to the Committee on Expenditures by Its Subcommittee on Investigations, US Senate, 81st Congress, 2d session, December 15, 1950.

36. Ibid.

37. Truman's White House did work behind the scenes to quash some extremes, as when chief counsel to the subcommittee Francis Flanagan tried to establish a central card index composed of the names of any person, whether or not a federal employee, who was suspected by any government agency of being a homosexual: David K. Johnson, *The Lavender Scare: The Cold War Persecution of Gays and Lesbians in the Federal Government* (Chicago: University of Chicago Press, 2004), p. 105. In 1950, however, Truman signed the Uniform Code of Military Justice, which included the regulation that homosexual service members must be discharged from the military.

38. Senator Clifford Case on *Face the Nation*, CBS, July 8, 1956: "News of Interest," *Washington Newsletter*, Mattachine Society, July 16, 1956, p. 3. A short-lived Washington, DC, branch of the Mattachine Society was formed in 1956. It was unrelated to Mattachine Society Washington, which Frank Kameny established in 1961.

39. Betty Deran, interview with Len Evans, May 7, 1983, Len Evans Papers, GLC9, box 1, folder 21, Gay and Lesbian Historical Society of Northern California Collection, San Francisco Public Library.

40. Routsong's original title for the novel was *A Place for Us*. Deran says the title and general story line derived from their experiences of having to leave DC and find "a place" where they could be together: Deran, interview with Evans.

41. Deran, interview with Evans.

42. Confidential memo from Humelsine, National Archives.

43. Deran, interview with Evans.

44. "Tydings Fires 2½ Hr. Blast at McCarthy from Floor," *Washington Post*, July 21, 1950, pp. 1ff.

45. McCarthy also practiced dirty tricks on Senator Lester Hunt, a much-loved liberal Democrat from Wyoming, whose son, Lester Jr., had been arrested for soliciting a male undercover agent. McCarthy and his henchman, New Hampshire senator Styles Bridges, told the senator that if he did not resign immediately, they would make sure that the incident became a public scandal. When he did not resign, they informed the media about the son's arrest and got Roy Blick to prosecute the twenty-year-old. The despondent senator committed suicide in 1954. The case is discussed at length in Rodger McDaniel, *Dying for Joe McCarthy's Sins: The Suicide of Wyoming Senator Lester Hunt* (Cody, WY: WordsWorth Press, 2013).

46. Senator Harry Cain, "I Could Not Remain Silent," as told to Tris Coffin, *Coronet*, November 1955, pp. 29–34.

47. Many were individuals whose jobs had nothing to do with "national security." For instance, Ian Nabishima, a Japanese American who'd gotten an honorable discharge from the US Army in 1951, was fired four years later from his job as a clerk-typist at the Public Health Service Hospital in San Francisco. An investigation had disclosed that the twenty-eight-year-old man "associated with known homosexuals under circumstances that raised serious questions about [his] moral conduct," and that he "frequented a place known as a homosexual hangout": "Before the United States Civil Service Commission Board of Appeals and Review: In the Matter of Ian A. Nabishima, Appellant," August 17, 1955; in Len Evans Papers, 93-98, box GLC-9, Gay and Lesbian Historical Society of Northern California Collection, San Francisco Public Library.

48. John Logan, "You're Fired!" *Mattachine Review* 2 (June 1956): pp. 27–29.

CHAPTER 3: NO ARMY OF LOVERS: TOWARD A HOMOSEXUAL-FREE MILITARY

1. Elizabeth Lutes Hillman, *Defending America: Military Culture and the Cold War Court-Martial* (Princeton, NJ: University of Princeton Press, 2005), pp. 114–19; and Victor Rabinowitz, *Unrepentant Leftist: A Lawyer's Memoir* (Champaign: University of Illinois Press, 1996), pp. 293–94.

2. "Kathryn Rising Navy Man's Bride," *New York Times*, April 4, 1937.

3. *U.S. v. Hooper*, 26 CMR 417 (1958); *Hooper, Plaintiff v. Hartman, Defendant*, no. 2027, 163 F. Supp. 437 (1958), US District Court, San Diego, CA, May 10, 1958; and *Hooper, Appellant v. Hartman, Appellee*, no. 16058, 274f, 2d 429, US Court of Appeals for the Ninth Circuit, December 4, 1959.

4. Quoted in "Trial by Military Court OKd for Retired Officers," *European Stars and Stripes*, September 28, 1958.

5. Hillman, *Defending America*, p. 117.

6. Ibid.

7. *Robert O. Bland v. C. C. Hartman*, Court of Appeals for the Ninth Circuit, 245f, 2d 311, May 3, 1957.

8. Quoted in "Navy Trial Upheld for Retired Officer," *New York Times*, September 27, 1958.

9. The October 19, 1949, DOD directive mandated that "An undesirable or blue discharge issued because of homosexual acts or tendencies generally will be considered as under dishonorable conditions and a bar to entitlements [of all veterans' benefits] under Public Law No. 2, 73rd Congress as amended, and Public Law No. 347, 78th Congress, as amended."

10. Lawrence P. Murphy, *Perverts by Official Order: The Campaign Against Homosexuals by the United States Navy* (New York: Haworth Press, 1988): see, for example, how investigators built their case against Samuel Neal Kent, pp. 77ff.

11. In 1951 the Articles of War were adapted into the Uniform Code of Military Justice.

12. Margot Canaday, *The Straight State: Sexuality and Citizenship in Twentieth Century America* (Princeton, NJ: Princeton University Press, 2009), p. 77.

13. Allan Berube, *Coming Out Under Fire: The History of Gay Men and Women in World War II* (New York: Simon & Schuster, 1990), chaps. 1 and 5.

14. Soon after the war, psychiatrist William Menninger sensibly guessed that for every homosexual who was detected by the military during World War II, "there were 5 or 10 who were never detected": William Menninger, *Psychiatry in a Troubled World* (New York: Macmillan, 1948), pp. 226–27.

15. Quoted in Eskridge, "Privacy Jurisprudence and the Apartheid of the Closet," pp. 703–888.

16. Three research teams of psychiatrists labored over surefire ways to distinguish the real from the phony homosexual using the Rorschach test: M. S. Bergmann, "Homosexuality on the Rorschach Test," *Bulletin of the Menninger Clinic* 9 (1945): pp. 78–83. The military was always reluctant to discharge self-confessed homosexuals in the midst of war. Colonel Zula Johnston, the head of nursing in an army hospital, recalls a trained medic who told his commander, "You can't send me to Vietnam. I'm gay." "If we got rid of all the homosexual medics in the army," the commander answered, "we wouldn't have any medics": Zula Johnston, interview with author, Olympia, WA, May 29, 2012.

17. "Medicine: Sanity in the Subs," *Newsweek*, August 11, 1947; and Berube, *Coming Out Under Fire*, ch. 10.

18. Memorandum: Department of Defense to Secretaries of the Army, Navy and Air Force, October 11, 1949, in *Report of the Board Appointed to Prepare and Submit Recommendations to the Secretary of the Navy for the Revision of Policies, Procedures, and Directives Dealing with Homosexuals*, March 15, 1957.

19. For a brief history of military regulations against homosexuality see Major Jeffrey S. Davis, "Military Policy Toward Homosexuals: Scientific, Historical, and Legal Perspectives, *Military Law Review* 131 (January 1991): pp. 55–108.

20. In the navy, for example, there were 483 discharges for homosexuality in 1950, during the Korean War. The year the armistice was signed, in 1953, the number had almost tripled to 1,353: in Randy Shilts, *Conduct Unbecoming: Gays and Lesbians in the U.S. Military* (New York: St. Martins, 1993), p. 70.

21. Carlita "Lee" Durand, interview with author, San Diego, August 3, 2012.

22. Captain Barbara M. S. Pratt, USAF Commander, 3629th School Squadron, Lackland Air Force Base, "Statement," November 23, 1959, in the private collection of Carlita "Lee" Durand.

23. Dasil C. Smith, MD, "Certificate" re. Carlita K. Durand, October 22, 1959, in the private collection of Carlita "Lee" Durand.

24. Memorandum, October 11, 1949.

25. Durand was able to get her discharge upgraded to honorable in 2008, after a half century of feeling disgraced. She'd turned to alcohol, had been rescued by Alcoholics Anonymous, and became a swimming champion in the Senior Olympics: Durand, interview with author.

26. Sue Young, interview with author, San Diego, July 13, 2012.

27. Canaday, *The Straight State*, pp. 199–200.

28. *Fannie Mae Clackum v. United States*, 296f, 2d, no. 246-56, United States Court of Claims, January 20, 1960. The *Clackum* case was first brought to my attention by Jonathan Ned Katz's *Gay American History: Lesbians and Gay Men in the U.S.A.* (New York: Thomas Y. Crowell, 1976), pp. 119–23.

29. Ibid.

30. Ibid.

31. Ibid.

CHAPTER 4: AMERICA PROTECTS ITS YOUNGSTERS

1. "Idaho Underworld," *Time*, December 12, 1955. *Time* fanned the flames of panic nationwide by its sensationalistic references to "a widespread homosexual underworld" that had been "preying on hundreds of teenage boys for the past decade." The Boise witch hunts are the subject of a full-length book by John Gerassi, *The Boys of Boise: Furor, Vice, and Folly in an American City* (New York: Macmillan, 1966).

2. Ralph H. Major Jr., "New Moral Menace to Our Youth," *Coronet*, September 1950, pp. 101–8.

3. Jim Duggins interviews with Ralph Neugebauer, August 13, 1994; Bud Robbins, July 20, 1994, and August 16, 1994; and Scott Boxwood, October 8, 1994, and December 3, 1994: "Uncles Project," San Francisco GLBT Historical Society. All three men were students at the University of Missouri in the late 1940s and were victims of the witch hunts.

4. Milton E. Hahn and Byron H. Atkinson, "The Sexually Deviant Student," *School and Society* (September 17, 1955): pp. 85–87; Kathleen Weiler, "The Case of Martha Deane: Sexuality and Power at Cold War UCLA," *History of Education Quarterly* 47, no. 4 (November 2007): pp. 470–96.

5. Daniel Tsang, "Gay Ann Arbor Purges," *Midwest Gay Academic Journal* 1, nos. 2 and 3 (1977).

6. Ron McCrea, "Madison Gay Purge," *Midwest Gay Academic Journal* 1, no. 3 (1977); Lewis Bosworth, interview with Scott Seyforth, Madison's LGBT Community, 1960s–Present, Oral History Program, interview 940, University of Wisconsin, Madison, Archives.

7. Barry Werth, *The Scarlet Professor: A Literary Life Shattered by Scandal* (New York: Random House, 2001).

8. Ibid.

9. The University of Texas witch hunt preceded the one at the University of Missouri: "University Row Laid to Homosexuals," *Los Angeles Times*, November 18, 1944, p. 4; "Education: In the Lone Star State," *Time*, November 27, 1944.

10. Mabel Norris Chesley, "The High Cost of Snooping," a series of ten articles about expenditures and methods of the Florida Legislative Investigation Committee in the *Daytona Beach (FL) Morning Journal*, December 1962: in John Egerton Collection, University of South Florida, box 3, folder 8.

11. Emmett Peter Jr., "The Sergeant," *Daily Commercial* (Leesburg, FL), April 2, 1963.

12. Sydney P. Freedberg, "The Story of Old Sparky," *St. Petersburg (FL) Times*, September 25, 1999.

13. Clip of Senator Johns speaking in film documentary *Behind Closed Doors: The Dark Legacy of the Johns Committee*, by Allyson A. Beutke, 2000.

14. Mabel Norris Chesley, "Johns Committee Does Little, Spends Lots," *Daytona Beach (FL) Morning Journal*, December 10, 1962.

15. Emmett Peter Jr., "Johns Committee: A Balance Sheet," *Daily Commercial* (Leesburg, FL), March 31, 1963.

16. Florida Legislative Investigation Committee Papers, box 8, folder 15, June 1, 1960, Florida State Archives, Tallahassee.

17. James T. Sears, *Lonely Hunters: An Oral History of Lesbian and Gay Southern Life, 1948–1968* (Boulder, CO: Westview Press, 1997), p. 57.

18. Ruth Perry Papers, John Egerton Collection, box 1, folder 6, University of South Florida.

19. "3 Witnesses Go Mum at NAACP Probe," *Fort Pierce (FL) News-Tribune*, February 27, 1958, p. 12.

20. Johns in documentary *Behind Closed Doors*.

21. "'NAACP Control High Court'—Johns," *Miami (FL) News*, February 24, 1959.

22. Johns did not cease his investigations into "integrationist groups" totally. His committee took complaints from right-wing groups such as Florida States Rights, the White Sentinel, and the Un-American Committee of the American Legion, and investigated groups such as the Congress for Racial Equality and the Independent Citizens Committee for Arts, Sciences, and Professions in 1960: Correspondence, August 31, 1960, and September 12, 1960, in the Florida Legislative Investigation Committee Papers, box 3, folder 11, Florida State Archives, Tallahassee. However, the primary focus of the Johns Committee by then was "cleaning up" public education.

23. The professor's protests had been triggered by an invitation to sociologist Jerome Davis, who'd been denied tenure at Yale because of his leftist sympathies.

24. Mabel Norris Chesley, "What Started Investigations of Educational Institutions?," *Daytona Beach (FL) Morning Journal*, December 14, 1962. Johns did not totally cease Red-baiting on campuses, despite AAUP resistance. For instance, an offer to a retired Vanderbilt professor to teach part-time at USF in fall 1962 was withdrawn under pressure from the Johns Committee when it was discovered he'd written a left-leaning book on the Cold War. AAUP blacklisted USF over the case: John Egerton, "The Stormy 1960s at the University of South Florida," unpublished manuscript, Egerton Papers, box 1, folder 1A, University of South Florida Special Collections.

25. Bonnie Stark, "McCarthyism in Florida: Charley Johns and the Florida Legislative Investigation Committee, July 1956 to July 1965" (master's thesis, University of South Florida, 1985), p. 92.

26. The American Association of University Professors claimed that the Johns Committee "libeled" faculty members by making "tenuous and unproved homosexual 'smears.'" But it never asserted the *right* to be a homosexual: Statewide AAUP meeting, Saint Petersburg: "Academic Freedom and the Johns Committee

Investigations," T. Terrell Sessums Papers, box 24, Special Collections, University of South Florida.

27. None of the university professors fired for homosexuality fought back in the courts, though three high school teachers did. The Florida Supreme Court declared that the firings of the high school teachers were illegal because confessions were obtained by threats; their teaching licenses were restored: John Egerton, "The Controversy" (unpublished manuscript), pp. 145–46, Egerton Papers, box 3, University of South Florida.

28. Peter Jr., "The Sergeant."

29. Johns bullied administrators, and they were often cowed by him. For example, on several occasions, he told the University of Florida's president, Wayne Reitz, that he must help Johns's "good friend" who was being mistreated by his supervisor (November 9, 1956); that Reitz must hire Mr. O. C. Gay, an air-conditioning maintenance man, to service the new university hospital's air-conditioning (June 21, 1957); that Reitz must raise the salary of Johns's "warm personal friend" who was employed in the Soils Department (August 20, 1959); that he must rehire a man who was fired after being charged with a DUI (February 20, 1959); and that he must "talk with the Dean Maloney and see if there is a way to pull up the grades to a desired level" of the son of a friend of Johns's (January 5, 1964): Office of the President Papers, series P14a, box 40, Department of Special and Area Studies Collections, George A. Smathers Libraries, University of Florida.

30. Florida Legislative Investigation Committee Papers, series 1486, box 7, folder 19, Florida State Archives, Tallahassee. The names of the investigated have been redacted in the FLIC files.

31. Many of the men caught by the Johns Committee were married to women and did not have a homosexual identity. Their same-sex sexual experiences were with anonymous partners in public places.

32. Egerton, "The Controversy"; and editorial, *Daily Commercial* (Leesburg, FL), April 23, 1963.

33. Charley Johns was not present at this particular interrogation, though he came to many of them.

34. Series 1486 (FLIC), box 7, folder 19, Florida State Archives, Tallahassee.

35. Eunice Maude Disney died at the age of forty-nine in 1967, a few years after she'd been forced out of her position at UF.

36. The University of Florida's dean of women, Marna Brady, who lived in a long-term relationship with another woman, Norma Olson, was untouched by the Johns Committee, as were, undoubtedly, other discreet (and lucky) lesbians on the faculty and in administration at UF and other state-supported institutions: Rita Irene Herron, "'True Spirit of Pioneer Traditions': An Historical Analysis of the University of Florida's First Dean of Women, Marna Brady" (PhD dissertation, Florida State University, 2004). Author Rita Mae Brown, who was a student at the University of Florida during the Johns witch hunts, presents a fictional version of Marna Brady, a hypocritical lesbian dean who cancels the autobiographical lesbian character's scholarship when she's caught with another

woman student: *Rubyfruit Jungle* (Plainfield, VT: Daughters Press, 1973); and Rita Mae Brown, interview with author, Charlotteville, VA (telephone), January 12, 2015.

37. R. J. Strickland to chair of the Florida Legislative Investigation Committee, letter, "Personal and Confidential," October 16, 1959, series 1486 (FLIC), box 3, folder 9, Florida State Archives, Tallahassee.

38. At least twenty-seven public school teachers were finally purged on the charge of lesbianism. Fifty-three male teachers and seven additional teachers whose gender can't be determined from the transcripts were also purged on the charge of homosexuality: Karen L. Graves, *And They Were Wonderful Teachers: Florida's Purge of Gay and Lesbian Teachers* (Champaign: University of Illinois Press, 2009), p. 22.

39. James Schnur, "Cold Warriors in the Hot Sunshine: The Johns Committee's Assault on Civil Liberties in Florida, 1956–1965" (master's thesis, University of South Florida, 1995), pp. 124–25.

40. October 20, 1960, series 1486 (FLIC), box 8, folder 43, Florida State Archives.

41. Names have been redacted on most FLIC documents, although occasionally the redactor missed a name: Investigation transcript, June 2, 1962, series 1486 (FLIC), box 10, folder 42, Florida State Archives, Tallahassee.

42. Ibid.

43. The woman's name is redacted in most of the files but appears in testimony of May 20, 1960, series 1486 (FLIC), box 8, folder 11, Florida State Archives, Tallahassee.

44. Debriefing of May by R. J. Strickland, May 9, 1960, series 1486 (FLIC), box 8, folder 7, Florida State Archives, Tallahassee.

45. Ibid.

46. March 20, 1960, series 1486 (FLIC), box 8, folder 3, Florida State Archives, Tallahassee.

47. March 20, 1960, series 1486 (FLIC), box 8, folder 4, Florida State Archives, Tallahassee.

48. R. J. Strickland to FLIC chairman, letter, September 21, 1959, series 1486, box 3, folder 9, Florida Legislative Investigation Committee Papers, Florida State Archives, Tallahassee. Requests for payments to informants were also made by Strickland in October and November: ibid.

49. "Senator Johns Offers to Quit; Probe Committee Rapped," *News Tribune* (Fort Pierce, FL), April 19, 1963, p. 3; Jerry Mock, "Shakeup Appears to Be Drawing Near in Johns Committee," *Panama City (FL) Herald*, May 21, 1963, p. 5.

50. United Press International, "Evans Named to Johns Committee," *Panama City (FL) Herald*, November 19, 1963, p. 1.

51. Florida Legislative Investigation Committee, *Homosexuality and Citizenship in Florida: A Report of the Florida Legislative Investigation Committee* (Tallahassee: FLIC, 1964).

52. Harold Rummel, "Nationwide Sale of Florida Homo Pamphlet!" *Evening Independent* (Saint Petersburg, FL), June 25, 1964.

53. Ibid.

54. Paul Welch, "Homosexuality in America," *Life*, June 26, 1964, pp. 66–74ff.

55. "Officials to Map Drive on Deviates," *Miami (FL) News*, July 15, 1964.

56. Karl Wickstrom, "The Life of a Homosexual Is Sad, Not Gay," *Miami Herald*, August 9, 1964.

CHAPTER 5: MATTACHINE

1. The most extensive biography of Harry Hay is Stuart Timmons, *Trouble with Harry Hay: Founder of the Modern Gay Movement* (Boston: Alyson, 1990).

2. Harry Hay, *Radically Gay: Gay Liberation in the Words of Its Founder*, ed. Will Roscoe (Boston: Beacon Press, 1996), p. 60. Christopher Bram points out that within days of the publication of the Kinsey Report on male sexuality, Gore Vidal's *The City and the Pillar* and Truman Capote's *Other Voices, Other Rooms* were also published. Bram observes hyperbolically that "The gay revolution began as a literary revolution": *Eminent Outlaws: The Gay Writers Who Changed America* (New York: Twelve, 2012). But the brutal crackdowns on homosexuals in that same year (see prologue and part 1 of this book) surely had as much and more to do with triggering what became, years later, the "gay revolution."

3. Harry Hay, "Birth of a Consciousness," *Harvard Gay and Lesbian Review* (Winter 1995).

4. Karl Ulrichs had tried to start an even earlier homosexual civil rights movement in Germany, in 1867, declaring he would unite "urnings" (homosexuals) into a mass, and they would "champion" their human rights: see Hubert Kennedy, *Ulrichs: The Life and Work of Karl Ulrichs, Pioneer of the Modern Gay Movement* (Boston: Alyson, 1988).

5. Timmons, *Trouble with Harry Hay*, p. 43.

6. The Society for Human Rights's charter is reproduced in Jonathan Ned Katz, *Gay American History: Lesbians and Gay Men in the U.S.A.* (New York: Crowell, 1976), pp. 385–88.

7. Edward Sagarin (aka Donald Webster Cory), "Structure and Ideology of an Association of Deviants" (PhD dissertation, New York University, 1966; reprinted, New York: Arno Press, 1975), pp. 64–67. The Veterans Benevolent Association continued until 1954. Other homosexual organizations were established in Europe during the 1940s, such as the Dutch Center for Culture and Leisure (COC), and the Danish "Furbundet af 1948" ("the League of 1948"), both started primarily to fight against laws that criminalized homosexuality.

8. In the 1984 documentary *Before Stonewall: The Making of a Gay and Lesbian Community*, Hay claimed, "We didn't know at that point, none of us knew, that there had been a gay organization anywhere in the world before."

9. Harry Hay, "In Memory of the Mattachine Foundation," unpublished manuscript, Mattachine Society Project Collection, box 1, folder 26, ONE National Gay and Lesbian Archives, University of Southern California Libraries.

10. Ibid.

11. Timmons, *Trouble with Harry Hay*, p. 140.

12. The school was deemed a "Communist front" by the Tenney Committee: Edward

L. Barrett Jr., *The Tenney Committee: Legislative Investigation of Subversive Activities in California* (Ithaca, NY: Cornell University Press, 1951), pp. 105–121.

13. In a 1984 Christmas letter to Don Slater, Jennings talks about his younger years when he was "a loud-mouthed commie," but there is no evidence of his having belonged to the party: in C. Todd White, "Dale Jennings (1917–2000): ONE's Outspoken Advocate," in *Before Stonewall: Advocates for Gay and Lesbian Rights in Historical Context*, ed. Vern L. Bullough (Binghamton, NY: Harrington Park Press, 2002), p. 84.

14. Hieronymous K. (pseudonym for Dale Jennings), "The Mattachine," *ONE*, January 1953, pp. 18–19.

15. Three years later, when Dale Jennings was far less smitten with Hay than he'd been at the beginning, he questioned the concept of homosexuals as a "cultural minority." In his essay "Homosexuals Are Not a People," written under the pseudonym Jeff Winters, Jennings characterized as simplistic the idea of a homosexual "ethic" or single distinct homosexual "culture." He echoed Alfred Kinsey's observation that humanity is not divided simply into homosexual and heterosexual (cf. Kinsey's 0 to 6 scale), and he was a proponent for "sexual freedom" for everyone: *ONE*, March 1953, pp. 2–6.

16. Chuck Rowland, interview with Eric Marcus in *Making History: The Struggle for Gay and Lesbian Equal Rights, 1945–1990* (New York: HarperCollins, 1992), p. 31.

17. John D'Emilio, *Sexual Politics, Sexual Communities: The Making of a Homosexual Minority in the United States, 1940–1970* (Chicago: University of Chicago Press, 1983), p. 64.

18. Faderman and Timmons, *Gay L.A.*, p. 128.

19. Gruber later changed his first name to John, claiming he did it so he could stop hearing in his head his mother's call of "Jimmy! Jimmy!" He and Stevens were leather men and early members of the first gay motorcycle club, the Satyrs, founded in Los Angeles in 1954. The history of their early participation in Mattachine is recounted in Chuck Rowland, "Opening Talk: California State Constitutional Convention of the Mattachine Society," April 11, 1953, Donald Lucas Papers, box 2, folder 20, San Francisco GLBT Historical Society.

20. Jim Kepner, "Why Can't We All Get Together, and What Do We Have in Common?" (1997) in *Great Speeches on Gay Rights*, ed. James Daley (Mineola, NY: Dover Publications, 2010), p. 93. Hay's recollections about when Bernhard joined the group differ from Kepner's but are vague and confused. In *Radically Gay*, Hay recalled that she was introduced to Mattachine in "approximately September of 1951" by two actors, "Paul Bernard" and Phil Jones (p. 76), but he told Stuart Timmons that Jones brought Bernhard to a meeting, and Bernhard later brought "Paul Bernard": *Trouble with Harry Hay*, p. 154. Jim Kepner was taken to his first Mattachine meeting in December 1952 by another woman, Betty Perdue, who was known by the pseudonym Geraldine Jackson.

21. Faderman and Timmons, *Gay L.A.*, p. 128; and Timmons, *Trouble with Harry Hay*, p. 154. Harry Hay told Timmons that Bernhard "volunteered to work with the Fifth Order, becoming number eight and the most active woman in Mattachine."

But Hay's own brief written history of the Fifth Order ("In Memory of the Matta-chine Foundation") does not mention Bernhard. Nor have I been able to find evidence that she was present during some of the most crucial Fifth Order meetings, such as the one in which the members decided to form the Citizens Committee to Outlaw Entrapment to raise funds for the Dale Jennings trial. (See below.)

22. Eann MacDonald (pseudonym for Harry Hay), "Preliminary Concepts," July 7, 1950, box 1, folder 21, ONE National Gay and Lesbian Archives, University of Southern California Libraries.

23. Hay, "In Memory of the Mattachine Foundation."

24. Joseph Hansen, *A Few Doors West of Hope: The Life and Times of Dauntless Don Slater* (Los Angeles: Homosexual Information Center, 1998), p. 23.

25. Harry Hay, interview with Jonathan Ned Katz in *Gay American History*, p. 414.

26. Hay, "Preliminary Concepts."

27. *Homophile* became the preferred term in the 1950s because it took the emphasis off of sex, as in *homosexual.*

28. Mattachine's FBI file consists of almost a thousand pages and is available online through the FBI's Freedom of Information Act—Subject: Mattachine Society. The file begins on May 21, 1953, with information given to the FBI by "a confidential informant of known reliability." As Dan Siminoski points out, the May 21, 1953, memo is "seemingly in mid-text," indicating that surveillance of Mattachine had at some earlier date been assigned a "highly classified internal security C status, given only to the most important FBI cases in this period." (*C* generally indicated Communist and left-wing groups): Dan Siminoski, un-titled paper, Dan Siminoski Collection, "FBI Surveillance of Gays and Lesbians," box 16, folder 13, ONE National Gay and Lesbian Archives, University of Southern California Libraries.

29. "Sense of Value," discussion notes by "Howard," September 20, 1951, Mattachine Society Project Collection, 2008-016, box 1, folder 11, ONE National Gay and Lesbian Archives, University of Southern California Libraries.

30. "Social Directions of the Homosexual," discussion notes by "Harry," October 4, 1951, ibid.

31. Dale Jennings, "To Be Accused Is to Be Guilty," *ONE*, January 1953, p. 10.

32. The version of this story that Harry Hay repeated to Stuart Timmons was some-what different from Jennings's version in "To Be Accused Is to Be Guilty," and makes Jennings clearly complicit: see Timmons, *Trouble with Harry Hay*, p. 164. Of course, the truth can never be known. Jennings wrote in "To Be Accused Is to Be Guilty" that even if he had "done all the things which the prosecution claimed," he wouldn't have deserved punishment: "I would have been guilty of no unusual act [that is, heterosexuals, too, have oral and anal sex], only an illegal one in this society."

33. Brochure, *Victory!*, Mattachine Society Project Collection, box 1, folder 14, ONE National Gay and Lesbian Archives, University of Southern California Libraries.

34. Jennings, "To Be Accused Is to Be Guilty."

35. Recounted in brochure, *Victory!*, Mattachine Society Project Collection.

36. Hansen, *A Few Doors West of Hope*, p. 23.
37. C. Todd White, *Pre-Gay L.A.: A Social History of the Movement for Homosexual Rights* (Urbana: University of Illinois Press, 2009), p. 24.
38. Ibid.
39. Harry Hay to Donald Webster Cory (aka Edward Sagarin), letter, April 1952, Mattachine Society Project Collection, box 1, folder 10, ONE National Gay and Lesbian Archives, University of Southern California Libraries.
40. White, *Pre-Gay L.A.*, p. 24.
41. The year before, Hay had read in Donald Webster Cory's book *The Homosexual in America* that "the American Civil Liberties Union had evinced an interest in the unconstitutionality of entrapment for the purpose of self-incriminating the victim," as he wrote to Cory, complaining that the Los Angeles ACLU refused to help Jennings and asking for Cory's assistance.
42. Hay to Cory, letter, April 1952.
43. Leaflet, "NOW Is The Time to Fight," Mattachine Society Project Collection, box 1, folder 14, ONE National Gay and Lesbian Archives, University of Southern California Libraries. As brave as Mattachine's words were, the Fifth Order continued to exercise considerable caution. This first leaflet asked that checks be made payable to "Miss Jean Dempsey, Treasurer," to an address on Oak Crest Drive, where Harry Hay's mother lived. (Subsequent leaflets specified that checks be made payable to Miss Romayne Cox.) Most of the literature distributed by the Citizens Committee to Outlaw Entrapment carefully placed Jennings's case in the context of LAPD's harassment of all minorities—for example, "SO LONG AS ONE MINORITY GROUP IS THUS HARRIED AND HOUNDED, NO MINORITY GROUP OR COMMUNITY GROUP IS SAFE: An Anonymous Call to Arms from the Citizens' Committee to Outlaw Entrapment," ibid.
44. The trial is described in Harry Hay's letter to Jay Clark, October 6, 1952, Mattachine Society Project Collection, box 1, folder 10, ONE National Gay and Lesbian Archives, University of Southern California Libraries.
45. Ibid.
46. Jennings's victory did not, of course, end vice squad entrapment of homosexual men in California or anywhere else.
47. Hay to Clark, letter, October 6, 1952.
48. Gerard G. Brissette to Mattachine Foundation, letter, February 15, 1953, Mattachine Society Project Collection, box 1, folder 9, ONE National Gay and Lesbian Archives, University of Southern California Libraries.
49. Jennings, "To Be Accused Is to Be Guilty," p. 13.
50. Brochure, *Victory!*, Mattachine Society Project Collection.
51. Timmons, *Trouble with Harry Hay*, p. 174.
52. Hay, "In Memory of the Mattachine Foundation."
53. "Official Statement of Policy on Political Questions and Related Matters," February 1953, Mattachine Society Project Collection, box 1, folder 16, ONE National Gay and Lesbian Archives, University of Southern California Libraries.
54. Hay, "In Memory of the Mattachine Foundation."

55. Paul Coates, "Well, Medium and Rare: Where Is Romayne?" *Daily Mirror* (Los Angeles), March 12, 1953.

56. Mrs. Henry Hay to Marilyn Rieger, February 23, 1953, and Marilyn Rieger to Mrs. Henry Hay, February 26, 1953, Don Lucas Papers, box 1, folder 3, GLBT Historical Society. I am grateful to Dr. Linda Garber for helping me locate this material.

57. Marilyn Rieger to Paul Coates, March 13, 1953, ibid.

58. Marilyn Rieger to the Mattachine Foundation, letter, March 23, 1953, Mattachine Society Project Collection, folder 8, ONE National Gay and Lesbian Archives, University of Southern California Libraries.

59. "Mrs. Henry Hay" to Marilyn Rieger, letter, April 14, 1953, Mattachine Society Project Collection, box 1, folder 8, ONE National Gay and Lesbian Archives, University of Southern California Libraries.

60. D'Emilio, *Sexual Politics, Sexual Communities*, p. 78.

61. Richard H. Gwartney, MD, "Reorganization Study," March 1953, box 1, folder 18, ONE National Gay and Lesbian Archives, University of Southern California Libraries.

62. Sears, *Behind the Mask of Mattachine*, p. 141.

63. "A Call to All Members of the Mattachine Society," Mattachine Society Project Collection, box 1, folder 19, ONE National Gay and Lesbian Archives, University of Southern California Libraries.

64. In Hay's recollections, he sometimes presented the convention that booted the Fifth Order from power in rosy terms: for example, "This wasn't the period when you hugged much yet, but nevertheless there was an awful lot of hugging going on that first weekend": quoted in Timmons, *Trouble with Harry Hay*, p. 177.

65. Rowland, "Opening Talk: California State Constitutional Convention of the Mattachine Society."

66. Harry Hay's speech is reprinted in "Are You Now or Have You Ever Been a Homosexual?" *ONE*, April 1953, pp. 6–7.

67. Resolution, Second Mattachine Constitutional Convention, May 23, 1953, Donald Lucas Papers, box 2, folder 21, GLBT Historical Society, San Francisco.

68. Marilyn Rieger to delegates of the convention, letter, May 23, 1953, Mattachine Society Project Collection, ONE National Gay and Lesbian Archives, University of Southern California Libraries.

69. Marcus, *Making History*, p. 36.

70. Harry Hay, interview with Peter Adair in Nancy Adair and Casey Adair, *Word Is Out: Stories of Some of Our Lives* (San Francisco: New Glide Publications, 1978), p. 242.

CHAPTER 6: THE DAUGHTERS

1. Daniel Winunwe Rivers, *Radical Relations: Lesbian Mothers, Gay Fathers, and Their Children in the United States Since World War II* (Chapel Hill: University of North Carolina Press, 2013), p. 28.

2. In 1971 Martin was one of the founders of the pioneering Lesbian Mother's Union.

3. Phyllis Lyon, "Del Martin (1921–)," in *Before Stonewall*, p. 162.

4. Phyllis Lyon, in film documentary *No Secret Anymore: The Times of Del Martin and Phyllis Lyon*, directed by Joan E. Biren (JEB), 2003.

5. Del Martin and Phyllis Lyon, interview with David Mixner and Dennis Bailey in *Brave Journeys: Profiles in Gay and Lesbian Courage* (New York: Bantam Books, 2000), p. 19.

6. In the 1950s, few heterosexuals knew that *gay* meant homosexual, but it was by then a widely used term among urban homosexuals.

7. Nan Alamilla Boyd, *Wide Open Town: A History of Queer San Francisco to 1965* (Berkeley: University of California Press), p. 92.

8. Del Martin and Phyllis Lyon, *Lesbian/Woman* (New York: Bantam, 1972), p. 238.

9. Martin and Lyon, *Lesbian/Woman*, pp. 238–39.

10. Del Martin and Phyllis Lyon, interview with author, San Francisco, August 14, 1987.

11. Martin and Lyon, *Lesbian/Woman*, pp. 239–42.

12. See p. 100.

13. The statement of purpose was reprinted, with little change, at the front of every issue of *The Ladder*, until July 1968, when the magazine was taken over by Barbara Grier and separated from Daughters of Bilitis.

14. "History of DOB" (1976), in June Mazer Lesbian Collection: Daughters of Bilitis Collection, box 1, folder 7, Special Collections, UCLA.

15. Natalie Lando (San Francisco DOB member who typed *The Ladder* for several years), interview with author, Oakland, April 4, 2012.

16. Letter to Del Martin, January 2, 1957, Daughters of Bilitis Papers, box 3, folder 1, June Mazer Lesbian Collection, Special Collections, UCLA.

17. Phyllis Lyon, "Ann Ferguson Is Dead!" *Ladder*, January 1957, p. 7. At DOB meetings, a "greeter" would stand by the door, introduce herself to new women, and tell them, "You don't have to give me your real name, not even your real first name": in Sidney Abbott and Barbara Love, *Sappho Was a Right-On Woman: A Liberated View of Lesbianism* (New York: Stein and Day, 1972), p. 100.

18. Lyon and Martin, interview with author. There were a few professionals who braved the risk and even became active members of DOB, such as public school special education teacher Billye Talmadge, partner of DOB president Jaye Bell.

19. Ann Ferguson, "Your Name Is Safe!" *Ladder*, November 1956, p. 10. The article was reprinted in several issues, including February 1958.

20. Informants' names have been redacted from the FBI files available under the Freedom of Information Act.

21. US Department of Justice, FBI Report, November 15, 1966, LA File, no. 7, Dan Siminoski Collection of FBI Surveillance of Gays and Lesbians, box 1, folder 2, ONE National Gay and Lesbian Archives, University of Southern California Libraries.

22. Ibid. The memo refers to Mattachine as well as DOB but makes little distinction

between the two groups except to say that DOB was an organization for female homosexuals. Mattachine had denounced Communists in the 1953 upheaval, and its policy was to discourage political "subversives" from joining.

23. FBI memos: April 22, April 29, April 30, June 19, 1964, Dan Siminoski Collection, box 1, folder 3, ibid.

24. June 19, 1964 memo, ibid.

25. "Homosexual Women Hear Psychologists," *New York Times*, June 21, 1964.

26. Ann Ferguson, "Your Name Is Safe!" *Ladder*, November 1956, p. 10.

27. Del Martin, "The Homosexual Vote," *Ladder*, July 1960, pp. 4–5.

28. "San Francisco Police Raid Reveals Lack of Knowledge of Citizen's Rights," *Ladder*, November 1956, p. 5; "Citizen's Rights," *Ladder*, December 1956, pp. 2–3; Martin, "Gay Bar—Whose Problem Is It?," *Ladder*, December 1959, pp. 4–13ff. "Revise Vagrancy Law, Say Experts," and "An Open Letter to Assemblyman John A. O'Connell," *Ladder*, September 1958, pp. 4–6. A 1959 article by Barbara Stephens, "Homosexuals in Uniform," *Ladder*, June 1959, pp. 17–20, surprisingly focused on the harassment of homosexual men in the military with not a word about the brutal treatment of lesbians.

29. Del Martin, "The Homosexual Vote," *Ladder*, January 1962, pp. 4–5.

30. The ONE Midwinter Institutes were sponsored by the ONE Institute of Homophile Studies, which was developed by Dorr Legg and, starting in 1955, offered the first "gay studies program" in America: See Faderman and Timmons, *Gay L.A.*, pp. 120–21.

31. Dorr Legg, interview with Paul D. Cain in *Leading the Parade: Conversations with America's Most Influential Lesbians and Gay Men* (Lanham, MD: Scarecrow Press, 2002), p. 3.

32. Hansen, *A Few Doors West of Hope*, p. 18; and White, *Pre-Gay L.A.*, p. 91.

33. "Homosexual Bill of Rights Sizzles and Fizzles," *Ladder*, March 1961, pp. 18 19.

34. Del Martin, "How Far Out Can We Go?" *Ladder*, January 1961, p. 4. Harry Hay opposed the bill too but, as he wrote in a wishful editorial for *The Ladder*, he was against it because homosexuals shouldn't have to ask for rights. In a republic, civil rights "are, and must ever be, INDIVISBLE . . . ALL have the obligation to apply them to each alike, without reservations, or to none! [*sic*]": Harry Hay, "Masculine Viewpoint," *Ladder*, July 1961, pp. 16–23.

35. Marci M. Gallo, *Different Daughters: A History of the Daughters of Bilitis and the Rise of the Lesbian Rights Movement* (New York: Carroll and Graf), p. 9.

36. "Homosexual Bill of Rights Sizzles and Fizzles," p. 24.

37. Ibid.

38. Helen Sanders, "Impressions," *Ladder*, June 1960, p. 6.

39. Sten Russell, "DOB Convention: A Look at the Lesbian," *Ladder*, July 1960, pp. 6–14.

40. See p. 8.

41. Russell, "DOB Convention."

42. Sanders, "Impressions."

43. Del Martin, "The Philosophy of DOB—Evolution of an Idea," *Ladder*, June 1962, pp. 4–8.

44. According to Randy Wicker, *The Homosexual in America* was considered by activists of the 1950s and early 1960s as "the bible of the early homosexual rights movement": in video of a panel discussion at the Stonewall Inn, June 4, 2007. I am grateful to Randy Wicker for sharing this video with me. Cory had written in 1951, "Until we are willing to speak out openly and frankly in defense of our own activities and identify ourselves with the millions pursuing those activities, we are unlikely to find the attitudes of the world undergoing any significant change": Donald Webster Cory, *The Homosexual in America: A Subjective Approach* (1951; reprinted, New York: Paperback Library, 1963), p. 14.

45. Donald Webster Cory was a pseudonym of Edward Sagarin, a bisexual man, who in his later work, beginning with *The Homosexual and His Society* (1963), effectively renounced the theories that had made him important to early activists.

46. Barbara Gittings, interview with author, Philadelphia, October 7, 1987.

47. Lyon, interview with Cain, *Leading the Parade*, p. 61.

48. Gittings, interview with author.

49. Ibid.

50. D'Emilio, *Sexual Politics, Sexual Communities*, pp. 89–90.

51. Gittings, interview with Katz, *Gay American History*, p. 424.

52. Gittings, interview with Marcus, *Making History*, p. 113.

53. "Tobin" was a pseudonym. She resumed using her real name, Lahusen, in the late 1970s.

54. Gittings, interview with author.

55. Ibid.

56. *Ebony* magazine did feature blues singer Gladys Bentley in April 1952, in a ghostwritten sensationalistic article in which she disavowed her lesbianism: "I Am a Woman Again," pp. 92–98.

    An African American woman, Pat "Dubby" Walker, became president of the San Francisco DOB in 1960. Cleo Bonner (who used the pseudonym Cleo Glenn), also an African American woman, became president of National DOB in 1963: Phyllis Lyon and Del Martin, "Cleo Glenn (Bonner) (Dates Unknown)," in *Before Stonewall*, pp. 189–90; and Del Martin with Leslie Warren, "Pat Walker (1938–1999)," in *Before Stonewall*, pp. 191–92. But *The Ladder* never published a feature on either of them, perhaps because both women were careful in the 1960s about protecting their identities.

57. Barbara Gittings and Kay Tobin, "Proposals to General Assembly," 1964, Daughters of Bilitis Papers, box 2, folder 9, June Mazer Lesbian Collection, Special Collections, UCLA. Gittings and Tobin also tried to convince DOB to change the name of the organization and to change the DOB "statement of purpose," which appeared unchanged from its inception in every issue of *The Ladder*. They were voted down: "Minutes of the DOB General Assembly Meeting, 1964," box 2, folder 9, ibid.

58. Gittings, interview with author.

59. Barbara Gittings, editorial, *Ladder,* June 1964, pp. 4–5.

60. Ibid., pp. 5–6.

61. Frank Kameny, "Does Research Into Homosexuality Matter?" *Ladder,* May 1965, pp. 14–19.

62. Kay Tobin, "Picketing: The Impact and the Issues," *Ladder,* September 1965, pp. 4–8.

63. "Cross-Currents," *Ladder,* August 1963, p. 11. See pp. 146–50 for a discussion of Scott's case.

64. Kay Tobin, "Homosexual Voting Bloc Puts Pizzazz in Politics," *Ladder,* November 1965, pp. 13–14.

65. Del Martin, Phyllis Lyon, and Cleo Glenn to Barbara Gittings et al., letter, June 7, 1965, Daughters of Bilitis Papers, box 1, folder 13, June Mazer Lesbian Collection, Special Collections, UCLA. Martin and Lyon were encouraged in this position by Reverend Ted McIlvenna of the newly formed Council on Religion and the Homosexual (see pp. 102–8), who wrote Barbara Gittings, in support of their antipicketing position, that if picketing happens at all, it should be "community directed"—that is, directed not by homosexuals but by groups in the larger community that are supportive of them: see Barbara Gittings to Reverend Ted McIlvenna, letter, September 22, 1965, Phyllis Lyon and Del Martin Papers, 1993-13, box 17, folder 12, GLBT Historical Society, San Francisco.

66. Frank Kameny to DOB president and governing board, letter, June 8, 1965, Daughters of Bilitis Papers, box 1, folder 13, June Mazer Lesbian Collection, Special Collections, UCLA.

67. Gallo, *Different Daughters,* pp. 95–96.

68. Gittings, interview with author.

69. Gallo, *Different Daughters,* p. 131. Gittings confided to her friends about tensions between her and Del Martin: for example, a letter from Barbara Gittings to Barbara Grier, May 8, 1964: "La Martin is all but persona non grata with us, confidentially . . . Her standards are simply different, and actually we disagree with her almost across the board on political matters as well," in Barbara Gittings /Kay (Tobin) Lahusen Gay History Papers and Photographs Collection, no. 6397, box 57, New York Public Library. In a letter written two months later, July 3, 1964, Gittings refers to Martin as a "prejudiced and frumpy thinker" and says that "DOB will never grow unless it can break from the grip of Del Martin," ibid. I am grateful to JoAnne Passet for calling these letters to my attention.

70. "History of DOB" (1976), in Daughters of Bilitis Papers, box 1, folder 7, June Mazer Lesbian Collection, Special Collections, UCLA.

71. In 1962, for example, there were only 130 dues-paying members of DOB nationally: Del Martin to the DOB governing board, letter, October 26, 1962, in Daughters of Bilitis Papers, box 1, folder 10, June Mazer Lesbian Collection, Special Collections, UCLA.

72. Robin Tyler (Arlene Chernick), first interview with author, Los Angeles, September 29, 2013.

73. See p. 410.

CHAPTER 7: JOUSTS WITH THE FOUR HORSEMEN

1. Dorr Legg, interview with Brad Mulroy, c. 1975, W. Dorr Legg Papers, Collection 2010-004, box 1, folder 6, ONE National Gay and Lesbian Archives, University of Southern California Libraries.

2. They were unaware of an earlier effort by another Angeleno, Edythe Eyde (Lisa Ben), who published *Vice Versa*, a typed and carbon-copied lesbian magazine, between June 1947 and February 1948.

3. Hansen, *A Few Doors West of Hope*, p. 22; and Joseph Hansen, "Don Slater (1923–1997)," in *Before Stonewall*, p. 106.

4. Block interview in Martin F. Block Papers, 2006-001, box 1, folder 7, ONE National Gay and Lesbian Archives, University of Southern California Libraries.

5. Ibid. Martin Block recollected that the meeting was not at Dorr Legg's home but at the home of Johnny Button and his lover, Alvin Novak: Block interview in Martin F. Block Papers. Dorr Legg says that Johnny Button quit after declaring "upon reflection that the whole idea was unintelligent, philosophically untenable, and useless": William Lambert, "How ONE Began," *ONE*, February 1955, pp. 8–15.

6. Lambert, "How ONE Began."

7. ONE's Articles of Incorporation were signed by Jennings, Block, and Slater's lover, Antonio Sanchez, a Mexican American flamenco dancer who worked at a restaurant in Olvera Street, a touristy re-creation of early Mexican-dominated Los Angeles. Sanchez used the pseudonym "Reyes." ONE got through the State of California's incorporation process because it promised to "aid in the social integration and rehabilitation of the sexual variant."

8. Ernie Potvin, "Kepner Remembered: Pioneer Gay Journalist, Historian, and Archives Founder Departs at 74," *ONE/IGLA Bulletin*, Summer 1998, pp. 1ff.

9. Wayne R. Dynes, "W. Dorr Legg (1904–1994)," in *Before Stonewall*, p. 98.

10. "Ann Carll Reid & the Feminine Viewpoint," *ONE*, December 1957, pp. 16–17.

11. Stella Rush, interview with author, Los Angeles, November 10, 2004.

12. Dorr Legg, interview with Paul D. Cain, March 12, 1994. I thank Mr. Cain for sharing a transcript of this interview with me.

13. Rush, interview with author.

14. Legg, interview with Mulroy, ONE National Gay and Lesbian Archives; and "ONE and the Supreme Court," *Ladder*, September 1958, pp. 10–13.

15. Eric Julber, interview with Stuart Timmons, June 24, 2005, in Faderman and Timmons, *Gay L.A.* The *Los Angeles Daily News* headline announced "Police Brutality Victim Acquitted."

16. Legg, interview with Mulroy, ONE National Gay and Lesbian Archives, University of Southern California Libraries.

17. E. B. Saunders, "Reformer's Choice: Marriage License or Just License?" *ONE*, August 1953, pp. 10–12.

18. "ONE and the Supreme Court," *Ladder*, p. 10.

19. ONE's Legal Counsel, "The Law of Mailable Material," *ONE*, October 1954, pp. 4–6.

20. *ONE, Inc., Appellant v. Otto K. Olesen, Postmaster of the City of Los Angeles, Appellee,* February 27, 1957, US Court of Appeals for the Ninth Circuit, 241 F. 2d 772.

21. Joyce Murdoch and Deb Price, *Courting Justice: Gay Men and Lesbians v. the Supreme Court* (New York: Basic Books, 2001), p. 31.

22. Julber, interview with Timmons, *Gay L.A.*, p. 119.

23. David I. Freeman, "How Much Do We Know About the Male Homosexual?" *ONE,* November 1955, pp. 4–6.

24. The handwriting is identified in a memo from Agent Jones to Agent Nichols, February 10, 1956, FBI file, Mattachine Society, Dan Siminoski Collection, box 4, ONE National Gay and Lesbian Archives, University of Southern California Libraries.

25. See, for example, Athan G. Theoharis and John Stuart Cox, *The Boss: J. Edgar Hoover and the Great American Inquisition* (Philadelphia: Temple University Press, 1985); Anthony Summers, *Official and Confidential: The Secret Life of J. Edgar Hoover* (New York: Putnam, 1993); Jennifer Terry, *An American Obsession: Science, Medicine, and Homosexuality in Modern Society* (Chicago: University of Chicago Press, 1999); and Thomas Doherty, *Cold War, Cool Medium: Television, McCarthyism, and American Culture* (New York: Columbia University Press, 2003).

26. J. Edgar Hoover to Los Angeles office, letter, January 27, 1956, FBI file, Mattachine Society, Dan Siminoski Collection, box 4, ONE National Gay and Lesbian Archives, University of Southern California Libraries.

27. Memo to Mr. Nichols, February 10, 1956, ibid.

28. Memo from A. M. Jones to Mr. Nichols, February 7, 1956, ibid.

29. *ONE, Inc., Appellant v. Otto K. Olesen, Postmaster of the City of Los Angeles, Appellee,* February 27, 1957, US Court of Appeals for the Ninth Circuit, 241 F. 2d 772.

30. Ibid.

31. Ibid.

32. Evelyn Hooker, interview with Bruce Shenitz in "The Grande Dame of Gay Liberation," *Los Angeles Times Magazine,* June 10, 1990.

33. Evelyn Hooker, interview with Laud Humphreys in *Alternative Lifestyles* 1, no. 2 (1978): 191–206.

34. Edwin S. Schneidman, "Evelyn Hooker (1907–1996)," obituary, *American Psychologist* 53, no. 4 (April 1998): 480–81.

35. Ibid.

36. Hooker, interview with Shenitz.

37. Murdoch and Price, *Courting Justice,* p. 144.

38. Evelyn Hooker, "Reflections of a 40-Year Exploration: A Scientific View of Homosexuality," *American Psychologist* 48, no. 4 (April 1993): 450–53.

39. Sharon Valente, "Evelyn Gentry Hooker (1907–1996)," in *Before Stonewall,* p. 347.

40. Ibid., p. 348

41. Shenitz, "The Grande Dame of Gay Liberation."

42. Hooker's presentation to the American Psychological Association was printed the

following year in "The Adjustment of the Male Overt Homosexual," *Journal of Projective Techniques* 21 (1957): 18–31. Hooker had published an earlier paper, "A Preliminary Analysis of Group Behavior of Homosexuals," *Journal of Psychology* 42 (1956), 217–225, in which she presented not only her first findings but also homosexuals' inchoate ideas about a civil rights struggle: "Many homosexuals are beginning to think of themselves as constituting a minority, sharing many of the problems of other minority groups, having to struggle for their rights against the prejudices of a dominant heterosexual majority."

43. Hooker, interview with Humphreys.

44. Dr. Judd Marmor, quoted in Shenitz, "The Grande Dame of Gay Liberation." The struggle to get the APA to remove homosexuality from the *DSM* is discussed at length in chapter 16, "How Gays and Lesbians Stopped Being Crazies."

45. Cecil Williams and Janice Mirikitani, *Beyond the Possible: 50 Years of Creating Radical Change in a Community Called Glide* (New York: HarperOne, 2013), pp. 63–64.

46. According to John D'Emilio, the League for Civil Education's *LCE News*, circulated only in San Francisco gay bars, had a printing of seven thousand by 1962, which exceeded the nationwide readership of *ONE, Mattachine Review*, and *The Ladder. Sexual Politics, Sexual Communities*, p. 189.

47. Del Martin, "History of S.F. Homophile Groups," *Ladder*, October 1966, pp. 7–13.

48. Del Martin to Governing Board, January 28, 1964, "An Invitation of Mr. Ted McIlvenna, Methodist Minister to Young Adults," Daughters of Bilitis Papers, box 1, folder 12, June Mazer Lesbian Collection, Special Collections, UCLA.

49. Ibid.

50. Martin and Lyon, interview with author.

51. Ted McIlvenna, interview with Mark Bowman, January 4, 2005, LGBT Religious Archives Network.

52. "How It Started," manuscript, Phyllis Lyon and Del Martin Papers, 1993-13, box 17, folder 14, GLBT Historical Society, San Francisco.

53. Martin and Lyon, interview with author.

54. Kay Tobin, "After the Ball," *Ladder*, February/March 1965, pp. 4–5.

55. "Clergy Shatter Taboo," *Christian Century*, December 23, 1964.

56. "Church Channel to Homosexuals," *Christianity Today*, March 4, 1966.

57. Report: *Council on Religion and the Homosexual, 1964–1968* (San Francisco: Glide Memorial Church, 1968), pp. 7–9.

58. Del Martin to the DOB governing board, letter, August 26, 1964, Del Martin and Phyllis Lyon Papers, box 1, folder 12, June Mazer Lesbian Collection, Special Collections, UCLA.

59. Del Martin to DOB governing board, handwritten letter, January 13, 1965, Martin and Lyon Papers, box 1, folder 13, June Mazer Lesbian Collection, Special Collections, UCLA.

60. Williams and Mirikitani, *Beyond the Possible*, p. 106.

61. Tobin, "After the Ball," p. 5.

62. Williams and Mirikitani, *Beyond the Possible*, p. 107.

63. Tobin, "After the Ball," p. 4.

64. "Chronology of Events Occurring in Connection with Arrest of above Individuals on January 1, 1965," p. 2, Evander Smith Collection, GLC box 46, folder 4, Gay and Lesbian Historical Society of Northern California Collection, San Francisco Public Library.

65. Williams and Mirikitani, *Beyond the Possible*, pp. 105–107.

66. Evander Smith, interview with Marcus, *Making Gay History*, p. 148.

67. Herbert Donaldson and Evander Smith, interview with Marcus, *Making Gay History*, p. 149.

68. "Chronology of Events," p. 6.

69. Evelyn Williams, quoted in Mixner and Bailey, *Brave Journeys*, p. 37.

70. "Chronology of Events," pp. 6–9.

71. Del Martin, untitled manuscript draft, January 14, 1965, Martin and Lyon Papers, box 1, folder 13, June Mazer Collection, Special Collections, UCLA.

72. Del Martin, untitled manuscript draft, January 14, 1965.

73. In Phyllis Lyon and Del Martin Papers, 1993-13, box 17, folder 8, GLBT Historical Society, San Francisco.

74. The National Planning Conference established the North American Conference of Homophile Organizations (NACHO).

75. Del Martin to Marge McCann, Del Shearer, and Barbara Gittings, letter, June 7, 1965. This is the same letter in which Martin said that DOB would withdraw from ECHO over the picketing controversy: Martin and Lyon Papers, box 1, folder 13, June Mazer Lesbian Collection, Special Collections, UCLA.

76. Minutes, National Planning Conference of Homophile Organizations Kansas City, Missouri, February 19–20, 1966, p. 12: Special Collections, Gay/Lesbian, Shields Library, UC Davis; and John Marshall, "Nationwide Attack on Draft Injustices," *The Homosexual Citizen*, 1/7 (July 1966), 5–7.

77. "U.S. Homophile Movement Gains National Strength," *Ladder*, April 1966, pp. 4–5.

78. Don Slater, "Protest on Wheels," *Tangents*, May 1966; Peter Bart, "War Role Sought for Homosexuals," *New York Times*, April 17, 1966.

79. "U.S. Homophile Movement Gains National Strength."

80. Bart, "War Role Sought for Homosexuals": the article was reprinted in newspapers all over America.

81. Daughters of Bilitis, Mattachine, Tavern Guild, Society for Individual Rights, and Guy Strait's latest homophile iteration, Citizen News.

82. Slater, "Protest on Wheels."

83. Timmons, *Trouble with Harry Hay*, p. 221.

84. Peter Welch, "Homosexuality in America," *Life*, June 26, 1964, pp. 66–74, 78–80.

85. Joseph Hansen's affectionate term for Slater in Hansen, *A Few Doors West of Hope*.

86. Paul Coates, "Problem for Army," *Los Angeles Times*, April 24, 1966. Thirteen years earlier, Coates had been the columnist who'd fired the first shot that had ended Harry Hay's life in Mattachine. See pp. 67–68.

87. Slater, "Protest on Wheels."

88. "War Role Sought for Homosexuals."

CHAPTER 8: SLIVERS OF SPACE AND JUSTICE

1. The term *transgender* didn't come into wide use until the 1990s. See p. xx.

2. John Rechy, interview with Stuart Timmons, Los Angeles, August 29, 2005, in Faderman and Timmons, *Gay L.A.*, pp. 1–2.

3. The Janus Society had previously been the Mattachine of Philadelphia; but when Mattachine ceased to be a national organization in 1961, the Philadelphia group renamed itself Janus after the two-faced Roman god of beginnings and change.

4. Marc Stein, *City of Sisterly and Brotherly Loves: Lesbian and Gay Philadelphia, 1945–1972* (Chicago: University of Chicago Press, 2000), pp. 245–46.

5. Address by Clark Polak to the National Planning Committee of Homophile Organizations, Kansas City, Missouri, February 20, 1966: Special Collections, Gay/Lesbian, Shields Library, UC Davis.

6. The following year, Rodwell opened the Oscar Wilde Memorial Bookshop in Greenwich Village, the first gay and lesbian bookstore in America. That same year, the Adonis Bookstore was opened by Mattachine Society president Hal Call in San Francisco; but Call's store was devoted largely to gay male erotica, while Rodwell's store featured political and literary works about gays and lesbians.

7. Dick Leitsch, interview with author, New York (telephone), May 19, 2013.

8. Lucy Komisar, "3 Homosexuals in Search of a Drink," *Village Voice*, May 5, 1966.

9. At a third bar, the Waikiki, the three men were joined by Randy Wicker. They were also served there without incident.

10. Panel at the Stonewall Bar, June 4, 2007 (video). I am grateful to Randy Wicker for giving me a copy of this video. Craig Rodwell claimed that police entrapment of homosexuals in Greenwich Village bars was sometimes like an assembly line. The police would "send plainclothesmen in fluffy sweaters and sneakers" to sit at a bar and proposition likely homosexual suspects. The Morals Squad kept a room at the Hotel Albert, Rodwell said. "They would just take people from the bars over to the hotel, and there would be a cop waiting in the room." After the arrest was made, the undercover officer would "go back and get somebody else. Then they'd get them all together and take them down and book them": Craig Rodwell, interview with Tina Crosby, "The Stonewall Riot Remembered" (unpublished paper, January 16, 1974), New York Public Library Manuscripts and Archives Division.

11. The picture appeared with the Lucy Komisar article "3 Homosexuals in Search of a Drink."

12. Thomas A. Johnson, "3 Deviates Invite Exclusion by Bars: But They Visit Four Before Being Refused Service in a Test of the S.L.A.," *New York Times*, April 22, 1966. Leitsch was perennially hoping for fair treatment from the mainstream media, and he made himself widely available for interviews, but almost always he was "burned," as he complained: "Public Relations," *New York Mattachine Newsletter*, January/February 1967, in Mattachine Collection, box 12, folder 4, ONE National Gay and Lesbian Archives, University of Southern California Libraries. One of the first mainstream newspaper articles to appreciate the struggle for gay and lesbian civil rights appeared in the July 17, 1968, *Wall Street Journal*: Charles

Alverson, "U.S. Homosexuals Gain in Trying to Persuade Society to Accept Them: With a Growing Militancy, They Battle Discrimination on Social, Legal, Job Lines," though it featured somewhat lurid subheadlines such as "Against the Morals of the Public."

13. Dick Leitsch, interview with Scott Simon, "Remembering a 1966 'Sip-in' for Gay Rights," NPR, June 28, 2008; and Sharyn Jackson, "Before Stonewall: Remembering That Before the Riots There Was a Sip-in," *Village Voice*, June 17, 2008, p. 1.

14. The following year, 1967, Tony Pastor's, another village bar, lost its liquor license because the management permitted the establishment to "become disorderly," allowing "homosexuals, degenerates, and undesirables" to "conduct themselves in an offensive and indecent manner": "Liquor License Is Revoked at Tony Pastor's Night Spot," *New York Times*, March 18, 1967.

15. *Screaming Queens: The Riot at Compton's Cafeteria*, a documentary by Susan Stryker and Victor Silverman, 2005; author correspondence with Susan Stryker, email, July 22, 2013; Susan Stryker, *Transgender History* (Berkeley, CA: Seal Press, 2008), p. 73; and Susan Stryker, interview with Erick Lyle in *On the Low Frequencies: A Secret History of the City* (Berkeley, CA: Soft Skull Press, 2008), pp. 134–36.

16. Jim Kepner, quoted in Donn Teal, *The Gay Militants* (New York: Stein and Day, 1971), p. 41.

17. The police raid and PRIDE protests at the Black Cat are discussed at greater length in Franklin Kameny, "Sad Celebration in L.A. Gay Bars," *The Homosexual Citizen*, March 1967, pp. 3–6; and in Faderman and Timmons, *Gay L.A.*, pp, 155 56.

18. See also Faderman and Timmons, *Gay L.A.*, pp. 157–58.

19. "Patch Fights Three-Way Battle," *Los Angeles Advocate*, August 1968, pp. 3ff.

20. Nancy Love, "The Invisible Society," *Philadelphia*, November 1967. This sensationalistic article informed lesbians in Philadelphia, who may not have heard of Rusty's before, of the bar's address. Of course, it also informed the Philadelphia police.

21. Marty Selnick, interview with author, Oakland, April 6, 2012; and Marge McCann and Carole (Meyers) Smith, interview with author, Kennett Square, PA (telephone), April 18, 2013.

22. Nancy Gertner, *In Defense of Women: Memoirs of an Unrepentant Advocate* (Boston: Beacon Press, 2012), p. 17.

23. McCann, interview with author.

24. Stein, *City of Sisterly and Brotherly Loves,* p. 275.

25. Selnick, interview with author.

26. No matter which DOB member wrote the letter, it was always signed "Ellen Collins," because nobody in the organization dared to use her own name.

27. Ada Bello, interview with author, Philadelphia, March 8, 2013.

28. Ibid.

29. As president of DOB New York, too, Willer believed "that any direct action is precluded by [DOB's] claim to existing exclusively as a social-service and educational organization": Jody Shotwell to Barbara Gittings, letter, June 11, 1965; and Barbara Gittings to Barbara Grier, letter, July 11, 1965, Barbara Gittings/

Kay (Tobin) Lahusen Gay History Papers and Photographs Collection, box 59, folder 17, New York Public Library. Willer refused to let New York DOB participate in the pickets that Frank Kameny and Barbara Gittings were organizing in 1965 in Washington, DC, and Philadelphia. I am grateful to JoAnne Passet for calling these letters to my attention.

30. *Homophile Action League Newsletter* 1, no. 1 (1968): 1, ONE National Gay and Lesbian Archives, University of Southern California Libraries.

31. In Los Angeles, the lesbian and gay Society of Anubis, founded in 1967, was also woman led, under the presidency of Helen Niehaus. The Society of Anubis was chartered by the state of California in 1969, stating on its application that its primary purpose was to work for "just and enlightened sex laws": *Anubis Bulletin*, March 1969, Anubis file, ONE National Gay and Lesbian Archives, University of Southern California Libraries.

32. Stein, *City of Sisterly and Brotherly Loves*, p. 310.

33. Mark Segal discusses Shapp's support of the gay community in "Governor Milton Shapp's Granddaughter," *The Bilerico Project*, March 21, 2013.

34. Randy Wicker, interview with author, Hoboken, NJ, March 11, 2013.

35. Wicker, interview with author.

36. Milton Bracker, "Homosexuals Air Their Views Here," *New York Times*, July 16, 1962.

37. Jack O'Brian, "Jack O'Brian Says," *New York Journal-American*, July 8, 1962.

38. "Cross-Currents," *Ladder*, August 1963, p. 20.

39. Picket description from Renée Cafiero, interview with author, Brooklyn, NY (telephone), May 20, 2013; Wicker, interview with author; Peter Golenbock, *In the Country of Brooklyn: Inspiration to the World* (New York: William Morrow, 2008), pp. 570–71; Betsy Kuhn, *Gay Power: The Stonewall Riots and the Gay Rights Movement, 1969* (Minneapolis: 21st Century Books, 2011), p. 56; and John Loughery, *The Other Side of Silence: Men's Lives and Gay Identities—A Twentieth Century History* (New York: Henry Holt, 1998), p. 269.

40. Cafiero, interview with author.

41. Wicker and Cafiero, interviews with author.

42. Frank Kameny to Clifford Norton, letter, July 11, 1969, Frank Kameny Collection, box 29, Norton folder, Manuscript Division, Library of Congress, Washington, DC.

CHAPTER 9: THROWING DOWN THE GAUNTLET

1. Dan Siminoski Collection, FBI files, box 7, folder 19, ONE National Gay and Lesbian Archives, University of Southern California Libraries.

2. *Franklin Edward Kameny v. Wilber M. Bruckner, Secretary of the Army, et al., Petition to the Supreme Court for a Writ of Certiorari,* filed January 27, 1961.

3. Ibid.

4. Dudley Clendinen and Adam Nagourney, *Out for Good: The Struggle to Build a Gay Rights Movement in America* (New York: Simon & Schuster, 1999), p. 112. In interviews with the authors, Kameny claimed that he'd merely been walking in

the park and had stopped to watch an arrest in progress when the police arrested him, too.

5. *Franklin Edward Kameny v. Wilber M. Bruckner, Secretary of the Army.*

6. Sears, *Lonely Hunters*, p. 201.

7. Donia Mills and Phil Gailey, "Kameny's Long Ordeal Personifies Wider Gay Struggles," *Washington Star*, April 10, 1981, p. A-8; and Frank Kameny, interview with authors in Kay Tobin and Randy Wicker, *The Gay Crusaders* (New York: Paperback Library, 1972), p. 93.

8. Tobin and Wicker, *Gay Crusaders*, p. 89.

9. *Petition to the Supreme Court for a Writ of Certiorari.*

10. Transcript: "50th Anniversary of the Mattachine Society of Washington: Panel Discussion, Lilli Vincenz and Paul Kuntzler, October 13, 2011. I am grateful to Philip Clark of the Rainbow History Project, Washington, DC, for sharing this transcript with me; also Warren D. Adkins (aka Jack Nichols), "Ex-Police Lieutenant Pleads Guilty to 'Fairy Shakes,'" *Gay Today*, January 29, 1998.

11. Jack Nichols's unpublished autobiography, Stephanie Donald Collection, pp. 46, 48. I am grateful to Ms. Donald for sharing Mr. Nichols's manuscript with me.

12. Ibid., p. 21.

13. Ibid., p. 73.

14. Kameny inherited enough money from his mother to buy a house in DC, but he was always financially strapped. Just a year before his death in 2011, the gay and lesbian DC group Helping Our Brothers and Sisters conducted a fund-raising campaign to keep his house from being auctioned off for back taxes. (I am grateful to Charles Francis for bringing this to my attention.) A young gay man also started a "Buy Frank Kameny a Drink" campaign, asking people to donate the $10 it would cost to buy a cocktail to a Facebook page on Frank Kameny's behalf, "to help Dr. Kameny get back on his feet": Lou Chibbaro Jr., "Kameny Facebook Page Formed to Help Activist," *Washington Blade*, December 30, 2010.

15. Frank Kameny, taped interview with Alison McKinney, May or June 1975, in the private collection of Pokey Anderson. I am grateful to Ms. Anderson for sharing the tape of this interview with me.

16. Frank Kameny, "Civil Liberties: A Progress Report," 1964 speech at Freedom House, reprinted in *New York Mattachine Newsletter*, 10/1 (July 1965), pp. 7–22.

17. Paul C. Jones to Frank Kameny, letter, August 28, 1962, Kamenypapers.org.

18. Charles E. Chamberlain to Frank Kameny, letter, August 30, 1962, ibid.

19. Dr. Franklin E. Kameny, president, Mattachine Society Washington, DC, to Robert F. Kennedy, attorney general, letter, June 28, 1962, FBI FOIA File HQ 100-403320 (Mattachine Society); and Gittings, interview with author.

20. "HR 5990," *Gazette* (Mattachine Society Washington), Spring 1964.

21. "Group Aiding Deviates Issued Charity License," *Washington Star*, September 16, 1962.

22. Ibid.

23. "The Mattachine Society of Washington: Extension of Remarks of Hon. John

Dowdy of Texas, in the House of Representatives," *Congressional Record:* Appendix, re. A4211, July 5, 1963.

24. "John Dowdy Is Indicted on Charges That He Took $25,000 in an Alleged Bribe Conspiracy," *New York Times,* April 1, 1970; and "Dowdy Loses Bid for Parole," *New York Times,* March 28, 1974.

25. Campaign ad, "Facts Speak for John Dowdy," paid for by Friends of John Dowdy, in *Malakoff (TX) News,* May 6, 1960.

26. John Dowdy, "Dear Friends," *Alto (TX) Herald,* May 9, 1963.

27. Statement of the president of the Mattachine Society of Washington before Subcommittee 4 of the District of Columbia, House of Representatives, August 8, 1963; and "HR 5990," *Gazette.*

28. Jack Nichols, unpublished autobiography, p. 47.

29. Statement of the president of the Mattachine Society.

30. "Piety by Fiat," *Washington Post,* August 8, 1963.

31. Transcript: "50th Anniversary of the Mattachine Society Washington."

32. Quoted in "HR 5990," *Gazette.*

33. Frank Kameny, 2003 interview with Amin Ghaziani, in "How the Militant Movement Began," *Gay and Lesbian Review Worldwide* 19, no. 1 (January/February 2012): pp. 11–14.

34. John D'Emilio discusses Rustin's homosexuality at length in *Lost Prophet: The Life and Times of Bayard Rustin* (Chicago: University of Chicago Press, 2004).

35. Jack Nichols, unpublished autobiography, pp. 49, 74.

36. Gittings, interview with author.

37. Don Slater, "Tangents" column, *ONE,* July 1965, p. 13.

38. Quoted in Jack Nichols, unpublished autobiography, p. 73.

39. Jack Nichols, November 1994 interview with Paul Cain in "Frank and Jack," *LGBT-Today* online.

40. Eva Freund, interview with author, Vienna, VA (telephone), February 9, 2013.

41. Kameny, "Civil Liberties: A Progress Report."

42. Ibid. Dick Leitsch, who became president of the New York Mattachine Society the next year and staged the Greenwich Village "sip-in" (see chap. 8) the year after that, credits Kameny's July 1964 speech with bringing him to an understanding of homosexuality as a political issue: in D'Emilio, *Sexual Politics, Sexual Communities,* p. 166.

43. Freund, interview with author.

44. Stein, *City of Sisterly and Brotherly Loves,* pp. 188–205, says that Philadelphia Mattachine, which was almost equally cogendered, was the exception to the rule. But Stein quotes a member of Philadelphia Mattachine who recalls that the women "were always the coffee makers and typists" (p. 205).

45. Kameny was also anxious to attract into the organization black gays and lesbians, and recruitment drives were held in DC African American gay bars such as Nob Hill. Mattachine members met to discuss topics such as "How Can We Bring the Negro into the Homophile Movement." (Johnson, *Lavender Scare,* p. 193.) But black membership was minuscule, despite the prominent participation and efforts

of Ernestine Eckstein, an African American woman, who was vice president of New York's Daughters of Bilitis and was brought into Mattachine Society Washington by Barbara Gittings.

46. The next day, Easter Sunday, the New York Mattachine Society staged a similar picket outside the United Nations, ostensibly protesting Cuba's incarceration of homosexuals.

47. Lilli Vincenz, interview with Mark Meinke, Rainbow History Project, Washington, DC, April 21, 2001. I am grateful to Philip Clark of the Rainbow History Project for sharing this transcript with me.

48. Transcript: "50th Anniversary of the Mattachine Society of Washington." Of course, not many of the mainstream press photographers thought that a homophile protest by ten people was newsworthy; but it was reported in the October 1965 issue of the scandal magazine *Confidential*, the cover of which announced, "Homos on the March: The Day They Picketed the White House." A photo of the picketers featured Kameny in the foreground. Homosexuals across America who had not known about Mattachine before knew about it now if they glanced at the magazine rack of their local supermarket or drugstore. The article even gave the address of Mattachine Society Washington headquarters, and the Mattachine office phone was soon ringing off the hook with inquiries from homosexuals in Iowa and Idaho and everywhere else in America. The *Confidential* article was the biggest publicity that Mattachine and the cause had gotten to date.

49. Gittings, interview with author.

50. Vincenz, interview with Meinke.

51. Kameny, who had nothing to lose, having already been fired from his government job, used his real name, as did Barbara Gittings.

52. Vincenz, interview with Meinke.

53. Jack Nichols, unpublished autobiography, p. 44. In 1967 Nichols left DC to move to New York with another lover, Lige Clarke. There his activism was focused more on "lifestyle" freedoms than on civil rights. He borrowed the Mattachine Society Washington magazine title *Homosexual Citizen* for a regular column that he and Clarke wrote for *Screw* magazine, but their primary emphasis was on encouraging open sexual expression.

54. Kameny, quoted in Rodger Streitmatter, *Unspeakable: The Rise of the Gay and Lesbian Press in America* (New York: Faber and Faber, 1995), p. 60.

55. Transcript: "50th Anniversary of the Mattachine Society."

56. Warren D. Adkins (pseudonym: Jack Nichols), "The Washington–Baltimore TV Circuit," *Homosexual Citizen*, May 1967, p. 6.

57. Gittings, interview with author.

58. Lilli Vincenz, interview with Jack Nichols, in "Lilli Vincenz: A Lesbian Pioneer," *Gay Today*, 2001.

59. Gittings, interview with author.

60. Cory had not yet disavowed his earlier militancy to argue, as he did in his 1963 book *The Homosexual and His Society*, that all homosexuals were pathologically disturbed.

61. History of East Coast Homophile Organizations: Frank Kameny to Richard Inman, letter, July 13, 1965, in Frank Kameny Collection, box 5, folder 11, Library of Congress Manuscript Division.

62. Leitsch, interview with author.

63. Kameny put himself in charge of the 1964 conference program, where he made sure that no "mental health professional" would be invited as a speaker. The theme of the 1964 conference was "Homosexuality: Civil Liberties and Social Rights."At subsequent ECHO conferences, Kameny saw to it that "there was not one single doctor, psychologist, psychiatrist, or MD of any sort on the program." Kameny to Inman, letter, July 13, 1965.

64. Paul Kuntzler in Transcript: "50th Anniversary of the Mattachine Society."

65. When Ellis delivered a similar speech the year before at a New York Mattachine Society meeting, he was given a standing ovation: David Carter, *Stonewall: The Riots That Sparked the Gay Revolution* (New York: St. Martin's, 2004), p. 37.

66. Gittings, interview with author.

67. Jody Shotwell, "ECHO Convention '63," *Ladder*, December 1963, p. 8.

68. Kay (Tobin) Lahusen, interview with author, Kennett Square, PA, March 9, 2013.

CHAPTER 10: THE HOMOSEXUAL AMERICAN CITIZEN TAKES THE GOVERNMENT TO COURT

1. The circumstances of Scott's arrest and his response are detailed in *Bruce C. Scott v. John W. Macy*, Civil Action no. 1050-63, US District Court for the District of Columbia, 1963: Mattachine Society Project Collection, box 9, folder 38, ONE National Gay and Lesbian Archives, University of Southern California Libraries; *Bruce C. Scott, Appellant v. John W. Macy, Jr., Chairman of the Civil Service Commission, et al., Appellees*, 349 F. 2d 182 (1965), US District Court of Appeals, District of Columbia Circuit, argued December 17, 1964; and *Bruce C. Scott, Appellant v. John W. Macy, Jr., Chairman, Civil Service Commission, et al., Appellees*, 402 F. 2d 644 131 U. S. App. D. C. 93, no. 20841, argued October 23, 1967; decided September 11, 1968.

2. *Scott v. Macy*, 1963.

3. "Cross-Currents," *Ladder*, August 1963, p. 19.

4. In *Scott v. Macy*, 1963.

5. For example, in 1951, in responding to a woman who'd asked for help after being discharged from the air force, the ACLU staff counsel declared that the ACLU believed that homosexuality was relevant to an individual's military service, and advised her to seek medical treatment that would enable her to "abandon homosexual relations": quoted in Allan Berube and John D'Emilio, "The Military and Lesbians During the McCarthy Years," in *The Lesbian Issue: Essays from Signs*, eds. Estelle Freeman et al. (Chicago: University of Chicago Press, 1985), pp. 290–95. In January 1957 the ACLU National Board of Directors affirmed that "homosexuality is a valid consideration in evaluating the security risk factor in sensitive positions," and "It is not within the province of the Union to evaluate the social

validity of the laws aimed at suppression or elimination of homosexuality": reported in "The ACLU Takes a Stand," *Ladder*, March 1957, pp. 8–9.

6. Jerry Kluttz, "Names of 200 Perverts Listed for Firing by U.S. Agencies," *Washington Post*, May 9, 1950, p. 1.

7. "Misplaced Morality," *Washington Post*, April 24, 1963.

8. *Scott v. Macy*, 1963.

9. King's real name was Robert Belanger, but he continued to use a pseudonym, even as Mattachine's president.

10. Johnson, *Lavender Scare*, p. 194.

11. David Rudenstine, *The Day the Presses Stopped: A History of the Pentagon Papers Case* (Berkeley: University of California Press, 1998), p. 391.

12. Franklin E. Kameny, "U.S. Government Clings to Prejudice," *Ladder*, January 1966, pp. 22–24.

13. *Washington Post*, June 17, 1965, p. 3.

14. *Scott v. Macy*, 1967.

15. John W. Macy Jr., oral history interview with Fred Holborn, May 29, 1964, p. 67, John F. Kennedy Library, Oral History Program.

16. John W. Macy, "A Citizen's Rights," speech delivered on May 22, 1968, to the Federal Bar Association, in *Vital Speeches of the Day* 34, no. 20 (August 1, 1968): p. 621. See also John W. Macy Jr., *Public Service: The Human Side of Government* (New York: Harper and Row, 1971).

17. Franklin Kameny, "U.S. Government Hides Behind Immoral Mores," *Ladder*, June 1966, pp. 17–20.

18. "Our President Speaks," *Gazette* (Mattachine Society Washington), Winter 1964, p. 6.

19. John Macy letter quoted in Franklin E. Kameny, "MSW Meets with Civil Service Commission," *Homosexual Citizen*, May/June 1966, pp. 7–8.

20. Ibid.

21. Picket photograph with Lilli Vincenz, cover of *Ladder*, October 1965.

22. Lilli Vincenz to Lawrence Meloy and Kimbell Johnson, "A Statement from a Member of the Mattachine Society Washington," 1965. I thank Charles Francis for sharing this statement with me.

23. Eva Freund, a Mattachine member who attended several of the meetings with government officials, said that Kameny orchestrated what would be said and who would speak: Freund, interview with Meinke.

24. Quoted in Lilli Vincenz to Lawrence Meloy and Kimbell Johnson. "A Statement from a Member of the Mattachine Society Washington."

25. "U.S. Government Hides Behind Immoral Mores."

26. John W. Macy Jr. to the Mattachine Society of Washington, letter, February 25, 1966, reprinted in *Homosexual Citizen*, May/June 1966, pp. 4–5. Macy's compendium of antihomosexual prejudices was so apt an illustration of historical discrimination against lesbians and gays that it was cited almost a half century later as an example of the blatant unreasonableness of such attitudes, in US District Court judge Vaughn Richard Walker's 2010 decision overturning California's

Proposition 8, which banned same-sex marriage: *Kristin Perry, et al. v. Arnold Schwarzenegger, et al.*, No. C 09-2292, "Findings of Fact," p. 96.

27. Editorial, "To Exist or Not Exist," *Homosexual Citizen*, May/June 1966, p. 3.

28. *Clifford L. Norton, Appellant v. John Macy, et al., Appellees,* US District Court of Appeals, District of Columbia Circuit, No. 21625, January 13, 1969, 417 F. 2d 1161.

29. *Clifford L. Norton, Appellant v. John Macy, et al., Appellees*, US District Court of Appeals, District of Columbia Circuit, No. 21625, 417 F. 2d 1161, argued January 13, 1969; decided July 1, 1969; petition for rehearing denied, October 20, 1969. The Sexual Revolution was well under way by now. In a few years, the United States Census Bureau would have to coin the term POSSLQ (persons of the opposite sex sharing living quarters) because cohabitation was so rife among unmarried heterosexual couples.

30. Clifford Norton to Frank Kameny, letter, July 6, 1969, Frank Kameny Collection, box 29, Norton folder, Manuscript Division of the Library of Congress.

31. Donald Rogers to Frank Kameny, July 7, 1969, ibid.

32. Frank Kameny to Clifford Norton, July 11, 1969, ibid.

33. Norton to Kameny, July 6, 1969.

34. Kameny to Norton, July 11, 1969.

35. Clifford Norton to Frank Kameny, letter, July 22, 1969, ibid.

36. US District Court of Appeals, *Norton v. Macy*.

37. David K. Johnson, *Lavender Scare*, p, 207.

38. Bulletin and Regulations quoted in *John F. Singer v. United States Civil Service Commission*, 530 F. 2d 247 Ninth Circuit, No. 74-2073, January 12, 1976.

39. Reported in "Rusk Probed on Picketing," *Ladder*, October 1965; and Clark Mullenhoff (syndicated column), "Homosexuals Charge Bias in Loss of Government Jobs," *Des Moines Register*, April 9, 1966.

40. "Rusk Probed on Picketing."

41. Kameny, interview in Tobin and Wicker, *Gay Crusaders*, p. 101.

42. Eva Freund, interview with author, Vienna, Virginia (telephone), February 9, 2013.

43. Frank Kameny, "Security Clearances for Homosexual Citizens," *Homosexual Citizen*, March 1966.

44. Colonial governor Benning Wentworth also granted large tracts of land to those who would become the founders of Vermont. Bennington was named after him. He was the subject of a scandal in 1760 when, at the age of sixty-four, he married his twenty-three-year-old housekeeper.

45. Frank Kameny to Don Slater, letter, December 9, 1967, Frank Kameny Papers, box 9, folder 7, Library of Congress, Washington, DC.

46. *Wentworth v. Laird, Secretary of Defense, et al.*, 348 F. supp. 1153 (D.D.C. 1972); *Wentworth v. Schlesinger, Secretary of Defense, et al.*, docket no. 71-1934, 490 F. 2d 740 (DC Circuit 1973); Charlayne Hunter, "Homosexual Seeks to Retain Security Clearance," *New York Times*, August 20, 1969.

47. Kameny to Slater, December 9, 1967.

48. Kameny, interview in Tobin and Wicker, *Gay Crusaders*, p. 106.

49. Associated Press, "Deviate, 31, Confesses in Bid to Retain Job," *Philadelphia Inquirer*, November 25, 1967.

50. Ibid.

51. Frank Kameny to Don Slater, December 9, 1967.

52. The hearing, Kameny's questions, and Wentworth's responses are recounted in Frank Kameny to Don Slater, December 9, 1967.

53. Department of Defense hearing (Office of the Assistant Secretary of Defense), transcript, docket 67-32, Federal Plaza, New York, August 19, 1969.

54. Tobin and Wicker, *Gay Crusaders*, p. 134.

55. *Wentworth v. Laird*. Judge Pratt ordered that Richard Gayer's and Otto Ulrich's clearances too must be restored.

56. *Wentworth v. Schlesinger*, op. cit. This court also found in favor of Gayer and Ulrich.

57. Ed O'Keefe, "Eye Opener: Apology for Frank Kameny," *Washington Post*, June 29, 2009. When Berry was confirmed by the Senate in 2009, he became the highest-ranking openly gay federal official in US history.

CHAPTER 11: THE RIOTS

1. Jim Fouratt, interview with author, New York (telephone), July 16, 2013.

2. Robert L. Pela, interview with Tony Coron, "Stonewall's Eyewitnesses," *Advocate*, May 3, 1994.

3. The Stonewall riots have been described extensively by eyewitnesses. Among the primary sources I used in this account are Dennis Eskow, "3 Cops Hurt as Bar Raid Riles Crowd," *Daily News* (New York), June 29, 1969; Lucian Truscott, IV, "Gay Power Comes to Sheridan Square," *Village Voice*, July 3, 1969; Howard Smith, "Full Moon over Stonewall (View from Inside)," *Village Voice*, July 3, 1969; Jerry Lisker, "Homo Nest Raided, Queen Bees Are Stinging Mad," *Daily News* (New York), July 6, 1969; Dick Leitsch, "The Hairpin Drop Heard Round the World," *New York Mattachine Newsletter*, July 1969; Dick Leitsch, "Gay Riots," *New York Mattachine Newsletter*, July 1969 Dick Leitsch, "Gay Riots in the Village," *New York Mattachine Newsletter*, August 1969; "The Night They Raided the Stonewall," *Gay Activist* 1, no. 3 (June 1971); interviews with eyewitnesses by David Isay, on "Remembering Stonewall," *Weekend All Things Considered*, NPR, July 1, 1989; interviews with eyewitnesses on "Stonewall Uprising," *American Experience*, PBS, 2011; and my own interviews with Jim Fouratt, John O'Brien, Perry Brass, Dick Leitsch, Frank Galassi, and Martha Shelley. Two full-length books devoted to the riots are Martin Duberman's *Stonewall* (New York: Dutton, 1993) and Carter's *Stonewall*.

4. The term *transgender* didn't yet have currency in 1969. See note on the history of changing terminology, p. xix. See also David Valentine, *Imagining Transgender: An Ethnography of a Category* (Durham, NC: Duke University Press, 2007), introduction.

5. Carter, *Stonewall*, p. 141.

6. A later raid at the Snake Pit, in March 1970, became a cause célèbre when an Argentine national, Diego Vinales, jumped from a window to escape the raiding police and was impaled on a fence below. Vinales survived, but the incident led to a massive gay march through the streets of Greenwich Village: see Jonathan Black, "The Boys in the Snake Pit: Games 'Straights' Play," *Village Voice*, March 19, 1970, p. 62.

7. Teal, *Gay Militants*, p. 20. There had also been a raid at the Stonewall the previous Tuesday, when the bar had fewer patrons: Eskow, "3 Cops Hurt as Bar Raid Riles Crowd." The police came back on a weekend night knowing that the bar would be packed. However, Inspector Seymour Pine and his assistant inspector Charles Smythe visited the New York Mattachine office on July 3 to discuss why the riot happened and to explain that there "had been no harassment of legitimate gay bars," but only an attempt to "go after places that serve liquor without a license. This has nothing to do with who forms the clientele of the place": "The Stonewall Riots: The Police Story," *New York Mattachine Newsletter*, August 1969.

8. In a 2004 talk for the New York Historical Society, Inspector Pine claimed that the real reason for the raid was that the police had received a tip that the Mafia was somehow involved in stolen European bonds, and the police believed that "after-hours clubs like the Stonewall were in on the operation. If we could close them down, we'd see what would happen to the bonds that were surfacing." However, he also admitted that the Public Morals Squad described gay bar raids as "We're going down to grab the fags": Pine's speech reported in Lincoln Anderson, "'I'm Sorry,' Says Inspector Who Led the Stonewall Raid," *Villager*, June 16–22, 2004.

9. Lisker, "Homo Nest Raided, Queen Bees Are Stinging Mad."

10. Lucian Truscott, "The Real Mob at Stonewall," *New York Times*, June 25, 2009. Truscott resigned his post at Fort Benning after a few months and wrote full-time for the *Village Voice* until 1975.

11. Though Truscott's and Smith's accounts were the most thorough of those in the straight media, they were often mocking of the gay rioters. Truscott, for example, writes of "the forces of faggotry" and says the rioters' "wrists were limp [and] hair was primped."

12. Smith, "Full Moon over Stonewall" and Truscott, "Gay Power Comes to Sheridan Square."

13. Fouratt, interview with author. Police records of the Stonewall arrests (which were not opened to the public until 2009) identify a "Marilyn Fowler" who was arrested that night. Fowler has been thought to be the woman in the police car: Sewall Chan, "Police Records Document Start of Stonewall Uprising," *New York Times*, June 22, 2009. Jim Fouratt, who witnessed the riot and who knew Marilyn Fowler, claims, however, that she was a slight woman and definitely not the "two-hundred-pound butch" who triggered the riot. In recent years, an urban legend has spread that African American butch lesbian Stormé DeLarverie, who'd been a professional drag king, was the woman in the police car. She's been dubbed the "Rosa Parks of the gay revolution": for

example, Jim Luce, "Gay Community's Rosa Parks Faces Death, Impoverished and Alone," *Huffington Post*, May 25, 2011. But as David Carter points out, De-Larverie was well known in the community and would have been recognized immediately; the woman who triggered the riot was unknown to those eye-witnesses whom Carter interviewed. Also, Carter says, DeLarverie's age, height, ethnicity, and physique do not match eyewitness descriptions of the lesbian who set off the riot: Carter, *Stonewall*, p. 309, and author's email correspondence with Carter.

14. The *Berkeley Barb*'s comment on the woman's participation was, "Ironically, it was a chick who gave the rallying cry to fight": Leo E. Laurence, "Gays Hit New York Cops," *Berkeley Barb*, July 4–10, 1969.

15. Truscott, "Gay Power Comes to Sheridan Square."

16. Smith, "Full Moon over Stonewall."

17. Duberman, *Stonewall*, p. 204.

18. Quoted in Duberman, *Stonewall*, p. 198. Stonewall historian David Carter does not give credence to Rivera's claim that she was at the riots: author's email correspondence with Carter, April 5, 2015.

19. Leitsch, "Hairpin Drop Heard Round the World."

20. Raymond Castro, interviewed in "Stonewall Uprising," *American Experience*.

21. John O'Brien, first interview with author, Los Angeles, July 25, 2012.

22. Ibid.

23. Martha Shelley, interview with author, Portland, OR (telephone), February 16, 2012.

24. Leitsch, interview with author.

25. Ibid.

26. *New York Mattachine Newsletter*, July 1969.

27. In Pine's speech, quoted in the *Villager*.

28. Smith, "Full Moon over Stonewall."

29. L. Craig Schoonmaker, interview with author, Newark, NJ (telephone), May 21, 2013; and L. Craig Schoonmaker, "Why *Homosexuals Intransigent!*?" *Homosexual Renaissance: Newsletter of HI!*, November 12, 1969. The charter for the group was approved April 1, 1969.

30. Schoonmaker, interview with author.

31. L. Craig Schoonmaker, "Homosexuality and Lesbianism: Parallel but Not the Same," *HI!*, October 1971. Schoonmaker's ideas were very much like those of Adolf Brand and Benedict Friedlaender, founders of the early-twentieth-century German homosexual group *Gemeinschaft der Eigene* (Community of the Special), with its cult of hypermasculinity. Schoonmaker had considered starting a branch of the Student Homophile League, which began at Columbia in 1967 and expanded to NYU and Cornell, but he decided finally to found *Homosexuals Intransigent!* because Homophile Student League included lesbians: Schoonmaker, interview with author..

32. Quoted in Jesse Monteagudo, "The Dream of a Gay Nation," *Gay Today*, September 13, 2004.

33. "Homo Revolt: Don't Hide It," *Berkeley Barb*, March 28–April 3, 1969.

34. "Militant March by S.F. Homosexuals," *San Francisco Chronicle*, April 10, 1969.

35. In addition to being fired from *Vector*, he was also fired from his paying job at KGO radio, an ABC affiliate in the Bay Area.

36. "Homo Revolt Blasting Off on Two Fronts," *Berkeley Barb*, April 11–17, 1969. Laurence repeated his accusations about SIR in a *Vector* article, in which he exonerated the organization's president, Larry Littlejohn, who wanted SIR to be more militant but was impeded by his "middle-aged uptight conservative" officers: Leo E. Laurence, "Gay Revolution," *Vector*, April 1969. In this prophetic article, Laurence declares, "1969 is our year. It's time to move, to be militant, to demand our rights."

37. Laurence, quoted in Teal, *Gay Militants*, p. 39.

38. "Homo Revolt Blasting Off on Two Fronts."

39. Ibid.

40. Leo E. Laurence, JD, interview with author, San Diego (telephone), May 31, 2013. Laurence says that when a carload of toughs drove by to menace the "faggot" picketers, he informed them he was calling the Panthers, with whom his group was tight, and the toughs zoomed off.

41. Leo E. Laurence, "Gay Strike Hits Southern California," *Berkeley Barb*, May 2–8, 1970, p. 11.

42. Ibid.

43. Laurence became increasingly confrontational and radical. At a West Coast Gay Liberation conference held at UC Berkeley, December 26–30, 1969, he predicted that as soon as "gay power" made itself felt, "the pigs will be after us," and he thought that gays would soon need to stockpile ammunition—"We have to defend ourselves": quoted in Teal, *Gay Militants*, p. 110.

44. Wittman's essay was finally published in the December 1969 issue of the *San Francisco Free Press*.

45. Seymour Pine, interview with Isay, "Remembering Stonewall."

46. Pine and others have estimated the crowd at two thousand or more. The *New York Times* estimated four hundred.

47. It was never definitely determined why each call was immediately disconnected, though Inspector Pine later suggested that the Sixth Precinct was unhappy with the First Division for not having informed them that they would be conducting a raid in their area that night. Pine didn't inform the Sixth Precinct because he suspected that policemen in the Sixth Precinct were taking payoffs from the Mafia owners (Arthur Bell, "Skull Murphy: The Gay Double Agent," *Village Voice*, May 8, 1978). Pine was also critical of the Sixth Precinct's effectiveness "in keeping these bars properly controlled": Anderson, "'I'm Sorry,' Says Inspector Who Led the Stonewall Raid."

48. Smith, "Full Moon over Stonewall."

49. Ibid.

50. David Isay interview with Howard Smith, "Remembering Stonewall."

51. In his interview for "Stonewall Uprising," on *American Experience,* Martin Boyce

recalled that a "drag queen" who went by the moniker Miss New Orleans was prominent in tearing up the parking meter; but John O'Brien (interview with author) recalls that only butch men participated.

52. "Full Moon over Stonewall." Pine had invited reporter Howard Smith to come inside the Stonewall with him and his officers. Smith's account is thus, as he subtitles his *Village Voice* article, the "View from Inside."

53. Anderson, "'I'm Sorry,' Says Inspector Who Led Stonewall Raid."

54. "Gay Riots in the Village," *New York Mattachine Newsletter*, August 1969.

55. Eyewitness account by J. E. Freeman to "Datebook," letter, *San Francisco Chronicle*, June 26, 2009.

56. Howard Smith interview, in "Stonewall Uprising," *American Experience*.

57. In "Stonewall Riot Police Report," June 28, 1969: OutHistory.org.

58. Chan, "Police Records Document Start of Stonewall Uprising."

59. Eskow, "3 Cops Hurt as Bar Raid Riles Crowd."

60. "Four Policemen Hurt in 'Village' Raid," *New York Times*, June 29, 1969.

61. Frank Galassi, interview with author, Los Angeles, April 22, 2013.

62. Ibid.

63. Marcia Chambers, "Ex-City Official Says He's Homosexual," *New York Times*, October 3, 1973. Because Brown resigned, Pearson never outed him.

64. Howard Brown, *Familiar Faces, Hidden Lives: The Story of Homosexual Men in America Today* (Boston: Houghton Mifflin, 1977), p. 20. Brown died of a heart attack in 1975. His book was published posthumously.

65. Brown's speech quoted in Randy Shilts's introduction to Brown, *Familiar Faces, Hidden Lives*, p. viii.

66. Dick Leitsch, though he was president of Mattachine in 1969, denied categorically that he was involved in posting the sign and pointed to his July 1969 article "The Hairpin Drop Heard Round the World" as evidence that he recognized the significance of the riot immediately: Leitsch, interview with author.

67. When Rodwell first used the words, he might not have intended their combative connotation: he'd coined the term in conjunction with a proposal for a directory of businesses friendly to gays, to be compiled by New York homophile organizations "as a significant step to unify the homosexual buying power": according to a February 1969 article in a Mattachine Society Washington newsletter, *The Insider* (eds. Dick Schaefer and Eva Freund). The September 1967 issue of the *Advocate* had a front-page article about a Washington, DC, meeting of the National Planning Conference of Homophile Organizations. It was headlined "U.S. Capital Turns on to Gay Power."

68. Craig Rodwell, interview in Tobin and Wicker, *Gay Crusaders*, p. 66.

69. Craig Rodwell, interview with Tina Crosby, in "The Stonewall Riot Remembered" (unpublished paper, January 16, 1974), Manuscripts and Archives Division, New York Public Library.

70. Carter, *Stonewall*, p. 178.

71. Leitsch, "Hairpin Drop Heard Round the World."

72. Edmund White to Ann and Alfred Corn, letter, July 8, 1969, in David Bergman,

ed., *The Violet Quill Reader: The Emergence of Gay Writing after Stonewall* (New York: St. Martin's, 1994).

73. Eyewitness J. Marks, quoted in Leo Laurence, "Gays Hit New York Cops," *Berkeley Barb*, July 4, 1969.

74. Ibid.

75. Leitsch, "Hairpin Drop Heard Round the World"; and Lige Clarke and Jack Nichols, Homosexual Citizen column, *Screw*, July 25, 1969.

76. Perry Brass, interview with author, New York, March 6, 2013.

77. Robert L. Pela, "Stonewall's Eyewitness," *Advocate*, May 3, 1994, p. 54. David Carter questions the veracity of this story: author's email correspondence with Carter.

78. Leitsch, "Hairpin Drop Heard Round the World."

79. White, letter to Ann and Alfred Corn.

80. Truscott, "Gay Power Comes to Sheridan Square." Truscott kept reminding the reader that he wasn't sympathetic to homosexuals with snide statements such as "It was the first time I had heard this crowd described as beautiful."

81. Fouratt, interview with author.

82. Leitsch, "Gay Riots in the Village."

83. "Hostile Crowd Dispersed Near Sheridan Square," *New York Times*, July 3, 1969.

84. Leitsch, "Gay Riots in the Village."

85. Flyer, "Get the Mafia and the Cops Out of Gay Bars" (1969), in Stonewall Collection, ONE National Gay and Lesbian Archives, University of Southern California Libraries.

86. Leitsch, "Gay Riots in the Village."

87. Jerry Lisker, "Homo Nest Raided, Queen Bees Are Stinging Mad," *Daily News* (New York), July 6, 1969.

88. Lige (Clarke) and Jack (Nichols), "N.Y. Gays: Will the Spark Die?" *Los Angeles Advocate*, September 1969.

CHAPTER 12: SAY IT PROUD—AND LOUD: NEW GAY POLITICS

1. FBI file, "Demonstrations of Homosexuals, Independence Hall, Philadelphia, Pennsylvania": Philadelphia Office, file 145-686.

2. Bello, interview with author.

3. Ad: "'Gay Is Good': Support the 5th Annual Reminder," in *Village Voice*, July 3, 1969, p. 53. The *Village Voice* became the target of the Gay Liberation Front's first protest because, though the paper accepted this July 3 ad, publisher Ed Fancher refused to accept subsequent ads with the word *gay* or *homosexual* in them, claiming that such words were "obscene" and that the *Voice* had a policy against printing obscenities. GLF picketed the *Voice* on September 12, 1969, carrying signs such as "*Village Voice* Won't Print 'Gay' in Ads but Calls Us 'Dikes' and 'Faggots'"—referring to the *Voice* articles on the Stonewall riots. Fancher called the protestors inside and capitulated immediately about running "gay" ads: "*Village Voice* Goes Down," *Come Out!*, November 14, 1969, p. 9.

4. Teal, *Gay Militants*, pp. 30–31; and Carter, *Stonewall*, pp. 216–17.

5. Renée Cafiero, who'd been at all the Reminder Day pickets and most of

Kameny's DC pickets, remembers that she and many others among the old picketers were actually relieved to see the new gays and lesbians challenging the stiff
style that Kameny had insisted upon: Cafiero, interview with author.

6. Price Dickenson, "What Is Gay Power?" *New York Mattachine Newsletter*, Septem-
    ber 1969, pp. 1–2.
7. Dick Leitsch to Frank Kameny, letter, July 9, 1965, Frank Kameny Papers, box 6,
    folder 11, Library of Congress.
8. Dick Leitsch to Frank Kameny, letter, September 30, 1965, Frank Kameny Papers,
    box 6, folder 11, Library of Congress.
9. Leitsch to Kameny, letter, July 9, 1965.
10. Tom Burke, "The New Homosexuality," *Esquire*, December 1969, pp. 178ff.
11. Rodwell quoted in Martin Duberman, *Stonewall* (New York: Dutton, 1993),
    p. 181.
12. In his September 30, 1965, letter to Frank Kameny, Leitsch claimed it was his
    involvement in the "New Left" that taught him "political savvy."
13. Leitsch to Kameny, letter, July 9, 1965.
14. Shelley, interview with author.
15. According to fellow Gay Liberation Front member Perry Brass: Brass, interview
    with author.
16. Shelley, interview with author.
17. Dick Leitsch to the *Clearing House Newsletter*, letter, directed to "All Homo-
    phile Organizations," September 12, 1967, in *New York Mattachine Newslet-
    ter*, file, 1964–67, ONE National Lesbian and Gay Archives, University of
    Southern California Libraries. Leitsch also wrote a scolding letter to Frank
    Kameny because he and Barbara Gittings had encouraged Donaldson to found
    a student Mattachine Society at Columbia: May 14, 1967, Frank Kameny Pa-
    pers, box 6, folder 11, Library of Congress. Donaldson's Student Homophile
    League was accredited by the Columbia University Committee on Student
    Organizations in April 1967. When accreditation was reported in the univer-
    sity paper, readers thought it was "an April Fool hoax." The *New York Times*
    considered it so controversial that there should be such an organization on
    a university campus that the story was given front-page coverage: Murray
    Schumach, "Columbia Charters Homosexual Group," *New York Times*, May 3,
    1967, pp. 1ff.
18. Eighteen-year-old Mark Segal quoted in Teal, *Gay Militants*, p. 32.
19. Dudley Clendinen and Adam Nagourney, *Out for Good: The Struggle to Build a
    Gay Rights Movement* (New York: Simon & Schuster, 1999), p. 26.
20. Duberman, *Stonewall*, p. 217.
21. Shelley, interview with author.
22. Eric Pace, "Policemen Forbidden to Entrap Homosexuals to Make Arrests," *New
    York Times*, May 11, 1966.
23. "City Lifts Job Curb for Homosexuals," *New York Times*, May 9, 1969, pp. 1, 23.
24. Shelley, interview with author.
25. Shelley says she doesn't recall whether or not she was the one to suggest "Gay

Liberation Front": Shelley, interview with author. Others who were there recall that she was indeed the one who came up with the name: Fouratt, interview with author.

26. Shelley, interview with author.

27. *Village Voice*, July 24, 1969.

28. The *Village Voice* estimated the crowd at five hundred: Jonathan Black, "Gay Power Hits Back," *Village Voice*, July 31, 1969—though people who were there, like Shelley, claim it was at least four times that number.

29. Ibid.

30. In Tobin and Wicker, *Gay Crusaders*, p. 167.

31. In Arthur D. Kahn, *AIDS, The Winter War: A Testing of America* (Philadelphia: Temple University Press, 1993), p. 5.

32. Black, "Gay Power Hits Back."

33. Ibid.

34. Donaldson also chaired NACHO's Committee on Youth that he'd started in 1967.

35. "A Radical Manifesto: The Homophile Movement Must Be Radicalized" (North American Conference of Homophile Organizations, Committee on Youth, 1969).

36. "N.A.C.H.O. '70—San Francisco," *New York Mattachine Society Newsletter*, September 1970, pp. 9–12.

37. Fouratt, interview with author; and Burke, "The New Homosexuality."

38. Fouratt, interview with author.

39. Years later, Fouratt apologized to Gittings, saying, "Now that I've become an older gay man to whom young gays won't listen, I realize I was too hard on the homophiles": Fouratt, interview with author.

40. Author's second interview with Kay (Tobin) Lahusen (telephone), Kennett Square, PA, May 12, 2013.

41. Ellen Broidy, interview with author, Santa Barbara, CA (telephone), June 2, 2013.

42. ERCHO convention reported in "ERCHO Fall Meeting," *New York Mattachine Society Newsletter*, December 1969, pp. 17–18.

43. What was seen as "Panther-style self-defense" was emulated literally by the Lavender Panthers, a San Francisco group started by gay Pentecostal Evangelist Reverend Ray Broshears. The Lavender Panthers patrolled the streets of the Castro, San Francisco's gay ghetto, armed with chains, billy clubs, and karate training in order to fight young toughs who invaded the area intending to "queer-bash": "The Sexes: The Lavender Panthers," *Time*, October 8, 1973.

44. GLF's Statement of Purpose, printed in *Rat* (underground New Left newspaper), August 12, 1969.

45. Fouratt, interview with author.

46. Nikos Diaman, interview with author, San Francisco (telephone), July 24, 2013.

47. Author's third interview with Kay (Tobin) Lahusen, Kennett Square, PA (telephone), May 29, 2013.

48. Karla Jay, who began attending GLF meetings in July 1969, gives her impression of the chaos as well as the exhilaration that she experienced at the meetings in

Tales of the Lavender Menace: A Memoir of Gay Liberation (New York: Basic Books), pp. 79ff.

49. Lois Hart, "GLF News," *Come Out!*, January 10, 1970, p. 16.

50. Lois Hart, "Some News and a Whole Lot'A Opinion," *Come Out!*, April/May 1970, p. 3.

51. Brass, interview with author

52. Ibid.

53. GLF dances described in Black, "Boys in the Snake Pit," p. 62.

54. Ellen Shumsky, interview with author, New York (telephone), March 13, 2013.

55. Los Angeles Gay Liberation Front, pamphlet: *Military Resistance for Gays*, Dan Siminoski Collection, box 7, folder 19, ONE National Gay and Lesbian Archives, University of Southern California Libraries.

56. Faygele ben Miriam, interview with Ruth Pettis, Northwest Lesbian and Gay History Museum Project, January 10, 2000.

57. Ibid.; and Paul Barwick, interview with Ruth Pettis, Northwest Lesbian and Gay History Museum Project, January 20, 2000.

58. Statement of Purpose, in Gay Liberation Front Los Angeles Records, Collection 2012.031, ONE National Lesbian and Gay Archives, University of Southern California Libraries.

59. John O'Brien, who became involved in the LA gay movement as soon as he moved west from New York, told the *Los Angeles Times* in 1988 that Kight came across as "a nice sweet old man, but if you turn your back you might find a knife through it": Paul Ciotti, "Morris Kight: Activist Statesman of L.A.'s Gay Community," *Los Angeles Times*, December 8, 1988.

60. GLF's Alpine County prank is discussed at length in Mary Ann Cherry, *The Kight Affect: The Liberating Life of a Gay Revolutionary*, forthcoming; Jacob Carter (University of Massachusetts, Boston), "Researching Stonewall Nation: Interdisciplinary Considerations for Lesbian, Gay, Bisexual, Transgender Historical Research" (unpublished), Second Annual History Graduate Student Conference, March 9, 2013; and Faderman and Timmons, *Gay L.A.*, pp. 177–79.

61. Don Jackson, "Brother Don Has a Dream," *Los Angeles Free Press*, August 14, 1970.

62. Del Whan, interview with author, Long Beach, CA (telephone), May 24, 2013.

63. Kight on "1989 Gay Day Celebration: 20 Years of Gay Liberation," IMRU (Pacifica Radio).

64. Ibid.

65. Associated Press, "Gay Front Alpine Visit," *Reno (NV) Evening Gazette*, November 26, 1970.

66. L. Craig Schoonmaker, interview with author, Newark, New Jersey (telephone), May 21, 2013.

67. Carolyn Weathers, interview with author, Long Beach, CA (telephone), May 24, 2013.

68. Associated Press, "Gays' Plan of Takeover Confirmed," *Long Beach (CA) Independent*, October 21, 1970.

69. Ibid.

70. Ibid.

71. United Press International, "County Vows to Resist Gay Takeover," *Argus* (Fremont, CA), October 19, 1970.

72. UPI photo, *Nevada State Journal* (Reno), November 27, 1970, p. 24.

73. United Press International, "Alpine County Residents Shrug at 'Gay' Invasion," *Nevada State Journal* (Reno), November 29, 1970, p. 14.

74. Associated Press, "Gay Liberationists Plan to Buy Town," *Bakersfield (CA) Californian*, April 1, 1971.

75. Fred Sargeant, "1970: A First-Person Account of the First Gay Pride March," *Village Voice*, June 22, 2010.

76. Diaman, interview with author; and Arnie Kantrowitz, *Under the Rainbow: Growing Up Gay* (New York: William Morrow, 1977), p. 154.

77. Reverend Troy Perry, interview with author, Los Angeles, June 20, 2012.

78. Morris Kight, "How It All Began," CSW Programme, ONE Subject File: Stonewall, ONE National Gay and Lesbian Archives, University of Southern California Libraries.

CHAPTER 13: LESS TALK AND MORE ACTION: THE GAY ACTIVISTS ALLIANCE

1. O'Brien, first interview with author.

2. Bob Kohler, quoted in Randy Wicker, "The Wicker Basket: GLF Gives $500 to Panthers and Bails Out Young Lords," *Gay*, August 24, 1970; and Diaman, interview with author. Gay radicals in other cities as well made common cause with the Panthers. In Washington, DC, for example, the newly opened gay bookstore Lambda Rising became the home of the Black Panther Defense Fund in 1970; in California, Leo Laurence reported that he was permitted to distribute gay liberation leaflets at a Black Panther rally in Oakland's Bobby Hutton Park: "The Panther official who okayed distribution of our leaflet said, 'Our Board of Control hasn't endorsed this, but we're for anyone who wants freedom, so go ahead'": in *Tangents*, August/September 1970.

3. Joseph P. Fried, "East Harlem Youth Explain Garbage Dumping Demonstration," *New York Times*, August 19, 1969.

4. Jim Owles, quoted in Teal, *Gay Militants*, p. 106.

5. Eugene McCarthy, Democratic senator from Minnesota, ran for president in 1968 on an anti–Vietnam War platform.

6. Jim Owles, interview in Tobin and Wicker, *Gay Crusaders*, p. 32.

7. Lois Hart, quoted in "Bob Kohler Recalling: Collecting Oral Histories with a West Village Legend," in *The Middle of the Whirlwind*, eds. Team Colors Collective (Journal of Aesthetics and Protest Press, 2008). Hart was somewhat disillusioned with the Panthers when she attended the Panthers' Revolutionary People's Constitutional Convention in September 1970 and asked from the floor whether there was "receptivity to women's and gay liberation." She was told, "We'll tolerate that crazy talk about thirty seconds, and you'll be asked to leave": Lois Hart, "Black Panthers Call Revolutionary People's Convention:

A White Lesbian Responds," *Come Out!*, September/October 1970. GLF-er Nikos Diaman recalls other examples of Panther hostility to gays at the convention: for example, when GLF-er Anna Sanchez, seated in the orchestra of the auditorium, kissed her girlfriend, she was startled at a voice from the balcony yelling, "You sick lezzie dykes!": Nikos Diaman, interview with author. The dramatic conflict between Panthers and lesbians at the convention is covered at length in "The Days Belonged to the Panthers," *Off Our Backs*, September 30, 1970, pp. 4–5.

8. Huey Newton, "A Letter from Huey to the Revolutionary Brothers and Sisters on the Women's Liberation and Gay Liberation Movements," *Black Panthers Newsletter*, August 21, 1970. The letter was delivered as a speech the previous week.

9. Clendinen and Nagourney, *Out for Good*, p. 49.

10. Arthur Evans, quoted in Tobin and Wicker, *Gay Crusaders*, p. 196.

11. Arthur Bell, *Dancing the Gay Lib Blues: A Year in the Homosexual Rights Movement* (New York: Simon & Schuster, 1971), p. 13.

12. Ibid., p. 14.

13. Arthur Evans, quoted in Linda Hirshman, *Victory: The Triumphant Gay Revolution* (New York: HarperCollins, 2012), p. 116.

14. Ibid.

15. (Tobin) Lahusen, interview with author.

16. Bell, *Dancing the Gay Lib Blues*, p. 17.

17. Ibid.

18. Ibid., p. 19.

19. The John Birch Society was a far-right, Christian, racist, anticommunist group that was in the news at the time. Kohler quoted in Teal, *Gay Militants*, p. 106.

20. Arnie Kantrowitz, who became an officer in the Gay Activists Alliance, characterizes the diversity of the membership as "long-haired radicals and short-haired conservatives": *Under the Rainbow*, pp. 128–29. But the "short hairs" were "conservative" only by contrast with the "radicals." Even the "short hairs" were militantly challenging homophobia in 1970.

21. Within a year or two, in other cities also, such as Washington, DC, Chicago, and even Louisville, Kentucky, and Columbus, Ohio, there were splits between flaming-radical Gay Liberation Front groups and more "moderately radical" organizations: for example, "Gays in Louisville Choosing Sides Over Liberation Groups," *Advocate*, October 14–27, 1970; and "Gay Lib: New Name and New Policies," *Ohio State Lantern*, October 28, 1971.

22. Evans, platform speech quoted in Tobin and Wicker, *Gay Crusaders*, p. 190.

23. GAA Constitution (December 21, 1969), GAA NY Collection 2010-002, box 1, folder 1, ONE National Gay and Lesbian Archives, University of Southern California Libraries. A later GAA pamphlet, *The GAA Alternative*, declared, contrasting itself with Mattachine style, "We dress as <u>we</u> please, without any regard for 'respectability.' No member of the group can be asked to stay behind the scenes because of his or her style of dress": GAA NY Collection 2010-002, box 1,

folder 1, ONE National Gay and Lesbian Archives, University of Southern California Libraries.

24. Gittings was brought into GAA New York through her partner, founding member Kay (Tobin) Lahusen.

25. As GAA president, Jim Owles sounded very much like Frank Kameny. Urging New York State legislators to pass a Homosexual Bill of Rights, for instance, Owles declared, "What we are demanding is our basic rights as American citizens and human beings. We do not ask for any respectability or sympathy from straight people. Their private opinion of us as individuals or as members of a group are [*sic*] of no interest to us except to the extent that these private bigotries are allowed to become public policy. We have been waiting almost 200 years for the reality of the phrase 'equal before the law'": Jim Owles, president, Gay Activists Alliance, to "Dear Legislator," letter, February 1, 1971, appended to "A Homosexual Bill of Rights Presented to the New York State Legislature by the Gay Activists Alliance," in GAA New York Collection, 2010-002, box 1, folder 7, ONE National Gay and Lesbian Archives, University of Southern California Libraries.

26. Lambda leaflet in GAA NY Collection 2010-002, box 1, folder 2, ONE National Gay and Lesbian Archives, University of Southern California Libraries. In a later GAA leaflet, it was explained that *lambda* was chosen to represent the organization because "The Greek letter lambda is a scientific symbol for activism."

27. Pamphlet, "What is GAA?" in Barbara Gittings Collection, box 1, folder 27, ONE National Gay and Lesbian Archives, University of Southern California Libraries.

28. Gay Activists Alliance, *The Fight for a Gay Civil Rights Law in New York City*, 1975, in GAA New York Collection 2010-002, box 1, folder 8, ONE National Gay and Lesbian Archives, University of Southern California Libraries.

29. Ibid.

30. Greitzer quoted in *Gay Activist: Newsletter of the Gay Activists Alliance*, April 1971.

31. Ibid.

32. Carter, *Stonewall*, pp. 248–49.

33. Clendinen and Nagourney, *Out for Good*, p. 54. Rivera quit GAA when the group refused to include "transvestites" (people now called *transgender*) in its civil rights agenda: David W. Dunlap, "Sylvia Rivera, 50, Figure in Birth of the Gay Liberation Movement," *New York Times*, February 20, 2002.

34. Despite her promise that night at the Village Independent Democratic Club, Greitzer delayed doing anything about the bill. In late 1970, two other members of the city council, Eldon Clingan and Carter Burden, were convinced by GAA's Fair Employment Committee to sponsor a gay rights bill. It did not pass. Gay rights bills came before the New York City Council almost yearly before one finally passed in 1986.

35. Leitsch, interview with author; and *Gay*, May 15, 1970, p. 144.

36. Lindsay's order was hardly "behind closed doors," since it was announced in the *New York Times*. In response to the order, the gratified Leitsch called Lindsay a "tremendous man" and promised that "homosexuals would vote 100%" for him

the next time he ran: Eric Pace, "Policemen Forbidden to Entrap Homosexuals to Make Arrests," *New York Times*, May 11, 1966.

37. Bell, *Dancing the Gay Lib Blues*.

38. GAA also used more conventional methods to demand gay civil rights. The GAA Ad Hoc 1970 Elections Committee sent questionnaires to candidates running for positions in state and federal legislatures and elective state executive officers, reminding them that "in certain areas of New York City close to thirty percent of the electorate is homosexual or bisexual," and asking questions such as "Would you work to oppose governmental collections of data on the sexual preference of individuals?" and "Do you favor total repeal of the New York State Sodomy and Solicitation laws?" The following year the GAA State and Federal Government Committee dispatched volunteers to gay and liberal neighborhoods, armed with voter registration forms and leaflets that explained the need for gay civil rights legislation. "Vote with the consciousness that we can be a bloc," the leaflets urged gays and gay sympathizers: "Gay Registration Drive," *Gay Activist: Newsletter of the Gay Activists Alliance*, September 1971.

39. Ron Gold, interview with author, New York, March 24, 2014.

40. Nathalie Rockhill, interview with author, Kirkfield, Ontario (Canada) (telephone), May 20, 2013.

41. Jack Nichols, unpublished autobiography, p. 138. I am grateful to Stephanie Donald for sharing this manuscript with me.

42. Gay Activists Alliance, "The Fight for a Gay Civil Rights Law in New York City."

43. Ibid.

44. Rich Wandel, interview with author, New York, March 12, 2013.

45. Flyer, "Total War on John V. Lindsay," in GAA New York Collection 2010-002, box 1, folder 10, ONE National Gay and Lesbian Archives, University of Southern California Libraries.

46. Ibid.

47. "GAA Finds a Home," *Gay Activist: Newsletter of the Gay Activists Alliance* 1, no. 2 (May 1971).

48. Wandel, interview with author; and Allen Roskoff, interview with author, New York (telephone), May 23, 2013.

49. Gold, interview with author.

50. Wandel and Roskoff, interviews with author.

51. Martin Tolchin, "Thousands of City Employees Attend Lindsay Benefit," *New York Times*, January 26, 1972.

52. Gold, interview with author.

53. Perrotta, along with another lesbian, Gale McGovern, and three GAA men, Jim Owles, Morty Manford, and John Paul Hudson, were arrested for zapping New York City's Board of Examiners for discriminatory policies against homosexual teachers: "Five Arrested in GAA Zap," *Gay Activist: Newsletter of the Gay Activists Alliance*, May 1970, pp. 1ff. Perrotta was again arrested, along with drag queen Sylvia Rivera and Charles Burch, and given a suspended sentence of fifteen days in jail plus a $250 fine for a zap at the office of the district attorney, protesting

police harassment in a gay bar: Charles Burch, "Gay Lib and the Police: Bad Day at Hauppauge," *Village Voice*, May 4, 1972, pp. 12ff.

54. Fair Employment Committee of the Gay Activists Alliance, "Employment Discrimination Against Homosexuals," Supplement 1, February 3, 1971: GAA New York Collection 2010-002, box 1, folder 6, ONE National Gay and Lesbian Archives, University of Southern California Libraries.

55. Tolchin, "Thousands of City Employees Attend Lindsay Benefit."

56. Roskoff, interview with author.

57. Press release, Gay Activists Alliance News and Media Relations Committee, October 4, 1972: GAA New York, Press Releases, 1972–1980, box 1, folder 4, ONE National Gay and Lesbian Archives, University of Southern California Libraries.

58. "Homosexuals in Revolt: The Year That One Liberation Movement Turned Militant," *Life*, December 31, 1971, pp. 62–73.

59. Gillen, quoted in Ruth Simpson, *From the Closet to the Courts* (New York: Viking Press, 1976), p. 123.

60. Wandel, interview with author; and "Employment Discrimination Against Homosexuals," supplement 1.

61. Simpson, *From the Closet to the Courts*, p. 124.

CHAPTER I 4: A PARALLEL REVOLUTION: LESBIAN FEMINISTS

1. Del Martin, "DOB Speaks for Lesbian," *Ladder*, October 1959, p. 19. With the rise of the feminist movement, Martin severed herself and DOB from all associations with the male homophiles. She declared in a 1967 editorial in *The Ladder* that "The Lesbian, after all, is first of all a <u>woman</u> [*sic*]," and the National Organization of Women [*sic*] is more pertinent to her than the male-dominated North America Conference of Homophile Organizations: "The Lesbian's Majority Status," June 1967, pp. 23–25. Her strongest farewell to coed organizations was her 1970 essay, "If That's All There Is," in which she rejects even her beloved Council on Religion and the Homosexual as "a bastion of male privilege . . . Be warned, my sisters, CRH spells only purgatory for you": *Ladder*, December 1970/January 1971, pp. 4–6.

2. The name of a popular feminist essay by bisexual writer Robin Morgan, "Goodbye to All That," first appeared in February 1970, in the underground paper *Rat*, which radical feminists had "liberated" from leftist males the month before. (*Good-Bye to All That* was also the name of poet/scholar Robert Graves's 1929 autobiography.)

3. Arlene Kisner, interview with author, New York (telephone), March 7, 2013.

4. Radicalesbians, "GLF Women," *Come Out!*, December 1969/January 1970, p. 10.

5. Shumsky, interview with author.

6. Ibid.

7. Martha Shelley, "Stepin Fetchit Woman," *Come Out!*, November 1969, p. 6.

8. Several GLF men were sensitive in the extreme to women's oppression. In 1972 ex-GLF-ers Kenneth Pitchford (then husband of bisexual radical feminist Robin Morgan), Steve Dansky, and John Knoebel started a group called the Effeminists,

whose purpose was to fight misogyny and "effemophobia": Kenneth Pitchford, interview with author, Flushing, NY, March 4, 2013; and Steven Dansky, "The Effeminist Moment," in *Smash the Church, Smash the State*, ed. Tommi Avicoli Mecca (San Francisco: City Lights Books, 2009).

9. See discussion of the controversy on pp. 210–11.

10. Flavia Rando, interview with author, New York (telephone), May 18, 2013.

11. Kisner, interview with author.

12. Jean O'Leary, interview with Jan Holden, in *Lesbian Nuns: Breaking the Silence*, eds. Rosemary Curb and Nancy Manahan (Tallahassee, FL: Naiad Press, 1985), pp. 231–40.

13. Jean O'Leary, interview with author, Los Angeles, February 18, 2004.

14. O'Leary, interview with author.

15. Jean O'Leary, interview with Eric Marcus, in *Making Gay History: The Half-Century Fight for Lesbian and Gay Equal Rights* (New York: HarperCollins, 2002), p. 157.

16. Rockhill, interview with author. Rockhill did join the Lesbian Liberation Committee and later Lesbian Women's Liberation, though she didn't drop out of GAA.

17. For example, Arthur Bell, "Sylvia Goes to College: Gay Is Proud at NYU," *Village Voice*, October 15, 1970.

18. Clendinen and Nagourney, *Out for Good*, p. 171.

19. Rita Mae Brown, "Take a Lesbian to Lunch," *A Plain Brown Rapper* (Oakland, CA: Diana Press, 1976).

20. Rita Mae Brown, interview with Tina Crosby, in "The Stonewall Riot Remembered" (unpublished paper, January 16, 1974), in New York Public Library, Manuscripts and Archives Division; and Rita Mae Brown, interview with author.

21. Brown, "Take a Lesbian to Lunch."

22. Ibid.

23. Edda Cimino, interview with author, Miami, October 14, 2012.

24. Rita Mae Brown, interview with author.

25. A blueprint for consciousness raising, "Radical Feminist Consciousness Raising," was laid out by Redstockings member Kathie Sarachild (pseudonym of Kathie Amatniek) at the 1968 National Women's Liberation Conference in Chicago. An expanded version appeared as "Consciousness-Raising: A Radical Weapon," in Redstockings, *Feminist Revolution* (New York: Random House, 1978), pp. 144–50.

26. Brown, "Take a Lesbian to Lunch."

27. Ivy Bottini, interview with author, Los Angeles, August 19, 2004; and Barbara Love, interview with author, New York (telephone), August 14, 2014.

28. Shumsky, interview with author.

29. Radicalesbians, "The Woman-Identified-Woman," reprinted in *Notes from the Third Year: Women's Liberation*, ed. Anne Koedt, 1971.

30. Vivian Gornick, "Lesbians and Women's Liberation: 'In Any Terms She Shall Choose,'" *Village Voice*, May 28, 1970, p. 5.

31. Ti-Grace Atkinson, "Strategy and Tactics: A Presentation of Political Lesbianism,"

January 1971; reprinted in *Amazon Odyssey: The First Collection of Writings by the Political Pioneer of the Women's Movement* (New York: Links Books, 1974).

32. In 1970 the essay became chap. 2 of her book *Sexual Politics*.

33. Ti-Grace Atkinson, "Lesbianism and Feminism: Justice for Women as 'Unnatural'" (December 1970, reprinted in *Amazon Odyssey*). Atkinson had written this piece as an op-ed for the *New York Times* after a December 14, 1970, article in *Time* magazine had exposed Kate Millett, author of *Sexual Politics*, as a "bisexual." Millett had been catapulted to fame when *Time* put her portrait on its August 31, 1970, cover. But the December article speculated that Millett's sexuality would "reinforce the views of those skeptics who routinely dismiss all liberationists as lesbians." Prominent feminists such as Atkinson, Flo Kennedy, and Gloria Steinem called a press conference at the Washington Square Methodist Church, where they strongly defended Millett and lesbians in general: Judy Klemesrud, "The Lesbian Issue and Women's Lib," *New York Times*, December 18, 1970.

34 Radicalesbians, "GLF Women," *Come Out!*, December/January 1970/71, p. 10.

35. Betty Friedan, "Up from the Kitchen Floor," *New York Times*, March 4, 1973.

36. Friedan, "Up from the Kitchen Floor." Friedan saw it as ironic that she'd been the one to "push forward" Atkinson as a NOW officer because "her ladylike blond image would counteract the man-eating specter" with which antifeminists tried to put down the women's movement.

37. Ibid.

38. Susan Brownmiller reiterated Friedan's Lavender Menace remark in *The New York Times Magazine*, announcing it to the world: "'Sisterhood Is Powerful': A Member of the Women's Liberation Movement Explains What It's All About," *New York Times Magazine*, May 15, 1970.

39. Donna Gottschalk, email correspondence with author, New York, November 14, 2013.

40. Ellen Broidy, interviews with author, Santa Barbara, CA (telephone), June 2, 2013, and November 11, 2013.

41. Love, interview with author.

42. Shumsky, interview with author; and Rita Mae Brown, interview with author.

43. Quoted in Teal, *Gay Militants*, p. 179. The demonstration is also described in Toby Marotta, *The Politics of Homosexuality: How Lesbians and Gay Men Have Made Themselves a Political and Social Force in Modern America* (Boston: Houghton Mifflin, 1981), pp. 248–49. After Lavender Menace disbanded, there were few all-lesbian direct action groups. Lesbian Avengers, the most prominent of them, was started twenty years later, in 1992, by activists Sarah Schulman and Maxine Wolfe: for a history of Lesbian Avengers see Kelly J. Cogswell, *Eating Fire: My Life as a Lesbian Avenger* (Minneapolis: University of Minnesota Press, 2014).

44. Shumsky, interview with author.

45. Karla Jay, *Tales of a Lavender Menace: A Memoir of Liberation* (New York: Basic Books, 1999), p. 143.

46. Radicalesbians, "The Lavender Menace Strikes," *Come Out!*, June/July 1970.

47. Shumsky, interview with author.

48. Friedan, "Up from the Kitchen Floor." Friedan repeated her allegations at the 1975 International Women's Year Conference in Mexico City, alleging that the CIA was acting as "agent provocateurs," pushing "pseudo-radical agendas" in the feminist movement to discredit it; and she warned against feminists becoming "anti-male," which, to her, signified "lesbian": "Betty Friedan Fears CIA Movement Role," *New York Times*, June 23, 1975.

49. Rita Mae Brown, "Take State Power!," *Lesbian Tide*, June 1974, p. 3.

50. Rita Mae Brown, "The Shape of Things to Come," *Women: A Journal of Liberation*, January 1972.

51. Brown, "Take State Power!"

52. Rita Mae Brown, *Rita Will: Memoirs of a Literary Rabble-Rouser* (New York: Bantam, 1999), pp. 253–54.

53. Charlotte Bunch, interview with author, New York (telephone), December 17, 2013; and Charlotte Bunch, "Learning from Lesbian Separatism" (1976); reprint, *Lavender Culture*, eds. Karla Jay and Allen Young (New York: Jove/HBJ, 1979), pp. 433–44.

54. Bunch, interview with author.

55. *Furies: Lesbian/Feminist Monthly* 1, no. 1 (January 1972): p. 1.

56. Charlotte Bunch, "Lesbians in Revolt: Male Supremacy Quakes and Quivers," *Furies* 1, no. 1 (January 1972): pp. 8–9; Barbry (Barbara Solomon), "Taking the Bullshit by the Horns," *Furies* 1, no. 3 (March/April 1972): pp. 8–9; Jennifer Woodul, "Darers Go First," *Furies* 1, no. 5 (June/July 1972): pp. 2–3.

57. Alix Dobkin, interview with Laurel Galana and Gina Covina, in *The New Lesbians: Interviews with Women Across the U.S. and Canada* (Berkeley, CA: Moon Books, 1977), p. 41.

58. Joyce Cheney, ed., *Lesbian Land* (Minneapolis: Word Weavers, 1985).

59. A 1973 national lesbian conference, held on the UCLA campus, was organized by Jeanne Córdova, who hoped to develop a "national lesbian agenda," which would include fighting for the rights of lesbian mothers in custody cases and for civil rights protection for lesbians in employment and housing. The conference was attended by two thousand lesbians, but as Córdova observes, the "cultural impact" of the conference was much more significant than the political impact: author's first interview with Jeanne Córdova, December 22, 2012, and email correspondence, February 24, 2014.

60. The term and concept were popularized by Jill Johnston, *Lesbian Nation: The Feminist Solution* (New York: Simon & Schuster, 1974).

61. Katherine English, "Lesbians Talk About Self-Help Law: Can We Create Our Own Courts?" *Pearl Diver*, May 1977, pp. 16–18.

62. Ibid.

63. Peter Stark, "Legal Row Over Son of Lesbian," *Age* (San Francisco), January 17, 1978.

64. Guy Gifford and Mary Jo Risher, *By Her Own Admission: A Lesbian Mother's Fight to Keep Her Son* (New York: Doubleday, 1977).

65. *Risher v. Risher*, no. 19067, Court of Civil Appeals (Dallas, Texas), 547 S.W. 2d 292 (1977).

66. Sue Levinkind, interview with author, Oakland (Skype), April 19, 2012.

67. Shan Ottey, interview with author, Seattle, May 10, 2012.

68. Anna Schlecht, interview with author, Olympia, WA, May 28, 2012.

69. "Combahee River Collective Statement" (1977), reprint, *Home Girls: A Black Feminist Anthology*, ed. Barbara Smith (New York: Kitchen Table Press, 1983).

70. Chirlane McCray, "I Am a Lesbian," *Essence*, September 1979.

71. Corky Culver, interview with author, Melrose, FL, October 25, 2012.

72. Bunch, "Learning from Lesbian Separatism."

73. See Bonnie Morris, *Eden Built by Eves: The Culture of Women's Music Festivals* (Los Angeles: Alyson, 1999).

CHAPTER 15: DRESSING FOR DINNER

1. Quoted in Robert S. Allen, "Inside Washington" (syndicated), *Clovis (NM) News-Journal*, July 3, 1972.

2. Bruce Voeller, "Notice: Elections '72 Strategy Meeting," GAA New York Collection, box 1, folder 11, ONE National Gay and Lesbian Archives, University of Southern California Libraries.

3. Voeller, "Notice: Elections '72 Strategy Meeting."

4. Morris Kight, "Gay Rights Plank," Morris Kight Collection, box 6, folder 21, ONE National Gay and Lesbian Archives, University of Southern California Libraries.

5. Fouratt had recently reminded GAA of its "rampant" offenses with regard to "chauvinism, sexism, and racism" by flyers he distributed at GAA meetings: for example, "GAA Effective But a Bummer Trip" (February 3, 1972), Morty Manford Papers, box 11, subject files: Jim Fouratt, Manuscript and Archives Division, New York Public Library.

6. A founding member of NACHO—bow tie–wearing, cigar-smoking, middle-aged Foster Gunnison—had remarked in 1966 on the necessity for a national organization, and how it would "prevent fringe elements, beatniks, and other professional nonconformists" from getting all the press: quoted in David Eisenbach, *Gay Power: An American Revolution* (New York: Carroll and Graf, 2006), p. 48.

7. Official Minutes: Strategy Planning Session, Washington, DC, May 5–7, 1972, National Coalition of Gay Organizations Papers, Gay/Lesbian Collection, Shields Library, UC Davis.

8. Allen, "Inside Washington."

9. National Political Affairs Committee, "Gay Presidential Politics: The Time to Act is Now," prepared by Steve Hoglund, National Coalition for Gay Organizations Papers, Gay/Lesbian Collection, Shields Library, UC Davis.

10. Mike Balduf, "Gays Want Representation at Democratic Convention," *Ohio State Lantern*, February 16, 1972.

11. On July 10 about five hundred demonstrators—veterans, SDS members, Yippies,

and radical gays—marched from Flamingo Park to the convention hall. They tried to tear down a metal fence that separated them from the convention hall. According to an FBI report, "A group of fifty policemen persuaded the demonstrators to remain outside." There was one slight injury—a portion of the fence fell on one of the officers: FBI memo, July 31, 1972, Dan Siminoski Collection, box 2, folder 7, ONE National Gay and Lesbian Archives, University of Southern California Libraries. Edda Cimino, who was the cocoordinator, with Morty Manford, of the radical gay and lesbian protests during the Republican National Convention that was held in Miami Beach the following month, recalls that the police were far less tempered at that convention. She witnessed police helicopters flying over Flamingo Park with regularity, and several incidents in which the police came into the park, beat up gay men, and used tear gas and pepper spray on them: Cimino, interview with author.

12. Rowland Evans and Robert Novak, "McGovern's Compromises" (syndicated), *Syracuse (NY) Post Standard*, June 28, 1972.
13. United Press International, "Dems Nix Abortion, 'Gay Lib' Planks," *Capital Times* (Madison, WI), June 27, 1972.
14. Virginia Payette, "Parties Need 'Sorting Out,'" *Lubbock (TX) Avalanche-Journal*, July 5, 1972.
15. Allen, "Inside Washington."
16. "The Protestors: Zippies, Arabs, Poor, Gay, Etc.," *San Antonio (TX) Express*, July 11, 1972.
17. "Gay Presidential Politics: The Time to Act Is Now," prepared by Steve Hoglund.
18. Allen, "Inside Washington." Frank Kameny also finagled a few minutes in front of the Republican Platform Committee's subcommittee on Human Rights and Responsibilities, before the Republican National Convention, which was to be held in Miami Beach on August 21–23. Kameny knew it was an exercise in futility, as he wrote Morty Manford: "Needless to say, we should not have expected much of a response from the Republicans." But, he admitted, his real purpose was to make gays visible to the media and to the "hundreds of gays who were there and had an important experience to share with other gays all around the country. A call to action": Frank Kameny to Morty Manford, September 13, 1972, Frank Kameny Papers, box 7, folder 2, Frank Kameny Collection, Library of Congress, Washington, DC.
19. Robert S. Allen, "McGovernites Divided on 'Gay' Rights Plank," (syndicated) *Charleston (WV) Daily Mail*, July 7, 1972.
20. Allen, "Inside Washington."
21. Associated Press, Odell Hanson, "McGovern Personally Lures Iowa Support, Visits Hawkeye Delegates," *Oelwein (IA) Daily Register*, July 10, 1972; John Lauritsen, "Gays to Demonstrate Against McGovern," *Militant*, July 28, 1972 (copy in FBI file, August 4, 1972; classification: 100-16589-94); and Gold, interview with author. Gold, who'd been a writer for *Variety*, recalls being rescued from the clutches of the McGovern aides by a convention delegate, the actress Shirley MacLaine, whom Gold had interviewed a few weeks earlier. MacLaine saw Gold

being manhandled, demanded the aides release him, and went back with him to the room where the South Dakota delegation had been meeting; but by then the delegates had adjourned. MacLaine had been on the platform committee and had signed the petition demanding that gays be given time on the convention floor: Allen, "Inside Washington."

22. Shilts describes the witch hunt of Foster in *Conduct Unbecoming*, pp. 167–68.

23. Clendinen and Nagourney, *Out for Good*, p. 132.

24. United Press International, "Delegates to Ballot Tonight," *Weirton (WV) Daily Times*, July 12, 1972.

25. Cronkite became a defender of gay rights soon after the convention, when he was zapped on his *CBS Evening News* program by nineteen-year-old gay rights activist Mark Segal; Cronkite showed up at Segal's trial and asked the young man to educate him about gay rights: Mark Segal, interview with author, Philadelphia, March 8, 2013. The incident is also discussed at length in Douglas Brinkley, *Cronkite* (New York: Harper Perennial, 2013).

26. Foster's speech may be heard in its entirety at sfspankycakes.tumblr.com/archive.

27. Madeline Davis, interview with Michel Martin (transcript), *Tell Me More*, NPR News, 2012.

28. Davis speech in transcript, Martin, *Tell Me More*.

29. Michael Ziegler, "City Woman Gives Report to Democrats," *Findlay (OH) Republican Courier*, July 13, 1972. Jim Foster and John Howard of New York GAA got to Mrs. Wilch soon after the speech and made her understand how hurtful it was to the gay community. The following day she issued an apology to gays, saying, "I was not aware the speech would imply homosexuals are child molesters," and she blamed the platform committee staff lawyer for the statement. Her apology was virtually absent from the mainstream press, though the *Advocate* printed it: "Text of Wilch Apology," *Advocate*, August 16, 1972, p. 3.

30. "Angry Gay Leaders Lie Down in McGovern Hotel Entrance," *Advocate*, August 2, 1972.

31. United Press International, "Dems Reject Homosexual Bid by Men, Women," *Lubbock (TX) Avalanche-Journal*, July 12, 1972; and "Opposition Speaker Says Women, Children Threatened," *Advocate*, August 2, 1972.

32. Associated Press, "Ohio Delegates Squabble," *Dover (OH) Times-Reporter*, July 12, 1972.

33. Official Minutes: Strategy Planning Session, Washington, DC, May 5–7, 1972. Demonstrations in Miami were minor, and none was reported anywhere else: "McGovern Gays Badly Shaken Up," *Advocate*, August 2, 1972, p. 3.

34. Rick Perlstein, *Nixonland: The Rise of a President and the Fracturing of America* (New York: Scribner, 2008), p. 698.

35. Albert Riley, "Former Gov. Griffin Plans to Vote for Nixon," *Thomasville (GA) Times-Enterprise*, August 11, 1972.

36. Perlstein, *Nixonland*, p. 695.

37. Associated Press, "McGovern Is Demo Nominee," *Hutchinson (KS) News*, July 13, 1972.

38. Wandel, interview with author.

39. Randy Shilts, "Political Lion or Paper Tiger," *Advocate*, May 31, 1978.

40. O'Brien, second interview with author.

41. Clendinen and Nagourney, *Out for Good,* p. 189. Ronald Gold, Voeller's confidant, also mentions other former GLF members, such as Brenda Howard and Jim Fouratt as triggering Voeller's anger and disdain: Gold, interview with author.

42. See p. 183 for my discussion of Howard Brown and the Stonewall Riots.

43. Chambers, "Ex-City Official Says He's a Homosexual."

44. Carlos A. Ball, *The Right to Be Parents: LGBT Families and the Transformation of Parenthood* (New York: New York University Press, 2012), p. 62.

45. Ralph Blumenthal, "Homosexual Civil-Rights Group Is Announced by Ex-City Aide," *New York Times*, October 16, 1973.

46. The name was dreamed up in the kitchen of Voeller's SoHo apartment by another former GAA member, Greg Dawson, who became NGTF's financial officer. Gold, Nathalie Rockhill, and Tom Smith, one of GAA's few black members, were also present at this first meeting: Gold, interview with author; and David Eisenbach, *Gay Power*, p. 244.

47. Rockhill, interview with author; and Gold, personal collection, speech at NGTF 10th Anniversary Bash, 1983. I thank Ronald Gold for sharing this material with me.

48. Murdoch and Price, *Courting Justice*, p. 181.

49. John D'Emilio, *The World Turned: Essays on Gay History, Politics, and Culture* (Durham, NC: Duke University Press, 2002), p. 101.

50. "Rights Struggle Shifts to Capitol Hill," *Advocate*, July 31, 1974.

51. "News from NGTF," February 7, 1975, National Gay Task Force Collection, box 1, folder 9, ONE National Gay and Lesbian Archives, University of Southern California Libraries.

52. Rockhill, interview with author.

53. Associated Press, "Bill Would Give Gays Equal Rights," *Corpus Christi (TX) Times*, March 26, 1975.

54. Rockhill, interview with author.

55. Marianne Means, "Viewpoint: Homosexuals out of the Closet" (syndicated), *Thomasville (GA) Times Enterprise*, April 7, 1975.

56. Ibid.

57. The organization's name wasn't changed to the National Gay and Lesbian Task Force until 1986. In 2014 it was changed again, to the National Gay, Lesbian, Bisexual, Transgender, and Queer Task Force.

58. Clendinen and Nagourney, *Out for Good*, p. 168.

59. Jean O'Leary and Bruce Voeller, PhD, coexecutive directors, NGTF, "Five Year Goal Proposal" (1976), National Gay Task Force Collection, box 1, folder 1, ONE National Gay and Lesbian Archives, University of Southern California Libraries.

60. D'Emilio, *The World Turned*, p. 103.

61. Secretary of the American Bar Association to Bruce Voeller, letter, December 21, 1973; and American Medical Association, letter of February 25, 1976;

unprocessed, Botts Collection of LGBT History, Houston. I am grateful to archivist Larry Criscione for bringing these materials to my attention.

62. "News from NGTF," February 7, 1975, NGTF Collection, box 1, folder 9, ONE National Gay and Lesbian Archives, University of Southern California Libraries.

63. Steve Endean, *Bringing Lesbian and Gay Rights into the Mainstream: Twenty Years of Progress*, ed. Vicki Lynn Eaklor (Binghamton, NY: Harrington Park Press, 2006). This is Endean's posthumously published autobiography. In 1985 the Gay Rights National Lobby merged with the Human Rights Fund to become the Human Rights Campaign. A couple of decades later, HRC was claiming six hundred thousand members and $30 million in donations: Sarah Wildman et al., "Tough Times at HRC," *Advocate*, February 29, 2005, p. 30. See also Bruce Bawer, *A Place at the Table: The Gay Individual in American Society* (New York: Simon & Schuster, 1993).

64. The *Advocate*'s circulation in 1974, when Michaels sold the publication to David Goodstein, was about forty-five thousand.

65. See p. 120; and Steve Ginsberg, "Pride Organizes Homophiles: New Group Wants Militant Civil Rights Drive," *Los Angeles Free Press*, 1966 (clipping), in PRIDE file, ONE National Gay and Lesbian Archives, University of Southern California Libraries. See also Faderman and Timmons, *Gay L.A.*, pp. 155–57, 159–62.

66. Editorial, "The Destroyers Strike!," *Advocate*, February 28, 1973, p. 36. When the National Gay Task Force was formed that year, Dick Michaels declared it "one of the most exciting developments in recent years . . . a national, professional, full-time gay civil rights organization" to replace the unprofessional, loose-cannon radicals: editorial, "Exciting News," *Advocate*, November 7, 1973. See also Michael Bronski's discussion of the *Advocate*'s opposition to radicalism: *Culture Clash: The Making of Gay Sensibility* (Boston: South End Press, 1984), pp. 148–51.

67. "Homosexuals in Uniform," *Newsweek*, June 9, 1947.

68. "Queer People," *Newsweek*, October 10, 1949.

69. "For the Emotionally Ill," *Newsweek*, December 26, 1955.

70. "Homosexuals: To Punish or Pity," *Newsweek*, July 11, 1960.

71. "Are Homosexuals Sick?" *Newsweek*, May 21, 1973.

72. Jerrold K. Footlick and Susan Agrest, "Gays and the Law," *Newsweek*, October 25, 1976.

73. *Virtually Normal* is the title of Andrew Sullivan's 1995 book, hugely controversial at the time, in which he argued that gays and lesbians would not be first-class citizens until they won the right to marry and the right to serve in the military.

74. Jim Foster to Frank Kameny, letter, September 1972, box 3, folder 8, Frank Kameny Papers, Library of Congress, Washington, DC.

75. Jim Foster to Frank Kameny, letter, January 29, 1974, ibid.

76. See p. 81.

77. Michael Grieg, "Gay Aide on City Staff," *San Francisco Chronicle*, March 27, 1975. In 1977 Feinstein even officiated at a lesbian commitment ceremony in the garden of her home, "wedding" Jo Daly to Nancy Achilles, a wealthy donor to Feinstein's campaigns. Del Martin and Phyllis Lyon were invited to be official

witnesses. Randy Shilts, *The Mayor of Castro Street: The Life and Times of Harvey Milk* (New York: St. Martin's, 1982), p. 181.

78. Quoted in Eskridge, *Dishonorable Passions*.

79. "Dymally Returns to Break Tie: Sex Liberalization Bill Ok'd," *Bakersfield (CA) Californian*, May 2, 1975.

80. David Mixner, interview with author, New York, March 4, 2013.

81. MECLA members Dana Hopkins and Jake Jacobson, interviews with author, Los Angeles, September 3, 2012, and August 25, 2012, respectively.

82. Hopkins, interview with author.

83. Roberta Bennett, interview with author, Los Angeles, December 18, 2004; and Diane Abbitt, interview with author, Los Angeles, October 17, 2005.

84. MECLA is also discussed at length in Faderman and Timmons, *Gay L.A.*, pp. 218–23.

85. Scott, quoted in David DeVoss, "Los Angeles: A Movement Sees Its Leaders Fall," *Los Angeles Times*, January 11, 1988.

86. Mixner, interview with author.

87. Jacobson, interview with author.

88. Irv Burleigh, "Ideological Root in Religious Belief," *Los Angeles Times*, July 7, 1975; and Dean Murphy, "Mr. Gibson: A Councilman of Deep Faith, Hard Work," *Los Angeles Times*, April 26, 1987.

89. Mixner, interview with author.

90. Sid Bernstein, "City Council Race Turns Bitter," *Los Angeles Times*, May 23, 1977.

91. In 1981 Ferraro engineered the election of his successor to the presidency: Joel Wachs, who was a gay man. See Greig Smith, "*If City Hall's Walls Could Talk*": *Strange and Funny Stories from Inside Los Angeles City Hall* (Bloomington, IN: Xlibris, 2010), pp. 43–48. In 1985 Councilman Wachs was responsible for the writing and passage of the first anti-AIDS-discrimination bill in the country.

92. Doyle McManus, "Gay Rights Group Displays Power," *Los Angeles Times*, March 18, 1979.

93. Pokey Anderson, interview with author, Puget Sound, Washington, May 31, 2012; and Pokey Anderson, interview with Erin Graham, July 25, 2006, Houston Oral History Project, University of Houston.

94. Anderson, interview with Graham.

95. Hugh Crell, "Point of View," *Pointblank Times* (Houston), October 1975, p. 3.

96. Frank Michelle interview with Fred Hofheinz, February 11, 2008, Mayor Bill White Collection, Houston Public Library.

97. "Fred," *Pointblank Times*, November 1975, pp. 1–2.

98. Associated Press, Linda Kramer, "Gays View Their Gains," *Oakland Tribune*, October 5, 1975.

99. Anderson, interview with Graham.

100. Quoted in John Goins, "Forging a Community: The Rise of Gay Political Activism in Houston," *Houston History Magazine*, March 25, 2010, pp. 38–42.

101. "Gays Seek to Gain Acceptance," *Houston Post*, July 1, 1975.

102. Fan Snodgrass, "Gays Form Political Caucus; Voter Registration Drive Set," *Daily Cougar* (University of Houston paper), July 3, 1975.
103. Quoted in *Van Ooteghem v. Gray*, 654 F. 2d 304, US Court of Appeals for the Fifth Circuit, August 24, 1981.
104. "Homosexual Vs. the Air Force," *New York Times*, June 1, 1975.
105. Murdoch and Price, *Courting Justice*, p. 217.
106. There were some members of HGPC opposed to Van Ooteghem's conservative style, such as Ray Hill, a street-smart, longtime Houston gay activist: Ray Hill, interview with author, Houston (telephone), April 16, 2012. James Sears discusses Hill at length in *Rebels, Rubyfruit, and Rhinestones: Queering Space in the Stonewall South* (New Brunswick, NJ: Rutgers University Press, 2001), chap. 20.
107. "GPC Ballot," *Pointblank Times*, November 1975, p. 8.
108. Goins, "Forging a Community."
109. Quoted in "GPC Ballot."
110. The *Houston Post* report was based on a survey in the *Advocate*, cited in Goins, "Forging a Community," p. 40.
111. William K. Stevens, "City Controller Expected to Unseat Mayor in Houston Election," *New York Times*, October 21, 1981.
112. Mayor Jim McConn to Gay Political Caucus, letter, October 11, 1978, unprocessed files: folder, GPC-Houston, 1978, Botts Collection of LGBT History, Houston.
113. William K. Stevens, "Houston Accepts New Political Force," *New York Times*, November 2, 1981.
114. See chapter 20.
115. Anderson, interview with author.
116. Ibid.
117. Flyer, "Frank Mann Is at It Again," October 27, 1979, unprocessed files: folder GPC-Houston, Botts Collection of LGBT History, Houston.
118. Steve Shiflett speech, November 20, 1979, unprocessed files: folder GPC-Houston, Botts Collection of LGBT History, Houston.
119. Stevens, "Houston Accepts New Political Force."

CHAPTER 16: HOW GAYS AND LESBIANS STOPPED BEING CRAZIES

1. Brass, interview with author; and Perry Brass, "Gay May Day," *Come Out!*, Spring/Summer 1971, pp. 6, 14ff.
2. Jack Baker was the newly elected (and very out) student-body president at the University of Minnesota. The panel also included Larry Littlejohn, president of San Francisco's Society for Individual Rights; Del Martin of DOB; and Lilli Vincenz of Mattachine Society Washington.
3. "GLF and Women's Lib Zap Shrinks," *Gay*, June 8, 1970, p. 3.
4. Poll cited on Alix Spiegel, "81 Words," *This American Life*, NPR, January 18, 2002.
5. Barbara Gittings, "Preface: Show-and-Tell," in *American Psychiatry and*

Homosexuality: An Oral History, ed. Jack Drescher and Joseph P. Merlino (Binghamton, NY: Harrington Park Press, 2007), p. xvii. DC GAA had been formed to support Frank Kameny's run for Congress in 1971.

6. Ronald Bayer, *Homosexuality and American Psychiatry: The Politics of Diagnosis* (New York: Basic Books, 1981), pp. 102–3. Starting in 1970, radical gay groups began staging such zaps whenever "mental health" professionals convened. In November 1970, for instance, the Los Angeles Gay Liberation Front descended on the Biltmore Hotel en masse—in bell-bottoms, army shirts, and roach-clip necklaces—to invade a session by Dr. M. P. Feldman, author of numerous articles on aversion therapy for "sexual deviation." Feldman was showing his fellow psychologists a film about his use of electroshock in curing homosexuality. As the screen flashed pictures of a male homosexual being given shocks while looking at the image of a naked man, the GLF-ers who were scattered among the 150 psychologists rose, stamped their feet, and shouted "We're not taking this anymore!" GLF member Don Kilhefner scuffled with Feldman for the microphone and won. Only one psychologist stormed out—"a pipe-smoking caricature of the profession"—GLF member Carolyn Weathers recalls. The rest let themselves be organized into small groups and actually listened to what the homosexuals had to say: Weathers, interview with author.

7. Spiegel, "81 Words."

8. Frank Kameny interview with John-Manuel Andriote, Andriote Collection, 1128, box 2, folder 31, Archives Center, National Museum of American History, Smithsonian Institution.

9. Mark Meinke, "Zapping the Shrinks: May 3, 1971," Rainbow History Project, Washington, DC.

10. Reported in *Newsweek*, August 23, 1971, p. 47; and Bayer, *Homosexuality and American Psychiatry*.

11. Frank Kameny to Morty Manford, May 10, 1971, letter, Frank Kameny Collection, Library of Congress, box 7, folder 2.

12. Thomas Szasz, *The Myth of Mental Illness* (New York: Harper and Row, 1961). In *The Manufacture of Madness* (New York: Harper and Row, 1970), Szasz was directly critical of the profession's misguided "preoccupation with the disease concept of homosexuality" and how it punishes homosexuals with a "stigmatizing label" that is nothing more than "a thinly disguised replica of the religious perspective which it displaced," pp. 168, 170.

13. Jack Nichols, letter, October 14, 1963, quoted in Nichols's unpublished autobiography, p. 50.

14. Frank Kameny statement, July 8, 2006, Rainbow History Project, Washington, DC.

15. Nichols's unpublished autobiography, p. 70.

16. Wicker, interview with author; and Kay Tobin, "'Expert' Challenged," *Ladder*, February/March 1965, p. 18.

17. "Cross Currents: The Homophile Community Versus Dr. Charles W. Socarides," *Ladder*, September 1968, pp. 29–30.

18. Kameny, interview in Tobin and Wicker, *Gay Crusaders*, pp. 98–99.

19. Frank Kameny, "Civil Liberties: A Progress Report," in *New York Mattachine News-letter*, July 1965, pp. 7–22.

20. Frank Kameny, "Does Research into Homosexuality Matter?" *Ladder*, May 1965, p. 15.

21. Barbara Gittings, interview with John-Manuel Andriote, Andriote Collection 1128, box 2, folder 5, Archives Center, National Museum of American History, Smithsonian Institution.

22. Kameny, "Does Research into Homosexuality Matter?" pp. 14, 20; also Frank Kameny, "Emphasis on Research Has Had its Day," *Ladder*, October 1965, pp. 10–14.

23. Ibid.; and Florence Conrad's answer to Kameny's rejection of "expert" opinions on homosexuality: "Research Is Here to Stay," *Ladder*, July/August 1965, pp. 15–21. Some Mattachine members were as cautious as Conrad was on the issue. The *New York Mattachine Newsletter*, for instance, published an article about Irving Bieber's 1962 book *Homosexuality* that criticized Bieber as "an abuser of behavioral science" and a perpetuator of lies about homosexuals. But an editor's note that followed the article disclaimed its bold views and called for "more research in the field of sexual deviation."

24. (Tobin) Lahusen, interview with author.

25. Spiegel, *This American Life.*

26. Ibid.

27. Ibid.

28. Lawrence Hartmann, interview with Jack Drescher, in Jack Drescher and Joseph P. Merlino, eds., *American Psychiatry and Homosexuality: An Oral History* (Binghamton, NY: Harrington Press, 2007), pp. 45–60.

29. Spiegel, *This American Life.*

30. Gittings, interview with Andriote.

31. Robert Seidenberg, "The Accursed Race," in *Homosexuality: A Changing Picture*, ed. Hendrik Ruitenbeek (London: Souvenir Press, 1973).

32. (Tobin) Lahusen, interview with author.

33. Gittings, interview with Andriote.

34. David L. Scasta, "John E. Fryer, M.D., and the Dr. H. Anonymous Episode," in *Journal of Gay and Lesbian Psychotherapy* 6, no. 4 (2003): pp. 73–84.

35. (Tobin) Lahusen, interview with author.

36. Ibid.

37. Fryer's speech is reprinted in "Dr. H. Anonymous Speaks," *Philadelphia Gay News*, May 17–23, 2002.

38. Press release by New York Gay Activists Alliance, "Gay Liberationists to Address Behaviorist, Psychiatric Conventions," October 12, 1972: in ONE National Gay and Lesbian Archives, University of Southern California Libraries, GAA NY Collection, box 1, folder 4; and flyer, "Heterosexual and Unhappy? Free Brainwashing Here," ibid.

39. Gold recalls that it had been agreed among GAA members that their president,

Rich Wandel, would lead the protest; but Wandel was absent, and the role fell to Gold: Gold, interview with author.

40. Ibid.

41. Robert L. Spitzer, interview with Jack Drescher, in Drescher and Merlino, eds., *American Psychiatry and Homosexuality*, pp. 99–100; and Gold, interview with author. Charles Silverstein also describes the Behavior Therapy zap in *For the Ferryman: A Personal History* (New York: Chelsea Station Editions, 2011), pp. 47–48.

42. Robert Jean Campbell, interview with Richard O. Hire, in Drescher and Merlino, eds., *American Psychiatry and Homosexuality*, pp. 63–80.

43. Robert L. Spitzer, interview with Jack Drescher, in Drescher and Merlino, eds., *American Psychiatry and Homosexuality*, p. 100.

44. Charles Silverstein, interview with author, New York (telephone), May 3, 2013. The group decided it would present a two-pronged approach. Mental health professionals Silverstein, Ray Prada, and Bernice Goodman would talk about scientific evidence that challenged the sickness theory, and Jean O'Leary and Ronald Gold would talk about how the sickness theory affected gays and lesbians: Gold, interview with author.

45. Gold, interview with author.

46. I am grateful to Charles Silverstein for sharing a copy of this speech with me.

47. Spitzer, interview with Drescher in *American Psychiatry and Homosexuality*, p. 100.

48. Irving Bieber, "A Symposium: Should Homosexuality Be in the APA Nomenclature?" printed in *American Journal of Psychiatry* 130, no. 11 (1973): pp. 1207–16; and Gold, interview with author.

49. Gold, interview with author. Irving Bieber later repeated to the *New York Times* the absurdly false point about there being no homosexuals in kibbutzim: "A.P.A. Ruling on Homosexuality: The Issue Is Subtle, the Debate Still On," December 23, 1973.

50. Judd Marmor, in "A Symposium: Should Homosexuality Be in the APA Nomenclature?"

51. Gold, interview with author. Drs. Robert Stoller and Richard Green, who were also on the panel, were "agnostics" on the subject of whether "homosexuality" belonged in the *DSM*.

52. Campbell, interview with Richard O. Hire.

53. Spitzer, interview with Jack Drescher.

54. Spiegel, "81 Words."

55. Spitzer, interview with Jack Drescher.

56. Robert Spitzer, "A Proposal About Homosexuality and the APA Nomenclature," in "Homosexual Orientation Disturbance: Proposed Change in *DSM-II*, APA Document," reference number 73008; Kay (Tobin) Lahusen attests to Kameny's authorship of the document: (Tobin) Lahusen, interview with author; and Memo, "Subject: Victory!!!! We have been cured!" December 15, 1973: Frank Kameny to "Those who contributed to my May 1973 trip to Honolulu to attend the meeting of the American Psychiatric Association." I am grateful to Ms. Lahusen for sharing with me her copy of this memo.

57. Spitzer, interview with Jack Drescher; and Gold, interview with author.

58. Ronald Bayer, in his book *Homosexuality and American Psychiatry*, suggests that the APA decision to declassify homosexuality in the *DSM* was "not a conclusion based on the approximation of scientific truth as dictated by reason, but was an action demanded by the ideological temper of the times" (pp. 3–4). It is surely true that "the ideological temper of the times" played a role in the APA's decision to declare that homosexuality is not an illness; but it is equally true, as Thomas Szasz has suggested, that the "ideological temper of the times" was responsible for the APA's original decision to declare that homosexuality *is* an illness.

59. Quoted in Silverstein, *For the Ferryman*, p. 45.

60. "A.P.A. Ruling on Homosexuality," *New York Times*.

61. The APA vote did not convince psychiatrists such as Bieber and Socarides to cease promulgating their theories, nor did it convince all medical professionals to stop listening to them. In 1976 the New York Academy of Medicine presented a panel, "Psychodynamics of Male Homosexuality," that included Bieber, Socarides, and Lionel Ovesey, the latter of whom, like his copanelists, had long proclaimed that homosexuality was pathological but could be cured by psychotherapy (*Homosexuality and Pseudohomosexuality*, New York: Science House, Inc., 1969). But organized gays did not tolerate such meetings. They invaded, shouting "Bigots!" and "No more shit!" They sat down on the conference room floor and refused to move even when the police arrived. They yelled out stories of the psychiatric oppression of gays. The meeting was adjourned before Bieber and Socarides had a chance to say a word: James Zepp, "S.O.B. Zap," *Gay Activist*, April/May 1976. The classification "ego-dystonic homosexuality" was finally removed from the *DSM-III-R* in 1987, but that did not prevent Socarides from founding the National Association for Research and Therapy of Homosexuality in 1992.

62. Frank Kameny to Jack Nichols, letter, April 24, 1975, Frank Kameny Papers, box 7, folder 10, Library of Congress.

CHAPTER 17: THE CULTURE WAR IN EARNEST

1. The invitees were Jean O'Leary, Bruce Voeller, William Kelley, Betty Powell, Charlie Brydon, Myra Riddell, Charlotte Spitzer, Ray Hartman, Pokey Anderson, George Raya, Frank Kameny, Reverend Troy Perry, Elaine Noble, and Charlotte Bunch: White House Meeting Agenda, March 26, 1977, in George Raya Collection, box 1, folder 17, ONE National Gay and Lesbian Archives, University of Southern California Libraries.

2. Perry, interview with author.

3. Charlie Brydon, interview with author, New Westminster, Canada (Skype), July 1, 2012.

4. Jurate Kazickas, "I'm Not in the Position Where I Need Permission to Do Anything," *Stars and Stripes*, June 27, 1977, p. 19.

5. Washington News Service, Saul Kohler, "The Presidency: Dirty Tricks," in *Beckley Raleigh (WV) Register*, September 20, 1977, p. 4.

6. United Press International, Lawrence McQuillan, "Midge Is Loud, Pushy, Etc.," *Salina (KS) Journal*, November 24, 1977, p. 18.

7. Garry Clifford, "As Midge Costanza Sees It, Her Cluttered Office Provides a Window to the President," *People*, March 21, 1977, pp. 32–34.

8. Robert Sheer, "The Playboy Interview: Jimmy Carter," *Playboy*, November 1976, pp. 63–86.

9. Kazickas, "I'm Not in the Position Where I Need Permission to Do Anything."

10. Charles F. Brydon Papers, MS 63, box 6, folder 27, Washington State Historical Society Archives.

11. Costanza had also had a secret affair for several years with a married business-man, whose secretary she'd been. He was influential in the New York Democratic Party, and he whetted her appetite for politics: Doreen J. Mattling and Ashley Boyd, "Bringing Gay and Lesbian Activism to the White House: Midge Costanza and the National Gay Task Force Meeting," *Journal of Lesbian Studies* 17, nos. 3–4 (2013): pp. 365–79; and Clendinen and Nagourney, *Out for Good*, p. 269.

12. Clifford, "As Midge Costanza Sees It."

13. Ibid.

14. Mattling and Boyd, "Bringing Gay and Lesbian Activism to the White House."

15. Kazickas, "I'm Not in the Position Where I Need Permission to Do Anything."

16. Agenda, National Gay Task Force/White House Meeting, March 26, 1977, George Raya Collection, box 1, folder 17, ONE National Gay and Lesbian Archives, University of Southern California Libraries.

17. The selection process caused some consternation among gays and lesbians who felt directly affected by government discrimination. Andrew Sullivan, who'd immigrated to the United States from Australia, had been fighting for several years for naturalization. He accused NGTF of "selling gay aliens down the river" by choosing cronies to attend the White House meeting rather than genuine experts in particular areas. Sullivan pointed especially to Charlotte Bunch, who "knew nothing about immigration, and had gained her berth by being on the NGTF board": Randy Shilts, "Political Lion or Paper Tiger," *Advocate*, May 31, 1978. But as Charlotte Bunch explains, there were no out gay or lesbian experts on immigration in 1977, and the role of the fourteen invitees was simply to raise the issues that troubled the gay and lesbian community: Bunch, interview with author.

18. Austin Scott, "Carter Aide Meets with Gay Activists," *Washington Post*, March 27, 1977.

19. "NGTF Meets with Bureau of Prisons Director" and "NGTF Wins Public Health Service Policy Change," *It's Time* (NGTF newsletter), May 1978. The summer after the White House meeting, the NGTF was informed by the IRS that its Fund for Human Dignity would be given tax-exempt status, with the proviso that the fund must not "advocate or actively seek to convince individuals" about sexual orientation: Robert T. Dodd, IRS, to Fund for Human Dignity, letter, July 27, 1977, in Human Sexuality Collection, Division of Rare and Manuscripts Collections, Cornell University Library.

20. United Press International, "Homosexual Leaders Meet at White House with

Presidential Aide to Discuss Discrimination in Federal Law," *New York Times*, March 27, 1977, p. 13.

21. Nancy Brown, "Protests Say: 'Gay Rights Now,'" *Young Socialist Review*, September 1977.

22. "Homosexual Leaders Meet at White House with Presidential Aide to Discuss Discrimination." From the start of his presidential ambitions, Carter had tried to do a balancing act on the issue of homosexual rights. When he campaigned for the presidency in Los Angeles, Reverend Troy Perry appeared in his audience and asked whether, if he were elected, he'd sign an executive order banning discrimination against homosexuals in housing, the military, immigration, and civilian jobs that required security clearances. Carter demurred only about security clearances for employees who were not "out in the open": Perry, interview with author. But when Reverend Perry tried to get a photo with Carter, the candidate sent his wife to pose in his place. Though Carter declared that he was "opposed to discrimination based on sexual orientation," the official line of his campaign was that he, a born-again Christian, was "not comfortable with homosexuality for personal reasons." His campaign committee blocked a plank in support of gay rights that activists had tried to put through at the Democratic National Convention. In the end, Carter did little for gay and lesbian civil rights: see J. Brooks Flippen, *Jimmy Carter, the Politics of Family, and the Rise of the Religious Right* (Athens: University of Georgia Press, 2011), pp. 83–85.

However, when Carter ran for reelection in 1980, the Carter-Mondale Presidential Committee quietly sought the gay vote. Robert Strauss, chair of the committee, responded to a National Gay Task Force query about the candidate's position on gay and lesbian civil rights, reminding the organization that "Three months after the inception of this administration, senior White House advisors met with representatives of the National Gay Task Force." Strauss also pointed out to NGTF that in 1978, Carter signed the Civil Service Reform Act, which prohibited "discrimination in federal personnel actions based on private, non-job-related behavior such as sexual orientation": Letter from Robert Strauss to NGTF, March 3, 1980, in NGTF Rhode Island Affiliate Newsletter, October 24, 1980, National Gay and Lesbian Task Force Collection, box 1, folder 8, ONE National Gay and Lesbian Archives, University of Southern California Libraries.

23. Midge Costanza in "Commemorating the 30th Anniversary of the White House Meeting," *NGLTF Newsletter*, March 26, 2007.

24. "Presidential Aide Meets Homosexual Leaders at White House to Discuss Discrimination."

25. Quoted in "Anita Bryant Scores White House Talk with Homosexuals," *New York Times*, March 28, 1977.

26. Ibid.

27. "Bryant Decries White House Gay Meeting," *Miami Herald*, March 28, 1977.

28. Friedan, "Up from the Kitchen Floor." *New York Times*, March 4, 1973.

29. Phyllis Schlafly, *A Choice, Not an Echo: How American Presidents Are Chosen* (Alton, Illinois: Pere Marquette Press, 1964).

30. Obituary: Martha Griffiths, *The Guardian,* April 28, 2003.

31. "Nation: New Victory in an Old Crusade," *Time,* August 24, 1970.

32. *Phyllis Schlafly Report* 5, February 1972, quoted in June T. Mansbridge, *Why We Lost the ERA* (Chicago: University of Chicago Press, 1986), p. 104.

33. Ann Lane interview with Jeanette Rodermyer, National Women's Conference, Houston, November 18, 1977, T-66, reel 1, side 1, sound recording, Hollis, Harvard Library.

34. "World Parlay on Women is Suggested at U.N." *New York Times,* January 20, 1974; "The Proceedings in the U.N. Today," *New York Times,* January 24, 1974; "Women's Year," *New York Times,* March 8, 1975.

35. The member nations kept the International Women's Year budget skimpy: $266,000 was voted for the two-week kickoff conference in Mexico City, compared with $3 million voted for a UN World Population Conference held that same year: Kathleen Teltsch, "U.N. Wants to Be More than a Ladies' Meeting," *New York Times,* May 10, 1974.

36. Quoted in Ruth Murray Brown, *For a Christian America: A History of the Religious Right* (Amherst, NY: Prometheus Books, 2002), p. 107.

37. *Eagle Forum Newsletter,* in *Phyllis Schlafly Report,* June 1976.

38. Jean O'Leary, interview with author.

39. Author's first interview and email correspondence with Córdova.

40. Mixner, interview with author; Bennett, interview with author, and email correspondence, December 10, 2013; Córdova, first interview with author, and email correspondence with author, December 9, 2013 and February 24, 2014; and Jeri Dilno, interview with author, San Diego, July 5, 2012. (All the women were delegates to the IWY National Women Conference.)

41. Jeanne Córdova, "Freedom Riders' Bus to Houston," *Lesbian Tide,* September/October 1977.

42. "Women at Utah Meeting Oppose Rights Proposal," *New York Times,* June 26, 1977.

43. "Women's Meeting Friday in Albany Will Have a National Focus," *New York Times,* July 5, 1977.

44. IWY Women for Racial and Economic Equality flyer: "Speak Out for Equality: Unseat the Mississippi Delegation," in Lesbian Legacy Collection, box 11, ONE National Gay and Lesbian Archives, University of Southern California Libraries. I am grateful to archivist Michael Oliveira for calling this flyer to my attention.

45. "Foes Leap on Women's Year," *Star News* (Pasadena, CA), August 23, 1977.

46. Christine Pattee, interview with author, Coventry, CT (telephone), November 21, 2013. Pattee, an open lesbian, was elected to the Iowa delegation with the highest number of votes, attesting to the participants' ready support of lesbian issues.

47. Pokey Anderson to Jean O'Leary, memo, Regarding Texas IWY, July 6, 1977, personal collection of Pokey Anderson; and Anderson, interview with Graham.

48. "Anti-ERA Forces Demand Probe of Balloting at Austin Women's Meeting," *Houston Post,* July 2, 1977.

49. Vicki Frierson and Ruthanne Garlock, "Christian, Be Watchful: Hidden Dangers in the New Coalition of Feminism, Humanism, Socialism, Lesbianism" (Dallas: Texas Eagle Forum, 1977).

50. Brown, *For a Christian America*, pp. 110–11.

51. "What Next for U.S. Women?" *Time*, December 5, 1977.

52. Quoted in Nancy Cohen, *Delirium: How the Sexual Revolution Is Polarizing America* (Berkeley, CA: Counterpoint, 2011), p. 69.

53. Quoted in Daniel K. Williams, *God's Own Party: The Making of the Christian Right* (New York: Oxford University Press, 2010), pp. 143–44.

54. Cited in "Women March on Houston," *Time*, November 28, 1977.

55. Mary Lu Abbott and John Kling, "No Apology for Blasting Women's Meet," *Houston Chronicle*, November 18, 1977, p. 1.

56. Gregory Shelton and Steve Brown, "Resurrections: The Early Years," *OutSmart* (Houston), April 1, 2007.

57. Deborah Diamond Hicks, "Lesbians Map Conference Strategy," *Daily Breakthrough* (Houston), November 19, 1977; and Bunch, interview with author.

58. Shelton and Brown, "Resurrections."

59. Jeanne Córdova Papers, box 16, folder 4, ONE National Gay and Lesbian Archives, University of Southern California Libraries; Córdova, email correspondence with author; and Bennett, interview with author, and email correspondence.

60. Betty Powell, interview with Kelly Anderson, July 7, 2004, Voices of Feminism Oral History Project, Sophia Smith Collection, Smith College.

61. See p. 303. Carter reiterated in a Father's Day 1977 interview that he didn't want to "involve" himself in the subject of homosexuality and said, "I'd rather not answer," when the interviewer asked him if homosexuals should be allowed to teach school or adopt: Associated Press, Ann Blackman, "Father's Day Chat: President Carter Talks About Problems Facing the American Family," *Daily News* (Bowling Green, KY), June 19, 1977, pp. 1, 22.

62. Quoted in Frierson and Garlock, "Christian, Be Watchful," p. 20.

63. Anderson, interview with author.

64. "First Ladies Out Front," *Time*, December 5, 1977.

65. Love, interview with author.

66. Anderson, interview with author.

67. Ibid.

68. Love, interview with author.

69. Ibid.

70. Del Martin, interview with Phyllis Lyon (both were delegates to the conference), "Del Martin (1921–)," in *Before Stonewall*, p. 166.

71. Anderson, interview with author.

72. Feldman, "Mississippi"; "What Next for U.S. Women?"; and Ruth Rosen, "Root of Our Division," *San Francisco Chronicle*, December 1, 2002.

73. "First Ladies Out Front."

74. Eagle Forum Newsletter, *Phyllis Schlafly Report*, January 1978; and Brown, *For a Christian America*, pp. 118–19.

75. "What Next for U.S. Women?"

CHAPTER 18: ENTER, ANITA

1. Bob Basker, interview with Jesse Monteagudo, *Weekly News*, October 7, 1998.

2. Bob Basker, interview with Keith Vacha, *Quiet Fire: Memoirs of Older Gay Men* (Trumansburg, NY: The Crossing Press, 1985).

3. "Emergency Bulletin from the Gay Activists Alliance," Robert Basker Collection (103-292 unprocessed), ONE National Gay and Lesbian Archives, University of Southern California Libraries.

4. Jesse Monteagudo, "Stephen Wayne Foster: Gay Activist and Scholar," *South Florida Gay News*, August 17, 2012.

5. See Berube, *Coming Out Under Fire*.

6. *Miami Herald*, August 10, 1954, sec. 2, p. 1; *Miami Herald*, August 13, 1954, sec. 1, p. 1; *Miami Herald*, September 2, 1954, sec. 1, p. 1. See also discussion in Fred Fejes, "Murder, Perversion, and Moral Panic: The 1954 Media Campaign Against Homosexuals and the Discourse of Civic Betterment," *Journal of the History of Sexuality* 9, no. 3 (July 2000): pp. 305–47.

7. Letter from Bob Barry, GAA president, to Capt. Eugene Gunn, Miami Police Department, May 7, 1972. Robert Basker Collection (103-292, unprocessed), ONE National Gay and Lesbian Archives, University of Southern California Libraries.

8. Bob Basker's presentation at the Hearings of the US Commission on Civil Rights, Miami, June 21, 1975, in Robert Basker Collection, ONE National Gay and Lesbian Archives, University of Southern California Libraries.

9. Letters to the Lesbian Task Force of NOW from Robert Basker, February 15, 1976, in Robert Basker Collection, ONE National Gay and Lesbian Archives, University of Southern California Libraries; and letter to Jack Campbell, president of the Alliance for Individual Rights, February 15, 1976, unprocessed collection, Stonewall National Museum and Archives, Fort Lauderdale, Florida.

10. "Campbell in Florida Race," *Advocate*, August 27, 1975, p. 15 and "Voter Apathy . . ." *Advocate*, December 3, 1975, p. 9.

11. Jesse Monteagudo, interview with author, Hollywood, FL, October 14, 2012.

12. Minutes of the Dade County Coalition for the Humanistic Rights of Gays, August 4, 1976, Robert Basker Collection, ONE National Gay and Lesbian Archives, University of Southern California Libraries.

13. Jack Campbell, interview with Fred Fejes, February 19, 1997, transcribed, Stonewall National Museum and Archives, Fort Lauderdale, FL.

14. Minutes of the Dade County Coalition for the Humanistic Rights of Gays, October 19, 1976, Robert Basker Collection, ONE National Gay and Lesbian Archives, University of Southern California Libraries.

15. Bob Kunst, interview with author, Miami Beach, FL, October 28, 2012.

16. Dade County Coalition Agenda Item No. 4 (a), 12-7-76, in Robert Basker

Collection, ONE National Gay and Lesbian Archives, University of Southern California Libraries.

17. Ruth Shack, interview with author, Miami, October 16, 2012.

18. Ron LaBrecque, "Metro to Examine Gay Bias Laws," *Miami Herald*, December 7, 1976.

19. Joe Baker, "The Unshakeable Ruth Shack," *Advocate*, September 28, 1978, p. 248.

20. Morton Lucoff, "Metro vote favors end to discrimination against homosexuals," *Miami News*, December 7, 1976.

21. Fred Fejes, *Gay Rights and Moral Panic: The Origins of America's Debate on Homosexuality* (New York: Palgrave, 2008), p. 109.

22. "Gays Don't Belong in Minority Camp," *Miami News*, December 10, 1976, p. 14a.

23. Steve Daily, "Daily Commentary," WINZ, December 7, 1976.

24. Bill Hutchinson and James R. Kukar, "Bryant/Kunst: Caught in the Middle," *Miami Magazine*, May 1977.

25. Anita Bryant, *The Anita Bryant Story: The Survival of Our Nation's Families and the Threat of Militant Homosexuality* (Old Tappan, NJ: Fleming H. Revell, 1977), pp. 13–14.

26. Jack Weatherly, "Anita Bryant Is Energetic Christian," *Courier News* (Blytheville, AR), May 1, 1976.

27. Shack, interview with author.

28. "Anita Bryant—Call from the Lord," *Oakland Tribune*, May 6, 1977, p. 16.

29. "Anita Bryant—Call from the Lord"; and Shack, interview with author.

30. *The Anita Bryant Story*, pp. 16–19.

31. Ibid.

32. Transcript of the Dade County Commission Meeting, "Public Hearing on Proposed Dade County Ordinance, January 18, 1977," Stonewall National Museum and Archives, Fort Lauderdale, Florida.

33. Shack, interview with author. Oral Is Moral was a motto adopted by Kunst in 1978, when he again campaigned for a gay rights amendment. Ms. Shack would, however, have been chagrined by the first words that Kunst actually did say at the hearing: "For a person to come out and accept oneself automatically means that he or she has to reject immediately church, faith, government, society, parents . . .": transcript of the Dade County Commission Meeting, Stonewall National Museum and Archives.

34. The comment was made to Stan Isaacs, *Newsday* reporter, on July 23, 1964: quoted in Rick Swaine, *The Integration of Major League Baseball: A Team by Team History* (Jefferson, NC: McFarland Publishing, 2009), p. 86.

35. Transcript of the Dade County Commission Meeting, Stonewall National Museum and Archives.

36. "Anita Bryant—Call from the Lord."

37. Theodore Stanger, "Dade Approves Ordinance Banning Bias Against Homosexuals," *Miami Herald*, January 19, 1977.

38. Morton Lucoff, "Metro Bans Bias against Homosexuals," *Miami News*, January 18, 1977.

39. "Anita Bryant—Call from the Lord."

40. *The Anita Bryant Story*, pp. 26–27; Brake, interview with Fejes, Stonewall National Museum and Archives.

41. Fejes, *Gay Rights and Moral Panic*, pp. 76–77; Brake, interview with Fejes, Stonewall National Museum and Archives.

42. "January 19, 1977: The Day it Snowed in Miami," *Miami Herald*, February 3, 2009.

43. Elinor Brecher and Steve Rothaus, "One-Time Discjockey Bob Green, Anita Bryant's Husband During the 1977 Gay-Rights Battle, Dies at 80," *Miami Herald*, February 26, 2012.

44. Joel Greenberg, "Singer Opens Drive to Repeal Gay Law, *Miami Herald*, February 12, 1977.

45. "Anita Bryant—Call from the Lord."

46. David W. Hacker, "Anita Bryant Tells Why She's Against Gay Rights," *The National Observer*, March 12, 1977.

CHAPTER 19: HOW TO LOSE A BATTLE

1. Shack, interview with author.

2. Morton Lucoff, "Metro Bans Bias Against Homosexuals," *Miami News*, January 18, 1977.

3. Monteagudo, interview with author. Monteagudo, who had been an early member of the coalition, recalls that the coalition "had no idea that the opposition was organizing" after the January hearing. See also his article "Anita and I: An Activist's Memoir," *Weekly News* (Miami), October 29, 1997.

4. *Miami Herald*, June 6, 1977.

5. *Miami Herald*, May 8, 1977.

6. Anita Bryant, *The Anita Bryant Story*, p. 117.

7. United Press International, "County in Florida Has Sex Problem," *Valley Morning Star* (Harlingen, TX), March 27, 1977, p. 20.

8. Associated Press, "Miami Split over Gay Rights," *Gastonia (NC) Gazette*, May 29, 1977, p. 7.

9. *The Anita Bryant Story*, p. 111.

10. John Arnold, "Dade Will Be Gay-Rights Battlefield," *Miami Herald*, April 20, 1977.

11. "Gay Rights Showdown in Miami," *Time*, June 13, 1977.

12. Knight News Service, "Countdown for Bryant's Anti-Gay War," *San Francisco Chronicle*, June 5, 1977.

13. B. Drummond Ayres Jr., "Miami Debate Over Rights of Homosexuals Directs Wide Attention to a National Issue," *New York Times*, May 10, 1977; and "Askew Would Vote No," *Miami Herald*, May 30, 1977.

14. Richard Cohen, "A Sober Note on the Gay Issue," *Washington Post* column reprinted in *Chicago Sun-Times*, June 6, 1977; and Richard Cohen, "Merit Badge for Bigotry?" *Washington Post*, July 18, 2012.

15. "Dade Will Be Gay-Rights Battlefield."

16. Monteagudo, interview with author.

17. Edda Cimino, interviews with author, Miami, October 14, 2012, and (telephone), November 16, 2012.

18. David W. Hacker, "Anita Bryant Tells Why She's Against Gay Rights," *National Observer,* March 12, 1977.

19. Monteagudo, interview with author; and Kunst, interview with author. The coalition joined the orange juice boycott *after* it lost at the ballot box and the amendment was repealed: "Florida Oranges Hit by National Boycott," *Palm Beach (FL) Post,* July 31, 1977.

20. Kurst, interview with author.

21. Jack Nichols, interview with Paul D. Cain. I am grateful to Mr. Cain for sharing the transcribed interview with me.

22. Kunst, interview with author.

23. Monteagudo, interview with author.

24. Associated Press, "Miami Split over Gay Rights," *Gastonia (NC) Gazette,* May 29, 1977, p. 7; and Bill Hutchinson and James R. Kukar, "Kunst/Bryant: Caught in the Middle," *Miami,* May 1977.

25. Monteagudo, interview with author.

26. George Mendenhall, "Miami Post-Mortem: Lessons from Losing—Four Perspectives of Dade County," *Advocate,* August 24, 1977.

27. David Goodstein, "Opening Space," *Advocate,* April 20, 1977.

28. Monteagudo, interview with author.

29. Cimino, interview with author; and Campbell, interview with Fejes.

30. John O'Brien, second interview with author, Los Angeles, July 26, 2012.

31. Sears, *Rebels, Rubyfruit, and Rhinestones,* p. 373.

32. O'Brien, second interview with author; and Sears, *Rebels, Rubyfruit, and Rhinestones,* pp. 241–42.

33. Paul D. Cain interview with Jack Campbell, November 26, 1994. I am grateful to Mr. Cain for sharing the transcribed interview with me.

34. Goodstein, "Opening Space."

35. Campbell, interview with Cain; and Fred Fejes interview with Campbell.

36. Ethan Geto, interview with author, New York, March 20, 2014. DeMilly came with Geto to Miami as his business partner.

37. Fred Fejes, *Gay Rights and Moral Panic: The Origins of America's Debate on Homosexuality* (New York: Palgrave, 2008), p. 119. The coalition was able to get public support from a few celebrities such as Jane Fonda and Rod McKuen.

38. Nicole Murray Ramirez, Grand Empress (emerita) of the transgender Imperial Court, says that the first money sent from California for the anti-Bryant campaign came out of a "drag ball": "We were having a coronation, and I got up at the mic," she recalls. "I told everyone there, 'A storm cloud is brewing across America. It's a black storm with thunderbolts aimed at the gay community. We're going to have to contend with this soon in California. It will sweep the nation. I

don't care if you can only give a dime, but *give*.' We passed the hat, and we raised thousands and thousands of dollars that we sent off to Miami." Nicole Murray Ramirez, interview with author, San Diego, June 29, 2012.

39. Geto, interview with author.
40. Kunst, interview with author.
41. "Anita Bryant—Call from the Lord."
42. Ibid.
43. Fejes, *Gay Rights and Moral Panic*, p. 97.
44. "GAA Launches Florida Citrus Boycott," *Gay Activist*, November/December 1977.
45. Perry, interview with author.
46. Love, interview with author.
47. Joe Baker, "Miami," *Advocate*, July 13, 1977.
48. *Advocate*, August 24, 1977, pp. 7–8. Geto recognized soon after the campaign that he and Foster "made the mistake of talking about abstract values, never putting a human face on it and never showing how this discrimination affects people": Geto, interview with author.
49. Campbell, interview with Paul Cain.
50. Monteagudo, "Anita and I."
51. Jesse Monteagudo, email correspondence with author, October 15, 2012.
52. "The Battle for Gay Rights," *Newsweek*, June 6, 1977, pp. 16–26.
53. Joe Baker, "Miami."
54. Cimino, interview with author; and Ardith Hilliard, "Battle Lines Drawn: Nation Awaits Gay Rights Verdict," *St. Petersburg (FL) Times*, June 6, 1977, p. 16.
55. Letter to Neil Rogers, March 21, 1977, in Robert Basker Collection (unprocessed), ONE National Gay and Lesbian Archives, University of Southern California Libraries. The violence was also physical: a man aimed a shotgun at Jim Foster's head and threatened to blow his brains out; Ethan Geto and Michelle DeMilly were sitting in campaign headquarters one evening when someone threw a Molotov cocktail through the window: Geto, interview with author.
56. Monteagudo, "Anita and I."
57. The irony would have been lost on these callers. B. Ruby Rich and Lourdes Arguelles quote Cuban émigrés as saying, "The only good thing about Castro is that he got rid of homosexuals," in "Homosexuality, Homophobia, and Revolution: Notes Toward an Understanding of the Cuban Lesbian and Gay Male Experience, Part 2," *Signs* 11, no. 1 (Autumn 1985): pp. 120–36.
58. Monteagudo, "Anita and I," and interview with author.
59. "First Victim of Bryant Crusade," *Bay Area Reporter*, March 31, 1977. See also Fejes, p. 129; and Rich and Arguelles.
60. "Enough! Enough! Enough!," *Time*, June 20, 1977, p. 69.
61. Monteagudo, interview with author; and Geto, interview with author.
62. United Press International, "'Gay Rights' Vote in Last-Ditch Battle," *Chicago Tribune*, June 6, 1977.
63. Ibid.; and "Ten Thousand Rally for Repeal," *Miami Herald*, May 23, 1977.

64. San Francisco mayor George Moscone was outraged at Save Our Children's slander of his city. He retorted, "We are proud that in San Francisco we know the meaning of the great American melting pot and that we have learned to live with our neighbors, regardless of the color of their skin, their economic status, their religious beliefs, or their sexual preference": "Moscone: Miami Voted on Issue That is Wrong," *San Francisco Examiner*, June 8, 1977.

65. "Dade Defeats Gay Rights Bill," *St. Petersburg Times*, June 8, 1977.

66. David Holmberg, "High Turnout Expected for Gay Rights Vote," *Miami News*, June 6, 1977.

67. Shack, interview with author.

68. David Holmberg, "Where Did the Liberals Go on the Gay Rights Issue?" *Miami News*, June 9, 1977.

69. Dr. Bobby Wright, director of Garfield Park Comprehensive Mental Health Center, quoted in *The Anita Bryant Story*, pp. 34–35.

70. Correspondence from Dade County Coalition for Human Rights administrative assistant Leanne Seibert to all office staff Regarding Victory Party 6/7/77: Robert Basker Collection, ONE National Gay and Lesbian Archives, University of Southern California Libraries.

71. Joe Baker, "Miami."

72. "Dade Defeats Gay Rights Bill."

73. "Enough! Enough! Enough!," p. 69.

74. Ibid.

75. "Dade Defeats Gay Rights Bill."

CHAPTER 20: GRAPPLING WITH DEFEAT

1. See chapter 31, note 2, regarding attempts by same-sex couples in the early and mid-1970s to marry.

2. "Gay Bills Pass Both Chambers," *Florida Times-Union* (Jacksonville), June 1, 1977. The Bryant antigay campaign influenced other state legislatures, too. In Arkansas, sodomy laws had been repealed in 1975. During the Dade County campaign, the Arkansas House of Representatives formally commended Anita Bryant, and on March 17, 1977, the legislature voted to reinstate sodomy laws.

3. *Journal of the Florida Senate*, May 11, 1977, pp. 370–71.

4. United Press International, "Florida Senate Votes Gay Marriage Ban," *Wisconsin State Journal*, May 10, 1977, p. 16.

5. "Denies Ban on Anita's OJ Commercials," *News Tribune* (Fort Pierce, FL), June 22, 1977.

6. "Florida Citrus Group Retains Anita Bryant," *New York Times*, July 20, 1977.

7. Associated Press, "Reluctant Citrus Unit Backs Anita," *Panama City (FL) News Herald*, November 17, 1977.

8. "Citrus Board Backs Anita," *News Tribune* (Fort Pierce, FL), November 17, 1977. The boycott continued, and sales of Florida orange juice plummeted so markedly that in 1979 the Citrus Commission gave up and allowed Bryant's contract to lapse.

The Florida orange growers then hired lawyers who argued all the way to the state Supreme Court that Florida identification should not be required on their product labels because "they did not want their product tied too closely to Miss Bryant": Associated Press, "People in the News," *Frederick (MD) News Post*, February 29, 1980.

9. United Press International, "Anita Bryant Says Homosexuals Lost Her Show," *El Paso (TX) Herald Post*, February 25, 1977.

10. Ibid.

11. Sears, *Rebels, Rubyfruit, and Rhinestones*, p. 236.

12. Letter from Joseph B. Flavin, chief executive officer of Singer Sewing Machines responding to Bryant supporters, March 9, 1977, in Robert Basker Collection (unprocessed), ONE National Gay and Lesbian Archives, University of Southern California Libraries. Despite Flavin's assurances, the series never aired.

13. Associated Press, "Anita Bryant to Stay Home Unless . . ." *Gadsden (AL) Times*, June 13, 1977.

14. Nathaniel Sheppard Jr., "After Repeal of Homosexual Bias Law, St. Paul Debates Implications," *New York Times*, April 27, 1978: First-term councilwoman Joanne Showalter observed, "The city has become divided over an issue it didn't even know it had until three months ago."

15. Angwin quoted in Clendinen and Nagourney, *Out for Good*, p. 327.

16. Nathaniel Sheppard Jr., "Measure Prohibited Discrimination on the Basis of Sexual Preference," *New York Times*, April 28, 1978.

17. United Press International, "Gay Rights Fought," *Radford (VA) News Journal*, April 30, 1978.

18. Fred Fejes, *Gay Rights and Moral Panic: The Origins of America's Debate on Homosexuality* (New York: Palgrave, 2008), p. 172.

19. Bryant canceled at the last minute claiming illness, but it is likely that she was worried about threats from the gay community. Authorities had announced that "normal precautions at the auditorium would be augmented by St. Paul police reserve units": United Press International, "Anita Bryant Hits the Campaign Trail," *Salina (KS) Journal*, April 19, 1978.

20. Sheppard, *New York Times*.

21. "Gay Rights Law Repealed in St. Paul," *Minnesota Daily*, April 28, 1978.

22. United Press International, "Preacher Fights Gays, Says Lifestyle is Immoral," *Santa Fe (NM) New Mexican,* April 28, 1978; and "Wichita Repeals Homosexual Law," *New York Times*, May 10, 1978.

23. Quoted in Fejes, p. 174.

24. "Rights Ordinance Gets a Setback," *Cincinnati Post*, April 24, 1978.

25. Tim Graham and Mike Graham, "City's Gay Rights Proposal Gets Strong Response; Anita's Waiting for Fight," *Cincinnati Post*, November 1, 1978.

26. The gay-and-lesbian-organized efforts to fight repeal in St. Paul, Wichita, and Eugene are discussed in Fejes, pp. 170–76, and Clendinen and Nagourney, pp. 323–28.

27. Eric Hoffer, *The True Believer: Thoughts on the Nature of Mass Movements* (1951; rpt. New York: Harper, 2002), p. 86.

28. "Thousands of Homosexuals March in Demonstration for Equal Rights," *New York Times*, June 27, 1977.

29. "San Francisco Gay Pride Parade," *Oakland Tribune*, June 25, 1977.

30. "Flags Honor Slain Homosexual," *New York Times*, June 25, 1977.

31. Shilts, *Mayor of Castro Street*, p. 163.

32. Ibid.

33. Shortly after Hillsborough's murder, the Save the Children Foundation, a Connecticut-based group that raised money for underprivileged children, sued Anita Bryant to stop calling her organization Save Our Children. A federal judge found in the foundation's favor, and Bryant changed the name of her group to Protect America's Children: "Anti-Homosexual Group Barred from Use of Name," *New York Times*, July 16. 1977.

34. "Mother of Slain Gay Sues Anita Bryant," *San Francisco Chronicle*, July 1, 1977. Robert Brake, the Miami lawyer who masterminded the petition to repeal the Dade County amendment, filed a motion on behalf of Bryant and Green to dismiss the case on the grounds of "lack of jurisdiction" in California. The judge agreed, and the case was dismissed: Robert Brake, interview with Fred Fejes, transcribed, May 28, 1997, Stonewall National Museum and Archives, Fort Lauderdale, FL.

35. Associated Press, "Miami Split over Gay Rights," *Gastonia (NC) Gazette*, May 29, 1977.

36. United Press International, "Gays' Walkout Makes Anita Bryant Cry," *Kingsport (TN) News*, June 10, 1977; "Anita Weeps as Gays Heckle Her," *Chicago Tribune*, June 10, 1977.

37. United Press International, "Gay Rights Activists Tune Up for Anita Bryant Protests," *News Tribune* (Fort Pierce, FL), June 19, 1977.

38. "1,800 Demonstrate Against Singer Here," *Atlanta Constitution*, June 12, 1978.

39. United Press International, "Bryant Accused at Church Service," *The New Mexican* (Santa Fe, NM), June 23, 1978.

40. Associated Press, "Gay Protesters Hounding Anita," *Bee* (Danville, VA), June 16, 1977.

41. "Gay Rights Activists Tune Up for Anita Bryant Protests"; and Hill, interview with author.

42. "Militant Gays Force Anita Bryant to Flee New York," *Gay Activist*, November/December 1977, p. 1.

43. "Anita Bryant Leaves New York Because of Threats on Her Life," *Citizen* (Ottawa, Canada), November 3, 1977.

44. Associated Press, "Anita Bryant: I'm Not Afraid to Continue Fighting," *Danville (VA) Register*, November 3, 1977.

45. *National Lampoon*, May 1977.

46. "The Gaycott Turns Ugly," *Time*, November 22, 1977, p. 55.

47. George Vecsey, "Secular Bookings Off, Anita Bryant Sings at Revivals," *New York Times*, February 21, 1978.

48. Ibid.

49. Green quoted in Associated Press, "Dade County Musters Little Enthusiasm for Gay Rights Again," *Courier News* (Blytheville, AR), October 24, 1978.

50. Anita Bryant Ministries Letter: Starr-PFLAG Collection, box 1, folder 21, ONE National Gay and Lesbian Archives, University of Southern California Libraries.

51. After her divorce, Bryant was interviewed in the *Ladies' Home Journal*, where she complained not only that her marriage had been bad from the start but also that the fundamentalist church was "sick" and cruel in its treatment of women. "There are some valid reasons why militant feminists are doing what they're doing," she said. Even more remarkable, Bryant announced in this interview that she'd had a change of heart toward gay people: she was now opposed to the fundamentalists' "personal vendetta about gays," and she claimed that she herself had become "more inclined to say live and let live": Cliff Jahr, "Anita Bryant's Startling Revelation," *Ladies' Home Journal*, December 1980, pp. 60–68.

52. Knight Ridder News Service, Barry Bearak, "Mutiny from the Bountiful: Who Squeezed Anita?," *Lakeland (FL) Ledger*, June 16, 1980.

CHAPTER 21: LEARNING HOW TO WIN

1. Author's second interview with Jeanne Córdova, Los Angeles, December 22, 2012.

2. See pp. 444–46.

3. Sharon McDonald, "9,500 March Against Bryant," *Lesbian Tide*, July/August 1977.

4. "State Senate Defeats Pro-Anita Resolution," *Daily Review* (Hayward, CA), June 16, 1977. See 715n2 for Arkansas's laudatory resolution.

5. Ibid.

6. Eskridge, *Dishonorable Passions*, p. 199.

7. Hayward, "State Senate Defeats Pro-Anita Resolution."

8. Cheryl Clark, "State Braces for Gay Rights Fight," *The Modesto Bee*, June 26, 1977, p. A12. In 1975 Briggs introduced a bill into the assembly that would have short-circuited the attempt to lift the California sodomy law. The bill, AB 2347, would have made sodomy and oral copulation legal only when committed by a man and wife. It was referred to the Committee on Criminal Justice on May 20, 1975, and it died in committee.

9. Randy Shilts cites a friendly encounter between Briggs and Harvey Milk, which led Milk to conclude that Briggs's antigay campaign was nothing but "a big joke" to Briggs: *Mayor of Castro Street*, p. 248.

10. In Ellen Goodman, "Proposition Fever," *Boston Globe*, September 28, 1978.

11. Clark, "State Braces for Gay Rights Fight."

12. Briggs petition drive flyer, "The California Legislature Refuses to Ban Openly Practicing Homosexual Teachers from Our Schools," Jim Gaylord's private collection, Olympia, WA. I am grateful to Mr. Gaylord for sharing this material with me.

13. Gallup poll quoted in "Should Homosexuals Be Allowed to Teach?" *McCall's*, March 1978.

14. Briggs had originally hoped to qualify his proposition for the June 1978 ballot, thinking it would bolster his votes for governor; but the petition was disqualified

because of a typographical error, and Briggs had to resubmit signatures in order to qualify for the November election.

15. Quoted in Peter Calamai, "After Tax Revolts, Morality by Referendum?" *Medicine Hat News* (Alberta, Canada), November 6, 1978.

16. "Homosexual Money" in Save Our Teachers Collection, no. 918, folder 12, Lambda Archives, San Diego.

17. "Protect Our Children" flyer in Save Our Teachers Collection, no. 918, folder 6, Lambda Archives, San Diego.

18. Randy Shilts, "The Life and Death of Harvey Milk," *Christopher Street*, March 1979, pp. 34–36. Shilts's book *Mayor of Castro Street* expands this article.

19. Quoted in Michael Ward and Mark Freeman, "Defending Gay Rights: The Campaign Against the Briggs Initiative in California," *Radical America* 13, no. 4 (July/August 1979): p. 16.

20. Ward and Freeman, "Defending Gay Rights," p. 13.

21. Shilts, *Mayor of Castro Street*, p. 222.

22. Ibid., pp. 70–77. Milk had no history of gay activism before he declared his candidacy, Foster insisted, telling Milk, "You don't get to dance unless you put up the chairs. I've never seen you put up the chairs," and "We take converts but we don't make them Pope the same day," ibid.

23. Cleve Jones, interview with author, San Francisco, April 12, 2013.

24. Ibid.

25. Sally Gearhart, interviews with author, Willits, CA, January 27 and 28, 2013; also Sally Gearhart eulogy for Harvey Milk, November 29, 1978, Temple Emanuel, San Francisco. I am grateful to Professor Gearhart for sharing this material with me.

26. Gearhart, interviews with author.

27. *Milk*, the 2008 biographical film about Harvey Milk, elided Sally Gearhart's important participation in San Franciscans Against Prop 6. Forty years after the campaign, the omission had the power to trigger angry protest among lesbians who accused Dustin Lance Black, the film's gay screenwriter and executive producer, of reverting to old gay male treachery.

28. Shilts, *Mayor of Castro Street*, p. 245.

29. Immediately after his election victory, Harvey Milk told the *New York Times*, "I represent the gay street people"; but his notion of gay radicalism was different from that of the gay "street people" such as those who'd been in the Gay Liberation Front. "Gay street people," Milk said in the same interview, "need a piece of the pie." He was seemingly oblivious to their conviction that the whole pie was rotten and needed to be thrown out: Herbert Gold, "A Walk on San Francisco's Wild Side," *New York Times*, November 6, 1977.

30. Save Our Teachers Collection, no. 918, folder 6, Lambda Archives, San Diego.

31. Ibid.

32. Diane Ehrensaft and Ruth Milkman, "Sexuality and the State: The Defeat of the Briggs Initiative and Beyond—An Interview with Amber Hollibaugh," *Socialist Review* 9, no. 3 (May/June 1979).

33. Ibid; and Michael Ward and Mark Freeman, "Defending Gay Rights: The Campaign Against the Briggs Initiative in California," *Radical America* 13, no. 4: July/ August 1979.

34. David Mixner, *Stranger Among Friends* (New York: Bantam, 1977), p. 143.

35. "Los Angeles Launches Drive for Gay Rights Ordinance!," *Lesbian Tide*, July/ August 1977.

36. Perry, interview with author.

37. "Troy Perry Fasts Against Bigotry," *AGN* (Tucson), September 23, 1977, p. 1.

38. Perry, interview with author; and "16-Day Fast: Reverend Troy Perry Gets $107,000 in Pledges," *Advocate*, November 2, 1977, p. 34.

39. Mixner, interview with author.

40. Ibid.

41. Ibid.

42. Save Our Teachers Collection, folder 6, Lambda Archives, San Diego.

43. "One Hell of a Campaign—and We Won!" *Southern California Women for Understanding Newsletter*, November/December 1978, SCWU Collection, June Mazer Lesbian Collection, Special Collections, UCLA.

44. Bottini, interview with author; and Mixner, interview with author.

45. Mixner, *Stranger Among Friends*, p. 146.

46. Mixner, interview with author.

47. Ibid. Pro-gay African American congressman Julian Dixon offered to donate furniture to the new headquarters, and Mixner hired a truck to pick it up. But when the furniture was unloaded, it was deemed "hideous" by Peter Scott and Gayle Wilson. Wilson enlisted two interior decorator friends, who convinced the Los Angeles and Beverly Hills design communities to donate attractive chairs, sofas, and decorative art to the campaign. It was widely agreed that the Los Angeles No on 6 office was the most beautiful political headquarters in history: Mixner, interview with author.

48. Córdova, second interview with author.

49. See p. 233.

50. Bottini, interview with author.

51. Quoted in Jeanne Córdova, "Teachers May Face Initiative," *Lesbian Tide*, September/October 1977.

52. Bottini, interview with author.

53. Córdova, second interview with author. Córdova also wrote to Morris Kight to assure him that "in the civil rights arena" coalition work "obviously with gay men" is a "top priority": Jeanne Córdova to Morris Kight, letter, May 31, 1978, Morris Kight Papers, Collection 2010-008, box 2, folder 1, ONE National Gay and Lesbian Archives, University of Southern California Libraries.

54. Robin Podolsky, interview with author, Los Angeles, April 6, 2004.

55. Aaron Goldstein, "Reagan and Milk: Who Did More to Stop Proposition 6?" *American Spectator*, February 26, 2009.

56. Mixner, interview with author.

57. Ibid.; and Stuart Timmons interview with Mixner, Los Angeles, September 4, 2005: Faderman and Timmons, *Gay L.A.*, pp. 227–28.

58. Sidney Crocker to Morris Kight, letter, July 24, 1978, Morris Kight Papers, Collection 2010-008, box 2, folder 1, ONE National Gay and Lesbian Archives, University of Southern California Libraries.

59. Mixner, interview with author.

60. Richard West, "Prop. 6 Dangerous, Reagan Believes," *Los Angeles Times*, September 23, 1978.

61. Bottini quoted in "One Hell of a Campaign."

62. Ehrensaft and Milkman, "Sexuality and the State," p. 2.

63. O'Brien, second interview with author, July 26, 2012.

64. United Press International, "Seattle Anti-Gay Fight: Cherished Ideals," *Altoona (PA) Mirror*, August 8, 1978.

65. "Officers Attack Gay Rights," *Walla Walla (WA) Evening Bulletin*, August 8, 1978.

66. By now, Bryant's new agent, Jackie Lee, was trying to disassociate Bryant from her connection to antihomosexual campaigns and to find her paying jobs. When news got out that Estes had issued the invitation, Lee told reporters, "Money has not been discussed . . . When Anita finds out more about the initiative out there, she may not want to go": Associated Press, "Bryant Receives Invitation," *Wilmington (NC) Morning Star*, March 3, 1978.

67. Radio ad sponsored by Save Our Moral Ethics, week of July 17–20, 1978, in Charles Brydon Collection, MS 63, box 10, folder 5, Washington State Historical Society Archives, Tacoma.

68. "Seattle Anti-Gay Fight."

69. Gary Atkins, *Gay Seattle: Stories of Exile and Belonging* (Seattle: University of Washington Press, 2003), p. 207.

70. Charlie Brydon, interview with author, New Westminister, Canada (Skype), July 1, 2012.

71. Ibid.

72. Transcript of Randy Henson interview with Roger Winters and Larry Knopp, Northwest Lesbian and Gay History Museum Project, Seattle, Washington, August 13, 2003. I am grateful to Ruth Pettis for calling this material to my attention.

73. "Ready When You Are, Anita: Brydon versus Bryant," *Seattle Weekly*, June 29–July 5, 1977.

74. Women Against Thirteen, "Anti-13 Actions and the Media," *Out and About*, August 1978, p. 8; and Jane Meyerding and Betty Johanna, "To Reach Beyond Words," *Out and About*, September 1978, p. 11.

75. Jane Meyerding, interview with Ruth Pettis (transcript), February 22, 1997, Northwest Lesbian and Gay History Museum Project.

76. Reprinted in the Seattle lesbian-feminist newsletter founded and edited by Jane Meyerding, "So Many Lives Have Been Lost," *Out and About*, July 1978, pp. 15–18.

77. Jane Meyerding and Betty Johanna, "To Reach Beyond Words," *Out and About*, September 1978, p. 8.

78. Jane Meyerding and Betty Johanna, "Blood on SOME: Thank You," *Out and*

About, August 1978, p. 3; and Johanna and Meyerding, "To Reach Beyond Words," pp. 8–11.

79. Randy Henson interview, Northwest Lesbian and Gay History Museum Project.
80. Associated Press, "Fatal Shooting of Suspect Defended by Police Chief," *Spokesman-Review* (Spokane, WA), August 22, 1978; and "Police Shot Victim Said Retarded," *Spokane (WA) Daily Chronicle,* August 23, 1978.
81. Denys Howard, "Seattle Retains Rights in Major Election Win," *Gaysweek,* November 8, 1978.
82. Ibid.; and Brydon interview in Eric Marcus, *Making Gay History: The Half-Century Fight for Lesbian and Gay Equal Rights* (New York: HarperCollins, 2002), p. 217.

CHAPTER 22: OF MARTYRS AND MARCHES

1. "Kathy Kozachenko," *Ann Arbor (MI) Sun,* March 22, 1974; and Glen Harris, "GOP Retains an Edge on City Council," *Ann Arbor (MI) News,* April 2, 1974, p. 1.
2. "Vote Scope," *Ann Arbor Sun,* March 22, 1974.
3. "Repubs Vote Big Mac," *Ann Arbor Sun,* February 22, 1974.
4. "$5 Tokes Triumph in A2, Colburn Crushed, HRP Squeaks By," *Ann Arbor Sun,* April 5, 1974.
5. Noble inspired Allen Spear, a gay man elected to the Minnesota State Senate in 1972, to come out two years later: "State Sen. Allan Spear Declares He's Homosexual," *Minneapolis Star,* December 1, 1974; and Elaine Noble, interview with David O'Brian, in "People, Politicians, and the Great Oz," *Advocate,* June 4, 1975. Spear won his reelection bids until he retired in 2000.
6. Mixner and Bailey, *Brave Journeys,* p. 91.
7. Elaine Noble, interview with author, Santa Rosa Beach, FL (telephone), September 29, 2012.
8. Eric Sauter, "Homosexual Legislator Ran on Dignity-for-All Platform," *Miami Herald,* November 8, 1974.
9. Quoted in Clendinen and Nagourney, *Out for Good,* p. 223.
10. Allen Young, "Noble Wins: First Open Gay in Legislature," *Advocate,* December 4, 1974.
11. Noble, interview with O'Brian, in "People, Politicians, and the Great Oz."
12. Associated Press, "Gay About Victory," *Star News* (Pasadena, CA), November 8, 1974; and "Wins on a Gay Ticket," *Biloxi (MS) Daily Herald,* November 7, 1974.
13. Noble, interview with author.
14. Quoted in Mixner and Bailey, *Brave Journeys,* p. 93.
15. Noble, interview with author; and Elaine Noble, interview with Larry Nichols, in *Windy City Times,* October 10, 2007. Fury at Noble was amplified because she also supported busing to end de facto school segregation.
16. Mixner and Bailey, *Brave Journeys,* pp. 97–98; and Elaine Noble, email correspondence with author, January 19, 2015.
17. Noble, interview with author.
18. Kronenberg married a man in 1986 but has continued to be active in gay and lesbian causes.

19. Jones, interview with author.
20. Film documentary *The Times of Harvey Milk*, produced and directed by Richard Schmeichen and Rob Epstein, 1984.
21. Shilts, "Life and Death of Harvey Milk," p. 37.
22. Paul D. Cain interview with Cleve Jones. I thank Mr. Cain for sharing a transcript of this interview with me.
23. Milk had been unpopular with mainstream gay political leaders such as Jo Daly, Jim Foster, Rick Stokes, and David Goodstein, who thought him too loud and too precipitous in seeking office (see note 22 on p. 719); in his taped will, he also named those he opposed as his successors (who would have been favored by the mainstream leaders): Scott Anderson, "A City Grieves Good Men Slain," *Advocate*, January 11, 1979.
24. Jones, interview with author.
25. Opening remarks of Douglas Schmidt, White's defense attorney: transcript is in Kenneth W. Salter, *The Trial of Dan White* (El Cerrito: Market and Systems Interface, 1991).
26. The most complete depiction of Dan White and his murder of Harvey Milk and George Moscone is Mike Weiss's *Double Play: The San Francisco City Hall Killings* (Reading, MA: Addison-Wesley, 1984). A 2010 edition, with a new subtitle, *The Hidden Passions Behind the Assassination of George Moscone and Harvey Milk*, includes a DVD of White's confession and several television interviews.
27. Film documentary *Times of Harvey Milk*.
28. John Geluardi, "Dan White's Motive: More About Betrayal than Homosexuality," *SF Weekly*, January 30, 2008.
29. "Gay Rights Law OK'd by Supervisors," *San Francisco Chronicle*, March 21, 1977.
30. Les Ledbetter, "Bill on Homosexual Rights Advances in San Francisco," *New York Times*, March 22, 1978.
31. Ledbetter, "Bill on Homosexual Rights Advances in San Francisco"; and film documentary *Times of Harvey Milk*.
32. *Times of Harvey Milk*.
33. Lenny Giteck, "Milk: Up-Front and Committed," *Advocate*, January 11, 1979.
34. Ramirez, interview with author.
35. Sasha Gregory-Lewis, "Milk Gets Canned But Keeps on Running," *Advocate*, April 7, 1976.
36. Duffy Jennings, "Several Jurors Weep in Court," *San Francisco Chronicle*, May 22, 1979, pp. 1, 18.
37. Willie Brown, *Basic Brown: My Life and Our Times* (New York: Simon & Schuster, 2008), p. 130; and "Brown Remembers Close Call on Tragic Day," *San Francisco Chronicle*, November 18, 2008, A21.
38. Shilts, *Mayor of Castro Street*, p. 272.
39. Transcript of Daniel White's taped confession, November 27, 1978, 12:05, "People's exhibit 54 in the trial of Daniel White."
40. Christian Arthur Bain, "A Short History of Lesbian and Gay Labor Activism in the United States," in *Laboring for Rights: Unions and Sexual Diversity*

Across Nations, ed. Gerald Hunt (Philadelphia: Temple University Press, 1999), pp. 63–64.

41. Jones, interview with author.

42. Ibid.

43. Ibid.

44. Tom Ammiano, interview in film documentary *Times of Harvey Milk.*

45. Proposition 7, authored by John Briggs, expanded the list of "special circumstances" that warranted the death penalty. Seventy-one percent of the California electorate voted in its favor, in the same November 1978 election in which they rejected the Briggs initiative on homosexual teachers.

46. Paul Krassner, "On the Scene at the Dan White Trial," *San Francisco Bay Guardian,* May 17, 1978, p. 5.

47. Jim Wood, "Heavy Strategy Behind White's Light Sentence," *San Francisco Examiner,* May 22, 1979, pp. 1, 14.

48. Transcript of Daniel White's taped confession.

49. Transcripts of trial testimonies are published in Salter, *Trial of Dan White.*

50. Duffy Jennings, "Several Jurors Weep in Court."

51. White would serve only five years of his sentence. He was released from prison on January 7, 1984. He committed suicide on October 22, 1985.

52. "The Shocked Jurors Defend Their Verdict," May 23, 1979, *San Francisco Chronicle,* p. 7.

53. Jones, interview with author.

54. Ibid.; Katy Butler, "A Bloody Protest at City Hall," *San Francisco Chronicle,* May 22, 1979, pp. 1, 18; Katy Butler, "Anatomy of Gay Riot," *San Francisco Chronicle,* May 23, 1979, pp. 1, 14; Mike McWhinney, "Violence Erupts from White Jury Decision," *San Francisco Progress,* p. 1; and Richard Saltus and Peter H. King, "Gay Plea: We Must Keep Cool Tonight," *San Francisco Examiner,* May 22, 1979, p. 14.

55. Jones, interview with author.

56. Gearhart, interview with author; and Saltus and King, "Gay Plea."

57. Jones, interview with author.

58. Warren Hinckle, "How Cops Waded into Castro Street," *San Francisco Chronicle,* May 23, 1979, p. 7.

59. "Britt's 'Gay Anger' at Dan White Verdict," *San Francisco Examiner,* May 22, 1979, p. 2.

60. Anderson, "A City Grieves Good Men Slain."

61. Amin Ghaziani, *The Dividends of Dissent: How Conflict and Culture Work in Lesbian and Gay Marches on Washington* (Chicago: University of Chicago Press, 2008), pp. 43–46.

62. Robin Tyler, second interview with author, North Hills, CA, January 6, 2014; flyer: "Robin Tyler, Feminist Comedienne, in a Benefit for St. Paul's Citizens for Human Rights"; and Joan Lopotko, "Robin Tyler Fights Back," *Lesbian Feminist Organizing Committee Newsletter,* April 22, 1978. I thank Robin Tyler for sharing these materials with me.

63. Committee for the March on Washington, "An Idea Whose Time Has

Come . . . ," 1978: National March on Washington for Lesbian and Gay Rights, Records of 1978–1979, box 1, folder 1, ONE National Gay and Lesbian Archives, University of Southern California Libraries.

64. Tyler, second interview with author.

65. The debate raged in correspondence among March Committee officials Barbara-Jean Metzger, Alisa Balterman, D. J. Munro, Don Bausch-Green, and Jim Hesley, in National March on Washington for Lesbian and Gay Rights, Records of 1978–79, box 1, folder 1, ONE National Gay and Lesbian Archives, University of Southern California Libraries; and Tyler, second interview with author.

66. Joyce Hunter, interview with author, New York, March 11, 2013.

67. Anderson, "A City Grieves Good Men Slain."

68. Steve Ault, interview with author, New York, March 4, 2013.

69. Minutes of the National Conference for the March on Washington, DC, February 23–25, 1979, unprocessed March on Washington file, Botts Collection of LGBT History, Houston.

70. Hunter, interview with author.

71. Perry, interview with author; Tyler, first interview with author; and album *The National March on Washington for Lesbian and Gay Rights*, produced by Jok Church and Adam Ciesielski, Magnus Records, 1979.

72. Jo Thomas, "Estimated 75,000 Parade Through Washington, DC, in Homosexual Rights March," *New York Times*, October 15, 1979. Estimates of the number of marchers were later revised upward to as many as 150,000.

73. "Homosexuals to March," *Cedar Rapids (IA) Gazette*, October 14, 1979.

74. "Gays Rights Supporters March on Washington, *Odessa (TX) American*, October 15, 1979.

75. "75,000 March for National Gay Rights," *Clearfield (PA) Progress*, October 15, 1979.

76. See, e.g., Shilts, *Mayor of Castro Street*, pp. 346, 363, 375, etc.

77. Arlie Scott's speech, reported in "Gays March in DC, Urge Rights Legislation," *Galveston (TX) Daily News*, October 15, 1979.

CHAPTER 23: THE PLAGUE

1. Michael Gottlieb, "Pneumocystis Pneumonia: Los Angeles," *Morbidity and Mortality Weekly Report* 30 (June 5, 1981): pp. 250–52. Dr. Lawrence Mass had written an earlier article about his observations of a mysterious disease among gay men, published May 18, 1981, in the gay paper *New York Native*. But the editor misleadingly titled it "Disease Rumors Largely Unfounded." The CDC's *Morbidity and Mortality Weekly Report* overlooked the cases of five previously healthy New York women, four of them IV drug users, one the sexual partner of an IV drug user; four of the women were heterosexual and one was bisexual: Between 1975 and 1981 all were diagnosed with depressed immune function and pneumocystis carinii pneumonia. By 1982, when their cases were reported in a medical journal, three had died: Henry Masur et al., "Opportunistic Infection in Previously Healthy Women," *Annals of Internal Medicine* 97, no. 4 (October 1, 1982): pp. 533–39.

2. "Kaposi's Sarcoma and Pneumocystis Pneumonia Among Homosexual Men—New York City and California," *Morbidity and Mortality Weekly Report* 30 (July 4, 1981): pp. 306–08.

3. Lawrence K. Altman, "Rare Cancer Seen in 41 Homosexuals," *New York Times*, July 3, 1981.

4. Robin Morantz Henig, "AIDS: A New Disease's Deadly Odyssey," *New York Times Magazine*, February 6, 1983.

5. Patrick J. Buchanan, "Nature Exacts Retribution" (syndicated column), *Roswell (NM) Daily Record*, May 24, 1983, p. 4.

6. Address by Melvin Boozer, Candidate for the Democratic Nomination for Vice President of the United States, Democratic National Convention, New York City, 1980.

7. Buchanan, "Nature Exacts Retribution," p. 7.

8. Transcript of White House Press Briefing, October 15, 1982, Ronald Reagan Presidential Library, quoted in Julie Eilperin, "How Attitudes Toward AIDS Have Changed in the White House and Beyond," *Washington Post*, December 14, 2013. Speakes continued to be jocular about AIDS in 1983 and 1984 press conferences. See Jon Cohen, *Shots in the Dark: The Wayward Search for an AIDS Vaccine* (New York: W. W. Norton, 2001), ch. 1.

9. "Reagan Would Not Ease Stand on Homosexuals," *New York Times*, August 18, 1984. If Senator Jesse Helms can be believed, even after Rock Hudson's death, Reagan was not sympathetic to safe sex practices involving homosexuals. Helms told the Senate that in 1987 he showed the president a comic book that Gay Men's Health Crisis, which had received federal funding for AIDS education, had produced. The comic book pushed the use of condoms by depicting two men being sexual together. Helms said that Reagan "looked at a couple of pages, shook his head, and hit the desk with his fist": Associated Press, "Senate Votes No Promotion of Homosexuality," *Frederick (MD) Post*, October 15, 1987.

10. Henig, "AIDS: A New Disease's Deadly Odyssey."

11. Larry Kramer, "1,112 and Counting," *New York Native*, March 14–27, 1983.

12. Maureen Dowd, "For Victims of AIDS, Support in a Lonely Siege," *New York Times*, December 5, 1983.

13. Interview with Dr. Barbara Starrett, in film documentary *How to Survive a Plague*, directed by David France, 2012.

14. Dowd, "For Victims of AIDS, Support in a Lonely Siege."

15. For a more extensive discussion of AIDS Project Los Angeles and its volunteers, see Faderman and Timmons, *Gay L.A.*, pp. 303–8.

16. Bill Higgins, "Gala AIDS Fundraiser Is Sedate but Still Starry," *Los Angeles Times*, February 16, 1998.

17. Randy Shilts, *And the Band Played On: Politics, People, and the AIDS Epidemic* (New York: St. Martin's Press, 1987), pp. 120–23.

18. Charles Garfield, *Sometimes My Heart Goes Numb: Love and Caregiving in a Time of AIDS* (San Francisco: Jossey-Bass, 1995).

19. "Chavez, UFW Endorse AB-1," *GLLU Unidad*, April/May 1983: pp. 1–2. Cesar

Chavez had also expressed support for San Francisco gays in the 1970s, when Harvey Milk got the board of supervisors to endorse UFW boycotts.

20. Roland Palencia, interview with author, Los Angeles, August 26, 2012.

21. Kramer, "1,112 and Counting."

22. Ibid.

23. John-Manuel Andriote, *Victory Deferred: How AIDS Changed Gay Life in America* (Chicago: University of Chicago Press, 1999), p. 212.

24. Andy Humm, interview with author, New York, March 5, 2013.

25. Larry Kramer, interview with Jonathan Katz, "In Conversation," Brooklyn Museum, December 1, 2011.

26. Phil Miller, interview with Jim Duggins, October 24, 1995, Nephews Project, OHP 95-95, San Francisco GLBT Historical Society.

27. Shilts, *And the Band Played On,* p. 334.

28. Dan Bernstein and Dale Maharidge, "These Are Dangerous Times, Gays Insist," *Sacramento (CA) Bee,* July 20, 1986.

29. William F. Buckley, "Crucial Steps in Combatting the AIDS Epidemic: Identify All Carriers," *New York Times,* March 18, 1986.

30. Less than a month before the election, only 26 percent of voters told pollsters they would vote against Proposition 64; most said they knew nothing about the initiative or were undecided: "Bradley Sees Prop 64 Peril for Minorities," *Los Angeles Times,* October 15, 1986. Proposition 64 lost by a vote of 71 percent to 29 percent after a last-minute blitz effort by the gay community and their friends—though two million Californians did vote in its favor.

31. *New York Post,* October 2, October 7, October 17, November 7, 1985.

32. Amy Bauer, who'd been a member of GLAAD and went on to direct civil disobedience actions for ACT UP, recalls that GLAAD leaders often discouraged Robinson's zaps, protesting, "No, no, no, you can't do that!" but his group would do it anyway: Amy Bauer, interview with Sarah Schulman, transcript, ACT UP Oral History Project, interview 48, March 7, 2004.

33. Michael Petrelis, interview with author, San Francisco (telephone), January 24, 2014.

34. Ibid.

35. Philip M. Boffey, "Homosexuals Applaud Rejection of Mandatory Testing for AIDS," *New York Times,* February 26, 1987. Mainstream gay organizations—National Gay and Lesbian Task Force, Lambda Legal Defense Fund, and Gay Men's Health Crisis—were also present and held a press conference after the convention. The Mobsters zapped them too, shouting in front of reporters that people were dying while the mainstream groups continued to be polite instead of angry: ibid.

36. Petrelis, interview with author.

37. Quoted in David France, "Pictures from a Battlefield," *New York,* April 2, 2012, p. 36.

38. Bill Bahlman, interview with Sarah Schulman, transcript, ACT UP Oral History Project, interview 112, March 10, 2010.

39. Ibid.

40. Maxine Wolfe, interview with Laraine Sommella, in "This Is About People Dying: The Tactics of Early Act Up and Lesbian Avengers in New York City," in *Queers in Space: Communities, Public Places, Sites of Resistance*, eds. Gordon Brett Ingram, Anne-Marie Bouthillette, and Yolanda Retter (Seattle: Bay Press, 1997), p. 412.

41. The mainstream media consistently underestimated the number of marchers: for example, Lena Williams, "200,000 March in Capital to Seek Gay Rights and Money for AIDS," *New York Times*, October 12, 1987; the progressive *In These Times* estimated the number of marchers at over a half million: Anne-Christine d'Adesky, "Gay and Lesbian March Signals New Credibility of Rights Movement," *In These Times*, October 21–27, 1987. Organizers noted that the front of the march left the staging area at the Eclipse at noon and the end of the march didn't arrive at the rally site until more than three hours later, which would indicate there were well over a half million marchers: Michelle Crone, one of the march producers, interview with author, Provincetown, MA (telephone), May 28, 2013; and Karlyn Barker and Linda Wheeler, "Hundreds of Thousands March for Gay Rights," *Washington Post*, October 12, 1987, p. 1.

42. Crone, interview with author; Lena Williams, "600 Gay Demonstrators Arrested at Supreme Court," *New York Times*, October 14, 1987; Karlyn Barker and Linda Wheeler, "Gay Activists Arrested at High Court," *Washington Post*, October 14, 1987, p. 1; and Mike Neufeld, "Gay Rights Activists Move on High Court," *Washington Times*, October 14, 1987, p. 1.

43. Jones, interview with author.

44. James Wentzy, documentary film *Fight Back, Fight AIDS: Fifteen Years of ACT UP*, 2003.

45. Mark Allen, "Why I Think *How to Survive a Plague* Is Going to Be Huge," *Huffington Post*, September 21, 2014.

46. Bauer, interview with Sarah Schulman.

47. Associated Press, "Demonstrators Demand Easier Access to AIDS Drugs," *Daily Herald* (Chicago), October 12, 1988.

48. Ann Northrop, interview with author, New York, March 12, 2013.

49. Ibid.

50. Sean Strub, *Body Counts: A Memoir of Politics, Sex, AIDS, and Survival* (New York: Scribner, 2014), p. 1.

51. Petrelis, interview with author.

52. Strub, *Body Counts*, p. 1.

53. Richard Perez-Feria, "Update: Tom Keane," *Poz*, April/May 1994.

54. Jason DeParle, "111 Held in St. Patrick's AIDS Protest," *New York Times*, December 11, 1989.

55. Northrop, interview with author.

56. Ibid.

57. For example, "AIDS Protestors Enter Sets of Two Newscasts," *New York Times*, January 23, 1991; "AIDS Activists Disrupt CBS, PBS Newscasts," *Los Angeles Times*, January 23, 1991; Associated Press, "'Fight AIDS, Not Arabs,'" *Hutchinson*

(KS) News, January 23, 1991; Associated Press, "AIDS Activists Invade Studios," *Galveston (TX) Daily News,* January 23, 1991.

58. Mark Harrington, with Jim Eigo, David Z. Kirschenbaum, and Dr. Iris Long, *A Glossary of AIDS, Drug Trials, Testing, and Treatment* (New York: ACT UP Outreach Committee, 1988).

59. Associated Press, "Senate Votes No Promotion of Homosexuality," *Frederick (MD) Post,* October 15, 1987.

60. Senate majority leader, Maine Democrat George Mitchell, countered that the government provides money through Medicare to treat people whose smoking caused lung cancer and heart disease, or whose reckless driving caused injury: Associated Press, "Helms Seeking to Block $600 Million AIDS Relief Bill," *Frederick (MD) Post,* May 16, 1990.

61. Associated Press, "Helms Unprotected from AIDS Protestors," *Daily Herald* (Chicago), September 6, 1991; and Sean Strub, "Condomizing Jesse Helms' House," *Huffington Post,* July 17, 2008.

62. Dr. Anthony Fauci, interview with Eli Adashi, "HIV Turns 30: Reflections from Dr. Anthony Fauci of the National Institute of Allergies and Infectious Diseases," *Medscape One-On-One,* June 2, 2011.

63. Jason DeParle, "Rude, Rash, Effective: ACT UP Shifts AIDS Policy," *New York Times,* January 3, 1990.

64. Ibid.

65. Philip J. Hilts, "AIDS Drug's Maker Cuts Price by 20%," *New York Times,* September 19, 1989.

66. Petrelis, interview with author.

67. There was some infighting: for instance, the Treatment and Data Committee broke off from ACT UP and formed the independent Treatment Action Group in 1992, because an ACT UP contingent, led by radical psychologist Maxine Wolfe, accused the committee of neglecting women with AIDS and being too caught up in "traditional U.S. medicine and . . . the capitalist system of profit": Wolfe, interview with Sommella, in "This Is About People Dying," p. 424.

68. Staley quoted in France, *Pictures from a Battlefield,* p. 41.

69. France, *How to Survive a Plague.*

CHAPTER 24: FAMILY VALUES

1. Wayne Sunday, interview with author, New York (telephone), May 16, 2013; Roskoff, interview with author; Geto, interview with author; and Phil Katz, "The Inner Circle Affair," *Gay Activist,* May/June 1972, p. 1.

2. Roskoff, interview with author; and Assistant Director Malone, New York, to Director, FBI, memo, April 20, 1972, Dan Siminoski Collection of FBI Surveillance of Gays and Lesbians, box 1, folder 12, ONE National Gay and Lesbian Archives, University of Southern California Libraries. Roskoff was arrested and charged with "trespassing": Morty Manford to Arthur Evans, letter, June 27, 1972, Morty Manford Papers, box 11, subject file: Arthur Evans, Manuscript and Archives Division, New York Public Library.

3. Les Ledbetter, "Homosexuals File Assault Charges Against Maye and 6 Others," *New York Times*, April 19, 1972.

4. "Mickey Maye Story," *Village Voice*, May 18, 1972.

5. Roskoff, interview with author; and Katz, "Inner Circle Affair."

6. Ethan Geto, interview with author, New York, March 20, 2014; "Manford Says Trial Witness 2nd Assailant," *Advocate*, August 2, 1972; and Randy Wicker, "Manford Efforts May Get Union Official Into Court," *Advocate*, August 30, 1972.

7. Eric Pace, "Official Accuses Maye of Assault," *New York Times*, April 25, 1972.

8. It was Manford who led an unsuccessful suit against the banquet guests who'd assaulted the gay men. Both McCormack and Maye were exonerated in the courts (*In the Matter of Morty Manford, Petitioner, and David McCormack, Respondent*, Criminal Court of the City of New York, November 6, 1972, 72 Misc 2d, 53; and Randy Wicker, "Maye Acquitted: Judges Say Testimony 'Far from Clear,'" *Advocate*, August 2, 1972.) Some GAA members later disputed the extent of Manford's injuries: Wayne Sunday recalled that Manford would show up at some press conferences with a patch on his left eye and at other conferences with a patch on his right eye (Sunday, interview with author). But Ethan Geto vouches that Manford, who was his roommate, was "unconscious and bloody," and that he himself took Manford by cab to St. Luke's Hospital to be treated for his injuries: Geto, interview with author; and draft letter to the editor, November 18, 1974, "Michael's Thing," Morty Manford Papers, box 23, subject file: Ethan Geto, Manuscript and Archives Division, New York Public Library. The assaults and the lawsuit were covered extensively by New York media.

9. Jeanne Manford, letter to the editor, "A Fair Chance," *New York Post*, April 29, 1972.

10. Ralph Blumenthal, "March Is Staged by Homosexuals," *New York Times*, June 26, 1972. Blumenthal also reported to his millions of readers that Mrs. Manford told him, "I'm proud of my son. I'm not ashamed of him."

11. Newspaper Enterprise Association, Ellie Grossman, "Parents of Gays Groups That Want to Help," July 23, 1979; and "Working Together We Can Make a Change: PFLAG, an Historical Snapshot," p. 2, in Adele Starr PFLAG Collection, box 1, folder 35, ONE National Gay and Lesbian Archives, University of Southern California Libraries.

12. Randy Wicker, "Parents of Gays Organizing," *Gay*, April 23, 1973, in Jeanne Manford Papers, box 1, clippings folder 1, Manuscript and Archives Division, New York Public Library.

13. Memo on Parents of Gays letterhead, June 11, 1977, Morty Manford Papers, box 23, Manuscripts and Archives Division, New York Public Library.

14. Jeanne Manford's speech at the first national congressional briefing and teach-in on Civil Rights of Gay People, quoted in Marcus, *Making Gay History*.

15. The logo paraphrases founding member Sarah Montgomery, the mother of a gay man: in Jeanne Manford Papers, box 1, folder 1, Manuscript and Archives Division, New York Public Library.

16. "Parents of Gays March," *Hutchinson (KS) News*, October 14, 1979.

17. Quoted in obituary: "Adele Starr Dies at 90: Unflagging Gay Rights Activist," *Los Angeles Times*, December 12, 2010.

18. James Brooke, "Colorado Is Engine in Anti-Gay Uproar," *New York Times*, October 11, 1995.

19. Michael Crowley, "James Dobson: The Religious Right's New Kingmaker," *Slate*, November 12, 2004.

20. Paul Cameron, interview with David Parkman, *The David Parkman Show* (syndicated on radio and TV), February 25, 2014.

21. "Our Mission," Family Research Institute home page. Various statewide groups that were "pro-family" and antigay mushroomed too: for instance, the "Illinois Family Association" pledged to protect the "natural family" by fighting same-sex domestic partnerships, and to protect kids who needed adoption or fostering by making sure they weren't placed in "homosexual households." Florida's "American Family Political Committee" had a similar goal: to stop the "homosexual agenda," which included "allowing homosexual couples to adopt children." The purpose of "Concerned Maine Families" was to abolish all city and state ordinances that bestowed any sort of legal protections on homosexuals.

22. Karen Thompson, interview with author, Clearwater, MN (Skype), July 2, 2012. The Sharon Kowalski case is also discussed in two full-length books: Karen Thompson and Julie Andrzejewski, *Why Can't Sharon Kowalski Come Home* (San Francisco: Aunt Lute Books, 1988), and Casey Charles, *The Sharon Kowalski Case: Lesbian and Gay Rights on Trial* (Lawrence: University of Kansas Press, 2003).

23. Thompson, interview with author.

24. Betty Cuniberti, "Just Whose Life Is It? Family and Lover Battle over the Care of a Paralyzed Woman," *Los Angeles Times*, August 5, 1988.

25. Thompson, interview with author.

26. Quoted in Karen D. Thompson, "More Than Same-Sex Marriage: Law, Health, and Defining Family," *Hastings Women's Law Journal* 25, no. 1 (Winter 2014): p. 15.

27. Cuniberti, "Just Whose Life Is It?"

28. Facts of the case and court judgments are in *In Re. Guardianship of Sharon Kowalski*, Appellant Court Case no. C1-85-1502, August 1, 1985; *In Re. Guardianship of Sharon Kowalski*, 382 N.W. 2d (Minn. Ct. App. 1986), cert. denied, 475 US 1085 (1986); *In Re. the Matter of Guardianship of Sharon Kowalski*, Ward no. C2-91-1047 (Minn. Ct. App., Brief and Appendix, August 5, 1991); and Judge Jack Davies, *In Re. Guardianship of Sharon Kowalski, Minnesota Court of Appeals*, 478 N.W. 2d 790, December 17, 1991.

29. During this period, Thompson began a relationship with Patty Bresser, with the understanding that Thompson and Sharon Kowalski were a "package deal"—that Thompson had a lifelong commitment to Kowalski. Bresser agreed to be part of that commitment and participate in Kowalski's care if she were permitted to come home. The three women have lived together since Kowalski's return in 1992: Thompson, interview with author.

30. Tamar Lewin, "Disabled Woman's Care Given to Lesbian Partner," *New York Times*, December 18, 1991.

31. The testimony of Debra Kowalski is summarized in Judge Jack Davies, *In Re. Guardianship of Sharon Kowalski, Minnesota Court of Appeals*, 478 N.W. 2d 790, December 17, 1991.

32. Nadine Brozan, "2 Sides Are Bypassed in Lesbian Case," *New York Times*, April 26, 1991.

33. Thompson, interview with author.

34. *In Re. the Matter of Guardianship of Sharon Kowalski*, Brief and Appendix, August 5, 1991.

35. *In Re. Guardianship of Sharon Kowalski, Minnesota Court of Appeals*, 478 N.W. 2d 790, December 17, 1991.

36. Wallace Turner, "Partnership Law Vetoed on Coast," *New York Times*, December 10, 1982.

37. *Brinkin v. Southern Pacific Transportation Company*, no. A034147, (Cal. Ct. App., 1987).

38. "W. Hollywood to Recognize Non-Married Partnerships," *Los Angeles Times*, February 23, 1985.

39. The state of Hawaii established a domestic partner registry two years earlier, in 1997.

40. Philip S. Gutis, "How to Define a Family: Gay Tenant Fights Eviction," *New York Times*, April 27, 1989.

41. Michael Weber, "Yellow Iris Farm: The Northern New Jersey Retreat of Leslie Blanchard," *Architectural Digest*, June 1986.

42. The Braschi rent-control suit is discussed at length in Carlos A. Ball, *From the Closet to the Courtroom: Five LGBT Rights Lawsuits That Have Changed Our Nation* (Boston: Beacon Press, 2011).

43. *Braschi v. Stahl Associates*, 143 A.D. 2d44, N.Y. App. Div. (1988).

44. *Braschi v. Stahl Associates*, 74 N.Y. 2d201 (1989).

45. Philip S. Gutis, "New York Court Defines Family to Include Homosexual Couples," *New York Times*, July 7, 1989.

46. Bauer quoted in Suzanne Fields, "Protect the Real Meaning of 'Family'" (syndicated), *Daily Herald* (Chicago), July 15, 1989.

47. Miguel Braschi died of AIDS in 1990, but the appeals court's decision in his case was used almost immediately as a precedent to argue other cases in New York. In August 1989 three teachers in New York City sued the New York City Board of Education, claiming that teachers' health care plans must cover their domestic partners. The three couples were teacher Ronald Madson and his partner Richard Deitz; teacher Ruth Berman and her partner Connie Kurtz; and teacher "Jane Doe" and her anonymous partner. The three couples won their suit in the New York State Supreme Court in 1993. Soon after, New York mayor David Dinkins created a "domestic partner registry" as one of his last acts before relinquishing office to Rudolph Giuliani: Ruth Berman and Connie Kurtz, interview with author, Hollywood, FL, October 28, 2012; "They Share Everything but Her Health Benefits," *Doylestown (PA) Intelligencer*, August 16, 1989; Milt Freudenheim, "Rising Worry on 'Partner' Benefits, *New York Times*, August 16, 1989; and Jonathan P.

Hicks, "A Legal Threshold Is Crossed by Gay Couples in New York," *New York Times*, March 2, 1993. In 1998 the New York City Council voted to give domestic partners the same rights and obligations under city law as those given to heterosexual married couples: "Domestic Partners' Banner Day," *Daily News* (New York), June 25, 1998. Ruth Berman and Connie Kurtz were among the first to register for domestic partnership in New York City.

48. Beverly LaHaye, fund-raising letter, 1993, Concerned Women for America, MS 63, box 1, folder 18, Washington State Historical Society Archives.

49. For example, "No Special Rights Committee" materials, Wilsonville, OR, November 13, 1992; and American Family Political Committee of Florida fundraising materials, c. 1992, MS 63, box 1, folder 18, Washington State Historical Society Archives.

50. The phrase was coined by evangelical minister Ted Haggard: James Brooke, "Gay Life Thrives Where Ballot Fight Began," *New York Times*, May 28, 1996. The site of the "Vatican of Evangelical Christians" was a fifty-seven-acre business development for religious organizations. Many of the "Vatican"'s leaders had come to Colorado Springs from California and had worked on the Briggs initiative. (See chapter 21.) Haggard was the pastor of a fourteen-thousand-member megachurch, New Life Church, in Colorado Springs, and headed the thirty-million-member National Association of Evangelicals during the Amendment 2 campaign. When a scandal broke in 2006 involving male prostitute Mike Jones, whom Haggard had paid for sex and crystal methamphetamines during the three preceding years, the pastor was forced to resign from both his church and the NAE: Dan Harris, "Haggard Admits Buying Meth," *ABC News*, November 3, 2006; and Bill Forman, "The Resurrection of Pastor Ted," *Colorado Springs (CO) Independent*, October 1, 2009.

51. Michael Booth, "The Man Who Sold Amendment 2," *Denver Post Magazine*, March 21, 1993, pp. 11–14. To demonstrate the dangers of homosexuals not staying in the closet and the false claims by gay people that homosexuality is genetic, Perkins presented a "cautionary tale" in the interview for this article. When he was an adolescent, he didn't like girls; he liked sports and "liked guys." If a homosexual counselor or acquaintance had told him "You're one of us. That's the way we are," he "could have been into that lifestyle, never having made a conscious decision, and said I was born that way."

52. Booth, "The Man Who Sold Amendment 2."

53. Gay groups such as the Equal Protection Ordinance Coalition in Denver had lobbied to get city councils to add gays and lesbians to nondiscrimination ordinances. The Denver ordinance was passed and then signed by Mayor Federico Pena on October 18, 1990. Right-wingers immediately petitioned to get a referendum on the ballot to repeal it. But in May 1991 Denver residents voted against repeal: Donaciano Martinez (member of the Equal Protection Ordinance Coalition) to Gerald Gerash, letter, June 30, 2008. I am grateful to Mr. Gerash for sharing this material with me.

54. Cara DeGette, "10 Republicans Who've Kept Us in Business," *Colorado Springs (CO) Independent*, August 7, 2003.

55. Dirk Johnson, "Colorado Justices Strike Down a Law Against Gay Rights," *New York Times*, October 12, 1994.

56. Editorial, "Vote Yes on Amendment 2," *Colorado Springs (CO) Gazette*, October 27, 1992; and video, *Romer v. Evans*, produced by Thomas Metzloff et al., Voices of American Law Series, 2008, Duke University School of Law, Durham, NC. The other major leaders in Colorado for Family Values were David Noebel, head of Summit Ministries, who'd written a 1977 book, *The Homosexual Revolution*, which tied homosexuality to Communism, atheism, and pedophilia; and Tony Marco, a direct-mail fund-raiser for the Christian Broadcasting Network. In his younger days, Marco had been a Marxist-Leninist, but he had a conversion (Jeffrey Rosen, "Sodom and Demurrer," *New Republic*, November 29, 1993). Marco was the architect of Amendment 2. Another leader in CFV was University of Colorado football coach Bill McCartney, founder of the Christian men's "family values" movement, Promise Keepers. McCartney was fond of saying that homosexuals were "an abomination of almighty God": video, *Romer v. Evans*, 2008.

57. C. J. Janovy, "The Gay Nineties," *Denver Westword News*, November 25, 1999.

58. "The CFV Philosophical Model" (a blueprint for other right-wing groups planning an assault on gay rights laws), II-6, MS 63, box 1, folder 20, Washington State Historical Society Archives.

59. Booth, "The Man Who Sold Amendment 2."

60. Associated Press, Nancy Shulins, "Anti-Gay Rights Proposals Meet With Mixed Results," *Stars and Stripes*, November 5, 1992.

61. See p. 251.

62. Will Perkins, "The Drive for Homosexual Rights Undermines the Family," *Denver Post*, May 23, 1992; and Booth, "The Man Who Sold Amendment 2."

63. Associated Press, Carl Hilliard, "Petitions Blocking Gay Rights Turned In," *Denver Post*, March 21, 1992.

64. Leaflet: "Equal Rights—Not Special Rights," MS 63, box 4, folder 6, Washington State Historical Society Archives,

65. Ibid. In ostensible contradiction to CFV's theme that homosexuals were pedophiles, they sometimes claimed that the ultimate goal of the gay rights movement was marriage, which would "erode traditional family structures, sap resources from legitimate traditional families (by increasing disease-driven insurance rates, and so on), and cause measureless misery to helpless children who would be the wretched victims of such 'marriages'": in CFV leaflet "Target: Children," quoted in Ellen Ann Andersen, *Out of the Closets and into the Courts: Legal Opportunity Structure and Gay Rights Litigation* (Ann Arbor: University of Michigan Press, 2005), p. 155.

66. Jean Dubofsky, interview with Marvin B. Woolf, 2008, transcript, Maria Rogers Oral History Program, Boulder Library, Colorado.

67. Brooke, "Colorado Is Engine in Anti-Gay Uproar."

68. Documentary *The Gay Revolt at the Denver City Council and How It Changed Our World*, produced by Jerry Gerash, 2010.

69. Jean Dubofsky, interview with author, Boulder, CO (telephone), March 10, 2014.

70. Dubofsky, interview with author.
71. Thaddeus Herrick, "Gay Rights Opponents Follow Colorado's Lead," *Rocky Mountain News* (Denver), April 3, 1993. Colorado for Family Values also reported to Herrick that the organization had been contacted by "individuals from at least 33 states seeking information on how to fight homosexuality." CFV published a how-to pamphlet for them: MS 63, box 1, folder 20, Washington State Historical Society Archives.
72. Video, *Romer v. Evans*, 2008.
73. Richard Evans, one of the seven plaintiffs, was a gay man who'd been a member of the Equal Protection Ordinance Coalition, which was responsible for getting the Denver City Council to pass a nondiscrimination ordinance. Evans was an aide to the mayor of Denver.
74. Jeffrey Rosen, "Sodom and Demurrer," *New Republic*, November 29, 1993.
75. Associated Press, Carl Hilliard, "Anti-Gay Amendment Leader Said He Wasn't Trying to Block Civil Rights," *Denver Post*, October 15, 1993. Amendment 2 and the various court cases around it are also discussed in Evan Gerstmann, *The Constitutional Underclass: Gays, Lesbians, and the Failure of Class-Based Equal Protection* (Chicago: University of Chicago Press, 1999); Murdoch and Price, *Courting Justice*; Andersen, *Out of the Closets and into the Courts*; and Lisa Melinda Keen and Suzanne Beth Goldberg, *Strangers to the Law: Gay People on Trial* (Ann Arbor: University of Michigan Press, 2000).
76. Dubofsky was assisted by lawyers Greg Eurich, Jeanne Winer, and Rick Hills.
77. Dirk Johnson, "Ban on Gay Rights Laws Is Put on Hold in Colorado," *New York Times*, January 16, 1993.
78. Dubofsky, interview with Woolf.
79. *Evans v. Romer*, 854 P.2d 11270 (Colo. 1993); and Dirk Johnson, "Colorado's Anti-Gay Measure Set Back," *New York Times*, July 20, 1993.
80. In 2001 Norton would give the Sierra Club fits after George W. Bush named her secretary of the interior, and it was clear that she'd support oil drilling in Alaska.
81. "Colorado Judge Overturns Initiative Banning Gay Rights," *New York Times*, December 15, 1993.
82. *Evans v. Romer*, 882 P.2d 1335 (Colo. 1994); and Dirk Johnson, "Colorado Justices Strike Down a Law Against Gay Rights," *New York Times*, October 12, 1994.
83. *Romer v. Evans*, 116 S Ct. 1620 (1996). (Oral arguments in the case were designated no. 94 1039.)
84. Dubofsky, interview with Woolf.
85. Suzanne Goldberg, interview with author, New York (telephone), May 28, 2014.
86. Dubofsky, interview with author.
87. Ibid.
88. Arthur S. Leonard, "Kennedy and the Gays, Again," *New York Native*, December 7, 1987.
89. Clay Wirestone, "In 1987, the New Hampshire Legislature Targeted Gay People as Unfit for Parenting," *Concord (NH) Monitor*, June 29, 2013.
90. *Romer v. Evans*; and Linda Greenhouse, "U.S. Justices Hear, and Also Debate, a

Gay Rights Case," *New York Times*, October 11, 1995. In his written dissent, Scalia characterized Amendment 2 as an answer to the *Kulturkampf* started by gays. The "elite class, from which members of this institution [SCOTUS] are selected," go along with them, Scalia said. But most Americans agree that "It's our moral heritage to consider certain conduct reprehensible," including murder, polygamy, cruelty to animals, and homosexuality.

91. Rosen, "Sodom and Demurrer."
92. Dubofsky, interview with author.
93. *Romer v. Evans.*
94. Laurie Asseo, "High Court Dumps Anti-Gay Law," *Oregonian* (Portland), May 20, 1996, p. 1.
95. David W. Dunlap, "The Gay Rights Ruling Signals More Fights to Come," *New York Times*, May 21, 1996. A few right-wing groups, including Focus on the Family, National Legal Foundation, and Phyllis Schlafly's Eagle Forum, did make some attempts to lead an impeachment drive: Steven W. Fitschen, "Impeaching Federal Judges: A Covenantal and Constitutional Response to Judicial Tyranny," *Regent University Law Review* (Spring 1998). But their campaign never got much traction.

CHAPTER 25: NEW GAYS AND LESBIANS VERSUS THE OLD MILITARY

1. Mike Hippler, *Matlovich: The Good Soldier* (Boston: Alyson Books, 1989), pp. 11–15; and Leonard Matlovich, radio interview with Ron Gold, on WBAI, New York, August 26, 1975. I am grateful to Michael Bedwell, longtime housemate and confidant of Leonard Matlovich, for calling this interview to my attention.
2. *Time* cover, September 8, 1975.
3. *Time* presented an anonymous homosexual man on the cover of its October 31, 1969, issue, which contained a hostile cover article, "The Homosexual in America."
4. After he became an icon in the gay rights movement, Matlovich declared, "Everything I am today, or even hope to be, I owe to black Americans": Hippler, *Matlovich*, p. 41.
5. Ibid., pp. 37–38.
6. Once Matlovich's homosexuality became known through the media, he was "disfellowshipped" and then excommunicated from the Mormon Church by an ecclesiastical court.
7. Hippler, *Matlovich*, p. 55.
8. Leonard Matlovich, interview with Mary Ann Humphrey, in *My Country, My Right to Serve* (New York: HarperCollins, 1990), p. 151.
9. Matlovich, radio interview with Gold.
10. Marianne Lester, "Homosexuals in Uniform," *Air Force Times*, March 27, 1974, pp. 4–9ff.
11. Kameny mentions the April 8 phone call in a letter to Matlovich dated April 11, 1974. Matlovich had asked Kameny for a list of gay books. Kameny sent him

the *Gay Bibliography* published by a gay and lesbian task force of the American Library Association: Frank Kameny to Leonard Matlovich, letter, April 11, 1974, Frank Kameny Collection, box 53, folder 2, Manuscript Division, Library of Congress. I am grateful to Manuscript Division librarian Jennifer Brathovde for calling this letter to my attention.

12. Martin Duberman, "The Case of the Gay Sergeant," *New York Times Magazine,* November 9, 1975.

13. Matlovich, radio interview with Gold.

14. Michael Bedwell, email communication with author, March 12, 2014.

15. Hippler, *Matlovich,* p. 45.

16. AFM 39-12, chap. 2, sec. H, par. 2-104.

17. Leonard Matlovich to the secretary of the air force, through Captain Dennis M. Collins, letter, March 6, 1975: Leonard Matlovich Papers, box 2, folder 39, GLC 6, 88-1, Gay and Lesbian Historical Society of Northern California Collection, San Francisco Public Library. The letterhead of this communication was "Lawyers Military Defense Committee of the American Civil Liberties Union."

18. Matlovich, radio interview with Gold.

19. "The Sexes: The Sergeant v. the Air Force," *Time,* September 8, 1975.

20. Lieutenant Colonel Charles Ritchie to Leonard Matlovich, letter acknowledging receipt of Matlovich's letter and advising him to seek military counsel, March 13, 1975: Leonard Matlovich Papers, box 2, folder 32, GLC 6, 88-1, Gay and Lesbian Historical Society of Northern California Collection, San Francisco Public Library.

21. Matlovich, interview with Humphrey, in *My Country, My Right to Serve,* p. 153.

22. Leonard Matlovich to James H. Ramberger (OSI), letter, April 25, 1975, Leonard Matlovich Papers, box 2, folder 47, GLC 6, 88-1, Gay and Lesbian Historical Society of Northern California Collection, San Francisco Public Library.

23. Lieutenant Colonel Charles Ritchie to Leonard Matlovich, letter, May 20, 1975, Leonard Matlovich Papers, box 2, folder 35, GLC 6, 88-1, Gay and Lesbian Historical Society of Northern California Collection, San Francisco Public Library.

24. "The Sergeant v. the Air Force," *Time.*

25. "Homosexual vs. the Air Force," *New York Times,* June 1, 1975.

26. "A Phil Donahue fan" to Leonard Matlovich, letter, November 21, 1975, North Dakota, Leonard Matlovich Papers, box 1, folder 33, 88-1, Gay and Lesbian Historical Society of Northern California Collection, San Francisco Public Library. Leonard Matlovich was man of the hour, a gay hero—but only to some gays. Those at Langley guessed correctly that to be seen being friendly with a known homosexual would trigger harassment by the boys from the Office of Special Investigations; and they gave him wide berth. Radical gays, fresh from the era of antiwar protests, also gave him wide berth; they didn't want to be represented by anyone who defended the military. Some even called him "baby killer" and "war criminal": Email correspondence with Michael Bedwell.

27. "Homosexual Sergeant Described by Doctor as No Risk to Security," *New York Times,* September 19, 1975.

28. Statement of Sergeant Armando Lemos: Leonard Matlovich Papers, box 2, folder 47, GLC 6, 88-1, Gay and Lesbian Historical Society of Northern California Collection, San Francisco Public Library.

29. Wayne King, "Homosexual G.I.'s Ouster Recommended by Panel," *New York Times*, September 20, 1975.

30. Letter of Evaluation, Major Arthur Patton, March 31, 1975, Leonard Matlovich Papers, box 2, folder 33, GLC 6, 88-1, Gay and Lesbian Historical Society of Northern California Collection, San Francisco Public Library.

31. Major Jeffrey S. Davis, "Military Policy Toward Homosexuals," *Military Law Review* 131 (January 1991): p. 78. Exceptions to the air force policy on discharge could be made if a service member engaged in a homosexual act only because he'd been drunk; or he'd experimented as a kid but had given it up; or he vowed he'd never do it again.

32. King, "Homosexual G.I.'s Ouster Recommended by Panel."

33. Ibid.

34. Secretary of the Air Force John McLucas upgraded Matlovich's discharge to honorable, but he still would not be eligible for severance pay or pension benefits.

35. Email correspondence with Michael Bedwell.

36. Hippler, *Matlovich*, pp. 79–81.

37. *Doe v. Commonwealth's Attorney of Richmond*, 425 US 901 (1976). See discussion on p. 540.

38. *Leonard P. Matlovich v. Secretary of the Air Force and Col. Alton J. Thogersen*, US Court of Appeals, 591 F. 2d 852. David Addlestone came back into the case independently to help Boggan.

39. As a result of this case, in 1981 the Department of Defense issued DOD Directive 1332.14, which made a policy of total exclusion of homosexuals (no exceptions) uniform throughout the military.

40. Vernon "Copy" Berg to Mr. White, American Armed Forces Association, letter, November 17, 1975, Vernon "Copy" Berg Papers, box 3, folder 4, Manuscripts and Archives Division, New York Public Library.

41. E. Lawrence Gibson, *Get Off My Ship: Ensign Berg Vs. the U.S. Navy* (New York: Avon Books, 1978), p. 138.

42. Vernon "Copy" Berg to Vernon Berg II, letter, September 17, 1975, Vernon "Copy" Berg Papers, box 3, folder 3, Manuscripts and Archives Division, New York Public Library.

43. Vernon "Copy" Berg, interview with Mary Ann Humphrey, in *My Country, My Right to Serve*, p. 74.

44. "The Bisexual and the Navy," *Time*, February 2, 1976.

45. Vernon "Copy" Berg, interview with Eric Marcus, *Making History*, p. 270.

46. Vernon "Copy" Berg to Greg, letter, July 25, 1975, Vernon "Copy" Berg Papers, box 3, folder 4, Manuscripts and Archives Division, New York Public Library.

47. Gibson set to work almost immediately. *Get Off My Ship: Ensign Berg Vs. the U.S. Navy* was published in 1978, three years before the final judgment of Berg's case.

48. Vernon "Copy" Berg to Ellen, letter, December 8, 1975, Vernon "Copy" Berg

Papers, box 3, folder 4, Manuscripts and Archives Division, New York Public Library.

49. Shilts, *Conduct Unbecoming*, p. 250.

50. Berg to Mr. White, letter.

51. Vernon "Copy" Berg to Military Ministers, United Presbyterian Church, Washington, DC, letter, November 17, 1975, Vernon "Copy" Berg Papers, box 3, folder 4, Manuscripts and Archives Division, New York Public Library.

52. Gibson, *Get Off My Ship*, pp. 46–48.

53. Vernon Berg II to Vernon "Copy" Berg III, n.d. (in response to Copy's letter of September 17, 1975), letter, Vernon "Copy" Berg Papers, box 3, folder 1, Manuscripts and Archives Division, New York Public Library.

54. The testimonies are recounted at length in Gibson, *Get Off My Ship*.

55. Shilts, *Conduct Unbecoming*, pp. 311–12.

56. The following year, soon after President Carter took office, Midge Costanza, riding high in her White House post, pressured the Pentagon to upgrade certain less-than-honorable discharges, and Copy Berg's discharge was changed to Honorable: Marcus, *Making History*, p. 279.

57. *Vernon E. Berg III v. W. Graham Claytor, Jr., Secretary of the Navy*, 436 F. Supp. 76 (1977).

58. *Vernon E. Berg III v. W. Graham Claytor, Jr. Secretary of the Navy*, 591 F.2d 849 (1978); and "The Homosexual in Uniform," *New York Times*, December 12, 1978.

59. "Navy Endorses Non-Repeating Members," *Body Politic*, April 1978, p. 9. A 1981 Department of Defense directive would again make the dismissal of homosexuals more draconian: See p. 478.

60. "U.S. Navy Will Pay Cash to Ousted Berg," *Advocate*, March 19, 1981, p. 10.

61. Murdoch and Price, *Courting Justice*, p. 390.

62. Miriam Ben-Shalom, interview with Paul Cain, in *Leading the Parade: Conversations with America's Most Influential Lesbians and Gay Men* (Lanham, MD: Scarecrow Press, 2002), p. 350.

63. Miriam Ben-Shalom, interview with Steve Estes, in *Ask and Tell: Gay and Lesbian Veterans Speak Out* (Durham: University of North Carolina Press, 2007), p. 195.

64. Ben-Shalom, interview with Cain, p. 344.

65. Shilts, *Conduct Unbecoming*, p. 228.

66. *Ben-Shalom v. Secretary of the Army*, 489 F. Supp. 964 (D. Wisc. 1980).

67. Shilts, *Conduct Unbecoming*, p. 264.

68. Martha Neil, Obit: "Long-Time 7th Circuit Judge Terence Evans," *ABA Journal*, August 11, 2011.

69. *Ben-Shalom v. Secretary of the Army*, 489 F. Supp. 964 (D. Wisc. 1980). Judge Evans, liberal as he was, preferred not to grapple with the notion of lesbian or gay sex: "It cannot be assumed that all who have personalities oriented toward homosexuality necessarily engage in homosexual conduct," he declared in his judgment.

70. Ibid.

71. *Ben-Shalom v. Secretary of the Army*, 826 F.2d 722, argued May 22, 1987; decided August 18, 1987.

72. AR 140-111, table 4-2.

73. Michael Kiefer, "Out of the Air Force Closet: How a Model Sergeant Came to Admit His Homosexuality on National TV," *New Times* (Phoenix), August 12, 1992.

74. *Miriam Ben-Shalom v. John O. Marsh, Secretary of the U.S. Army*, 703 F. Supp. 1372, January 10, 1989. The case of Staff Sergeant Perry Watkins ran parallel to that of Miriam Ben-Shalom. In 1967, during the Vietnam War, Watkins, an African American who'd identified as homosexual since childhood, was drafted into the army despite his having checked the box declaring his homosexuality. He was allowed to reenlist three times and was regularly promoted, though it was no secret that he performed in drag as "Simone" on his army base and in army clubs throughout Europe. Watkins even received a security clearance after arguing that he couldn't be blackmailed because he was gay. But when he tried to reenlist in 1984 during the Reagan administration, he was turned down. As in Ben-Shalom's case, a district court ordered that he be readmitted, but the army refused. The US Court of Appeals heard his case in 1989. That court would not rule on whether the army's rejection of Watkins violated his Fourteenth Amendment Equal Protection rights (as his lawyers had argued); but it did rule that the Army could not bar his enlistment solely on the grounds that he was a homosexual. In 1990 the Bush I administration appealed the case to the US Supreme Court. SCOTUS refused to hear it, letting the appeals court decision stand. Like Matlovich and Berg, Watkins accepted a settlement ($135,000) rather than reinstatement. He was also awarded an honorable discharge, full pension, and retroactive promotion from staff sergeant to sergeant first class: *Watkins v. U.S. Army*, 875 F.2d 699 (Ninth Circuit, 1989); and Perry Watkins Collection, accession 1991.03, box 1, Lambda Archives, San Diego. Other cases in which service members who were discharged after they admitted they were homosexual and then reinstated by civil courts that found their Equal Protection rights had been violated include Army Reserve captain Dusty Pruitt, discharged in 1983 and ordered reinstated and promoted to major by the Ninth Circuit Court of Appeals in 1991 (*Dusty Pruitt, Captain, USAR v. Richard Cheney, Secretary of Defense*, 963 F.2d 1160); and navy pilot Keith Meinhold, discharged in 1992, reinstated by District Judge Terry Hatter in 1993, and reinstatement upheld by the Ninth District Court of Appeals in 1997 (*Meinhold v. Department of Defense*, no. 9656094). In rendering his decision, Judge Hatter declared, "Gays and lesbians have served, and continue to serve, the United States military with honor, pride, dignity, and loyalty. The Department of Defense's justification for its policy banning gays and lesbians from military service are based on cultural myths and false stereotypes. These justifications are baseless and very similar to the reasons offered to keep the military racially segregated in the 1940s."

75. "Bush Administration Decision to End the Practice of Consulting the ABA About Potential Nominees for Federal Judgeships," National Public Radio, March 23, 2001.

76. *Miriam Ben-Shalom v. John O. Marsh, Secretary of the Army*, 881 F.2d 454, argued May 18, 1989; decided August 7, 1989.

77. "Lesbian Struggles to Serve in Army," *New York Times*, August 10, 1989; "Court Upholds Army in Its Refusal to Enlist Lesbian Drill Sergeant," *New York Times*, August 11, 1989. Ben-Shalom also insisted to the media that though she is a homosexual, she doesn't engage in homosexual acts. Her stance was thus less challenging to the military than that of Matlovich and Berg, who refused to deny that they were sexual beings and would remain so.

78. John Balzar, "Lesbian Army Officer Wins Battle in Court," *Los Angeles Times*, June 2, 1994.

79. Colonel Margarethe Cammermeyer, interview with author, Whidbey Island, WA, June 1, 2012.

80. Colonel Margarethe Cammermeyer, interview with Jan Secor, January 11, 1999, Pierce County Gay History Project, Washington. I am grateful to Gloria Stancich for sharing this material with me.

81. Margarethe Cammermeyer with Chris Fisher, *Serving in Silence* (New York: Viking, 1994), chapter 8.

82. Cammermeyer, interview with author.

83. Ibid.

84. Ibid.

85. Ibid.

86. "Statement of Subject," April 28, 1989, in the private papers of Margarethe Cammermeyer. I am grateful to Colonel Cammermeyer for sharing this document with me.

87. The lore of Cammermeyer's Norwegian childhood said that the only way to get into Valhalla, the Viking heaven, was to show up with sword in hand: Colonel Margarethe Cammermeyer, interview with Jan Secor.

88. Quoted in *Cammermeyer v. Perry*, US Court of Appeals, 97 F.3d 1235 (1996).

89. Cammermeyer with Fisher, *Serving in Silence*, p. 274.

90. *Cammermeyer v. Aspin*, 850 F. Supp. 910 (1994); and Cammermeyer, *Serving in Silence*, pp. 275–76.

91. See note 74 above.

92. *Cammermeyer v. Aspin*.

93. *Cammermeyer v. Perry*, US Court of Appeals, 97 F. 3d 1235 (1996).

CHAPTER 26: DON'T ASK, DON'T TELL, DON'T SERVE

1. Video: Bill Clinton Rally, the Hollywood Palace, May 18, 1992. I am grateful to Karen Ocamb for sharing this video from her private collection with me; and Ronald Brownstein, "Clinton Addresses 600 at Rally of Gays, Lesbians," *Los Angeles Times*, May 19, 1992.

2. Melanie Mayson et al., "Gay Political Donors Move from Margin to Mainstream," *Los Angeles Times*, May 13, 2012; and Mixner, interview with author.

3. Video: Bill Clinton Rally. Clinton courted and received the backing of organized gays all over America, including the increasingly prominent Human Rights Campaign that had morphed out of the Gay Rights National Lobby and by 1992 had become a multimillion-dollar concern. "Bill Clinton not only asks for our

support, he's earned it," HRC declared in the run-up to the presidential election: "Defining Moment for Gays and Lesbians: A High Profile and a Sympathetic Candidate Make for a Breakthrough," *Philadelphia Inquirer*, July 19, 1992.

4. Video: Bill Clinton Rally.

5. Congressman Barney Frank, interview with author, Washington, DC, November 15, 2012.

6. Buchanan's August 17, 1992, Republican National Convention speech is available through the C-Span video library.

7. Hattoy's and Achtenberg's July 14, 1992, Democratic Convention speeches are available through the C-Span video library.

8. Roberta Achtenberg, interview with author, San Francisco, April 9, 2012; and "Democratic Party Platform: A New Covenant with the American People," July 13, 1992.

9. "Nonconforming Sexual Orientations and Military Suitability" (PERS-TR-89-002), prepared by Theodore Sarbin, PhD, and Kenneth Karols, PhD, Defense Personnel Security Research and Education Center, 1988. Clinton referred to the report as having influenced him at his May 18, 1992, fund-raiser at the Hollywood Palace: Video, Bill Clinton Rally.

10. *Report of the Board Appointed to Prepare and Submit Recommendations to the Secretary of the Navy for Revision of Policies, Procedures, and Directives Dealing with Homosexuality* (aka *The Crittenden Report*), March 15, 1957.

11. Colin J. Williams and Martin S. Weinberg, *Homosexuals and the Military: A Study of Less than Honorable Discharge* (New York: Harper and Row, 1971).

12. Michael A. McDaniel, *Pre-Service Adjustment of Homosexual and Heterosexual Military Accessions* (Monterey, CA: Defense Personnel Security Research and Education Center, June 1989).

13. Eric Schmitt, "Clinton Set to End Ban on Gay Troops," *New York Times*, January 21, 1993.

14. Associated Press, Robert Burns, "Armed Services Begin Adjusting to Clinton's Interim Gay Policy," *Gettysburg (PA) Times*, February 3, 1993.

15. David Evans, "Has Clinton Thought This Issue Through?" *Baltimore Sun*, November 13, 1992; and Karen deYoung, *Soldier: The Life of Colin Powell* (New York: Alfred Knopf, 2006), p. 230. When Congressman Barney Frank asked the general whether he thought gays really didn't do a good job in the military, Powell responded that he thought they did, but it was the problem of "unit cohesion" that worried him: Frank, interview with author.

16. Harry G. Summers, "Clinton's Gay Policy Proves He's a 'Brass Hat,'" *Stars and Stripes*, February 10, 1993.

17. Documentary *Ask Not*, directed by Johnny Symons, Persistent Films, 2008; and Paul Cameron, "Medical Consequences of What Homosexuals Do," *Family Research Council Newsletter*, 1997.

18. Frank, interview with author.

19. "Gays and the Military," *Newsweek*, February 1, 1993, p. 53.

20. Congressman Barney Frank felt he paid back Nunn for his outrageous

"prudence" in 1996, when George Stephanopoulos, Clinton's senior advisor for policy and strategy, called Frank to ask what he thought of Clinton's idea to name Sam Nunn as his secretary of state. Frank's response was, "He can't do that to us!" Nunn fell out of the running for the position: Frank, interview with author.

21. Mixner, interview with author.

22. "Gays and the Military," *Newsweek.*

23. Summers, "Clinton's Gay Policy Proves He's a 'Brass Hat.'"

24. The hearings were held over nine days, March 29, 31; April 29; May 7, 10, 11; July 20, 21, 22: *Policy Concerning Homosexuality in the Armed Forces: Hearings Before the Committee on Armed Services*, United States Senate, 103rd Congress, 2nd Session (US Government Printing Office, January 1, 1994).

25. Bill McAllister, "Both Sides Oppose Military Job Limits on Gays," *Washington Post*, March 25, 1993.

26. McAllister, "Both Sides Oppose Military Job Limits on Gays."

27. Frank, interview with author.

28. United Press International, "Sailors Tell Senators 'Keep Ban on Homosexuals,'" *Stars and Stripes*, May 11, 1993; and *Policy Concerning Homosexuality in the Armed Forces: Hearings Before the Committee on Armed Services.*

29. *Policy Concerning Homosexuality in the Armed Forces: Hearings Before the Committee on Armed Services*; and Associated Press, "Ex-General Argues Against Gays in the Military," *Cedar Rapids (IA) Gazette*, April 30, 1993.

30. Gannett News Service, "Highly Charged Debate over Gays in Military Heads for Hill," *Colorado Springs (CO) Gazette Telegraph*, March 29, 1993.

31. *Policy Concerning Homosexuality in the Armed Forces: Hearings Before the Committee on Armed Services,* p. 492.

32. "Ex-General Argues Against Gays in the Military."

33. Charles Moskos, op-ed: "Does America Need a 'G.I. Bill' for Youth?" *New York Times*, April 15, 1989; and Charles C. Moskos, *A Call to Civic Service: National Service for Country and Community* (Riverside, NJ: Free Press, 1988).

34. Winston Williams, "U.S. Aide Says Allies Criticize Blacks in Army," *New York Times*, June 6, 1982.

35. Douglas Martin, "Charles Moskos, Policy Advisor, Dies at 74," *New York Times*, June 5, 2008; and Joe Holley, "Charles Moskos, 74, Created the Military's Don't Ask, Don't Tell," *Washington Post*, June 4, 2008.

36. Moskos in a 1993 *Chicago Tribune* interview, quoted in Martin, "Charles Moskos."

37. Paul F. Horvitz, "'Don't Ask, Don't Tell, Don't Pursue' Is White House Compromise," *New York Times*, July 20, 1993.

38. Miriam Ben-Shalom, who participated in the protest, was forced by the park police to take off the medals she was wearing and place them in their container. "This is the last time I'll ever wear these," Ben-Shalom wept: Patricia Ireland (one of the organizers of the DADT protest), interview with author, Miami, October 15, 2012.

39. Bridget Wilson, interview with author, San Diego, July 31, 2012.

40. Ibid.; and Bridget Wilson, interview with Daniel Redman and Ilona Turner, in "Don't Ask, Don't Tell—Anyone, Anywhere," *Nation*, November 16, 2010.

41. Diana Wickman and Judy (J. P.) Persall, interview with author, Port Townsend, WA, May 31, 2012.

42. Thom Shanker, "'Don't Ask, Don't Tell' Hits Women Much More," *New York Times*, June 25, 2008.

43. *Margaret Witt v. Department of the Air Force*, 739 F. Supp. 2d 1308 (Western District, Washington, 2010).

44. Margaret Witt, interview with author, Gig Harbor, WA, May 12, 2012.

45. Margaret Witt, interview with author.

46. *Margaret Witt v. Department of the Air Force*, 444 F. Supp. 2d 1138 (Western District Washington 2006).

47. *Margaret Witt v. Department of the Air Force*, 527 F.3d 806 (Ninth Cir. 2008). Subsequent DADT cases, such as *Log Cabin Republicans v. United States*, built on this appeals court decision, which placed the burden on the military to show that a service member's homosexuality had adverse effects on his or her unit. Federal district court judge Virginia Phillips, applying what came to be known as the "Witt standard" in her *Log Cabin Republicans* decision on October 12, 2010, ruled that DADT was unconstitutional.

48. Associated Press, "Former Colleagues Back Lesbian Nurse Discharged from U.S. Air Force," *Guardian* (UK), September 14, 2010.

49. *Margaret Witt v. Department of the Air Force*, 739 F. Supp. 2d 1308 (Western District, Washington, 2010).

50. Margaret Witt, interview with author; *Margaret Witt v. Department of the Air Force*, 739 F. Supp. 2d 1308 (Western District, Washington, 2010); and Gene Johnson, "Margaret Witt, Air Force Major Discharged Under DADT, Expects Reinstatement by January," *Huffington Post*, November 30, 2010.

51. "Don't Ask, Don't Tell: Retreating," *Los Angeles Times*, August 16, 2009.

52. Associated Press, "Admirals, Generals: 'Let Gays Serve Openly,'" *NBC News*, November 18, 2008.

53. Gallup News Service, Lydia Saad, "Tolerance for Gay Rights at High-Water Mark," May 29, 2007.

54. Tom Shanker and Patrick Healy, "A New Push to Pull Back 'Don't Ask, Don't Tell'," *New York Times*, November 30, 2007.

55. "Admirals, Generals: 'Let Gays Serve Openly.'"

56. Shanker and Healy, "A New Push to Roll Back 'Don't Ask, Don't Tell'."

57. Quoted in Judith Davidoff, "Move Afoot to Repeal Don't Ask, Don't Tell," *Madison (WI) Capital Times*, March 4, 2009.

58. Reuters, "Time to Review Policy on Gays in the U.S. Military: Powell," July 5, 2009.

CHAPTER 27: "GET 'DON'T ASK, DON'T TELL' DONE!"

1. Shanker and Healy, "A New Push to Roll Back 'Don't Ask, Don't Tell'."

2. Steve Ralls, "Primary Questions," *The Bilerico Project*, February 28, 2008.

3. Kerry Eleveld, "Obama Talks All Things LGBT with *The Advocate*," *Advocate*, April 10, 2008.

4. Obama recalled his January 2009 White House meeting with Gates and Mullen in a second interview with Kerry Eleveld, "Obama: Prepared to Implement," *Advocate*, December 22, 2010.

5. Robert M. Gates, *Duty: Memoirs of a Secretary at War* (New York: Alfred Knopf, 2014), p. 298.

6. Kimberly Maul interview with Kerry Eleveld, "Journalist Q&A: Kerry Eleveld, *The Advocate*," *PR Week* (trade magazine for the public relations industry), August 21, 2009.

7. Richard Socarides, "Ask Obama About Don't Ask, Don't Tell," *Wall Street Journal*, January 24, 2010.

8. The 1993 poll was conducted by NBC/*Wall Street Journal*; 2009 poll conducted by *USA Today*/Gallup. By March 2010, 78 percent of Americans favored gay men and lesbians serving openly: Eric Zimmerman, "Poll: 78% Favor Repealing Don't Ask, Don't Tell," *The Hill*, March 25, 2010.

9. Quoted in Socarides, "Ask Obama About Don't Ask, Don't Tell."

10. Quoted in Aaron Belkin et al., "One Year Out: An Assessment of 'Don't Ask, Don't Tell' Repeal's Impact on Military Readiness," Palm Center, UCLA, September 20, 2012.

11. Gates, *Duty*, p. 333.

12. Gates, *Duty*, p. 332.

13. Ibid.

14. Defense Manpower Data Center, DRS 16291, February 2010.

15. Congresswoman Tammy Baldwin, interview with author, Washington, DC, November 16, 2012. Baldwin had been elected to the Senate ten days earlier.

16. Congressman Patrick Murphy, interview with David Welna, "Veterans Call Out Obama on 'Don't Ask, Don't Tell,'" *NPR Morning Edition*, July 9, 2009.

17. Roxanne Tiron, "Skelton Opposes Repeal of Don't Ask, Don't Tell," *The Hill*, January 15, 2010.

18. "He'd Rather Not Talk About 'Don't Ask, Don't Tell,'" *New York Times*, June 28, 2010.

19. Lesley Clark, "Lawmaker Backs Off Effort to Fight Don't Ask, Don't Tell," *Miami Herald*, July 28, 2009; and Congressman Alcee Hastings, interview with author, Washington, DC, November 15, 2012. Hastings recalled that most of the forty-one members of the Congressional Black Caucus had been strongly in favor of repeal.

20. Hastings, interview with author; and Clark, "Lawmaker Backs Off Effort."

21. Associated Press, Christine Simmons, "Obama HRC Speech: 'I Will End Don't Ask, Don't Tell,'" *Huffington Post*, October 10, 2009.

22. Gates, *Duty*, p. 433.

23. Julian Barnes, "Marine Commandant Opposes Ending Ban on Gays Serving Openly in the Military," *Stars and Stripes*, February 25, 2010. The chair of the Joint Chiefs of Staff, Admiral Mullen, had testified a few weeks earlier before the committee. Despite his legal advisor's having said that repeal was a bad idea in the midst of fighting a war, the admiral, making it clear he was "speaking for

myself and myself only," told the committee, "No matter how I look at the issue, I cannot escape being troubled by the fact that we have in place a policy which forces young men and women to lie about who they are . . . It comes down to integrity, theirs as individuals and ours as an institution": Tony Romm, "Admiral Mullen: 'Repealing "Don't Ask, Don't Tell" Is the Right Thing to Do,'" *The Hill*, February 2, 2010.

24. Craig Whitlock, "Gay, Straight Marines Couldn't Share Rooms with Don't-Ask Repeal," *Washington Post*, March 27, 2010.

25. Perry Bacon Jr. and Ed O'Keefe, "House Votes to End 'Don't Ask, Don't Tell' Policy," *Washington Post*, May 28, 2010.

26. Frank, interview with author; and Bacon and O'Keefe, "House Votes to End 'Don't Ask, Don't Tell' Policy."

27. Bacon and O'Keefe, "House Votes to End 'Don't Ask, Don't Tell' Policy."

28. Ben Smith, "White House Delaying 'Don't Ask' Repeal," *Politico*, April 19, 2010.

29. John Schwartz, "Judge Rules That Military Policy Violates Rights of Gays," *New York Times*, September 9, 2010.

30. This was exactly what President Obama did in February 2011, when he instructed the Justice Department not to challenge a judicial decision striking down a part of the Defense of Marriage Act: "Letter from the Attorney General to Congress on Litigation Involving the Defense of Marriage Act," press release, Department of Justice, February 23, 2011.

31. Michael D. Shear, "Gibbs: Our Defense of Don't-Ask Is Pro Forma," *New York Times*, September 24, 2010.

32. Ed O'Keefe, "Air Force Officer Fights Discharge Under Military 'Don't Ask, Don't Tell' Rule," *New York Times*, August 13, 2010.

33. With the repeal of DADT the following year, Fehrenbach was able to complete his twentieth year before retiring: Victor Fehrenbach with Damien Lewis, *Out of the Blue* (London: Endeavor Press, 2013).

34. "John McCain, Prisoner of War: A First Person Account," *U.S. News & World Report*, May 14, 1973.

35. John Gerstein, "McCain Call for 'DADT' Hearings Dims Repeal Chances," *Politico*, November 14, 2010.

36. Chris Geidner, "Looking for Leadership on DADT," *Metro Weekly* (Washington, DC), May 2, 2010.

37. Geidner, "Looking for Leadership."

38. Smith, "White House Delaying 'Don't Ask' Repeal."

39. Charles Keyes, "End of 'Don't Ask, Don't Tell' Brings Relief," *CNN*, September 20, 2011.

40. Mark Thompson, "Dismay over Obama's 'Don't Ask, Don't Tell' Turnabout," *Time*, June 9, 2009.

41. Dan Choi, interview with author, San Francisco (telephone), August 28, 2014.

42. Admiral Alan Steinman (ret.), interview with author, Joint Base Lewis-McChord, WA, May 12, 2012.

43. Admiral Steinman, interview with author.

44. John Files, "Ex-Gay Officers Say 'Don't Ask, Don't Tell' Doesn't Work," *New York Times*, December 10, 2003.

45. Admiral Steinman, interview with author.

46. Eric Alva's autobiography, coauthored with Sam Gallegos, is *Once a Marine: A Memoir of Coming Out Under Fire* (Los Angeles: Alyson, 2010).

47. Eve Conant, "Exclusive: Dan Choi on his Arrest over DADT," *Newsweek*, March 21, 2010.

48. Robin McGehee, interview with author, Fresno, CA, April 27, 2012.

49. McGehee, interview with author. The irony wasn't lost on the gay press that a radical organization was funded by a "major donor": for example, Bil Browning, "Behind the Veil: Is Get Equal the New HRC?" *The Bilerico Project*, June 2, 2010.

50. Choi, interview with author.

51. Ibid.

52. McGehee and Choi, interviews with author.

53. Choi, interview with author; and "Arrest of Lt. Dan Choi," *Oklahoma Citizen* (Henryetta, OK), March 18, 2010.

54. Sarah Toce, "White House DADT Protest—Thirteen Arrested," *Seattle Lesbian*, November 15, 2010. All the arrested but Dan Choi agreed to plead guilty after the prosecutor promised they wouldn't be sent to jail. Choi refused the plea and demanded a federal trial: *U.S. v. Choi*, 10-739-11, August 29, 2011. The case was settled March 28, 2013; Choi was fined $100.

55. Stephen C. Webster, "Protesting 'Don't Ask, Don't Tell' Gay Activists Arrested," *Raw Story*, November 15, 2010.

56. Mattilda Bernstein Sycamore, "Community Spirit: The New Gay Patriot and the Right to Fight in Unjust Wars," in *Against Equality: Don't Ask to Fight Their Wars*, ed. Ryan Conrad (Lewiston, ME: Against Equality Publishing Collection, 2011). The collection includes essays by ten LGBT activists opposed to gays and lesbians serving in the military.

57. Mattilda Bernstein Sycamore, "A Fine Romance: Democracy Now's Amy Goodman and Lieutenant Dan Choi," *The Bilerico Project*, August 5, 2010.

58. "Election 2010: Nevada Senate," *Rasmussen Reports*, June 9, 2010.

59. Choi, interview with author; Stephanie Condon, "Reid Makes a Promise to Dan Choi for Gay Rights," *CBS News*, July 24, 2010; and Shaun Knittel, "Discharged Gay Army Lieutenant Dan Choi Confronts Reid," *Seattle Gay News*, July 30, 2010.

60. Jonathan L. Lee, a member of the group, discusses the study's methods and conclusions in "The Comprehensive Review Working Group and the 'Don't Ask, Don't Tell' Repeal at the Department of Defense," *Journal of Homosexuality* 60, nos. 2–3 (February 2013), pp. 282–311.

61. Ed O'Keefe and Greg Jaffe, "Sources: Pentagon Group Finds There is Minimal Risk in Lifting Gay Ban During War," *New York Times*, November 11, 2010.

62. Quoted in O'Keefe and Jaffe.

63. "McCain Takes Shot at 'Don't Ask, Don't Tell' Repeal," *CNN*, December 2, 2010.

64. Frank, interview with author.

65. Jennifer Steinhauer, "Senate Stalls Bill to Repeal Gay Policy in Military," *New York Times*, December 9, 2010.

66. Persall and Wickman, interview with author.

67. The president signed the bill in December 2010, but it "gestated" for nine months as the military prepared for gays and lesbians to serve openly. Repeal of Don't Ask, Don't Tell went into effect in September 2011.

68. William Dobbs, interview with author, New York, March 6, 2013; and Anemona Hartocollis, "For Some Gays, a Right They Can Forsake," *New York Times*, July 30, 2006.

69. Author on-site observation; "Members of Military March in San Diego Gay Pride Parade," *Los Angeles Times*, July 22, 2012; Associated Press, "Troops in Uniform March in San Diego Gay Pride Parade," *Jacksonville (NC) Daily News*, July 22, 2012; "Policy Reviewed on Troops at Gay Pride Event," *Marine Times*, July 26, 2012; "Are Military Uniforms OK in Gay Pride Parades?" *San Diego Union-Tribune*, August 5, 2012. Leon Panetta, who'd been a congressman from California, had become Obama's secretary of defense in 2011; Panetta permitted a onetime dispensation for troops to march in uniform in the 2012 San Diego Pride Parade, in celebration of the repeal of Don't Ask, Don't Tell the previous year. But in 2014 the Department of Defense permitted the color guard of the US Armed Forces Military District of DC to lead Washington's Pride Parade: Aaron C. Davis, "U.S. Armed Forces Color Guard to March in Gay Pride Parade in D.C.: Called a First Nationwide," *Washington Post*, June 5, 2014.

CHAPTER 28: HOW LESBIANS AND GAYS
STOPPED BEING SEX CRIMINALS

1. Frank Kameny to Jim Foster, letter, September 8, 1972, Frank Kameny Papers, box 3, folder 8, Library of Congress.

2. *Laws of Illinois*, p. 1983, enacted July 28, 1961, effective January 1, 1962.

3. Frank Kameny to George Painter, letter, January 21, 1992, Frank Kameny–George Painter Correspondence, Rainbow History Project, Kiplinger Research Library, Washington, DC.

4. "Sodomy Laws," *New York Mattachine Newsletter*, September 1969; and "The Buchanan Case," *New York Mattachine Newsletter*, July 1970.

5. Associated Press, Michael Graczyk, "After Dallas D.A.'s Death, 19 Convictions Are Undone," *USA Today*, July 29, 2008.

6. *Buchanan v. State*, 471 S.W. 2d 401 (1971).

7. United Press International, "Despite Ruling, Judge Refuses to Release Homosexual," *Lubbock-Avalanche (TX) Journal*, February 6, 1970. Buchanan appealed his sentence in the court of criminal appeals, which reversed his conviction for the Sears, Roebuck offense because that was committed behind the closed doors of the toilet stall; but the court upheld his conviction for the park offense because that was committed in an open stall: *Buchanan v. State*, 471 S.W. 2d 401 (1971).

8. Frank Kameny correspondence with Jim Foster: Foster to Kameny, September 5,

1972; Kameny to Foster, September 8, 1972; Frank Kameny Papers, box 3, folder 8, Library of Congress.

9. Gudron Fonfa, "Most Wanton Women," *Lesbian Tide*, July 1974, p. 8; Jeanne Córdova, *When We Were Outlaws* (Denver: Spinsters Ink, 2011), pp. 52ff; Perry, interview with author; and Córdova, second interview with author.

10. *John Doe v. Commonwealth's Attorney for the City of Richmond*, 403 F. sup. 1199 (1975).

11. Ibid.

12. *John Doe v. Commonwealth's Attorney for the City of Richmond*, 425 US 901 (1976).

13. B. Drummond Ayers, "Judges' Decision in Custody Case Raises Concerns," *New York Times*, September 9, 1993.

14. *Sharon Bottoms v. Kay Bottoms*, 457 S.E. 2d 102 (1997). For an example of a judge refusing custody to a homosexual father, see *Catherine Roe v. David Roe*, 324 S.E. 2d 691 (1985).

15. *Baker v. Wade*, 553 F. Supp. 1121 (1982).

16. Ibid.

17. David Fagan, "Texas Anti-Gay Statute (21.06) Goes to Court," *UpFront America*, April 11, 1980. I am grateful to Becky Smith for bringing this article to my attention; and "Post Trial Briefs Filed in 21.06," *Montrose Voice* (Houston), August 14, 1981.

18. *Baker v. Wade*, 553 f. Supp. 1121 (1982).

19. "Law: They Call Him Dr. Death," *Time*, July 1, 1981.

20. *Baker v. Wade*, 553 f. Supp. 1121 (1982).

21. Ibid.

22. Eduardo Paz Martinez, "Federal Court Rules Against Homosexuals," *Houston Post*, September 9, 1985.

23. *Baker v. Wade* et al., 769 F.2d 289 (1985).

24. Peter Irons interview with Michael Hardwick, in *Lesbians, Gay Men, and the Law*, William B. Rubenstein, ed. (New York: New Press, 1993), pp. 125–31; and Murdoch and Price, *Courting Justice*, chap. 11.

25. *Williams v. Wallace*, 240 F. Supp. 100 (M.D. Alabama 1965); and Burke Marshall, "In Remembrance of Judges Frank M Johnson, Jr. and John Minor Wisdom," *Yale Law School Legal Scholarship Repository*, 2000.

26. *Hardwick v. Bowers*, 760 F.2d 1202.

27. Quoted in Murdoch and Price, *Courting Justice*, p. 286.

28. Brennan, Marshall, and Stevens. Stevens started on the court as a conservative, but his voting record during his tenure was largely liberal. Justice Harold Blackmun, too, began his service on the court as a conservative but became increasingly liberal, and he provided the fourth vote in favor of Hardwick. Tribe had also counted on the vote of Justice Lewis Powell, a moderate who sometimes voted with the liberals. After Powell retired from SCOTUS, he did speak of "having made a mistake" in the Hardwick case: Nat Hentoff, "Infamous Sodomy Law Struck Down," *Village Voice*, December 22, 1998. (Hentoff's title refers to the Georgia Supreme Court striking down the state sodomy law on November 23, 1998.)

29. Evan Wolfson, "Bowers v. Hardwick," *Advocate*, November 12, 2002. Wolfson, a junior attorney at the time, worked with Tribe on the case.

30. *Bowers v. Hardwick*, 478 US 186 (1986).

31. Quoted in Wolfson, "Bowers v. Hardwick."

32. Groups such as Lambda, Gay and Lesbian Advocates and Defenders, and the ACLU had started meeting together a couple of times a year as the "Round Table," in order to discuss strategies for overturning the sodomy laws: Evan Wolfson, interview with author, New York, March 6, 2013.

33. *Lawrence v. Texas*, 539 US 558 (2003); and Dale Carpenter, *Flagrant Conduct: The Story of Lawrence v. Texas* (New York: Norton, 2012). Carpenter's is the most complete account of the story behind *Lawrence v. Texas*.

34. Garner was arrested for assault again in fall 1998, in the midst of appealing his sodomy conviction. He and Robert Eubanks were living together in a hotel, and after a night of drinking, Garner swatted Eubanks with a belt. Eubanks, as was his wont, called the police: Lisa Teachey, "Defendant in Sodomy Case Out of Jail After Assault Charges Dismissed," *Houston Chronicle*, November 25, 1998.

35. Joseph Landau, "Ripple Effect: Sodomy Statutes as Weapons," *New Republic*, June 23, 2003.

36. Douglas Martin, "Tyron Garner, 39, Plaintiff in Pivotal Sodomy Case, Dies," *New York Times*, September 14, 2006.

37. Goldberg, interview with author.

38. Associated Press, "State Sodomy Law Ruled Constitutional by Appeals Court," *Texas City (TX) Sun*, March 16, 2001.

39. Associated Press, "High Court Hears Case on Texas Sodomy Law," *Odessa (TX) American,* March 27, 2003.

40. Martin, "Tyron Garner."

41. Goldberg, interview with author.

42. Ibid.; "Justices Hear Anti-Sodomy Case," *USA Today*, March 27, 2003; and Linda Greenhouse, "Court Seems Set to Reverse a Sodomy Law," *New York Times*, March 27, 2003.

43. Greenhouse, "Court Seems Set to Reverse a Sodomy Law."

44. Brian Rogers, "Rosenthal Cites Prescription Drugs in Resignation as DA," *Houston Chronicle*, February 15, 2008.

45. Mark Tushnet, *A Court Divided: The Rehnquist Court and the Future of Constitutional Law* (New York: Norton, 2005), p. 170. Suzanne Goldberg (interview with author) speculates that Texas might have sent Chuck Rosenthal to the Supreme Court to argue the case because the state was not committed to defending the law.

46. Tushnet, *A Court Divided*, p. 170.

47. Quoted in Greenhouse, "Court Seems Set to Reverse a Sodomy Law."

48. Charles Lane, "Justices Overturn Texas Sodomy Ban," *Washington Post*, June 27, 2003.

49. *Lawrence v. Texas*, 539 US 558 (2003).

CHAPTER 29: "THE FIRST LAW IN AMERICAN HISTORY THAT BEGINS THE JOB OF PROTECTING LGBT PEOPLE"

1. Stephen Holden, "The Brandon Teena Story: A Rape and Beating, Later 3 Murders, and Then a Twist," *New York Times*, September 3, 1998.
2. Documentary, *The Brandon Teena Story*, directors Susan Muska and Greta Olafsdottir, 1998.
3. Rogers Worthington, "Deadly Deception," *Chicago Tribune*, January 17, 1994.
4. *JoAnn Brandon (representing estate of Teena Brandon, deceased) v. County of Richardson, Nebraska and Charles B. Laux, Sheriff*, Supreme Court of Nebraska, no. S-00-022, April 20, 2001.
5. Aphrodite Jones, *All She Wanted* (New York: Pocket Books, 1996), p. 228; and *The Brandon Teena Story*.
6. *The Brandon Teena Story*.
7. *JoAnn Brandon v. County of Richardson, Nebraska and Charles B. Laux, Sheriff*, Supreme Court of Nebraska.
8. Eric Bishop and Jeff Slowikowski, "Fact Sheet 29: Hate Crime," August 1995, National Criminal Justice Reference Service. Thanks to the pressure of activist groups, in 1990 the Department of Justice had begun keeping statistics on hate crimes based on the victim's "sexual orientation": Hate Crime Statistics Act of 1990, 28 U.S.C., paragraph 534.
9. *JoAnn Brandon v. County of Richardson, Nebraska and Charles B. Laux, Sheriff*, 653 NW 2nd 829 (2002). The court ordered that Teena's mother be paid $98,000.
10. Ibid.
11. "Deputy Wanted to Arrest Two Suspects Before Alleged Murder," *McCook (NE) Daily Gazette*, October 27, 1994.
12. Dr. Reena Roy, interview with author, State College, PA (telephone), July 13, 2014.
13. In 2007, with Lotter still on death row and Nissen serving a life sentence, Nissen claimed that he was responsible for having fired the shots that killed all three people: "Nissen: I Am the Person Who Shot and Stabbed Tina Brandon," *Lincoln (NE) Journal Star*, September 19, 2007. As of January 2015, Lotter was still on death row.
14. *JoAnn Brandon v. County of Richardson, Nebraska and Charles B. Laux, Sheriff*, Supreme Court of Nebraska; and Memorandum and Order (for a writ of habeas corpus): *John L. Lotter, Petitioner v. Robert Houston, Warden, Tecumseh State Correctional Center*, filed in US District Court, Nebraska, 4:04CV3187, doc. 83, March 18, 2012.
15. The 1998 documentary *The Brandon Teena Story* preceded *Boys Don't Cry* but received far less media attention.
16. The term, which came into use in the transgender community in the 1990s, refers to people who experience no discrepancy between the sex they were assigned at birth and their own gendered sense of themselves.
17. FBI Report: "Hate Crime Statistics," 1998.
18. James Brooke, "Gay Man Beaten and Left for Dead; 2 Are Charged," *New York*

Times, October 10, 1998; and James Brooke, "Gay Man Dies from Attack, Fanning Outrage and Debate," *New York Times*, October 13, 1998.

19. James Brooke, "Witnesses Trace Brutal Killing of Gay Student," *New York Times*, November 21, 1998; and Melanie Thernstrom, "The Crucifixion of Matthew Shepard," *Vanity Fair*, March 1999.

20. Gallup News Service, Mark Gillespie, "Americans Support Hate Crime Legislation That Protects Gays," April 7, 1999.

21. Rachel Martin interview of Stephen Jimenez, *Weekend Edition*, NPR, October 6, 2013.

22. Stephen Jimenez, *The Book of Matt: Hidden Truths About the Murder of Matthew Shepard* (Hanover, NH: Steerforth Press, 2013).

23. Luke Brinker, "Debunking Stephen Jimenez's Effort to De-Gay Matthew Shepard's Murder," *Equality Matters Blog*, October 2, 2013; see also the almost five hundred comments posted in response to James Nichols, "Matthew Shepard Murdered by Bisexual Lover and Drug Dealer, Stephen Jimenez Claims," *Huffington Post*, September 12, 2013.

24. Senate Bill 1529 (105th Congress), Hate Crimes Prevention Act of 1998, November 13, 1997.

25. Hearst Syndicate, Jennifer Corbett Dooren, "Gay Student's Mom: 'Expand U.S. Hate Law,'" *Sun-Sentinel* (Miami), May 12, 1999.

26. Debate transcript, "The Second Gore-Bush Presidential Debate," October 11, 2000, Commission on Presidential Debates.

27. See Michael Crowley, "James Dobson: The Religious Right's New Kingmaker," *Slate*, November 12, 2004; and David Kirkpatrick, "Evangelical Leader Threatens to Use Political Muscle Against Some Democrats," *New York Times*, January 1, 2005.

28. See p. 446.

29. Dan Gilgoff, "New Report Tallies Conservative Christian Visits to Bush White House," *U.S. News & World Report*, September 14, 2009.

30. Quoted in "Special Report: U.S. Senate Approves Hate Crimes Legislation," North Carolina Family Policy Council, June 16, 2004.

31. "House Favors Expanding Hate Crime Law to Protect Gays," *Washington Post*, September 15, 2005.

32. Frank, interview with author; and Baldwin, interview with author.

33. Frank, interview with author.

34. Stefen Styrsky, "Decision Day on Trans Rights," *Gay City News* (New York), August 5–11, 2004.

35. Frank and Baldwin, interviews with author.

36. David Stout, "House Votes to Expand Hate Crime Protection," *New York Times*, May 4, 2007.

37. Dobson quoted in Associated Press, "White House Threatens to Veto Hate Crimes Bill," NBC News, May 3, 2007. The bill specifically protected all First Amendment freedoms, which would include even hate speech.

38. Quoted in "House Passes LGBT-Inclusive Hate-Crimes Bill," *Advocate*, May 4, 2007.

39. Kerry Eleveld, "Shepard Bill Reception Proves Emotional," *Advocate*, October 28, 2009.

40. Richard Kim, "The Truth About Hate Crime Laws," *Nation*, July 12, 1999; Joey L. Mogul, Andrea J. Ritchie, and Kay Whitlock, *Queer (In)Justice: The Criminalization of LGBT People in the U.S.* (Boston: Beacon Press, 2011), chap. 6, "False Promises"; Dobbs, interview with author; William Dobbs, "Justice, Not Vengeance for Hate Crimes," *New York Times*, April 16, 2012; and Michael Bronski, Ann Pelligrini, and Michael Amico, "Hate Crime Laws Don't Prevent Violence Against LGBT People," *Nation*, October 2, 2013.

41. See also Wade Henderson (head of the national Leadership Conference on Civil and Human Rights, a coalition of two hundred rights organizations), "Bias Laws Ensure Action Against Hate," *New York Times*, March 7, 2012.

42. Sheriff Randy Houser, interview with Stephanie Fairyington, in "Two Decades After Brandon Teena's Murder, a Look Back at Falls City," *Atlantic Monthly*, December 2013.

43. Quoted in Deb Price, "Savor the Moment," Creators Syndicate, October 28, 2009.

CHAPTER 30: A FORTY-YEAR WAR: THE STRUGGLE FOR WORKPLACE PROTECTION

1. Al Kamen, "Frank's Greatest Hits: A Collection of the Massachusetts Democrat's Notable Jokes and Putdowns," *Washington Post*, November 30, 2011.

2. Former congressman Bob Bauman, who'd been a "family values" foe of gays, had failed in his 1980 reelection bid after the FBI let it be leaked to the media that sitting in his car in a gay DC cruising area, with a license plate that said "U.S. Congress 1," he'd solicited a sixteen-year-old male hustler. In 1986 Bauman published *The Gentleman from Maryland: The Conscience of a Gay Conservative*, in which he talked of Barney Frank attending the annual DC Gay Pride Parade "in a tank top, with his usual young companion."

3. John Robinson, "Frank Discusses Being Gay: Says It's 'Not Relevant to the Job'," *Boston Globe*, May 30, 1987. Barney Frank, interview with Jeffrey Toobin, in "Barney's Great Adventure," *New Yorker*, January 12, 2009; Stuart B. Weisberg, *Barney Frank: The Story of America's Only Left-Handed, Gay, Jewish Congressman* (Amherst: University of Massachusetts Press, 2009).

4. Paul Norton, "Anti-Gay Attack by Greer Ignites Campaign Battle," *Madison Capital Times*, July 10, 1998.

5. Jeff Mayers, "Baldwin's Win over Musser Historic," *Wisconsin State Journal*, November 4, 1998.

6. See p. 261.

7. Tanya Domi, "Remembering Ted Kennedy's Work on ENDA," *Pam's House Blend*, August 27, 2009.

8. Reuters, "Gay Marriage Opposed in Polls," *Boston Globe*, February 7, 1994.

9. Robert P. Jones and Daniel Cox, "Two Decades of Polling on Gay and Lesbian Issues at Pew: An Overview and Assessment," Public Religion Research Institute, August 8, 2010.

10. Don Feder, "Gay Rights Lobby Stakes Hopes on House Gambit," *Colorado Springs (CO) Gazette Telegraph*, June 28, 1994.

11. Senator Edward Kennedy, introducing Senate Bill 2238, June 23, 1994.

12. "Employment Non-Discrimination Act," *Civil Rights Monitor* 9, no. 1 (Winter 1997).

13. "The Senate's Votes on Gay Rights," *New York Times*, September 13, 1996.

14. "Employment Non-Discrimination Act," *Civil Rights Monitor*.

15. HR 2015 specified protections for "gender-related identity, appearance, or mannerisms, or other gender-related characteristics of an individual."

16. I am grateful to Diego Sanchez, Congressman Frank's legislative assistant, for providing me with copies of HR 2015 and all ENDA bills that were introduced by Frank.

17. By 2007, there were already numerous transgender rights groups, such as the National Transgender Advocacy Coalition, Transgender Foundation of America, Sylvia Rivera Law Project, and National Coalition for Transgender Equality. An annual Transgender Day of Remembrance had been started in 1998 to honor the memory of transgender people killed in hate crimes. There'd also been a spate of books by transgender activists that were passed from hand-to-hand in the LGBT community, including Kate Bornstein's *Gender Outlaw: On Men, Women and the Rest of Us* (New York: Routledge, 1994); Leslie Feinberg's *Transgender Warriors: Making History from Joan of Arc to Dennis Rodman* (Boston: Beacon Press, 1996), and Feinberg's *Trans Liberation: Beyond Pink or Blue* (Boston: Beacon Press, 1999); as well as a seven-hundred-page compendium (beginning with Richard von Krafft-Ebing's nineteenth-century musings on "men trapped in women's bodies" and "women trapped in men's bodies"), edited by Susan Stryker and Stephen Whittle, *The Transgender Studies Reader* (New York: Routledge, 2006).

18. Stephen Mark Beaudoin, "Frankly Speaking: U.S. Rep. Barney Frank to Trans Community: 'Get Your Own Train,'" *Just Out*, May 2, 2008.

19. Frank, interview with author.

20. Baldwin, interview with author.

21. Ibid.

22. Frank, interview with author.

23. Frank also introduced a separate "gender-identity"-only bill at that time, HR 3686. He had no hopes for its passage, but he wanted to begin a discussion in Congress that would educate lawmakers for a future vote. It died in committee.

24. Paul Schindler, "HRC Alone in Eschewing No-Compromise Stand," *Gay City News* (New York), October 4, 2007.

25. The largest survey of transgender people, taken in 2011, reported that 90 percent said they'd experienced "harassment and mistreatment at work," compared with 37 percent of lesbians and gays who reported work harassment: in Jennifer Pizer et al., "Evidence of Persistent and Pervasive Workplace Discrimination Against LGBT People," *Loyola of Los Angeles Law Review*, March 2012, p. 721.

26. Jenny Pizer, Lambda Legal law and policy director, interview with author, Los Angeles (telephone), August 6, 2014.

27. Quoted in Lisa Keen, "Gloves Come Off in Fight over ENDA," *Between the Lines News*, October 18, 2007.

28. Keen, "Gloves Come Off in Fight over ENDA," *Between the Lines News*.

29. NGLTF Press Release, "Update on ENDA," October 11, 2007. The stance that rights organizations took on a trans-inclusive ENDA was not without consequences. Jon Davidson, legal director of Lambda Legal, recalled several phone calls and letters from donors who said, "Why is a gay group doing this? Gays have nothing in common with transgender people," or "You're interfering with a bill that's much needed by gays and lesbians, and there are many more of us than there are trans people": Jon Davidson, interview with author, Los Angeles (telephone), August 12, 2014.

30. John Aravosis, "How Did the T Get in LGBT?" *Salon*, October 8, 2007.

31. Quoted in Chris Geidner, "Then and Now," *Metro Weekly* (Washington, DC), March 8, 2012.

32. Diego Sanchez, interview with author, Washington, DC (telephone), August 7, 2014.

33. Ibid.; and Jordy Yager, "I Was Not a Pretty Girl, and I Felt Like a Man," *Hill*, March 10, 2009. The appointment of Sanchez was the start of the LGBT community's reinvigorated romance with Barney Frank: see, for example, Autumn Sandeen, "Diego Sanchez Is Rep. Frank's New Legislative Advisor," *Pam's House Blend,* December 18, 2008.

34. House Committee on Education and Labor: hearing regarding HR 3017, Employment Non-Discrimination Act, September 23, 2009.

35. Vandy Beth Glenn had come out as transgender to her immediate supervisor on Coming Out Day, October 11, 2006. The supervisor, who was supportive, suggested that that Halloween she come to the office dressed as who she felt she was. "It will serve as a trial balloon," the supervisor said: Vandy Beth Glenn, interview with author, Decatur, GA (telephone), September 7, 2014.

36. Glenn, interview with author.

37. House Committee on Education and Labor: hearing regarding HR 3017, Employment Non-Discrimination Act, September 23, 2009; and Glenn, interview with author.

38. Christian Boone, "Hired as a Man, Fired as a Woman," *Atlanta Journal-Constitution*, November 5, 2009. Glenn sued Brumby and the Georgia Assembly. Represented by Lambda Legal, she claimed that her constitutional right to equal protection had been violated (*Glenn v. Brumby*, et al., 724 Supp. 2d 1284 [N.D. Ga. 2010]). She won in both the US District Court and the US Court of Appeals.

39. Hearing regarding HR 3017.

40. Tico Almeida, "A Game Plan for ENDA," *Metro Weekly* (Washington, DC), March 31, 2011. Almeida went on to found Freedom to Work, a lobbying group devoted to getting legislation passed for LGBT workplace protections.

41. See p. 516.

42. HR 3017, introduced June 24, 2009.

43. Quoted in Lisa Keen, "ENDA Introduced in Senate," *Bay Area Reporter*, August 6, 2009.

44. Chris Geidner, "ENDA Vote May Be Near," *Metro Weekly* (Washington, DC), March 29, 2010.

45. Chris Geidner, "Not the ENDA Road," *Metro Weekly* (Washington, DC), March 19, 2010.

46. Chris Johnson, "Pelosi Endorses Executive Order Against LGBT Job Discrimination," *Washington Blade*, July 21, 2011.

47. Editorial Board, "The President Should Extend Workplace Protections for Sexual Orientation," *Washington Post*, February 6, 2012.

48. The poll was taken by Greenberg Quilan Rosner Research: in Jeff Krehely, "Polls Show Huge Public Support for Gay and Transgender Workplace Protections," *American Progress*, June 2, 2011.

49. Sam Hanane, "Obama's Gay Appointees Smash Record," *Huffington Post*, October 26, 2010.

50. Kevin Johnson and Joan Biskupic, "Obama Team Won't Defend Defense of Marriage Act," *USA Today*, February 24, 2011.

51. Laura Meckler, "Obama Won't Issue Ban on Gay Discrimination," *Wall Street Journal*, April 11, 2012.

52. On April 6, 2012, during his last year in office, Barney Frank had again reintroduced a trans-inclusive ENDA, HR 1397. It fizzled.

53. Peter Wallsten, "Obama Delays Ban on Discrimination by U.S. Contractors, Disappointing Gay Rights Advocates," *Washington Post*, April 12, 2012.

54. Meckler, "Obama Won't Issue Ban on Gay Discrimination."

55. Ibid.

56. Kylar Broadus, interview with author, Washington, DC (telephone), July 31, 2014.

57. Amanda Terkel, "Jeff Merkley Takes Up Mantle of LGBT Equality from Ted Kennedy," *Huffington Post*, November 4, 2013.

58. Amanda Terkel, "Bill Nelson Backs ENDA," *Huffington Post*, October 29, 2013.

59. US Senate Health, Education, Labor and Pensions Committee Hearing on ENDA, Dirksen Senate Building, June 12, 2012.

60. Broadus, interview with author; US Senate Health, Education, Labor and Pensions Committee Hearing on ENDA, Dirksen Senate Building, June 12, 2012; and Souleo, "On the Job: Gender Identity and Sexuality Discrimination in the Office," *Black Enterprise*, February 17, 2011.

61. Sunnivie Brydum, "In Historic First, Senate Approves ENDA," *Advocate*, November 7, 2013.

62. Amanda Terkel and Michael McAuliff, "John McCain Worried ENDA Will Be Like Busing," *Huffington Post*, October 29, 2013.

63. Juliet Eilperin, "Cindy McCain Petitions Husband to Back Gay Rights Bill," *Washington Post*, October 25, 2013.

64. Press Release, "Statement by Senator John McCain on ENDA," November 7, 2013.

65. Religion News Service, Lauren Markoe, "Hobby Lobby Boycotts Jewish Hanukkah and Passover," October 2, 2013.

66. *Sylvia Burwell, Secretary of Health and Human Services, et al. v. Hobby Lobby Stores, et al.*, 573 US (2014).

67. Aaron Blake, "A Lot of People Could Be Affected by the Supreme Court's Birth Control Decision—Theoretically," *Washington Post,* June 30, 2014.

68. Eli Clifton, "Hobby Lobby's Secret Agenda: How It's Quietly Funding a Vast Right-Wing Movement," *Salon*, March 27, 2014.

69. Ruth Bader Ginsburg, dissent, *Burwell v. Hobby Lobby*, 573 US (2014).

70. Jenny Pizer, law and policy director of Lambda Legal, quoted in Gabriel Arana, "Fighting the Religious Right Exacts a Toll," *Salon*, July 23, 2014.

71. Molly Ball, "How Hobby Lobby Split the Left and Set Back Gay Rights," *Atlantic*, July 20, 2014.

72. Amanda Terkel, "Barney Frank Sharply Criticizes Gay Rights Groups' Flip on ENDA," *Huffington Post*, August 5, 2014.

73. Faith letter to president defending executive order, c/o Melissa Rogers, executive director, White House Office of Faith-Based and Neighborhood Partnerships, July 8, 2014.

74. Quoted in Julie Hirschfeld and Erik Eckholm, "Faith Groups Seek Exclusion from Bias Rule," *New York Times*, July 8, 2014. The Christian right was mired in a slough of despond as a result of the two executive orders. "This is a "post-Christian America," they lamented, where "traditional religious believers are pushed ever more fully out of the public sphere." They complained that the president of the United States had just told them, "Drop dead!" Now, they said—co-opting the rhetoric of the outraged victim—"religious groups that feed the poor will have to decide between Christ and Caesar": Rod Dreher, "Obama to Religious 'Bigots': 'Drop Dead,'" *American Conservative*, July 18, 2014.

75. In 2002 President George W. Bush had also amended Johnson's executive order by E.O. 13279, which said that a religious corporation, association, educational institution or society could favor people of that religion in hiring.

CHAPTER 31: "THE STATUS THAT EVERYONE UNDERSTANDS AS THE ULTIMATE EXPRESSION OF LOVE AND COMMITMENT"

1. Carol Ness, "Lesbians Crusade for Same-Sex Marriage," *San Francisco Examiner*, April 30, 1995.

2. In the 1970s, there'd been a spate of high-profile attempts by same-sex couples to marry, beginning in 1970 with Jack Baker and Michael McConnell in Minnesota (*Baker v. Nelson*, Minnesota Supreme Court, 191 N.W. 2d, 185); and Marjorie Jones and Tracy Knight in Kentucky (United Press International, "Marriage License Asked by 2 Women," *Middlesboro [KY] Daily News*, July 8, 1970; and *Jones v. Hallahan*, Kentucky Court of Appeals, 501 S.W. 2d, 588). One of the most high-profile cases was that of radical GLF-er John (Faygele) Singer, who teamed up with Paul Barwick, a buddy and fellow zapper, and demanded a marriage license in Seattle. Their case went all the way to the Washington Court of Appeals: *Singer*

v. Hara, Washington Court of Appeals, 247, 522P. 2d, 1187; and "'We Can Fight It from Within': Non-Believers Seek License to Wed," *Advocate*, November 10, 1971. The 1975 marriage case of Richard Adams, a naturalized American citizen from the Philippines, and Anthony Sullivan, an immigrant from Australia, also got considerable media attention (*Adams v. Howerton*, Ninth Circuit, 673 F.2d, 1036 (1982); Peter Nardi, "The Endless Debate on Gay Union," *Baltimore Sun*, February 20, 1996; and documentary *Limited Partnership*, directed by Tom Miller, 2014).

3. Paula Ettelbrick, "Since When Is Marriage the Path to Liberation?," *Out/Look*, Fall 1989. In the same issue of *Out/Look*, Tom Stoddard, who was Lambda Legal's executive director, wrote a promarriage piece, "Why Gay People Should Seek the Right to Marry," but it was Ettelbrick's view that held sway in 1989. Another attorney articulating widely disseminated lesbian-feminist views of marriage at the time was Nancy Polikoff: see, for example, "We Will Get What We Ask For: Why Legalizing Gay and Lesbian Marriage Will Not 'Dismantle the Legal Structure of Gender in Every Marriage,'" *Virginia Law Review* 79 (1993): pp. 1535–50.

4. William E. Woods, "Marriage's Grass Roots," *Advocate*, May 11, 2004; and John Gallagher, "Marriage, Hawaii Style," *Advocate*, February 4, 1997.

5. Denby Fawcett, "Looking Back with Ninia Baehr on the Early Struggle for Same-Sex Marriage," *Huffington Post*, October 31, 2013.

6. Associated Press, "Judge in Hawaii Set to Rule on Landmark Same-Sex Marriage Case," *Walla Walla (WA) Union Bulletin*, December 3, 1996.

7. *Baeher v. Lewin*, No. 91-1394-05 (Haw. Cir. Ct. October 1, 1991).

8. Evan Wolfson, "Same-Sex Marriage and Morality: The Human Rights Vision of the Constitution," April 1983, Harvard Law School. This 140-page "final paper" became the basis of Wolfson's book *Why Marriage Matters: America, Equality, and Gay People's Right to Marry* (New York: Simon & Schuster, 2004). Wolfson had felt like a lone voice crying in the wilderness until he read Andrew Sullivan's "Here Comes the Groom: A (Conservative) Case for Gay Marriage," *New Republic*, August 28, 1989, one of the first published serious arguments for same-sex marriage.

9. Wolfson, interview with author; and Richard Socarides, "Q&A: Evan Wolfson on Winning the Gay Marriage Fight," *The New Yorker*, December 2, 2013.

10. The case brought public attention to the existence of gay youth and sparked a 2013 revision of BSA's gay exclusion. *Boy Scouts of America v. Dale*, 530 US 640 (2000).

11. "High Court Justice Will Be Stepping Down," *Star-Bulletin* (Honolulu), October 15, 2008.

12. *Baehr v. Lewin*, 852 P.2d 44 (Hawaii 1993).

13. Mary Bonauto, quoted in David J. Garrow, "Toward a More Perfect Union," *New York Times*, May 4, 2004.

14. Carey Goldberg, "Hawaii Judge Ends Gay Marriage Ban," *New York Times*, December 4, 1996.

15. By now Lewin had been replaced as director of the State Health Department. The suit was retitled *Baehr v. Miike*, 910 P.2d 112 (1996).

16. Press release: "The Birth of a Gay, Lesbian, Bisexual Movement in South Dakota," National Gay and Lesbian Task Force, February 22, 1995.

17. David W. Dunlap, "Some States Trying to Stop Gay Marriages Before They Start," *New York Times*, March 15, 1995.

18. Alan Matsuoka, "Gay Unions Score Low in *Star-Bulletin* Poll," *Star-Bulletin* (Honolulu), March 29, 1996.

19. "Defense of Marriage Act," *Capitol Words*, 142/103 (July 12, 1996), pp. H7480–7506.

20. "Defense of Marriage Act," *Capitol Words*, 142/102 (July 11, 1996), pp. H7441–7449.

21. "Defense of Marriage Act," HR 3396, 104th Congress, 2d Session.

22. House of Representatives, 104th Congress, 2d Session, *Report* 104-664, July 9, 1996.

23. Congressional Record, 103rd Congress, Senate, May 24, 1993, p. S6333. Helms asked that an article, "The Homosexual Lobby: The $5 Million Clout," from the *Washington Post Weekly Edition*, February 1–7, 1993, be put into the Congressional Record.

24. Achtenberg, interview with author; Michael Ross and Elizabeth Shogren, "Gay Activist Nomination Hotly Debated," *Los Angeles Times*, May 20, 1993; Clifford Krauss, "Housing Nominee Is Attacked," *New York Times*, May 21, 1993; and "Lesbian Confirmed in Housing Position with Votes to Spare," *New York Times*, May 25, 1993.

25. David W. Dunlap, "Clinton Names First Liaison to Gay and Lesbian Groups," *New York Times*, June 14, 1996.

26. Richard Socarides, "Why Bill Clinton Signed the Defense of Marriage Act," *New Yorker*, March 8, 2013.

27. "Gay Revolution Comes Out," *Rat*, August 12–26, 1969. In "Refugees from Amerika: A Gay Manifesto" (1970), which became a gay bible in radical circles, Carl Wittman dubbed marriage "a rotten, oppressive institution."

28. Michael Warner, *The Trouble with Normal: Sex, Politics, and the Ethics of Queer Life* (Cambridge, MA: Harvard University Press, 2000).

29. Michael Bronski, interview with author, Cambridge, MA, March 15, 2013.

30. Nicole Murray-Ramirez, interview with author, San Diego, June 29, 2012.

31. Urvashi Vaid, interview with author, New York, March 24, 2014; Urvashi Vaid, *Irresistible Revolution: Confronting Race, Class, and the Assumptions of LGBT Politics* (New York: Magnus, 2012); and Urvashi Vaid, *Virtual Equality: The Mainstreaming of Gay and Lesbian Liberation* (New York: Doubleday, 1995).

32. Dobbs, interview with author.

33. *Against Equality: Queer Critiques of Gay Marriage*, ed. Ryan Conrad (Lewiston, ME: Against Equality Publishing Collective, 2010).

34. Garrow, "Toward a More Perfect Union."

35. Czech word for "mother."

36. Mary Bonauto, interview with author, Portland, ME (telephone), March 18, 2013.

37. Garrow, "Toward a More Perfect Union."

38. A year earlier, in 1993, the Supreme Judicial Court of Massachusetts had granted

a "second-parent adoption" of the three-year-old daughter of celebrity doctor Susan Love to her partner, Dr. Helen Cooksey: *Adoption of Tammy*, 619 NE.2d 315 (Mass. 1993); and Susan Love and Helen Cooksey, interview with author, Pacific Palisdes, CA, December 23, 2014.

39. *Baker v. Vermont*, 744 A.2d 864 (Vermont 1999).

40. Bonauto, interview with author.

41. Mary L. Bonauto, "Goodridge in Context," *Harvard Civil Rights-Civil Liberties Law Review* 40, no. 1 (2005): pp. 1–70.

42. Bonauto, interview with author; and *Goodridge v. Department of Public Health*, 798 NE.2d 941 (Mass. 2003).

43. Bonauto, "Goodridge in Context."

44. Kathleen Burge, "Judge Dismisses Same-Sex Marriage Suit," *Boston Globe*, May 2, 2002.

45. *Goodridge v. Department of Public Health*.

46. The gay and lesbian community got a hint of where Marshall stood on the subject of same-sex marriage a few years earlier, when she was the speaker at the 1999 annual dinner of the Massachusetts Lesbian and Gay Bar Association. Marshall told her audience they ought to learn from the examples of other countries: Sweden, Norway, and Denmark all had state recognition of same-sex relationships; the Netherlands was about to legalize same-sex marriage: Joseph Barri, past president of the Massachusetts Lesbian and Gay Bar Association, interview with author, Boston (telephone), March 16, 2013.

47. Quoted in *Goodridge v. Department of Public Health*. The win was strongly contested before same-sex marriages could take effect: Governor Mitt Romney supported a constitutional amendment that would overrule the court decision. Conservatives demanded a constitutional convention—a joint meeting of the Massachusetts House and Senate—which they hoped would lead to legislators blocking the court's order or, at the least, substituting "civil unions" for marriage. If the legislators wouldn't overturn the court decision, conservatives hoped to put a constitutional amendment banning same-sex marriage on the 2006 ballot. But politically savvy groups and individuals made sure that Goodridge got implemented. They were led by the Massachusetts Gay and Lesbian Political Caucus, cochaired by Arline Isaacson, a polished and stylish lesbian who'd been lobbying for gay and lesbian causes since the 1980s; Massachusetts Equality's executive director, Marc Solomon, a cerebral strategist who knew how to mobilize the troops; and Marty Rouse, a politico hired by Mass Equality after he'd helped Vermont legislators overcome their constituents' ire for their support of same-sex relationships. They not only lobbied legislators but also encouraged Massachusetts gays and lesbians, who were coming out on a large scale, to play an active role, even to knocking on legislators' door themselves: "Tell them your personal story. Bring your family. Bring your parents," Marty Rouse instructed them. At the State House, where the constitutional conventions were held, the leaders orchestrated dramatic vigils: gays and lesbians waving twelve-foot flags and singing "America, the Beautiful" and "This Land Is Your Land" in the halls and at the door of the chamber where

legislators were meeting. They outscreamed the Right—bused in from antigay churches all over the country—who'd come to chant "Let the people vote!" and demand a referendum: Marc Solomon, interview with author, New York, March 6, 2013; Arline Isaacson, interview with author, Brookline, Massachusetts, March 14, 2013; and Marty Rouse, interview with author, Washington, DC (telephone), February 2, 2013. In the end, there was no referendum, Governor Romney failed to block the court's decision, and gay and lesbian couples started marrying in Massachusetts in May 2004. Right-wing efforts to ban same-sex marriage in the state continued for a time but slowed after thousands of gay and lesbian couples had married and the sky over Massachusetts hadn't fallen. See also a discussion of the Massachusetts marriage battle in Marc Solomon, *Winning Marriage: The Inside Story of How Same-Sex Couples Took On the Politicians and Pundits— and Won* (Lebanon, NH: Fore Edge/University Press of New England, 2014).
48. See p. 551.

CHAPTER 32: GETTING IT RIGHT, AND WRONG, IN THE WEST

1. Charlene Strong, interview with author, Seattle, May 9, 2012
2. Ibid.; and David Hoffman, "The Making of an Activist," *Washington Blade*, September 23, 2010.
3. Strong, interview with author.
4. The bill permitted heterosexual couples over sixty-two who didn't want to marry (for reasons such as loss of social security benefits) to register their partnership, too.
5. Senator Ed Murray, interview with author, Seattle, May 10, 2012; and documentary *For My Wife: The Making of an Activist for Marriage Equality*, directed by David Rothmiller, 2010.
6. Nevertheless, all but one Republican senator voted against the bill. It would bring "a threat to traditional marriage," they argued. The one Republican senator to vote for it, Dale Broadland from Bellingham, said that hearing Charlene Strong's testimony affected him deeply. "I couldn't face my children saying I voted against this," he told the Unitarian minister when she thanked him for his vote: Reverend Carol McKinley, interview with author, Olympia, WA, May 29, 2012; and Associated Press, "Senate Passes Domestic Partnership Measure," *Walla Walla (WA) Union-Bulletin*, March 2, 2007.
7. Governor Christine Gregoire, interview with author, Olympia, WA (telephone), June 26, 2012.
8. Representative Jamie Pedersen, interview with author, Seattle, May 10, 2012.
9. Evan Wolfson, "Marriage Equality and Some Lessons for the Scary Work of Winning," *Law and Sexuality* 135, no. 14 (2005).
10. Chris McGann, "A Long Awaited Win for Gay Rights," *Seattle Post-Intelligencer*, January 27, 2006.
11. Gregoire and Murray, interviews with author.
12. Pedersen, interview with author.
13. Gregoire, interview with author.
14. Molly Ball, "The Marriage Plot: Inside This Year's Epic Campaign for Gay

Equality," *Atlantic*, December 11, 2012; and "Gay Marriage Bill a Go in Washington State," *Los Angeles Times*, January 23, 2012.

15. Joel Connelly, "Ed Murray-Michael Shiosaki: A 22-Year Trip to the Altar," *Seattle Post-Intelligencer*, August 9, 2013.

16. William Yardley, "Washington State Senate Passes Gay Marriage Bill," *Los Angeles Times*, February 1, 2012.

17. Representative Laurie Jinkins, interview with author, Tacoma, WA, May 12, 2012.

18. Representative Maureen Walsh, interview with author, Walla Walla, WA, May 8, 2012. In 2008, she'd been censured by Republican leaders in her district because she'd cosponsored the domestic partnership bill; 70 percent of the electorate in her district had voted to overturn the bill.

19. Walsh, interview with author.

20. Rachel LaCorte, "Washington House Passes Gay Marriage Bill," *Huffington Post*, February 8, 2012.

21. Senator Pete Knight, television interview with Leon Worden, SCVTV (Santa Clarita, CA), April 1, 2004.

22. Ellen Goodman, "Who Needs Robertson? GOP Has Knight" (syndicated), *Daily Herald* (Chicago), March 3, 2000.

23. David Knight, "My Father Is Wrong on Gays," op-ed piece, *Los Angeles Times*, October 14, 1999.

24. "Failed Bill Author Says Son is Gay," *Orange County Register* (California), September 12, 1996.

25. Ellen Goodman, "Who Needs Robertson?"

26. In 2004 Valentine's Day fell on a Saturday, when the courthouse would be closed. Avoiding Friday the thirteenth, the couples requested marriage licenses on Thursday, February 12. The Metropolitan Community Church had been conducting Valentine's Day demonstrations at the courthouse since Knight's Prop 22 passed in 2000.

27. Tyler, first interview with author; Perry, interview with author; and Gloria Allred, interview with author, Los Angeles, August 20, 2012.

28. Statement reprinted in Matthew Fleischer, "California Supreme Court Set to Consider Gay Marriage: Meet the L.A. Four Who Started All the Trouble," *L.A. Weekly*, February 27, 2008.

29. Gloria Allred, press release: "Same Gender Marriage and Valentine's Day: Lesbian Couple and Their Attorney, Gloria Allred, Who Sued Los Angeles County for Denying Them a Marriage License, Will Once Again Apply for the License at the Beverly Hills Courthouse." I am grateful to Ms. Allred for sharing this document with me.

30. Perry and DeBlieck were already legally married, but only in Canada. Their marriage in Toronto's Metropolitan Community Church, performed in 2003, as soon as the Canadian government legalized same-sex marriage, wasn't recognized anywhere in the United States.

31. Michael A. Lindberger, "From Gay Marriage's Ground Zero," *Time*, June 17, 2008.

32. Rachel Gordon, "The Battle Over Same-Sex Marriage," *San Francisco Chronicle*, February 15, 2004.

33. Ilene Lelchuk, "Son of Gay Marriage Foe Weds in San Francisco," *San Francisco Chronicle*, March 10, 2004.

34. Senator Pete Knight, television interview with Leon Worden.

35. Quoted in Lee Romney and Maura Dolan, "Judge Rules State Can't Ban Gay Marriage," *Los Angeles Times*, March 15, 2005.

36. John Wildermuth, "Governor Demands End to Gay Marriage; Lockyer Told to Act against S.F.'s Same-Sex Licenses," *San Francisco Chronicle*, February 21, 2004.

37. *Lockyer v. City and County of San Francisco* (2004) 33 Cal. 4th 1055.

38. Lawyer Shannon Minter, quoted in Donna Domino, "Same-Sex Marriage," *San Francisco Attorney*, Winter 2008.

39. Governor Wilson had sparked gay riots up and down the state in 1992 when he refused to sign a bill passed by the assembly that would prohibit workplace discrimination against gays.

40. *Marriage Cases*, Superior Court of the City and County of San Francisco, Judicial Council Coordination Proceeding, no. 4365.

41. Domino, "Same-Sex Marriage"; and Neal Riley, "Judge Richard Kramer Reflects on the Gay Marriage Fight," *San Francisco Chronicle*, August 11, 2013.

42. Accusation against Lockyer in *Proposition 22 Legal Defense and Education Fund v. City and County of San Francisco*, Supreme Court of California, Case No. S147999, p. 3.

43. *In Re. Marriage Cases*: 143 Cal. App. 4th 873.

44. "California High Court Grants Review of Same-Sex Marriage Ban," *Jurist*, December 21, 2006.

45. *In Re. Marriage Cases*: 43 Cal. 4th 757 (2008).

46. Democratic strategists complained in a postmortem that the No on 8 Campaign was run by a committee that wouldn't take advice from professional strategists: Chris Cillizza and Sean Sullivan, "How Proposition 8 Passed in California, and Why It Wouldn't Today," *Washington Post*, March 26, 2013.

47. Pope Benedict XVI declared that homosexuality was "an intrinsic moral evil" (Cardinal Ratzinger [who would become Pope Benedict], "Letter to the Bishops of the Catholic Church on the Pastoral Care of Homosexual Persons," 1986); and that "clear and emphatic opposition to homosexual unions is a duty" (Pope Benedict, Doctrinal Document: "Considerations Regarding Proposals to Give Legal Recognition to Unions Between Two Homosexual Persons," 2003).

48. Tony Semerad, "Leaked Memos: Gay Rights Group Makes New Charges Over LDS Prop 8 Role," *Salt Lake Tribune*, March 19, 2009.

49. "Catholic Effort Launched to Support California Proposition Defending Marriage," Catholic News Agency, August 14, 2008; Matthai Kuruvila, "Catholics, Mormons Allied to Pass Prop 8," *San Francisco Chronicle*, November 10, 2008; Jesse McKinley and Kirk Johnson, "Mormons Tipped Scale in Ban on Gay Marriage," *New York Times*, November 14, 2008; Tony Semerad, "Utah Money Helped Push Prop 8 Spending to Historic Levels," *Salt Lake Tribune*, November 21, 2008; Documentary *8: The Mormon Proposition*, directed by Reed Cowan, 2009.

50. The California Supreme Court ruled on March 26, 2009, that the 18,000 married same-sex couples could stay married.

51. Michael Rothfeld and Tony Barboza, "Governor Backs Gay Marriage," *Los Angeles Times*, November 10, 2008.

CHAPTER 33: THE EVOLUTION OF A
PRESIDENT AND THE COUNTRY

1. Senator Obama's response to author's question, Miami Book Fair International, November 18, 2006.

2. "Open Letter from Barack Obama to the LGBT Community," reprinted in *The Bilerico Project*, February 28, 2008.

3. The letter is reprinted in John Wildermuth, "Obama Opposes Proposed Ban on Gay Marriage." *San Francisco Chronicle*, July 2, 2008.

4. Rick Warren, video message to Saddleback Church members, October 23, 2008.

5. Saddleback Presidential Candidates Forum, aired August 17, 2008, CNN.

6. Roper Public Opinion Archives: "How Groups Voted in 2008."

7. William Harless, "How Important Is the Gay and Lesbian Vote for the Upcoming Election?" *PBS News Hour*, July 16, 2012.

8. See chapter 31, note 8.

9. Quoted in Alexander Mooney, "Obama's Inaugural Choice Sparks Outrage," CNN, December 18, 2008.

10. *Arthur Smelt and Christopher Hammer v. United States of America, State of California, and Does 1 through 1000*, US District Court for the Central District of California, Southern Division, Case No. SACV09-0086.

11. *Reply Memorandum in Support of Defendant United States of America's Motion to Dismiss*, Case No. SACV 09-00286 DOC, August 17, 2009.

12. Lindsey Ellerson, "Obama Justice Department Defends Defense of Marriage Act," *ABC News*, June 12, 2009.

13. "Marriage: Historical Trends": Gallup.

14. Scott Keeter et al., "Young Voters in the 2008 Election," Pew Research Center, November 13, 2008.

15. Nate Silver, "How Opinion on Same-Sex Marriage Is Changing, and What It Means," *FiveThirtyEight*, March 26, 2013.

16. Harvey Milk, "That's What America Is," Gay Freedom Day speech, San Francisco, June 25, 1978.

17. See p. 263.

18. Tim Appelo, "THR Poll: *Glee* and *Modern Family* Drive Voters to Favor Marriage—Even Republican Voters," *Hollywood Reporter*, October 29, 2012.

19. Ibid.

20. Quoted in Jo Becker, *Forcing the Spring: Inside the Fight for Marriage Equality* (New York: Penguin, 2014). Becker's book and David Boies and Theodore B. Olson, *Redeeming the Dream: The Case for Marriage Equality* (New York: Viking, 2014), both present extensive insider views of the struggle around Proposition 8.

21. Romney's proposal for a constitutional amendment wouldn't have been

unpopular in all states. On May 8, 2012, the day before Obama announced his "evolution," 61 percent of North Carolina voters ticked *yes* to a ballot question asking whether the state constitution should be amended by the statement, "Marriage between one man and one woman is the only domestic legal union that shall be valid or recognized in this State." Nevertheless, Obama won North Carolina in 2012 by a four-point margin, capturing not only 93 percent of the African American vote but also 55 percent of the women's vote and 60 percent of the youth vote.

22. Evan Wolfson, head of Freedom to Marry, was identified by Molly Ball as "the architect of the strategy," having briefed White House officials on the talking points that his group found most effective: Molly Ball, "The Marriage Plot: Inside This Year's Epic Campaign for Gay Equality," *Atlantic*, December 11, 2012. In *Forcing the Spring*, Jo Becker says that George W. Bush's former campaign manager and a Republican National Committee Chair, Ken Mehlman—a gay man who'd been closeted until he was inspired to come out in 2010 by Republican lawyer Ted Olson agreeing to take on the Prop 8 challenge—strategized Obama's declaration that he supported same-sex marriage.

23. The following year Robin Roberts made public that she was a lesbian and had a partner of ten years.

24. Anugrah Kumer, "Polls Show Sudden Increase for Gay Marriage," *Christian Post*, November 10, 2012.

25. Transcript: *ABC News Special Report*, May 9, 1012.

26. Richard Socarides, "Forcing Obama's Hand on Gay Marriage," *The New Yorker*, April 6, 2014.

27. *Strauss v. Horton*, 46 Cal. 4th 364 (2009).

28. John Schwartz, "California High Court Upholds Gay Marriage Ban," *New York Times*, May 26, 2009.

29. Olson and Boies tell the story of how they became cocounsel on the Prop 8 case in *Redeeming the Dream*. Griffin is depicted at length in Becker's *Forcing the Spring*.

30. Two years later, David Blankenhorn, like President Obama, had evolved, as he wrote in an op-ed: "How My Views on Gay Marriage Changed," *New York Times*, June 22, 2012. He now believed, he said, in "the equal dignity of homosexual love."

31. *Perry, et al. v. Schwarzenegger, et al.*, U.S. District Court for Northern California, no. C 09-2292 (2010).

32. Eunice Oh, "Stars Celebrate Overturning of Gay Marriage Ban," *People*, August 4, 2010.

33. See pp. 463–67.

34. *Perry, et al. v. Brown, et al.*, US Court of Appeals for the Ninth Circuit, no. 10-16696 (2012).

35. *Hollingsworth, et al. v. Perry, et al.*, 133 S. Ct. 2652 (2013). The lead plaintiff was Dennis Hollingsworth, a former Republican California Senate minority leader who'd spent much time in the Senate on bills about monitoring and prosecuting sex offenders. Hollingsworth, who'd become the head of ProtectMarriage.com,

had also led an unsuccessful charge to annul the marriages of the eighteen thousand same-sex couples that had wed before Prop 8 passed.

36. Geoffrey A. Fowler, "The Other Lawyer in the Gay-Wed Case," *Wall Street Journal*, March 26, 2013.

37. The Ninth Circuit Court of Appeals did grant the anti-same-sex marriage leaders "standing" based on their argument that they'd been the Proposition 22 Defense and Education Fund "sponsors, organizers, financial supporters and volunteers."

38. Nathaniel Persily, Jack Citrin, and Patrick J. Egan, *Public Opinion and Constitutional Controversy* (New York: Oxford University Press, 2008), p. 82.

39. Transcript of oral arguments: *Hollingsworth v. Perry*, Supreme Court of the United States, no. 12-144, March 26, 2013.

40. *Hollingsworth, et al. v. Perry, et al.*, 133 S. Ct. 2652 (2013).

41. Michael Winter and Elizabeth Weise, "Same-Sex Marriages Resume in California," *USA Today*, June 29, 2013.

42. Edie Windsor, interview with author, Southampton, NY (telephone), July 15, 2014; and David W. Dunlap, "A Marriage Born Where Tables for 2 Women Are Common," *New York Times*, March 26, 2013.

43. Documentary *Edie and Thea: A Very Long Engagement*, directed by Susan Muska and Greta Olafsdottir, 2009.

44. Windsor, interview with author.

45. Ibid.

46. Ariel Levy, "The Perfect Wife: How Edith Windsor Fell in Love, Got Married, and Won a Landmark Case for Gay Marriage," *New Yorker*, September 30, 2013.

47. The Massachusetts residency requirement for a marriage license was repealed in 2008.

48. *Edie and Thea: A Very Long Engagement*; and Levy, "The Perfect Wife."

49. Windsor, interview with author.

50. Julie Bolcer, "Fight of Her Life," *Advocate*, October 2012.

51. Windsor, interview with author.

52. Quoted in David J. Garrow, "Toward a More Perfect Union," *New York Times*, May 4, 2004.

53. *Dennis Hernandez, et al. v. Victor Robles, City Clerk, et al.*, 794 N.Y.S. 2d 579, decided July 6, 2006.

54. Roberta "Robbie" Kaplan, quoted in "One Year Later," *Metro Weekly*, June 25, 2014.

55. Kaplan, interview with author, New York (telephone), May 27, 2014.

56. John Schwartz, "U.S. Marriage Act Is Unfair to Gays, Court Panel Says," *New York Times*, October 18, 2012.

57. Kaplan, interview with author; and Levy, "The Perfect Wife."

58. Kaplan, interview with author. Bonauto, who agreed with Kaplan's instinct by the time the Windsor case was accepted in the Supreme Court, signed on as cocounsel.

59. Kaplan, interview with author.

60. *United States v. Edith Schlain Windsor*, Oral Arguments, no. 12-307, March 27, 2013.

61. Adam Liptak and Peter Baker, "Justices Cast Doubt on Benefits Ban in U.S. Marriage Law," *New York Times*, March 27, 2013.

62. *United States v. Edith Schlain Windsor*, Opinion, no. 12-307, June 26, 2013.

EPILOGUE

1. White, *Pre-Gay L.A.*, p. 220.

2. Franklin Kameny, "A Celebration of Jim Kepner's Life: May 22, 1998," in *Speaking for Our Lives: Historic Speeches and Rhetoric for Gay and Lesbian Rights (1892–2000)* (New York: Routledge, 2004).

3. Lou Chibbaro Jr., "Kameny Honored in Memorial Service on Capitol Hill," *Washington Blade*, November 16, 2011.

4. Judge Richard Posner, in *Marilyn Rae Basker, et al. v. Penny Bogan, et al; Virginia Wolf, et al. v. Scott Walker, et al.*, US Court of Appeals for the Seventh Circuit, no. 14-2386, decided September 4, 2014.

5. Wedding announcements: "Tess Bridgeman and Elizabeth George," *New York Times*, August 31, 2014.

6. JoAnne Viviano, "Backers Rally for Fired Gay Teacher," *Columbus (OH) Dispatch*, April 17, 2013.

7. Jeanne R. Roe, obituary, *Columbus (OH) Dispatch*, February 25, 2013.

8. Quoted in John Seewer, "Carla Hale Update: Gay Catholic School Teacher in Ohio Fights Firing," *Huffington Post*, April 29, 2013.

9. Trudy Ring, "Ohio Catholic School Fires Lesbian Teacher," *Advocate*, April 17, 2013.

10. JoAnne Viviano, "Fired Lesbian Teacher Won't Get Job Back in Deal with Diocese," *Columbus (OH) Dispatch*, August 16, 2013.

11. Associated Press, "Lesbian Teacher at Ohio School Won't Get Her Job Back," *Omaha World-Herald*, August 15, 2013.

12. *Hosanna-Tabor Evangelical Lutheran Church and School v. Equal Employment Opportunity Commission*, Supreme Court of the United States, no. 10-555 (January 11, 2012).

13. JoAnne Viviano, "Catholic Diocese Adds Morality to Guidelines," *Columbus (OH) Dispatch*, June 5, 2014.

14. *Jonathan R. Robicheaux, et al. v. James D. Caldwell, Louisiana Attorney General, et al.*, US District Court, Eastern District of Louisiana, no. 13-5090 C/W, July 16, 2014.

15. According to some pundits, Republican wins were unrelated to conservative orthodoxy on social issues: e.g., Thomas B. Edsall and Molly Worthen, "Election 2014," *New York Times,* November 4, 2014.

16. *April DeBoer, et al. v. Richard Synder, Governor of Michigan,* etc., 14-1341, etc., US Court of Appeals for the Sixth Circuit, November 6, 2014.

17. Center for American Progress, *We the People*, forthcoming report, quoted in Katy Steinmetz, "A Comprehensive LGBT Bill Is Coming," *Time*, December 10, 2014.

18. Marc Benioff, quoted in "Salesforce Relocating Employees Out of Indiana," *Indianapolis Star*, April 3, 2015.

19. "FIX THIS NOW," *Indianapolis Star*, March 31, 2015.

20. ABC News/*Washington Post* poll, taken the week of April 16–23, 2015.

PHOTO CREDITS

1. *Joplin Globe*, May 29, 1948. Reprinted with permission.
2. Photo by Bernie Cleff, courtesy of the Collections of the University of Pennsylvania Archives.
3. From *Real: The Exciting Magazine for Men*, December 1953. Courtesy of the ONE National Gay and Lesbian Archives.
4. Photo by Melanie Bell, 2011. Reprinted with permission.
5. Photo courtesy of Kendra A. Mon.
6. Photo courtesy of Renée Cafiero.
7. Photo by Robert Giard; © Estate of Robert Giard. Reprinted with permission.
8. Photo by Fred W. McDarrah. Reprinted with permission from Getty Images.
9. Photo by Kay Tobin; © Manuscripts and Archives Division, New York Public Library. Reprinted with permission.
10. Photo by Kay Tobin; © Manuscripts and Archives Division, New York Public Library. Reprinted with permission.
11. Photo by Kay Tobin; © Manuscripts and Archives Division, New York Public Library. Reprinted with permission.
12. Photo by Fred W. McDarrah. Reprinted with permission from Getty Images.
13. Photo by Diana Davies; © Manuscripts and Archives Division, New York Public Library. Reprinted with permission.
14. Photo by Rich Wandel. Courtesy of the LGBT Community Center National History Archive.
15. Photo by Rich Wandel. Courtesy of the LGBT Community Center National History Archive.

16. Photo by Rich Wandel. Courtesy of the LGBT Community Center National History Archive.

17. Photo by Rich Wandel. Courtesy of the LGBT Community Center National History Archive.

18. Photo by Kay Tobin; © Manuscripts and Archives Division, New York Public Library. Reprinted with permission.

19. Photo courtesy of the San Francisco Gay, Lesbian, Bisexual, Transgender Historical Society.

20. From the Walter "Butterfly" Blumoff Papers; photo courtesy of the San Francisco Gay, Lesbian, Bisexual, Transgender Historical Society.

21. Photo reprinted with permission from PFLAG National.

22. From the private collection of John O'Brien. Photo courtesy of John O'Brien.

23. Photo by Diana Davies; © Manuscripts and Archives Division, New York Public Library. Reprinted with permission.

24. From the personal papers and images of Jeanne Córdova. Reprinted with permission.

25. From the personal papers and images of Jeanne Córdova. Reprinted with permission.

26. From the private collection of Elaine Noble. Reprinted with permission.

27. From the Marie Ueda Collection. Photo courtesy of the San Francisco Gay, Lesbian, Bisexual, Transgender Historical Society.

28. Photo by Kay Tobin; © Manuscripts and Archives Division, New York Public Library. Reprinted with permission.

29. Photo by Bill Bland. National Gay and Lesbian Task Force Records #7301. Reprinted with permission from the Division of Rare and Manuscript Collections, Cornell University Library.

30. From the Marie Ueda Collection. Photo courtesy of the San Francisco Gay, Lesbian, Bisexual, Transgender Historical Society.

31. Photo by Peter Gridley. Reprinted with permission from Getty Images.

32. Copyright by Bless Bless Productions. Reprinted with permission.

33. Photo from the private collection of David Mixner. Courtesy of David Mixner.

34. Photo from the private collection of Karen Thompson. Courtesy of Karen Thompson.

35. Photo courtesy of Lambda Legal.

36. Photo courtesy of Michael Bedwell @ www.leonardmatlovich.com.

37. Photo courtesy of Eric Alva.

38. Photo courtesy of Margaret Witt.

39. Photo by Daniel Richard Arant. Courtesy of Margarethe Cammermeyer.

40. Photo courtesy of Robin McGehee.

41. Photo by Marta Evry. Reprinted with permission.

42. Photo by Michael Key, *Washington Blade*. Reprinted with permission.

43. Photo by Larry Downing. Reprinted with permission of Reuters.

44. Photo by Luis Sinco. © 2008 by the Los Angeles Times. Reprinted with permission.

INDEX

ABOUT THE AUTHOR

LILLIAN FADERMAN is the author of several award-winning books of LGBT history, including *Surpassing the Love of Men, Odd Girls and Twilight Lovers, To Believe in Women,* and *Gay L.A.* (with Stuart Timmons). She has also published two memoirs, *Naked in the Promised Land* and *My Mother's Wars*.